Endorsements

'*Internet of Things and the Law* is an impressive work on several levels. It exposes inadequate consumer safeguards in the current "contractual quagmire" and complex, overlapping regulatory regimes governing the IOT. Noto La Diega masterfully analyzes the relevant privacy, intellectual property, telecommunications, competition, and internet laws as he explicates their implications and proposes reforms. But like an artist sweeping away an intricate mandala after he has completed it, Noto La Diega boldly recognizes the limits of law and proposes a utopian horizon for IOT governance based on a deep engagement with studies in political economy and social theory. This book not only advances our understanding of IOT policy but also serves as a model for future work in the law and political economy of technology policy.'

Professor Frank Pasquale, *Brooklyn Law School,*
author of the bestseller The Black Box Society

'*Internet of Things and the Law: Legal Strategies for Consumer-Centric Smart Technologies* is a thorough exposition of the regulation of the Internet of Things which starts by expertly defining 'the Things' and the regulatory puzzles around them. Keeping the consumer front and centre, the book engages with a broad range of issues starting with 'Netflix Law, GeoBlocking and the personal/non-personal data binary. A strong case is made for a non-binary approach to regulation and for legal approaches, including contract law, consumer law, privacy law and intellectual property law, that mitigate the imbalances and vulnerabilities consumers are exposed to. Ultimately, Nota La Diega argues that the Commons for a Collectivised and Open IoT will take society beyond the limitations of these legal approaches. This is a timely and brilliant addition to scholarship that should inform forward-thinking regulatory approaches.'

Professor Caroline B Ncube, *Professor and SARChI*
Research Chair in Intellectual Property, Innovation
and Development, University of Cape Town

'A wonderfully informative and deeply reflective study of the Internet of Things from a socio-legal perspective, presented to us by one of the leading experts in the field. Dr Guido Noto La Diega convincingly argues for an open IoT and points to some hopeful signs. The book should be read especially by those interested in how European law might effectively regulate an Internet dominated by 'Things' and how people acting collectively can harness their power to reshape the future.'

*Professor **Megan Richardson**, Professor of Law,*
University of Melbourne, and Chief Investigator in the
ARC Centre of Excellence for Automated
Decision-Making and Society

'The only comprehensive and thorough legal analysis of IoT available as yet, which beautifully combines technological savvy with an admirable love for polemics'

*Professor **Marco Ricolfi**, Co-Director of the Nexa Centre*
for Internet & Society; Professor of Commercial Law,
Università degli Studi di Torino; Equity Partner
at Weigmann Studio Legale

Internet of Things and the Law

Internet of Things and the Law: Legal Strategies for Consumer-Centric Smart Technologies is the most comprehensive and up-to-date analysis of the legal issues in the Internet of Things (IoT). For decades, the decreasing importance of tangible wealth and power – and the increasing significance of their disembodied counterparts – has been the subject of much legal research. For some time now, legal scholars have grappled with how laws drafted for tangible property and predigital 'offline' technologies can cope with dematerialisation, digitalisation, and the internet. As dematerialisation continues, this book aims to illuminate the opposite movement: rematerialisation, namely, the return of data, knowledge, and power within a physical 'smart' world. This development frames the book's central question: can the law steer rematerialisation in a human-centric and socially just direction? To answer it, the book focuses on the IoT, the sociotechnological phenomenon that is primarily responsible for this shift. After a thorough analysis of how existing laws can be interpreted to empower IoT end users, Noto La Diega leaves us with the fundamental question of what happens when the law fails us and concludes with a call for collective resistance against 'smart' capitalism.

Dr Guido Noto La Diega (he/they) is an award-winning Scotland-based Sicily-born academic with a passion for law and technology. They are Associate Professor of Intellectual Property and Privacy Law at the University of Stirling, Faculty of Arts and Humanities. At Stirling, Noto La Diega leads the Royal Society of Edinburgh Research Network SCOTLIN (Scottish Law and Innovation Network); is Deputy Chair of the Faculty's Equality, Diversity, and Inclusion Committee; and carries out research at the Centre for Research into Information, Surveillance, and Privacy (CRISP). Currently, they are leading the AHRC-DfG-funded international research project 'From Smart Technologies to Smart Consumer Laws: Comparative Perspectives from Germany and the United Kingdom', in partnership with the universities of Osnabrück, Warwick, and Bonn. Outside of Stirling, Noto La Diega is Member of the European Commission's Expert Group on AI and Data in Education and Training, Fellow of the Nexa Center for Internet and Society, Research Associate at the UCL Centre for Blockchain Technologies, and Co-Convenor of the Open Section of the Society of Legal Scholars, the oldest and largest society of law academics in the UK and the Republic of Ireland. Noto La Diega's main expertise is in Internet of Things, artificial intelligence, cloud computing, robotics, and blockchain. Their work is animated by the conviction that the law should be pivotal to human-centric, and socially just sustainable technologies.

Routledge Research in the Law of Emerging Technologies

Biometrics, Surveillance and the Law
Societies of Restricted Access, Discipline and Control
Sara M. Smyth

Artificial Intelligence, Healthcare, and the Law
Regulating Automation in Personal Care
Eduard Fosch-Villaronga

Health Data Privacy under the GDPR
Big Data Challenges and Regulatory Responses
Edited by Maria Tzanou

Regulating Artificial Intelligence
Binary Ethics and the Law
Dominika Ewa Harasimiuk and Tomasz Braun

Cryptocurrencies and Regulatory Challenge
Allan C. Hutchinson

Regulating Artificial Intelligence in Industry
Edited by Damian M. Bielicki

The Law of Global Digitality
Edited by Matthias C. Kettemann, Alexander Peukert and Indra Spiecker gen. Döhmann

Internet of Things and the Law
Legal Strategies for Consumer-Centric Smart Technologies
Guido Noto La Diega

Internet of Things and the Law

Legal Strategies for Consumer-Centric
Smart Technologies

Guido Noto La Diega

Routledge
Taylor & Francis Group

LONDON AND NEW YORK

First published 2023
by Routledge
4 Park Square, Milton Park, Abingdon, Oxon OX14 4RN

and by Routledge
605 Third Avenue, New York, NY 10158

Routledge is an imprint of the Taylor & Francis Group, an informa business

© 2023 Guido Noto La Diega

British Library Cataloguing-in-Publication Data
A catalogue record for this book is available from the British Library

ISBN: 978-1-138-60479-7 (hbk)
ISBN: 978-1-032-30579-0 (pbk)
ISBN: 978-0-429-46837-7 (ebk)

DOI: 10.4324/9780429468377

Typeset in Times New Roman
by Apex CoVantage, LLC

To James: will you marry me?

Contents

Introduction   1

1   IoT Law: Obstacles and Alternatives in the Regulation of a Non-Binary Sociotechnological Phenomenon   9

    1.1   Introduction   9

    1.2   The IoT Today: Related Concepts, Definitions, and Core Features   11

    1.3   Two Reasons That It Is Difficult to Regulate   15

    1.4   Some Regulatory and Policy Options for an Interconnected World   40

    1.5   Overcoming Regulatory Binaries, Coregulation, and Supervisory Authority   61

    1.6   Interim Conclusion   66

2   The Internet of Spying Sex Toys, Killer Petrol Stations, and Manipulative Toasters: A View of Private Ordering from the Contractual Quagmire   68

    2.1   Scope of Chapter and Private Ordering   68

    2.2   A Four-Pronged Methodology   69

    2.3   Consumer Benefits   72

    2.4   The Main Risks Encountered by Consumers of Things   74

    2.5   Fantastic Legals and Where to Find Them: Understanding Private Ordering through Amazon Echo's Contractual Quagmire   83

    2.6   Interim Conclusion   115

3   The Internet of Contracts: The Tension between Consumer Contract Laws and IoT Imbalance   117

   3.1   Scope of the Chapter 117

   3.2   The IoT Overcomes Yet Another Binary: Unfairness of Substance and Unfairness of Form in the Smart Home 118

   3.3   Private Ordering 'by Bricking': Can IoT Traders Deprive Consumers of their Things' Smartness? 142

   3.4   Precontractual Duties to Inform Under the CRD in a Hyperconnected, Interface-Free World 167

   3.5   Interim Conclusion 181

4   The Internet of Vulnerabilities: Tackling Human and Product Vulnerabilities through Noncontractual Consumer Laws   184

   4.1   Introduction 184

   4.2   What's in a Product? EU Product Liability Laws and the Challenge of a Defective IoT 185

   4.3   Can We Trust the Internet of Personalised Things? 200

   4.4   Interim Conclusion 233

5   The Internet of Loos, the General Data Protection Regulation, and Digital Dispossession under Surveillance Capitalism   235

   5.1   Introduction: The Erosion of Privacy and Data Protection in the Global Private-Public Surveillance Network 235

   5.2   The GDPR: From Confidentiality to Data Control 237

   5.3   Data Protection Issues in the IoT 239

   5.4   Surveillance Capitalism and IoT Apparatus: From Prediction to Execution 251

   5.5   Looking into Alexa's Black Box 258

   5.6   Can the GDPR Counter IoT-Powered Digital Dispossession? 264

   5.7   Interim Conclusion: Data Protection Law and the 'Smart' Proletariat 274

6   The Internet of Things (You Don't Own) under Bourgeois Law: An Integrated Tactic to Rebalance Intellectual Property   275

   6.1   Introduction: Intellectual Property and Rentier Capitalism 275

   6.2   An Overview of the IP Issues and Themes in the IoT 277

6.3 *Death of Ownership: To Strengthen Property Rights and Empower IoT Users-Digital Peasants or to Counter Bourgeois Property? 285*

6.4 *Intra-IP Limitations: IP Exceptions or the Piecemeal Protection of Public Interest 295*

6.5 *IP Overlaps and the Erosion of IP Exceptions in the 'Smart' World 313*

6.6 *Extra-IP Limitations: Are Standard Essential Patents on Fair, Reasonable, and Nondiscriminatory Terms IoT-FRANDly? 323*

6.7 *Interim Conclusion 339*

Conclusion: When the Law Fails Us: The Commons for a Collectivised and Open IoT   341

Index   360

Introduction

> [T]he establishment of the political state and the dissolution of civil society into
> independent individuals – whose relations with one another depend on law . . . is
> accomplished by one and the same act.
>
> Marx, *On the Jewish Question*

For decades, the decreasing importance of tangible wealth and power – and the increasing significance of their intangible counterparts – has been the subject of much legal analysis.[1] This evolution predates the digital economy (bonds, shares, etc.), but it is in the context of the current pervasive digitalisation that intellectual property (IP) has risen to the role of a prevalent form of wealth, which – combined with contractual and technological measures – allows for the control of key immaterial resources, such as software, algorithms, and even data itself. For some time now, legal scholars have grappled with how laws drafted for tangible property and predigital 'offline' technologies cope with demate-rialisation, digitalisation, and the internet.[2] This debate is far from reaching a definitive conclusion, as the frenzy surrounding non-fungible tokens (NFTs) is showing.[3]

---

1 See e.g. Alexander Peukert, *Güterzuordnung als Rechtsprinzip* (Mohr Siebeck 2008); Jan Jacob, *Ausschließlichkeitsrechte an immateriellen Gütern: eine kantische Rechtfertigung des Urheber-rechts* (Mohr Siebeck 2010). More modestly, this was also the subject of Guido Noto La Diega, 'Il paradigma proprietario e l'appropriazione dell'immateriale' (PhD thesis, Università degli Studi di Palermo 2014).

2 See M Scott Boone, 'Ubiquitous Computing, Virtual Worlds, and the Displacement of Property Rights' (2008) 4 ISJLP 91. On the challenges of cloud computing to right to property see Guido Noto La Diega, 'Il Cloud Computing. Alla Ricerca Del Diritto Perduto Nel Web 3.0' (2014) 2 Europa e diritto privato 577. More broadly on issues of 'new' property without control see Aaron Perzanowski and Jason M Schultz, *The End of Ownership: Personal Property in the Digital Economy* (The MIT Press 2016). The crucial issue of how traditional principles about jurisdiction apply online see Julia Hörnle, *Internet Jurisdiction: Law and Practice* (OUP 2021).

3 Joshua Fairfield, 'Tokenized: The Law of Non-Fungible Tokens and Unique Digital Property' (2022) 97(4) Indiana Law Journal 1261; Ifeanyi E Okonkwo, 'NFT, Copyright; and Intellectual Property Commercialisation' (2021) 29(4) IJLIT 296.

DOI: 10.4324/9780429468377-1

As the dematerialisation continues, this book aims to illuminate the opposite development: rematerialisation,[4] namely, the return of data, knowledge, and intangible power – that we tend to conceive as disembodied and displaced in cyberspace – to the physical world. This move begs the question whether the law steers rematerialisation in a human-centric and socially just direction. To answer it, I will focus on the sociotechnological phenomenon that is primarily responsible for this shift: the Internet of Things (IoT).[5]

With smart devices (in this book referred to as 'Things') outnumbering human beings and with European spending in smart technologies exceeding EUR200 billion in 2021,[6] the IoT is now past the hype. This sociotechnological reality promises to considerably improve our lives through a network of sensors and actuators deployed in the most disparate sectors, from healthcare through agriculture to transport and entertainment. In an IoT world, every Thing is connected to the internet, communicates automatically with other Things, transforms every aspect of our lives into computable information, and uses this information to act on the physical reality and produce often unforeseeable changes in the 'real' world. Some incidents attracted some publicity, e.g. hackers screaming at children through unsecured baby monitors,[7] killer connected cars,[8] and the transformation of hundreds of Things into remotely controlled bots to bring down a domain registration

4   See Jennifer Gabrys, 'Re-Thingifying the Internet of Things' in Nicole Starosielski and Janet Walker (eds), *Sustainable Media: Critical Approaches to Media and Environment* (Routledge 2016) 180; Henriikka Vartiainen and others, 'Rematerialization of the Virtual and Its Challenges for Design and Technology Education' (2020) 27 Techne Serien – Forskning i slöjdpedagogik och slöjdvetenskap 52.

5   The renewed centrality of tangibles goes beyond the IoT, see e.g. 3D printing, but with the IoT it acquires an unparalleled scale. Climate change and sustainability considerations are also leading to a new awareness of the materiality of assets that would otherwise be regarded as intangible, see e.g. the energy consumptions concerns associated to the blockchain. See Jon Truby, 'Decarbonizing Bitcoin: Law and Policy Choices for Reducing the Energy Consumption of Blockchain Technologies and Digital Currencies' (2018) 44 *Energy Research & Social Science* 399; Dinusha Kishani Mendis, Mark A Lemley and Matthew Rimmer (eds), *3D Printing and beyond: Intellectual Property and Regulation* (Edward Elgar Publishing 2019).

6   'Worldwide Internet of Things Spending Guide' (*IDC*, 9 June 2021) <www.idc.com/tracker/show-productinfo.jsp?containerId=IDC_P29475>.

7   Department for Digital, Culture, Media & Sport, *Code of Practice for Consumer IoT Security* (UK Gov 2018) <www.gov.uk/government/publications/code-of-practice-for-consumer-iot-security/code-of-practice-for-consumer-iot-security>.

8   The first death occurred in Florida in May 2016, when a Tesla Model S's autopilot sensors mistook a white tractor-trailer crossing the highway for the sky, thus killing its 'driver.' In March 2018, a Volvo car that Uber had been using to test its self-driving technology killed a cyclist in Arizona as its operator was distracted watching *The Voice*. The operator was charged in September 2020, whereas surprisingly prosecutors decided that there was no basis for criminal liability for the corporation, despite the vehicle's automatic systems' failure to identify the victim and her bicycle as an imminent collision danger due to sensor and software issues (National Transportation Safety Board, 'Preliminary Report Released for Crash Involving Pedestrian, Uber Technologies, Inc., Test Vehicle' (*NTSB*, 24 May 2018) <www.ntsb.gov/news/press-releases/Pages/NR20180524.aspx>). In August 2019, a Tesla car in autopilot killed a fifteen-year-old in California. More recently, in April 2021, a Tesla car killed its own passengers in Texas. Cf Antonio Davola, 'A Model for Tort Liability in a World

service provider.[9] One can only imagine what would happen if malicious players exploited the 'smartness' of Things to remotely control a petrol station, a pacemaker, or an army of drones. The higher the degree of a Thing's autonomy, the higher the risks. For example, in March 2021 the UN Security Council revealed that for the first time a lethal autonomous weapon system had attacked a human target without being told to.[10] Alongside security and privacy, the IoT poses a threat to other fundamental values, from self-determination through dignity to freedom of expression and equality.

While there is growing interest for the IoT,[11] existing analyses tend to focus on individual issues – mainly privacy,[12] cybersecurity,[13] and competition law.[14] More comprehensive studies are US-centric,[15] targeted at practitioners,[16] or no longer current, considering the speed of technological evolution and legal change.[17] Some contributions have also explored the IoT alongside artificial intelligence (AI) and other technologies of the 'Fourth Industrial Revolution.'[18] Against this

---

of Driverless Cars: Establishing a Framework for the Upcoming Technology' (2018) 54 Idaho Law Review 591.

9 'The State of DDoS Weapons' (*A10*, 2020) <www.a10networks.com/resources/reports/state-ddos-weapons/>.

10 UN Security Council, 'Letter Dated 8 March 2021 from the Panel of Experts on Libya Established Pursuant to Resolution 1973 (2011) Addressed to the President of the Security Council' (S/2021/229).

11 In terms of nonlegal literature, key references are Jeremy Rifkin, *The Zero Marginal Cost Society: The Internet of Things, the Collaborative Commons, and the Eclipse of Capitalism* (Palgrave Macmillan 2015); Philip N Howard, *Pax Technica: How the Internet of Things May Set Us Free or Lock Us Up* (YUP 2015); Bruce Schneier, *Click Here to Kill Everybody* (Norton 2018).

12 See e.g. Rolf H Weber, 'Internet of Things – New Security and Privacy Challenges' (2010) 26 Computer Law & Security Review 23; Aurelia Tamò-Larrieux, *Designing for Privacy and Its Legal Framework: Data Protection by Design and Default for the Internet of Things* (Springer 2018); Jatinder Singh and others, 'Accountability in the IoT: Systems, Law, and Ways Forward' (2018) 51 Computer 54; Nóra Ni Loideain, 'A Port in the Data-Sharing Storm: The GDPR and the Internet of Things' (2019) 4 Journal of Cyber Policy 178.

13 See e.g. J Singh and others, 'Twenty Security Considerations for Cloud-Supported Internet of Things' (2016) 3 IEEE Internet of Things Journal 269; David Lindsay and Evana Wright, 'Regulating Security for the Consumer Internet of Things (IoT)' (2020) 3 REDC 541.

14 See e.g. Marco Ricolfi, 'IoT and the Ages of Antitrust' (Nexa Center for Internet & Society 2017) Working paper nr 4/2017; Rupprecht Podszun, 'Standard Essential Patents and Antitrust Law in the Age of Standardisation and the Internet of Things: Shifting Paradigms' (2019) 50 IIC 720.

15 Joshua AT Fairfield, *Owned: Property, Privacy, and the New Digital Serfdom* (CUP 2017); Brett M Frischmann and Evan Selinger, *Re-Engineering Humanity* (CUP 2018); Shoshana Zuboff, *The Age of Surveillance Capitalism: The Fight for a Human Future at the New Frontier of Power* (PublicAffairs 2019); Cynthia H Cwik and others (eds), *The Internet of Things: Legal Issues, Policy, and Practical Strategies* (ABA 2019).

16 Cwik and others (n 15); Thaddeus Hoffmeister, *Internet of Things and the Law* (Practising Law Institute 2020).

17 Rolf H Weber and Romana Weber, *Internet of Things. Legal Perspectives* (Springer Berlin Heidelberg 2010).

18 Mireille Hildebrandt, *Smart Technologies and the End(s) of Law: Novel Entanglements of Law and Technology* (Elgar 2015); Frischmann and Selinger (n 15); Eduardo Magrani, *Laws and Ethics of Internet of Things and Artificial Intelligence* (Lambert 2019); Sebastian Lohsse, Reiner Schulze

backdrop, *Internet of Things and the Law* differs to existing works as it is an updated comprehensive reflection on the IoT from a European sociolegal perspective and targeted at academics and law students. While this is first and foremost a research monograph, I believe that it can be of use to students as well. Indeed, nowadays it has become impossible to understand internet governance and information technology law without a thorough comprehension of the IoT. First, the IoT is a rapidly expanding area of the web, as suggested inter alia by the fact that IoT patents grow nearly seven times faster than other technologies.[19] Second, in recent years a deluge of laws (including standards and soft laws) has been introduced to regulate the IoT, directly or indirectly: these range from the Regulation on the Free Flow of Non-Personal Data to the UK's Code of Practice for Consumer IoT Security. Therefore, ignoring these laws would provide only a partial understanding of how the internet is governed.

This book builds on those contributions that have regarded the new extractive practices of the IoT as illustrative of the current stage of development of capitalism. Most famously, Shoshana Zuboff in her *Surveillance Capitalism* shed light on a new form of power generated by big data, an unprecedented threat to democratic values as it exiles persons from their own behaviour by creating new markets of behavioural prediction and modification.[20] Zuboff creates a parallel with the industrial capitalism studied by Marx, but she posits that whereas the old capitalism fed on labour, IoT-powered capitalism 'feeds on every aspect of every human's experience.'[21] In fact, there is uninterrupted continuity between the old and the new capitalism, and the point of the IoT is to appropriate the previously uncapturable, thus transforming every aspect of human experience into labour. Indeed, it is now accepted that data is the main commodity, and we, as IoT users, can be regarded as data producers. By appropriating this commodity and controlling the means of production, surveillance capitalists treat us as industrial capitalists treat their workers – except now we are no longer aware of being workers.

IoT power, and the way big tech uses it, cannot be comprehended without looking also at those subjected to it. Humans use Things and are increasingly used – and transformed – by Things. This is where another major recent contribution to contemporary scholarship, *Re-engineering Humanity* by Brett Frischmann and Evan Selinger, steps is. The authors focus on how these companies use new technologies, including the IoT – rebranded 'smart techno-social environment' – to change those subjected to power: us. The IoT risks erasing the '*freedom to be off*, to be free from systemic, environmentally architected human engineering.'[22] Building on this analysis, it is vital to understand how to de-engineer humanity.

---

and Dirk Staudenmayer (eds), *Liability for Artificial Intelligence and the Internet of Things: Münster Colloquia on EU Law and the Digital Economy IV* (Hart 2019).

19 Intellectual Property Office, 'Eight Great Technologies. The Internet of Things. A Patent Overview' (2014) UKIPO 6.

20 Zuboff (n 15) 8.

21 ibid 16.

22 Frischmann and Selinger (n 15) 124.

To this end, alongside understanding power and its subjects, one needs to closely scrutinise how the law mediates the relationship. In this sense, an unavoidable reference is to the germinal book *Between Truth and Power* by Julie E. Cohen, who focuses on how the law is changing in the networked information age. Law is closely intertwined with code (or design) and political economy: 'through their capacities to authorize, channel, and modulate information flows and behaviour patterns, code and law *mediate* between truth and power.'[23] This approach builds on a tradition that goes back to Lawrence Lessig's *Code*,[24] which famously regarded code – the binary code that shapes the internet – as a new form of regulation. More recently, Roger Brownsword and Karen Yeung observed that we need to reimagine legal rules as one element of a larger regulatory environment of which technological management is also part.[25] While building on these three streams of literature, this book further advances knowledge by understanding power, humans, law, and technology as inextricably connected and each capable of affecting and being affected by the others.

The impact of the IoT on the law is not limited to the rethinking of the concept of law to include techno-regulation. The IoT disrupts many of the dichotomies upon which the law was built, most notably good-service, hardware-software, tangible-intangible, consumer-trader, consumer-worker, human-machine, security-cybersecurity, online-offline. As noted by Mireille Hildebrandt, smart environments engender novel types of regulation, which usher in the 'onli*fe*' world: the IoT is not simply a technological infrastructure; it is 'a transformative life world, situated beyond the increasingly artificial distinction between online and offline.'[26] The IoT's smartness means that Things will be executing their own programs and negotiating with each other to achieve their own goals. This makes it imperative to 'address [smart] environments or their constitutive elements as agents that we need to hold responsible for the harm they cause, for their *lack of fairness*.'[27] More generally, the fact that the IoT is troubling the binary categories that underpin the law calls for a rigorous legal analysis to critically assess whether the law can be 'queered'. By 'queering' the law, I mean the overcoming of the the aforementioned binaries through interpretation, legal design, or law reform. A queer approach requires also that the power dynamics hidden behind the 'smart' world be brought to life, which in turn means asking oneself whether traditional legal changes adequately curb the power of IoT capitalists or a more radical upheaval would be desirable.

Rematerialisation, the internal dynamics within the power-humans-law triad, the regulatory function of IoT code, and the tension between a non-binary

---

23 Julie E Cohen, *Between Truth and Power: The Legal Constructions of Informational Capitalism* (OUP 2019) 13.

24 Lawrence Lessig, *Code* (Version 2.0, Basic Books 2006).

25 Roger Brownsword and Karen Yeung (eds), *Regulating Technologies: Legal Futures, Regulatory Frames and Technological Fixes* (Hart 2008); Roger Brownsword, *Law, Technology and Society: Re-Imagining the Regulatory Environment* (Routledge 2019); Karen Yeung and Martin Lodge (eds), *Algorithmic Regulation* (OUP 2019).

26 Hildebrandt (n 18) 8.

27 ibid 27.

sociotechnological phenomenon and dichotomic regulatory mechanisms are only some of the reasons that made me embark on this writing journey. A final, crucial factor played a role. Internet studies have long explored the challenges and opportunities of the collection and use of information. The EU General Data Protection Regulation (GDPR)[28] and prominent surveillance scandals have led to an abundance of research on data management, data science, and data ethics. These laudable endeavours have mostly focused on 'incoming data,' namely, on the transformation of real-world information into strings of code. However, to study the IoT means to account not only for how machines sense the world but also for how they act on it. As will be seen in the next chapter, being equipped with actuators is a core feature of Things. An example is provided by the automated border control systems that decide whether to open the door based on the matching of the passport's biometric data and facial recognition data. More trivial illustrations include a turning on of the lights based on location data, or a smart sprinkler watering the plants based on weather data. Zooming out, one starts to see how this constant two-directional flow – real world being transformed into computable information, information being used to change the real world – shows how the IoT is, at once, a global network of surveillance and a global infrastructure for the collective organisation of IoT users-cum-data producers-cum-workers. With the IoT, the factory becomes distributed and every aspect of one's life is commodified and rendered reprogrammable. Similar to industrial capitalists collectively organising labour in the factory, IoT big tech extracts value from our data by organising our digital labour at a systemic level.

This leads to the explanation of why I have adopted a methodology that can be loosely regarded as Marxist. At a higher level, as technological artefacts have politics[29] – the most popular Things' politics being clearly neoliberal – and given that the IoT has been convincingly framed as the epitome of the current stage of capitalism,[30] it makes only sense to adopt a Marxist lens. Indeed, Marxism remains the most compelling and comprehensive critical approach to capitalism, and Marx was the first to argue that technology is the primary influence on human social relations and organisational structure.[31] I would also put forward that a Marxist legal research method demands a sociolegal 'law in action' approach. As Roscoe Pound put it, lawyers need not to regard the law as 'the beginning of wisdom and the eternal jural order;'[32] rather, we should 'look the facts of human conduct in the face (and) cease to assume that jurisprudence is self-sufficient.'[33] While Pound was mainly preoccupied with the relationship between common law and legislation, 'law in action' is nowadays construed as a nonnormative

---

28 Regulation 2016/679 on the protection of natural persons with regard to the processing of personal data and on the free movement of such data [2016] OJ L 119/1.

29 Langdon Winner, 'Do Artifacts Have Politics?' (1980) 109 Daedalus 121.

30 Cohen (n 23).

31 For a nuanced analysis of technological determinism and Marxism, see Bruce Bimber, 'Karl Marx and the Three Faces of Technological Determinism' (1990) 20 Social Studies of Science 333.

32 Roscoe Pound, 'Law in Books and Law in Action' (1910) 44 Am L Rev 12, 35.

33 ibid 35–36.

understanding of the many forms the law can take and operate in the real world. This is in line with the Marxist refusal of 'legal fetishism,' a common attitude whereby the law is depicted as a 'unique phenomenon which constitutes a discrete focus of study.'[34] The view that the law is only 'one aspect of a variety of political and social arrangements concerned with the manipulation of power and the consolidation of modes of production of wealth'[35] for me is no reason not to study the nature of legal phenomena. Rather, it is an incentive to reflect on how power and socio-economic factors shape the law and how the latter governs – or, one may say, is governed by – emerging technologies, which in turn have become personalised regulatory tools in the hands of private rule-makers: the 'smart' platforms. To understand this new law in action, I have adopted a multipronged methodology, including semistructured interviews, subject access requests, text analysis of contracts, and autoethnography, as elucidated at the beginning of each chapter.

My approach can also be defined loosely as Marxist as it reconciles the historical materialist tenet that human behaviour is conditioned by external factors (mainly socio-economic ones) with the acknowledgement of the importance of conscious action in the transformation of societies. As the epigraph shows, the law had a crucial role in creating the state while dissolving – and depoliticising – civil society.[36] While the law imposed by the dominant classes is one of the factors that condition human behaviour, this does not mean that there is no room for organised action. In shedding light on how the IoT threatens humanity, and on the limitations of the law in dealing with it, this book intends to raise awareness – to heighten class consciousness, one would say in Marxist terms – about the risks of technologically driven capitalism, with the ultimate goal of a call to action to refute techno-legal solutionism and transform the IoT into an open and collective vision for a more just society.

With this in mind, I will endeavour to answer the following overarching question: how does the law mediate the power dynamics between IoT big tech and the end users, and can the law steer the development of the IoT in a human-centric and socially just direction?

* * *

Like all knowledge, a book is a collective endeavour. I wish to thank Northumbria University for granting my sabbatical request, and the University of Stirling for a generous research allocation, and for funding the publication of Chapter 6 in open access. Thank you to the library and administrative staff at both universities for their outstanding professionalism. I am much obliged to Siobhán Poole, Sanjo Joseph Puthumana, Richard George and everyone at Routledge for believing in this project and being patient while I was missing all the deadlines partly due to deadly viruses, relocations, and job changes.

---

34 Hugh Collins, *Marxism and Law* (OUP 1984) 11.
35 ibid 13.
36 On the interdependence between the emergence of the autonomous state and the nonpolitical civil society in Marx, see Justin Rosenberg, *The Empire of Civil Society: A Critique of the Realist Theory of International Relations* (Verso 1994) 69.

I owe a debt of gratitude to my *Maestro*, Luca Nivarra, and to all those who selflessly mentored me over these years, namely – in alphabetical order – Ray Arthur, Eva-Marina Bastian, Frances Burton, Enrico Camilleri, Lilian Edwards, Sue Farran, Martin Kretschmer, Dave McArdle, Christopher Millard, Lars Mosesson, Andrew Murray, Marina Nicolosi, Michele Perrino, Fabrizio Piraino, Jenny Preston, Chris Reed, Megan Richardson, Marco Ricolfi, Michael Stockdale, Alain Strowel, Elaine Sutherland, Ian Walden, Jason Whalley, Tony Ward, and Hong-Lin Yu. Thanks for leading by example!

In the years I have worked on this book, my students, PhD students, research assistants, supervisees and mentees have been a source of constant inspiration. Many of them have meanwhile become successful colleagues. It is impossible to name them all, but I wish to single out Rachel Allsopp, Valentina Borgese, Paolo Burdese, Luca Dell'Atti, Cameron Giles, Arletta Gorecka, Zoi Krokida, Zihao Li, Daria Onitiu, Alessia Palladino, Samantha Rasiah, David Sinclair, James Stacey, Pete Tiarks, and Giuseppe Zago. *Homines dum docent discunt.*

I wish to acknowledge the crucial role played by my research participants. An honourable mention goes to IoT leaders Alexandra Deschamps-Sonsino, Laura James, Joshua Montgomery, Peter Bihr, and Alasdair Davies. Thanks to you, I gained a better understanding of the IoT and of the importance of opening it up.

This book would not have been possible without the love and support of my family. Thank you, *madre* and *babbo*, for regarding my weirdness as uniqueness, for teaching me to embrace it and celebrate it. I wish to thank Dr James Crawford Bell, my amazing partner, who stood by me despite my erratic behaviour while working on this book, including waking up in the middle of the night to scribble confused ideas, most of which never made it into the final draft, fortunately. I could not have chosen a better (lockdown or otherwise) companion. Thank you for expressing your love through 'extensive notes.'

1 IoT Law

Obstacles and Alternatives in the Regulation of a Non-Binary Sociotechnological Phenomenon

In the medieval guilds the master was prevented from becoming a capitalist by the guild regulations.

Marx, *Economic Manuscript of 1861–63*

1.1 Introduction

The IoT promises to improve our lives and realise the vision of a fully interconnected world, where we are constantly online, with easy access to a vast range of digital services and unprecedented new opportunities in every sector, from defence to healthcare. However, the IoT raises a number of issues that existing laws do not properly address for a number of reasons, most notably the reliance on outdated dichotomies (e.g. good-service) and principles (e.g. copyright's territoriality). These issues would require better and IoT-aware regulations to address questions of utmost importance, ranging from the problem of covert, ubiquitous surveillance to the liability for the harms produced by the unintended and automated interactions within and between IoT systems.

When I started writing this book, I was reading Marx's *Economic Manuscript 1861–63*,[1] from which the epigraph of this chapter is taken. The manuscript plays a 'very important'[2] role in the development of Marx's critique of political economy, a process that starts with the *London Notebooks of 1850–53*[3] and ends with the *Capital*.[4] Entitled by Marx *Zur Kritik der Politischen Ökonomie* (*A Contribution to the Critique of Political Economy*) and consisting of 23 notebooks, the

---

1 Karl Marx, 'Economic Manuscript of 1861–63. A Contribution to the Critique of Political Economy' in Karl Marx and Friedrich Engels (eds), *Collected Works*, vol 30 (Progress 1988).
2 Alex Callinicos, 'Marx's Unfinished But Magnificent Critique of Political Economy' (2018) 82 Science & Technology 139, 140.
3 These remain unpublished, but they are included in the Marx-Engels-Gesamtausgabe (MEGA) project and are set to be published in *MEGA* IV/7–11 according to Lucia Pradella, *Globalisation and the Critique of Political Economy: New Insights from Marx's Writings* (Routledge 2015) 6.
4 In this book, I will mainly refer to the Italian translation of *Capital* and in particular to Karl Marx, *Il Capitale (1867)*, vol 1 (Bruno Maffi tr, Aurelio Macchioro and Bruno Maffi, UTET 2008); Karl Marx, *Il Capitale (1885)*, vol 2 (Bruno Maffi ed, UTET 2009); Karl Marx, *Il capitale (1894)*, vol 3 (Bruno Maffi tr, Bruno Maffi, UTET 2009).

DOI: 10.4324/9780429468377-2

'path-breaking'[5] manuscript can be regarded as the first systematic draft of all four volumes of *Capital*.[6] I was drawn to it for two reasons. First, the idea that the existence of regulations prevented feudal masters from becoming capitalists. If one compares it to the current regulation of the IoT, its piecemeal, outdated, and often unenforceable character reduces the ability to rein in IoT capitalism. Second, one of the key features of the *1861–63 Manuscript* is Marx's interest in the role of technology in the passage from manufacture to 'mechanical workshop' or industrial factory.[7] The difference between these stages lies in the technological revolution that, thanks to the passage from 'tool' to 'machine,' enabled the capitalist mode of production. The difference is pithily explained by Marx himself:

> [O]nce the *tool is itself driven by a mechanism*, once the tool of the worker, his implement, of which the efficiency depends on his own skill, and which needs his labour as an intermediary in the working process, is converted into the tool of a mechanism, the machine has replaced the tool.[8]

The replacement of humans with machines in the handling of the tools is 'the material essence of the revolution of "mode of production."'[9] The all-consuming labourer-machine relationship isolates the former, who confronts 'capital as an isolated individual, standing outside the social connection with his fellow workers;'[10] the labourer confronts a thing, rather than the person of the capitalist. The machine is the labourer's '*aggregate body, which exists outside him . . .* Human beings are merely the living accessories . . . of the unconscious but uniformly operating machinery.'[11] Under smart capitalism, this isolation and passivity of workers is worsened by the fact that the machine is no longer only the external body of the labourer when working in the factory: the machine is all around us, in our smart cities; reaches our most private spaces, in the smart home; and enters our own body under the guise of smart health. In a society where data is the most sought-after commodity, IoT users become round-the-clock workers as they produce big data, thus generating value, whether they are aware of it or not.

Against this backdrop, this chapter will critically evaluate whether existing regulations do enough to protect us from the extractive practices of the IoT, whether they can rebalance our relationship vis-à-vis these ubiquitous 'smart' machines, whether they can prevent hyperconnectivity from making us feel like disconnected

5 Enrique Dussel, *Towards an Unknown Marx: A Commentary on the Manuscripts of 1861–63* (Yolanda Angulo tr, Routledge 2001) 2.
6 Institute of Marxism-Leninism, 'Economic Manuscripts: Theories of Surplus-Value. Preface' <www.marxists.org/archive/marx/works/1863/theories-surplus-value/preface.htm>.
7 Dussel (n 5) 169.
8 Marx, 'Economic Manuscript of 1861–63. A Contribution to the Critique of Political Economy' (n 1) 423. Italics added.
9 Dussel (n 5) 170.
10 Marx, 'Economic Manuscript of 1861–63. A Contribution to the Critique of Political Economy' (n 1) 478.
11 ibid 489. Italics added.

machines. In doing so, it will tackle the book's overarching research question by answering the following subquestion: *what are the hurdles in the regulation of the IoT, and how is the EU rising to the challenge?*

PART 1 – IOT DEFINITION AND REGULATORY DIFFICULTIES

1.2 The IoT Today: Related Concepts, Definitions, and Core Features

The core idea that underpins the 'Internet of Things' can be traced back to 1926, when Nikola Tesla imagined that devices simpler and more mobile than the traditional telephone would convert the Earth into a brain. One needs to wait until the seventies for the first 'Thing' to be developed. It was a Coke vending machine at the Carnegie Mellon Computer Science Department, and its microswitches enabled users to remotely double-check whether the machine was empty or full.[12] Flash forward thirty years, Kevin Ashton coined the phrase 'Internet of Things' in a 1999 presentation for Procter & Gamble, where he linked the use of radio frequency identification (RFID) in that company's supply chain and the internet as a new, more reliable way for computers to collect data about the physical world with little, if any, human involvement.[13]

Despite a not-so-recent history, there is no single commonly accepted definition of the IoT.[14] For the purpose of this book, and building on the Microsoft Cloud Computing Research Centre's approach[15] to the IoT, a 'Thing' is:

> *An inextricable mixture of hardware, software, service, digital content, and data with (inter)connectivity, sensing, and actuating capabilities and interfacing the physical world.*

Although the IoT is an ever-changing and contested concept, this definition encompasses the main features that lawyers and regulators need to keep in mind:

a) *Physicality*. Whilst for decades innovation has been software-driven, with the IoT there is a return to the physical objects, now enhanced with computational

---

12 Jay Patel, 'The Timeline of Things' (2015) 22 XRDS: Crossroads, The ACM Magazine for Students 13). Others claim that the first Thing was a 1991 camera-equipped coffee pot at the Trojan Lab at Cambridge University (Paul Ford, 'It's All Connected' [2013] United Hemispheres, as cited by Keith Marzullo, in Federal Trade Commission, 'Internet of Things: Privacy and Security in a Connected World' (2015) 15–16).

13 Kevin Ashton, 'That "Internet of Things" Thing' (2009) 22 RFID Journal 97.

14 Hugh Boyes and others, 'The Industrial Internet of Things (IIoT): An Analysis Framework' (2018) 101 Computers in Industry 1; Theo Lynn and others, 'The Internet of Things: Definitions, Key Concepts, and Reference Architectures' in Theo Lynn and others (eds), *The Cloud-to-Thing Continuum: Opportunities and Challenges in Cloud, Fog and Edge Computing* (Palgrave Macmillan 2020) 1.

15 Noto La Diega and Walden (n 24).

power, connectivity, and sensing/actuating capabilities. If one overlooks the physical element, there is the risk of ignoring the issues that are specific to the IoT, which is increasingly enabled by – but should be kept distinct from – cloud computing, edge computing, AI, big data, and more recently, blockchain technologies.

b) *(Inter)connectivity*. As the name IoT suggests, Things are connected to the internet, usually wirelessly.[16] This raises a number of issues exemplified by the hacker who threatened to kidnap a child using a 'smart' baby monitor and a Nest camera.[17] Interconnectivity also means that for the full realisation of the IoT's potential, it is pivotal that Things communicate with other Things and with humans. This raises questions of interoperability, as well as liability, when an IoT system reconfigures and a harm is produced as a consequence of the unforeseen interaction between the Things (so-called 'repurposing'). For example, there are clear tensions between IoT's repurposing, the GDPR's principle of purpose limitation,[18] and the concept of foreseeability in tort law.[19]

c) *Equipment with sensors and actuators*.[20] Sensors play a crucial role in enabling the acquisition of data from the real world and transforming it into actions. Their importance is evidenced by the fact that over half of ISO's standards on the IoT are dedicated to sensor networks.[21] Actuators are as important because they make the Things act based on the information received by the sensors. Actions can be fully automated (e.g., lights switching on if movement is detected) or may require some human intervention (e.g., a wireless sensor network detects a problem in a factory and humans fix it). However, current IoT systems are still 'mostly unprepared for handling human actuation as an inherent component of the system.'[22] Therefore, it is likely that

16 Gil Reiter, 'Wireless Connectivity for the Internet of Things' (2014) 433 Europe 868MHz.
17 '"I'm in Your Baby's Room": A Hacker Took Over a Baby Monitor and Broadcast Threats, Parents Say' (*Washington Post*, 20 December 2018) <www.washingtonpost.com/technology/2018/12/20/nest-cam-baby-monitor-hacked-kidnap-threat-came-device-parents-say/>.
18 Personal data has to be 'collected for specified, explicit and legitimate purposes and not further processed in a manner that is incompatible with those purposes' (GDPR, art 5(1)(b)). One could argue that IoT's repurposing means that a larger range of purposes becomes compatible with the original purposes.
19 For example, in English law there are three elements in the tort of negligence: duty of care, breach of the duty, and damages. The reasonable foreseeability of harm is a key component of the duty of care as per *Caparo Industries Plc v Dickman* [1990] 2 AC 605. The argument could be put forward that if the manufacturer of a Thing could not reasonably foresee that an interaction with third-party Things would lead to damage, then there would be no duty of care and no negligence. However, it could also be argued that the IoT – because of its repurposing potential – by its nature widens the scope of what can be reasonably foreseen.
20 ISO and IEC (n 18) 42.
21 'ISO/IEC JTC 1/SC 41 – Internet of Things and Digital Twin' (*ISO*) <www.iso.org/committee/6483279/x/catalogue/p/1/u/0/w/0/d/0>.
22 Nunes, Silva and Boavida (n 37) 32.

liability issues will arise from the interaction between non-human actuators and human ones.

d) *Things as an inextricable mixture of hardware, software, service, digital content, and data.* Existing legal regimes are predicated on the software-hardware, goods-services, and online-offline dichotomies.[23] Four examples will suffice. First, the rules on liability for defective products were tailored for traditional hardware products and may need tweaking[24] to accommodate defects related to software, service, or data.[25] Second, the exclusion from patentability of computer programs 'as such' relied on a clear distinction between hardware and software, in principle patentable and nonpatentable, respectively. Therefore, with the blurring of the distinction produced by the IoT, the exclusion risks have become meaningless.[26] Third, international trade law is organised around the goods-services dichotomy, and current rules, drafted in the nineties, are not entirely fit for a 'world of talking teapots and connected cars.'[27] Increasingly, governments take measures against IoT manufacturers that are based not only on the hardware but also on the digital features of the products.[28] If Things are regarded as goods, the relevant controversies will fall under the General Agreement on Tariffs and Trade[29] and under the Agreement on Technical Barriers to Trade.[30] Conversely, if Things are services, the General Agreement on Trade in Services[31] will govern the litigation.[32] Finally, the online-offline dichotomy provided a justification for the digital libertarian

---

23 There are recent exceptions. Under the Consumer Rights Act, section 16, goods do not conform to the contract if 'the goods are *an item that includes digital content*' and the digital content does not conform to the contract. For an analysis of this regime, see Siobhan McConnell, 'Product Quality and the Internet of Things: Are the New EU Laws "Smart" Enough?' [2020] SI REDC.

24 In Noto La Diega and Walden (n 24), we argued that current product liability rules are flexible enough to deal with IoT defects. While I confirm that view, amendments that expressly addressed IoT defects would increase legal certainty.

25 The European Commission has set up a group of experts entrusted with the task of reviewing Council Directive 85/374/EEC of 25 July 1985 on the approximation of the laws, regulations, and administrative provisions of the member states concerning liability for defective products (Product Liability Directive) [1985] OJ L 210/ 29. One of the main issues that are under consideration is how to amend the product liability rules for nonhardware defects. See European Commission, 'Report from the Commission to the European Parliament, the Council and the European Economic and Social Committee on the Application of the Council Directive on the Approximation of the Laws, Regulations, and Administrative Provisions of the Member States Concerning Liability for Defective Products (85/374/EEC)' COM/2018/246 final.

26 More on this in Guido Noto La Diega, 'Software Patents and the Internet of Things in Europe, the United States and India' (2017) 39 EIPR 173.

27 Anupam Chander, 'The Internet of Things: Both Goods and Services' (2019) 18 World Trade Review 1.

28 ibid 3.

29 1867 U.N.T.S. 187 (GATT).

30 1868 U.N.T.S. 120 (TBT).

31 1869 U.N.T.S. 183 (GATS).

32 While the IoT complicates the classifications at the heart of international trade law, the latter 'may yet prove more adaptable than might have been expected' (Chander (n 58) 14).

claim that the internet had to be immune from the regulation of the offline.[33] This political option permeates the e-Commerce Directive,[34] which grants online intermediaries some immunities for the illegal activities carried out by their users (so-called safe harbours).[35] As an increasing number of traditionally offline intermediaries are embracing the IoT, thus becoming at least in principle eligible for the safe harbours, the scope of platform immunity could become much wider than originally foreseen.[36]

A feature that may not refer to all Things but that can have important legal repercussions is that most Things are made of several components (they are composite or compound). Even limiting the analysis to the hardware in itself, the Things' components have different manufacturers responsible for different aspects of any 'Thing of Things,' such as a smartphone,[37] 'a composite, multi-purpose Thing, with component Things embedded in it including its touchscreen, microphone, and other sensors.'[38] For example, should a plane equipped with 20,000 sensors be treated as a single Thing?[39] This creates huge issues of accountability, because it could be virtually impossible for a consumer to understand which component of the Thing caused harm and who is responsible for it. The manufacturer of the final Thing may try to use the composite and system-of-systems nature of the Thing to try to disclaim liability.[40] As a practical example of the legal ramifications of the Things' composite nature, one can think of wireless modules and the difficulties of complying with the relevant EU laws once these modules are no longer implemented only in laptops and mobile phones, but in any . . . Thing. Many manufactures of Things that embed third-party wireless modules which comply with the Radio Equipment Directive[41] 'assume that because these wireless modules are compliant as an independent unit, no further action is required, but this may not be the case.'[42] Indeed, the integration of a wireless module into

33 Wanshu Cong, 'Understanding Human Rights on the Internet: An Exercise of Translation?' (2017) 22 Tilburg Law Review 138.
34 Directive 2000/31/EC on certain legal aspects of information society services, in particular electronic commerce, in the Internal Market ('eCommerce Directive') [2000] OJ L 178/1.
35 eCommerce Directive, arts 12–14.
36 It must be said, however, that the current trend is towards a narrowing of the safe harbours. See e.g. Giancarlo F Frosio, 'The Death of "No Monitoring Obligations": A Story of Untameable Monsters' (2017) 8 JIPITEC <www.jipitec.eu/issues/jipitec-8-3-2017/4621>.
37 Noto La Diega and Walden (n 24).
38 W Kuan Hon, Christopher Millard and Jatinder Singh, 'Twenty Legal Considerations for Clouds of Things' [2016] Queen Mary University of London, School of Law Legal Studies Research Paper No 216/2016.
39 Bernard Marr, 'That's Data Science: Airbus Puts 10,000 Sensors in Every Single Wing!' (*Data Science Central*, 9 April 2015) <www.datasciencecentral.com/profiles/blogs/that-s-data-science-airbus-puts-10-000-sensors-in-every-single>.
40 On these issues, see Singh and others (n 40).
41 Directive 2014/53/EU on the harmonisation of the laws of the member states relating to the making available on the market of radio equipment [2014] OJ L 153/62.
42 Jean-Louis Evans, 'IoT Must Learn to Operate in a World of Wireless Regulations' [2015] Electronics Weekly 14.

a Thing 'changes the regulatory requirements,'[43] as the host product as a whole must comply with this directive and the relevant standards,[44] especially in terms of health and safety and electromagnetic compatibility.[45]

Whereas to understand – and to regulate – the IoT it is important to agree on its core technical features, one should avoid exclusively technical conceptualisations.[46] The IoT is a sociotechnological phenomenon for a twofold reason. First, in order to fully comprehend the IoT, one needs to focus on the interaction between the technology, human actors, and human processes.[47] In this vein, the European Commission High-Level Expert Group on Artificial Intelligence's *Ethics Guidelines for Trustworthy AI*[48] deal with 'socio-technical systems' and accordingly put forward that technological trustworthiness not only concerns the AI system itself 'but requires a holistic and systemic approach, encompassing the trustworthiness of all actors and processes that are part of the system's socio-technical context.'[49] Second, especially now that the IoT is beyond the hype, it is clear that it is affecting society profoundly. This is related to its being an advanced form of technological management. Indeed, as noted by Brownsword,[50] societal behaviour is increasingly managed by technological means. He underlined that technological management should not be allowed to run out of public control and called on tomorrow's jurists to 'rise to the challenge by helping their communities to grapple with the many questions raised by the accelerating transition from law (especially from the primary rules of law) to technological management.'[51] With this book, I aspire to rise to that challenge.

1.3 Two Reasons That It Is Difficult to Regulate

There are several reasons that the IoT can be seen as a phenomenon too complex to regulate.[52] The following subsections will focus on three of them that seem particularly important:

   (i) The impossibility to agree on *one* IoT taxonomy as a consequence of the many and diverse application domains and enabling technologies;

---

43 ibid 14.
44 Equipment which complies with the Harmonised Standards for this Directive is presumed to comply with the requirements of the Radio Equipment Directive. These are available at <https://ec.europa.eu/growth/single-market/european-standards/harmonised-standards/red_en>.
45 Radio Equipment Directive, art 3.
46 A recent literature review of existing IoT definitions correctly pointed out that there are two main conceptualisations of the IoT: technical and sociotechnical. Lynn and others (n 14) 2.
47 Donghee Shin, 'A Socio-Technical Framework for Internet-of-Things Design: A Human-Centered Design for the Internet of Things' (2014) 31 Telematics and Informatics 519.
48 High-Level Expert Group on Artificial Intelligence, 'Ethics Guidelines for Trustworthy AI' (2019) European Commission.
49 ibid 5.
50 Roger Brownsword, *Law, Technology and Society: Re-Imagining the Regulatory Environment* (Routledge 2019).
51 ibid 30.
52 See Noto La Diega (n 12).

(ii) The intrinsically transnational character of Things, which are located in many places at the same time (e.g. if the company providing the service is not the same as the manufacturer) and are highly mobile, as they can be carried, worn, implanted, etc.;

(iii) The 'relational black box,' i.e. the IoT's complex supply chain and intricate ecosystem that lead Thing users to enter into several relationships with different actors without necessarily being aware of it.

These factors that render difficult to regulate the IoT will be explored in the next chapter in turn.

1.3.1 A Kaleidoscope of Taxonomies: Sectoral Fragmentation and Enabling Technologies

If the IoT were a homogenous phenomenon with clear boundaries, it would be relatively easy to regulate. However, the IoT is an amorphous mass that has applications in radically different domains, relies on a number of enabling technologies, pursues a diverse range of business objectives, and has several architectural requirements, platform types, and network topologies (Figure 1.1).

For the purposes of this book, it is sufficient to focus on the first two complexities, starting off with the 'sectoral fragmentation,' i.e. the heterogeneity in IoT application domains. The regulation of other technologies is a relatively easy task when it is clear what the main sectors or applications are, as is the case, for example, with FinTech.[53] However, the IoT is used in manifold sectors, and each of them has different characteristics and raises different issues. The main IoT domains are transportation, e.g. driverless cars; domotics, popularly yet incorrectly dubbed 'smart home'; healthcare, e.g. implantable and ingestible Things; energy, e.g. smart grids; city development, i.e. so-called 'smart cities'; manufacturing, e.g. industrial robots; distribution, e.g. RFID tracking; retail, e.g. contactless payment systems; agriculture, e.g. irrigation systems; fitness, e.g. quantified-self Things; and leisure, e.g. augmented reality wearables.[54] Accordingly, it has been noted that whereas the IoT is being and will be shaped by the success of communications policy and regulation, as well as information policies, 'the IoT is likely to be applied in so many ways that policy and practice

---

53 However, the blockchain is increasingly multipurposed. See Michèle Finck, *Blockchain Regulation and Governance in Europe* (CUP 2018).

54 On some regulatory issues stemming from the IoT being a cross-technology and cross-application phenomenon, see H Song, GA Fink and S Jeschke, 'Overview of Security and Privacy in Cyber-Physical Systems' in *Security and Privacy in Cyber-Physical Systems: Foundations, Principles, and Applications* (IEEE 2017); Russ Banham, 'IoT Complexity' (2016) 63(6) Risk Management 38.

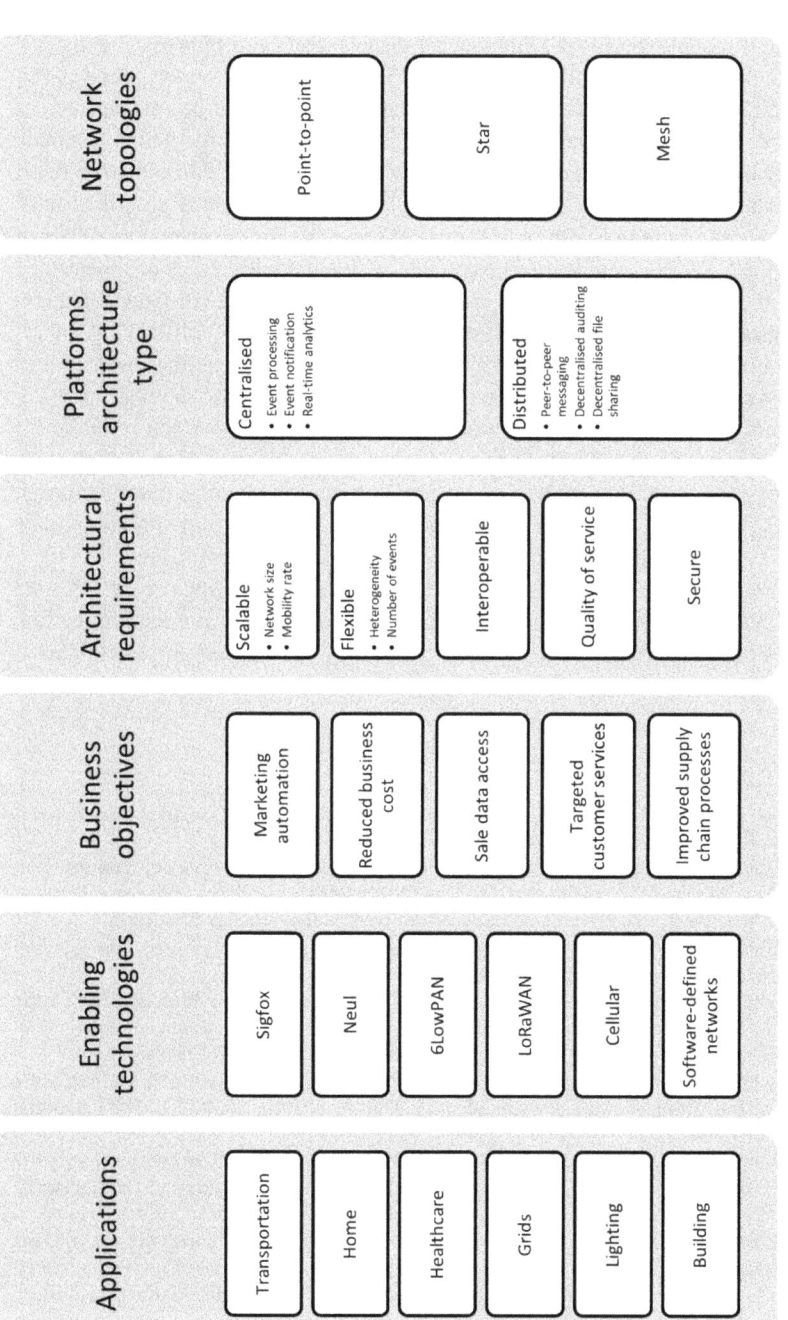

Figure 1.1 Some taxonomies of the Internet of Things. The visualisation is mine; the source of the data is I Yaqoob and others, 'Internet of Things Architecture: Recent Advances, Taxonomy, Requirements, and Open Challenges' (2017) 24 IEEE Wireless Communications 10.

will be reconfigured across nearly every sector of government, business and industry.'[55]

Whilst the deployment of Things in all these sectors can improve our lives,[56] it nonetheless raises several issues that are specific to each sector, albeit partly overlapping. For example, privacy and security are likely to be relevant across the board, but with different issues, depending on whether the Thing is inside our body or in a field of daffodils.[57] Moreover, these sectors fall under the remit of different regulators that usually operate without any form of coordination.[58] To get a sense of the problem, one should observe the fragmented approaches of Ofcom, the UK's communications regulator, in dealing with issues of spectrum;[59] Ofgem, the energy regulator, with smart meters;[60] the Centre for Connected and Autonomous Vehicles (UK Department for Transport) with self-driving cars;[61] and the UK Civil Aviation Authority with drones.[62] This begs the question if a holistic regulation is at all possible or sectoral regulations are the way forward. The status quo seems to suggest that the latter is the only option, although it is highly unsatisfactory because the IoT sectors overlap and many Things can be deployed in several sectors (e.g. are robots to be regulated as manufacturing, domotics, healthcare, leisure?). At the end of this chapter, a third way to regulate the IoT – not properly holistic, not entirely sectoral – will be proposed.

The fragmentation of the IoT does not depend only on the Things being designed for deployment in several sectors. Things can be made and/or provided for certain purposes but may end up serving other potentially unforeseen purposes. This is a consequence of what I call 'repurposing,'[63] i.e. a critical characteristic of IoT

---

55 Dutton (n 74) 4.

56 I Yaqoob and others, 'Internet of Things Architecture: Recent Advances, Taxonomy, Requirements, and Open Challenges' (2017) 24 IEEE Wireless Communications 10, 12.

57 In the field of domotics, see Department for Digital, Culture, Media & Sport, *Code of Practice for Consumer IoT Security* (UK Gov 2018) <www.gov.uk/government/publications/code-of-practice-for-consumer-iot-security/code-of-practice-for-consumer-iot-security>.

58 An exception is constituted by the *Comitato permanente per i servizi di comunicazione Machine to Machine*, which will be dealt with at the end of this chapter.

59 IoT spectrum is available on a licence-exempt basis or through a Wireless Telegraphy Act licence. Ofcom, 'VHF Radio Spectrum for the Internet of Things' (2016). Unlicensed spectrum creates because it 'requires efficient spectrum sharing among IoT devices and fair coexistence with other wireless networks' (Ghaith Hattab and Danijela Cabric, 'Unlicensed Spectrum Sharing for Massive Internet-of-Things Communications' [2019] arXiv:1903.01504 [cs] <http://arxiv.org/abs/1903.01504>).

60 Energy suppliers must take all reasonable steps to roll out smart meters to all their domestic and small business customers by the end of 2020 (Gas Supplier Standard Licence Condition 33 and Electricity Supplier Standard Licence Condition 39). See Ofgem, 'Licence Guide: Smart Metering' (2019).

61 Centre for Connected and Autonomous Vehicles, 'Code of Practice: Automated Vehicle Trialling' (2019) Department for Transport.

62 The main provisions about drones (or small unmanned aircraft) are under the Air Navigation Order, arts 94, 94A, 94B, 95, and 241.

63 Guido Noto La Diega, 'Clouds of Things: Data Protection and Consumer Law at the Intersection of Cloud Computing and the Internet of Things in the United Kingdom' (2016) 9(1) Journal of Law & Economic Regulation 69.

systems, dependent on their (inter)connectivity and system-of-systems dimension. 'Repurposing' can be understood as the phenomenon whereby an IoT system ends up being used for purposes other than those originally foreseen in two scenarios:

(i)   The communication within the relevant subsystem and among subsystems can lead the system to perform actions and produce information which the single Thing was incapable of or that could not be foreseen by its manufacturers; and

(ii) Under certain conditions (e.g. an emergency) the system may reconfigure either in an automated fashion or a user-initiated one.

A sectoral approach to regulation presupposes a static and isolated view of Things as devices that can be used only for foreseeable purposes and that are not part of a system of Things or of a system of systems. This is not the case, and for example, a wristband designed for leisure and sport purposes can become a health device, depending on the context and the interactions with other Things.

The technical complexity is another reason of the difficulty to agree on a single IoT taxonomy. At a higher level, this means that despite the IoT being advertised as making things simple,[64] the technologies involved are often unknown to the general public, which may now be familiar with the meaning of cloud computing but could still not understand what the meaning of RFID, Near-Field Communication (NFC),[65] Low Energy Bluetooth (LEB), and ZigBee is.[66] Education is needed to raise awareness on, and therefore trust in, the IoT. Technical complexity also means that computer scientists and engineers are still struggling with some technical aspects, for instance, those related to hardware constraints (small interfaces, reduced energy autonomy, difficulties in encryption), multitenancy (every Thing can be controlled by several people in numerous – potentially conflicting – ways), and the importance of tracking data throughout the systemic flow, thus ensuring integrity and validity (e.g. information flow control,[67] sticky policies,[68] etc.). The

---

64 Case C-311/11 P *Smart Technologies ULC v Office for Harmonisation in the Internal Market (Trade Marks and Designs) (OHIM)* (CJEU, 12 July 2012). In this case, regarding the mark '*Wir machen das Besondere Einfach*' (we make special things simple), the court observed that OHIM does not need ad hoc evidence when taking well-known facts into consideration in its assessment; one of them is that many undertakings assert in their advertising for smart technologies that their products are simple to use (ibid [15]).

65 Popularised by Apple Pay and Google Pay, near-field communication, or NFC, is a 'form of contactless, close proximity, radio communications based on radio-frequency identification (RFID) technology' (Rick Ayers, Sam Brothers and Wayne Jansen, Guidelines on Mobile Device Forensics) (National Institute of Standards and Technology 2014) NIST SP 800–101r1, 70). For an example of use of NFC in an IoT context, see Daniel Palma and others, 'An Internet of Things Example: Classrooms Access Control over Near Field Communication' (2014) 14 Sensors 6998.

66 ZigBee is a proprietary standard which defines a set of communication protocols and is suitable for applications with low cost, low data rate, and long battery life requirements.

67 These decentralised systems allow the controlled exchange of data between Things in compliance with pre-established policies.

68 These are machine-readable policies that 'stick' to data to define allowed usage and obligations. Sticky policies are particularly useful in the IoT because they enable a secure and privacy-compliant processing and storing of data at edges of the network.

technical complexity of the IoT begs some foundational questions. Can regulation resolve the technical problems of the IoT? Is it wise to regulate a phenomenon that is too complex to be fully understood and that has not reached maturity yet? Should regulation prevent the deployment of Things whose underlying technologies are still in their early stages and thus vulnerable? Some solutions may be provided by the technology itself; others will require legal change. It seems increasingly clear that any strategy that relies either only on technological solutions or on legal solutions would be affected by reductionist regulatory trends that go by the name of techno-legal solutionism.[69]

Understanding the enabling technologies of the IoT is important for a proper regulation of the phenomenon. Among these, connectivity deserves separate attention because it is crucial for the existence itself of the IoT and it is linked to interoperability (or lack thereof); that is one of the main reasons that it is important, yet difficult, to regulate. Things that do not connect and are not interoperable lead to what we can call the Internet of Silos, which is due mainly to two factors. First, IoT data is often held in 'silos' that are 'difficult to integrate without time-consuming data discovery and licensing.'[70] Second, IoT platforms can be vendor- and industry-specific, with few opportunities for smaller businesses to join.[71] Things are heterogeneous, and for their connectivity to function, 'different networking and communication technologies are used,'[72] such as software-defined networking,[73] cellular,[74] low-range wireless area network,[75] IPv6 over

---

69 cf Lina Dencik and Arne Hintz, 'Civil Society in an Age of Surveillance: Beyond Techno-Legal Solutionism?' (*Civil Society Futures*, 26 April 2017) <https://civilsocietyfutures.org/civil-society-in-an-age-of-surveillance-beyond-techno-legal-solutionism/>.

70 Brown (n 79) 14.

71 ibid 19.

72 Yaqoob and others (n 112).

73 Also known as SDN, this is 'a technology that allows separation of control and data planes and brings network programmability to the realm of advanced data forwarding mechanisms' (Khalid Halba and Charif Mahmoudi, 'In-Vehicle Software Defined Networking: An Enabler for Data Interoperability' *Proceedings of the 2nd International Conference on Information System and Data Mining – ICISDM '18* (ACM Press 2018)). SDN enables heterogeneous data flows to be exchanged and is therefore useful in an IoT context.

74 For long-distance operations, Things often rely on GSM, 3G, and 4G. This is seen as 'the most ideal for the sensor-based low-bandwidth-data projects' (Yaqoob and others (n 62) 12). On spectrum scarcity and cross-technology interference, see Vijay K Shah and others, 'Designing Green Communication Systems for Smart and Connected Communities via Dynamic Spectrum Access' (2018) 14 ACM Transactions on Sensor Networks 1.

75 Hailed as a key enabler of the IoT (Nicolas Ducrot and others, *LoRa Device Developer Guide* (Orange Connected Objects & Partnerships and Actility 2016)), LoRaWAN is one of the most successful technologies in the low-power wide area networking (LPWAN) space. Like all LPWAN technologies, it is characterised by low data rate and robust modulation to achieve a multikilometre communication range (Ferran Adelantado and others, 'Understanding the Limits of LoRaWAN' (2017) 55 IEEE Communications Magazine 34). Thanks to its low data rate, it features low power consumption, whilst a single gateway can cover a range of tens of kilometres and serve up to thousands of Things (ibid 40).

Low-Power Wireless Personal Area Networks,[76] Neul,[77] and Sigfox.[78] One of the reasons of this proliferation is that in the IoT, 'there is not a single solution for all the possible connectivity needs.'[79]

The Internet of Silos constitutes a threat to the functioning of the IoT – for example, if Amazon Echo cannot control noninteroperable lightbulbs. However, it goes beyond this, and it can affect the security of the IoT and, hence, user safety. Autonomous cars provide a useful case study, in that a lack of communication between the Things inside the vehicle can lead to high degree of vulnerability. If the radar system does not trigger the electronic stability control, the car may not be able to ensure user safety in high-risk situations.[80] The lack of interoperability is often due to the adoption of proprietary systems (e.g. Apple)[81] and to the limited development of generally accepted standards.[82] On the face of it, the former may be dealt with from an antitrust perspective, for example, arguing an abuse of dominant position[83] by the owner of a standard essential patent (SEP), as

76 6LowPAN is 'an adaptation layer for IPv6 that addresses device limitations by means of header compression and protocol optimizations' (The British Standards Institute, 'Intelligent Transport Systems – Communications Access for Land Mobiles (CALM) – 6LoWPAN Networking' (2016) BS ISO 19079:2016, v). IPv6, or Internet Protocol version 6, is a data communication protocol towards which traditional internet protocols (IPv4) are migrating. Since the pool of public addresses in IPv4 exhausted in 2011, the shift to the new version, which has 128-bit address, will allow every Thing to be uniquely identifiable. See International Electrotechnical Commission, 'Power Systems Management and Associated Information Exchange – Part 200: Guidelines for Migration from Internet Protocol Version 4 (IPv4) to Internet Protocol Version 6 (IPv6)' (2015) IEC TR 62357–200 6. 6LoWPAN allows several Things to be deployed in local wireless sensor networks using the 'address space of IPv6 for data and information harvesting through the Internet' (Anhtuan Le and others, '6LoWPAN: A Study on QoS Security Threats and Countermeasures Using Intrusion Detection System Approach' (2012) 25 International Journal of Communication Systems 1189).

77 Neul is a 'weightless wide range wireless networking technology designed to support IoT' (Yaqoob and others (n 62) 12).

78 As noted by Radek Fujdiak and others, 'On Track of Sigfox Confidentiality with End-to-End Encryption' *Proceedings of the 13th International Conference on Availability, Reliability and Security – ARES 2018* (ACM Press 2018), like all LPWANs, proprietary communication technology SigFox is low-cost, low-power, long-range, and it can harvest information from millions of nodes. Although it has some security issues, it strikes a balance between security, performance, and low cost (Thomas Eisenbarth and others, 'A Survey of Lightweight-Cryptography Implementations' (2007) 24 IEEE Design & Test of Computers 522).

79 Adelantado and others (n 81) refer to the low-power M2M fragmented connectivity space, but the assertion can be applied to IoT connectivity more generally.

80 Halba and Mahmoudi (n 129).

81 This is a common issue, as exemplified by Google's domotics brand Nest, which warns users that they should use Nest products (e.g. the thermostat) only with Things designated by Nest as compatible. Third-party Things that do not carry such designation may not work or may have limited functionality, and Nest disclaims all liability related to the use of unauthorised Things. See Nest Terms of Service as updated on 23 May 2018, para 4(q) <nest.com/legal/terms-of-service/>.

82 Jack Moore, 'Will Government Regulation Kill the Internet of Things?' (*Nextgov.com*, 8 December 2014) <www.nextgov.com/emerging-tech/2014/12/will-government-regulation-kill-internet-things/100695/>.

83 Giuseppe Mazziotti, 'Did Apple's Refusal to License Proprietary Information Enabling Interoperability with Its IPod Music Player Constitute an Abuse under Article 82 of the EC Treaty?' (2005) 28 World Competition 253.

will be explored in Chapter 6. As to the latter, in September 2018, ISO published the world's first standard reference architecture for the IoT.[84] This document describes the generic characteristics of IoT systems,[85] a conceptual model outlining the key concepts of the IoT,[86] a reference model,[87] and a set of architecture views, i.e. functional, system, networking, and usage view. Thus, it guides those who develop IoT systems and 'aims to give a better understanding of IoT systems to the stakeholders of such systems, including device manufacturers, application developers, customers and users.'[88] This standard is a positive development, and it may lead to the adoption of a common language in the IoT world, thus ultimately favouring interoperability and overcoming the Internet of Silos. However, four critiques can be moved to this laudable effort.

First, there is a fragmented approach to the 'law by design' question. By 'law by design' we mean the adoption of technical and organisational measures to comply with relevant laws, from the initial moments of the design of the product or service. An example of this approach is data protection by design principle that has been mandated by the GDPR.[89] The new ISO standard imperfectly deals with the 'law by design' question. For example, the standard considers compliance as one of the characteristics of an IoT system, and it refers to 'a variety of laws, policies or regulations.'[90] However, this standard regards as relevant for the IoT only the regulations that deal with interoperability, safety, radio frequencies, and consumer protection. Surprisingly, especially given the rise of the data protection by design principle, data protection laws are not considered in the compliance section. They are, conversely, separately dealt with as trustworthiness-related characteristics. Another drawback of the standard is that it refers to 'personally identifiable information' (PII), a typically American way to refer to personal data.[91] This is problematic because PII is 'any information that (a) can be used to establish a link between the information and the natural person to whom such information relates,

---

84 ISO and IEC (n 38).
85 These are divided into trustworthiness, architecture, and functional characteristics. See ibid 13.
86 These are entity, digital entity, physical entity, IoT-user, network, identity, and domain. Entities can be a person, an organisation, a Thing, a subsystem, or a combination thereof. Entities are subdivided in the Thing (physical), the IT systems (digital), the user (IoT-user), and communication networks (network). Entities are associated with identifiers that allow them to communicate with other entities. IoT systems are analysed as subsystems, where entities are grouped based on a common purpose, i.e. a domain. Subsystems and entities within a domain interact with each other and with subsystems and entities from other domains. ibid 33.
87 The overall structure of the architecture's elements is broken down into an entity-based reference model and a domain-based one. More information ibid 42–44.
88 ibid 10.
89 GDPR, art 25.
90 ISO and IEC (n 18) 25.
91 On the differences between the US and the EU approach to data protection and a proposal to bridge them, see Paul M Schwartz and Daniel J Solove, 'Reconciling Personal Information in the United States and European Union Essay' (2014) 102 California Law Review 877.

or (b) is or can be directly or indirectly linked to a natural person.'[92] Conversely, in the EU, *personal data* is broader in that it refers to 'any information relating to an identified or identifiable natural person.'[93] To determine whether a natural person is identifiable, in the EU, account must be taken of 'all the means reasonably likely to be used, such as singling out, either by the controller or by another person to identify the natural person directly or indirectly.'[94] This suggests that compliance with the standard may expose the IoT controller to a violation of EU data protection laws.

Second, it is important to keep in mind that often, despite the existence of standards, if the market is oligopolistic, there can be issues of lack of interoperability linked to proprietary software, network effects, and lock-in.[95] These could be partly resolved by tweaking the Software Directive[96] in order to expressly allow the 'sharing of interface specifications obtained by decompilation.'[97] However, this does not necessarily resolve the problems created by other intellectual property rights (e.g. trade secrets), as well as by technological protection measures and contracts.[98]

Third, even though in theory this standard is 'neutral,' as it is usable by anyone in any context, it owes much to previous standards that were developed for different applications and stakeholders,[99] namely, smart grids,[100] transport,[101] and cities;[102] thus, the result is necessarily affected and not genuinely neutral. Finally, several entities keep working on IoT standardisation in an uncoordinated fashion. These include AIOTI – the European Alliance for Internet of Things Innovation;

---

92 ISO and IEC, 'Information Technology – Security Techniques – Code of Practice for Protection of Personally Identifiable Information (PII) in Public Clouds Acting as PII Processors' (2019) r ISO/IEC 27018:2019(E) 3.2.

93 GDPR, art 4(1). Although different, the element of the 'link' has some relevance also in our jurisdiction, as exemplified by *Efifiom Edem v Information Commissioner and Financial Services Authority* [2014] EWCA Civ 92. In *Edem*, it was decided that the biographical significance and focus tests, whereby data is personal only if it has biographical significance and focuses on the individual affecting their privacy, apply only when the data requested is not obviously about an individual or clearly linked to them. Thus, the court restricted the applicability of those tests as laid out in *Durant v Financial Services Authority* [2003] EWCA Civ 1746.

94 GDPR, recital 26.

95 Sally Weston, 'Improving Interoperability by Encouraging the Sharing of Interface Specifications' (2017) 9 Law, Innovation and Technology 78.

96 Directive 2009/24/EC on the legal protection of computer programs [2009] OJ L 111/16, art 6.

97 ibid 78.

98 cf Josef Drexl, 'Designing Competitive Markets for Industrial Data. Between Propertisation and Access' (2017) 8 JIPITEC 257; Guido Noto La Diega, 'Artificial Intelligence and Databases in the Age of Big Machine Data' (2019) 25 AIDA 2018 93.

99 Brown (n 79) 13.

100 There are thirteen international standards on smart grids. See e.g. PD IEC TS 62872–1:2019 and BS IEC SRD 62913–1:2019.

101 There are eight international standards on smart transport. See e.g. BS ISO 37154:2017 and 18/30350145 DC.

102 There are fourteen international standards on smart cities. See e.g. BS ISO/IEC 30182:2017 and PAS 184:2017.

IIC – the Industrial Internet Consortium; ISO/IEC JTC 1 – Working Group 10 on the Internet of Things; ITU-T – International Telecommunications Union Joint Coordination Activity on Internet of Things and Smart Cities and Communities; as well as W3C – the World Wide Web consortium and their Web of Things interest group.[103]

The difficulty to identify one IoT taxonomy, because of the sectoral fragmentation and the technological complexity, is not the only reason that regulating the IoT is a complicated matter. Indeed, the intricacy of the supply chain is a key factor to consider.

A second element contributes to explain the difficulties in regulating the IoT and in understanding how existing laws apply to it: the intrinsically transnational character of the Things.

1.3.2 Where Are the Things? Regulation, Law, and Jurisdiction in Intrinsically Transnational Systems

As Bauman put it, in modern times, '(*p*)*ower can move with the speed of the electronic signal* – and so the time required for the movement of its essential ingredients has been reduced to instantaneity. For all practical purposes, *power has become truly exterritorial*.'[104] With the IoT, power becomes fluid in the sense that it is both territorial and extraterritorial at the same time.

To understand who should regulate the IoT, which laws apply, and which court has jurisdiction, one should geographically locate the Thing at issue. This is no easy task, given that we are talking about an inextricable mixture of hardware, software, service, and data. To respond to the question 'Where is the Thing?' it is useful to go back to the beginning of the internet, when the legitimacy of national laws to regulate cyberspace was first called into question. Being that the IoT is a species of the genus 'Internet,' it inherits the issues of the latter,[105] although they can be exacerbated, as is the case with the matter at hand.

When the internet was invented, it was perceived as a stateless space where any traditional law had to be avoided because it could have nipped in the bud a nascent industry; traditionally territorial legal categories, it was argued, could not apply to the internet.[106] Those days are long gone; the internet has become centralised and controlled by few transnational corporations that are often more powerful than states, and the latter have reacted with a proliferation of attempts to regulate the internet, with national authorities endeavouring to enforce domestic law beyond

103 Henri Barthel et al., 'GS1 and the Internet of Things' (2016).

104 Zygmunt Bauman, *Liquid Modernity* (Polity Press; Blackwell 2000) 10–11. Emphasis added.

105 ITU (n 18).

106 See, e.g. the calls on the government to leave cyberspace alone and the claim that the former had no sovereignty online, in John Perry Barlow, 'Declaration of Independence for Cyberspace.' For a criticism of his rhetorical strategies, see Aimée Hope Morrison, 'An Impossible Future: John Perry Barlow's "Declaration of the Independence of Cyberspace"' (2009) 11 New Media & Society 53.

their territories.[107] The change in the industry legitimates a change in regulatory attitudes, but it does not justify the current attempts that are often uncoordinated, not technologically aware, bordering on vexatious. Internet regulation brings to mind the pamphlet *Yet Another Effort, Frenchmen, before You Call Yourselves Republicans*, included by the Marquis de Sade in his 1795 book *Philosophy in the Bedroom*.[108] There, one can find a passionate attack on universal laws, regarded as absurd and necessarily exceptional: 'the punishment of a man for violating a law which he cannot observe is no more just than the punishment of a blind man for failing to differentiate colors.'[109] It is fair to say that the many laws of the internet are intricate – and their attempts to extraterritorial enforcement so contradictory – that many companies operating online cannot be reasonably expected to comply with all the cyberlaws, whose colours, to recall de Sade's metaphor, they cannot see. Expecting such compliance would often require that these companies infringe upon Aristotle's principle of noncontradiction.[110]

The IoT contributes to overcoming the depiction of the internet as stateless and lawless inasmuch as that depiction was predicated on the dichotomy between online and offline.[111] The rationale that the internet is a separate world where separate (no) rules apply becomes untenable when all of us have become constituent parts of the infosphere,[112] constantly online through our Things,[113] nodes of the internet infrastructure.[114] This has been regarded as a positive shift with potential for increased solidarity, empathy, and democratisation of the internet.[115] However, risks of loss of autonomy, self-determination, and privacy should not be overlooked.

Whereas there are good reasons to regulate the IoT, it is difficult to identify which authority has legitimacy to regulate, what the applicable law is, and which courts have jurisdiction[116] in a context where hardware, software, service, and data are inextricably mixed and simultaneously online and offline, with each component and subcomponent potentially being owned, controlled, or provided by several private and public entities located in different countries. The task to

---

107 Reed and Murray (n 20).
108 Marquis de Sade, *Philosophy in the Bedroom (1795)*, vol 1 (Paul J Gillette tr, Holloway House 2008).
109 ibid 283.
110 The principle (or law) of noncontradiction predates Aristotle, but its traditional source is in Aristotle's *Metaphysics* (Michael V Wedin, 'The Scope of Non-Contradiction: A Note on Aristotle's "Elenctic" Proof in Metaphysics Gamma 4' (1999) 32 Apeiron 231). Under the logical version of the principle, '(t)he most certain of all basic principles is that contradictory propositions are not true simultaneously' (Aristotle, *Metaphysics*, ll 1011b13–14).
111 Dan Jerker Svantesson, *Private International Law and the Internet* (Wolters Kluwer Law & Business 2016).
112 Floridi (n 21).
113 Svantesson (n 193).
114 Jeremy Rifkin, *The Zero Marginal Cost Society: The Internet of Things, the Collaborative Commons, and the Eclipse of Capitalism* (Palgrave Macmillan 2015).
115 ibid.
116 See, in general, Reed and Murray (n 20).

resolve complex cross-border issues has been traditionally undertaken by private international law.[117] However, perhaps surprisingly, most states' private international laws do not provide for jurisdictional claims over any internet content that can be accessed in their respective territories, let alone the application of their own laws.[118] For this reason, this section will focus on four attempts to regulate the IoT in a way that accounts for the Things' intrinsically transnational dimension. These attempts regard data protection, cross-border portability of online content, geoblocking, and free flow of nonpersonal data.

When the legal issues in the IoT started being investigated, it became clear that a problem of utmost importance concerned cross-border data flows, 'which occur when IoT devices collect data about people in one jurisdiction and transmit it to another jurisdiction with different data protection laws for processing.'[119] Whilst this problem is not specific to the IoT, it becomes more pressing with Things that generate 'big machine data'[120] and are intrinsically cross-border due to their architecture and supply chain. For example, these Things can automatically connect to other Things[121] and transmit information across borders,[122] which begs the question, to what extent can liability be placed on those who cannot predict the data flows?[123] This has practical consequences also in light of the case law epitomised by *Dow Jones & Co. Inc. v. Gutnic*[124] based on the presumption that online publication is targeted to all states on the fact that '[h]owever broad may be the reach of any particular means of communication, those who make information accessible by a particular method do so knowing of the reach that their informa-

---

117 On internet jurisdiction from a private international law perspective, see Kohl (n 9) 14–19, 75–87, and, more comprehensively, Svantesson (n 193); Faye Fangfei Wang, *Internet Jurisdiction and Choice of Law: Legal Practices in the EU, US and China* (CUP 2010). For an updated analysis see Fabrício Bertini Pasquot Polido and Lucas Costa dos Anjos (eds), *Jurisdiction and Conflicts of Law in the Digital Age. Regulatory Framework of Internet Regulation* (Institute for Research on Internet and Society 2017).

118 Svantesson (n 193).

119 Karen Rose, Scott Eldridge and Lyman Chapin, 'The Internet of Things: An Overview' (*Internet Society* 2015) 3.

120 *Big machine data* refers to big data generated and processed by machines (e.g. IoT and AI) and usually considered nonpersonal (also called 'industrial data'). Noto La Diega, 'Artificial Intelligence and Databases in the Age of Big Machine Data' (n 154).

121 As noted by the FBI, Things use Universal Plug and Play protocol to remotely connect and communicate to a network automatically without authentication; 'this protocol is designed to self-configure when attached to an IP address, making it vulnerable to exploitation' FBI, 'Internet of Things Poses Opportunities for Cyber Crime' (10 September 2015) <www.ic3.gov/media/2015/150910.aspx>.

122 ibid 35.

123 In the IoT, other privacy-related issues of territorial laws regard forensics. Indeed, it may happen that a forensic investigator is in one jurisdiction and the data reside in another jurisdiction, where the privacy laws are not harmonised. On this point, see S. Zawoad and R. Hasan, 'FAIoT: Towards Building a Forensics Aware Eco System for the Internet of Things' *2015 IEEE International Conference on Services Computing* (2015).

124 [2002] HCA 56 [39]), as cited in Case C-618/15 *Concurrence Sàrl v Samsung Electronics France SAS and Amazon Services Europe Sàrl* [2016] ECR, Opinion of AG Wathelet [64].

tion may have.'[125] Such foreseeability would seem to be less certain in a time of automated IoT communications.

A well-known way to deal with the issue is the GDPR's very broad extraterritorial application clause.[126] Whilst the GDPR's extraterritorial clause could be seen as an extreme way of dealing with the transnational nature of many sociotechnological phenomena, including the IoT, the following section will deal with three understudied and overall more moderate strategies, all of which fall under the so-called Digital Single Market (DSM).[127] The idea dates back to 2005, when the European Commission launched i2010, a strategy aiming primarily to 'establish a European information space, i.e. a true single market for the digital economy.'[128] Only three years later, however, during the midterm review, the Commission identified new themes to consider for a longer-term agenda for the EU that included, for the first time expressly, 'the DSM.'[129] The latter became a goal of the EU in 2015, when the *DSM Strategy*[130] was launched with the aim to create a single market where 'the free movement of goods, persons, services and capital is ensured and where individuals and businesses can seamlessly access and exercise online activities,' irrespective of nationality or residence, pursuant to fair competition, consumer protection, and data protection. The pillars of the DSM strategy are access, environment, economy, and society. First, the implementation promises to lead to better access for consumers and businesses to digital goods and services across Europe. For example, the new Payment Services Directive[131] made sure that new providers of innovative payment services could compete on equal terms,[132] while ensuring high levels of security through strong customer authentication.[133] Second,

---

125 ibid.
126 GDPR, art 3. For an in-depth analysis of this provision, see European Data Protection Board, 'Guidelines 3/2018 on the Territorial Scope of the GDPR (Article 3)' (2018) Text <https://edpb. europa.eu/our-work-tools/public-consultations/2018/guidelines-32018-territorial-scope-gdpr-article-3_en>; Brendan Van Alsenoy, 'Reconciling the (Extra) Territorial Reach of the GDPR with Public International Law' in Gert Vermeulen and Eva Lievens (eds), *Data Protection and Privacy under Pressure* (Maklu 2017).
127 European Commission, 'Communication "A DSM Strategy for Europe"' (2015) COM/2015/192 final.
128 European Commission, 'Communication "Preparing Europe's Digital Future. I2010 Mid-Term Review" (I2010 Annual Information Society Report 2008), COM(2008)199' (2008) [1].
129 European Commission, 'Commission SWD – Europe's Digital Competitiveness Report: Main Achievements of the I2010 Strategy 2005–2009 (SEC/2009/1060 Final)' (2009).
130 European Commission, 'Communication "A DSM Strategy for Europe" (COM/2015/192 final)' (2015).
131 Directive (EU) 2015/2366 on payment services in the internal market ('PSD2') [2015] OJ L 337/35.
132 PSD2, art 35.
133 This is multifactor authentication based on two or more of the following: something only the user knows (e.g. password), something only the user possesses (e.g. one's own phone), and biometric data. See Elizabeth Kennedy and Christopher Millard, 'Data Security and Multi-Factor Authentication: Analysis of Requirements under EU Law and in Selected EU Member States' (2016) 32 CLSR 91.

it aims to create the right conditions and a level playing field for digital networks and innovative services to flourish (e.g. the end of roaming charges).[134] Third, it wants to maximise the growth potential of the digital economy.[135] For example, since 2019 online marketplaces and search engines must disclose the main parameters they use to rank goods and services.[136] Whilst the DSM strategy may greatly benefit IoT stakeholders, it seems vitiated by the reliance on the same dichotomies that the IoT disrupted. The idea itself of a separate 'digital' strategy, for example, reflects the outdated view of a divide between online and offline.

The strategy has led to 28 legislative interventions,[137] the most (in)famous[138] of which is the EU reform of copyright,[139] introducing the so-called upload filter[140] and a new publishers' right.[141] Whilst sharing the concerns that this reform risks being useless if not dangerous,[142] the DSM Copyright Directive does not tackle any of the cross-border issues that are important for the IoT. Therefore, the focus of this section will be on three other DSM measures that are relevant from a cross-border and IoT perspective: the reforms of portability of online content services, geoblocking, and free flow of nonpersonal data.

In 2020, the DSM strategy was rebranded 'European Digital Strategy' and led, most famously, to the Digital Services Act and the Digital Markets Act.[143]

---

134 Regulation (EU) 2015/2120 laying down measures concerning open internet access [2015] OJ L 310/1, art 1(2).
135 European Commission, 'A DSM Strategy for Europe' (n 286).
136 Regulation (EU) 2019/1150 on promoting fairness and transparency for business users of online intermediation services [2019] OJ L 186/57, art 5.
137 See 'Shaping the DSM' (*European Commission*, 29 October 2020) <https://ec.europa.eu/digital-single-market/en/shaping-digital-single-market>.
138 See e.g. Lionel Bently et al., 'EU Copyright Reform Proposals Unfit for the Digital Age. Open Letter to Members of the European Parliament and the Council of the European Union' (24 February 2017) <www.create.ac.uk/wp-content/uploads/2017/02/OpenLetter_EU_Copyright_Reform_24_02_2017.pdf>; Marco Ricolfi et al., 'Academics against Press Publishers' Right: 169 European Academics Warn Against It' (26 April 2018) <www.ivir.nl/publicaties/download/Academics_Against_Press_Publishers_Right.pdf>; João Quintais, 'The New Copyright in the DSM Directive: A Critical Look' [2019] EIPR.
139 Directive (EU) 2019/790 of 17 April 2019 on copyright and related rights in the DSM and amending Directives 96/9/EC and 2001/29/EC [2019] OJ L 130/92 ('C-DSM Directive').
140 C-DSM Directive, art 17.
141 C-DSM Directive, art 15.
142 See Ted Shapiro, 'EU Copyright Will Never Be the Same: A Comment on the Proposed Directive on Copyright for the DSM (DSM)' (2016) 38 EIPR 771; Giuseppe Colangelo and Mariateresa Maggiolino, 'ISPs' Copyright Liability in the EU DSM Strategy' (2018) 26 International Journal of Law and Information Technology 142.
143 Proposal for a Regulation of the European Parliament and of the Council on a Single Market For Digital Services and amending Directive 2000/31/EC (Digital Services Act or DSA) COM/2020/825 final; Proposal for a Regulation of the European Parliament and of the Council on contestable and fair markets in the digital sector (Digital Markets Act or DMA) COM (2020) 842. At the time of writing, a political agreement has been reached with regard to both of them but they have not been published in the Official Journal of the European Union. For a critical appraisal see e.g. Martin Senftleben and Christina Angelopoulos, 'The Odyssey of the

*1.3.2.1 Netflix Law: The Cross-Border Service Portability Regulation
and the Indirect Reform of Copyright's Territoriality:
Ubiquitous Access to Online Content Services for
Ubiquitous Computing*

Whereas providers of traditional 'offline' services have been relying on the EU Treaties' freedoms since at least 1974,[144] until recently the same was not always true for online services.[145]

The resulting fragmentation of the audiovisual media market was – and to some extent still is – mainly due to the principle of territoriality of copyright, including broadcasting rights.[146] Most Europeans access copyright content, such as films and music online, increasingly through Things other than computers.[147] Therefore, the resulting discriminatory practices adversely affected IoT providers and consumers, since the whole point of buying (or renting) a Thing and not a traditional device is to access its 'smart' components, which often entail audiovisual content. This is reflected in the rise of the concept of complex multimedia product in European jurisprudence.[148] If a consumer travels from one member state to another and, by doing so, can no longer use the Thing because the audiovisual content becomes unavailable, this would profoundly affect the Thing as a whole. Let us imagine that a consumer buys an Amazon Echo in the UK and then relocates to Italy to write a book about the IoT; if the consumer can no longer access Echo's services, they are left with an expensive Coke can–shaped speaker.

A reform of copyright's principle of territoriality would have been the ideal way to overcome some of these issues. Instead, in June 2017 the EU introduced the Cross-Border Service Portability Regulation.[149] This recognised that the 'proliferation of portable devices such as laptops, tablets and smartphones are increasingly facilitating the use of online content services by providing access to

Prohibition on General Monitoring Obligations on the Way to the Digital Services Act: Between Article 15 of the E-Commerce Directive and Article 17 of the Directive on Copyright in the DSM' (*SSRN*, 22 October 2020) <https://papers.ssrn.com/abstract=3717022>.

144 Since Case 33/74 *van Binsbergen v Bestuur van de Bedrijfsvereniging voor de Metaalnijverheid* [1974] ECR 1299 [26], the Court of Justice recognised the direct effect of Article 56 TFEU (then Article 49 Treaty establishing the European Community [2002] OJ C 325/33) insofar as it seeks to abolish restrictions on the freedom to provide services stemming from the fact that the service provider is established in a member state other than that in which the service is to be provided.

145 Regulation (EU) 2017/1128 on cross-border portability of online content services in the internal market [2017] OJ L 168/1 ('Cross-Border Service Portability Regulation'), recital 1.

146 Benjamin Farrand, 'The EU Portability Regulation: One Small Step for Cross-Border Access, One Giant Leap for Commission Copyright Policy?' (2016) 38 EIPR 321; Giuseppe Mazziotti and Felice Simonelli, 'Another Breach in the Wall: Copyright Territoriality in Europe and Its Progressive Erosion on the Grounds of Competition Law' (2016) 18 info 55.

147 Kantar Public, *Flash Eurobarometer 477a. Report 'Accessing Content Online and Cross-Border Portability of Online Content Services'* (European Commission 2019).

148 More on this in Chapter 6.

149 The Cross-Border Service Portability Regulation is applicable as of 20 March 2018.

them regardless of the location of consumers.'[150] Accordingly, it introduced the cross-border portability of online content services, by ensuring that subscribers to portable, paid-for[151] online content services (e.g. Netflix and Spotify) 'which are lawfully provided in their Member State of residence can access and use those services when temporarily present in a Member State other than their Member State of residence.'[152] Thus, the regulation overcame the main barrier to the free movement of audiovisual content throughout the EU, which stemmed from the fact that the 'rights for the transmission of content protected by copyright or related rights, such as audiovisual works, are often licensed on a territorial basis.'[153] This hinders the DSM because the acquisition of a licence for relevant rights is not always possible, in particular when rights in content are licensed on an exclusive basis.[154]

From this book's perspective, this regulation is relevant for at least six reasons. First, although this regulation does not have a provision on the territorial scope of the jurisdiction, it can be inferred that it only applies to the companies with an establishment in a member state and providing online content services to consumers in the European Economic Area.[155] Hence, a moderate approach to jurisdiction without overreaching risks. Second, more generally, it acknowledges the importance of ensuring ubiquitous access to audiovisual contents, broadcasts, and other protected works in an IoT world. Third, allowing lawful users of audiovisual content and broadcasts to retain access to the relevant online services if temporarily abroad is an insufficient response to the problems connected to copyright's territoriality, which would have been better resolved in the context of a copyright reform. The territoriality of copyright laws is still an issue that, if not adequately resolved, will keep preventing the IoT from growing.[156] Indeed, a more organic and ideally international reform of copyright, including territoriality and subject matter,[157] is needed because we live in an age where copyright materials circulate through digital flows that cross border continuously; in such an age, some pre-internet principles are no longer fit for their purpose.[158] Fourth, this regulation for

---

150 Cross-Border Service Portability Regulation, recital 2.
151 The regulation applies to paid online content services; free services are free to decide whether or not to provide portability to their subscribers (art 6).
152 Cross-Border Service Portability Regulation, recital 2.
153 Cross-Border Service Portability Regulation, recital 4.
154 Cross-Border Service Portability Regulation, recital 10.
155 This is confirmed by the fact that the regulation no longer applies to UK-EEA travel. As of January 2021, UK customers visiting the EEA and vice versa may see restrictions to the content available to them. 'Cross-Border Portability of Online Content Services' (*Gov.UK*, 30 January 2021) <www.gov.uk/guidance/cross-border-portability-of-online-content-services>.
156 A first comprehensive analysis of the intersection between copyright and telecommunications law can be found in Monica Horten, *The Copyright Enforcement Enigma: Internet Politics and the "Telecoms Package"* (Palgrave MacMillan 2012).
157 E.g. sport events are not protected by copyright or related rights under Union law but are sometimes protected nationally by copyright, related rights, or other specific legislation. Cross-Border Service Portability Regulation, recital 5.
158 Farrand (n 188) sees this regulation as an indirect reform of copyright and expresses the wish for a proper EU copyright reform.

the first time openly confesses the real purpose of consumer laws, that is, not protecting consumers as such. Consumers are protected only as a means to the actual end of realising a more competitive market.[159] Indeed, the opening of the regulation is adamant in stating that the reasons for ensuring seamless access to online content services throughout the EU are 'the smooth functioning of the internal market and . . . the effective application of the principles of free movement of persons and services.'[160] Fifth, the Cross-Border Service Portability Regulation, like the GDPR,[161] recognises that private ordering by means of contracts (including copyright licences) can frustrate the public interest, be it the fundamental rights to privacy and data protection or, in this instance, the principle of free competition. Indeed, it provides that '[a]ny *contractual provisions* . . . which are contrary to this Regulation, including those which prohibit cross-border portability of online content services or limit such portability to a specific time period, shall be *unenforceable.*'[162] This legal innovation explains Netflix's vaguely worded terms of use, whereby

> You may view the Netflix content primarily within the country in which you have established your account and only in geographic locations where we offer our service and have licensed such content. The content that may be available to watch will vary by geographic location and will change from time to time.[163]

These terms must be interpreted as not allowing restrictions for intra-EEA travellers. The unenforceability of contractual circumventions echoes similar provisions whereby contracts that purport to circumvent copyright defences are null and void.[164] These are becoming increasingly common, as illustrated by the copyright in the DSM Directive. Nor are they limited to copyright and business-to-consumer contracts in the audiovisual market. For example, as of July 2020, the

---

159 The idea that consumer laws have the chief (hidden) purpose of fostering 'perfect' competition has already been argued by many scholars. See Luca Nivarra, *Diritto Privato e Capitalismo: Regole Giuridiche e Paradigmi Di Mercato* (Editoriale Scientifica 2010) 97; Armando Plaia, 'Profili Evolutivi Della Tutela Contrattuale' [2018] Eur Dir Priv 69. See the latter also for some useful bibliographic references (ibid 71, fn 8).

160 Cross-Border Service Portability Regulation, recital 1.

161 cf Case C-210/16 *Unabhangiges Landeszentrum fur Datenschutz Schleswig-Holstein v Wirtschaftsakademie Schleswig-Holstein GmbH* [2019] 1 WLR 119.

162 Cross-Border Service Portability Regulation, art 7. Italics added.

163 Netflix Terms of Use, as of 1 January 2021 <https://help.netflix.com/legal/termsofuse>.

164 See e.g. Directive 2009/24/EC of 23 April 2009 on the legal protection of computer programs ('Software Directive') [2009] OJ L 111/16, art 8; Directive 96/9/EC of 11 March 1996 on the legal protection of databases ('Database Directive') [1996] OJ L 77/20, art 15. Positively, in introducing exceptions for text and data mining for research purposes, cross-border teaching, and preservation of cultural heritage, the C-DSM Directive provided that '[a]ny contractual provision contrary to the(se) exceptions . . . shall be unenforceable' (art 7).

Platform to Business Regulation[165] imposes fairer and transparent terms in the relationships between business users and providers of online intermediation services. Non-compliant terms and changes without notice are 'null and void, that is, deemed to have never existed, with effects *erga omnes* and *ex tunc*.'[166] Although this prevalence of statutory provisions on contractual terms does not apply across the board, it is hoped that it will become a standard feature of the regulation of online relationships as it contributes to tackling a power imbalance that the IoT has nothing but exacerbated.

Finally, the Cross-Border Service Portability Regulation's scope relies on the divide between free and paid-for services.[167] The rationale of the exclusion of providers of online content services that are provided without payment of money is that these companies could not afford the 'disproportionate costs'[168] of compliance, for example, to implement a mechanism to verify the member state of residence of the subscribers.[169] This may sound naive to those who are aware that, with the advent of the business models that have replaced subscription fees with the harnessing of the users' personal data, the free/paid-for distinction no longer holds.[170]

Another measure that tackles the tension between transnationality of Things and territoriality of laws is the Geoblocking Regulation,[171] which can be seen as complementing the right to service portability.

1.3.2.2 The EU Ban on Unjustified Geoblocking or the Illusion of Realising a DSM without Reforming Intellectual Property Laws

Applicable as of 3 December 2018, the Geoblocking Regulation ensures that consumers can access goods and services online without worrying about discrimination or geographically based restrictions. Traders would adopt geoblocking and other discriminatory practices that denied or limited access to goods or services by customers wishing to engage in cross-border transactions. Geoblocking occurs when these customers have no or limited access to other member states' traders' online interfaces (e.g. unavailable websites and apps).[172] For example, an Echo Show bought in the UK may not provide access to Amazon's shopping interface

---

165 Regulation (EU) 2019/1150 of 20 June 2019 on promoting fairness and transparency for business users of online intermediation services (P2B Regulation) [2019] OJ L 186/57.

166 Platform-to-Business Regulation, recital 20; art 3(3).

167 Cross-Border Service Portability Regulation, art 6.

168 Cross-Border Service Portability Regulation, recital 20.

169 Cross-Border Service Portability Regulation, recital 20.

170 cf Sarah Spiekermann and others, 'The Challenges of Personal Data Markets and Privacy' (2015) 25 Electronic Markets 161.

171 Regulation (EU) 2018/302 of 28 February 2018 on addressing unjustified geoblocking and other forms of discrimination based on customers' nationality, place of residence or place of establishment within the internal market and amending Regulations (EC) No 2006/2004 and (EU) 2017/2394 and Directive 2009/22/EC [2018] OJ L 60I/1 (Geoblocking Regulation).

172 Cross-Border Service Portability Regulation, recital 1.

if the user carried the device to Italy.[173] 'Other discriminatory practices,' in turn, occurs when, despite the absence of objective reasons, certain traders apply different general conditions of access to their goods and services with respect to such customers from other member states.[174] Linking back to the IoT, this would be the case if Google Home used the GPS sensor to offer personalised pricing.

To tackle the more general underlying problem, the Geoblocking Regulation introduced four main provisions, i.e. the prohibition to:

(i) Block or limit consumers' access to an online interface;
(ii) Redirect consumers to a version of an online interface based on their nationality or place of residence that is different from the online interface to which the consumers first sought access;
(iii) Apply different general conditions of access when selling goods or providing services in situations laid down in the Geoblocking Regulation; and
(iv) Accept payment instruments issued in another member state on a discriminatory basis.

Overall, if implemented and enforced adequately, the Geoblocking Regulation may benefit IoT stakeholders and consumers because it prevents fragmentation and overcomes the online-offline divide, in that it applies to both online and offline sales of goods and services, 'as well as cases where these two channels are integrated.'[175] However, there are at least three reasons for criticism.

First, the regulation does not outlaw geoblocking and discriminatory practices as such, but only to the extent and in the event that they are not objectively justified. What an *objective justification* means is not entirely clear. Article 4 defines certain situations 'where there can be no justified reason,'[176] but it does not define the concept of 'objective justification.' For instance, traders are never justified when they discriminate against customers that seek to receive services from a trader, other than electronically supplied services, in a physical location within the territory of a member state where the trader operates.[177] Even in these scenarios where the discrimination is considered unjustified by the regulation, geoblocking or differential treatment may still be allowed where an EU or national legal requirement (in compliance with EU law) obliges the trader to block access to the goods or services offered.[178] If understanding which discriminatory practices are unjustified is difficult, having a grasp of what is 'objectively justified' is a Sisyphean task. The regulation does not say much apart from the fact that '[d]ifferent

---

173 It is worth noting that this regulation no longer applies to the UK as of 1 January 2021.
174 Cross-Border Service Portability Regulation, recital 1.
175 European Commission, *Questions & Answers on the Geo-Blocking Regulation in the Context of e-Commerce* (European Union 2018) 10.
176 ibid 7.
177 Geoblocking Regulation, art 4(1)(c).
178 European Commission, *Geo-Blocking Regulation in the Context of e-Commerce* (n 335) 8, that makes the example a French website subject to an order issued by the French courts that prevents access to its website because of litigation on the use of trademarks in France.

treatment . . . should be based only on objective and well justified reasons.'[179] The European Commission's guidance[180] does not meaningfully elaborate on this point. It tells the reader that the general prohibition of discrimination on grounds of nationality[181] is specified by the Services Directive,[182] which allows differences in the conditions of access where those differences are directly justified by objective criteria. Examples of these are the lack of the required IPRs in a particular territory and the additional costs incurred because of the distance involved or the technical characteristics of the provision of the service.[183] To understand what can be objectively justified, one can also consider EU antitrust case law on discrimination of consumers by nationality and/or residence.[184] For example, in the *Deutsche Post AG* case,[185] the world's largest courier company was held to be abusively imposing discriminatory pricing to letter mail coming from the UK as 'different tariffs . . . cannot be justified on the basis of objective economic factors [as they do not have] sufficient or reasonable relationship to real costs or to the real value of the service provided.'[186] The lack of guidance affects that same legal certainty that the regulation wanted to improve.[187] For example, it is difficult to foresee how Alibaba's Transaction Service Agreement will play out in European courts as much as it provides that

> The types of Online Transactions and other benefits, features and functions of the Transaction Services available to a registered member may vary for different countries and regions. No warranty or representation is given that the same type and extent of transactions, benefits, features and functions will be available to all members.[188]

This agreement cannot be interpreted as giving the Chinese e-commerce giant discretion as to carry out discriminatory practices, including geoblocking: they have to be based on objective and well-justified reasons.

---

179 Geoblocking Regulation, recital 33.
180 European Commission, *Geo-Blocking Regulation in the Context of e-Commerce* (n 335).
181 TFEU, art 18; Charter of Fundamental Rights of the EU, art 21(2).
182 Art 20(2).
183 Directive 2006/123/EC of 12 December 2006 on services in the internal market ('Services Directive') [2006] OJ L 376/36, recital 95; European Commission, 'SWD with a View to Establishing Guidance on the Application of Article 20(2) of Directive 2006/123/EC on Services in the Internal Market ('the Services Directive')' (2012) SWD/2012/0146 final.
184 More on this case law in Wolf Sauter, 'Discrimination of Consumers in EU Competition Law' (2019) 40 ECLR 511.
185 2001/892/EC: Commission Decision of 25 July 2001 relating to a proceeding under Article 82 of the EC Treaty (COMP/C-1/36.915 – *Deutsche Post AG – Interception of Cross-border mail*) [2001] OJ L331/40.
186 ibid [127], [167].
187 Geoblocking Regulation, recital 2.
188 Alibaba Transaction Services Agreement, as of 16 January 2021, point 2.3 <https://rule.alibaba.com/rule/detail/2054.htm>.

Second, with regards to the prohibition to apply different general conditions to the access to goods and services, the weak point is that the provision does not apply to 'services the main feature of which is the provision of access to and use of copyright protected works or other protected subject matter.'[189] The regulation is designed not to affect the rules applicable in the field of copyright and neighbouring rights.[190] It follows that copyright and other intellectual property rights (IPRs) may also nullify the effect of other geoblocking-related prohibitions. For example, the provision that allows the block of the access to online interfaces and the redirection when 'necessary in order to ensure compliance with a legal requirement'[191] may be interpreted as meaning that said block and redirection are permitted when they have the purpose of protecting copyright materials. Given the fact that many aspects of a Thing are covered by IPRs,[192] it is fair to say that copyright – including licences and technical protection measures – may be used to factually reintroduce discriminatory access conditions for Thing users based on their nationality, residence, or establishment, thus effectively sidestepping the prohibition of geoblocking and other discriminatory practices. If the Cross-Border Service Portability Regulation was open to criticism because it constituted an indirect and imperfect way to reform copyright's territoriality, the Geoblocking Regulation is worse in that it rests on the illusion that IP-enabled discriminatory practices can be resolved without dealing with IP in the first place. Along the same lines, the latter regulation excludes audiovisual services from the scope of the regulation.[193] This means that IoT manufacturers could geoblock some of their services, thus affecting the 'smartness' of the Thing as a whole. In November 2020, the Commission reported on the evaluation of this regulation.[194] This could have been the opportunity to extend it to copyright content and audiovisual services; this would have greatly benefitted IoT stakeholders and consumers. Instead, the Commission concluded that, despite the potential benefits for consumers, the inclusion of copyright-protected content needs to be further assessed,[195] and it

---

189 Geoblocking Regulation, art 4(1)(b).

190 Geoblocking Regulation, art 1(5).

191 Geoblocking Regulation, art 3(3).

192 Noto La Diega, 'Software Patents' (n 78).

193 Services Directive, art 2(2)(g). The Geoblocking Regulation, art 1(3), excludes from its scope the same services excluded by the Services Directive. Alongside audiovisual services, the directive – and hence the regulation – regrettably exclude a number of activities that are important in the DSM, such as transport and gambling. This has a direct impact on the sharing economy, since the Court of Justice has decided that Uber and the likes offer a service in the field of transport, hence excluded from the Services Directive, as well as Article 56 TFEU and the eCommerce Directive) [2000] OJ L 178/1 (Case C-434/15 *Elite Taxi v Uber* (CJEU, 20 December 2017).

194 European Commission, 'Report on the First Short-Term Review of the Geo-Blocking Regulation WD(2020)294final}' (2020) COM(2020) 766 final.

195 This decision was based on Richard Procee and others, 'Study on the Impacts of the Extension of the Scope of the Geo-Blocking Regulation to Audiovisual and Non-Audiovisual Services Giving Access to Copyright Protected Content' (2020) Directorate-General for Communications Networks, Content and Technology.

will launch a stakeholder dialogue with the audiovisual sector in order to improve consumers' access to audiovisual content across the EU.[196]

Third, the geographical scope of the Geoblocking Regulation is not entirely clear. A passage in one of the recitals[197] reads that the regulation aims to further clarify the Services Directive by defining certain situations where different treatment based on nationality, place of residence, or place of establishment cannot be justified. However, geoblocking 'can also arise as a consequence of actions by traders established in third countries, which fall outside the scope of that Directive.'[198] This, coupled with the fact that – unlike the Cross-Border Service Portability Regulation[199] – 'service' is defined by referring to Article 57 TFEU and not also to Article 56 (only the latter refers to an establishment in the EU), creates the risk that the regulation may be interpreted as applicable to all online provision of goods and services within the European Economic Area (EEA) regardless of the establishment. Only purely internal situations, where all the relevant elements of the transaction are confined within one single member state, would be out of the scope.[200] Should this be the case – as suggested by the European Commission's[201] and industry guidance[202] – this would be an instance of jurisdictional overreach similar to the GDPR. By contrast, the DSM measure that will be analysed in the next section constitutes a more moderate solution to IoT's transnationality.

1.3.2.3 *The Free-Flow of Nonpersonal Data Regulation between the Ban on Data Localisation Laws and the Outdated Personal/ Nonpersonal Data Binary*

To realise the DSM, the Commission felt that ensuring service portability and geoblocking was not enough. There was the need to address the portability of data as such; without it, there was the risk that, practically, IoT users could not avail themselves of service portability because services may be, in principle, portable, but data would still be locked in. It has been noted that '[l]imited user access to raw IoT data reduce(d) ability to switch providers (and to understand privacy implications).'[203] To overcome this issue, the EU adopted another DSM measure:

---

196 Annette Broocks and others, 'Geo-Blocking: A Literature Review and New Evidence in Online Audio-Visual Services' (2020) JRC Digital Economy WP 2020–01.
197 Geoblocking Regulation, recital 4.
198 ibid.
199 Art 2(5).
200 Geoblocking Regulation, art 1(2).
201 As pointed out in European Commission, Geo-Blocking Regulation in the Context of e-Commerce (n 335) 13, traders established in non-EU countries that operate in the EU are therefore subject to the Geoblocking Regulation.
202 See e.g. Fabian Fechner et al., 'FAQ on the Implementation of the Geoblocking Regulation' (*Eurocommerce EU*) <www.eurocommerce.eu/media/155816/eurocommerce_faq_on_the_ implementation_of_the_geoblocking_regulation_readonly.pdf>.
203 Brown (n 108) 20.

the Free Flow of Non-Personal Data Regulation, applicable as of 28 May 2019, introducing some IoT-relevant news. Unlike the GDPR, it does not apply to the processing of data of generic 'data subjects who are in the Union'; instead, it applies only to those who formally reside or have an establishment in the EU. Moreover, the 'offering of goods or services' does not trigger EU jurisdiction; only the provision of services of electronic processing of nonpersonal data does.

The main innovation is that nonpersonal data can now be stored and processed anywhere in the EU, and accordingly, '[d]ata localisation requirements shall be prohibited.' For example, laws such as the Danish Bookkeeping Act imposing the storage of financial data of Danish citizens in Denmark or other Nordic country may need to be amended. This is important because Things produce considerable amounts of nonpersonal data (so-called industrial data),[204] and data localisation laws would prevent the availability of all those Things whose data constantly flows from one member state to another and where storage (including cloud storage) may well take place in a country other than the manufacturer's. For example, if one uses an Amazon Thing, e.g. Echo or Kindle, the '[i]nformation provided to Amazon may be processed in the cloud to improve [one's] experience and [Amazon's] products and services, and may be stored on servers outside the country in which [one] live[s].'[205]

Another provision of interest for IoT stakeholders aims to make it easier for professional users to switch cloud service providers. It was felt that whereas consumer law already smoothens switching in business-to-consumer transactions,[206] there were not similar provisions for business-to-business relationships. Therefore, the Free Flow of Non-Personal Data Regulation entrusted the Commission with the task of facilitating the adoption of codes of conduct that consider best practices for facilitating the switching of service providers and the portability of data in a structured, commonly used, and machine-readable format.[207] Outsourcing at least part of the processing to cloud providers is a common practice in the IoT (hence the 'Cloud of Things'),[208] and ensuring the possibility of switching providers and port data, especially in open standard formats, will be crucial for better-quality and interoperable Things.[209] The codes of conduct should mandate open standard formats, 'where required or requested by the service provider receiving the data.'[210] Since openness is pivotal to interoperability and the latter

---

204 As recognised by the Free Flow of Non-Personal Data, '(t)he expanding Internet of Things, artificial intelligence and machine learning, represent major sources of non-personal data, for example as a result of their deployment in automated industrial production processes' (recital 9).

205 Point 3(a) of Amazon Device Terms of Use <www.amazon.com/gp/help/customer/display.html?nodeId=202002080> accessed 20 September 2018.

206 See e.g. Directive (EU) 2019/944 on common rules for the internal market for electricity [2019] OJ L 158/125.

207 Free Flow of Non-Personal Data Regulation, art 6(1)(a).

208 Noto La Diega, 'Clouds of Things' (n 119).

209 Libing Wu and others, 'Efficient and Secure Searchable Encryption Protocol for Cloud-Based Internet of Things' (2018) 111 Journal of Parallel and Distributed Computing 152.

210 Free Flow of Non-Personal Data Regulation, art 6(1)(a).

is crucial for the IoT to avoid the 'Internet of Silos,' it can be argued that the IoT requires openness. Accordingly, the codes of conduct should recommend open standards at least when cloud services are provided in an IoT context.

Finally, the Free Flow of Non-Personal Data Regulation acknowledges that the IoT is 'raising novel legal issues surrounding questions of access to and reuse of data, liability, ethics and solidarity.'[211] Perhaps the regulation itself was not the best place to deal with these issues, but it is to be hoped that from their awareness specific initiatives will follow.

The combination of personal data portability,[212] service portability,[213] ban on unjustified geoblocking,[214] ban on data localisation requirements,[215] and the principle of exhaustion[216] may be useful for the development of the IoT, increasing user control over the Thing, facilitating its circulation throughout the EU, removing obstacles to full interoperability, and preventing lock-in. Full portability – of data, service, and content – will become even more important in the future IoT, when an increasing number of Things will be implanted in our body. If some of the components of one's smart insulin pump are not portable, this would ultimately impact the free movement of persons.

The strategy of complementing the GDPR with a separate ad hoc regulation on nonpersonal data could be criticised because of two dichotomies that the IoT is disrupting: personal-nonpersonal and good-service. This regulation relies on the assumption that whilst personal data should be protected, nonpersonal data are a commodity that should be subject to the usual free market imperatives.[217] This approach is predicated on the dichotomy between personal and nonpersonal data. The latter is untenable because anonymisation does not always prevent reidentification,[218] and in the IoT, ostensibly nonpersonal and even raw data can be combined to identify individuals.[219] And indeed, the guidance that the

---

211 Free Flow of Non-Personal Data Regulation, recital 1. Alongside the IoT, this recital refers to other emerging technologies, i.e. artificial intelligence, autonomous systems, and 5G.

212 GDPR, art 20.

213 Cross-Border Portability Regulation, art 3.

214 Geoblocking Regulation, arts 3–5.

215 Free Flow of Non-Personal Data Regulation, art 4.

216 Pursuant to the principle of exhaustion, IP holders cannot prohibit their use in relation to goods which have been put on the market in the Union by holder or with the latter's consent.

217 This is despite the European Commission's awareness that in the data economy, most datasets are a mix of personal and nonpersonal data, 'thanks to technological developments such as the Internet of Things (i.e. digitally connecting objects), artificial intelligence and technologies enabling big data analytics' (European Commission, 'Guidance on the Regulation on a Framework for the Free Flow of Non-Personal Data in the European Union' (2019) COM/2019/250 final [2.2]).

218 Paul Ohm, 'Broken Promises of Privacy: Responding to the Surprising Failure of Anonymization' (2009) 57 UCLA l. Rev. 1701. It does not leave entirely satisfied the precision that '[i]f technological developments make it possible to turn anonymised data into personal data, such data are to be treated as personal data, and Regulation (EU) 2016/679 is to apply accordingly' (Free Flow of Non-Personal Data Regulation, recital 9).

219 Lilian Edwards and Michael Veale, 'Slave to the Algorithm: Why a Right to an Explanation Is Probably Not the Remedy You Are Looking For' (2017) 16 Duke Law & Technology Review 18.

European Commission offered about the Free Flow of Non-Personal Data Regulation recognised that in an IoT world, most datasets are comprised of personal and nonpersonal data.[220] It has been convincingly argued[221] that the notion itself of nonpersonal data is problematic not only because datasets are mixed and the concept of personal data is fluid but also because there is the risk of firms exploiting regulatory rivalry, and data has economic value irrespective of its legal classification. Hopefully, the awareness that the personal/nonpersonal data dichotomy should be overcome will permeate future regulations and not only nonbinding guidelines.

As to the second critique – of relying on the good-service dichotomy – this applies in varying degrees also to the GDPR and other DSM measures, with the exception of the Geoblocking Regulation, which is the most IoT-friendly, at least from this standpoint. Indeed, it applies to activities regarding both services and goods,[222] the latter being defined as 'any tangible movable item.'[223] Accordingly, Things' providers and providers of subcomponents are not allowed to fragment the DSM and reduce consumer control over their Things by means of unjustified geoblocking measures. From the point of view of the goods-services dichotomy, the second most IoT-friendly regulation is the GDPR, which applies to the offering of goods and services.[224] However, there is no GDPR definition of *goods*; therefore, there is no certainty as to whether all Things will fall under this regulation, although it is likely that they will be regarded either as goods or as services or both. In third place, the Free Flow of Non-Personal Data Regulation only refers to services and does not mention goods.[225] Nonetheless, it can be argued that this regulation applies also to goods, because it applies not only to the processing of nonpersonal data provided as a service but also to the processing 'carried out by a natural or legal person residing or having an establishment in the Union for its own needs.'[226] This may be interpreted as encompassing also the provision of goods. Finally, the least IoT-friendly DSM regulation is the Cross-Border Portability Regulation, in that it refers only to services and excludes the online sale of goods.[227] This is consistent with other recent acts of digital regulation, such as the

---

220 European Commission, 'Free Flow of Non-Personal Data' (n 377). As example of mixed dataset, the guidance refers to 'data related to the Internet of Things, where some of the data allow assumptions to be made about identifiable individuals (e.g. presence at a particular address and usage pattern' (ibid [2.2]).
221 Inge Graef, Raphael Gellert and Martin Husovec, 'Towards a Holistic Regulatory Approach for the European Data Economy: Why the Illusive Notion of Non-Personal Data Is Counterproductive to Data Innovation' [2018] TILEC Discussion Paper No 2018–029 <https://papers.ssrn.com/sol3/papers.cfm?abstract_id=3256189>.
222 Geoblocking Regulation, arts 1, 2, 4.
223 Geoblocking Regulation, art 2(15); this provision excludes from the definition of goods only 'items sold by way of execution or otherwise by authority of law.'
224 GDPR, art 3(2)(a).
225 E.g. Free Flow of Non-Personal Data Regulation, art 2(1)(a).
226 Free Flow of Non-Personal Data Regulation, art 2(1)(b).
227 Cross-Border Portability Regulation, recital 16.

Digital Content Directive[228] and the new Sale of Goods Directive,[229] that are built on the dichotomies between goods-services and hardware-software; they will be analysed in Chapter 3.

In conclusion, the transnational nature of the IoT requires legal approaches that strike a balance between the need for cross-border enforcement and the avoidance of excessive compliance burdens. While the GDPR's extraterritoriality may be excessive, it seems to exemplify a trend in internet governance, as confirmed recently by the proposed Artificial Intelligence Act.[230] Some of the DSM measures appear to be more moderate. The new rules in matters of service portability, geoblocking, and free flow of nonpersonal data may benefit IoT stakeholders and consumers. However, they rely on a number of dichotomies, such as online-offline, personal-nonpersonal, goods-services, that the IoT has contributed to call into question. In this sense, they appear to be already obsolete.

PART II – THE EU IOT STRATEGY AND A CALL FOR A NON-BINARY APPROACH TO IOT REGULATION

1.4 Some Regulatory and Policy Options for an Interconnected World

The IoT's sectoral fragmentation, partially standardised complex technologies, relational black box, and transnational nature make it difficult for policy- and lawmakers to regulate it. In line with current regulatory theory,[231] in this book 'regulation' is construed in a broad sense: as a set of commands, as deliberate state influence, and as all forms of social or economic influence. The main focus will be on self-regulation, coregulation, and regulation.

There are several issues in the IoT that require better regulation. The main such issues[232] are interoperability,[233] the so-called contractual quagmire in which IoT

---

228 Directive (EU) 2019/770 on certain aspects concerning contracts for the supply of digital content and digital services ('Digital Content Directive') [2019] OJ L 136/1.

229 Directive (EU) 2019/771 of 20 May 2019 on certain aspects concerning contracts for the sale of goods, amending Regulation (EU) 2017/2394 and Directive 2009/22/EC, and repealing Directive 1999/44/EC (Sale of Goods Directive) [2019] OJ L 136/28. It shall be transposed by 1 January 2022.

230 Proposal for a regulation laying down harmonised rules on artificial intelligence ('Artificial Intelligence Act' or AI Act) (COM/2021/206 final), art 2(1).

231 Robert Baldwin, Martin Cave and Martin Lodge, *Understanding Regulation: Theory, Strategy, and Practice* (2nd edn, OUP 2012).

232 This list partly relies on Urquhart (n 108). See also Thomas Hoppner and Anastasia Gubanova, 'Regulatory Challenges of the Internet of Things' (2015) 21 Computer and Telecommunications Law Review (CTLR) 227; Hon, Millard and Singh (n 94).

233 Simon Deakin, Charlotte Sausman, Boni Sones and Carolyn Twigg, *The Internet of Things: Shaping Our Future* (Cambridge Public Policy 2015) 7.

users inadvertently find themselves,[234] privacy,[235] security,[236] market dominance and inadequate competition around firms,[237] insufficient spectrum and internet protocol (IP) addresses for devices,[238] lack of leadership on industry standards,[239] responsibility and liability for harm,[240] as well as technical education, appropriate regulation, and trust in the security of these systems.[241]

Whilst there is consensus as to the importance of at least some of these issues for the IoT to develop in a socially just way,[242] not all the countries and all the stakeholders agree on whether or not new regulations should be introduced, whether self-regulation may suffice, whether a body with IoT-related regulating and lawmaking powers would be needed, and if so, at which level, if national, regional, or international.[243]

There is a historical divide between the US and the EU about whether and how to regulate the internet.[244] It should come as no surprise that the same applies to the debate about the regulation of the IoT, although in recent years the EU seems to be increasingly fascinated by the North-American preference for nonbinding instruments that go by the name of 'soft laws.' For the purposes of this book, 'soft law' means '[r]ules of conduct which, in principle, have no legally binding force but which nevertheless may have practical effects.'[245] In this sense, the next section will deal with the soft laws on the IoT, as encompassing policy documents, self-regulation (e.g. industry codes of conduct), techno-regulation (code as law and law by design), and research funding.

1.4.1 Of Market-Led Self-Regulation, Soft Laws, Code, and Other Unsatisfactory Ways (Not) to Regulate the IoT

In November 2013, the US Federal Trade Commission (FTC) held a multistakeholder workshop on *The Internet of Things: Privacy and Security in a Connected*

---

234 Noto La Diega and Walden (n 24). This issue was not considered by Urquhart (n 108).
235 Christoph Krönke, 'Data Regulation in the Internet of Things' (2018) 13 Frontiers of Law in China 367.
236 Hoppner and Gubanova (n 392).
237 Brown (n 108).
238 ibid 19.
239 GSMA and KRC Research, 'The Impact of the Internet of Things – The Connected Home' (2015).
240 Rose, Eldridge and Chapin (n 201).
241 Mark Walport, 'Internet of Things: Making the Most of the Second Digital Revolution' (UK Government Office of Science 2014).
242 Urquhart (n 108).
243 Hoppner and Gubanova (n 392).
244 Filippo Maria Lancieri, 'Digital Protectionism? Antitrust, Data Protection, and the EU/US Transatlantic Rift' (2018) 7 Journal of Antitrust Enforcement 27.
245 Francis Snyder, 'Soft Law and Institutional Practice in the European Community' in *The construction of Europe* (Springer 1994) 198. The so-called internet bills of rights, such as the Italian *Dichiarazione dei Diritti in Internet*, are a form of soft law, as noted by Carmelita Camardi, 'L'eredità Digitale. Tra Reale e Virtuale' (2018) 2 Diritto dell'informazione e dell'informatica 65.

World.[246] The main perceived risks were unauthorised access and misuse of personal information, the potential for consumer-interfacing Things to facilitate attacks on other systems, and personal safety. However, the FTC reiterated the evergreen American idea that legislation stifles innovation.[247] This mantra has been blindly espoused by the UK government, which launched the Plan for Digital Regulation in July 2021. There, the government is adamant that deregulation and self-regulation are the way forward to promote innovation as '[p]olicymakers must *back innovation wherever they can by removing unnecessary regulation . . .* and considering non-regulatory measures.'[248] In some instances, overregulation may be seen as stifling innovation. However, if innovation is not regulated in a timely fashion, there is the real risk of 'cementing of socially undesirable outcomes when vested interests are left too long unchecked.'[249] Indeed, the window of time left in which to consider the manifold challenges of the IoT 'and to articulate a meaningful response to them . . . is closing.'[250] This does not seem to preoccupy the FTC that reaches the perhaps deterministic, albeit back then arguable, conclusion that 'IoT-specific legislation at this stage would be premature.'[251] The FTC nonetheless recommended that, in more sensitive areas, existing laws be strengthened. In particular, the FTC ambitiously called on Congress to enact 'strong, flexible, and technology-neutral federal legislation to strengthen its existing data security enforcement tools and to provide notification to consumers when there is a security breach.'[252] One year later, speaking at an event hosted by the Center for Data Innovation,[253] many representatives recognised that the US risks losing to China and other competitors if they do not update laws that had been passed before the time of videocassette recorders.[254] However, the concern 'not to snuff any of this great innovation out'[255] by means of strict security and privacy

---

246 The report summarising the workshop and providing recommendations is Federal Trade Commission (n 12).

247 Steve Taylor and Larry Hettick, 'Innovation and Legislation: The Conflict Continues; * Does Legislation Stifle Innovation?' [2006] Network World.

248 'New Plan to Make Britain Global Leader in Innovation-Focused Digital Regulation' (*GOV. UK*) <www.gov.uk/government/news/new-plan-to-make-britain-global-leader-in-innovation-focused-digital-regulation>. It should be said that the plan includes a reference to regulatory measure, namely, the Product Security and Telecommunications Infrastructure Bill. At the time of writing, the content of the bill is unknown, but based on the information available, it seems that it will have a narrow focus on cybersecurity issues.

249 Manwaring (n 66).

250 Adam Greenfield, *Everyware: The Dawning Age of Ubiquitous Computing* (New Riders 2010) 260.

251 Federal Trade Commission (n 12) vii.

252 ibid vii.

253 'How Can Policymakers Help Build the Internet of Things?' (Center for Data Innovation, Washington, DC, 4 December 2014). A report of the event can be found in Moore (n 138).

254 Sen. Deb Fischer, R-Neb., then member of the Commerce, Science and Transportation Committee. ibid.

255 Sen. Brian Schatz, D-Hawaii, then member of the Commerce, Science and Transportation Committee. ibid.

laws seemed to prevail. Regrettably, these concerns prevented any meaningful regulation of the IoT, and the US is still one of the few countries without comprehensive and modern privacy and security laws, let alone IoT-aware laws.

In line with its market-oriented tradition, the FTC seemed more favourable to self-regulating the IoT[256] rather than 'hard' solutions. This line seems to be prevailing. Currently, 'the regulation of the IoT is mainly based on self-regulation through business standards,'[257] such as GS1's[258] Electronic Product Code and the relevant standards,[259] which rest on concepts that are common in traditional regulations, such as consumer notice and consumer education.

For once, the EU pioneered this approach and favoured a 'soft' approach. This will be illustrated by reference to:

(1) The European research funding agenda;
(2) The launch of a Commission-backed IoT alliance;
(3) The attempt of impressing European values on the IoT;
(4) Ethical IoT; and
(5) Regulation by design.

First, a nonbinding way to indirectly regulate the IoT is through funding of research and innovation. Indeed, one can posit that shaping the research agenda can affect the stakeholders' behaviour as profoundly as actual regulations.[260] As noted by the US National Institute of Standards and Technology (NIST), the chief incentivising mode to regulate new technologies is the offer of research and development funding to help companies securely adopt new technologies.[261]

The first EU-coordinated effort to support IoT research was the European Research Cluster on the Internet of Things (IERC)[262] that groups EU-funded projects[263] aimed at defining 'a common vision and the IoT technology and development research challenges at the European level in the view of global development.'[264] Launched in 2010, IERC's vision is to support an open, vibrant, and innovative IoT ecosystem 'which brings together the research community with the private sector

---

256 Federal Trade Commission (n 266) 55.
257 Hoppner and Gubanova (n 254) 227.
258 GS1 is a not-for-profit organisation that develops global standards for business communication.
259 'Electronic Product Code/Radio Frequency Identification (RFID) Standards' <www.gs1.org/epc-rfid>.
260 E.g. it has been noted that 'funding is a key mechanism of change in the norm system since its reward structure influences the performance and evaluation of research' (Mats Benner and Ulf Sandström, 'Institutionalizing the Triple Helix: Research Funding and Norms in the Academic System' (2000) 29 Research Policy 291).
261 Moore (n 138).
262 'IERC-European Research Cluster on the Internet of Things' <www.internet-of-things-research.eu/about_ierc.htm>.
263 It brought together projects funded by the 7th European research framework programme (FP7) and national initiatives.
264 'IERC-European Research Cluster on the Internet of Things' (n 422).

companies and the end-users.'[265] One of the main outputs of this research has been the so-called cluster study.[266] The latter mapped IoT innovation clusters in the EU and identified four types of clusters: geographical, virtual, thematic, and institutionalised. The study recommended that the European Commission intervene in four strategic areas: the identification of IoT risks, the development of standards, the creation of EU-wide communities through support to technology development, transfer, and platforms, and finally, the development of IoT ecosystems.[267] So far, not much, if anything, seems to have followed from these recommendations in terms of actions and policies.

Another coordinated effort to regulate the IoT through research funding has been the IoT European Platform Initiative (IoT-EPI), which was launched in 2016 to promote open and accessible IoT platforms through projects funded by the Horizon 2020 Programme.[268] In order to achieve a vibrant and sustainable IoT ecosystem, the Commission funded seven projects that were seen as maximising the opportunities for platform development, interoperability, and information sharing.[269] Most notably, IoT-EPI comprises:

   (i) Inter-IoT, aiming at designing an open, cross-layer framework, an associated methodology, and tools to enable voluntary interoperability among heterogeneous IoT platforms;
  (ii) BIG IoT, addressing the interoperability gap by defining a generic, unified web application programming interface (API) for Thing platforms;
 (iii) AGILE, which builds a modular and adaptive gateway for Things;
 (iv) SymbIoTe, with the goal of devising an interoperability framework across existing and future IoT platforms;
  (v) TagItSmart!, having at its core the Smart Tag, which is a context-sensitive, printable QR code to convey life cycle information about mass-market Things;
 (vi) VICINITY, a platform and ecosystem that provides 'interoperability as a service' for IoT infrastructures; and
(vii) bIoTope, which intends to overcome the vertical silos problem[270] by building a platform that enables companies to easily create new IoT systems.

Like IERC, IoT-EPI confirms that private stakeholders are at the heart of the EU IoT strategy. Indeed, the initiative is marketed as having a partner network of

---

265 'Research & Innovation in Internet of Things' (*European Commission*, 28 April 2016) <https://ec.europa.eu/digital-single-market/en/research-innovation-iot>.
266 JIIP et al., 'Study on Mapping Internet of Things Innovation Clusters in Europe' (2019) European Commission.
267 ibid 4.
268 IoT-EPI, *Advancing IoT Platforms Interoperability* (River Publishers 2018).
269 'IoT European Platforms Initiative' (*IoT-EPI*) <http://iot-epi.eu>.
270 The IoT has stumbled into vertical data silos, and little to no integration between data exists. A Mazayev, JA Martins and N Correia, 'Interoperability in IoT Through the Semantic Profiling of Objects' (2018) 6 IEEE Access 19379.

120 established companies and organisations, and the funding calls are open for 'SMEs, startups, companies,'[271] and, last and least of all, research centres or universities. The influence of private, usually corporate, stakeholder in shaping the EU research agenda is akin to an informal – and rather opaque – form of coregulation of the IoT. More transparent coregulatory initiatives will be presented later in this chapter.

Second, in March 2015, the European Commission launched the Alliance for Internet of Things Innovation (AIOTI), to support the creation of 'an innovative and *industry driven* European Internet of Things ecosystem.'[272] This led to some noteworthy work about standardisation and policy, including the IoT LSP Standard Framework Concepts,[273] the IoT High Level Architecture,[274] and the AIOTI Position on Cybersecurity Act.[275] The former constitutes the alliance's main effort, and it has the aim to present the global dynamics and landscapes of standard-developing organisations and open-source software initiatives with ultimate goal of:

(i) Leveraging existing IoT standardisation, industry promotion, and implementation of standards and protocols;
(ii) Providing input for large-scale pilot standards framework and gap analysis; and
(iii) Presenting guidelines for the proponents of future project proposals associated with IoT-related calls financed by the EU.[276]

Whilst AIOTI has become an important IoT stakeholder in its own right and may play a crucial role in the development of a European IoT ecosystem, its mission currently seems far from being accomplished. Indeed, its work may lay the foundations for future standardisation initiatives and other soft laws, but it has not led, in itself, to proper standards. Nonetheless, AIOTI has been carrying out praiseworthy work in identifying standardisation gaps, which include operational strategies, such as deployment and its scalability, software update, sustainability and green technologies, and usability.[277]

Third, one year after the setting up of AIOTI, in the context of the Digitising European Industry initiative,[278] the European Commission published its main IoT-focused soft law instrument: *Advancing the Internet of Things in Europe.*[279]

---

271 'IoT European Platforms Initiative' (n 429).
272 'The Internet of Things' (*DSM – European Commission*, 1 October 2013) <https://ec.europa.eu/digital-single-market/en/policies/internet-things>. Italics added.
273 AIOTI WG03, 'IoT LSP Standard Framework Concepts' (2017) Release 2.8.
274 AIOTI WG03, 'High Level Architecture (HLA)' (2016) Release 2.1.
275 AIOTI WG04, 'AIOTI Position on the EU Cybersecurity Act Proposal' (2018).
276 AIOTI WG03, 'IoT LSP Standard Framework Concepts' (n 433).
277 AIOTI WG03, 'High Priority IoTStandardisation Gaps and Relevant SDOs' (2020) Release 2.0.
278 European Commission, 'Communication "Digitising European Industry Reaping the Full Benefits of a DSM"' (2016) COM/2016/0180 final.
279 European Commission, 'Advancing the Internet of Things' (n 159).

This Commission Staff Working Document specify the EU's IoT vision as based on a single market for the IoT, a thriving IoT ecosystem, and a human-centred IoT approach. First, the idea of an IoT single market translates into the commitment to make sure that Things can connect seamlessly and on a plug-and-play basis anywhere in the EU and scale up across borders.[280] Second, in order to achieve a thriving IoT ecosystem, open platforms used across vertical silos will help communities of developers to innovate and IoT deployments in selected lead markets will be supported.[281] Third, the Commission expressed the belief that Things must 'respect *European values, empowering people along with machines* and businesses, thanks to high standards for the protection of personal data and security, visible notably through a "Trusted IoT" label.'[282] This is problematic for four reasons:

(i) It is unlikely that consensus will be reached as to what exactly constitutes a 'European value' and, subsequently, to learn how to translate it into machine-readable commands.[283]

(ii) Since Things are designed for international (including extra-EU) mobility, the idea that a user in India should interact with Things embodying so-called European values may count as neocolonial digital imperialism. This trait was inherited by internet regulation more generally.[284] Indeed, benign efforts to wire the world 'in the name of an ostensibly universal/cosmopolitan vision of electronic democracy . . . emerge as a form of "computer-mediated colonization", i.e., an imposition of a specific set of cultural values and communicative preferences upon diverse cultures.'[285]

(iii) The suggestion that we should be 'empowering *people along with machines* and businesses' implies that machines need to be empowered and that people are on an equal footing with machines. One would have thought that machines need to be powered, people empowered. That phrase may perhaps be seen as a result of the regrettable anthropomorphism that increasingly characterises machines.[286]

---

280 European Commission, 'SWD Advancing the Internet of Things in Europe' (n 298) [2].

281 ibid [3].

282 European Commission, 'SWD Advancing the Internet of Things' (n 298) [1(3)]. Italics added.

283 See Guido Noto La Diega, 'The Artificial Conscience of Lethal Autonomous Weapons: Marketing Ruse or Reality?' [2019] Lexis Nexis Middle East Law, and Literature there cited.

284 It has been noted that 'the recent expansion of the Internet retraces the geography of Europe's first colonization of the globe from the late 15th century onwards' and underlines the similarities between early colonialism's rich trade and the internet in the marking out of status in hierarchical and differentiated societies (Martin Hall, 'Virtual Colonization' (1999) 4 Journal of Material Culture 39).

285 Charles Ess, 'Computer-Mediated Colonization, the Renaissance, and Educational Imperatives for an Intercultural Global Village' (2002) 4 Ethics and Information Technology 11, 12.

286 For example, it has been argued that if social robots are too similar to humans, this would have a negative impact on humans, as a group, and their identity more generally, because similarity blurs category boundaries, undermining human uniqueness (Francesco Ferrari, Maria Paola Paladino and Jolanda Jetten, 'Blurring Human – Machine Distinctions: Anthropomorphic Appearance in

(iv) The 'Trusted IoT' label, as a demonstration of compliance to the Network Information Security (NIS) Directive's requirements,[287] may be useful, although it must be kept in mind that labelling has often failed to achieve its objectives.[288]

Fourth, one of the clearest – and most concerning – recent trends in internet governance is the ethical turn, as shown by the increasing reliance on ethics charters and value-sensitive design to complement or even replace legislation and oversight.[289] While most ethical initiatives are not binding and can be criticised for this reason as they can do little to change corporate behaviour, a recent trend in internet governance is the enshrining of ethics into binding instruments. This can be seen most clearly in the field of AI, where the proposed Artificial Intelligence Act is the result of the commitment by the European Commission president to put forward *'legislative proposals* for a coordinated European approach to the human and *ethical implications of AI.'*[290] Published in April 2021, the proposed act can be regarded as the legislative codification of the *Ethics Guidelines for Trustworthy AI.*[291] The use of binding ethical instruments is open to criticism for many reasons. For the purposes of this section, suffice it to note that the unification of law and ethics is worrying from a historical perspective. Indeed, this unification served the Nazi jurists as a means of extending the authority and power of the state to the control of personal convictions.[292] Nazi law was based on the higher law of a declared Germanic sense of justice, which ended up liberating the judge from the 'inflexible framework of the law.'[293] Ultimately, as Hans Kelsen argued in *General Theory of Law and State*, if only 'just' law is law, legal systems are all morally justified.[294] Needless to say, the intentions underpinning the idea of legislating on ethical AI do not share anything with the intentions of Nazi lawmakers. Nonetheless, we should all be aware of the dangers of governing new technologies by transforming ethics into law.

Social Robots as a Threat to Human Distinctiveness' (2016) 8 International Journal of Social Robotics 287).

287 Directive (EU) 2016/1148 concerning measures for a high common level of security of network and information systems across the Union ('NIS Directive') [2016] OJ L 194/1.

288 Camilla C Erskine and Lyndhurst Collins, 'Eco-Labelling: Success or Failure?' (1997) 17 Environmentalist 125.

289 Lilian Edwards (ed), *Law, Policy and the Internet* (Hart 2019) ii.

290 'EU Guidelines on Ethics in Artificial Intelligence: Context and Implementation' (*European Parliament*, 19 September 2019) <www.europarl.europa.eu/thinktank/en/document.html?reference=EPRS_BRI(2019)640163>.

291 High-Level Expert Group on Artificial Intelligence (n 104).

292 Herlinde Pauer-Stauder, 'Law and Morality under Evil Conditions' (2012) 3 Jurisprudence 367, 370.

293 Christopher Theel, 'The Moral Rigour of Immorality: The Special Criminal Courts of the SS' in Wolfgang Bialas and Lothar Fritze (eds), *Nazi Ideology and Ethics* (Cambridge Scholars 2014) 343.

294 Hans Kelsen, *General Theory of Law and State* (Anders Wedberg tr, HUP 1945) 5.

Most manifestations of the ethical turn in technology governance are not binding. Ethical charters and manifestos abound in the field of the IoT. For example, researchers at ThingsCon,[295] a collective that promotes development of responsible IoT, have mapped around thirty 'ethical IoT' initiatives, such as the Arduino IoT Manifesto,[296] the Everyware Principles,[297] and the IoT Bill of Rights.[298] The use of ethics to "regulate" the IoT can be criticised for a number of reasons,[299] but for the purposes of this book, one need only focus on the fact that ethics has been weaponised 'in support of deregulation, self-regulation or hands-off governance.'[300] In this sense, 'ethics washing' acts as an ideological rhetoric device that lacks the strength of law and brings confusion to the regulatory discourse rather than solutions. However, the condemnation of ethics washing has led to a form of 'ethics bashing,' that is, 'the trivialization of ethics and moral philosophy now understood as discrete tools or pre-formed social structures such as ethics boards, self-governance schemes or stakeholder groups.'[301] If ethics is used to complement regulation and not as a substitute, and if it takes the form of evidence-based participatory best practice rather than vague charters drafted with opaque methods, there are reasons to be open to it. One such positive application is the Edinburgh Initiative, i.e. the work of an Action Group on Governance and Ethics in assessing the use of a new IoT infrastructure at the University of Edinburgh.[302] Participatory and involving diverse actors, this initiative was underpinned by the belief that ethical precepts can be translated into procedures, guidelines, training, reflection, and support, which in turn can be can be used to '*augment . . . the application of legal requirements*, for example, accountability and transparency by means of other instruments that may be more adaptable to rapidly changing technologies.'[303] In this initiative, ethics was instantiated by:

295 Laura James, 'Responsible and Trustworthy IoT' (*Medium*, 24 August 2018) <https://medium.com/the-state-of-responsible-iot-2018/responsible-and-trustworthy-iot-dcf8b05e8ea0>.

296 'Arduino IoT Manifesto' [2016] *Wired* <www.wired.com/beyond-the-beyond/2016/04/arduino-iot-manifesto/>.

297 'Adam Greenfield's Everyware Principles' (*Everwas*, 26 August 2006) <https://everwas.com/2006/08/adam_greenfields_everyware_principles/>.

298 Adafruit, 'Internet of Things Bill of Rights' (*GitHub*, 2014) <https://github.com/adafruit/iot-bill-of-rights>.

299 The most radical criticism is that ethical values are intrinsically subjective and relative to a particular society and time. What is even more worrying is when some attempt to crystallise ethics into the design of Things. Ethics by design produces ethically desensitised, deskilled, and re-responsabilised agents 'merely herded, mindlessly and non-responsibly, towards some pre-established options chosen by the designers of the environment' (Luciano Floridi, 'Tolerant Paternalism: Pro-Ethical Design as a Resolution of the Dilemma of Toleration' (2016) 22 Science and Engineering Ethics 1669, 1681).

300 Elettra Bietti, 'From Ethics Washing to Ethics Bashing: A View on Tech Ethics from within Moral Philosophy' *FAT 2020 Proceedings* (ACM 2020) 210.

301 ibid 211.

302 Andrés Domínguez and others, 'Ethical and Responsible IoT: The Edinburgh Initiative' (2020) 11 EJLT.

303 ibid 7.

(i) A city-wide communications network that was 'as open as possible,'[304] where it was possible to access, modify, and experiment with virtually any hardware and software component of the network;

(ii) The shift from consultation via a survey to codesign via focus groups in setting up – and assessing the privacy impact of – a system to identify unoccupied desks at the library repurposing student card data.

Initiatives such as this are praiseworthy, but one can doubt that they can easily be exported and applied to other IoT sectors for at least two reasons. First, universities have a strong incentive in listening to and engaging with its main stakeholders, its students, on whose satisfaction the financial sustainability of the institution depends. Chapter 2 will present a hierarchy of incentives that shows how IoT companies will not adopt fair data practices unless they have strong incentives, either in terms of public exposure or in terms of financial pressure. Second, universities have a tradition in research ethics and can source in-house the expertise that may be necessary for the evaluation of its own practices.[305] The same cannot be said for most commercial IoT applications. The Edinburgh initiative is also a reminder that the many instances of the ethical turn are 'often very siloed, when IoT is always a cross-cutting endeavour, with decisions about hardware, software, data, application area and users intertwined.'[306]

Lastly, the most recent and problematic form of self-regulation is the regulation by design.[307] This is connected to the idea of (binary) code as the law of cyberspace, as famously put forward by Lawrence Lessig and his followers.[308] The way the internet – and the IoT – is designed (e.g. which content Apple Watch's screen shows us or hides from us) affects us in a way that is similar to the way democratically produced laws impact citizens,[309] despite code being developed in an untransparent and undemocratic way.[310] IoT's code, in particular, being ubiquitous and hidden in seemingly harmless everyday objects, has the potential to

---

304 ibid 8.

305 This second limitation is clear to ibid 29.

306 James (n 455).

307 On code as a form of self-regulation, see Robert Pitofsky, 'Self Regulation and Antitrust' [1998] Anuario de la competencia 585; Mark A Lemley, 'Standardizing Government Standard-Setting Policy for Electronic Commerce' [1999] Berkeley Technology Law Journal 745.

308 Lawrence Lessig, *Code* (Version 2.0, Basic Books 2006). The idea is having a renaissance thanks to the blockchain becoming fashionable. See e.g. Primavera De Filippi, *Blockchain and the Law: The Rule of Code* (HUP 2018); Karen Yeung, 'Regulation by Blockchain: The Emerging Battle for Supremacy between the Code of Law and Code as Law' (2019) 82 MLR 207.

309 Lawrence Lessig, 'Law Regulating Code Regulating Law' (2003) 35 The Loyola University Chicago Law Journal 1; Lessig (n 304); Guido Noto La Diega, 'Grinding Privacy in the Internet of Bodies. An Empirical Qualitative Research on Dating Mobile Applications for Men Who Have Sex with Men' in Ronald Leenes et al. (eds), *Data Protection and Privacy: The Internet of Bodies* (Hart 2018).

310 O'Hara (n 64); Guido Noto La Diega, 'Against the Dehumanisation of Decision-Making – Algorithmic Decisions at the Crossroads of Intellectual Property, Data Protection, and Freedom of Information' (2018) 9 JIPITEC 3.

regulate the citizens' behaviour in unforeseeable ways. It may sound like a stretch to argue that the idea of technologically regulating through Things was written in cyberspace's DNA; however, it is a fact that 'cyberspace' comes from 'cybernetics,' which comes from *kybernetiké téchne*, the art of control at a distance through devices.[311] *Cybernetics* was coined by Norbert Weiner in 1948 to refer to the scientific study of control and communication in the animal and the machine.[312] And control – or regulation by code (or by design) – at a distance through Things is what is happening with the IoT, where private companies seek to 'promote techno-regulation through design, algorithms and market-based contracts.'[313]

The relationship between self-regulation and code is relevant for at least two reasons. First, the possibility of self-governance depends on architectural features of the internet, and these are not always developed in democracy-supporting ways.[314] Second, companies are increasingly expected to operate self-restraint 'by design.' This is perhaps best exemplified by the 'data protection by design' obligation under GDPR and by the UK government's *Code of Practice for Consumer IoT Security*.[315]

The former requires data controllers to implement technical and organisational measures that embed data protection principles from the outset, i.e. from the conception and design of a product or service,[316] Things included. This would mean, for example, that if the Thing contains cameras, these should not be hidden in order to prevent the Thing from becoming a means of covert surveillance.[317] 'Data protection by design' has its roots in the 'privacy by design'[318] approach, which was entirely voluntary. With the GDPR, it has become a binding obligation and could be regarded as a form of coregulation, where the lawmaker sets forth the high-level principles and the data controllers transform them into design rules.

The 'by design' trend, however, goes beyond data protection, and most of it still qualifies as a form of self-regulation. The *Code of Practice for Consumer IoT*

---

311 Kevin Kelly, *Out of Control: The New Biology of Machines, Social Systems, and the Economic World* (Hachette UK 2009).
312 Norbert Wiener, *Cybernetics or Control and Communication in the Animal and the Machine* (2nd edn, 10 Print, MIT Press 2000).
313 Eduardo Magrani, 'Threats of the Internet of Things in a Techno-Regulated Society: A New Legal Challenge of the Information Revolution' (2018) 9 International Journal of Private Law 4.
314 Henry H Perritt Jr, 'Cyberspace Self-Government: Town Hall Democracy or Rediscovered Royalism' (1997) 12 Berkeley Technology Law Journal 413.
315 Department for Digital, Culture, Media & Sport (n 113).
316 GDPR, art 25.
317 On data protection by design in the IoT, see Aurelia Tamò-Larrieux, *Designing for Privacy and Its Legal Framework: Data Protection by Design and Default for the Internet of Things* (Springer 2018). On transparency by design in sensor-equipped robots see Burkhard Schafer and Lilian Edwards, '"I Spy, with My Little Sensor": Fair Data Handling Practices for Robots between Privacy, Copyright and Security' (2017) 29 Connection Science 200.
318 Privacy by design is often regarded as first conceived by Ann Cavoukian, 'Privacy by Design: The 7 Foundational Principles' (2009) 5 Information and Privacy Commissioner of Ontario, Canada. However, the idea of privacy by design predates her; see Michael Veale, Reuben Binns and Jef Ausloos, 'When Data Protection by Design and Data Subject Rights Clash' (2018) 8 IDPL 105.

Security, based on the Secure by Design report,[319] is a prime example of this type. This code sets out steps for IoT manufacturers and other stakeholders to improve the security of consumer-interfacing Things by implementing thirteen guidelines, including no default passwords and minimisation of exposed attack surfaces.[320] The fact that many Things are sold with universal default usernames and passwords leads to serious security issues; therefore, the requirement to sell Things with unique passwords is a positive move.[321] As to the minimisation of exposed attack surfaces, Things should operate on the 'principle of least privilege';[322] therefore, unused ports shall be closed, hardware shall not unnecessarily expose access, services shall not be available if not used, and code shall be minimised to the functionality necessary for the Thing to work.[323] At its core, the Code of Practice is a traditional self-regulatory 'soft' measure in that it is 'outcome-focused, rather than prescriptive, giving organisations the flexibility to innovate and implement security solutions appropriate for their products.'[324] Whilst the effort may be laudable, it is peculiar to leave this to private companies' goodwill, as the security of Things 'is now as important as the physical security of our homes.'[325] The same can be said for the first globally applicable standard for consumer IoT security, released by the European Telecommunications Standards Institute in February 2019.[326] It includes provisions storage of security-sensitive data, software integrity, and system resilience.[327] Such important things should not be left to the discretion of private corporations.

As IoT companies use design/code to regulate us, it makes sense to 'regulate' them through design/code. However, the idea that technology will resolve the problems created by technology is excessively optimistic. There are grounds for scepticism when technological design is presented as *the* solution to human rights problems; in this sense, regulation by design can be regarded as antagonistic to

---

319 Department for Digital, Culture, Media & Sport, 'Secure by Design' (2018).

320 Department for Digital, Culture, Media & Sport (n 113).

321 ibid. Guideline No 1.

322 This principle is a cornerstone of good security engineering in general, although it becomes particularly important and needs to be partly rethought to make it fit for the IoT. Marcela S Melara, David H Liu and Michael J Freedman, 'Pyronia: Redesigning Least Privilege and Isolation for the Age of IoT' [2019] arXiv:1903.01950 [cs] <http://arxiv.org/abs/1903.01950>.

323 Department for Digital, Culture, Media & Sport (n 113). Guideline 6.

324 ibid. Introduction.

325 ibid.

326 European Telecommunications Standards Institute, 'Cyber Security for Consumer Internet of Things (ETSI TS 103 645)' (ETSI, 2019) <www.etsi.org/deliver/etsi_ts/103600_103699/10364 5/01.01.01_60/ts_103645v010101p.pdf>. At the time of publication, a new version of the standard has been published: European Telecommunications Standards Institute, 'Cyber Security for Consumer Internet of Things: Baseline Requirements' (2020) ETSI EN 303 645 v 2.1.1. This chapter's analysis is based on the previous version, but at cursory look, no relevant changes have been made.

327 European Telecommunications Standards Institute, 'Cyber Security for Consumer Internet of Things (ETSI TS 103 645)' (n 486) [4.4], [4.7], [4.9].

actual regulation.[328] Regulation by design suffers from a legitimacy gap. Indeed, as Langdon Winner[329] argued already in 1980, technologies embody power relations, and their design is an insufficiently democratic activity. The design of new technologies 'is so thoroughly biased . . . that it regularly produces results heralded as wonderful breakthroughs by some social interests and crushing setbacks by others,'[330] which is a strong argument for more participatory methodologies[331] – what is usually missing both in the ethical turn and in regulation by design. Whilst refusing techno-solutionism, this book has been written on the assumption that 'by design' solutions can and should complement – though never replace – more traditional, 'hard' regulatory responses.

Self-regulation and, more generally, soft initiatives have the benefit of being more flexible than traditional top-down regulation and to follow the principle of subsidiarity.[332] Under this principle, a central authority or a transgovernmental network has a subsidiary function in handling only those tasks that cannot be handled by the self-regulatory authority.[333] Self-regulation and minimal state involvement have been seen as more efficient in dynamic, innovative industries.[334] However, the question is inherently political and at least five arguments can be made against a soft approach to IoT regulation. First, letting the (binary) code regulate itself means assuming absolute technological neutrality, but technology's social impact cannot be regarded as neutral.[335] Second, the internet is characterised by economies of scale and network effects that have led to noncompetitive markets.[336] The failures of antitrust jurisprudence in addressing patent abuses are a good illustration of this issue and will be analysed in Chapter 6. Third, there is a democratic argument to regulate, since voters may 'not allow governments to ignore the social impact of this ubiquitous medium.'[337] Fourth, it is in the nature of self-regulation to be nonbinding; indeed, it can act only as a form of moral suasion

---

328 N van Dijk and others, 'Right Engineering? The Redesign of Privacy and Personal Data Protection' (2018) 32 International Review of Law, Computers & Technology 230.
329 Langdon Winner, 'Do Artifacts Have Politics?' (1980) 109 Daedalus 121.
330 ibid 125.
331 Justina Pila, 'Covid-19 and Contact Tracing: A Study in Regulation by Technology' (2020) 11 EJLT.
332 Hoppner and Gubanova (n 392).
333 Ian G Smith, *The Internet of Things 2012: New Horizons* (CASAGRAS2 2012) 238.
334 Ian Brown and Christopher T Marsden, *Regulating Code: Good Governance and Better Regulation in the Information Age* (The MIT Press 2013).
335 Chris Reed, 'Taking Sides on Technology Neutrality' (2007) 4 SCRIPTed 263; Egbert Dommering, 'Regulating Technology: Code Is Not Law' [2006] Coding Regulation: Essays on the Normative role of Information Technology 1; Christian Azar and Björn A Sandén, 'The Elusive Quest for Technology-Neutral Policies' (2011) 1 Environmental Innovation and Societal Transitions 135.
336 Jonathan Zittrain, *The Future of the Internet–and How to Stop It* (YUP 2008); Tim Wu, *The Master Switch: The Rise and Fall of Information Empires* (Vintage 2010); John Herrman, 'What If Platforms Like Facebook Are Too Big to Regulate?' *The New York Times Magazine* (8 October 2017) 14.
337 Brown and Marsden (n 308) 3.

and when certain conditions occur, such as sanctions under contract or association rules.[338] The flexibility of soft laws and self-regulation should not be the dominant factor in making decisions about regulation.[339] Indeed, this ideological stance causes 'regulatory inertia'[340] and 'legal procrastination'[341] that are difficult to break without a substantial and public failure.[342] Indeed, as IoT companies increasingly adopt business models based on big data and on the use of Things to further their marketing activities, 'their resistance to subsequent restriction of these activities will increase.'[343] Finally, even more radically, it can be argued that self-regulation is not actual regulation. Indeed, a commonly accepted definition of 'regulation' is 'the sustained and focussed attempt to *alter the behaviour of others* according to standards or goals with the intention of producing a broadly identified outcome or outcomes, which may involve mechanisms of standard-setting, information-gathering and behaviour modification.'[344] By definition, self-regulation cannot alter the behaviour of others as it is self-directed. Therefore, if we want IoT companies to act differently, external stimuli are needed.

Especially in markets where big tech such as Google, Apple, Facebook, and Amazon (GAFA) – and its Chinese counterparts, Baidu, Alibaba, Tencent, and Xiaomi (BATX) – dominate and have little or no incentives to self-restrict their behaviour, the argument can be put forward that hard laws are more suitable than soft laws. The need to regulate the behaviour of GAFA and BATX is a common thread in recent debates about how to counter illegal content online[345] and whether to 'break' these companies, since fines do not exert any meaningful deterrence function.[346] For example, in *United States v. Facebook*,[347] Facebook settled[348] with the FTC a number of privacy violations. Under the settlement, the social networking site will have to pay a record $5bn fine for data mishandling.

---

338 Hoppner and Gubanova (n 392).
339 Kayleen Manwaring, 'Will Emerging Technologies Outpace Consumer Protection Law? The Case of Digital Consumer Manipulation' [2018] Competition and Consumer Law Journal 141.
340 Daniel Gervais, 'The Regulation of Inchoate Technologies' (2010) 47 Houston Law Review 665.
341 David A Super, 'Against Flexibility' (2010) 96 Cornell Law Review 1375, 1382.
342 Manwaring (n 499).
343 ibid 181.
344 Julia Black, 'What Is Regulatory Innovation?' in Julia Black, Martin Lodge and Mark Thatcher (eds), *Regulatory Innovation* (Edward Elgar 2005) 11.
345 See Department for Digital, Culture, Media & Sport and Home Office, 'Online Harms White Paper' (2019) <www.gov.uk/government/consultations/online-harms-white-paper/online-harms-white-paper>, that proposed establishing in law a new duty of care towards online users, which will be overseen by an independent regulator. This was related also to the fact that '(p)ublic opinion is growing increasingly intolerant of the abuses which big tech companies have failed to eliminate' (House of Lords Select Committee on Communications, 'Regulating in a Digital World' (2019) 2nd Report of Session 2017–19, 5).
346 E.g. it has been stated that '[f]ines alone cannot solve structural challenges behind privacy lapses' (The Editorial Board, 'Fresh Thinking Needed to Keep Big Tech in Check' *Financial Times* (8 July 2019)).
347 [2019] Case 1:19-cv-02184 (US District Court Columbia).
348 Stipulated order for civil penalty, monetary judgement, and injunctive relief, *United States v Facebook Inc* [2019] Case No. 19-cv-2184.

However, Facebook reacted by immediately posting a $2.6bn profit, which led to a 3% rebound of its stocks.[349] Whilst this rise may be explained with the fact that the settlement would extinguish more than 26,000 consumer complaints against Facebook pending at the FTC,[350] it is not unreasonable to see this as the confirmation that thinking to regulate big tech by means of fines is not a winning strategy.

Consumers' choices are increasingly determined by the products and the information that GAFA and BATX show on the 'digital shelf' (e.g. Amazon's Buy Box).[351] With the IoT, this shelf is becoming smaller and smaller. Therefore, regulators should ask themselves new questions and think of new strategies to deal with abuses of power by IoT corporations. A good starting point would be to reflect on whether control over the design of the web and the underlying algorithms that attempt to monopolise our attention has become 'the latest tool in the landlord's toolbox.'[352] It would be naive to leave the regulation of the IoT to the market; indeed, GAFA, BATX, and other digital landlords that use algorithms and web design as the tools of a new enclosure tend to seek monopolistic rents and maximise profit at the expenses of smaller businesses and society at large. Schumpeter believed that technological innovation could cause a reduction in wealth and rent inequalities through powerful destruction.[353] However, he himself acknowledged that this innovation often leads to temporary rents, which can, over time, become traditional monopolistic rents.[354] Relying on the invisible hand of market to achieve the best good of all, without government interference, is a political choice that is no longer sustainable.[355]

In a context of IoT innovation dominated by few rent-seeking and fine-immune multinationals, transnational hard laws should be part of the regulatory strategy.

---

349 Jeff Horwitz and Deepa Seetharaman, 'Facebook Posts Strong Earnings, Revenue Growth' *Wall Street Journal* (24 July 2019) <www.wsj.com/articles/facebook-posts-strong-earnings-revenue-growth-11563999791>.

350 Also for this reason, privacy group EPIC has filed a motion to intervene in *Facebook* (n). The motion is available at <epic.org/privacy/facebook/EPIC-Motion-to-Intervene-FTC-Facebook-Settlement.pdf>.

351 The European Commission will investigate the role of the data collected by Amazon about the independent sellers hosted on the platform in the selection of the winners of the 'Buy Box' that is displayed prominently on Amazon and allows customers to add items from a specific retailer directly into their shopping carts. The vast majority of transactions are done through the Buy Box. See 'Antitrust: Commission Opens Investigation into Possible Anti-Competitive Conduct of Amazon' (*European Commission*, 17 July 2019) <https://ec.europa.eu/commission/presscorner/home/en>.

352 Tim O'Reilly, 'Antitrust Regulators Are Using the Wrong Tools to Break up Big Tech' (*Quartz*, 17 July 2019) <https://qz.com/1666863/why-big-tech-keeps-outsmarting-antitrust-regulators/>.

353 Joseph A Schumpeter, 'The Theory of Economic Development: An Inquiry into Profits, Capital, Credit, Interest, and the Business Cycle (1912/1934)' (1982) 1 Transaction Publishers. – 1982. – January 244.

354 O'Reilly (n 512).

355 Underlying how Adam Smith's invisible hand concept has been mostly misrepresented, Kaushik Basu has argued for a shift in focus from efficiency to fairness through collective action (Kaushik Basu, *Beyond the Invisible Hand. Groundwork for a New Economics* (PUP 2016). It does strike as peculiar that some scholars keep calling for a return to a classical liberal economic order free of interference from governments; see e.g. Deepak Lal, *Reviving the Invisible Hand* (PUP 2006).

1.4.2 *The EU Hard Law Approach to the IoT: The Case Study of the European Electronic Communications Code between Spectrum Management, Over-the-Top Services, High-Speed Connectivity, and Numbering*

While in principle top-down hard laws appear to be a suitable solution, much will depend on the method and the content. These laws should not be IoT-specific, rather 'IoT-aware,' i.e. they must be wary of how the IoT has changed our everyday life and challenged traditional concepts and binaries on which old laws still rest. Some examples of IoT-relevant, albeit only partly, IoT-aware top-down regulation have already been presented and fall under the DSM strategy. Whilst the new Sale of Goods Directive and Digital Content Directive will be analysed in Chapter 3, to complete the picture of EU IoT-related hard laws, one needs to mention the review of telecoms rules. In this context, the European Commission:

(i) Proposed that by 2025 the main providers of public services and digitally intensive enterprises shall have access to internet connections with 1GB/s speed;[356]
(ii) Set out a coregulatory framework for member states and industry to cooperate in the development of 5G wireless technologies;[357]
(iii) Supported public entities to offer free Wi-Fi[358]

The heart of the reform of telecommunications, however, is the European Electronic Communications Code (EECC),[359] which was due to be transposed by December 2020,[360] but 24 member states missed the deadline, which led the European Commission to open infringement proceedings in February 2021.[361]

The EECC sets EU-wide objectives and harmonised rules on how the telecom industry should be regulated,[362] with notable new provisions about spectrum management, over-the-top (OTT) or over-the-air services, high-speed connectivity, and numbering.

---

356 European Commission, 'Communication "Connectivity for a Competitive DSM – Towards a European Gigabit Society" COM(2016)587' (2016).
357 European Commission, 'Communication "5G for Europe: An Action Plan" COM(2016)588' (2016).
358 European Commission, 'Calls for Applications for the WiFi4EU Initiative (Promotion of Internet Connectivity in Local Communities), under the Connecting Europe Facility in the Field of the Trans-European Telecommunication Networks (Amended 2017 CEF Telecom Work Programme – Commission Implementing Decision C(2017) 7732) [2018] OJ C 168/1'.
359 Directive (EU) 2018/1972 of 11 December 2018 establishing the EECC [2018] OJ L 321/36.
360 The Code became effective on 20 December 2018.
361 'Commission Opens Infringement Procedures against 24 Member States for Not Transposing New EU Telecom Rules' (*European Commission*, 4 February 2021) <https://ec.europa.eu/commission/presscorner/detail/en/ip_21_206>.
362 Wolfgang Briglauer and others, 'The EECC: A Critical Appraisal with a Focus on Incentivizing Investment in next Generation Broadband Networks' (2017) 41 Telecommunications Policy 948.

Some telecoms-related issues in the IoT are linked to the capacity to handle a huge amount of highly diverse Things[363] and the need to securely identify them, as well as being able to discover them so that they can be plugged into IoT systems.[364] Therefore, an open and interoperable IoT numbering space for a universal Thing identification and an open system for Thing authentication become vital.[365] The EECC provides a partial answer to these problems, in particular with regards to some aspects of numbering.

The background of the code is that, as a consequence of fragmentation in telecoms laws, the EU was lagging behind the US, as exemplified by a three-year delay in the rollout of 4G technologies.[366] To avoid that, the European Commission recognised that the regulation of 5G technologies could not be treated as a purely domestic matter,[367] and it goes without saying that the prompt and coordinated 5G rollout is pivotal to the IoT, in light of the transnational and high-speed mobile connectivity-hungry nature of Things.

By 2025, in Europe, there will be 25 billion IoT connection.[368] Since these connections are mostly wireless, to accommodate the resulting traffic between Things, the amount of available spectrum will have to be increased,[369] shared more effectively, and underutilization will have to be avoided.[370] The code aims to stimulate investments throughout the EU through the release of spectrum frequencies on the same technical conditions, as well as long-lasting (20 years) and easy-to-renew licenses.[371] The code recommends that radio spectrum management adopts, 'where appropriate, a cross-sectorial approach to improve the efficient use of radio spectrum.'[372] Thus, it shows to be aware of the importance of spectrum for the IoT, and it is fit for the IoT's sectoral fragmentation.

---

363 S Singh and N Singh, 'Internet of Things (IoT): Security Challenges, Business Opportunities Reference Architecture for E-Commerce' *2015 International Conference on Green Computing and Internet of Things (ICGCIoT)* (2015).

364 M Ishino, Y Koizumi and T Hasegawa, 'Leveraging Proximity Services for Relay Device Discovery in User-Provided IoT Networks' *2015 IEEE 2nd World Forum on Internet of Things (WF-IoT)* (2015); B Da and others, 'Identity/Identifier-Enabled Networks (IDEAS) for Internet of Things (IoT)', *2018 IEEE 4th World Forum on Internet of Things* (2018).

365 Mehmet Bilal Ünver, 'Turning the Crossroad for a Connected World: Reshaping the European Prospect for the Internet of Things' (2018) 26 International Journal of Law and Information Technology 93.

366 'Late to Everything' (*The Verge*, 10 October 2011) <www.theverge.com/2012/3/27/2907104/uk-4g-lte-rollout>.

367 European Commission, 'Communication "5G for Europe: An Action Plan"' (n 517).

368 CBI, 'The European Market Potential for (Industrial) Internet of Things' (2021) <www.cbi.eu/market-information/outsourcing-itobpo/industrial-internet-things/market-potential>.

369 European Commission, 'SWD Advancing the Internet of Things' (n 159).

370 Distributed ledger technologies have been identified as key to more effective spectrum authorisation systems. See Cigdem Sengul, 'Distributed Ledgers for Spectrum Authorization' (2020) 24 IEEE Internet Computing 7.

371 EECC, arts 45 and 49.

372 EECC, recital 30, which expressly refers to the IoT as 'an illustration of how the radio signal conveyance underpinning electronic communications continues to evolve and shape societal and business reality.'

High-speed connectivity is fundamental for the development of the IoT in Europe.[373] To achieve this, the code offers telecoms operators with significant market power,[374] reduced price, and access regulation in exchange for investments in high-capacity broadband networks.[375] At the same time, national regulatory authorities may impose[376] on these operators obligations of transparency,[377] nondiscrimination,[378] accounting separation[379] in relation to interconnection or access, as well as obligations relating to cost recovery and price control,[380] and to meet reasonable requests for access to and use of civil engineering[381] and specific network elements.[382]

Finally, the previous telecoms regulatory framework dated back to 2002, when it was unthinkable that traditional phone calls and texts would have been replaced by so-called OTT voice and instant messaging services such as Skype and WhatsApp.[383] The EECC levels the regulatory playing field for OTT services with that of traditional telecoms services. To do so, it redefines electronic communications services – and hence the scope of telecoms regulations – not based on technical parameters but by taking a functional approach. Indeed, it recognises that traditional voice telephony, SMS, and email conveyance services are 'functionally equivalent (to) online services such as Voice over IP, messaging services and web-based e-mail services.'[384] Accordingly, the new definition of *electronic communications*[385] service refers – and the relevant regulations apply – to three partly overlapping types of services:

(i) *Internet access services.* This is not a new concept and refers to 'a publicly available electronic communications service that provides access to the internet, and thereby connectivity to virtually all end points of the internet, irrespective of the network technology and terminal equipment used.'[386]

---

373 European Commission, 'SWD "A DSM Strategy for Europe – Analysis and Evidence Accompanying the Document Communication from the Commission to the European Parliament, the Council, the European Economic and Social Committee and the Committee of the Regions A DSM Strategy for Europe" SWD(2015)100 Final' (2015) [2.2].

374 Undertakings have significant market power if, either individually or jointly with others, they enjoy 'a position equivalent to dominance, namely a position of economic strength affording (them) the power to behave to an appreciable extent independently of competitors, customers and ultimately consumers' (EECC, art 63).

375 EECC, art 76.

376 EECC, art 68.

377 EECC, art 69.

378 EECC, art 70.

379 EECC, art 71.

380 EECC, art 74.

381 EECC, art 72.

382 EECC, art 73.

383 Katarzyna Lasinska, 'IoT Update: The EECC' (*Global Policy Watch*, 10 August 2018) <www.globalpolicywatch.com/2018/08/iot-update-the-european-electronic-communications-code-developing-the-future-of-iot-in-the-eu/>.

384 EECC, recital 15.

385 EECC, art 2(4).

386 Regulation (EU) 2015/2120 of 25 November 2015 laying down measures concerning open internet access and amending Directive 2002/22/EC on universal service and users' rights relating to

(ii) *Interpersonal communications services*. This is a concept introduced by the code that defines them as 'services that enable interpersonal and interactive exchange of information . . . between a finite . . . number of natural persons, which is determined by the sender of the communication.'[387] This includes services like traditional voice calls between two individuals but also all types of emails, messaging services, or group chat. It should be noted that many IoT communications can be qualified as number-independent interpersonal communications, and these are subject to the code's obligations 'only where public interests require that specific regulatory obligations apply to all types of interpersonal communications services, regardless of whether they use numbers for the provision of their service.'[388]

(iii) *Services consisting wholly of or mainly in the conveyance of signals.*[389] These include transmission services used for the provision of M2M services and for broadcasting.

This reform has led to a change in scope for all the regulations regarding electronic communications services that henceforth will apply to both OTT and 'traditional' services. The code may prima facie be interpreted as narrowing the definition of *electronic communications services* by limiting them to those that are 'normally provided for remuneration,'[390] which may be seen as excluding all those IoT services that are paid by means of personal data.[391] For example, one can call through Amazon Echo without any pecuniary exchange. However, the reference to the remunerations is a merely ostensible limitation, because the preamble[392] of the code clarifies that 'remuneration' encompasses situations where:

(i) The provider of a service requests and the end user knowingly provides personal data or other data directly or indirectly to the provider;

(ii) The end user allows access to information without actively supplying it, such as personal data, including the IP address, or other automatically generated information, such as information collected and transmitted by a cookie;

---

electronic communications networks and services and Regulation (EU) No 531/2012 on roaming on public mobile communications networks within the Union [2015] OJ L 310/1, art 2(2), as referred to by EECC, art 2(4)(a)).

387 EECC, recital 17.
388 EECC, recital 18.
389 EECC, art 2(4).
390 EECC, art 2(4).n.
391 See Guido Noto La Diega, 'Data as Digital Assets. The Case of Targeted Advertising: Towards a Holistic Approach?' in Mor Bakhoum and others (eds), *Personal Data in Competition, Consumer Protection and Intellectual Property Law. Towards a Holistic Approach*? (Springer 2018) 445.
392 EECC, recital 16. On the important interpretive value of EU acts' preambles, see Richard Wainwright, 'Techniques of Drafting European Community Legislation: Problems of Interpretation' (1996) 17 Statute Law Review 7; Tadas Klimas and Jurate Vaiciukaite, 'The Law of Recitals in European Community Legislation' (2008) 15 ILSA Journal of International & Comparative Law 61; Llio Humphreys and others, 'Mapping Recitals to Normative Provisions in EU Legislation to Assist Legal Interpretation' (2015).

(iii) The end user is exposed to advertisements as a condition for gaining access to the service or situations in which the service provider monetises personal data it has collected.[393]

The broader scope resulting from the code's new definition will affect not only telecoms regulations but also all the other regulations that refer to the telecoms framework to define 'electronic communications services.' Most notably, these include the ePrivacy Directive,[394] with an option confirmed in the Draft ePrivacy Regulation.[395] From an IoT perspective, a regulation framework such as this, that is technologically agnostic yet technologically aware, thus not resting upon out-of-date distinctions, is a positive endeavour.

The identification of Things is necessary for a number of reasons, from allowing the communication itself to competition and law enforcement purposes. To this end, numbering can play a key role.[396] Under the EECC, member states should be able to grant rights of use for numbering resources to businesses other than providers of electronic communications networks or services 'in light of the increasing relevance of numbers for various Internet of Things services.'[397] Numbering plans remain managed by national authorities, but the code recognises that there may be the need for EU harmonisation of numbering resources to support 'new machine-to-machine-based services such as connected cars,'[398] in which case the Commission can take implementing measures with the assistance of the Board of European Regulators for Electronic Communications (BEREC). Nonetheless, BEREC rather surprisingly concluded that the scarcity of traditional numbers (so-called E.164) is merely alleged, and it would not constitute a barrier to the development of the IoT.[399] Should numbering become an issue, the reasoning goes, it would have to be solved by national authorities, e.g. by introducing a new numbering range for IoT

---

393 This is in line with Case 352/85 *Bond van Adverteerders and Others v The Netherlands State* [1988] ECR 2085 [7]; remuneration exists within the meaning of the TFEU, art 57 (then TEC, art 50), if the service provider is paid by a third party and not by the service recipient.

394 ePrivacy Directive, art 2. This is the reasonable inference of Rosa Barcelo and Matthew Buckwell, 'New EECC Means the Application of the ePrivacy Directive to OTTs' (*IAPP Privacy Tracker*, 21 December 2018) <https://iapp.org/news/a/new-european-electronic-communications-code-means-the-application-of-the-eprivacy-directive-to-otts/>.

395 Proposal for a Regulation concerning the respect for private life and the protection of personal data in electronic communications and repealing Directive 2002/58/EC ('Draft ePrivacy Regulation') COM/2017/10 final, art 4(1)(b).

396 Meriam Bouzouita and others, 'Estimating the Number of Contending IoT Devices in 5G Networks: Revealing the Invisible' (2019) 30 Transactions on Emerging Telecommunications Technologies e3513.

397 EECC, recital 250.

398 ibid.

399 BEREC, 'Guidelines on Common Criteria for the Assessment of the Ability to Manage Numbering Resources by Undertakings Other than Providers of Electronic Communications Networks or Services and of the Risk of Exhaustion of Numbering Resources If Numbers Are Assigned to Such Undertakings' (2019) BoR (19) 114.

services or increasing the mobile number resources.[400] In light of the transnational nature of the IoT, EU full harmonisation would be preferable.

Traditional regulation is far from perfect. Indeed, it has sometimes led to overregulation and forms of censorship.[401] Moreover, it has allowed industry stakeholders to lobby regulators in an opaque way; this has affected the resulting regulations[402] and sometimes led to the failure to adopt any legislation.[403] For example, in December 2020, a leaked document showed that Amazon endeavoured to 'kill' the reform of the ePrivacy Directive by pitting the EU institutions against each other.[404] Additionally, private stakeholders that are not collectively organised or do not have the means to lobby (e.g. IoT users) have limited or no influence on regulation, despite being often profoundly affected by it.[405] Although these arguments have some merit, there are good reasons to rely on actual laws rather than soft laws.

The legitimacy of hard laws and top-down regulation rests on a positive argument, as well as on a negative one. On the one hand, only states – and, to some extent, supranational institutions such as the EU[406] – are democratically elected and, therefore, have legitimacy to regulate such a pervasive and impactful socio-technological phenomenon. On the other hand, self-regulation, including ethical charters and code, lack constitutional checks and balances for private citizens.[407] It is fair to say that the regulation of the IoT should encompass top-down and self-regulation, hard and soft laws – the crucial point will be to find the right

---

400 BEREC, 'Report on Enabling the Internet of Things' (2016) BoR (16) 39, as cited by BEREC (n 559).

401 Rebecca MacKinnon, 'Consent of the Networked: The Worldwide Struggle for Internet Freedom' (2012) 50 Politique étrangère 432.

402 With records to the telecoms package and the so-called graduated response, Horten (n 315). The same could be said with regards to the Copyright in the DSM Directive. Indeed, in the process of passing this directive, 'MEPs have rarely or never been subject to a similar degree of lobbying before' ('Questions and Answers on Issues about the Digital Copyright Directive' (*European Parliament – JURI*, 27 March 2019) <www.europarl.europa.eu/news/en/press-room/20190111IPR23225/questions-and-answers-on-issues-about-the-digital-copyright-directive>). On the competing agendas pushing the DSM initiatives, see Simone Schroff and John Street, 'The Politics of the DSM: Culture vs. Competition vs. Copyright' (2018) 21 Information, Communication & Society 1305.

403 In the field of net neutrality, see Christopher T Marsden, *Net Neutrality: Towards a Co-Regulatory Solution* (A&C Black 2010).

404 Vincent Manancourt, 'Amazon Sought to Water down EU Privacy Rules' (*Politico*, 10 December 2020) <www.politico.eu/article/amazon-sought-to-water-down-eu-privacy-rules-document-shows/>.

405 Milton L Mueller, *Networks and States: The Global Politics of Internet Governance* (MIT Press 2010).

406 The view that the EU is a democratic institution is a disputed one, the main argument being that the European Parliament does not have proper legislative powers, although it would seem that over the years the democratic deficit has decreased. See Andrew Moravcsik, 'Reassessing Legitimacy in the European Union' (2002) 40 JCMS 603; Christophe Crombez, 'The Democratic Deficit in the European Union: Much Ado about Nothing?' (2003) 4 European Union Politics 101; Miriam Sorace, 'The European Union Democratic Deficit: Substantive Representation in the European Parliament at the Input Stage' (2018) 19 European Union Politics 3.

407 See, more widely, Hans-W Micklitz and others, *Constitutional Challenges in the Algorithmic Society* (Cambridge University Press 2021).

mix of the two. And to include all those hybrid initiatives that go by the name of coregulation.

1.5 Overcoming Regulatory Binaries, Coregulation, and Supervisory Authority

The main regulatory options explored for the IoT exist within a continuum from regulation to self-regulation.[408] Whereas the regulatory discourse is often polarised, non-binary approaches are possible, and on the face of it, this would be suitable for a non-binary phenomenon like the IoT. Between self-regulation – flexible but opaque and not binding – and regulation – binding but accused to stifle innovation – there is a variety of initiatives known as 'coregulation.' There is no agreed definition of coregulation, but most studies refer the term to those situations where 'the State and the private regulators co-operate in joint institutions.'[409] In this chapter, *coregulation* is understood broadly as including the so-called middle-out approach, i.e. all the models that sit between top-down and bottom-up regulation, such as 'monitored self-regulation, coordination mechanisms for good AI governance, and "wind-rose" models for the Web of Data.'[410] Coregulation seems to cope well with increasingly complex technological challenges, as it accommodates 'the uncertainties of innovation, imposing society's preferences on emerging innovation, while allowing us to capture expanding understanding of technological challenges with increasing regulatory granularity.'[411]

The incoming tide of internet coregulation should be read in the context of the increasing use of cost-benefit analysis in selecting and articulating regulatory initiatives.[412] Cost-benefit analysis counters pure self-regulation. Indeed, coregulation can protect democratic processes from interest groups that are pressing for a type of regulation despite the argument to support it being fragile.[413] It is not unreasonable to say that stakeholders should have some influence on the regulation that will affect them, but internet self-regulation does not provide sufficient incentives to shape big tech's behaviour and leaves out small and medium enterprises, including microenterprises, as well as excluding civil society. The latter exclusion constitutes a strong argument in favour of formally inclusive

---

408 Richard Posner, 'Theories of Economic Regulation' (1974) 5 Bell Journal of Economics 335.

409 Hans J Kleinsteuber, 'The Internet between Regulation and Governance' in Christian Moeller and Arnaud Amouroux (eds), *The Media Freedom Internet Cookbook* (OSCE 2004) 61, 63.

410 Ugo Pagallo, Pompeu Casanovas and Robert Madelin, 'The Middle-out Approach: Assessing Models of Legal Governance in Data Protection, Artificial Intelligence, and the Web of Data' (2019) 0 The Theory and Practice of Legislation 1.

411 ibid 25.

412 Christopher T Marsden, *Internet Co-Regulation: European Law, Regulatory Governance and Legitimacy in Cyberspace* (CUP 2011).

413 Cass R Sunstein, 'The Cost-Benefit State: The Future of Regulatory Protection' (American Bar Association 2002).

multistakeholder coregulation, which has been considered 'the best chance to reconcile market failures and constitutional legitimacy failures in self-regulation.'[414]

Interestingly, the first proper attempt to regulate the IoT in the EU can be seen
as a form of coregulation. In May 2009, the European Commission recommended
that industry should develop a framework for privacy impact assessments (PIA)
of RFID applications.[415] However, unlike the US, this framework would have to
be approved by the Article 29 Working Party, then the EU privacy advisory body,
now replaced by the European Data Protection Board. Such industry-led framework approved by a public law body well illustrates coregulation.[416] In July 2009,
an informal 'RFID workgroup' led by industry representatives, began working on
the definition of a PIA Framework, through regular meetings with stakeholders,
including consumer groups, standardisation bodies, and scholars.[417] The first version of the framework was not endorsed for the lack of a proper risk assessment
procedure and a number of issues, including the fact that the submission did not
address 'issues that could arise when tags are carried by individuals in everyday
life.'[418] The Article 29 Working Party was being prescient, if one considers how
the shift from RFID tags to the IoT has meant a proliferation of tracking devices
in our everyday life. In 2011, a revised version was approved,[419] with the purpose
of helping RFID operators 'uncover the privacy risks associated with an RFID
Application, assess their likelihood, and document the steps taken to address
those risks'[420] The framework goes beyond RFID tags to encompass back-end
systems and networked communication infrastructures;[421] therefore, it could be
adapted to more modern and complex IoT systems using RFID technologies. The
PIA Framework played an important role in the development of future initiatives,
such as the IoT Cluster and AIOTI.

An option that can be loosely regarded as coregulation, although it straddles
the coregulation-self-regulation line, is the so-called playground, nowadays more
commonly called regulatory sandbox, especially in the fintech world.[422] The playground, or sandbox, is a framework set up by a regulator to 'allow small scale, live
testing of innovations by private firms in a controlled environment (operating under
a special exemption, allowance, or other limited, time-bound exception) under the

---

414 Brown and Marsden (n 494).
415 European Commission, 'Commission Recommendation of 12 May 2009 on the Implementation
     of Privacy and Data Protection Principles in Applications Supported by Radio-Frequency Identi-
     fication' (2009) C(2009)3200 final.
416 cf Marsden (n 572).
417 Article 29 Working Party, 'Opinion 5/2010 on the Industry Proposal for a Privacy and Data Pro-
     tection Impact Assessment Framework for RFID Applications' (2010) 00066/10/EN WP 175 2.
418 Article 29 Working Party (n 276) 9.
419 Article 29 Working Party, 'Opinion 9/2011 on the Revised Industry Proposal for a Privacy and
     Data Protection Impact Assessment Framework for RFID Applications' (2011) 00327/11/EN WP
     180.
420 'Privacy and Data Protection Impact Assessment Framework for RFID Applications' (12 January
     2011) 3.
421 ibid 4.
422 Financial Conduct Authority, *Regulatory Sandbox* (FCA 2005).

regulator's supervision.'[423] In November 2020, the Council of the EU called on the Commission to consider regulatory sandboxes as a tool for an innovation-friendly, future-proof, sustainable, and resilient EU regulatory framework.[424] As noted by the associate director of Cyber-Physical Systems Program at NIST,[425] it could be possible to move away from the carrot-or-stick mode when it comes to internet regulation, and NIST is working to create a regulatory playground through the Global Cities Challenge programme.[426] The latter allows IoT players to work directly with local governments to test Things in the real world. In particular, it encourages local governments, not-for-profit organizations, academic institutions, technologists, and corporations from all over the world to form project teams to work on groundbreaking IoT applications within the city and community environment.[427] NIST, which is an agency of the US Department of Commerce, is to be praised for the initiative in that it allows meaningful public-private collaboration and oversight in a field that has not reached maturity. However, the more the IoT grows in complexity and pervasiveness, the more it becomes apparent that it is no longer time for playing with sandboxes.

Whilst stakeholder participation is important, it can be argued that consultations could be a sufficient tool to that end and that the case for having private parties (co)dictating the rules that should constrain them has not been done with sufficient strength. Even the direct involvement of civil society, and other weak actors, has raised significant questions as to the effectiveness, accountability, and legitimacy in representing the public interest.[428]

The fact that current laws are not always or entirely fit for the IoT, the unenforceability of self-regulation, and the insufficiency of coregulation led some scholars to argue that a new legal framework must be set up 'in order to allow for an effective introduction of the new information architecture (of the IoT) and therewith protect the developing new services,'[429] while ensuring a high level of cybersecurity, data protection, privacy, and competition.[430] Many believe that institutionalised control mechanisms aimed at policy coordination across sectors,

423 Ivo Jenik and Kate Lauer, 'Regulatory Sandboxes and Financial Inclusion' (2017) WP. Washington, DC: CGAP 1.

424 Council of the European Union, 'Conclusions on Regulatory Sandboxes and Experimentation Clauses as Tools for an Innovation-Friendly, Future-Proof and Resilient Regulatory Framework That Masters Disruptive Challenges in the Digital Age' (2020) 13026/20 BETREG 27.

425 Moore (n 138).

426 Kristy D Thompson, 'Global City Teams Challenge' (*NIST*, 30 June 2014) <www.nist.gov/el/cyber-physical-systems/smart-americaglobal-cities>.

427 Sokwoo Rhee and Martin Burns, 'Global City Teams Challenge 2018 Kickoff and IES-City Framework Workshop' (National Institute of Standards and Technology 2018) NIST SP 1900–201 <https://nvlpubs.nist.gov/nistpubs/SpecialPublications/NIST.SP.1900-201.pdf>.

428 William J Drake and Ernest J Wilson (eds), *Governing Global Electronic Networks* (MIT Press 2008); Mueller (n 565); Brown and Marsden (n 494).

429 Rolf H Weber, 'Accountability in the Internet of Things' (2011) 27 CLSR 133.

430 Helen Rebecca Schindler and others, 'Europe's Policy Options for a Dynamic and Trustworthy Development of the Internet of Things' (RAND 2013) SMART 2012/0053.

regions, and areas is needed.[431] This would be coherent with the inherently fragmented and non-binary nature of the IoT.

There is no agreement, however, on which institution should have a supervisory role in the IoT. Some see the European Commission as the natural holder of the relative powers,[432] and this would serve the purpose of strengthening an EU vision of the IoT. However, such a solution would ignore the genuinely global nature of the IoT, and it would provide stakeholders with opaque means to influence the process. Accordingly, others believe that an ad hoc nongovernmental international organisation would be a better fit for the role of IoT supervisory authority.[433] The latter would be composed of a 'mixture of governmental officials, representative of private sector and scholars.'[434] This option has been seen as more suitable, given that academic research could provide a sound empirical basis for the new body's actions and that 'the IoT is mainly used by private entities.'[435] This argument is open to a twofold criticism. First, public entities are increasingly part of the IoT world, as exemplified by the smart cities phenomenon.[436] Second, gun manufacturers are mostly private companies, but it does not mean that they get to supervise themselves.[437]

More generally, an ad hoc international authority would be cumbersome to set up; accordingly, the task could be given to an existing organisation, e.g. the World Trade Organization (WTO) or the Organization for Economic Co-operation and Development (OECD).[438] This solution would have a more rapid implementation, provided that the parties could agree on giving more resources (e.g. specialised staff) to the relevant body. The proposal has been criticised because private stakeholders cannot be elected to WTO and OECD committees.[439] Whilst for the aforementioned reasons the exclusion of the industry from the IoT supervisory body would not be necessarily negative, the main argument against this solution is that the regulation of the IoT would risk being affected by the specific mission of the relevant body. For example, a WTO committee as the prospective IoT authority would benefit from the enforcement actions ensured by the dispute settlement body. However, the resulting regulation would probably be trade-oriented: a focus on competition may obliterate other perspectives, e.g. sustainability and human rights.

Arguably, an international and cross-sector coordination between existing regulatory authorities would be an IoT-friendly solution. Italy's Permanent Committee

---

431 Rolf H Weber and Romana Weber, *Internet of Things. Legal Perspectives* (Springer Berlin Heidelberg 2010); Schindler and others (n 590).
432 Schindler and others (n 590).
433 Weber and Weber (n 591); Weber (n 589).
434 Weber and Weber (n 41) 29.
435 Hoppner and Gubanova (n 254) 228.
436 Wilson and Cali (n 108).
437 Asif Efrat, *Governing Guns, Preventing Plunder International Cooperation against Illicit Trade* (OUP 2012).
438 Weber and Weber (n 591).
439 Hoppner and Gubanova (n 392).

on M2M Communication could be a best practice that could be scaled up. This was set up in 2016 by Italy's Communications Authority (AGCOM) with the goal of ensuring the necessary exchanges between all IoT regulators so that the subsequent policies could be consistent with the other authorities' activities. Alongside AGCOM, whose president chairs the committee, other members are the Electric Energy, Gas, and Water Authority (AEEGSI), the Transportation Authority (ART), the Digital Italy Agency (AGID), and the Ministry for the Economic Development (MISE). Building on this experience, this book invites European and international authorities to consider the setting up of an International Regulation Coordination Organisation for the IoT (IRCOIOT). This would be along the same lines of one of the last brilliant ideas of Giovanni Buttarelli, the European Data Protection supervisor who passed away in August 2019. Buttarelli launched the idea of a 'Digital Clearinghouse,' a voluntary network of regulators involved in the enforcement of legal regimes in digital markets, with a focus on data protection, consumer, and competition law.[440] The European Parliament endorsed the initiative underlining the importance of deepening regulatory synergies to safeguard the rights and interests of individuals.[441] More recently, in issuing an opinion on online manipulation – rendered easier by the ubiquitous presence of Things[442] – Buttarelli reiterated the idea that 'no single regulatory approach will be sufficient on its own, and that regulators therefore need to collaborate urgently to tackle not only localised abuses but also both the structural distortions.'[443] In this vein, as of April 2021, the main digital regulators in the UK – Competition and Markets Authority, Information Commissioner's Office, Office of Communications, and Financial Conduct Authority – strengthened the coordination between their activities by pooling expertise and resources, working more closely together on online regulatory matters of mutual importance, and reporting on results annually.[444] The main drawbacks of this initiative is its overlooking the global dimension of internet governance and its having too broad a mandate (the regulation of digital and online services). IRCOIOT would learn from these experiences and constitute a stable cross-sectoral and cross-border organism entrusted with regulating the IoT in a coordinated manner. It could even be initially conceived as a unit within the Digital Clearinghouse.

---

440 European Data Protection Supervisor, 'EDPS Opinion on Coherent Enforcement of Fundamental Rights in the Age of Big Data' (2016) Opinion 8/2016.
441 European Parliament, 'Resolution of 14 March 2017 on Fundamental Rights Implications of Big Data: Privacy, Data Protection, Non-Discrimination, Security and Law-Enforcement (2016/2225(INI)) [2018] OJ C 263/82' (2017).
442 Natali Helberger, 'Profiling and Targeting Consumers in the Internet of Things – A New Challenge for Consumer Law' in Reiner Schulze and Dirk Staudenmayer (eds), *Digital Revolution: Challenges for Contract Law in Practice* (Nomos 2016).
443 European Data Protection Supervisor, 'EDPS Opinion on Online Manipulation and Personal Data' (2018) Opinion 3/2018. 7.
444 Digital Regulation Cooperation Forum, 'A Joined-up Approach to Digital Regulation' (*Gov.UK*, 10 March 2021) <www.gov.uk/government/news/a-joined-up-approach-to-digital-regulation>.

1.6 Interim Conclusion

As noted in the epitaph, it is thanks to the regulatory interventions of the medieval guilds that the master could not become a capitalist. The nature itself of the IoT calls into question whether it is possible to rein in the power of the IoT overlords. Regulating capitalists has always proved arduous for the simple reason that 'profit is the only regulator for capitalist production.'[445] The difficulty is augmented in the IoT due to the difficulty of defining it, its sectoral fragmentation, relational black box, and global nature. However, this state of things does not justify defeatist attitudes; conversely, it should push us to find better and more sophisticated legal – and nonlegal – solutions to some of the most pressing issues of our time.

In light of the risks of the IoT – from ubiquitous surveillance to consumer safety – fresh evidence is necessary to reassess if existing laws are still fit for purpose, if amendments or new laws are needed, and what regulatory strategy can steer the development of the IoT in a socially just direction. This book aspires to contribute to an evidence-based regulatory discourse. Whilst the case for IoT-specific laws has not been made, it does seem that many of the current laws that are relevant from an IoT perspectives are not fit for this sociotechnological phenomenon. Indeed, they tend to rely on those same dichotomies that the IoT is calling into question: online-offline, hardware-software, good-service, personal-nonpersonal. IoT-aware legal reforms are needed, and they should include top-down regulation. We are beyond the hype, and with IoT technologies reaching maturity, it does no longer make sense – if it ever did – to argue that regulating would stifle innovation. Hard, binding laws seem the most appropriate response to a market dominated by few fine-immune, rent-seeking US- and China-based large corporations. To regulate the IoT is no easy task. Whilst absolute extraterritoriality – such as the one enshrined in the GDPR and the AI Act – can be regarded as an excessive measure, more moderate solutions could adopt the model of some DSM measures. Coregulation is not to be dismissed, as long as (i) the ultimate responsibility for the framework rests with the lawmaker, (ii) it does not become the vehicle for private actors without democratic legitimacy writing their own rules, and (iii) consumers and workers can influence the process on an equal stand with IoT companies. In any event, coregulation is by itself insufficient and should be part of a wider strategy with hard laws at its core, and self-regulations (especially ethics and regulation by design) at its periphery.

Such an integrated and non-binary strategy is not miles away from what the EU is already doing, with a mix of regulations (e.g. on free flow of nonpersonal data), coregulation (the PIA Framework on RFID), and self-regulation (e.g. AIOTI and its industry-driven IoT ecosystem). The content of these regulations, policies, etc. is open to criticism, but the idea of a complex strategy, with a focus on 'traditional' regulation, is the most suitable for the IoT, although not in itself sufficient. Finally, given the global nature of the IoT, the sectoral fragmentation, and the

---

445 Marx, 'Economic Manuscript of 1861–63. A Contribution to the Critique of Political Economy' (n 1) 617.

multidisciplinary legal issues thereof, there would be the need for some form of international supervision. This should not be played by a specific IoT authority, be it ad hoc or within existing organisations. Instead, IRCOIOT is proposed, an International Regulation Coordination Organisation for the IoT, which brings together existing horizontal and vertical regulators in a cross-sector and cross-border way.

2 The Internet of Spying Sex Toys, Killer Petrol Stations, and Manipulative Toasters: A View of Private Ordering from the Contractual Quagmire

> *Outside contract, the very concepts of subject and will exist only as lifeless abstractions in the legal sense.*
>
> Pashukanis, *General Theory of Law and Marxism*

2.1 Scope of Chapter and Private Ordering

This chapter aims to answer the following research subquestion: *what are the main consumer threats in the IoT based on the analysis of the terms and conditions of Amazon Echo?* To this end, it will map the main consumer issues in the IoT and focus on how these are enabled by the fact that IoT companies exploit gaps, inadequacies, and obsolescence of existing laws to put in place dubious practices of 'private ordering'.

Private ordering will be mainly observed through the lens of the contractual quagmire, i.e. the instrumental use of contracts to control the Thing and, ultimately, its user. The contractual quagmire is a core component of private ordering that includes other legal, factual, and technical forms of rule-making by private stakeholders. This private ordering is the direct or indirect cause of virtually all the consumer issues considered in this book, and its contractual species justifies the empirical qualitative analysis of IoT contracts presented here. Private ordering has become a fashionable topic in the studies about digital platforms, which are becoming as powerful as states and are accordingly assuming quasi-lawmaking powers.[1] However, private ordering predates the rise of platforms and goes beyond them. When it comes to private ordering in the IoT, the starting point is that this sociotechnological phenomenon is moving at such a fast pace that existing laws struggle to keep up. This leaves ample room for private ordering, which is private companies' power to unilaterally regulate the IoT taking advantage of the lacunae and legacy issues in existing laws and of the slowness of the lawmaking process. The private agreements that instantiate private ordering

---

1 Rossana Ducato, 'Private Ordering of Online Platforms in Smart Urban Mobility: The Case of Uber's Rating System' in Michèle Finck and others (eds), *Smart Urban Mobility: Law, Regulation, and Policy* (Springer 2020) 301.

DOI: 10.4324/9780429468377-3

in the IoT can be regarded as eluding the law, but also as a form of response to a legislative framework that always (and inevitably) lags behind technological developments, often resulting in regulatory voids.[2] While the focus of this chapter is on contractual private ordering, technical private ordering is as problematic. The latter's paradigm is the ability of IoT traders to shape market relationships through the use of algorithms and other opaque technologies – Lessig's code as law and Brownsword's technological management, as seen in the previous chapter. Regrettably, the details of such 'technical' private ordering are kept hidden mainly through a combination of trade secrets and technical protection measures. As such, there is not sufficient data to attempt to analyse this type of private ordering. Conversely, data on 'contractual' private ordering is at least partly publicly available. The reference is to the numerous Terms of Service, privacy policies, etc. (collectively 'legals') that consumers are asked to accept if they want to use a Thing. This unilateral imposition is at odds with the principle of autonomy that is pivotal to the idea itself of contracts.

As Hegel put it:[3]

> Everyone, we are told, makes a contract with the sovereign, and he in turn with the subjects . . . But . . . the contract . . . originates in the arbitrary will of the person . . . in the case of the state, this is different from the outset, for the arbitrary will of individuals is not in a position to break away from the state, because the individual is already by nature its citizen.

The essence of a contract is the 'arbitrary will' of the contracting party and their ability to break away from the contract. It could be said that the relationship between IoT companies and their users is reminiscent of the relationship between states and citizens, rather than being of a genuinely contractual nature. Indeed, in IoT contracting there is no room for the arbitrary will of the IoT users, who are forced to accept a cascade of 'legals' when using their Things, following an increasingly common take-it-or-leave-it approach. In this sense, IoT users can be regarded as the subjects of the new 'smart' state under the rule of IoT's big players.

2.2 A Four-Pronged Methodology

This chapter adopts a four-pronged methodology. First, a desk-based literature review is carried out to map benefits and issues in the IoT. While the perspective is a European one, English law is considered in those areas that have not been harmonised. The UK has retained most of the EU acquis,[4] and although as of January 2021 the UK is no longer obliged to comply with EU law, it is likely that

---

2 See David Castle, *The Role of Intellectual Property Rights in Biotechnology Innovation* (Edward Elgar Publishing 2009).

3 Georg Wilhelm Friedrich Hegel, *Elements of the Philosophy of Right (1820)* (HB Nisbet tr, Allen W Wood, CUP 1991) [76].

4 European Union (Withdrawal) Act 2018, ss 2–4.

it will retain legislative and regulatory convergence with its main commercial partner due to the so-called Brussels effect.[5] This research has been carried out between Newcastle upon Tyne, Palermo, and Stirling. However, I have not taken an Italian law to increase the accessibility of the text, as most readers will not be able to access Italian sources. I have not taken a Scots law angle either because although some of the topics covered in this book impinge on devolved matters (e.g. human rights), the Scotland Act 1998 reserved to the UK Parliament legislative competence over internet services, IP, and much consumer protection and commercial law.[6]

Second, the chapter takes a case study approach and examines the complexity of the IoT through the lens of a specific series of products, i.e. the Echo 'family.' Its components varied over time, but at the time of writing, this series included Echo and Echo Plus, the can-shaped, voice-activated, web-connected speakers produced by Amazon and equipped with speech-controlled virtual assistant Alexa; Dot (its smaller and less-powerful version); Show (equipped with a display); Spot (alarm clock); Look (style assistant); Input (to bring Alexa to third-party speakers); Flex (plug-in speaker); Button (game buzzer); and Wall Clock. The terms of service, privacy policies, end user license agreements, etc. of these products (hereinafter 'Echo's legals') provide a good case study of IoT complexity because Echo and Alexa appear to be leading the smart home market.[7] To do so, the next sections will carry out a text analysis of Echo's legals. Any documents have been accessed in the UK in April 2020 from a desktop computer and an Android phone. Such a method was first used in 2016[8] when, looking at Google Nest Thermostat, it was found that for a single seemingly simple Thing, thousands of contracts would apply. Shoshana Zuboff underlined how this is a salient and worrying feature of surveillance capitalism.[9] I have replicated the Google Nest experiment to critically assess if the considerations that were made with regards to Nest are applicable to Echo, which would suggest their potential for generalisation. The choice of this case study is due to the fact that (i) consumer goods are the fastest-growing domain in the Fourth Industrial Revolution,[10] (ii) the Echo range is the clear market leader in the field of home automation,[11] (iii) Amazon's cloud

---

5 Anu Bradford, *The Brussels Effect: How the European Union Rules the World* (OUP 2020).

6 Scotland Act 1998, sch 5, C10, C4, C7. See Hector MacQueen, 'Intellectual Property in a Peripheral Jurisdiction' in David Vaver and Lionel Bently (eds), *Intellectual Property in the New Millennium* (CUP 2004) 58.

7 Andria Cheng, 'What Amazon is Doing to Keep Alexa in the Lead' (*Forbes*, 26 June 2018) <www.forbes.com/sites/andriacheng/2018/07/26/what-amazon-is-doing-to-keep-alexa-in-the-lead/>.

8 Guido Noto La Diega and Ian Walden, 'Contracting for the "Internet of Things": Looking into the Nest' (2016) 7 European Journal of Law and Technology <http://ejlt.org/article/view/450>.

9 Shoshana Zuboff, *The Age of Surveillance Capitalism: The Fight for a Human Future at the New Frontier of Power* (PublicAffairs 2019) 226.

10 European Patent Office, 'Patents and the Fourth Industrial Revolution: The Global Technology Trends Enabling the Data-Driven Economy' (2020) 9 <www.epo.org/service-support/publications.html?pubid=222#tab3>.

11 'Smart Speaker Shipments Worldwide by Vendor 2020' (*Statista*) <www.statista.com/statistics/796349/worldwide-smart-speaker-shipment-by-vendor/>.

services AWS seem to have become the de facto hidden infrastructure of cloud-enabled products and services in Europe,[12] and (iv) the use of data by Amazon is under increasing public scrutiny, as most recently epitomised by its being handed the largest fine to date under the GDPR.[13] The limitation of this method is that there is no sufficient data as to how these legals are implemented; therefore, it cannot be excluded that the actual practices diverge from the stated policies.

Third, Amazon's corporate group will be scrutinised. The data on Amazon's conglomerate is not public, but it is partly accessible through the European e-Justice Portal.[14] The analysis was carried out in April 2020 with a method developed to study Uber,[15] where the text analysis of Uber's legals was coupled with the interrogation of national and international databases held by Companies House and its counterparts. This time, I focused on the latest available version of the business register's documents and dedicated particular attention to the Annual Accounts of 2020.[16] Amazon EU S.à r.l.'s accounts did not contain a full list of subsidiaries; therefore, it was necessary to analyse the documentation of the ultimate parent, that is, Amazon.com Inc., based in Seattle (Washington). It should be noted that information available about US companies varies according to state law and detailed disclosure is often optional.[17] The state of Washington discloses very limited information (Figure 2.1).[18]

Fortunately, since Amazon's shares are traded publicly, they also need to register with the Securities and Exchange Commission (SEC), whose data policies are more open. Through SEC's database, it was possible to access Amazon.com Inc.'s annual report.[19] The information on the supply chain has also been sourced by Amazon's customer advisers, to whom I submitted queries by email and on through Amazon's live chat.

Finally, the chapter concludes with some autoethnographic remarks. *Autoethnography* is a 'research method and methodology which uses the researcher's personal

---

12 cf Ingrid Burrington, 'Why Amazon's Data Centers Are Hidden in Spy Country' (*The Atlantic*, 8 January 2016) <www.theatlantic.com/technology/archive/2016/01/amazon-web-services-data-center/423147/>.

13 Amazon.com, Inc., SEC Form-Q, for the quarterly period ended June 30, 2021 (US Securities and Exchange Commission file no 000–22513/2021) 13.

14 'European E-Justice Portal' (*e-Justice Europa*) <https://beta.e-justice.europa.eu/489/EN/business_registers__search_for_a_company_in_the_eu>.

15 Guido Noto La Diega and Luce Jacovella, 'UBERTRUST: How Uber Represents Itself to Its Customers Through Its Legal and Non-Legal Documents' (2016) 5 Journal of Civil and Legal Sciences 199.

16 Amazon EU S.à r.l., 'Registre de Commerce et Des Sociétés No RCS B101818; Référence de Dépôt L200046766; Déposé et Enregistré on 13 March 2020'.

17 Companies House, 'Overseas Registries' (*Gov.UK*, 5 June 2018) <www.gov.uk/government/publications/overseas-registries/overseas-registries>.

18 'Business Lookup' (*Washington State Department of Revenue*) <https://secure.dor.wa.gov/gteunauth/_/>.

19 Amazon.com, Inc., 'US Securities and Exchange Commission, Form 10-K No 000–22513 Annual Report for the Fiscal Year Ended on 31 December 2019' <www.sec.gov/ix?doc=/Archives/edgar/data/1018724/000101872420000004/amzn-20191231x10k.htm>.

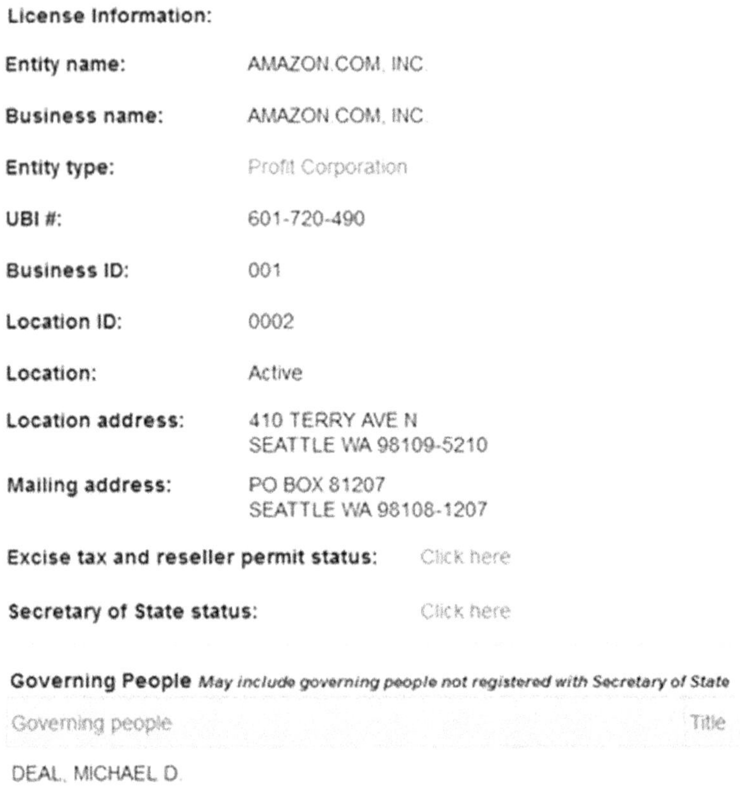

License Information:

Entity name:	AMAZON.COM, INC
Business name:	AMAZON.COM, INC
Entity type:	Profit Corporation
UBI #:	601-720-490
Business ID:	001
Location ID:	0002
Location:	Active
Location address:	410 TERRY AVE N SEATTLE WA 98109-5210
Mailing address:	PO BOX 81207 SEATTLE WA 98108-1207
Excise tax and reseller permit status:	Click here
Secretary of State status:	Click here

Governing People *May include governing people not registered with Secretary of State*

Governing people   Title

DEAL, MICHAEL D.

Figure 2.1 License information regarding Amazon.com Inc., obtained through the Washington State Department of Revenue's database on 4 April 2020.

experience as data to describe, analyze and understand cultural experience.'[20] By sharing one's personal experience, emotions, and interactions – in my case, oscillating between euphoria and frustration – autoethnography contributes to a richer and more meaningful understanding of the relevant phenomenon.

2.3 Consumer Benefits

It is beyond contention that the IoT has the potential to greatly benefit consumers and society at large. Compared to 'nonsmart' devices and systems, Things provide new functionalities thanks to their sensing, actuating, connectivity, and

---

20 Elaine Campbell, 'Exploring Autoethnography as a Method and Methodology in Legal Education Research' (2016) 3 Asian Journal of Legal Education 95, 96. The author refers to Tony E Adams, Stacy Linn Holman Jones and Carolyn Ellis, *Autoethnography* (OUP 2015).

communication capabilities.[21] Services that once were available only offline or by accessing a desktop computer are becoming decentralised and accessible from every Thing and on the go.[22] Complex Things such as driverless cars will allow human drivers to use their commute time for alternative, more useful activities[23] and will allow people who cannot or prefer not to drive a vehicle to travel more easily.[24] Saving costs and minimising the impact on the environment are other ways in which Things can be advantageous. For example, the new generation of thermostats automatically adjust the temperature, thus reducing the pollution and the costs associated with excessive heating.[25] By leveraging the big data produced by Things, traders can tailor their products and services and offer, for example, discounted insurance rates to consumers who allow the insurance company to remotely monitor car usage.[26] This granular information can also be used to show us personalised offers and more relevant advertising.[27] As noted optimistically in the influential *Zero Marginal Cost Society*, the IoT is 'pushing large segments of economic life to near zero marginal cost';[28] thus, it would usher into a future where Things are 'nearly free, and abundant, and no longer subject to market forces.'[29] Finally, the ability of manufacturers to remotely modify Things means that upgrades can be delivered over the air throughout the life cycle of the Thing, whose performance could endlessly improve.[30] Smarter can also mean safer. Indeed, Things can alert manufacturers of unsafe conditions or use, and the manufacturer could deactivate or 'brick' the unsafe Thing,[31] alert the consumers, and deliver fixes without necessarily recalling the Thing.[32] Safety issues may also be prevented upstream using RFID and other tracking technologies, including the

---

21 Consumers International, 'Connection and Protection in the Digital Age. The Internet of Things and Challenges for Consumer Protection' (2016).

22 Miryam Bianco, '"Take Care, Neo: The Fridge Has You": A Technology-Aware Legal Review of Consumer Usability Issues in the Internet of Things' (2016) Nexa Center for Internet & Society.

23 Department for Transport, *The Pathway to Driverless Cars* (UK Gov 2015) <https://nls.ldls.org. uk/welcome.html?ark:/81055/vdc_100063396695.0x000001>.

24 Jeffrey K Gurney, 'Sue My Car Not Me: Products Liability and Accidents Involving Autonomous Vehicles' [2013] University of Illinois Journal of Law, Technology & Policy 247.

25 OECD, 'Consumer Product Safety in the Internet of Things' (2018) OECD Digital Economy Paper no 267.

26 Scott R Peppet, 'Regulating the Internet of Things: First Steps Toward Managing Discrimination, Privacy, Security, and Consent' (2014) 93 Texas Law Review 85.

27 Natali Helberger, 'Profiling and Targeting Consumers in the Internet of Things – A New Challenge for Consumer Law' in Reiner Schulze and Dirk Staudenmayer (eds), *Digital Revolution: Challenges for Contract Law in Practice* (Nomos 2016).

28 Jeremy Rifkin, *The Zero Marginal Cost Society* (Palgrave Macmillan 2015) 3.

29 ibid.

30 OECD, 'The Internet of Things: Seizing the Benefits and Addressing the Challenges' (2016) OECD Digital Economy Papers 252 <www.oecd-ilibrary.org/science-and-technology/the-internet-of-things_5jlwvzz8td0n-en>.

31 Natasha Tusikov, 'Regulation through "Bricking": Private Ordering in the "Internet of Things"' (2019) 8 Internet Policy Review.

32 OECD (n 25).

blockchain,[33] to identify risks to the supply chains in real time and mitigate them promptly.[34]

This is only one side of the coin, however. The other side is a dark tale of spying sex toys, killer petrol stations, and manipulative toasters. Indeed, as examined in the next sections, consumers encounter risks that go well beyond invasions of privacy, due to the core features of IoT technologies, in particular their physicality, ubiquity, and invisibility.

2.4 The Main Risks Encountered by Consumers of Things

The main threats IoT consumers should be aware of are:

   (i) Surveillance capitalism and its challenges to privacy and data protection.
  (ii) The 'death of ownership' that transforms consumers into digital tenants because IoT traders either retain ownership of the Thing or retain control over it via IP rights, contracts, and technological measures.
 (iii) Private ordering 'by bricking,' that is, the IoT traders' ability to remotely monitor consumers and automatically downgrade the Thing, discontinue the service, remove functionalities, determine the lifespan of the Thing, and even deactivate or 'brick' it.
 (iv) Defective and vulnerable Things. Current legal regimes struggle to cope with new defects (e.g. software updates, inaccurate sensors, etc.) and vulnerabilities (e.g. the limitations stemming from software instructions and training datasets that affect the capacity to predict human behaviour in real-world scenarios).
  (v) IoT commerce and the limited opportunities to inform consumers who make transactions while immersed in hyperconnected interface-free environments.
 (vi) The Internet of Personalised Things. Things allow traders to personalise products, services, prices, and 'legals.' Situational data and granular knowledge of biases and human vulnerabilities allow these traders to manipulate consumers and even discriminate against them, thus hindering their trust.
(vii) The contractual quagmire, namely, the plethora of 'legals' that IoT consumers are forced to accept when using their Things.

Some of these issues are at the core of 'traditional' consumer law in the sense of that field of law that expressly regulates the relationship between consumers and traders. Within consumer law, some regimes deal with business-to-consumer contracts. These include the Consumer Sales Directive,[35] recently paired with

---

33 See Marco Conoscenti, Antonio Vetro and Juan Carlos De Martin, 'Blockchain for the Internet of Things: A Systematic Literature Review' (IEEE 2016).
34 OECD (n 25).
35 Directive 1999/44/EC of 25 May 1999 on certain aspects of the sale of consumer goods and associated guarantees [1999] OJ L 171/12.

the Digital Content Directive;[36] the Consumer Rights Directive;[37] and the Unfair Terms Directive.[38] The next chapter will critically assess whether they can tackle issues iii, v, vii, respectively. Other 'traditional' consumer laws protect consumers regardless of a contractual relationship, most notably Product Liability Directive[39] and the Unfair Commercial Practices Directive.[40] Chapter 4 will explore their suitability to deal with issues iv and v respectively. Finally, to successfully tackle the consumer issues in the IoT, it is crucial to adopt an integrated approach that encompasses also laws that are not normally regarded as consumer laws as the existence of a consumer is not a precondition for their application. In particular, Chapter 4 will consider whether data protection and intellectual property law can protect consumers against IoT traders' abuses, as epitomised by i and ii, respectively.

2.4.1 Surveillance Capitalism and the Insufficiency of a Privacy-Only Approach

The vast majority of legal studies on the IoT have a privacy focus.[41] When everything that we wear, hold, ingest, or that surrounds us collects granular data about us, sends it back to the manufacturer, and shares it with an unknown number of third parties, there is no doubt that our privacy is at stake. Indeed, as Shoshana Zuboff asserts, we do live in the age of surveillance capitalism.[42] It is also true that, even though the GDPR may increase the level of the protection of the right to privacy in the EU, it has a number of shortcomings, such as its focus on rights that individuals do not have the time and resources to invoke and fines that do not appear to have a deterrence effect on the main corporate players.[43] At the same time, the GDPR penalises smaller businesses by imposing unaffordable compli-

---

36 Directive (EU) 2019/770 of 20 May 2019 on certain aspects concerning contracts for the supply of digital content and digital services [2019] OJ L 136/1.

37 Directive 2011/83/EU of 25 October 2011 on consumer rights, amending Council Directive 93/13/EEC and repealing Council Directive 1999/44/EC and repealing Council Directive 85/577/EEC and Directive 97/7/EC Text with EEA relevance [2011] OJ L 304/64.

38 Council Directive 93/13/EEC of 5 April 1993 on unfair terms in consumer contracts [1993] OJ L 95/29.

39 Council Directive 85/374/EEC of 25 July 1985 on the approximation of the laws, regulations, and administrative provisions of the member states concerning liability for defective products [1985] OJ L 210/29.

40 Directive 2005/29/EC of 11 May 2005 concerning unfair business-to-consumer commercial practices in the internal market and amending Council Directive 84/450/EEC, Directives 97/7/EC, 98/27/EC and 2002/65/EC and Regulation (EC) No 2006/2004 [2005] OJ L 149/22.

41 See e.g. Burkhard Schafer and Lilian Edwards, '"I Spy, with My Little Sensor": Fair Data Handling Practices for Robots between Privacy, Copyright and Security' (2017) 29 Connection Science 200; Aurelia Tamò-Larrieux, *Designing for Privacy and Its Legal Framework: Data Protection by Design and Default for the Internet of Things* (Springer 2018).

42 Zuboff (n 9).

43 W Gregory Voss and Hugues Bouthinon-Dumas, 'EU General Data Protection Regulation Sanctions in Theory and in Practice' (2020) 37 Santa Clara High Technology Law Journal.

ance burdens.[44] Chapter 5 will investigate this further. Justifiable as it may be, the privacy angle has obfuscated other equally important threats to consumers, as well as keeping in the shadow other legal regimes that could play a key role in empowering consumers and making sure that the IoT remains human-centric.[45]

There are three reasons that a privacy-only approach does not help IoT consumers. They have to do with weakness of consent as a justification for processing, the death of ownership, and the contractual quagmire. First, data protection laws require a legal basis for personal data processing, and this is usually interpreted as an obligation to seek the data subject's consent, though only a minority of companies obtain a consent that would comply with the high standards set by data protection laws.[46] The other go-to legal basis is legitimate interest, but it is not available when data is used in ways individuals reasonably expect and which have a minimal privacy impact;[47] therefore, it will not be of much help in many IoT scenarios, where it is hard to understand how data is (re)used and where sensor data is recombined in privacy-invasive ways.[48]

Consent-based approaches have proved to be useless, especially when data controllers hold 'data power,'[49] a multifaceted form of power arising from the control over data flows.[50] Thanks to IoT data power, traders can impose unlawful, opaque, or otherwise unfair data practices – and the data subjects are forced to accept. The take-it-or-leave-it approach has both a contractual and technical basis. The former is exemplified by *Deroo-Blanquart v Sony Europe*,[51] when the CJEU considered fair the practice whereby Sony obliged its laptops' consumers to accept the operating system's EULA. The latter is best expressed in Lessig's words about code as the law of cyberspace, where individuals are deprived of the choice of whether to conform to this new 'law':

> One obeys these laws as code not because one should; one obeys these laws as code because one can do nothing else. There is no choice about whether

44 Craig McAllister, 'What about Small Businesses' (2017) 12 Brooklyn Journal of Corporate, Financial & Commercial Law 187. cf CMS, 'GDPR Enforcement Tracker – List of GDPR Fines' (*Enforcement Tracker*) <www.enforcementtracker.com>.

45 Consumers International (n 21); Bianco (n 22); Kayleen Manwaring, 'Emerging Information Technologies: Challenges for Consumers' (2017) 17 Oxford University Commonwealth Law Journal 265; Tusikov (n 31).

46 Martino Trevisan and others, '4 Years of EU Cookie Law: Results and Lessons Learned' (2019) 2019 Proceedings on Privacy Enhancing Technologies 126.

47 See e.g. Agencia Española de Protección de Datos, decision 17 October 2020 No 72167.

48 cf Lokke Moerel and Corien Prins, 'Privacy for the Homo Digitalis: Proposal for a New Regulatory Framework for Data Protection in the Light of Big Data and the Internet of Things' [2016] SSRN <https://papers.ssrn.com/abstract=2784123>.

49 Orla Lynskey, 'Grappling with "Data Power": Normative Nudges from Data Protection and Privacy' (2019) 20 Theoretical Inquiries in Law 189.

50 ibid. refers it to digital platforms. Whilst in that context data power is particularly evident, this data power is held also by all the IoT traders the control data flows throughout the supply chain, without necessarily qualifying as platforms.

51 Case C-310/15 *Deroo-Blanquart v Sony Europe* [2016] 1 WLR 4538.

to yield to the demand for a password; one complies if one wants to enter the system.[52]

The other two reasons that privacy-only approaches are insufficient coincide with distinct, albeit overlapping, consumer issues in the IoT and will be therefore analysed in the following sections.

2.4.2 The Death of Ownership in the New Rentier Capitalism

The 'death of ownership' phenomenon refers to the fact that we do not own our Things – we are digital tenants.[53] Even when we formally own 'our' Things, IP rights, contracts, and technological measures prevent us from having control over them.[54] The death of ownership has repercussions on most consumer rights, as seen in Joshua Fairfield's *Owned*,[55] which opens with a story of spying sex toys. In 2016, a class action lawsuit was brought against smart erotic massage manufacturer Standard Innovation.[56] This Thing had been collecting its users' most intimate data, including date and time of usage and temperature. Standard Innovation would collect data via the We-Connect app and use it for market research purposes. The embedded software would secretly send the users' data onto the manufacturer's servers. Standard Innovation was able to argue that this practice was lawful because users had accepted the EULA, which disclosed the relevant processing activities and because the company could use their copyright on the embedded software to factually control the Thing in its entirety. The fact that IP and contract law have 'crowded out everyday property ownership'[57] led Fairfield to conclude that we must restore such ownership, else we are owned.[58] Although this solution will be contested in Chapter 6, *Owned* provides a good analytical framework to understand the power dynamics underpinning the IoT. The shift in control illuminated by the death of ownership cannot be addressed solely through data protection. Despite the GDPR's emphasis on restoring consumer control over data, it does not seem adequately equipped to counter the death of ownership, as it provides limited tools to rebalance IP-related and contractual imbalances. For example, the GDPR concedes that IP rights may prevail data subject rights, although it does not clarify how the conflict should be resolved.[59]

---

52 Lawrence Lessig, 'The Zones of Cyberspace' (1995) 48 Stanford Law Review 1403.
53 Joshua AT Fairfield, *Owned: Property, Privacy, and the New Digital Serfdom* (CUP 2017).
54 Bianco (n 22).
55 Fairfield (n 53).
56 *N.P. v. Standard Innovation (US)*, Corp., case number 1:16-cv-08655. The dispute was settled.
57 Fairfield (n 53) 2.
58 cf Christina Mulligan, 'Personal Property Servitudes on the Internet of Things' (2015) 50 Georgia Law Review 1121.
59 GDPR, arts 15(4) and 20(4), read jointly with recital 63. We provided guidance on this in Guido Noto La Diega and Cristiana Sappa, 'The Internet of Things at the Intersection of Data Protection and Trade Secrets. Non-Conventional Paths to Counter Data Appropriation and Empower Consumers' [2020] REDC 419.

The erotic Thing case study is also illustrative of a third reason that privacy-only approaches are inadequate, as well as a consumer issue in its own right: the 'contractual quagmire.'

2.4.3 Private Ordering by 'Bricking'

A third issue is private ordering by 'bricking.' This is a manifestation of the aforementioned 'technical' private ordering, that is, the phenomenon whereby private companies take advantage of legal gaps and of the slowness of the lawmaking process to impose their own rules on consumers of new technologies. This can be done in subtle ways, for example, by using opaque algorithms to manipulate our emotions.[60] Some forms of technical private ordering are kept secret. However, other forms can be inferred by the legals and by the observation of common practices. Private ordering by 'bricking' refers to manufacturers and third parties having control over the Thing or over some of its components, and thus being able to downgrade it, remotely delete contents, discontinue software updates, prevent lawful and fair uses by design, and determine the Thing's lifespan. *Bricking* here means deactivating, as in depriving a Thing of its 'smartness.'

The ability to do so stems from the joint operation of the non-binary nature of the IoT – not entirely goods, not entirely services – the death of property, the data power held by IoT traders, the remote-monitoring capabilities of the Things, and the contracts providing a dubious legal basis for abusive practices.

The phenomenon has been regarded as a form of 'private regulation by bricking'[61] by an author who has focused on the deliberate impairment or destruction of software (and discontinuation or downgrading of services) with the aim of negatively affecting product functionality. As she correctly considered, this is a form of techno-regulation *à la* Brownsword, that is, a type of regulation of cyberspace that does not limit itself to recognising 'code as part of the regulatory repertoire; it does not simply make use of CCTV, forensic data bases, tracking devices, and the like; instead, it relies entirely on design.'[62] This book shares the view that IoT private power is allowing traders to reshape the governance of Things and gives them the 'unfair capacity to impose their preferred policies unilaterally, automatically, and remotely.'[63]

Bricking can take the form of programmed obsolescence, which is a reminder of how the IoT can negatively affect the environment. In an effort to contribute to the circular economy, the EU in 2019 adopted ten implementing regulations[64]

---

60 Lilian Edwards, '"With Great Power Comes Great Responsibility?" The Rise of Platform Liability' in Lilian Edwards (ed), *Law, Policy and the Internet* (Hart 2019).

61 Tusikov (n 31).

62 Roger Brownsword, 'Code, Control, and Choice: Why East Is East and West Is West' (2005) 25 Legal Studies 1. See, more broadly, Roger Brownsword, *Law, Technology and Society: Re-Imagining the Regulatory Environment* (Routledge 2019).

63 Tusikov (n 31).

64 The full list is available at <https://ec.europa.eu/energy/topics/energy-efficiency/energy-label-and-ecodesign/regulation-laying-down-ecodesign-requirements-1-october-2019_en?redir=1>.

that complement and update the Ecodesign Directive,[65] which introduced design requirements aiming at improving the environmental performance of products, with a focus on household appliances' energy efficiency. The 2019 implementing regulations can be regarded as introducing a solution to the issue of programmed obsolescence by providing something akin to a 'right to repair,' meaning that as of March 2021, household appliance manufacturers must make appliances longer-lasting and supply spare parts for up to ten years. The solution is only partial due to the fact that the 'right to repair' is available only to professional repairers and that it applies only to lighting, washing machines, dishwashers, and fridges.[66] From an IoT perspective, it is particularly worrying that there is no requirement for manufacturers to continue updating software throughout the lifetime of a product. Hopefully, the current increased sensitivity towards issues of climate change and sustainability, alongside the desire for the IoT to unleash its potential, will lead to a more ambitious adoption of a universal right to repair in Europe and globally.[67]

2.4.4 The Vulnerability of Things

A crucial consumer concern is ensuring that Things are free of defects and, more generally, secure. Having surveyed 1,000 consumers in Australia, Canada, France, Japan, UK, and the US, a 2019 study found that 60% of consumers believe that IoT traders have an obligation to ensure their Things are secured.[68] Yet only 22% of cybersecurity personnel believe that such security is achievable.[69] This could seriously hinder the IoT uptake, since security concerns are as determinant as the price when it comes to the consumer's decision to purchase a Thing.[70] To get a sense of the dangers associated to IoT vulnerabilities, one need only consider the driverless cars' industry. In 2016, Tesla reported the first death of a driverless car's passenger; the sensors did not distinguish a white tractor-trailer crossing the highway against a bright sky. The top of the vehicle was torn off by the force of the collision.[71] In 2018, a driverless Uber car killed a woman in the first ever fatal crash involving a pedestrian. She was walking outside of the crossroads, and

---

65 Directive 2009/125/EC of 21 October 2009 establishing a framework for the setting of ecodesign requirements for energy-related products ('Ecodesign Directive') [2009] OJ L 285/10.

66 Carl Dalhammar, Leonidas Milios and Jessika Luth Richter, 'Ecodesign and the Circular Economy: Conflicting Policies in Europe' in Yusuke Kishita and others (eds), *EcoDesign and Sustainability I: Products, Services, and Business Models* (Springer 2021).

67 See Chloé Mikolajczak, 'New Ecodesign Regulations: 5 Reasons Europe Still Doesn't Have the Right to Repair' (*Right to Repair Europe*, 1 March 2021) <https://repair.eu/news/new-ecodesign-regulations-5-reasons-europe-still-doesnt-have-the-right-to-repair/>.

68 Consumers International and Internet Society, 'The Trust Opportunity: Exploring Consumers'Attitudes to the Internet of Things' (2019).

69 John Pescatore, 'Securing the "Internet of Things" Survey. A SANS Analyst Survey' (2014). Future research should replicate this study, because it would surprising if the IoT security readiness had not improved in the last six years.

70 Consumers International and Internet Society (n 68).

71 John Baruch, 'Steer Driverless Cars towards Full Automation' (2016) 536 Nature News 127.

the car hit her without even attempting to slow down.[72] These events suggest that the IoT disrupts yet another dichotomy: this time the lines that blur are the ones between cybersecurity and security. The two overlap and often coincide.[73] Virtual attacks and software vulnerabilities can have serious consequences in the physical world. It would be hard to achieve consensus around whether the remotely triggered explosion of a smart petrol station would be a security issue or a cybersecurity one. Things, especially complex ones, such as cars, can be a threat to the life and integrity of consumers for a number of reasons. These include defective sensors, the lack of instinctual reactions, and the incapability to predict behaviour beyond the training dataset – Uber did not predict that pedestrians can, and often do, walk outside of the zebra crossing.

It should be questioned if these types of failures qualify as a harm for which IoT traders can be found liable. To trust that the IoT is not defective and vulnerable, consumers can rely on a wide array of legal tools. The relevant, and rather-complex, legislative framework revolves around the Product Liability Directive, the soon-to-be-replaced Machinery Directive,[74] the GDPR, and the Network Information Security Directive.[75] Recent calls to strengthen the security of Things resulted in the proposal to pass a delegated act to allow the Radio Equipment Directive[76] to apply to software that has been added to the Thing after it has been put on the market[77] and in the discussion on the introduction of horizontal cybersecurity legislation to be coordinated with the certification framework set forth by the Cybersecurity Act.[78] Tools to increase IoT security can also be found in 'soft' instruments, such as codes of practice, certification schemes, and standards. The most notable examples are, respectively, the UK's *Code of Practice for Consumer IoT Security*,[79] ENISA's efforts to draft the first EU cybersecurity certification

---

72　cf Michael Cameron, *Realising the Benefits of Driverless Vehicles: Recommendations for Law Reform* (The Law Foundation 2018).

73　Guido Noto La Diega, 'The Artificial Conscience of Lethal Autonomous Weapons: Marketing Ruse or Reality?' [2019] Lexis Nexis Middle East Law.

74　Directive 2006/42/EC of 17 May 2006 on machinery, and amending Directive 95/16/EC [2006] OJ L 157/24, which is being reformed also to cover the safety risks stemming from the IoT.

75　Directive (EU) 2016/1148 of 6 July 2016 concerning measures for a high common level of security of network and information systems across the Union [2016] OJ L 194/1.

76　Directive 2014/53/EU of 16 April 2014 on the harmonisation of the laws of the member states relating to the making available on the market of radio equipment and repealing Directive 1999/5/EC [2014] OJ L 153/62.

77　'Radio Equipment Directive (RED)' (*European Commission*, 14 September 2020) <https://ec.europa.eu/growth/sectors/electrical-engineering/red-directive_en>.

78　Council of the European Union, 'Conclusions on the Cybersecurity of Connected Devices' (2020) 13629/20 [7]; Regulation (EU) 2019/881 of 17 April 2019 on ENISA and on information and communications technology cybersecurity certification and repealing Regulation (EU) No 526/2013 ('Cybersecurity Act') [2019] OJ L 151/ 15.

79　Department for Digital, Culture, Media & Sport, *Code of Practice for Consumer IoT Security* (UK Gov 2018) <www.gov.uk/government/publications/code-of-practice-for-consumer-iot-security/code-of-practice-for-consumer-iot-security>.

schemes,[80] and ETSI's TS103645,[81] the first globally applicable standard for consumer IoT security. Laudable, albeit nonenforceable, efforts to make our Things less vulnerable.

2.4.5 IoT Commerce: Contracting in Immersive, Hyperconnected, Interface-Free Environments

Moving on to the fifth consumer issue in the IoT, the starting point is that consumer laws oblige traders to inform consumers about key aspects of the relevant transactions and products (so-called mandated disclosures or consumer notices).[82] The IoT is increasingly used to communicate information to us, collect our information, and facilitate transactions. Communicating information is problematic because the IoT is ubiquitous, invisible, and interface-free.[83] The shift from e-commerce to IoT-commerce means that we live immersed in a world that is hyperconnected and supposedly smart; here, the information costs rise vertically. Indeed, because 'almost anything can now be designed to run software, the amount of resources a person must expend to learn how to appropriately use the devices in their possession will increase, whether the objects in fact run software or not.'[84] The time, attention, and resources that this absorbs adversely affect the time, attention, and resources that are needed to read and understand the consumer notices and the legals more generally. Things are increasingly used for e-commerce purposes, as exemplified by Amazon Echo and Google Home; this means that consumer contracts are concluded not only without any paper information but also without even a digital visual copy of the information. This is because, in IoT commerce, traditional interfaces become smaller, mutate, and even disappear.[85] The Consumer Rights Directive[86] mandates the communication of certain information before the conclusion of a contract. This notice-and-consent approach may be regarded as unfit for an interface-free world, where purchases are actioned by voice, buttons, and eye blinks, as will be shown in the next chapter, which will look at a German decision on Amazon Dash Button.

---

80 ENISA, 'Cybersecurity Certification. EUCC, a Candidate Cybersecurity Certification Scheme to Serve as a Successor to the Existing SOG-IS' (2020) v. 1.0. ENISA is the European Union Agency for Cybersecurity.

81 European Telecommunications Standards Institute, 'Cyber Security for Consumer Internet of Things (ETSI TS 103 645)' (ETSI, 2019) <www.etsi.org/deliver/etsi_ts/103600_103699/103645/01.01.01_60/ts_103645v010101p.pdf>.

82 These information requirements can be found in many EU instruments, but the main reference is to the Directive 2011/83/EU of 25 October 2011 on consumer rights [2011] OJ L 304/64.

83 Eliza Mik, 'The Disappearing Computer: Consent in the World of Smart Objects' [2020] REDC.

84 Mulligan (n 58) 1148.

85 cf Mark Weiser, 'The Computer for the 21st Century' (1999) 3 SIGMOBILE Mobile Computing Communications Review 3.

86 Arts 5 and 6.

2.4.6 The Internet of Personalised Things and Consumer Manipulation

A sixth consumer issue in the IoT is the 'Internet of Personalised Things.' The IoT could be the key disruptor of e-commerce not only because of the ubiquitous and 'always-on' access to purchasing facilities but also because Things are the cookies of tomorrow. Whereas we can delete or block the cookies hoping that this will prevent companies from tracking us, what can we do when our smart devices themselves are used to identify us, track us, and profile us? Things can be used to profile and target consumers with unparalleled precision and efficacy. This is confirmed by an empirical study that concluded that the ability to profile and target IoT consumers is one of the key trends in the future development of IoT for businesses.[87] The granular, situational, and often sensitive data collected by Things and their ability to follow the consumer and target them at the best time and in the best context all contribute to the IoT being a very powerful weapon of manipulation. IoT-enabled profiling can allow personalised ads, personalised products, personalised prices, even personalised terms of service.[88] The line between personalisation and manipulation is a fine one. Big data analytics is increasingly less about predicting consumer behaviour and more about influencing it.[89] IoT-generated data, Thing analytics, profiling, and targeting can be used to actively influence and change consumer behaviour through personalised nudges.[90] More data and more advanced tools to influence the consumers enable IoT traders to utilise cognitive biases, vulnerabilities, and proclivities to shape consumer perceptions and behaviour.[91]

2.4.7 The Contractual Quagmire

In the IoT, consumers find themselves in a contractual quagmire in the sense that countless legals are attached to every Thing, and these are difficult to find, read, and understand. Stuck in the quagmire, the consumer feels that they do not have other choice but accepting all the legals, regardless of how unfair, opaque, and potentially unenforceable they may be.

The phrase 'contractual quagmire' was coined by Jennifer Belcher[92] in 2004, but it had a radically different meaning. Indeed, Belcher used it to criticise the US Supreme Court's decision in *Archer v Warner*[93] that stated that bankruptcy courts

---

87 Euan Davis, 'The Rise of the Smart Product Economy' (2015) Cognizant and EIU.
88 Helberger (n 27).
89 Guido Noto La Diega, 'Some Considerations on Intelligent Online Behavioural Advertising' (2018) 66 Revue du droit des technologies de l'information 53.
90 cf Cass R Sunstein, 'Impersonal Default Rules vs. Active Choices vs. Personalized Default Rules: A Triptych' [2013] Active Choices vs. Personalized Default Rules: A Triptych (May 19, 2013).
91 Jon D Hanson and Douglas A Kysar, 'Taking Behavioralism Seriously: Some Evidence of Market Manipulation' [1999] Harvard Law Review 1420; Helberger (n 27).
92 Jennifer Belcher, 'Archer v. Warner: Circuit Split Resolution or Contractual Quagmire?' (2004) 61 Washington and Lee Law Review 1801.
93 *Archer v Warner (In re Warner)*, 538 U.S. 314 (2003).

should 'look behind' privately contracted settlements to determine if the underlying and completely released original debt was obtained by fraud. The author critically concluded that the court had merely 'created a contractual quagmire for those parties seeking settlement of fraud claims.' Transactions are often accompanied by a plethora of contracts, but the IoT exacerbates existing problems.[94] As Things are a mixture of software, hardware, service, data, and due to an elaborate supply chain (the 'relational black box'), consumers of seemingly simple Things like a thermostat or a speaker find themselves submerged by dozens of legals. These are used by IoT traders to purport to retain full control of the Thing and yet disclaim all liability. And they do so with overly long, illegible, and inconsistent documents that few read, let alone understand.[95] Therefore, consumers have little control over their Things, are deprived of most of their rights, and are practically left without redress – either because, in the quagmire, they cannot identify who the defendant would be or because they were forced to accept foreign, inaccessible jurisdiction.[96]

To conclude, the IoT may benefit consumers, but only if they are aware of the risks and if the law provides effective incentives for IoT companies to treat consumers fairly. The analysis above had, therefore, the aim of raising awareness of some consumer threats in the IoT and to reflect on the issues that existing laws need to grapple with. To complete the picture, the next sections of this chapter will focus on an empirical analysis of Amazon Echo's 'legals.' Its findings will be of help to understand what 'legal' private ordering is and how, if at all, we can counter it.

2.5 Fantastic Legals and Where to Find Them: Understanding Private Ordering through Amazon Echo's Contractual Quagmire

In order to assess if and how EU laws can assist IoT consumers, it is important to look at the 'legals.' This methodological option is based on two considerations. First, IoT traders take advantage of the lacunae left by non-IoT-aware laws to heavily regulate and restrict the behaviour of consumers, which gives rise to a form of contractual private ordering. This makes it important to empirically analyse the contracts, as they can even take precedence on formal laws when it comes to determining the actual rights and obligations of the IoT actors.[97] Second, the unfairness of a contractual term is assessed 'by referring . . . to all the other terms of the contract or of another contract on which it is dependent.'[98] Therefore, it is imperative to have a clear picture of the overall applicable contractual framework.

---

94 Noto La Diega and Walden (n 8).
95 cf Jonathan A Obar and Anne Oeldorf-Hirsch, 'The Biggest Lie on the Internet: Ignoring the Privacy Policies and Terms of Service Policies of Social Networking Services' [2018] Information, Communication & Society 1.
96 cf Dale M Clapperton and Stephen G Corones, 'Unfair Terms in 'clickwrap' and Other Electronic Contracts' (2007) 35 Australian Business Law Review 152.
97 Noto La Diega and Walden (n 8).
98 Unfair Terms Directive, art 4.

Many consumer issues stem precisely from the interactions between these networks of contracts.[99]

2.5.1 *Amazon's Forest of Terms and Conditions: The 'Core Legals'*

A consumer that uses a speaker does not expect to face a legal mountain. However, if one wants to have a comprehensive picture of the rights, obligations, and responsibilities associated with the use of Amazon Echo, one must read at least 246 'legals.' These include terms of use, terms of service, terms and conditions, conditions of use, conditions of sale, notices, agreements, policies, certifications, guidelines, usage rules, warranties, licenses, requirements, lists, codes of conduct, statements, warnings, choices, legal information, addendums, and additional terms. They are referred to as legals and not as contracts because in some jurisdictions their contractual nature is disputed.[100] I have focused on the UK legals for language reasons and because during the data collection, I was mostly based in the UK; however, users from other member states face the same amount of legals. US consumers have to accept partly different legals both in their content (e.g. to take account of the unenforceability of certain clauses under EU consumer law) and in their number. For example, in Europe we do not have the Children's Privacy Disclosure,[101] which regards the way Amazon collect information from children under the age of 13. The reason for this difference is that in the US, children are expressly targeted as customers, whereas Amazon's European companies rely on the fiction, whereby they 'sell children's products for purchase by adults.'[102]

The following 24 legals are 'core' in the sense that they are the most likely to directly affect rights, risks, and obligations in Echo's ecosystem.

The main issues that the aforementioned table shows are as follows.

(i) The subject matter of each of the document remains usually unclear either because a document's title refers to an aspect of the Thing, but it covers also other aspects (e.g., Amazon Device Terms dealing with software) or because it provides a definition of 'services' and 'products' that changes from document to document.

(ii) The contractual parties are often left wholly or partly unidentified, or they are set to change over time without notice.

---

99 The issue is not new; see the category of *Vertragsnetze* (networks of contracts) in Marc Amstutz and Gunther Teubner, 'Editorial zum Schwerpunkt Vertragsnetze: Rechtsprobleme vertraglicher Multilateralität' (2006) 89 KritV Kritische Vierteljahresschrift für Gesetzgebung und Rechtswissenschaft 103.

100 Thomas B Norton, 'The Non-Contractual Nature of Privacy Policies and a New Critique of the Notice and Choice Privacy Protection Model' (2016) 27 Fordham Intellectual Property, Media & Entertainment Law Journal 181.

101 Last updated on 28 August 2019 <www.amazon.com/gp/help/customer/display.html?nodeId=202185560>.

102 Amazon Privacy Notice, last updated on 23 September 2019 <www.amazon.co.uk/gp/help/customer/display.html?nodeId=201909010>.

Table 2.1 Amazon Echo's Core 'Legals'

Name	Parties	Subject Matter	Issues
Amazon Device Terms of Use[103]	Amazon EU S.à r.l., Amazon Media S.à r.l. and their affiliates	Kindle e-readers, Fire tablets, Fire TV devices, the Echo series, Smart Plug, Dash Button, Dash Wand, and any Amazon accessories	Although it purports to regulate the use of the device as hardware, it ends up covering also digital content (e.g. e-books), services (e.g. wireless connectivity), and software (the program running in an Echo).
Alexa Terms of Use[104]	Amazon Media EU S.à r.l. and its affiliates	Virtual assistant Alexa either in its immaterial form or embedded in an 'Alexa-Enabled Product'[105]	'Alexa-enabled product' refers typically to Echo but also to mobile apps, thus suggesting a new concept of 'product', potentially free of its hardware substratum.
Conditions of Use and Sale[106]	Amazon Europe Core S.à r.l., Amazon EU S.à r.l., and their affiliates	'Amazon Services,' including website features and other products and services provided on Amazon.co.uk, Amazon devices, products, or services, Amazon applications for mobile, or software provided by Amazon	A new concept of service, traditionally distinct from devices, products, and software, but here included in it.
Privacy Notice[107]	Amazon Europe Core S.à r.l., Amazon EU S.à r.l., Amazon Services Europe S.à r.l., Amazon Media EU S.à r.l., and Amazon Digital UK Limited	Processing of personal data through Amazon websites, devices, products, services, stores, and apps that reference the Privacy Notice	It deals with 'Amazon Services,' which are not defined in the same way as the Conditions of Use and Sale, where, by contrast, service encompasses software provided by Amazon. It is unsure which document governs that type of personal data processing. It is also unknown if this is the same privacy policy that applies to Amazon's mobile apps, since the app's link to the policy does not work.[108]

103 Last updated on 4 September 2019 <www.amazon.co.uk/gp/help/customer/display.html?nodeId=202002080>.
104 Last updated on 11 June 2019 <www.amazon.co.uk/gp/help/customer/display.html?nodeId=201809740>.
105 Preamble to the Alexa Terms of Use.
106 Last updated on 10 July 2019 <www.amazon.co.uk/gp/help/customer/display.html?nodeId=1040616>.
107 Last updated on 23 September 2019 <www.amazon.co.uk/gp/help/customer/display.html/ref=hp_left_v4_sib?ie=UTF8&nodeId=201909010>.

(Continued)

Table 2.1 (Continued)

Name	Parties	Subject Matter	Issues
Cookies[109]	Unspecified	Tracking and profiling	The document does not identify the contractual party.
Interest-Based Ads[110]	Unspecified	Tracking, profiling, and targeted advertising	In addition to the issue of nonidentification, 'interest-based advertising' could be regarded as the mere rebranding of 'targeted advertising.'
Privacy Shield Certification[111]	Unspecified	EU-US data transfers	It covers only five of Amazon's companies;[112] it excludes, for example, Twitch.tv and IMDb. When the analysis was first conducted, the scheme covered seven companies. It is unclear if the companies who are no longer certified have meanwhile ceased to exist, no longer qualify as data importers, or lost the certification, which may indicate that they do not protect personal data in an adequate way. After the *Schrems II* case,[113] Amazon no longer relies on the Privacy Shield but still refers to this certification as they 'continue to keep to the commitments . . . that [they] made when [they] certified to the Privacy Shield'[114]
Amazon Payments Europe User Agreement – Personal Accounts[115]	Amazon Payments Europe s.c.a.	Wallet services, which enable consumers to pay users with merchant accounts using internet- or mobile-based services and applications	
Amazon Assistant Conditions of Use[116]	Amazon Europe Core S.a.r.l. and its affiliates	A suite of software applications that supplement the online shopping experience by comparing products from Amazon as one shops on retailer websites	

Alexa Communication Usage Guidelines[117]	Unspecified	Communication through Alexa	It does not identify the contractual party, and it does not define 'communication.'
One-Year Limited Warranty for Amazon Devices[118]	Amazon EU S.à r.l.	Repair, replacement, or refund should defects in materials and workmanship arise within one year from the purchase of most Amazon devices	The warranty applies '*only to hardware components*' of the Device that are not subject to accident' or other external causes.
Limited Warranty for Amazon Accessories[119]	Amazon EU S.à r.l.	90-day warranty; applies to some Things such as Echo Buttons and Echo Wall Clock	These Things are qualified as 'accessories' despite the line between them and the rest of Amazon's devices being blurred. Hardware-only protection.
Amazon Fire Game Controller 90-Day Limited Warranty[120]	Amazon EU S.à r.l.	Amazon Fire game controller	Amazon groups the main legals in a page.[121] This document is linked there, but the link does not work.[122] It was found by accident via a link in the return policies.

108 Accessed from an Android phone on 2 October 2019.
109 Last updated on 23 May 2018 <www.amazon.co.uk/gp/help/customer/display.html?nodeId=201890250>.
110 Last updated on 23 May 2018 <www.amazon.co.uk/gp/help/customer/display.html?nodeId=201909150>.
111 Original certification date 16 August 2017 <www.privacyshield.gov/participant?id=a2zt0000000TOWQAA4>.
112 As of 2 January 2020, Amazon's traders that are Privacy-Shield-certified are Amazon.com, Inc., Amazon Advertising LLC, Amazon Web Services. Inc., Audible, Inc., and Amazon.com Services LLC.
113 Case C-311/18 *Data Protection Commissioner v Facebook Ireland Limited and Maximillian Schrems* (CJEU, 16 July 2020). Although this case is popularly known as *Schrems II*, it should be more correctly referred to as *Schrems III* as the second Schrems case is Case C-498/16 *Schrems v Facebook Ireland* [2018] 1 WLR 4343.
114 Privacy notice, clause 12.
115 Last updated on 6 August 2019 <pay.amazon.co.uk/help/201751590>.
116 Last updated on 8 October 2015 <www.amazon.co.uk/gp/help/customer/display.html?nodeId=202055080>.
117 Last updated on 11 June 2019 <www.amazon.co.uk/gp/help/customer/display.html?nodeId=202143060>.
118 Unknown date <www.amazon.co.uk/gp/help/customer/display.html?ref=hp_left_ac?ie=UTF8&nodeId=201311110>.
119 Unknown date <www.amazon.co.uk/gp/help/customer/display.html?nodeId=201606430>.
120 Unknown date <www.amazon.co.uk/gp/help/customer/display.html?nodeId=201484900>.
121 <www.amazon.co.uk/gp/help/customer/display.html?nodeId=201483110>.
122 The link to the ghost legal is <www.amazon.co.uk/gp/help/customer/display.html?nodeId=00000>.

(Continued)

Table 2.1 (Continued)

Name	Parties	Subject Matter	Issues
Worry-Free Guarantee (Two-Year Limited Warranty)[123]	Amazon EU S.à r.l.	Fire HD Kids Edition Tablet, Fire Kids Edition Tablet with Kid-Proof Case, and Kindle Kids Edition	It purports to cover only hardware defects.
Alexa Voice Remote 90-Day Limited Warranty[124]	Amazon EU S.à r.l.	Fire's remote if purchased separately	It purports to cover only hardware defects.
One-Year Limited Warranty (Waterproof Devices)[125]	Amazon EU S.à r.l.	Kindle Oasis and Kindle Paperwhite	It purports to cover only hardware defects.
Amazon Premium Headphones 90-Day Limited Warranty[126]	Amazon EU S.à r.l.	Amazon Premium Headphones	It purports to cover only hardware defects. It is unclear why there should be 7 distinct warranties.
Amazon Prime Terms and Conditions[127]	Amazon EU S.à r.l., Amazon Media EU S.à r.l., Amazon Video Limited, and their affiliates	Prime, the membership program whose main benefits are fast shipping and discounted prices	
Amazon Music Terms of Use[128]	Amazon Digital UK Ltd.	Services, this time defined as unlimited, Prime Music, Amazon Music (free with ads), the Store, and the Music Library Service	It provides a long list of Amazon traders that may be the consumer's counterparty depending on the location, but regrettably it refers to a further page[129] for the identification of the actual party. 'Services' are given each time a different meaning.

Amazon Photos Terms of Use[130] **(previously Amazon Drive Terms of Use)**	Amazon Media EU S.à.r.l. and its affiliates	Both services and software, and in particular storage, retrieval, management, and access features and functionality for photos, videos, and other files	
Amazon Prime Video Terms of Use[131]	Amazon Digital Services LLC, Amazon Digital UK Limited, and their affiliates	Personalised service that offers consumers discovery of digital movies, television shows, and other video content	The party may change over time. 'Your Amazon Prime Video service provider may change from time to time, with or without prior notice.'[132]
Amazon Prime Video Usage Rules[133]	Unspecified	The ways to watch (e.g. streaming or downloading) and the viewing period of the video contents depending on whether the video was purchased, rented, accessed on a subscriptions basis, etc.	The document does not identify the contractual parties. This confirms also the aforementioned idea of death of ownership and its practical and legal ramifications.

123 Unknown date <www.amazon.co.uk/gp/help/customer/display.html/ref=hp_left_v4_sib?ie=UTF8&nodeId=201606410>.

124 Unknown date <www.amazon.co.uk/gp/help/customer/display.html/ref=hp_left_v4_sib?ie=UTF8&nodeId=201484910>.

125 Unknown date <www.amazon.co.uk/gp/help/customer/display.html/ref=hp_left_v4_sib?ie=UTF8&nodeId=202197860>.

126 Unknown date <www.amazon.co.uk/gp/help/customer/display.html/ref=hp_left_v4_sib?ie=UTF8&nodeId=201555510>.

127 Last updated on 25 March 2019 <www.amazon.co.uk/gp/help/customer/display.html?nodeId=200198240>.

128 Last updated on 1 October 2019 <www.amazon.co.uk/gp/help/customer/display.html?nodeId=201380010>.

129 Amazon Music Service Provider Information and Applicable Terms and Policies, unknown date <www.amazon.co.uk/gp/help/customer/display.html?nodeId=2007389 50&view-type=content-only>.

130 Last updated on 4 September 2018 <www.amazon.co.uk/gp/help/customer/display.html?nodeId=201376540>.

131 Last updated on 5 February 2019 <www.primevideo.com/help?nodeId=202095490&view-type=content-only>.

132 Amazon Prime Video Terms of Use.

133 Unknown date <www.primevideo.com/help?_encoding=UTF8&nodeId=202095500>.

(Continued)

Table 2.1 (Continued)

Name	Parties	Subject Matter	Issues
Third Party Software[134]	Unspecified	Use, in Amazon's video services, of Microsoft PlayReady™, a copy prevention technology embedded in software and hardware that allows control over the video content displayed on Amazon's Things. The document includes also the Open Source Notices for Amazon Video.[135]	Linked to the death of ownership is the idea of a private ordering 'by bricking' thanks to IP rights on different aspects of Thing. It includes the threat that the only alternative to accepting PlayReady™ is no longer being able to access the content. The keen consumer may find the Third Party Software Licenses in a separate page.[136]
Amazon Devices Return Policies[137]	Unspecified	How to return Echo and other Amazon Things within 30 days.	This 'legal' regards also the return of nonhardware products, namely, Kindle books, as well as services, namely, Kindle subscriptions, thus confirming the untenability of the attempts to regulate the Things' components as if they were not interdependent.

134 Last updated on 26 July 2019 <www.amazon.co.uk/gp/help/customer/display.html?nodeId=201422780>.
135 In the US, there is a separate document for these namely Notice Relating to Open Source Software, unknown date <www.amazon.com/gp/BIT/thirdpartylicenses 1/>.
136 Unknown date <www.amazon.co.uk/gp/help/customer/display.html?nodeId=201420340>.
137 Unknown date <www.amazon.co.uk/gp/help/customer/display.html?nodeId=201818950>.

(iii) Only some of the legals are grouped in an ad hoc 'legals section' on the IoT trader's website. The others are often hidden in other parts of the website or hyperlinked in one of the 'grouped' legals.

(iv) Every layer of the Thing is heavily controlled by the IoT trader in a proprietary way; the consumer is accordingly left with little control over the Thing, qualifying more as a tenant rather than an owner.

 (v) The prohibitive number of legals that an IoT consumer is expected to find and read.

The number itself of the legals is an issue, because it makes it unlikely for consumers to find them, let alone read them and understand them. The situation is worsened by the high length and low readability of these documents. Echo's core legals amount to 457 pages,[138] 114,292 words (well above the average PhD dissertation), 733,665 characters. They contain 23,667 complex words[139] and are therefore as readable as Machiavelli's *The Prince* and as long as *Harry Potter and the Prisoner of Azkaban* (Figure 2.2). This means that, should the consumer find all the legals promptly, they would need approximately 20 hours to read them.[140] Such breach of the principle of transparency is likely to be contrary to the direc-

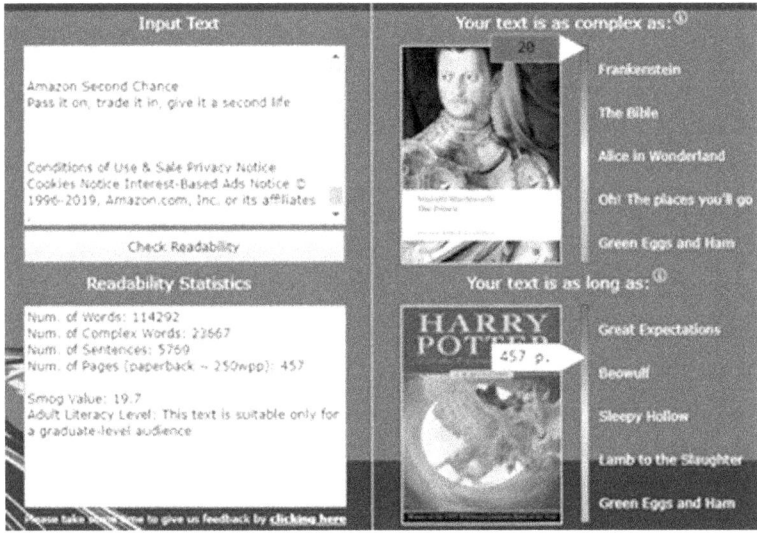

Figure 2.2 The Literatin add-on analyses the readability of texts by comparing their complexity and length to famous books.

138 This is considering 250 words per page, as in Stuart Moran, Ewa Luger and Tom Rodden, 'Literatin: Beyond Awareness of Readability in Terms and Conditions' (ACM 2014).
139 I used the 'Literatin ' add-on designed by ibid.
140 This calculation was made on the assumption that one reads 100 words per minute and can read uninterrupted.

tive on Unfair Terms[141] and Unfair Commercial Practices,[142] the GDPR,[143] as well as general contract law.[144] The next chapter will consider the issue of contractual transparency as a fairness issue.

2.5.2 The Mountain Behind the Mountain: The Incontrollable Multiplication of the Legals

In and of themselves, the 'core' legals justify the suggestion that IoT users find themselves stuck in a contractual quagmire. Should the keen consumer climb this legal mountain and find, read, and understand these 24 documents, they will soon realise that another mountain is hiding behind them. Countless other legals remain to be considered for at least five reasons:

   (i) A multilayered supply chain. This is due to a gargantuan corporate structure and to the widespread reliance on 'affiliates.' These are left unidentified, and Amazon disclaims liability for their activities, despite the fact that they provide key portions of Amazon's offerings.

  (ii) 'Things-as-a-service' or hyperservitisation, as in the ubiquitous presence of services everywhere and in every Thing, as well as the provision of the Thing itself as a mere service.

 (iii) Controlled interoperability. IoT traders use contracts to regulate the interactions of their Things with umpteen third-party Things, services, and software.

 (iv) The overcoming of the trader-consumer dichotomy through the rise of prosumers. Consumers' roles become fluid; they can identify as a trader, albeit temporarily.

  (v) The increasing shift from the IoT to the Cloud of Things.

 (vi) The wave of sustainability and corporate social responsibility (CSR) measures.

2.5.2.1 A Journey in Amazon's Multilayered Supply Chain

As the analysis of the core legals shows, Echo's consumers are in a contractual relationship with a number of companies that belong to Amazon's corporate structure or are in some way associated to it. It is important to have a comprehensive picture of who these companies are for a fourfold reason. First, to identify the defendant in a potential action. No breach can be actioned if the claimant cannot identify a defendant who has standing. Second, this omission may fall foul of duties of precontractual information[145] and may qualify as an

---

141 *Kásler* (n 27).
142 Case C-388/13 *Nemzeti Fogyasztovedelmi Hatosag v UPC Magyarorszag Kft* [2015] Bus L R 946.
143 Art 12.
144 *Spreadex Ltd v Cochrane* [2012] EWHC 1290 (Comm).
145 Consumer Rights Directive, arts 5(1)(b) and 6(1)(b).

unfair commercial practice.[146] Third, to resolve questions of applicable law and jurisdiction – keeping in mind that, under unfair terms laws, consumers 'should not normally be prevented from starting legal proceedings in their local courts.'[147] This explains why Echo's consumers accept the jurisdiction of the courts of the district of Luxembourg City only in nonexclusive terms and retain the right to sue in the member state where they live.[148] Fourth, 'Amazon Europe shares customers' information . . . with Amazon.com, Inc. and the subsidiaries that Amazon. com, Inc. controls.'[149] Some of them may be subject to Amazon's publicly available Privacy Notice; some others are not. These companies are declared to put in place data practices 'at least as protective as those described in this Privacy Notice,'[150] but due to corporate secrecy, there is no way to make sure that all the companies in Amazon's supply chain stand by this commitment. At the time of writing, international data transfers could be justified if covered by an adequacy decision, such as the EU-US Privacy Shield.[151] Most of Amazon's subsidiaries were established in the US, but only five of them were Privacy Shield–certified, which meant that it was unclear whether the transfers of EU residents' personal data to the US had a legal basis. This is all the more true after the recent *Schrems II*[152] ruling that invalidated the Privacy Shield, leaving companies with no clear legal basis for international data transfers. Adequacy decisions are not the only method to justify international transfers. The main alternatives are agreements between public entities, binding corporate rules, standard contractual clauses, and approved codes of conduct. Amazon relies on 'adequacy decisions or use contracts with standard safeguards published by the European Commission.'[153] However, this is not satisfactory. Indeed, although the CJEU in theory upheld the validity of standard contractual clauses, it has shifted the emphasis on the supplementary technical, contractual, and organisational measures that controllers must put in place when 'the law or practice of the third country . . . may impinge on the effectiveness of the appropriate safeguards,'[154] as is arguably the case with US law, where redress against state surveillance is not always available.[155]

---

146 Unfair Commercial Practices Directive, art 7(4)(b).
147 Competition & Markets Authority, *Unfair Contract Terms Guidance. Guidance on the Unfair Terms Provisions in the Consumer Rights Act 2015* (CMA 2015) [5.29.7].
148 Conditions of Use & Sale, clause 14.
149 Amazon UK Privacy Notice, last updated 23 September 2019.
150 ibid.
151 An *adequacy decision* is a decision whereby the European Commission finds that the third country's level of data protection is adequate. The Privacy Shield instantiated this with regard to EU-US transfers.
152 (n 113).
153 Privacy Notice, clause 5.
154 EDPB, 'Recommendations 01/2020 on Measures That Supplement Transfer Tools to Ensure Compliance with the EU Level of Protection of Personal Data' (2020) [30].
155 *Schrems II* (n 113) [115]. To assist data exporters and importers in assessing when the surveillance laws of a third country interfere with privacy rights and potentially invalidate the transfer, the European Data Protection Board has also adopted EDPB, 'Recommendations 02/2020 on the European Essential Guarantees for Surveillance Measures' (2020).

Controllers must identify these supplementary measures on a case-by-case basis[156] – which Amazon fails to do.

In light of the importance of identifying the parties involved in this network of contracts, the analysis below will, first, attempt to present a picture of Amazon's gargantuan corporate conglomerate and then explore the concept of 'affiliate.'

Starting the journey in Luxembourg, where Amazon has its main European headquarters, we find nine companies, namely Amazon EU S.à r.l., Amazon Eurasia Holdings S.à r.l., Amazon Business EU S.à r.l., Amazon Payments Europe SCA, Amazon International Services S.à r.l., Amazon Services Europe S.à r.l., Amazon Media EU S.à r.l., Amazon Europe Core S.à r.l., and Amazon Web Services EMEA S.à r.l.

Amazon EU S.à r.l. is the main European company, and it has registered branches in the UK, Italy, Germany, France, Spain, and the Netherlands. It also holds interests in other companies. There is no publicly available list of all the subsidiaries, but the main[157] affiliated undertakings, whose share capital is held in its entirety by Amazon EU S.à r.l., are Amazon UK Services Limited, Amazon Data Services Ireland Limited, Amazon Fulfillment Poland sp. z o.o., and Amazon Italia Logistica s.r.l.

Finally, the US parent company Amazon.com Inc., the ultimate parent company, has dozens of partly unidentified subsidiaries. The most significant ones are Amazon Services LLC, Amazon Digital Services LLC, Amazon.com Services Inc., and Amazon Technologies Inc.[158] It is impossible to know exactly which companies are part of Amazon.com Inc.'s corporate family. By mere accident, while I was browsing the section of Amazon's website dedicate to prospective employees, I stumbled upon a page referring to 17 'companies you might not realise are part of Amazon's family,'[159] including AbeBooks.com, Audible, Goodreads, IMDb, Twitch, and Whole Foods. I thought I could get a more complete picture of Amazon's corporate structure if I could read the group's consolidated financial statements. However, they 'are available at 410 Terry Avenue North, Seattle'; this makes it rather impractical for the average consumer – or the average academic, for that matter – to retrieve the relevant information.

In order to better understand with whom a consumer has a contractual relationship, it is also important to understand the repeated reference, found in many of Echo's legals, to unidentified 'affiliates.' For example, under the Conditions of Use and Sale, 'Amazon Europe Core S.à r.l., Amazon EU S.à r.l. *and/or* their affiliates ("Amazon") provide website features and other products and services to you.'[160] Even after reading the legals, browsing Amazon's website, and inquiring

---

156 EDPB (n 154) [46].
157 These are the main European subsidiaries in terms of carrying account, as reported in Amazon EU S.à r.l., 'Registre de Commerce et Des Sociétés No RCS B101818; Référence de Dépôt L200046766; Déposé et Enregistré on 13 March 2020.'
158 Amazon.com, Inc. (n 19).
159 'Subsidiaries' (*amazon.jobs*) <www.amazon.jobs/en-gb/business_categories/subsidiaries>.
160 Conditions of Use & Sale, preamble.

the customer support centre, I am not sure who these affiliates are and which functionalities, products, and services they provide. It would be important to answer
these questions mainly for two reasons. First, Amazon disclaims all liability for
the affiliates' actions, products, and contents.[161] Second, the affiliates' legals will
apply too, and Amazon expects you to 'carefully review their privacy statements
and other conditions of use.'[162] After some digging, I came to the conclusion that
'affiliate' may mean one of two things. It may refer to all those traders that become
an 'associate' of Amazon for advertising purposes, e.g. by inserting Amazon ban-
ners on their website or linking to part of Amazon's catalogue. The Amazon Affiliate Resource Centre[163] provides the relevant information; the Associates Program
Operating Agreement[164] and the Associates Program Policies[165] refer to affiliates
and associates indistinctly. One of Amazon's customer service advisers (Adviser
X),[166] consulted via live chat, confirmed that these are the affiliates referred to in
the 'legals,' although they did not have a list of who precisely the affiliates were
and which services, products, and functionalities they were responsible for. If this
were the case, there may be potentially thousands of affiliates that play an important role in the consumers' experience, access their data, and come with thousands
of legals of their own. The second possible concept of 'affiliate' would refer to
Amazon's subsidiaries and those companies that provide some of Amazon's products, services, and functionalities on the basis of stable arrangements. This interpretation is supported by four arguments. First, whereas the UK legals do not name
any company that counts as an affiliate, the US legals do. In particular, under the
US version of the Alexa Terms of Use,[167] AMCS LLC is the affiliate that 'may
offer you certain Alexa-related communication, services, such as the ability to
send and receive messages and calls and connect with other Alexa users.'[168] These
are core functionalities of Amazon Echo (and of all the Alexa-enabled apps and
Things) and are provided by a company that does not exist on any openly accessible traders directory, whose terms we are expected to nonetheless read and agree
to, and for whose activities Amazon disclaims liability. Second, at the bottom of
IMDb Conditions of Use, one can find a list of 'Amazon Affiliates,' namely, Prime

---

161 'Amazon does not assume any responsibility or liability for the actions, product, and content' of
     third parties, including the affiliated traders. Conditions of Use & Sale, point 11.
162 ibid.
163 <amazon-affiliate.eu/en/?pk_campaign=ukacbottomfotter>.
164 Associates Program Operating Agreement, last updated on 6 September 2019 <affiliate-program.
     amazon.co.uk/help/operating/agreement>.
165 These are eight documents: Associates Program – Fee Statement; Associates Program – Participation
     Requirements; Associates Program – Products Statement; Associates Program – Mobile Appli-
     cation Policy; Associates Program – Trademark Guidelines; Associates Program – IP License;
     Associates Program – Amazon Influencer Program Policy; DE Associate Program Comparison
     Shopping Engine Requirements. These policies are undated and with unspecified parties but,
     positively, can be found all at <affiliate-program.amazon.co.uk/help/operating/policies >.
166 I have contacted Adviser X on 1 October 2019 using Amazon's live chat.
167 Last updated on 14 June 2019 <www.amazon.com/gp/help/customer/display.html?nodeId=
     201809740>.
168 ibid, point 3.8.

Video to stream movies and TV; Amazon UK, Amazon Germany, Amazon Italy, Amazon France, and Amazon India to buy DVDs; DPReview for digital photography; and Audible for audio books. All these traders are part of Amazon's corporate group. Third, another clue comes from the comparison between the sections 'Make Money with Us' in the UK and in the US (Figure 2.3).

The UK's Associates Programme corresponds to 'Become an Affiliate' in the US. This would suggest that the references to 'affiliates' in the UK legals may be a legacy problem. Indeed, it is common practice for US companies who operate in Europe to regulate the relationship with European consumers with legals that are nearly identical to the US version, with minor changes to the limited extent imposed by the law and by spelling conventions.[169] The last argument in favour of 'affiliates' as subsidiaries and traders with stable arrangements with Amazon is based on a second interaction with Amazon customer support, this time with the 'Associate Team' (*affiliati* in Italian)[170] and by email. Adviser Y from this team did not answer my questions on who the affiliates are and which services, products, and functionalities they provide. After I asked that the matter be escalated, Adviser Z[171] replied that Amazon Europe Core S.à.r.l., Amazon EU S.à.r.l. Italia,

Figure 2.3 The 'Make Money with Us' section at the bottom of Amazon.co.uk (left) and Amazon.com (right).[172]

169 Noto La Diega and Walden (n 8).
170 The exchange took place on 1 October 2019 with I., an advisor from the *Programma Affiliazione* (the Italian equivalent of the Associate Programme).
171 Email exchange of 1 October 2019 with Amazon's advisor Z.
172 The screenshot on the left was captured on 1 October 2019 at www.amazon.co.uk/gp/help/customer/display.html?nodeId=201809740; the screenshot on the right at <www.amazon.com/gp/help/customer/display.html?nodeId=201809740>.

Amazon Services Europe S.à.r.l., and Amazon Media EU S.à.r.l. 'are responsible for providing functionalities, products, and services,' but neither did they clarify if this list is exhaustive nor shed light on which services, products, and functionalities those traders are responsible. Adviser Z only clarified that Amazon Europe Core S.à.r.l is responsible for the main website, but other services are provided by other affiliates, 'for example Amazon's MP3 Service is provided by Amazon Media EU S.à r.l.' Although this only partly answered my question, it did have an unintended positive consequence. Indeed, I had not previously found the conditions of use of AutoRip,[173] Amazon's service to convert purchased CDs into MP3s.

Based on these four arguments, though no conclusive answer has been found, it is fair to assume that the unidentified affiliates that are party to most legals Amazon Echo consumers accept and for which Amazon disclaims liability are its subsidiaries or other companies with which it has stable arrangements to provide certain services, products, or functionalities. In theory, consumers would be expected to find and read also the affiliates' 'legals,' but since even identifying them is virtually impossible, it is safe to say that consumers cannot be assumed to be bound by any obligations under them and Amazon's liability disclaimers should be deemed to be unenforceable. This may depend on the rules on unfairness in consumer contracts, as elaborated in the next chapter, or on the rules on vagueness in general contract law. Vague clauses 'are not in general enforced in English law'[174] and in all those jurisdictions where courts tend to refrain from rewriting contracts on behalf of the parties.[175] Under *Scammell v Ouston*,[176] leading authority in the field, when a phrase is 'so vaguely expressed that it cannot, standing by itself, be given a definite meaning,'[177] the relevant clause must be regarded as too uncertain to be enforceable. There are two scenarios in which courts may decide to give enforceable content to vague clauses. First, when case-specific contextual factors apply. For example, in *Shamrock v Storey*,[178] a *contract* referred to unspecified 'terms of usual colliery guarantee,' and there were three forms of colliery guarantee; however, since all of them contained the same provision on the relevant point (the loading time in a contract for the sale of coal), duties and rights were in fact clear. In our scenario, despite my efforts, it was impossible to identify the 'affiliates,' and therefore, the relevant duties remaining unclear, the clause should be deemed unenforceable. The same applies to the second set of contextual factors that courts may consider to enforce vague clauses, namely, commercial usage. Expressions such as 'reasonable' and 'best endeavours' are vague and yet customary in commerce. They make for flexible and enforceable

---

173 AutoRip Terms & Conditions, last updated on 1 October 2019.
174 TT Arvind, *Contract Law* (OUP 2017) 249.
175 See e.g. Alessandro D'Adda, 'La Correzione Del "Contratto Abusivo": Regole Dispositive in Funzione "Conformativa" Ovvero Una Nuova Stagione per l'equità Giudiziale?' in Alessandro Bellavista and Armando Plaia (eds), *Le invalidità nel diritto privato* (Giuffrè 2011) 394.
176 [1941] AC 251.
177 Ibid [254] per Viscount Simon.
178 (1899) 81 LT 413.

contracts; however, 'straying beyond these established types of clauses can lead to the contractual provisions . . . becoming unenforceable,'[179] which is the case with Amazon's contractual quagmire.

The AudioRip example leads us nicely to the second reason that the number of Echo's legals is considerably higher than the 24 core legals: the growth of 'Things-as-a-service' or hyperservitisation.[180]

2.5.2.2 Things-as-a-Service

Whilst traditional markets were focused on the sale of goods, with the dematerialisation that followed the digital revolution, the key has become the provision of services. *Servitisation* refers to 'manufacturing firms developing the capabilities they need to provide services and solutions that supplement their traditional product offerings'[181] and has been a trend for many years now. Forty-eight percent of traders profiting from servitisation leverage data from the IoT.[182] By calling into question the very ideas of 'goods' and 'ownership,' the IoT ushers in the 'Thing-as-a-service' era.[183] With the advent of cloud computing, companies no longer need to have certain resources in-house; resources are virtualised and are accessed remotely on-demand.[184] Services are structured according to their level of abstraction, typically resulting in the three layers, namely, software-as-a-service, platform-as-a-service, and infrastructure-as-a-service.[185] With the IoT, services become so pervasive that a forth layer should be considered, namely, the 'Thing-as-a-service.'[186] Thing-as-a-service means both that (i) the Thing is provided as if it were a service, namely, under a subscription contract, rather than a sale, and that (ii) the service component of the Thing instantiates the core of the

179 Arvind (n 174) 249.
180 Guido Noto La Diega, 'Can Artificial Intelligence and the Internet of Things Be Governed to Achieve the UN Sustainable Development Goals? An Intellectual Property Law Perspective' *WTO Public Forum, AIPPI's Working Session "New Digital Technologies: the Protagonists of a Change in Perspective in the Global Supply Chain* (2019) <https://papers.ssrn.com/abstract=3505247>.
181 Charles Rathmann, 'Industrial Servitization and Field Service Technology' (2018) IFS White Paper.
182 ibid.
183 Christiane Wendehorst, 'Consumer Contracts and the Internet of Things' in Reiner Schulze and Dirk Staudenmayer (eds), *Digital Revolution – Challenges for Contract Law in Practice* (Nomos 2016) 189.
184 ME Khalil, K Ghani and W Khalil, 'Onion Architecture: A New Approach for XaaS (Every-Thing-as-a Service) Based Virtual Collaborations' *2016 13th Learning and Technology Conference (L&T)* (2016); Guido Noto La Diega, 'Il Cloud Computing. Alla Ricerca Del Diritto Perduto Nel Web 3.0' (2014) 2 Europa e diritto privato 577.
185 D Androcec and N Vrcek, 'Thing as a Service Interoperability: Review and Framework Proposal' *2016 IEEE 4th International Conference on Future Internet of Things and Cloud (FiCloud)* (IEEE 2016).
186 This is akin to the idea of Everything as a Service (XaaS), but with an IoT focus. Y Duan, Y Cao and X Sun, 'Various "AaS" of Everything as a Service' *2015 IEEE/ACIS 16th International Conference on Software Engineering, Artificial Intelligence, Networking and Parallel/Distributed Computing (SNPD)* (IEEE 2015).

Thing, the essential functionality that the consumer expects. The IoT enables new and ubiquitous services that can be accessed by an increasing number of Things in close proximity to the end user.[187] Whilst this hyperservitisation can benefit consumers, the more the services – and the more they are distributed and hidden in countless Things – the higher the complexity to untangle, and the more the legals to find, read, and make sense of. To map Echo's legals, one would need to have a clear idea of all the services that the speaker's consumers can access. This is impossible, however.

As provided with baffling vagueness in the Conditions of Use and Sale, Amazon offers 'a wide range of Amazon Services, and sometimes additional terms may apply.'[188] Amazon does not clarify when additional terms indeed apply, nor do they provide a full list of such services; they only make the 'example [of] Your Profile, Gift Cards or Amazon applications for mobile.' It would be important to find these additional terms because '[i]f these Conditions of Use are inconsistent with the Service Terms, those Service Terms will control.'[189] Alarmed by this clause, I ventured to search for additional terms. Whilst I could not find the terms applicable to Your Profile, after some digging I managed to find the following 55 Thing-as-a-service-related legals.

The Thing-as-a-service-related legals confirm issues of:

(i) Incontrollable multiplication of legals;
(ii) Difficulty to find the legals;
(iii) Unclear contractual parties, partly due to the gargantuan corporate structure and the reliance on affiliates;
(iv) Unclear subject matter;
(v) Control of every layer through IP rights and corresponding death of ownership;
(vi) Difficulty to distinguish between hardware, software, service, and data;
(vii) Untenable resting on the dichotomy between personal data and nonpersonal ones.

It should be noted that it is unclear why all these services need ad hoc separate legals and why they are not listed by Amazon in its 'Legal Policies' section of the website, which currently shows only seven legals.[190] To give a sense of how difficult it is to find all the relevant legals, see Figure 2.4, which follows, about Amazon Now's terms. The consumer will have to open the app, click on the 'hamburger button,' then click 'Help & About,' followed by 'About,' 'Legal information,' and 'Additional terms.' All this happens in-app. Finally, one has to open a browser and search for HERE

---

187 Anna Rymaszewska, Petri Helo and Angappa Gunasekaran, 'IoT Powered Servitization of Manufacturing – an Exploratory Case Study' (2017) 192 International Journal of Production Economics 92.
188 Conditions of Use, preamble.
189 Conditions of Use & Sale, preamble to the conditions of use.
190 www.amazon.co.uk/gp/help/customer/display.html/ref=hp_bc_nav?ie=UTF8&nodeId=GWFZQ 8U37JV9AUT5>.

Table 2.2 Amazon Echo's Legals Related to Thing-as-a-Service

Name	Parties	Subject Matter	Issues
Amazon.co.uk Gift Card Content Submission Terms and Conditions[191]	Unspecified	Submission of digital images for display on a gift voucher	
Amazon.co.uk Promotional Code and Promotional Credit Terms and Conditions[192]	Unspecified	Certain promotional offers, as defined on the landing page of the relevant promotion	I did not find this document initially, but I was intrigued by Amazon Prime Terms and Conditions' passage whereby 'Prime Terms trial or other promotional memberships . . . are subject to these Terms except as otherwise stated in the promotional membership terms.'[193]
Qualified Promotions Terms and Conditions[194]	Unspecified	Promotions available to consumers who take qualifying actions, such as spending a minimum amount or buying one product to receive another product for free	
Amazon Dash Replenishment Terms of Use[195]	Amazon EU S.à r.l. and its affiliates	Service of reordering supplies of consumer goods through a physical or virtual button or auto-detection capabilities	It covers both the software and the hardware components of the button. However, the latter is mainly governed by the aforementioned Amazon Device Terms of Use.[196]
Amazon Discount Voucher Terms and Conditions[197]	Unspecified	Discount vouchers	

Twitch Terms of Service[198]	Twitch Interactive Inc. (bought by Amazon. com in 2014) and its affiliates	Gaming and interactive entertainment	These are complemented by 16 separate documents carrying the Privacy Notice[199] and Choices,[200] the Community Guidelines,[201] DMCA Guidelines,[202] Trademark Policy,[203] Trademark Guidelines,[204] Terms of Sale,[205] Developer Agreement,[206] Affiliate Program Agreement,[207] Supplemental Fees Statement,[208] Ad Choices,[209] Channel Points Acceptable Use Policy,[210] Bits Acceptable Use Policy,[211] Cookie Policy,[212] Photosensitive Seizure Warning,[213] and Events Code of Conduct[214]

(Continued)

191 Unknown date <www.amazon.co.uk/gp/help/customer/display.html?nodeId=201971000>.

192 Unknown date <www.amazon.co.uk/gp/help/customer/display.html?nodeId=201895970>.

193 Amazon Prime Terms and Conditions, point 3.5.

194 Unknown date <www.amazon.co.uk/gp/help/customer/display.html?nodeId=201622460>.

195 Last updated on 24 May 2018 <www.amazon.co.uk/gp/help/customer/display.html?nodeId=201730770>.

196 Last updated on 4 September 2019 <www.amazon.co.uk/gp/help/customer/display.html?nodeId=202002080>.

197 Unknown date <www.amazon.co.uk/gp/help/customer/display.html?nodeId=201896080>.

198 Last updated on 16 April 2019 <www.twitch.tv/p/legal/terms-of-service/>.

199 Last updated on 10 August 2018 <www.twitch.tv/p/legal/privacy-policy/>.

200 Last updated on 9 September 2019 <www.twitch.tv/p/legal/privacy-choices/>.

201 Last updated on 12 September 2019 <www.twitch.tv/p/legal/community-guidelines/>.

202 Last updated on 27 March 2019 <www.twitch.tv/p/legal/dmca-guidelines/>.

203 Last updated on 9 February 2017 <www.twitch.tv/p/legal/trademark-policy/>.

204 Last updated on 11 July 2018 <www.twitch.tv/p/legal/trademark/>.

205 Last updated on 10 September 2019 <www.twitch.tv/p/legal/terms-of-sale/>.

206 Last updated on 19 July 2019 <www.twitch.tv/p/legal/developer-agreement/>.

207 Last updated on 8 June 2018 <www.twitch.tv/p/legal/affiliate-agreement/>.

208 Last updated on 18 December 2018 <www.twitch.tv/p/legal/supplemental-fees-statement/>.

209 Last updated on 30 May 2013 <www.twitch.tv/p/legal/ad-choices/>.

210 Last updated on 3 September 2019 <www.twitch.tv/p/legal/channel-points-acceptable-use-policy/>.

211 Last updated on 23 April 2018 <www.twitch.tv/p/legal/bits-acceptable-use/>.

212 Last updated on 22 February 2019 <www.twitch.tv/p/legal/cookie-policy/>.

213 Last updated on 5 July 2014 <www.twitch.tv/p/legal/seizure-warning/>.

214 Last updated on 20 June 2019 <www.twitch.tv/p/legal/events-code-of-conduct/>.

Table 2.2 (Continued)

Name	Parties	Subject Matter	Issues
Kindle Store Terms of Use[215]	Amazon Media EU S.à r.l. and its affiliates	Kindle content and software, Kindle store and support	It includes matters that would traditionally qualify as services, as well as software and data.
Audible Service Conditions of Use[216]	Audible Limited, whose immediate parent company is Audible Inc.; Amazon.com Inc. is their holding company[217]	Spoken-word audio entertainment services through Audible's websites and apps	This document includes the Audible Purchase Terms and Conditions, Audible Terms and Conditions for Gift and Promotional Codes and Vouchers, Audible Plan Terms, Additional Software Terms, and Great Listen Guarantee Terms and Conditions. Separate policies regard privacy[218] and cookies.[219]
IMDb Conditions of Use[220]	IMDb.com Inc. and its affiliates. The company was acquired by Amazon.com in 1998.	IMDb services that include products, software, and apps provided by the online movie database	In separate pages, the eager consumer may find the IMDb Privacy Notice,[221] the Third Party Licensing Notices for iOS[222] and Android,[223] and the policy on Interest-Based Ads.[224] The latter, albeit hosted on Amazon's main website and seemingly referring to all of Amazon's services and products, is different from the Interest-Based Ads policy mentioned above, which raises the issue of how to reconcile the inconsistencies. For example, IMDb's policy does not contain a commitment not to associate consumer 'interactions on unaffiliated sites with personally identifiable information.'
Amazon Appstore for Android Terms of Use[225]	Amazon Media EU S.à r.l. and its affiliates	Amazon Appstore for Android and associated software, services, and purchases	
Additional Terms Relating to Amazon Apps Software[226]	Unspecified	Licensed use of third-party software in Amazon's apps	

| **Amazon Coins Terms**[227] | Amazon Media EU S.à r.l. and its affiliates | Amazon Coins, a cryptocurrency that allows consumers to purchase digital products (apps, games, and in-game items) on Amazon Appstore | |
| **Amazon App Suite Legal Notices**[228] | Unspecified | Virtually any aspect of Amazon's apps is covered by patents, trademarks, copyright, or other forms of IP | It evidences the phenomena of death of ownership and digital dispossession. |

215 Last updated on 23 May 2018 <www.amazon.co.uk/gp/help/customer/display.html?nodeId=201014950>.

216 Last updated on 4 December 2018 <www.audible.co.uk/legal/conditions-of-use?moduleId=201654400&ie=UTF8#p7>.

217 Audible Limited Report and Financial Statements, Year ended 31 December 2018, retrieved from the Traders House directory, whose servere are interestingly hosted by Amazon itself.

218 Audible Privacy Help Page, unknown date <www.audible.co.uk/ep/privacyfaq>.

219 Cookies Notice, last updated on 23 May 2018 <www.audible.co.uk/legal/cookies-and-advertising?moduleId=201654420&pf_rd_p=8b988335-dfd9-4b60-bde4-28fd204e4999&pf_rd_r=Y7NE7V4D1MB9PMPHB56C&ref=mn_anon-h_f6_ca>.

220 Unknown date <www.imdb.com/iphone_app/conditions/?pf_rd_m=A2FGELUUNOQJNL&pf_rd_p=89741122-4d15-4fc0-b4b2-7bc3d5403f19&pf_rd_r=NT58F7QFWDBSQGH3SEG3&pf_rd_s=center-1&pf_rd_t=60601&pf_rd_i=iphone_app.terms&ref=fea_lw_1>.

221 Last updated on 8 February 2018 <www.imdb.com/iphone_app/privacy/?pf_rd_m=A2FGELUUNOQJNL&pf_rd_p=89741122-4d15-4fc0-b4b2-7bc3d5403f19&pf_rd_r=NT58F7QFWDBSQGH3SEG3&pf_rd_s=center-1&pf_rd_t=60601&pf_rd_i=iphone_app.terms&ref=fea_lw_2>.

222 Unknown date <www.imdb.com/iphone_app/terms_thirdparty_ios/?pf_rd_m=A2FGELUUNOQJNL&pf_rd_p=89741122-4d15-4fc0-b4b2-7bc3d5403f19&pf_rd_r=NT58F7QFWDBSQGH3SEG3&pf_rd_s=center-1&pf_rd_t=60601&pf_rd_i=iphone_app.terms&ref=fea_lw_3>.

223 Unknown date <www.imdb.com/iphone_app/terms_thirdparty_android/?pf_rd_m=A2FGELUUNOQJNL&pf_rd_p=89741122-4d15-4fc0-b4b2-7bc3d5403f19&pf_rd_r=NT58F7QFWDBSQGH3SEG3&pf_rd_s=center-1&pf_rd_t=60601&pf_rd_i=iphone_app.terms&ref=fea_lw_4>.

224 Unknown date <www.amazon.com/b/?node=516028011&ref=fea_lw_5>.

225 Last updated on 23 May 2018 <www.amazon.co.uk/gp/help/customer/display.html?nodeId=201485660&_encoding=UTF8&ref=mas_help_legacy_legal_doc_page>.

226 Last updated on 30 August 2012 <www.amazon.co.uk/gp/feature.html/ref=amb_link_170954367_4?ie=UTF8&docId=1000662743&pf_rd_m=A3P5ROKL5A1OLE&pf_rd_s=center-2&pf_rd_r=03AVGH5RA9MNZ21CFKP5&pf_rd_t=1401&pf_rd_p=500480187&pf_rd_i=1000065093>.

227 Last updated on 23 May 2018 <www.amazon.co.uk/gp/help/customer/display.html/ref=hp_left_v4_sib?ie=UTF8&nodeId=20143452>.

228 Unknown date <www.amazon.co.uk/gp/help/customer/display.html/ref=hp_left_v4_sib?ie=UTF8&nodeId=20135769()>.

(Continued)

Table 2.2 (Continued)

Name	Parties	Subject Matter	Issues
Amazon GameCircle Terms of Use[229]	Amazon Media EU S.à.r.l. and its affiliates	Amazon GameCircle (game-related features, e.g. storage of game data on the cloud) and associated software and service	Echo can be used to control Fire TV, and the latter's app is available on Echo Show. Therefore, Fire TV's legals will apply.
Amazon Fire TV App Terms of Use	Amazon Media EU S.à.r.l. and its affiliates	Mobile app and software associated to Amazon Fire TV app, through which Things can be used to control Amazon Fire TV devices	
Amazon Silk Terms and Conditions[230]	Amazon EU S.à.r.l.	Amazon Silk browser software and related services	The link to these terms is broken, and one needs to resort to external search engines to find them.
Fire for Kids Unlimited and Kindle for Kids Terms and Conditions[231]	Amazon Media EU S.à.r.l., Amazon Video Limited, and their affiliates	Digital content (e-books, movies, games, etc.) for children aged 3 to 12 years old	
Amazon App Legal Notice[232]	Unspecified	It contains a patent notice, a notice and take-down procedure for copyright infringement, an open-source software notice, and third parties copyright licenses	It is available only on the Fire TV mobile app and cannot be found anywhere else.
Legal Here Service Terms[233]	HERE Global B.V.	Unclear. HERE is Amazon's licensor that provides unspecified 'portions of the Amazon Service,'[234] in particular Prime Now, which offers household items and essentials with 2-hour delivery.	Subject matter's lack of definition. Additionally, it is unclear – although I would be inclined to answer in the positive – whether also the other HERE legals would apply, namely, End User License Agreement,[235] Terms for HERE Products and Services,[236] HERE Mobility Terms,[237] Open Location Platform Terms,[238] Other legal information and notices,[239] HERE XYZ Pro Beta Terms and Conditions.[240]

Amazon Maps Terms of Use[241]	Amazon Media EU S.à.r.l. and its affiliates	Maps service, data, and associated software	Unlike the other legals, these terms do not refer to the main privacy policy. The reason may be the erroneous conviction that location data is not personal data and the resting on the outdated dichotomy between personal and nonpersonal data. Inasmuch as the service involves personal data processing, Amazon's Privacy Notice should apply. For example, since 'map data' are defined as including 'reviews, and other related information,'[242] these could well identify a data subject.
AutoRip Terms and Conditions[243]	Amazon EU S.à r.l. and Amazon Digital UK Ltd	AutoRip (provision of MP3 versions of eligible physical albums) and Amazon Music library	I found this document only because one of Amazon's advisers mentioned it in passing as an example of a service provided by one of Amazon's affiliates.

229 Last updated on 23 May 2018 <www.amazon.co.uk/gp/help/customer/display.html?nodeId=201283870>.
230 Last updated on 26 December 2017 <www.amazon.co.uk/gp/help/customer/display.html?nodeId=200775270>.
231 Last updated on 4 June 2019 <www.amazon.co.uk/gp/help/customer/display.html?nodeId=201222340>.
232 Unknown date, unknown parties, and unknown URL. The Fire TV app has been accessed on 2 October 2019 from an Android phone.
233 Last updated on 12 April 2015 <legal.here.com/en-gb/terms>.
234 Prime Now App's Additional Terms, available only in-app.
235 Updated on 8 March 2016 <legal.here.com/en-gb/terms/end-user-license-agreement>.
236 Last updated on 13 June 2019 <legal.here.com/en-gb/terms/terms-for-here-products-and-services>.
237 Last updated on 4 June 2019 <legal.here.com/en-gb/terms/here-mobility-terms>.
238 Last updated on 7 June 2019 <legal.here.com/en-gb/terms/open-location-platform-terms>.
239 Last updated on 7 June 2019 <legal.here.com/en-gb/terms/other-legal-information-and-notices>.
240 Last updated on 8 July 2019 <legal.here.com/en-gb/HERE-XYZ-Pro-Beta-Terms-and-Conditions>.
241 Last updated on 23 May 2018 <www.amazon.co.uk/gp/help/customer/display.html?ref=hp_left_v4_sib?ie=UTF8&nodeId=201544030>.
242 ibid.
243 Last updated on 1 October 2019 <www.amazon.co.uk/gp/help/customer/display.html?nodeId=201420350>.

Figure 2.4 'Screens' to go through before accessing all of Prime Now's legals.

Global B.V.'s terms. Regrettably, these legals teem with casting-net provisions, that is, 'mean-spirited contract provision[s that] cast . . . a wide net that captures other contracts, leaving the consumer with the daunting task of reconciling possibly conflicting terms.'[244] IoT consumers are bounced from one document to another, which questions whether consumers can be deemed to be bound by these terms.

2.5.2.3 Controlled Interoperability

This hyperservitisation leads to a multiplication of legals that is only matched by another characteristic of the IoT, namely, the interactions with third parties' Things, software, and service. In the context of Echo, this takes the form of the

---

244 Nancy S Kim, *Wrap Contracts: Foundations and Ramifications* (OUP 2013) 67.

Works with Alexa–certified products and the Alexa-compatible brands.[245] Interoperability is regulated both by technological means (e.g. communication protocols) and by contractual ones (e.g. EULA).[246] If this regulation is too strict, it can lead to closed systems that cannot work together, that is, the Internet of Silos. Unrestrained interoperability, conversely, can be perceived as leading to uncontrolled actions and data flows, with harms whose liability cannot be easily allocated.

Amazon Echo can be controlled, control, and share data with over 60,000 third parties' Things (e.g. Google Nest Thermostat and Samsung's cleaning robot Powerbot) from more than 7,400 brands. Therefore, a consumer who would like to have a clear picture of their rights, obligations, and risks would be expected to find and read also these thousands of third parties' legals. It is not very likely that this will happen, because the consumer would have to spend months, if not years, just looking for the legals and then try to understand their content, the relationships between them, and to endeavour to reconcile the inconsistencies.

Controlled interoperability explains why another set of legals should be taken into account, namely, the developers' legals. They govern how third parties' developers can enable access to Amazon products and services in their own apps and devices. This contractual thicket has an influence on how personal data is processed, liability allocated, etc. They are also important because they regulate the interoperability of Amazon Echo with third-party products and services. Intricate liability issues stem from these (sometimes unforeseen) interactions. Of the twelve 'developer legals,' Table 2.3 focuses on the main documents consumers should be aware of.

Other 'developer legals' include the Alexa Built-In Trademark Usage Guidelines,[247] Mobile Ad Network Program Participation Requirements,[248] Mobile Ad Network Publisher Agreement,[249] Works with Alexa – Program Guidelines,[250] Works with Alexa – Trademark Usage Guidelines,[251] Certified for Humans – Program Guidelines,[252] Program Materials License Agreement,[253] Trademark, Brand, and Marketing Guidelines,[254] and Amazon Developer Services Portal Terms of Use.[255] Their separate analysis is not necessary because they affect consumer rights only indirectly.

---

245 The list is available at <developer.amazon.com/en-GB/alexa/connected-devices/compatible>.
246 Developers must make sure that their app's EULA complies with the requirements of the Amazon Developer Services Agreement (see clause 4(a)).
247 Unknown date <developer.amazon.com/support/legal/alexa_built_in_trademark_usage_guidelines>.
248 Last updated on 31 August 2015 <developer.amazon.com/support/legal/mobileads/participation-requirements>.
249 Last updated on 14 May 2018 <developer.amazon.com/support/legal/mobileads/terms-and-agreements>.
250 Unknown date <developer.amazon.com/support/legal/wwa-program-guidelines>.
251 Unknown date <developer.amazon.com/support/legal/wwa-trademark-usage-guidelines>.
252 Unknown date <developer.amazon.com/support/legal/certified-for-humans-program-guidelines>.
253 Last updated on 22 August 2018 <developer.amazon.com/support/legal/pml>.
254 Last updated on 17 May 2018 <developer.amazon.com/support/legal/tuabg>.
255 Last updated on 24 May 2018 <developer.amazon.com/support/legal/tou>.

Table 2.3 Amazon Echo's Key Developer Legals

Name	Parties	Subject Matter	Issues
Amazon Developer Services Agreement[256]	Amazon Digital Services LLC, Amazon Media EU S.a.r.l., Amazon Services International Inc., Amazon Servicos de Varejo do Brasil Ltda., Amazon.com Int'l Sales Inc., Amazon Australia Services Inc., Amazon Mexico Services Inc., and their affiliates	All the apps, digital content, and Things that embed Amazon's service or software	In Amazon's lingo, these are called 'skills.' For example, LG is likely to have agreed to this contract when developing its ThinQ Alexa-enabled fridges.
Alexa Voice Service Program Requirements[257]	Unspecified	More detailed rules regarding Alexa Voice Service (AVS) Products and AVS Components	Products are Alexa-powered third-party devices and apps; the requirements apply also to these devices and apps' components.
Alexa Device Requirements[258]	Unspecified	'[A]ll Devices, including AVS Products, AVS Components, and Alexa Gadgets'[259]	Very broad scope, ranging from the prevention of unlawful content, e.g. pornography, to the prevention of activities, e.g. unauthorised gambling.

The developers' legals present similar issues to the ones analysed in previous passages, that is, the multiplication of legals, the difficulty to find them, the lack of clarity as to the contractual parties, and the overcoming of traditional concepts of service and product. Additionally, their intricate web heavily controls interoperability in a proprietary and closed way. To exemplify this, suffice it to say that developers are prevented from using open-source software, insofar as it requires

256 Last updated on 14 February 2019 <developer.amazon.com/support/legal/da>.
257 Unknown date <developer.amazon.com/support/legal/alexa/alexa-voice-service/terms-and-agreements>.
258 Unknown date <developer.amazon.com/support/legal/alexa_device_requirements>.
259 ibid.

Amazon to disclose or make available any software and materials.[260] It would be excessive to qualify Amazon's approach as leading to the Internet of Silos. Indeed, the use of open source is, in principle, allowed.[261] Nonetheless, it is a fundamentally proprietary system that, as such, deprives consumers of the benefits of generalised interoperability. From the fact that Things are an amalgam of software, service, etc. follows that each component must be open for the Thing and the system to be open.[262] Open software will not suffice if it is not complemented by open hardware and open data.

Understanding the interactions between Echo and third parties' Things, software, and service is important to consumers also due to the rise of 'prosumers,' that is, the fourth determinant of the multiplication of legals in the IoT.

2.5.2.4 Overcoming the Trader-Consumer Dichotomy: The Time of Prosumers

We live in the time of prosumers, who 'refuse the two-polar definition of growth economy knowing that every producer is also a consumer and every consumer is a producer.'[263] The overcoming of the consumer-trader binary – particularly evident in the 'smart' economy[264] – is also recognised by EU consumer laws that encompass dual-purpose contracts. Such a contract is concluded for purposes that are partly within and partly outside the person's trade, if 'the trade purpose is so limited as not to be *predominant* in the overall context of the contract.'[265] As Jeremy Rifkin put it, by leveraging the IoT, '[p]rosumers can . . . accelerate efficiency, dramatically increase productivity, and lower the *marginal cost of producing and sharing a wide range of products and services to near zero, just like they now do with information goods.*'[266] In light of the key role of prosumers in the IoT, Amazon Echo's consumers, acting even temporarily in a professional capacity, will have to consider also the following 56 legals.

These legals confirm the aforementioned issues and are of particular relevance to understand the death of ownership, as considered in Chapter 6.

2.5.2.5 The Cloud of Things

The fifth determinant of the staggering number of legals is the shift from IoT to the Cloud of Things, namely, the increasing reliance of Things on cloud computing. In light of the limited processing capabilities of most commercially available

---

260 Amazon Developer Services Agreement, 4(c).
261 ibid 10(f).
262 cf Alexander Kotsev and others, 'Next Generation Air Quality Platform: Openness and Interoperability for the Internet of Things' (2016) 16 Sensors 403.
263 Uygar Özesmi, 'The Prosumer Economy–Being Like a Forest' [2019] arXiv preprint arXiv:1903.07615.
264 Rifkin (n 28) 163.
265 Consumer Rights Directive, recital 17.
266 Rifkin (n 28) 3.

Table 2.4 Amazon Echo's Legals for Prosumers

Name	Parties	Subject Matter	Issues
Non-Disclosure Agreement[267]	Amazon EU S.à.r.l. and its affiliates	Confidential information disclosed to those who are engaged in or considering a business relationship with Amazon	
Non-Exhaustive List of Amazon Trademarks[268]	Unspecified	Registered trademarks	Especially for prosumers, it is useful to know that Amazon has 237 trademarks in the UK, including arguably not very distinctive signs, such as 'bottom of the page'[269] and '1-click'[270]
Non-Exhaustive List of Applicable Amazon Patents and Applicable Licensed Patents[271]	Unspecified	The list includes 104 patents that apply to Amazon.com and to the features and services accessible via the site.	Patents monopolise both tangible and intangible inventions. See e.g. a '[s]ecure method and system for communicating a list of credit card numbers over a non-secure network.'[272]
Amazon Services Europe Business Solutions Agreement[273]	Amazon Services Europe S.à.r.l.	Optional seller services, including selling on Amazon, sponsored ads, and selling partner API	This agreement is complemented by 52 policies, agreements, guidelines, etc.[274] that I will not analyse because the agreement will usually prevail on them[275] and because they are less directly relevant to consumers.

267 Unknown date <www.amazon.co.uk/gp/help/customer/display.html/ref=hp_left_v4_sib?ie=UTF 8&nodeId=20202992>.

268 Unknown date <www.amazon.co.uk/gp/help/customer/display.html?nodeId=200952730>.

269 EU003367935, priority date 26 March 2003, owned by Amazon Europe Core S.à r.l.

270 EU000865527, priority date 2 January 1998, owned by Amazon Europe Core S.à r.l.

271 Last updated on 21 January 2011 <www.amazon.co.uk/gp/help/customer/display.html?nodeId= 201909270>.

272 US5715399 (A) — 1998–02–03, invented by Jeff Bezos and owned by Amazon.com, Inc.

273 Last updated on 1 October 2019 <sellercentral.amazon.co.uk/gp/help/external/201190440? language=en_GB&ref=efph_201190440_cont_521>.

274 Unknown date <sellercentral.amazon.co.uk/gp/help/external/help-page.html?itemID=521& language=en_GB&ref=efph_521_bred_201190440>.

275 'If there is any conflict between these General Terms and the applicable Service Terms and Program Policies, the General Terms will govern and the applicable Service Terms will prevail over the Program Policies' (Amazon Services Europe Business Solutions Agreement, general terms).

Table 2.5 Amazon Echo's Cloud-Related Legals

Name	Parties	Subject Matter	Issues
AWS Customer Agreement[276]	Amazon Web Services EMEA S.à.r.l.	Service offerings defined as 'the Services (including associated APIs), the AWS Content, the AWS Marks'.[277]	Despite the contractual party being Amazon Web Services EMEA S.à.r.l., affiliates are responsible for making available some contents, e.g. APIs. The document contains casting-net provisions as it refers to the AWS Service Terms for the definition of 'services.'
AWS Service Terms[278]	Unspecified	It deals with 89 services, including Alexa.	It lists the services, but it does not define them. Some of the services come with additional terms.[279]
AWS Acceptable Use Policy[280]	Amazon Web Services Inc. and its affiliates	Prohibits certain uses of the services and of AWS. Amazon.com	Broad scope, ranging from IP infringement to child pornography.
AWS Privacy Notice[281]	Amazon Web Services EMEA S.à r.l.	Data processing in relation to any AWS websites, applications, products, services, and events	Refers to the now-invalidated Privacy Shield, while declaring not to rely on it and stating that extra-EEA data transfers are done 'in accordance with the terms of this Privacy Notice and applicable data protection law.'[282]

276 Last updated on 20 April 2019 <aws.amazon.com/agreement/>.
277 ibid, point 14.
278 Last updated on 27 September 2019 <aws.amazon.com/service-terms/>.
279 AWS services include inter alia Alexa Web Services, AI Services, and IoT 1-Click.
280 Last updated on 16 September 2019 <aws.amazon.com/aup/>.
281 Last updated on 10 December 2018 <aws.amazon.com/privacy/>.
282 ibid, para 'Additional Information for Certain Jurisdictions.'

(Continued)

Table 2.5 (Continued)

Name	Parties	Subject Matter	Issues
AWS GDPR Data Processing Addendum[283]	Unidentified 'applicable Amazon Web Services contracting entity'[284]	Standard Contractual Clauses providing a legal basis for cross-border data transfers[285]	Not mentioned in the AWS Privacy Notice, referred to only in the AWS Service Terms. It relies on the Standard Contractual Clauses without the identification of the supplementary measures mandated by *Schrems II*.[286] The Addendum provides that the Standard Contractual Clauses will not apply 'if AWS has adopted Binding Corporate Rules . . . or an alternative recognised compliance standard,'[287] but it does not inform the reader whether AWS has indeed adopted these rules, let alone explaining what this compliance standard is.
AWS Site Terms[288]	Amazon Web Services Inc. and its affiliates	Use of AWS.Amazon.com.	
AWS Trademark Guidelines[289]	Amazon Web Services Inc. *or* its affiliates	It grants a limited licence to use of AWS-related trademarks	
AWS Elemental Appliances and Software Terms of Service[290]	Elemental Technologies LLC (subsidiary of Amazon Web Services)	Encoding, packaging, and delivery of video assets on premises	

283 Unknown date <d1.awsstatic.com/legal/aws-gdpr/AWS_GDPR_DPA.pdf>.
284 ibid.
285 European Data Protection Board, 'Information Note on Data Transfers under the GDPR in the Event of a No-Deal Brexit' (12 February 2019) <https://edpb.europa.eu/sites/edpb/files/files/file1/edpb-2019-02-12-infonote-nodeal-brexit_en.pdf>.
286 (n 113).
287 AWS GDPR Data Processing Addendum, 12(2).
288 Last updated on 30 August 2019 <aws.amazon.com/terms/>.
289 Last updated on 14 September 2019 <aws.amazon.com/trademark-guidelines/>.
290 Last updated on 6 August 2019 <aws.amazon.com/legal/elemental-appliances-software-agreement/>.

Things and of the wealth of data they produce, cloud computing appears to be the go-to solution for optimal processing capabilities.[291] In our case study, this takes the form of Amazon Web Services (AWS), which maintain the network-connected hardware required for cloud-enabled services; AWS are both provided to third parties and used internally in many of Amazon's services. For example, alongside Alexa, another cloud-powered app is Amazon Chime, tool for online meetings and videoconferencing. This means that consumers will have to find, read, and understand also the following 97 legals.

Additionally, one would need to consider the Service Level Agreements for each of the 89 AWS services,[292] such as the Alexa for Business Service Level Agreement.[293]

Alongside the number of the cloud-related legals, their opaqueness, and their inconsistencies when it comes to international data transfers, the main criticisms are that they are US contracts – there is no UK- or EU-tailored version – and that they cannot be found in Amazon's main legal policies section.

2.5.2.6 *The Wave of Sustainability*

Not all the determinants of the high number of legals in the IoT shed light on a concerning aspect of this sociotechnological phenomenon. Sustainability-related legals constitute a prime example of this. The idea of sustainability dates back to the eighties.[294] Most notably, in 1987 the World Commission on Environment and Development referred to it as a form of 'development that meets the needs of the present without compromising the ability of future generations to meet their own needs.'[295] This meant, for private companies, an increasing pressure to embrace forms of corporate social responsibility (CSR), whereby social, environmental, and economic issues are strategically integrated into all companies' operational and capital investments decisions.[296] In recent years, thanks to the increased awareness of the imperative to tackle climate change, sustainability has become more central, and it has been linked to state and nonstate actors' obligations to enforce and abide by human rights.[297] An important role is being played

---

291 See e.g. W Kuan Hon, Christopher Millard and Jatinder Singh, 'Twenty Legal Considerations for Clouds of Things' [2016] Queen Mary University of London, School of Law Legal Studies Research Paper No 216/2016; Guido Noto La Diega, 'Clouds of Things: Data Protection and Consumer Law at the Intersection of Cloud Computing and the Internet of Things in the United Kingdom' (2016) 9(1) Journal of Law & Economic Regulation 69.

292 <aws.amazon.com/legal/service-level-agreements/>.

293 Last updated on 19 March 2019 <aws.amazon.com/alexaforbusiness/sla/>.

294 See Geir B Asheim, *Sustainability* (World Bank Publications 1994).

295 World Commission on Environment and Development, *Our Common Future* (OUP 1987) 43.

296 Michael Hopkins, *CSR and Sustainability: From the Margins to the Mainstream: A Textbook* (Routledge 2017) <https://search.ebscohost.com/login.aspx?direct=true&scope=site&db=nlebk&db=nlabk&AN=1592603>.

297 See e.g. Gerhard Bos and Marcus Düwell (eds), *Human Rights and Sustainability* (Routledge 2016).

by the UN and their Guiding Principles on Business and Human Rights.[298] IoT traders can play an important role to make sustainability a reality, for example, by adopting circular economy principles. Marco Ricolfi makes the example of self-driving cars, 'not to be sold but leased, so that in accordance with the tenets of what is designated as "predictive maintenance" the supplier, who retains property, constantly receives all the information required to optimize product life cycles, including repairs, maintenance, replacements, etc.'[299] At the same time, the IoT constitutes a challenge for sustainability. The proliferation of Things can lead to a vertical increase in nonrecycling waste. More generally, IoT traders have been criticised for putting in place rather-unstainable practices. Amazon provides an excellent example of this. In 2013, a BBC investigation found that Amazon makes its staff work under unbelievable pressure in slave camp conditions.[300] In 2018, there was evidence that Amazon workers were forced to urinate in bottles or skip bathroom breaks because fulfilment demands were too high.[301] These incidents are not isolated. For example, in 2019 Amazon's supplier Foxconn was found to employ over 1,000 schoolchildren, who were reported to work night shifts and overtime.[302]

This means that IoT traders have an interest to include in the contractual quagmire documents that evidence their commitment to sustainability. In this context, the main legals that an Amazon Echo's consumer will have to find and read are:

- Supplier Code of Conduct.[303] A typical CSR measure, this code aims at making sure that Amazon's suppliers respect human rights and the environment and protect the fundamental dignity of workers.[304] The failure to comply with the code can lead to Amazon terminating the relationship with the supplier.[305]
- Modern-Day Slavery Statement.[306] Unlike most CSR measures, this is a legal requirement, in particular imposed by the UK Modern Slavery Act.[307] The latter obliges traders with a global turnover of at least £36 million, who carry

---

298 United Nations Human Rights Council, resolution 17/4 of 16 June 2011.
299 Marco Ricolfi, 'IoT and the Ages of Antitrust' (Nexa Center for Internet & Society 2017) Working paper nr 4/2017 6.
300 Dave Lee, 'Amazon Workers Face "Illness Risk"' *BBC News* (25 November 2013) <www.bbc.com/news/business-25034598>.
301 James Bloodworth, *Hired: Six Months Undercover in Low-Wage Britain* (Atlantic Books 2019).
302 China Labor Watch, 'Amazon's Supplier Factory Foxconn Recruits Illegally' (2019) <www.chinalaborwatch.org/upfile/2019_08_07/Amazon%20English%20Report%2008.09.pdf>.
303 Unknown date <d39w7f4ix9f5s9.cloudfront.net/4d/80/9e681da64536a287f9e658216ff9/amazon-supplier-code-of-conduct-2019-09-18-2.pdf>.
304 These standards are derived from the UN Guiding Principles on Business and Human Rights, the Core Conventions of the International Labour Organization (ILO), and the UN Universal Declaration of Human Rights.
305 Amazon Supply Chain Standards, point 2.
306 Unknown date <www.amazon.co.uk/gp/help/customer/display.html/ref=hp_left_v4_sib?ie=UTF8&nodeId=202151760>.
307 S 54.

on a business or part of a business in the UK, to produce a slavery and human trafficking statement for each financial year.[308]

These documents will be of interest to the 'ethical' consumer who believes in sustainable consumption and demands human rights–compliant supply chains.

Keeping public attention high is pivotal to ensuring that IoT multinationals deliver on their commitments to sustainability, human rights, and antislavery, which is in turn fundamental for a socially just IoT.

2.6 Interim Conclusion

I will conclude with some autoethnographic remarks. It took me over two weeks to identify the legals consumers are expected to find, read, and understand when using a Thing as simple as a speaker. Whilst Amazon's 'Legal Policies' section groups seven legals,[309] consumers are left . . . to their own devices in their search for the remaining 24 core legals, to which one needs to add 55 Thing-as-a-Service-related legals, 12 developers' legals, 56 legals for the prosumer, 97 cloud-related, and two that regard sustainability, for a total of 246 legals. And this is not even the full picture, because consumers should also take into account the legals of 7,400 third parties providing 60,000 Things that interact with Echo. Additionally, consumers should pierce the corporate veil and understand which of the hundreds of subsidiaries and affiliates is responsible for each functionality, service, etc. I found it impossible to have a clear picture of who these companies are and what they are responsible for, let alone finding their Echo-relevant legals. The analysis prior showed not only the issue of the staggering number of legals in the IoT but also two related issues, namely, the difficulty to identify the contractual parties – that amongst other things is crucial to successfully bring an action – and the fluidity of the contractual subject matter. Some legals purport to regulate the Thing by separating its hardware, software, service, and data components, but the way these components are on each occasion (re)defined – often by qualifying as 'service' what would normally count as software, data, or hardware – confirms the initial thesis that Things are an inextricable mixture of these components. This is perhaps best illustrated by the Amazon Device Terms of Use, which would, in theory, regard the product as hardware, but most of their clauses are about services or data.[310] Similarly, Alexa Terms of Use regard the software and service components of Echo, but they affect the Thing as a whole, including its hardware

---

308 *Transparency in Supply Chains Etc. A Practical Guide. Guidance Issued under Section 54(9) of the Modern Slavery Act 2015* (Home Office 2015).

309 These are the Non-Disclosure Agreement, the Modern-Day Slavery Statement, Miscellaneous Reporting, Conditions of Use Sale, Non-Exhaustive List of Applicable Amazon Patents and applicable Licensed Patents, Amazon.co.uk Privacy Notice, Non-Exhaustive List of Amazon Trademarks.

310 For example, under the Amazon Device Terms of Use, point 2.b. 'Some Services may be unavailable, vary (e.g.by device or geography), be offered for a limited time, or require separate subscriptions.'

and data components. Indeed, should Amazon exercise its contractual power to discontinue Alexa at any time and at their sole discretion,[311] it would end up 'bricking' the speaker in its entirety. Echo as a whole would be affected because, without Alexa, Echo's consumers would be left with a 'dumb' speaker. These conclusions about the number of 'legals,' the impossibility to identify the parties, and the inextricability of software, hardware, service, and data are in line with the findings of the similar study that in 2016 analysed Google Nest's legals.[312]

These weeks spent looking for Amazon Echo's legals have seen me oscillating between the excitement of finding something that could benefit consumers and the psychophysical discomfort over Amazon's opaque private ordering of our lives. Every time I thought I found all the Echo-related legals, I was astonished by the realisation that new documents would frequently pop up, often even by accident, e.g. the stumbling upon an alarming passage in one of the core legals or an unclear sentence from a customer support adviser. These feelings of discomfort and astonishment made me interrupt this exploration many times, and I cannot imagine any user who would be willing to go through this experience.

IoT traders invest considerable resources in the design of their interfaces to improve the user experience.[313] The key principle in web design is the principle of least astonishment, whereby '[i]f a necessary feature has a high astonishment factor, it may be necessary to redesign the feature.'[314] Based on this chapter's analysis, it is recommended that IoT traders apply this principle also to their legals. This will mean to redesign the legals to reduce their number, group them in one place, increase their readability, decrease their length, improve their clarity (e.g. specifying who the contractual parties are and what the document's subject matter is), their consistency (e.g. when it comes to international data transfers), and their fairness (e.g. by avoiding casting-net provisions).

Building on this picture of the IoT's consumer issues, the next chapter will investigate whether EU consumer contract laws can counter them, rebalance the business-to-consumer relationship, and ultimately empower consumers.

---

311 Alexa Terms of Use, point 3.2.
312 Noto La Diega and Walden (n 8).
313 Claire Rowland and others, *Designing Connected Products: UX for the Consumer Internet of Things* (O'Reilly 2015).
314 MF Cowlishaw, 'The Design of the REXX Language' (1984) 23 IBM Systems Journal 326, 333.

3 The Internet of Contracts

The Tension between Consumer Contract Laws and IoT Imbalance

The law can never be higher than the economic structure of society and the cultural development conditioned by it.

K. Marx, *Critique of the Gotha Programme*

3.1 Scope of the Chapter

Despite the great benefits that the IoT can bring to consumers, the previous chapter has shown how this sociotechnological phenomenon threatens consumers' safety, autonomy, self-determination, and privacy. This is done through a combination of 'technological' private ordering (e.g. opaque algorithms) and 'legal' private ordering, whereby private companies use contracts to take advantage of legal lacunae and the slowness of the lawmaking process, thus imposing unilaterally their own rules to market relationships. It becomes therefore crucial to critically assess whether IoT contracts can be re-engineered so as to better protect consumers.

Over the years, EU laws have greatly contributed to rebalance business-to-consumer relationships mainly in two ways. Some laws have focused on consumer contracts, by imposing precontractual duties of information, banning unfair terms, and obliging traders to make sure that the product matches what was promised in the contract. Other laws have looked beyond the contract and tried to address the power imbalance in business-to-consumer relationships, especially by holding manufacturers liable for the defects in their products, regardless of any fault and of the existence of a contractual relationship, and by outlawing unfair commercial practices.

This chapter will focus on the former set of laws, namely, EU consumer contract laws; the latter will be analysed in the next chapter. The next sections will first consider whether the Unfair Terms Directive can be invoked to tackle the IoT's contractual quagmire. This chapter will then explore whether the issue of private ordering 'by bricking' can be addressed by consumer sales law, especially after a recent reform that is replacing the First Consumer Sales Directive[1] and pairing

---

1 Directive 1999/44/EC on certain aspects of the sale of consumer goods and associated guarantees ('First Consumer Sales Directive') [1999] OJ L 171/12 will be replaced by Directive 2019/771

DOI: 10.4324/9780429468377-4

it with the Supply of Digital Content Directive.[2] Finally, it will be questioned whether the precontractual duties to inform under the Consumer Rights Directive (CRD) can address the challenges of 'IoT Commerce' to mandated disclosures, i.e., the tension between text-based notice-and-consent mechanisms and the reality of immersive, hyperconnected, interface-free transactional environments.

With this in mind, this chapter will answer the following subquestion: *can consumer contract laws curb the power imbalance in IoT business-to-consumer transactions?*

3.2   The IoT Overcomes Yet Another Binary: Unfairness of Substance and Unfairness of Form in the Smart Home

IoT-generated data enables traders to personalise goods and services, thus potentially benefitting consumers. Amazon e.g. can 'personalise content and features . . . including by showing you recommendations (as well as) continuously improve the Amazon devices and services.'[3] However, this wealth of granular knowledge also 'facilitates data-driven exploitative contracting.'[4] This is exemplified by Facebook Australia allowing its advertisers to target unstable and vulnerable teenagers.[5] Correspondingly, there has been a decrease in the amount of knowledge that consumers have about the traders, who increasingly rely on technical and legal secrecy (e.g. 'black box' AI algorithms and trade secrets).[6] This exacerbates information asymmetry and, hence, power imbalance, which can lead to the imposition of unfair contractual terms. Arguably, the contractual quagmire is both the cause and the effect of such power imbalance. The following sections will investigate whether the contractual quagmire as such, as well as individual terms in Echo's legals, fall foul of unfair terms laws. These laws focus on the balance of rights and obligations established between the seller or supplier of the product (hereinafter 'trader')[7] and the consumer. The rules proceed on the assumption, corroborated by behavioural studies, that the consumer is in a weak

---

on certain aspects concerning contracts for the sale of goods ('Second Consumer Sales Directive) [2019] OJ L 136/28 as of 1 January 2022.

2 Directive 2019/770 on certain aspects concerning contracts for the supply of digital content and digital services (Digital Content Directive) [2019] OJ L 136/1.

3 Amazon Coins Terms, point 5 <www.amazon.co.uk/gp/help/customer/display.html?nodeId= 201434520> accessed 23 May 2018.

4 Philipp Hacker, 'Personal Data, Exploitative Contracts, and Algorithmic Fairness: Autonomous Vehicles Meet the Internet of Things' (2017) 7 International Data Privacy Law 266.

5 Sam Machkovech, 'Report: Facebook Helped Advertisers Target Teens Who Feel "Worthless"' (*Ars Technica*, 5 January 2017) <https://arstechnica.com/information-technology/2017/05/facebook-helped-advertisers-target-teens-who-feel-worthless/>.

6 Guido Noto La Diega, 'Against the Dehumanisation of Decision-Making – Algorithmic Decisions at the Crossroads of Intellectual Property, Data Protection, and Freedom of Information' (2018) 9 JIPITEC 3.

7 'Seller or supplier' is the EU wording, 'trader' the UK one. Even though this book takes an EU perspective, I prefer the simpler and more encompassing 'trader.'

position both in their bargaining power and their level of knowledge,[8] and provide a public law framework to remedy private law failings. These rules tackle both terms that are unfair in their content – unfairness 'of substance' – and terms whose form renders them unfair, typically because untransparent – unfairness 'of form.'

3.2.1 Scope of the Unfair Terms Directive and Its Consequences for the Contractual Quagmire

In the EU, the primary legislative reference in the field is Directive 93/13/EEC 'on unfair terms in consumer contracts,' as amended by Directive 2019/2161 (Omnibus Directive).[9] Transposed in November 2021, the national implementation measures will apply from 28 May 2022.[10] This reform is part of the 'New Deal for Consumers' package,[11] which includes a directive on class actions for the protection of the collective interests of consumers (Representative Action Directive).[12] This directive will have to be transposed by December 2022 and will oblige member states to put in place effective procedural mechanisms to allow qualified entities (e.g. consumer organisations or public bodies) to bring class actions, including the right to obtain injunctions and compensation.[13]

With the goal of updating and making consumer protection more effective,[14] the main innovations of the Omnibus Directive are to have member states introduce effective penalties for infringements and fines of up to 4% of the trader's annual turnover or, if the relevant information is not available, EUR 2 million.[15] To this end, it amended the Unfair Terms Directive, the Unfair Commercial Practices Directive, the CRD, and the Price Indication Directive,[16] though no provision on fines was inserted in the latter. With regards to the Unfair Terms Directive, the reform only introduced an obligation to introduce penalties and the aforementioned rule on fines.[17] These are not particularly relevant from this book's perspective and therefore will not be analysed, but more will be said on the reform when dealing with the CRD and the Unfair Commercial Practices, which are more profoundly affected by it.

---

8 Case C-484/08 *Caja de Ahorros v Ausbanc* [2010] 3 CMLR 43.
9 Directive 2019/2161 amending Council Directive 93/13/EEC and Directives 98/6/EC, 2005/29/EC and 2011/83 as regards the better enforcement and modernisation of Union consumer protection rules ('Omnibus Directive') [2019] OJ L 328/7.
10 Omnibus Directive, art 7.
11 European Commission, 'Communication "A New Deal for Consumers"' (2018) COM/2018/183 final.
12 Directive 2020/1828 on representative actions for the protection of the collective interests of consumers and repealing Directive 2009/22/EC [2020] OJ L 409/1.
13 Representative Actions Directive, arts 7–9, 24.
14 Omnibus Directive, recitals 1, 2, and 25.
15 Omnibus Directive, art 1 (with regards to the Unfair Terms Directive), 3(6) (with regards to the Unfair Commercial Practices Directive), and 4(13) (with regards to the CRD).
16 Directive 98/6/EC on consumer protection in the indication of the prices of products offered to consumers [1998] OJ L 80/27.
17 Unfair Terms Directive, art 8b, as inserted by Omnibus Directive, art 1.

The Unfair Terms Directive tackles the unfairness of standard contracts; it does not apply to terms that have been negotiated individually.[18] Indeed, this instrument aims at offsetting the weak position consumers find themselves vis-à-vis traders, as such position, the CJEU reiterated in *de Grote*, 'leads to the consumer agreeing to terms drawn up in advance by the seller or supplier without being able to influence the content of those terms.'[19] Most online transactions appear not to be negotiated individually, and this is exacerbated by the IoT, which leads to an increased distance 'between consumers and the contract formation process.'[20] Preformulated standard contracts, such as Echo's legals (and most IoT 'legals'), are the primary object of this regime – this was recently confirmed by the CJEU in *VKI v Amazon*,[21] regarding the unfairness of Amazon.de's general terms and conditions.

Unfair terms are not binding on the consumer unless the consumer objects.[22] Consumers can initiate judicial proceedings or rely on forms of public enforcement through actions by regulators, e.g. the Competition and Markets Authority and Trading Standards Services. Whilst the term that is found to be unfair is declared nonbinding, the rest of the contract retains its validity, unless the agreement is not capable of continuing in existence without the unfair term.[23] This was the case in *GT v HS*[24] when the unfair term defined the main subject matter of the agreement; accordingly, its unfairness was at the core of the contract and invalidated it in its entirety. The recent *Abanca Corporación Bancaria*[25] well illustrates the consequence of a finding of unfairness. The case regarded a mortgage loan contract that provided for the early termination in the event that the debtor missed a single monthly loan repayment (so-called accelerated repayment clause). The referring court questioned whether, should an early repayment clause be deemed unfair, it might nonetheless be maintained in part, with the elements which made it unfair removed. The court moved from the observation that the directive remedies the weakness of the consumer by considering unfair and hence nonbinding terms that are contrary to good faith, imbalanced, and/or intransparent.[26] There is no doubt in the case that the early termination and repayment of the loan where the debtor missed a single monthly repayment is not in good faith, and it leads to a significantly imbalanced relationship. Therefore, it is unfair. The problem was

---

18 Unfair Terms Directive, art 3(2).
19 Case C-147/16 *Karel de Grote – Hogeschool Katholieke Hogeschool Antwerpen VZW v Susan Romy Jozef Kuijpers* [2018] 5 WLUK 320 [54].
20 Stacy-Ann Elvy, 'Contracting in the Age of the Internet of Things: Article 2 of the UCC and Beyond' (2015) 44 Hofstra Law Review 839.
21 Case C-191/15 *Verein für Konsumenteninformation v Amazon EU Sàrl* [2016] 7 WLUK 797 [63].
22 Case C-618/10 *Banco Español de Crédito v Calderón Camino* [2013] CEC 182 [65].
23 Unfair Terms Directive, art 6(1).
24 Case C-38/17 *GT v HS* (CJEU, 5 June 2019) [37], [43].
25 Joined Cases C-70/17 and C-179/17 *Abanca Corporación Bancaria v García Salamanca Santos* [2019] 3 WLUK 424.
26 ibid [49], [50].

that, according to case law dating back to *Banco Español de Crédito*,[27] national law cannot allow national courts to modify that contract by revising the content of the unfair term. Such power is seen as adversely affecting the 'dissuasive effect' of the Unfair Terms Directive in that traders

> would still be tempted to use those terms in the knowledge that, even if they were declared invalid, the contract could nevertheless be modified, to the extent necessary, by the national court in such a way as to safeguard the interest of those (traders).[28]

It follows, in the CJEU's reasoning, that the early repayment clause is invalid in its entirety and the mere removal of the ground for termination, with the rest of the term remaining binding, would 'ultimately be tantamount to revising the content of those terms by altering their substance.'[29] However, national courts have some replacing powers when the invalidity of the unfair term would lead to annul the entire contract, thus exposing the consumer to 'particularly *unfavourable consequences*.'[30] In such scenarios, the court can replace the term 'with a supplementary provision of national law'[31] that in *Abanca Corporación Bancaria* made it possible for mortgage loan contracts to be terminated prematurely after the debtors failed to pay at least three monthly repayment instalments.[32]

This is consistent with the directive's objective to re-establish equality between the parties, not to annul all contracts containing unfair terms. Equally, this is consistent with the aforementioned 'dissuasive effect,' because should this judicial power to replace unfair terms not be recognised – hence the invalidity of the entire loan contract – the consumer would have to transfer the outstanding balance forthwith. This would penalise the consumer rather than the lender, who, 'as a consequence, might not be dissuaded from inserting such terms in its contracts.'[33] There is no definition of the 'unfavourable consequences' that allow courts to replace unfair terms – as opposed to simply declaring them nonbinding, with potential invalidity of the contract as a whole. However, the argument could be put forward that once a consumer builds a smart home around Alexa and Echo, if its legals are declared invalid because one or more of its terms are unfair, the downgrading that would follow from being cut out of all the smart home-related benefits could amount to such 'unfavourable consequence,' creating margins of judicial manoeuvre. Therefore, courts may intervene to replace unfair terms with fair ones in order to preserve the 'smartness' of the Thing or of the IoT system (e.g. smart home).

---

27 (n 22) [73]; Case C-26/13 *Árpád Kásler and Hajnalka Káslerné Rábai v OTP Jelzálogbank Zrt* [2014] Bus L R 664 [73]; *Abanca Corporación Bancaria* (n 25) [53].
28 *Abanca Corporación Bancaria* (n 25) [54] and case law cited therein.
29 ibid [55].
30 ibid [61], emphasis added.
31 ibid [56].
32 Law No 1/2000 on Civil Procedure of 7 January 2000, art 693(2).
33 ibid [58].

Consumers are not expected to contest a term's unfairness; indeed, the CJEU held in *Pannon*[34] and confirmed in *Bucura*[35] that national courts must examine, of their own motion, the unfairness of a contractual term if they have available to them the legal and factual elements necessary for that task. The rationale of this principle – called *ex officio* control of unfair terms – is to compensate for the structurally weaker position of consumers, who may not be aware of their rights and may, consequently, not raise the unfairness of contract terms.[36] The court's obligation to assess unfair contract terms of its own motion applies also to the terms that are connected to the subject matter of the dispute, as recently decided in *Lintner*. According to the CJEU, a court must examine of its own motion 'those *terms which are connected to the subject matter of the dispute*, as delimited by the parties.'[37] This means that national courts must take into account all the contractual terms – arguably in all the legals, even the unchallenged ones – to assess the unfairness of the term forming the basis of the claim, but they do not have to examine of their own motion whether or not all those terms are unfair. In the IoT, this judicial power is likely to be useful as it will allow courts to examine the whole web of legals, thus freeing the consumer from the contractual quagmire.

The rule of the own-motion review has one exception that has to be construed narrowly,[38] namely, if the term reflects a specific and mandatory statutory or regulatory provision, as stated in *Aqua Med*[39] applying *OTP Bank*.[40] These are two distinct requirements, as ruled in *Kanyeba*[41] and *Gómez del Moral Guasch*.[42] First, the contractual term must reflect a statutory or regulatory provision, and secondly, that provision must be mandatory. These provisions are defined as 'provisions of national law that apply between the parties to the contract independently of their choice and to provisions that apply by default, that is to say, in the absence of other arrangements established by the parties in that regard.'[43] Terms reflecting these provisions are outside the scope of the directive.[44] For example, in *Roundlistic Ltd v Jones*,[45] under the Leasehold Reform, Housing and Urban Development

34 Case C-243/08 *Pannon v Sustikné Győrfi* [2009] ECR I-4713 [35].
35 Case C-348/14 *Bucura v SC Bancpost* [2015] 10 Europe 42.
36 European Commission, 'Notice – Guidance on the Interpretation and Application of Council Directive 93/13/EEC on Unfair Terms in Consumer Contracts' (2019) OJ C 323/4 [5.2.1].
37 Case C-511/17 *Györgyné Lintner v UniCredit Bank Hungary Zrt* (CJEU, 11 March 2020) [50], emphasis added.
38 Case C-51/17 *OTP Bank Nyrt. v Ilyés* [2018] 4 Dir com scambi internaz 643.
39 Case C-266/18 *Aqua Med v Skóra* [2019] 3 CMLR 1 [31].
40 (n 38) [52].
41 Cases C-349/18 to C-351/18 *Kanyeba* (CJEU, 7 November 2019) [60].
42 Case C-125/18 *Gómez del Moral Guasch v Bankia* (CJEU, 3 March 2020) [31].
43 ibid [33].
44 Unfair Terms Directive, art 1(2).
45 [2016] UKUT 325 (LC). It is important to look at national cases as it is for the national courts to determine whether this exemption applies. See e.g. Case C-779/18 *Mikrokasa v XO* (CJEU, 26 March 2020) [51].

Act 1993, the lessor was obliged to grant a new lease; the UK regulations that transposed the Unfair Terms Directive did not apply.[46]

Therefore, in principle courts faced with the alleged unfairness of terms in IoT legals have to examine of their own motion the entire network of contracts as it is likely that a large number of terms in the IoT's contractual quagmire are in some way connected to the subject matter of the dispute. Indeed, we have seen in the previous chapter how in IoT contracting casting-net provisions abound and that virtually all legals affect the Thing as a whole, despite their attempt of regulating only one of its components, e.g. software. In intervening *ex officio*, courts will have to be open to rewrite the term – not simply to declare it nonbinding – as the more the IoT becomes an integral part of our life, the more being cut out of it must be regarded as an unfavourable consequence that calls for judicial re-engineering of contracts.

The directive elaborates two different, albeit intertwined, types of unfairness: 'of substance' and 'of form.'[47] Prima facie, the main focus of the directive is on the former, that is, on the assessment of whether the content of a contractual term signals a significant imbalance of rights and obligations.[48] Unfairness of form, in turn, looks more closely at issues of transparency.[49] The next section will consider issues of substance, whilst those of form will be analysed in the following one.

3.2.2   Unfairness of Substance: Terms That, Contrary to the Requirement of Good Faith, Cause a Significant Imbalance in the Parties' Rights and Obligations

A term is considered unfair if, 'contrary to the requirement of good faith, it causes a significant imbalance in the parties' rights and obligations arising under the contract, to the detriment of the consumer.'[50] The European Commission[51] breaks the unfairness test into two requirements: lack of good faith and significant imbalance.

Good faith embodies a 'fair and open dealing'[52] principle, with regards to how the contract is drafted, presented, negotiated, and carried out. As observed in *Aziz*,[53] there is good faith if the trader, 'dealing fairly and equitably with the consumer, could reasonably assume that the consumer would have agreed to such a term in individual contract negotiations.'[54] The concept of good faith is not a

---

46 The reference is to the Unfair Terms in Consumer Contracts Regulations 1999, repealed by the Consumer Rights Act 2015 (CRA), sch 4, para 34.

47 Gintautas Šulija, *Standard Contract Terms in Cross-Border Business Transactions: A Comparative Study from the Perspective of European Union Law* (P Lang 2011).

48 Unfair Terms Directive, arts 3(1) and 3(3); Annex.

49 Unfair Terms Directive, arts 4(2) and 5.

50 Unfair Terms Directive, art 3(1).

51 European Commission (n 36).

52 *Director General of Fair Trading v First National Bank* [2001] UKHL 52 [17] per Lord Bingham of Cornhill.

53 Case C-415/11 *Aziz v Catalunyacaixa* [2013] All E R (EC) 770.

54 Case C-186/16 *Andriciuc v Banca Românească* [2017] 9 WLUK 313 [57].

subjective one, in the sense that courts do not need to assess if the trader was aware that a contractual term could harm the consumer.[55] It is an objective concept, 'linked to the question of whether, in light of its content, the contract term in question is compatible with fair and equitable market practices.'[56] The directive[57] makes it clear that good faith and significant imbalance are closely intertwined, as in making an assessment of good faith, courts must have regard:

(i) To the strength of the bargaining positions of the parties;
(ii) Whether the consumer had an inducement to agree to the term and whether the goods or services were sold or supplied to the special order of the consumer; and
(iii) Whether the trader dealt fairly and equitably and took into account the consumer's legitimate interests.

In the IoT context, and keeping in mind the empirical analysis in the previous chapter, there is little doubt that IoT traders' data power put them in a strong bargaining position, and it weakens the consumers' position, as traders can exploit consumers' vulnerabilities and biases.[58] It can also be said that unilaterally submerging the consumer with countless legals is not an open and equitable practice and disregards the consumer's interests. Arguably, therefore, the IoT's contractual quagmire is contrary to good faith, and the first requirement of the unfairness test is made out.

It has been suggested[59] that the requirements are so closely linked that, at a closer look, good faith is not a separate condition for the unfairness of a contract term, and what matters is only the significant imbalance. However, the CJEU and Commission do not support this interpretation;[60] therefore, the significant imbalance requirement will be separately considered.

There is a significant imbalance, as stated in *Director General of Fair Trading v First National Bank*, 'if a term is so weighted in favour of the (trader) as to tilt the parties' rights and obligations under the contract significantly in (the former's) favour.'[61] An example of imbalance provided in *Andriciuc*[62] is a loan agreement where the exchange rate risk is borne entirely by the consumer. A good indication that this requirement is made out is when the term places the consumer in a legal position that is less favourable than the one ordinarily provided for by the law.[63]

---

55 The difference between good faith in an objective sense and in a subjective one is a crucial one, especially in European civil law jurisdictions. See Fabrizio Piraino, *La buona fede in senso oggettivo* (Giappichelli 2015).
56 European Commission (n 36) [3.4.1].
57 Recital 16.
58 cf Hacker (n 4).
59 Case C-34/18 *Lovasné Tóth v ERSTE Bank Hungary* [2019], Opinion of AG Hogan [56]–[62].
60 *Andriciuc* (n 54); European Commission (n 36).
61 *Director General of Fair Trading* (n 52) [17] (Bingham of Cornhill L).
62 (n 54).
63 *Aziz* (n 53).

Courts have to compare the relevant contract term with any rules of national law which would apply in the absence of the contract term.[64] For example, the fact that a contract deviates from a law setting out conditions under which penalties, such as default interest, may be requested may indicate a significant imbalance.[65] Where there are no such statutory provisions, the imbalance will be assessed in light of other points of reference, such as 'fair and equitable market practices or a comparison of the rights and obligations of the parties under a particular term.'[66] As held in *Constructora Principado*,[67] the chief question is whether the significant imbalance results from a 'sufficiently serious impairment of the legal situation in which the consumer . . . is placed by reason of the relevant national provisions.'[68] This does not necessarily refer to an economic imbalance. For instance, a term that imposes the payment of a tax on a consumer, whereas under national law this tax should be borne by the trader, qualifies as significant imbalance, regardless of the amount that the consumer will have to pay.[69] The imbalance can be also nonfinancial, e.g. if a privacy policy allows the trader to pass on information it holds on the consumer more widely than it would be permitted under the GDPR.[70]

Although there is no EU guidance on whether the detriment to the consumer is a distinct requirement, at a national level the prevailing option is that actual harm is not required. This is the case in the UK, where the Competition and Markets Authority[71] clarified that what matters is that the imbalance is practically significant and therefore a potential harm will suffice. Terms can be challenged if they could be used to cause consumer detriment, regardless of whether they are being used so as to produce that outcome in practice. This is also the case in Italy. Whilst the Italian version of the directive refers to '*danno*' (damage, harm), the relevant implementation measure[72] more generically provides that the significant imbalance must regard the consumer ('*a carico*'), which means that a significant imbalance that is contrary to good faith is presumed to be inherently harmful.[73]

The unfairness of a term has to be assessed taking into account:[74]

(i) The nature of the goods or services to which the contract relates;
(ii) All the other terms of the contract or of another contract on which the former is dependent;
(iii) All the circumstances attending the conclusion of the contract.

---

64 Case C-226/12 *Constructora Principado v Menendez Alvarez* [2014] 1 WLUK 197 [21]; [59].
65 This was the case in *Aziz* (n 53) [74].
66 European Commission (n 36) [3.4.1].
67 *Constructora Principado* (n 64).
68 ibid [23].
69 ibid [26].
70 Part 5A of Competition & Markets Authority, *Unfair Contract Terms Guidance. Guidance on the Unfair Terms Provisions in the CRA* (CMA 2015).
71 ibid.
72 Decreto legislativo 6 settembre 2005, n. 206 'Consumer Code' ('*Codice del Consumo*').
73 Consumer Code, art 33(1).
74 Unfair Terms Directive, art 4(1).

If we apply the first factor to the IoT, all points in the direction of a likelihood of a finding of unfairness. IoT contracts regard products that are complex to understand and that can be used to increase and leverage the power imbalance between trader and consumer. In the contractual quagmire, one needs to consider the connection between a term and all the other terms provided in extremely long and countless legals. Coming to the circumstances attending the conclusion of the contract, as stated in *Andriciuc*,[75] they have to be interpreted broadly, as inclusive of all the 'circumstances which *could have been known* to the (trader) at that time . . . taking account, in particular of the *expertise and knowledge* of the (trader).'[76] IoT traders have a wealth of knowledge about both the Thing and the consumer – Amazon e.g. may know if you have a tendency to impulsive buying[77] and could leverage it. The higher the knowledge on the side of the company, the stricter the assessment of the unfairness of the terms.

The directive is accompanied by a list of terms that may be considered unfair.[78] An example is terms that limit a trader's liability in the event of a consumer's death or personal injury to the latter resulting from an act or omission of that trader.[79] Although the inclusion in the list is an essential element on which the unfairness assessment may be based, courts have to verify if the good faith and significant imbalance requirements are made out on a case-by-case basis.[80] This is usually referred to as 'grey list,'[81] to distinguish it from the blacklist of terms that are unfair in all circumstances, without the need for a case-by-case assessment. Indeed, since the directive follows the principle of minimum harmonisation, member states can introduce stricter rules.[82] Belgium, Bulgaria, Czech Republic, Germany, Greece, Spain, France, Italy, Luxembourg, Hungary, the Netherlands, Austria, Portugal, Slovakia, and the UK provide such blacklists.[83] Under the UK Consumer Rights Act 2015 (CRA),[84] contract terms seeking to exclude or restrict statutory rights and any remedies are not binding on the consumer without the need to apply the fairness test.

In our scenario, it is worth noting that, in the grey list, we find also terms 'irrevocably binding the consumer to terms with which (they) had no real opportunity

---

75 (n 54) [54].

76 ibid [58], emphasis added.

77 Georgiana Bighiu, Adriana Manolică and Cristina Teodora Roman, 'Compulsive Buying Behavior on the Internet' (2015) 20 Procedia Economics and Finance 72.

78 Annex to the Unfair Terms Directive.

79 Unfair Terms Directive, Annex, para 1(a).

80 Case C-472/10 *Nemzeti Fogyasztovedelmi Hatosag v Invitel Tavkozlesi Zrt* [2012] 3 CMLR 1 [25]–[26]; *Pannon* (n 34) [37]–[38]; Case C-76/10 *Pohotovosť s.r.o. v Iveta Korčkovská* [2010] ECR I-11557 [56], [58]; Case C-478/99 *Commission v Sweden* [2002] ECR I-4147 [22].

81 Case C-143/13 *Bogdan Matei and Ioana Ofelia Matei v SC Volksbank România SA* [2015] 2 WLUK 837 [60].

82 Unfair Terms Directive, art 8.

83 'Notifications under Article 8a of Directive 93/13/EEC' (*European Commission*, 31 May 2019) <https://ec.europa.eu/info/notifications-under-article-8a-directive-93-13-eec_en>.

84 Ss 31, 47, and 57.

of becoming acquainted before the conclusion of the contract.'[85] This provision seems particularly suitable for the contractual quagmire, where traders expect their terms to be binding, despite the fact that they are hard to find and read, let alone understand. Grey-listed terms merely indicate terms that may be unfair, but one needs still to assess whether they are contrary to good faith and lead to a significant imbalance of rights and obligations. Indeed, as held in *Freiburger Kommunalbauten*,[86] it is for the national authorities to assess the unfairness of specific contract terms in light of the specific circumstances of each case. Therefore, to answer the question of whether the contractual quagmire instantiates unfairness of substance, the next section will look at how UK authorities have dealt with the unfairness of Amazon's legals.

3.2.3 *The Competition and Market Authority's Review of Cloud Storage Unfair Terms and the Incentives Hierarchy*

Between 2015 and 2017, the UK Competition and Market Authority reviewed whether cloud storage providers were complying with consumer protection law.[87] This led Amazon Media EU S.a.r.l., provider of the cloud storage service then branded as Amazon Drive (now Photos), to commit to rewrite its contract terms. The company recognised that certain terms needed to be changed to make Amazon Drive (now Photos) Terms of Use fair.[88] The main problem with this initiative is that it focused only on one of the 'legals,' ignoring the way the legals interrelate within Amazon's web of contracts. It is also problematic that the enquiry targeted only one of Amazon's traders, without considering the role played by subsidiaries and affiliates. The new provisions introduced in Amazon Drive Terms of Use as a consequence of the Competition and Markets Authority's review can be used as analytical tool to assess if unfair terms are still present in other Echo legals. The focus will be on two crucial points: changes to service and liability.

1. *Material changes to the service can only be made for valid reasons clearly set out in the contract terms.* As a consequence of the enquiry of the Competition and Markets Authority, the Drive Terms have been amended and now permit changes to the services only 'for legal or regulatory reasons; for security reasons; to enhance features of the Services; to reflect advancements in technology; to make reasonable technical adjustments to the Services; and to ensure the ongoing operability of the Services.'[89] A similar provision is

---

85 Annex to Unfair Terms Directive, para 1(i).
86 Case C-237/02 *Freiburger Kommunalbauten GmbH Baugesellschaft & Co. KG v Ludger Hofstetter and Ulrike Hofstetter* [2004] ECR I-3403.
87 'Cloud Storage: Consumer Compliance Review' (*GOV.UK*) <www.gov.uk/cma-cases/cloud-storage-consumer-compliance-review>.
88 'Amazon Media EU S.à.r.l.' <https://assets.publishing.service.gov.uk/media/58a6c4ee40f0b67ec 500001e/summary-of-undertakings.pdf>.
89 Amazon Photos Terms of Use, point 5.1.

now present in Prime Terms;[90] however, the same does not apply to the other legals. For example, under the Device Terms: 'We may change, suspend, or discontinue the Services, or any part of them, at any time. We may amend any of this Agreement's terms *at our sole discretion*.'[91] Similarly, in Alexa Terms of Use[92] and in the Conditions of Use,[93] there is no setting out of valid reasons.

2. *Consumers shall receive reasonable advance notice of material changes to the service.* On this point, Amazon responded to the enquiry by amending the Drive Terms, which now provide that '[they] will inform [users] a reasonable period in advance of any material changes becoming effective.'[94] A similar provision, albeit less favourable to the consumer, can be found in Prime Terms, where Amazon commits to 'inform [users] *in due form and time*.'[95] This is less favourable because the information does not have to be provided necessarily before or with the changes. The Device Terms and the Alexa Terms are even less favourable as thereunder changes are not communicated; they are simply made 'by posting the revised terms on the Amazon.co.uk website.'[96] At the bottom, in terms of the degree of fairness, are the Conditions of Use: they do not even require the posting of the changes. Indeed, users 'will be subject to the terms and conditions, policies and Conditions of Sale in force at the time that [they] order products from [Amazon].'[97] This term is complemented by the caveat 'unless any change . . . is required to be made by law.'[98] These generic terms do not meet the transparency requirements, and as their language is not plain and intelligible, courts will be able to assess the unfairness of the main subject matter of the contract and of the price. They could also be regarded as unenforceable under general contract law, as they are vague.[99]

3. *Consumers who do not wish to accept material changes to the service must be able to cancel the contract and obtain a refund for services not yet provided.* After the intervention of the Competition and Markets Authority, the Drive Terms have been changed, and now consumers can reject the changes to the service by terminating the contract, and they will receive a prorated refund of any fees paid.[100] This can be seen as equivalent to Prime Terms'

---

90 Amazon Prime Terms and Conditions, point 5. The changes may occur also to add additional features to the Prime Service.
91 Amazon Device Terms of Use, point 3.b.
92 Point 3.2.
93 Conditions of Use & Sale, point 15.
94 Amazon Photos Terms of Use, point 5.1.
95 Amazon Prime Terms and Conditions, point 5.
96 Amazon Device Terms of Use, point 3.b; Alexa Terms of Use, point 3.2.
97 Conditions of Use & Sale, point 9.
98 Conditions of Use & Sale, point 9.
99 *Scammell v Ouston* [1941] AC 251.
100 Amazon Photos Terms of Use, point 5.1.

'partial refund of this membership fee based on benefits usage.'[101] No refund, conversely, is provided by Device Terms,[102] Alexa Terms,[103] Conditions of Use.[104]

The new Drive Terms' provisions regarding the changes to the service (points 1, 2, and 3 prior) 'shall prevail over . . . the Amazon.co.uk Conditions of Use to the extent of any conflict or inconsistency between the two terms.'[105] This is another casting-net provision that would require the consumer to find and read two separate 'legals' and compare them to try to understand if they are consistent. Better would have been if Amazon directly changed all its legals to ensure consistency and fairness across all the provisions regarding changes to service.

Unilateral and arbitrary changes are likely to be unfair, and the prior analysis inter alia confirmed the accuracy of the prediction whereby the IoT will 'likely lead businesses to further take advantage of consumer ignorance and apathy by including one-sided contract terms, such as unilateral amendment provisions.'[106] Whilst there is not sufficient evidence that consumers are indeed apathetic, it can be accepted that the IoT's data flood is increasing the opportunities to impose unfair unilateral terms – and, correspondingly, disenfranchising consumers who do not feel like they can challenge IoT traders' practices.[107]

4   *Amazon's liability will not be excluded or limited if it fails to provide the service with reasonable skill and care.* Since the terms that regard liability in the main Echo legals refer to the Conditions of Use, it can be useful to start by looking at the latter. Amazon disclaims liability for interrupted and flawed services, blaming it on 'the nature of the internet'[108] (*sic!*). They also refuse liability for losses that are not cause of a breach on their part, business losses, indirect or consequential losses. The exclusion of consequential losses can be regarded as unfair because the legal meaning of 'consequential' is different to the ordinary one; this divergence may mislead consumers into thinking that 'they have no claim for any loss which is a consequence of a trader's breach of contract.'[109] Moreover, it is unfair to exclude certain losses only because they do not flow directly and naturally from the trader's breach; e.g. the consumer is entitled to compensation if they told the trader about a risk and the

---

101 Amazon Prime Terms and Conditions, point 5.
102 Amazon Device Terms of Use, point 3.b.
103 Alexa Terms of Use, point 3.2.
104 Conditions of Use & Sale, point 9.
105 Amazon Photos Terms of Use, point 5.1.
106 Elvy (n 20).
107 This issue goes beyond the IoT and has manifold causes; e.g. arguably 'awarding consumer rights without properly regulating the consumer's access to the court system renders these rights to be unenforceable' (Marco Loos, 'Individual Private Enforcement of Consumer Rights in Civil Courts in Europe' [2010] <www.ssrn.com/abstract=1535819>.).
108 Conditions of Use & Sale, point 13.
109 Competition & Markets Authority (n 70) 76.

latter did not put in place measures to avoid them. Conversely, Amazon's disclaimer of liability for breach of contract is not necessarily unfair if it is limited to the breach arising 'from any cause which is beyond [Amazon's] reasonable control.'[110] Indeed, terms excluding rights to redress for breach of contract may be unfair, but only if such exclusion is inappropriate;[111] the exclusion of liability for breaches beyond the trader's control seems appropriate. Similarly, it is fair to limit liability for death or personal injury to negligence or wilful misconduct. It may be useful to recall that, under the grey list of terms that may be unfair, traders can exclude or limit liability for death or personal injury, as long as these do not result from an act or omission of the trader.[112] The closing, finally, is both unfair and lacking transparency,[113] in that it merely refers to the fact that the laws of some countries may not allow some liability limitations, in which case 'you might have additional rights.'[114] This is in violation of *RWE Vertrieb*,[115] inasmuch as it outlawed the practice to refer generically, without any details, to laws determining rights and obligations.

In the review conducted by the Competition and Market Authority, it was agreed that it would be unfair to exclude or limit liability if the company fails to provide the service with reasonable skill and care.[116] Accordingly, the revised version of the Drive Terms reads:

> Amazon will exercise reasonable care and skill in providing the Services to you and . . . we will not limit our liability to you in respect of losses you incur that arise as a direct result of our failure to do so.[117]

Here Amazon only partly followed up to its commitments with the Competition and Markets Authority; indeed, the quoted term is caveated by 'unless otherwise excluded below.'[118] This means that the broader, and partly conflicting, disclaimer of warranties and limitation of liability in the Conditions of Use may prevail on the Drive Terms, thus affecting liability in the provision of Cloud of Things services. What is worse, the Drive Terms add other limitations, e.g. for the losses that are not excluded, 'Amazon's liability to you for *compensation (including any statutory right* to obtain a refund) will be limited to the *amount*

---

110 ibid, point 13.
111 Unfair Terms Directive, Annex, para 1(b); CRA, sch 2, para 2.
112 Unfair Terms Directive, Annex, para 1(a); CRA, sch 2, para 1.
113 Competition & Markets Authority (n 70) 33.
114 Conditions of Use & Sale, point 13.
115 Case C-92/11 *RWE Vertrieb AG v Verbraucherzentrale Nordrhein-Westfalen eV* [2013] 3 CMLR 10.
116 'Cloud Storage: Consumer Compliance Review' (n 87).
117 Amazon Photos Terms of Use, point 6.5.
118 Amazon Photos Terms of Use, point 6.5.

you paid (if any) for your then current Service Plan.'[119] Under the Prime Terms, in turn, Amazon accepts liability for gross negligence, wilful misconduct, and breach of its obligations under the terms 'which are essential for the provision of Prime and which you rely on when joining Prime,'[120] with the exclusion of unforeseeable losses. At a first look, this is a fair term, but it refers generically to the Conditions of Use, and therefore it may be construed as inclusive of the latter's disclaimers and limitations. The precision that 'your statutory rights as a consumer'[121] will not be affected is of little help; as noted by the Competition and Markets Authority, the 'mere addition of a statement that statutory rights are unaffected, without explanation, cannot make such a term acceptable.'[122] The terms are even more unfair in the remaining legals. Under the Device Terms, the device 'may be subject to a limited warranty,' unless 'otherwise provided by Amazon.' A vague and arguably unenforceable provision that is paired with a compensation cap of £50, in addition to 'the amount you paid for your Amazon Device,'[123] without specifying whether Amazon is liable for lack of skill and care. These terms are without prejudice to the disclaimers and limitations of the Conditions of Use, and so are the Alexa Terms, which carry a liability provision that resembles the Device Terms' one, this time with a £50 cap. Caps on available compensation limit on the trader's liability, and if 'a contract is to be fully and equally binding on both trader and consumer, each party should be entitled to full compensation where the other fails to honour its obligations.'[124] Therefore, these caps, although not automatically blacklisted as unfair, are 'under strong suspicion of unfairness.'[125]

Public enforcement and, more generally, public scrutiny over IoT platforms' private ordering are a positive step in the direction of a more trustworthy IoT. However, initiatives such as the UK Competition and Markets Authority's review of cloud storage contracts have their drawbacks. First, they do not consider that the cloud is integrated in more complex services and products. Having traders change their cloud contracts without intervening on the rest of legals does not help consumers, because the latter's rights and obligations remain negatively affected by the interrelations with those legals that are left untouched. Second, the assessment of the fairness of Echo's legals suggests that there is a hierarchy of incentives IoT traders respond to (Figure 3.1). Indeed, as seen above, it has been noted that the Drive Terms present the highest degree of fairness, followed by Prime Terms, Device Terms, Alexa Terms, and Conditions of Use. This suggests that there is a hierarchy of incentives, in the sense that IoT traders are:

---

119 Amazon Photos Terms of Use, point 6.5.
120 Amazon Prime Terms and Conditions, point 6.
121 Amazon Prime Terms and Conditions, point 6.
122 Competition & Markets Authority (n 70) 73.
123 Amazon Device Terms of Use, point 3.e.
124 Competition & Markets Authority (n 70) 74.
125 ibid 74.

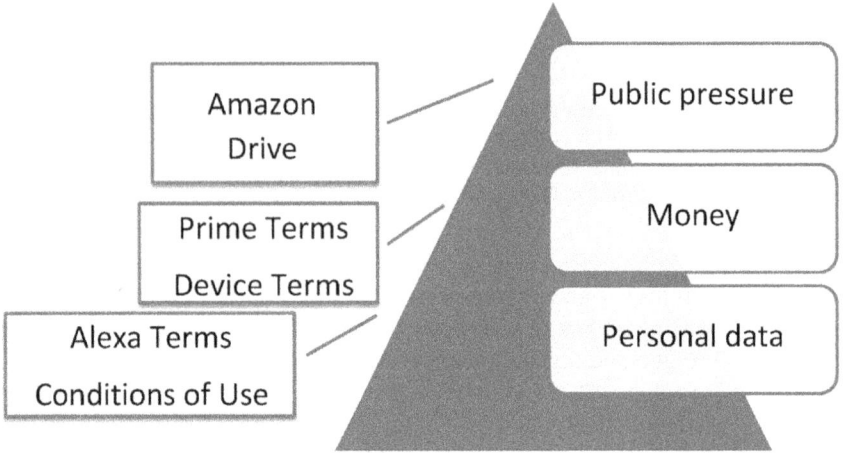

Figure 3.1 The IoT's hierarchy of incentives.

(i)   More likely to treat consumers fairly as a response to public pressure (e.g. a regulator publicly reviewing their terms, see the Drive Terms);

(ii) Somehow likely to be fair as a response to financial incentives (e.g. the Prime subscription and the price of the Thing, see Prime Terms and Device Terms respectively); and

(iii) Less likely to be fair to the average consumer that 'pays' with their personal data (Alexa Terms and Conditions of Use).

Lawmakers and regulators should keep into account the above analysis when choosing how to intervene to make IoT transactions fairer. Public pressure (reviews, inquiries, etc.) seems more likely to obtain a positive result, provided that they are aware of the IoT's contractual quagmire and, in particular, of the interactions between the components of the Thing, between Things within an IoT system, and between the relevant providers that may be subsidiaries of the main trader or hardly identifiable third parties. Positively, public actions leading to changes in contractual terms are becoming more common. In October 2019, the European Data Protection Supervisor published the preliminary results of its enquiry underlining 'serious concerns over the compliance of the relevant contractual terms with data protection rules and the role of Microsoft as a processor for EU institutions.'[126] After a month, working with the Dutch Ministry of Justice, which had reached similar conclusions,[127]

---

126 European Data Protection Supervisor, 'EDPS Investigation into IT Contracts: Stronger Cooperation to Better Protect Rights of All Individuals' (*EDPS Europa*, 21 October 2019) <https://edps.europa.eu/press-publications/press-news/press-releases/2019/edps-investigation-it-contracts-stronger_en>.

127 'Data Protection Impact Assessments DPIA's Office 365 ProPlus, Windows 10 Enterprise, Office 365 Online and Mobile Apps' (2019) Rijksoverheid <www.rijksoverheid.nl/documenten/rapporten/2019/06/11/data-protection-impact-assessment-windows-10-enterprise>.

Microsoft updated its privacy provisions in the Microsoft Online Services Terms[128] in their commercial cloud contracts.[129] Arguably, the company took advantage of the policymakers' lack of awareness of the IoT's contractual quagmire – and the relevant interconnection between contracts – therefore, the update of only some provisions of one of the 'legals' risks being ineffective.

This analysis illustrated some of the manifestations of unfairness 'of substance' in the IoT. Instances of unfairness 'of form' are no less concerning, as the next section will show.

3.2.4 The Importance to Design the Legals in a Plain and Intelligible Way

In addition to the fairness test (good faith and significant imbalance) and the non-exhaustive grey list, the Unfair Terms Directive contains transparency requirements. They have a threefold function:

(i) Terms that are not drafted in plain, intelligible language have to be interpreted in favour of the consumer.[130]

(ii) The main subject matter of the contract or the adequacy of the price and remuneration are normally excluded from the unfairness test. However, the fairness of these 'core' terms will be open to assessment if they are not in plain, intelligible language.[131]

(iii) The lack of transparency can be an element in the assessment of the unfairness of a given contract term[132] and can even indicate unfairness – unfairness 'of form.'[133]

Although transparency plays an important role, member states do not have an obligation under the directive to regard opaque terms as unlawful per se.[134] Conversely, in the UK, transparency is also a 'requirement in its own right, breach of which can lead to enforcement action.'[135] Similarly, the German Civil Code expressly links the lack of transparency and significant imbalance.[136] Under EU law, opaque terms can be fair,[137] and transparent terms can be unfair.[138]

---

128 This document is available at <www.microsoft.com/en-us/licensing/product-licensing/products>.

129 'Introducing More Privacy Transparency for Our Commercial Cloud Customers' (*Microsoft Blog*, 18 November 2019) <https://blogs.microsoft.com/eupolicy/2019/11/18/introducing-privacy-transparency-commercial-cloud-customers/>.

130 Unfair Terms Directive, art 5.

131 Unfair Terms Directive, art 4(2).

132 *Nemzeti* (n 80) [30]–[31]; *Constructora Principado* (n 64) [27].

133 *Verein für Konsumenteninformation v Amazon EU Sàrl* (n 21) [65]–[71].

134 European Commission (n 36).

135 Competition & Markets Authority (n 70) [2.4]. See CRA, s 68.

136 BGB, § 307(1) ('An unreasonable disadvantage may also arise from the provision not being clear and comprehensible.').

137 Case C-421/14 *Banco Primus SA v Gutierrez Garcia* [2017] 2 CMLR 26 [62]–[67].

138 Case C-342/13 *Sebestyen v Zsolt Csaba Kovari* [2014] 4 WLUK 165 [34].

Transparency means that terms should be drafted in a way that ensures 'that consumers can make informed choices.'[139] Arguably, Things may appear as simple entities, but in reality, they are complex due to their reliance on new technologies, their being a mixture of hardware, software, service, and data, and their multilayered supply chain. Their complexity makes it difficult for consumers to understand them and to make an informed transactional decision. In addition, they provide IoT traders with unprecedented opportunities to track, profile, influence, and exploit consumers. This requires careful contractual drafting to ensure transparency and a balance of rights and obligations.

The unfairness 'of form' is linked to the duty to draft terms 'in plain intelligible language.'[140] These issues are 'of form' in the sense that it is the manner in which the contract is presented to the customer that is being considered. Contrary to popular belief, 'formal unfairness' is in fact of the essence. Indeed, as mentioned above with regards to the second function of the transparency requirement, the assessment of the unfair nature of the terms does not 'relate neither to the definition of the main subject matter of the contract nor to the adequacy of the price and remuneration, on the one hand, as against the services or goods supplies in exchange, on the other.'[141] An example of a term that would usually escape an unfairness assessment is a term in a loan agreement that determines how the amount of the loan is to be established, as was the case in *GT v HS*.[142] However, if these 'core' terms are not drafted in plain, intelligible language, the unfairness assessment will include both the definition of the main subject matter and the adequacy of the price. As recently held in *Gómez del Moral Guasch*,[143] regardless of whether a member state availed itself of the option to provide that the assessment of the unfairness of a term is not to relate to the definition of the main subject matter of the contract, its courts must verify that the term is plain and intelligible. This is a positive indication that the way legals are designed plays a crucial role in assessing their unfairness.

Whilst many European and national cases regard unfairness of substance, there is a growing body of cases that deal with issues of form. They are mostly linked to the fact that if the language is not plain and accessible, the unfairness assessment can concern also the main object of the contract and the price.[144] While a finding that a term lacks transparency may not in itself be sufficient to render the term unfair, any uncertainty about the meaning arising from the lack of transparency should be interpreted in a manner most favourable to the consumer.[145]

As observed in *OFT v Foxtons*,[146] to assess if a term in the 'small print' is fair, one needs to look at consumer expectations and manner of presentation. The

---

139 Competition & Markets Authority (n 70) 30.
140 Unfair Terms Directive, art 4(2).
141 Unfair Terms Directive, art 4(2).
142 *GT* (n 24).
143 (n 42).
144 See e.g. *Andriciuc* (n 54).
145 Competition & Markets Authority (n 70).
146 *The Office of Fair Trading v Foxtons Ltd* [2009] EWHC 1681 (Ch).

expectation of the average consumer is that the legals contain 'things which are not of everyday concern to the consumer – it contains various clauses which are thought by the supplier to be necessary but which are not usually relied on.'[147] In theory, the average consumer is circumspect and therefore will read all the 'legals,' but 'the practice is that even the circumspect (consumer) will be unlikely to do so with a great degree of attention.'[148] Therefore, provisions containing important obligations should not 'be tucked away in the "small print" only, with no prior flagging, notice or discussion';[149] otherwise, they become a 'trap, or a *time bomb.*'[150] Accordingly, IoT providers should make sure that their 'legals' are easily accessible to consumers. An indicator of this is the readability coefficient, which is usually measured through the Flesch-Kincaid test. The higher the score, the higher the readability of the text. Some US states have introduced an obligation to draft contracts that meet prescribed Flesch-Kincaid scores; e.g. in South Carolina[151] loan contracts must have a Flesch-Kincaid score of 70–80, which corresponds to a US school level of seventh grade (13-year-olds). Echo's core legals have a Flesch-Kincaid readability score of 43, which means that they are difficult to read and are accessible only to consumers who have a college education. This is in line with the readability level of most sign-in-wrap agreements, which are as readable as academic journals.[152] However, such prevalence does not make the practice any fairer.

Most consumers do not read the 'legals,'[153] and the IoT, by exacerbating information and power asymmetries, 'further *encourage(s) consumers' failure to read and understand contract* terms prior to contracting.'[154] The hypothetical avid reader of Echo's legals will need 78 hours to read them. Improving the readability of the 'legals' is important not only to consumers but also to providers, given that, if the 'legals' are not 'written in plain English, then they may not be legally binding – or at least the parts that are not transparent won't be.'[155]

Transparency must be understood broadly as going beyond the mere comprehensibility of the term. It is a requirement for obligations and rights to be set out fully, to put 'the consumer into a position where (they) can understand (the terms') practical significance.'[156] The leading case is *Kásler*,[157] where the CJEU

---

147 ibid [92].
148 ibid.
149 ibid.
150 ibid.
151 South Carolina Consumer Protection Code, s 37–3–202.
152 Uri Benoliel and Shmuel I Becher, 'The Duty to Read the Unreadable' (2019) 60 Boston College Law Review 2255.
153 Guido Noto La Diega, 'Grinding Privacy in the Internet of Bodies. An Empirical Qualitative Research on Dating Mobile Applications for Men Who Have Sex with Men' in Ronald Leenes et al. (eds), *Data Protection and Privacy: The Internet of Bodies* (Hart 2018).
154 Elvy (n 20).
155 Kathy Conklin and Richard Hyde, 'If Small Print "Terms and Conditions" Require a PhD to Read, Should They Be Legally Binding?' (*The Conversation*) <http://theconversation.com/if-small-print-terms-and-conditions-require-a-phd-to-read-should-they-be-legally-binding-75101>.
156 Competition & Markets Authority (n 70) 19.
157 (n 27).

decided that 'plain intelligible language' cannot 'be reduced merely to (the terms) being formally and grammatically intelligible.'[158] Rather, it must be understood in a broad sense, on the basis of an 'average consumer, who is reasonably well informed and reasonably observant and circumspect'[159] and who should be able to 'assess the potentially significant economic consequences for (them),'[160] as confirmed in *Van Hove*[161] and *Andriciuc*.[162]

These principles have been reiterated in the recent *EOS*[163] case, where the CJEU held that the fact that a consumer credit agreement does not mention the annual percentage rate of charge and contains only a mathematical formula for its calculation without the information necessary to make that calculation is decisive evidence in assessing if the terms relating to the total cost of the credit are drafted in plain, intelligible language. The key is that a plain, intelligible contract should give the consumer '*full knowledge* of the terms of the future performance of the agreement entered into at the time of concluding such an agreement'[164] and of the extent of the consumer's liability.[165] Arguably, such a full knowledge is not provided by Echo's legals, as exemplified by the Amazon Device Terms of User, under which Amazon 'may amend any of this Agreement's terms at our sole discretion,'[166] or by Alexa Terms of Use, under which they 'may change, suspend, or discontinue Alexa, or any part of it, at any time.'[167] This is contrary to the principle of transparency, and as such, it allows courts to assess the unfairness of substance of main subject matter of the contract and the adequacy of the remuneration. Similarly, the extent of Echo's consumer's liability is hard to grasp. Indeed, Amazon may terminate the agreement or restrict, suspend, or terminate your use of the services at any time, including if they 'determine that *your use . . . is improper . . . or differs from normal use* by other users.'[168] As a sanction, consumers 'may be unable to access the Services and (they) may not receive any refund of fees or any other compensation.'[169] Even less intelligibly, then, 'to the extent permitted by applicable law you agree to accept responsibility for all activities that occur under your account or password.'[170] These terms do not provide a clear picture of the consumer's liability – when does one's use differ from the normal use? – and, hence, cannot be considered transparent, plain, and intelligible.

158 ibid [71]; *Matei* (n 81) [73].
159 *Kásler* (n 27) [74]. This wording has been inserted into the UK CRA, s 64(5).
160 ibid [74].
161 Case C-96/14 *Jean-Claude Van Hove v CNP Assurances SA* [2015] 3 CMLR 31.
162 (n 54) [44].
163 Case C-448/17 *EOS KSI Slovensko s.r.o. v Ján Danko and Margita Danková* [2018] 9 WLUK 230.
164 ibid [67], emphasis added.
165 ibid.
166 Amazon Device Terms Of Use, point 3.b.
167 Alexa Terms of Use, point 3.2.
168 Amazon Music Terms of Use, point 5.2.
169 Amazon Music Terms of Use, point 5.2.
170 Conditions of Use & Sale, point 7.

In *RWE Vertrieb*,[171] the court noted that it was not sufficient, for transparency to be achieved, to include a 'mere reference, in the general terms and conditions, to a legislative or regulatory act determining the rights and obligations of the parties.'[172] It is fundamental, indeed, that 'the consumer is informed . . . of the content of the provisions concerned.'[173] This interpretation could have significant implications for contractual drafting in Europe.[174] In Echo's scenario, many legals refer to generic legislative or regulatory acts. Amazon e.g. 'reserve the right to accept or refuse your (Prime) membership, *to the extent permitted by applicable law*'[175] and 'will inform you of any decision to restrict, suspend or terminate the Service Plan, *to the extent that [they] are legally permitted to do so.*'[176] Similarly, after introducing a wide liability disclaimer, Amazon points out that '*[t]he laws of some countries do not allow some or all of the limitations* described above. If these laws apply to you, some or all of the above limitations may not apply to you and *you might have additional rights.*'[177] Such wide exclusions 'qualified merely by a statement that the trader's liability is excluded only to the extent permitted by statute'[178] are both unfair and lacking transparency, as underlined by the UK Competition and Markets Authority. Whilst this type of phrasing is not uncommon,[179] this does not make these terms any less unfair, also given that the IoT exacerbates the imbalance of bargaining power and the knowledge asymmetries that are at the core of the unfair terms' regime. Indeed, the 'legion of IoT data expected to be generated about consumers and their preferences will *worsen preexisting information asymmetry* in consumer contracts to the benefit of traders.'[180] Therefore, IoT providers must comply with higher transparency standards.

The transparency ensured by the use of plain and intelligible language, broadly understood, means that courts cannot consider the term in isolation. They have to assess it in its relationship to the connected terms in the rest of the contract as well as in the connected legals. In *Bogdan Matei*[181] e.g. the court pointed out that defendant should have set out clearly not only the reasons for a particular term (unilateral alteration of interest rate) but also its relationship to the other terms 'relating to the lender's remuneration, so that the consumer can foresee, on the basis of clear, intelligible criteria, the economic consequences for him which derive

---

171 *RWE Vertrieb* (n 115).
172 ibid [50].
173 Ibid [50].
174 Candida Leone, 'Transparency Revisited – on the Role of Information in the Recent Case-Law of the CJEU' (2014) 10 European Review of Contract Law 312.
175 Amazon Prime Terms and Conditions, point 3.6.
176 Amazon Photos Terms of Use, point 5.3.
177 Conditions of Use & Sale, point 13.
178 Competition & Markets Authority (n 70) 33.
179 Similar provisions can be found in Google Nest legals. Guido Noto La Diega and Ian Walden, 'Contracting for the "Internet of Things": Looking into the Nest' (2016) 7 European Journal of Law and Technology <http://ejlt.org/article/view/450>.
180 Elvy (n 20).
181 (n 81).

from it.'[182] The imperative to a comprehensive assessment gets to the point that the contract must be considered as whole, including the terms that have been meanwhile annulled, as ruled in *OTP Bank*.[183] Also, documents that may not strictly qualify as contracts must be considered, 'including the promotional material and information provided . . . in the negotiation.'[184] This is important because under general contract law, these documents may not qualify as contracts. This provision has wider consequences because it means that in drafting the 'legals,' including those that may not strictly qualify as contracts, e.g. guidelines, Amazon and other IoT traders must make sure that consumers can understand both the terms and their interrelations so as to assess its 'actual effects.'[185] It does not seem that such an assessment is possible in the IoT's contractual quagmire.

Under EU law, there is currently no express obligation for member states to assess the unfairness of terms included in noncontractual documents: these documents will be considered in the assessment of contractual terms but not assessed in themselves to determine their own unfairness.[186] However, some member states have introduced stronger consumer protections by providing a judicial power to assess the unfairness of terms in those legals that do not qualify as contracts but as mere 'notices.' This is the case of the UK, which subjects consumer notices to control for unfairness. They are defined as 'notices, announcements, communications or purported communications that relate to rights or obligations between a trader and a consumer, or appear to exclude or restrict a trader's liability to a consumer.'[187] This approach is fit for the IoT, where consumers find themselves in a forest of 'legals' that take a number of forms, including noncontractual ones. The inclusion of consumer notices allows courts to assess the unfairness of privacy policies that in some jurisdictions may not qualify as contracts[188] and yet contain some of the most important provisions about rights, obligations, and liability in IoT transactions.

Regardless of whether individual terms in the contractual quagmire are opaque, it should be questioned whether the practice of submerging consumers with countless legals that are difficult to find, read, and understand falls in itself foul of the Unfair Terms Directive. One should answer in the positive for a twofold reason.

First, the directive requires that 'the consumer should actually be given an opportunity to examine all the terms.'[189] Whilst this statement is contained in a recital and is as such not binding, the CJEU in the recent *Profi Credit Polska*[190]

---

182 *Matei* (n 81) [74].

183 *OTP Bank* (n 38) [91].

184 *Matei* (n 81) [75].

185 *OTP Bank* (n 38) [92], *Andriciuc* (n 54) [51].

186 Under the Unfair Terms Directive, art 4(1).

187 CRA, s 61(4).

188 Thomas B Norton, 'The Non-Contractual Nature of Privacy Policies and a New Critique of the Notice and Choice Privacy Protection Model' (2016) 27 Fordham Intellectual Property, Media & Entertainment Law Journal 181.

189 Unfair Terms Directive, Recital 20.

190 Joined Cases C-419/18 and C-483/18 *Profi Credit Polska S.A. v Bogumiła Włostowska and others; Profi Credit Polska S.A. v OH* (CJEU, 7 November 2019).

case underlined the importance of the circumstance that the 'consumer has actually been given the opportunity to examine (the term's) content.'[191] Moreover, official guidance provided by the European Commission set out the factors to consider when assessing if a term is plain and intelligible. Two factors stand out:

(i) The consumer had the real opportunity of becoming acquainted with a contract term before the conclusion of the contract; 'this includes the question of whether the consumer had access to and was given the opportunity to read the contract term(s).'[192] Only eight of the 246 Echo's legals are grouped in an easily accessible ad hoc section. They total 963 pages and 440,547 words; therefore, atop the two weeks that it takes to locate them, one would need over three days to read them. One could hardly argue that consumers are given a real opportunity to read.

(ii) Contract terms whose impact can only be understood when reading them jointly should not be presented in such a way that their joint impact is not manifest. The abundance of casting-net provisions in Echo's legals means that the application of this factor will point towards a finding of lack of transparency.

The second reason that the contractual quagmire as a whole may be regarded as instantiating unfairness of form is the link between the latter and the good faith requirement, which mandates openness. As ruled in *Director General of Fair Trading*, terms should be 'expressed fully, clearly and legibly, containing no concealed pitfalls or traps. Appropriate prominence should be given to terms which might operate disadvantageously'[193] to the consumer. Such prominence is usually given by capitalising the disadvantageous terms or writing them in bold or separately.[194] Amazon does not follow this best practice, as exemplified by the Conditions of Use and Sale that bury the limitations to liability in the text without any differentiated formatting.[195] Openness means that consumers should not be assumed to be able themselves to identify (particularly in longer contracts) terms which are important or which may operate to their disadvantage. In *Spreadex v Cochrane*,[196] a factor rendering a term unfair was the fact that it was buried in long 'legals' (49 pages, four documents) that were 'click-wrap' and contained closely printed and complex paragraphs so that it 'would have come *close to a miracle* if (the consumer) had read the (unfair term), let alone appreciated its purport or implications, and it would have been quite irrational for the claimant to assume that (they) had.'[197]

---

191 ibid [58].
192 European Commission (n 36) [3.3.1].
193 *Director General of Fair Trading* (n 52) [17].
194 Noto La Diega and Walden (n 179).
195 Conditions of Use & Sale, point 13.
196 (n 144).
197 ibid [21]

At a closer look, the distinction between unfairness 'of substance' and 'of form' is not clear-cut. This was confirmed in *VKI v Amazon*.[198] Until mid-2012, Amazon.de's general terms and conditions read, 'Luxembourg law shall apply, excluding [the Convention on the International Sale of Goods].' The question was whether such a term, under which the contract is to be governed by the law of the member state in which the trader is established, is unfair. Choice-of-law terms are not unfair as such. Under the Rome I Regulation on the law applicable to contractual obligations,[199] the condition for the legality of these terms is that they do not deprive 'the consumer of the protection afforded to (them) by provisions that cannot be derogated from by agreement by virtue of the law (of the country of the consumer's habitual residence).'[200] It is up to the national court to decide which statutory provisions cannot be derogated, but what matters is the guidance offered by the CJEU is assessing the unfairness of choice-of-law terms and, arguably, most otherwise-lawful nonnegotiated terms. Such terms may be unfair only insofar as they display *'certain specific characteristics inherent in (their) wording or context* which cause a significant imbalance in the rights and obligations of the parties.'[201] So in order to ascertain whether an imbalance occurs, the key is to look at wording and context. This link between substance and form is even more clearly spelled out in the subsequent passage, where the court states that unfairness may result 'from a formulation that does not comply with the requirement of being drafted in *plain and intelligible language.'*[202] Applying *Van Hove*,[203] the CJEU points out that this 'formal' requirement must be interpreted broadly, 'having regard to the consumer's weak position vis-à-vis (Amazon) with respect to (their) level of knowledge.' *VKI* has broader consequences for IoT contracting and many online transactions. Indeed, the low level of knowledge inherent to IoT transactions – at once causing and caused by the contractual quagmire – means that IoT traders must adopt higher standards of contractual drafting. Otherwise, terms that would normally be lawful, such as choice-of-law terms, could be found to be unfair. In *VKI*, the term was not intelligible because it gave the consumer the impression that only the law of Luxembourg applied, without informing them that they also enjoy 'the protection of the mandatory provisions of the law that would be applicable in the absence of that term,'[204] in that case Austrian law.

After the ruling, the term has been changed and now reads, 'Luxembourg law applies, excluding the UN Sales Convention (CISG) and the conflict of laws. . . . If you are a consumer with habitual residence in the EU, you also enjoy protection

198   (n 21).
199   Regulation (EC) No 593/2008 of 17 June 2008 on the law applicable to contractual obligations (Rome I) [2008] OJ L 177/6.
200   Rome I Regulation, art 6(2).
201   *VKI* (n 21) [67], emphasis added.
202   ibid [68].
203   (n 161) [40].
204   (n 21) [71].

of the mandatory provisions of the law of your state of residence.'[205] Therefore, the courts of the district of Luxembourg City, which have nonexclusive jurisdiction, will have to apply the statutory provisions of the consumer's country of residence. If one compares this provision to the US terms, it becomes immediately clear how stronger EU consumer laws are. Indeed, in the US any dispute is 'resolved by binding arbitration, rather than in court . . . and court review of an arbitration award is limited';[206] the arbitrator will exclusively apply 'Federal Arbitration Act, applicable federal law, and the laws of the state of Washington.'[207] If a similar clause were to be found in a European contract, it would fall within the scope of one of the grey-listed terms in the Unfair Terms Directive, that is, 'terms which have the object or effect of excluding or hindering the consumer's right to take legal action or exercise any other legal remedy.'[208] In principle, therefore, they would be unfair and not binding, as clarified in *Océano Grupo Editorial*.[209] Moreover, under *Aqua Med*,[210] terms that leave it to the trader to decide whether to bring an action before the court of the place of performance rather than consumer's domicile may be considered unfair if the distance would make it too expensive for the consumer to participate in the trial. This would be in violation of the right to defence, as enshrined both in the European Convention of Human Rights and the Charter of Fundamental Rights of the EU.[211]

The above analysis shows that many of Echo's terms – and the contractual quagmire as a whole – can be regarded as unfair and opaque. The IoT contributes to overcoming the form-substance binary and to fully embrace transparency as a key component of fairness. In a way, it could be said that the IoT corroborates a key tenet of Marxist legal theory, that is, that the 'bourgeois law'[212] rewrites the traditional form-content dichotomy.[213] EU law, especially compared to US law, provides stronger protections against unfair terms, but it relies on judicial actions brought by individuals who lack the time, resources, and knowledge to inchoate the file relevant to the lawsuits or on public enforcement that is partly ineffective due to a limited understanding of the technology and of private ordering. IoT

---

205 Amazon.de Allgemeine Geschäftsbedingungen, point 14 <www.amazon.de/gp/help/customer/display.html/ref=hp_left_v4_sib?ie=UTF8&nodeId=201909000> accessed 26 June 2019.

206 Amazon US Conditions of Use <www.amazon.com/gp/help/customer/display.html?ie=UTF8&nodeId=508088&ref_=footer_cou> accessed 21 May 2018.

207 Amazon US Conditions of Use, 'Applicable Law.'

208 Annex, para 1(q).

209 Joined Cases C-240/98 to C-244/98 *Océano Grupo Editorial SA v Roció Murciano Quintero* [2000] ECR I-4941 [21], [24].

210 (n 39).

211 Arts 6 and 48, respectively.

212 This is the law under capitalism; its main goal is to regulate the 'distribution of products and the distribution of social labour' (Evgeny Bronislavovich Pashukanis, 'A Course on Soviet Economic Law (1935)' in Piers Beirne and Robert Sharlet (eds), Peter B Maggs (tr), *Pashukanis: Selected Writings on Marxism and Law* (Academic Press 1980) 323.) Bourgeois law relies on the misunderstanding whereby equal standards can be applied to unequal individuals.

213 On this depiction of the contribution of Marxism to legal theory, see Luca Nivarra, *La grande illusione: come nacque e come morì il marxismo giuridico in Italia* (G Giappichelli 2015).

traders, in light of the complexity of the IoT and of the imbalances in terms of power and information, must comply with more stringer requirements of fairness, with a particularly urgent need to redraft the IoT legals to make them easy to find, read, and understand. From this point of view, EU regulators may learn something from the US counterparts and introduce obligations to draft 'legals' that reach at least a Flesch-Kincaid readability score that does not require a college education to understand them.

The analysed regime aims to curb power imbalance by making imbalanced terms nonbinding on the consumer. Another way to curb such imbalance is to make sure that traders stand by their contractual commitments by giving consumers the right to bring the product in line with the contract. This is the domain of consumer sales law, which will be analysed in the following section to critically assess whether it can be used to empower consumers, in particular by tackling the issue of private ordering 'by bricking.'

3.3 Private Ordering 'by Bricking': Can IoT Traders Deprive Consumers of their Things' Smartness?

One day Luke Kurtis, Quartz's tech contributor, woke up and found that Apple locked him out of its walled garden. That day, he understood the consequences of going 'smart' without reading the 'legals.'[214] For an unfounded suspect of fraud, Apple had permanently disabled his account and the customer advisers told him that there was no way to review the decision, which they felt they were entitled to make under the terms and conditions. All the Things he purchased over the years became unusable, a music collection built over 15 years became unavailable, his boarding pass unretrievable during a family emergency trip. That was when he realised that, if he had read Apple's 'legals,' he would have understood that whilst technically he was buying Things, factually he was just 'renting for a while.'[215] He understood that the IoT's hyperservitisation is sustained by new business models that allow traders to lock consumers into the services they offer exclusively for those Things.[216]

This anecdote illustrates what happens when IoT traders take advantage of the contractual quagmire to deprive consumers of their Things' 'smartness.' Usually, the intangible components of a Thing, as opposed to its hardware, make the Thing 'smart' and thus determine the decision to purchase that particular Thing, as opposed to its nonsmart counterpart. However, IoT traders can deprive consumers of their Things' smartness by remotely controlling them, downgrading them, and even deactivating them or 'bricking' them. This is what the previous chapter called private ordering by bricking.

---

214 Luke Kurtis, 'Apple Locked Me Out of Its Walled Garden' (*Quartz*, 13 August 2019) <https://qz.com/1683460/what-happens-to-your-itunes-account-when-apple-says-youve-committed-fraud/>.

215 ibid.

216 Mike Murphy, 'Apple Continues to Thrive in Its Q3 2019 Earnings' (*Quartz*, 30 July 2019) <https://qz.com/1678569/apple-continues-to-thrive-in-its-q3-2019-earnings/>.

It is crucial that the IoT trader does not discontinue or otherwise adversely affect the service, software, and data components of the Thing. Indeed, this would downgrade the Thing to a nonsmart device that would be radically different to what was promised in the contract or otherwise expected. EU consumer sales law aims to ensure that goods are as promised or expected. Therefore, next section will investigate if these laws can be invoked to tackle the issue of private ordering by bricking or if they are unfit for the IoT. In other words, can IoT traders deprive consumers of their Things' 'smartness' or bricking instantiates an unlawful lack of conformity?

3.3.1 EU Consumer Sales Law and the Lack of Conformity of the Thing to the 'Legals'

Directive 1999/44/EC (First Consumer Sales Directive) was introduced to tackle the issue of faulty products by requiring traders of consumer goods to guarantee that the goods are in conformity with the contract for at least two years after their delivery.[217] This is the main principle of EU consumer sales law.

Conformity – one of the key concepts of modern contract law[218] – is not defined. The directive refers to four scenarios where conformity is presumed (presumptions of conformity or types of conformity).[219]

(i) *As described.* The goods comply with the description given by the trader and possess the qualities of the sample or model.
(ii) *Particular purpose.* The goods are fit for the purpose which the consumer made known to the trader when concluding the contract and that the trader accepted.
(iii) *Usual purpose.* The goods are fit for the purpose for which goods of the same type are normally used.
(iv) *Reasonably expected quality and performance.* The goods show the quality and performance which are normal in goods of the same type and which the consumer can reasonably expect. This expectation depends on the nature of the goods and the trader's public statements, including advertising and labelling.[220]

In the event of lack of conformity, in addition to the general remedies in tort and contract,[221] consumers have a right to have the goods repaired, replaced, reduced

---

217 First Consumer Sales Directive, arts 2, 3, 5.
218 Reiner Schulze, 'Supply of Digital Content – A New Challenge for European Contract Law' in Alberto De Franceschi (ed), *European Contract Law and the Digital Single Market – The Implications of the Digital Revolution* (Intersentia 2016) 127.
219 First Consumer Sales Directive, art 2(2).
220 Unless the trader was not, and could not reasonably be, aware of the statement, corrected it timely, or the purchasing decision could not have been influenced by the statement, the burden of proof is on the trader. First Consumer Sales Directive, art 2(3).
221 Angelo Luminoso, *La compravendita* (9th edn, Giappichelli 2018).

in price, or the contract terminated.[222] Repair and replacement must be free of charge;[223] as the CJEU stated in *Quelle*, the rationale for this is that if 'a seller delivers goods which are not in conformity, it fails correctly to perform the obligation which it accepted in the contract of sale and must therefore bear the consequences of that faulty performance.'[224] The most important news in the directive is not the introduction of repair and replacement as remedies to the breach of contract, which had already been introduced by the Convention on the International Sale of Goods.[225] Rather, it is the hierarchy between these remedies.[226] This means that the consumer must in first instance ask for repair or replacement, and only if these are impossible or disproportionate will they have to opt between reduction of price and contract rescission.[227] Finally, a commercial guarantee must be set out in plain, intelligible language and indicate what rights it gives *on top* of the legal guarantee.[228]

The right to repair is the most likely to be relevant in the context of a strategy against private ordering by bricking. Indeed, if an IoT trader recalls some smart functionalities, downgrades the Thing, bricks it, etc., they are making it nonconforming to the contract or to consumers' expectations. In this context, the right to repair can be interpreted as a right to have the smartness of the Thing restored. As smartness is mostly intangible, it can be, in principle, restored remotely, without the need to recall the Thing and replace it. This interpretation was codified in domestic laws, such as the UK's CRA, where the good is considered as nonconforming if it includes digital content and said content does not conform to the contract,[229] hence the right to repair it, which means that a Thing's digital components must match the description of the contract.[230] The main issue is that the right to repair the digital content, i.e. the right to restore the smartness, does not apply if consumers 'have expressly agreed a change to the description with the consumer.'[231] In light of the power imbalance that such a provision would exacerbate, one could argue that it could be considered both an unfair term and an unfair commercial practice.

These rights cannot be waived or restricted through agreements concluded before the lack of conformity is brought to the trader's attention – such agreements will not be binding on the consumer.[232] The hierarchy of remedies – with

---

222 First Consumer Sales Directive, art 3.
223 First Consumer Sales Directive, art 3(3).
224 Case C-404/06 *Quelle AG v Bundesverband der Verbraucherzentralen und Verbraucherverbände* [2008] ECR I-2685 [41].
225 Salvatore Mazzamuto, 'La Vendita Di Beni Di Consumo' in Carlo Castronovo and Salvatore Mazzamuto (eds), *Manuale di diritto privato europeo*, vol 2 (Giuffrè 2007).
226 The literature on the point is abundant, see e.g. Salvatore Mazzamuto and Armando Plaia, *I rimedi nel diritto privato europeo* (Giappichelli 2012).
227 First Consumer Sales Directive, arts 3(3)-3(5).
228 First Consumer Sales Directive, art 6.
229 S 16.
230 CRA, s 19.
231 Department for Business Innovation & Skills, *CRA: Digital Content. Guidance for Business* (Crown 2015) 22.
232 First Consumer Sales Directive, art 7.

the prevalence of specific performance over compensatory remedies[233] – and the unenforceability of the agreements to the contrary constitute evidence that EU consumer sales law not only does not have the objective to protect consumers but also pursues 'a specific idea of market,'[234] where the sale's traditional exchange function gives way to a consumeristic imperative.

The realisation of a certain idea of market is somehow hindered by the fact that the First Consumer Sales Directive is a measure of minimal harmonisation, and therefore, amongst other things, member states are not obliged to introduce a hierarchy of remedies.[235] Member states can introduce more business-friendly regimes and e.g. subject this directive's rights to the consumer's communication to the trader about the lack of conformity – this is the case of Italy, although this requirement does not apply if the trader acknowledged the existence of said lack or hid it.[236] Member states can also introduce more stringent rules,[237] as did the UK by applying the general six-year limitation period for contract claims in England, Wales, and Northern Ireland (five years in Scotland),[238] as opposed to the general EU limitation of liability to the lacks that become apparent within two years from the delivery.[239]

From an IoT perspective, probably the most problematic aspect is to determine to what extent Things can be goods and, correspondingly, if the nonhardware components' lack of conformity can trigger the rights of the consumers under the First Consumer Sales Directive. Additionally, there is the problem of whether most IoT contracts can be qualified as 'sale' and, even before that, as 'contracts.' Indeed, the directive sets forth the laws on contracts of sale of consumer goods;[240] therefore, consumers could not invoke it to counter private ordering by bricking, if IoT contracts do not qualify as sale.

3.3.1.1 Are Things 'Goods'?

Starting off with the concept of goods, this refers to 'any tangible movable item,'[241] which would suggest that most Things, having physicality as a definitional feature, may qualify as goods.[242] However, the argument could be put forward that when the tangible component is minimal and the prevalent components are software, service,

---

233 The First Consumer Sales Directive's preference for performance has been seen as a point of convergence between common law and civil law jurisdictions by Noto La Diega and Walden (n 26).
234 Mazzamuto and Plaia (n 225) 74.
235 First Consumer Sales Directive, art 8.
236 Italy's Consumer Code, art 132(2). See the critical commentary by Lorenzo Racheli, 'Profili problematici della vendita dei beni di consumo (art. 1519 bis ss. c.c.)' (2005) 5(2) Giust CIV 20.
237 First Consumer Sales Directive, art 8(2).
238 Explanatory notes to the CRA – Commentary on Sections, s 19.
239 First Consumer Sales Directive, art 5(1).
240 First Consumer Sales Directive, arts 1(1) and 2(1).
241 First Consumer Sales Directive, art 1(2).
242 Immovable Things, such as a smart home as a whole, will be excluded – but its movable components will not.

and data, then Things are not necessarily 'goods.' For example, Echo Input's core is the computer program that, once Input is plugged in a traditional speaker, transforms the latter in an Alexa-enabled speaker. The interpretation of good whereby products such as Input are not goods because their intangible components arguably prevail on their tangible ones is not convincing, for a twofold reason. First, this interpretation would be inconsistent with the First Consumer Sales Directive's objective to 'strengthen consumer confidence and enable consumers to make the most of the internal market.'[243] Such arbitrary exclusion would adversely affect consumer confidence as it would potentially leave out a large quantity of goods whose tangible element is ancillary, as their smartness is dictated by their intangible elements. Second, it would decrease legal certainty as one could hardly predict if a Thing fell within or beyond the scope of sale of goods law. Indeed, it is unclear who would decide when the tangible component of a Thing would be prevalent. Therefore, any Thing will qualify as good under the First Consumer Sales Directive, regardless of how prevalent the tangible component is.

Despite the fact that since Things are tangible, this limitation is unlikely to be problematic in the IoT, it is important to underline that the applicability of this regime to only tangible, movable goods can lead to unreasonable discriminatory effects, as epitomised by *St Albans City and District Council v International Computers Ltd.*[244] In the Sale of Goods Act 1979, now mostly replaced by the CRA, *goods* include all 'personal chattels other than things in action and money.'[245] In turn, 'personal chattels' refers to 'tangible movable property.'[246] The defendant in *St Albans* argued that this meant that since the consumer's problem was caused by a defective computer program, the latter was distinct from the tangible disc, and therefore, it could not be said that they had not supplied 'goods' of satisfactory quality. The argument was rejected because *hardware* and *software* cannot be seen as distinct:

> *By itself hardware can do nothing.* The really important part of the system is the software. Programs are the instructions or commands that tell the hardware what to do. The program itself is an algorithm or formula. It is of necessity contained in a physical medium.[247]

Perhaps paradoxically, *St Albans* ended up being used for the opposite purpose, namely, to deprive the consumers of their protection whenever digital products are supplied over a network, as opposed to a tangible format (e.g. a CD). This distinction effectively weakens the protection of consumers and makes little sense

243 First Consumer Sales Directive, recital 5.
244 [1996] EWCA Civ 1296.
245 Sale of Goods Act 1979, s 61.
246 Inheritance and Trustees' Powers Act 2014, s 3.
247 The court of appeals refers to the cited passage in the first-instance decision per Scott Baker J (*St Albans City and District Council v International Computers Ltd* [1994] 10 WLUK 8, emphasis added), that in turn took it from *Toby Constructions Products Ltd v. Computer Bar Sales Pty Ltd* [1983] 2 N.S.W.L.R. 48, 51.

from an economic perspective, as stated in *UsedSoft*.[248] A distinction that is out-dated, since CDs and downloads are increasingly replaced by the mere access of the program on the cloud (software-as-a-service),[249] as the IoT is shifting towards the Cloud of Things.[250] These problems have been resolved by the CRA, which has effectively extended the remedies traditionally provided for consumer goods to contracts for the supply of digital content,[251] defined broadly as 'data which are produced and supplied in digital form.'[252] The solution is only partial because whilst the tangible medium is not required if the consumers paid a monetary price for the digital content, 'free' content (including content 'paid' through personal data) will fall within the scope only under certain circumstances. In particular, if it was supplied with goods ('tangible moveable items'),[253] services, or other digital content for which the consumer paid a price,[254] and if the content would not be otherwise generally available to consumers.[255] The reference to money may be seen as including cryptoassets,[256] but not personal data, thus excluding the content provided by traders adopting one of the most common business models of today. Positively, this Act shows awareness of the fact that content, goods, and services are increasingly bundled. Accordingly, the attempt from businesses to limit or disclaim liability by arguing that a Thing's tangible and intangible components are separate shall be unsuccessful. It is to be hoped that the reference to 'goods,' defined as necessarily tangible, will not allow the survival of the *St Albans* juris-prudence with its focus on the physical medium: intangible goods (digital content) are today on an equal standing with tangible goods.

3.3.1.2 Does 'Bricking' Instantiate a Lack of Conformity?

A more intricate question is whether the nonhardware components' lack of conformity can trigger the rights of the consumers under the First Consumer Sales

---

248 (n 103) [61].
249 The CJEU has not dealt with the issue of software accessed and used on the cloud, but it can be argued that under *UsedSoft*, 'agreements on the delivery of software have to be qualified as licence agreements – irrespective of whether online technologies or offline "sales" apply' (Reto M Hilty, Kaya Köklü and Fabian Hafenbrädl, 'Software Agreements: Stocktaking and Outlook – Lessons from the UsedSoft v. Oracle Case from a Comparative Law Perspective' (2013) 44 IIC – International Review of Intellectual Property and Competition Law 263).
250 Guido Noto La Diega, 'Clouds of Things: Data Protection and Consumer Law at the Intersection of Cloud Computing and the Internet of Things in the United Kingdom' (2016) 9(1) Journal of Law & Economic Regulation 69.
251 CRA, s 33.
252 CRA, s 2(9).
253 CRA, s 2(7).
254 CRA, s 33(2)(a).
255 CRA, s 33(2)(b).
256 On the nature of cryptocurrencies, see *AA v Persons Unknown* [2019] EWHC 3556 (Comm); *B2C2 Ltd v Quoine Pte Ltd* [2019] SGHC(I) 03; *Vorotyntseva v Money-4 Limited, trading as Nebeus.com* [2018] EWHC 2598 (Ch)); *Liam David Robertson v Persons Unknown* (unreported 15th July 2019).

Directive. As seen above, there are four types of conformity (or presumptions of conformity): 'as described,' fit for a particular purpose, fit for the usual purpose, and 'as reasonably expected.'

First, if the description of the Thing, the sample, or the model included its intangible components, consumers would have to be entitled to their rights to repair, replace, etc. if these components are not *as described* or sampled. For example, Alexa Terms of Use describe Amazon's virtual assistant as 'a continuously improving service that you control with your voice.'[257] If an Echo's Alexa stops improving or can no longer be controlled by the consumer's voice, the latter will be able to invoke their rights under the First Consumer Sales Directive, in particular the right to repair as right to have the smartness restored.

Second, the rights to repair, replace, etc. should be available if the *particular purpose* cannot be achieved due to a fault or issue in the Thing's intangible components. For example, if the consumer tells the trader that they will use the phone for videoconferences but the phone turns out to be unable to do so, then it is not fit for the particular purpose. On the one hand, one could expect this type of lack of conformity to be less relevant in the context of the IoT, where nonnegotiated and unilaterally imposed legals prevail and hence the consumer may not have the opportunity to communicate with the trader about the particular purpose for which the Thing is purchased. On the other hand, IoT traders have a wealth of knowledge about potential customers, and therefore one could argue that they are aware of the particular purpose of the Thing, for example, if they track and profile customers for direct marketing purposes. Yet this type of conformity is not relevant if the trader does not accept the particular purpose, which makes it unlikely to be relevant in an IoT context.

A third type of conformity is the fitness to the *usual purpose*. This book defined the *Thing* as capable of (inter)connectivity, sensing, and actuating. Therefore, if a Thing does not exhibit these capabilities, e.g. it does not connect to the internet, then it is unlikely to be fit for its usual purpose. In Echo's case study, its usual purpose includes giving information about the weather, listening to music, and controlling other Things. If Echo is no longer available to do this, for example for interoperability issues, consumers have the right to have the smartness restored, regardless of whether the issue regards the hardware components of the Thing or not. In considering whether this presumption of conformity applies, one needs to recall that 'repurposing' is one the IoT's crucial features.[258] As seen in Chapter 1, *repurposing* is the phenomenon whereby an IoT system is designed for a purpose but ends up being used for purposes other than those originally foreseen, in two scenarios: (i) the communication within the relevant subsystem and among subsystems can lead the system to perform actions and produce information which the single Thing was incapable of or that could not be foreseen by its manufacturers,

---

257 Alexa Terms of Use, point 1.3.
258 Guido Noto La Diega, 'British Perspectives on the Internet of Things. The Clouds of Things-Health Use Case' in *Internet of Things: Legal Issues and Challenges Towards a Hyperconnected World* (Seoul National University 2015).

and (ii) under certain conditions (e.g. an emergency) the system may reconfigure either in an automated fashion or a user-initiated one. Since repurposing is a common feature of IoT systems, the relevant traders should be aware that a Thing's 'usual purpose' can vary over time. Therefore, IoT traders should make sure that the Thing is fit for the new purposes, thus stretching the concept of foreseeability.

Fourth, courts will look at which qualities and performance consumers can *reasonably expect*. As the CJEU recently noted in *Bosch*,[259] consumers expect Things to have either a normal connection to a network or to allow for the interconnection between goods. This type of conformity is likely to be the most relevant to counter private ordering by bricking. Indeed, IoT traders may leverage their data power to impose legals that allow them to deprive consumers of their Things' 'smartness.' However, since smartness is an IoT consumer's reasonable expectation – and since consumers cannot reasonably be expected to read the legals – it can be concluded that private ordering by bricking instantiates a lack of conformity of this type. To assess what can be reasonably expected, courts will also look at the nature of the goods and the public statements.[260] As to the nature of Things, smartness is at their core. As to the public statements, we have seen that in Echo's legals there is the commitment that Alexa will learn over time. Continuous learning is a reasonable expectation of Echo's consumers. As an example of statements that are not found in the legals but only in advertising – that is relevant because it qualifies as public statement – Amazon advertises Echo Show primarily as a clock (Figure 3.2), so the fact that an update made it virtually impossible to use it as a clock, as lamented in some customers' reviews,[261] means that Echo Show lacked conformity to Amazon's public statements.

All four conformity presumptions – as described, particular purpose, usual purpose, as reasonably expected – apply to the IoT. Therefore, consumers can counter 'bricking' and related practices by exercising their rights to have the Thing repaired or replaced, the price reduced, or the contract rescinded. What is changing is how these rights work in practice: the nature of the IoT means that most Things can be repaired remotely, and their intangible components replaced remotely. Traders can avoid repairing and replacing if these are impossible or disproportionate. Fixing the intangible components of a Thing remotely – e.g. through an over-the-air update – seems by definition always possible. *Disproportionate*, in turn, means unreasonably expensive, which does not seem to be the case for the repair and replacement of Things due to intangible issues. For example, Amazon patched remotely a Wi-Fi vulnerability in Echo and Kindle

259 Cases T-251/17 and T-252/17 *Bosch v EUIPO* (CJEU, 28 March 2019) [12].
260 First Consumer Sales Directive, art 2(2)(d).
261 E.g. on 20 July 2019, customer Capt_paranoia, in giving Echo Show a 1/5 star rating, rhetorically asked, 'Why have something which has a clock built in and the clock can't be displayed constantly? . . . Ok you can in don't disturb mode, but I've had one of those since the 80s it's called an alarm clock.' The review is available at <www.amazon.co.uk/gp/customer-reviews/R1H1QY18LEKX5C/ref=cm_cr_arp_d_rvw_ttl?ie=UTF8&ASIN=B07KD7TJD6>.

Figure 3.2 The first of the images used by Amazon to advertise Echo Show 5.[262]

that enabled man-in-the-middle attacks.[263] Consequently, most of the times IoT consumers will be able to demand specific performance, being difficult for the traders to prove that repairing and replacing are disproportionate or impossible. In a way, it could be said that the IoT reinforces the EU lawmaker's preference for an idea of market where repair and replacement prevail because they keep the contract alive and they foster the new consumeristic function of the sale of consumer goods, which is the cornerstone of a perfectly competitive internal market.[264]

3.3.1.3 Are IoT Contracts 'Sales'?

The qualification of Things as goods and the issue of intangible conformity are not the only reasons that the application of the First Consumer Sales Directive to the IoT, and to the private ordering by bricking, is problematic. The directive has a relatively narrow scope regarding 'certain aspects of the sale of consumer goods and associated guarantees.'[265] If there is no contract of sale, including contracts

---

262 <www.amazon.co.uk/Introducing-Echo-Show-Compact-display/dp/B07KD7TJD6/ref=cm_cr_arp_d_product_top?ie=UTF8>.

263 Kate O'Flaherty, 'New Amazon Echo Warning As Wi-Fi Cyberattack Risk Confirmed' (*Forbes*, 17 October 2019) <www.forbes.com/sites/kateoflahertyuk/2019/10/17/new-amazon-echo-warning-as-wi-fi-hack-risk-confirmed/>.

264 Cf Mazzamuto and Plaia (n 225); Luca Nivarra, *Diritto Privato e Capitalismo: Regole Giuridiche e Paradigmi Di Mercato* (Editoriale Scientifica 2010).

265 First Consumer Sales Directive, art 1(1).

for the supply of consumer goods to be manufactured or produced,[266] the directive and the relevant rights and remedies will not apply.

Since there is no harmonised definition of sale, one should refer to the national rules on contract of sale that will apply to the sale of consumer goods inasmuch as compatible with the First Consumer Sales Directive.[267] As a generally accepted definition of *sale*, one can refer to the most ambitious attempt to build a common set of private laws in the EU,[268] namely, the Draft Common Frame of Reference,[269] whereby a contract for the 'sale' of goods is a contract under which one party, the seller, undertakes to another party, the buyer, to transfer the ownership of the goods to the buyer, or to a third person, either immediately on conclusion of the contract or at some future time, and the buyer undertakes to pay the price.[270]

The key element is the transfer of ownership. The Amazon Device Terms of Use do not clarify if the ownership is transferred to the consumer, but it expressly excludes the application of the Convention on the International Sale of Goods.[271] This term could be construed as meaning that consumer sales laws that are not expressly excluded, such as the First Consumer Sales Directive and its national implementations, should apply. The Device Terms, moreover, refer to the Conditions of Use and links to its page that is titled 'Conditions of Use & *Sale*.'[272] The Conditions of Sale constitute the second part of the latter, and they 'govern the sale of products by Amazon EU SARL to you'[273] – of all products, including Echo. Under these conditions, Amazon 'conclude the contract of sale for a product ordered by you, when we dispatch the product to you.'[274] Whereas this is an argument in favour of the qualification of some of Echo's legals as a sale, one needs also to consider that Amazon does not transfer ownership of Echo's intangible components; indeed, it grants only 'a limited, non-exclusive, non-transferable, non-sublicensable licence to access and make personal and non-commercial use of the Amazon Services.'[275] Moreover, such services are defined broadly as encompassing devices, products, services, mobile apps, and software provided by Amazon in connection with any of the foregoing.[276] Since all 'rights not expressly granted to you in these Conditions of Use or any Service Terms are reserved and retained

---

266 First Consumer Sales Directive, art 1(4).

267 Luminoso (n 220).

268 Gerhard Wagner (ed), *The Common Frame of Reference: A View from Law & Economics* (Sellier 2009).

269 Christian von Bar and others (eds), *Principles, Definitions and Model Rules of European Private Law: Draft Common Frame of Reference (DCFR)* (Outline, Sellier 2009).

270 ibid, Book IV, A. – I:202.

271 Amazon Device Terms of Use, point 3(d).

272 <www.amazon.co.uk/gp/help/customer/display.html?ie=UTF8&nodeId=201909000&ref_=foo ter_cou#GUID-189D34BF-F756-4879-B149-0D73223A3BFD__SECTION_DE289546269C-476B94AC853787C5CF48>.

273 Conditions of Use & Sale, conditions of sale's preamble.

274 Conditions of Use & Sale, point 1.

275 Conditions of use & Sale, point 6.

276 Conditions of use & Sale, preamble.

by Amazon,'[277] some may argue that consumers are only renting Echo, namely, using it under the terms of a license but not owning it. This line of thought may be supported by the fact that Amazon purports to disclaim liability if Echo's digital contents become unavailable[278] – which may be seen as proof that the consumer did not own them in the first place, and that some of legals and services can be changed without warning and at Amazon's sole discretion.[279]

Whilst there are arguments both in favour and against the qualification of an IoT sale as proper sale for all purposes, in light of the broad wording of the First Consumer Sales Directive and its objectives, it can be concluded that as long as the contract is either expressly qualified as a sale or transfers the ownership of the Thing as a whole, then it will be a 'sale' at least for the purposes of the aforementioned directive, whose rights and remedies will be available in most business-to-consumer IoT transactions.

A separate, albeit closely interwoven, issue is which contract one needs to look at in assessing the lack of a Thing's conformity. Whilst the existence of a contract of sale or of a guarantee is necessary for a dispute to fall under the First Consumer Sales Directive,[280] in the IoT's contractual quagmire, the legals must be considered jointly, in their interrelationships. The directive seems flexible enough to accommodate this because the parameter of the conformity, or lack thereof, is not necessarily to be found in the contract of sale: it can depend also on 'any public statements on the specific characteristics of the goods made about them by seller.'[281] Whilst this passage primarily refers to advertising and labelling, the mountain of legals that consumers have to accept when using a Thing can be deemed to fall at least within the concept of public statement. Consequently, consumers can invoke the rights to have the Thing's smartness restored not only when it lacks conformity with the contract of sale but also with the other connected legals that create a reasonable expectation that the Thing has certain qualities or performance. For example, even though Echo's Conditions of Sale do not contain a commitment that Alexa will learn continuously, if Alexa stops improving, this may be regarded as a lack of conformity because Amazon committed to it in Alexa Terms of Use.

To conclude, the First Consumer Sales Directive is, in principle, flexible enough for the IoT, and it can be invoked to counter private ordering by bricking through a right to repair construed as a right to have the Thing's smartness restored. The main limitation of this regime is that traders are liable 'for any lack of conformity which exists *at the time the goods were delivered.*'[282] Arguably, if a trader bricks the Thing after the delivery, that lack of conformity did not exist when the Thing was delivered. This issue is partly offset by the fact that, if the lack (e.g. the brick-

---

277 Conditions of use & Sale, point 6.
278 Prime Video Conditions of Use, point 3(I).
279 Conditions of use & Sale, point 3(b).
280 First Consumer Sales Directive, art 2(1).
281 First Consumer Sales Directive, art 2(2)(d).
282 First Consumer Sales Directive, art 3(1), emphasis added.

ing) manifests itself within six months, the consumer will not have to prove that it existed at the time of delivery.[283] However, traders can rebut this presumption.[284] Moreover, after the six months, the burden of proof will be on the consumer.[285] As to said burden, the CJEU in *Faber*[286] clarified that the consumer has to prove the lack of conformity, not 'the cause of that lack of conformity or to establish that its origin is attributable to the (trader).'[287] IoT consumers may find it difficult to prove that the deprivation of the smartness existed at the time of delivery. A solution could be to construe 'delivery' broadly. Indeed, since in the IoT the good's key components are intangible, and given that the intangible components are delivered throughout the Thing's life cycle, any deprivation of smartness will, by definition, take place at the time of delivery. Directive 2019/771 ('Second Consumer Sales Directive), which will replace the First Consumer Sales Directive, expressly embraces this solution.[288] Indeed, it provides that, in the case of goods with digital elements, where the sales contract provides for a continuous supply of the digital content or digital service over a period of time, the seller shall also be liable for any lack of conformity of the digital content or digital service that occurs or becomes apparent within the period during which the content or service is to be supplied.[289] The next section will deal with this new directive that, alongside the new Digital Content Directive, has been welcomed as the 'main development in European contract law and consumer contract law'[290] of the last twenty years.

3.3.2 The EU Reform of the Laws on Consumer Sales and Supply of Digital Content and Digital Services

Unlike a minority of member states such as the UK,[291] Germany,[292] and the Netherlands,[293] EU consumer laws still rely on the tangible-intangible dichotomy, despite the increasing awareness of its untenability. Under EU law, there is no obligation to recognise the right to repair, replace, etc. faulty intangible products,

---

283   Unless this presumption is incompatible with the nature of the goods or the nature of the lack of conformity. First Consumer Sales Directive, art 5(3).
284   See e.g. UK's CRA, s 19(15)(a); Italy's Consumer Code, art 132(3).
285   First Consumer Sales Directive, art 5(3).
286   C-497/13 *Froukje Faber v Autobedrijf Hazet Ochten BV* (CJEU, 4 June 2015).
287   ibid [75].
288   Second Consumer Sales Directive, recital 37.
289   Second Consumer Sales Directive, art 10(2).
290   Jorge Morais Carvalho, 'Sale of Goods and Supply of Digital Content and Digital Services – Overview of Directives 2019/770 and 2019/771' [2019] EuCML 194.
291   cf Paula Giliker, 'Regulating Contracts for the Supply of Digital Content: The EU and UK Response' in Tatiana – Eleni Synodinou and others (eds), *EU Internet Law. Regulation and Enforcement* (Springer 2017) 101.
292   BGB, § 453.
293   In 2014, the Dutch Implementation Law on CRD (*Implementatiewet richtlijn consumentenrechten*) amended the Civil Code of the Netherlands (*Burgerlijk Wetboek*) to extend the rules on consumer sales to contracts on the supply of digital content without durable medium.

but this will change soon as a result of the adoption of Directive 2019/771 ('Second Consumer Sales Directive')[294] and Directive 2019/770 ('Digital Content Directive'), collectively 'the EU reform.' Member states will have to implement these directives (collectively 'the EU reform') by 1 July 2021, and the implementing measures will apply from 1 January 2022.[295] Whilst some authors[296] argue that the First Consumer Sales Directive applies to digital content and that the characteristics of the medium are not relevant, with the reform, for the first time expressly,[297] the conformity requirements will apply also to digital content and digital services. This reform aims to modernise the existing rules on the lack of conformity of goods to the contract and complement them with a similar regime regarding digital content and digital services.[298] This is fundamental because at 'the heart of the digital revolution is the way digital content is utilised,'[299] and the IoT calls for the convergence of rules on intangible goods and tangible ones.

Derived from the failed Common European Sales Law project[300] and part of the Digital Single Market strategy,[301] these directives follow the principle of maximum harmonisation,[302] which sets them apart from the First Consumer Sales Directive, which aimed at minimum harmonisation.[303] This notwithstanding, some provisions leave room for national tailoring; for example, member states can decide whether or not to extend the subjective scope of application, e.g. by including natural or legal persons that are not consumers, such as nongovernmental organisations, start-ups, and small and medium enterprises.[304] Such an extension would be positive in light of the rise of prosumers and to address power

---

294 Directive 2019/771 of 20 May 2019 on certain aspects concerning contracts for the sale of goods, amending Regulation (EU) 2017/2394 and Directive 2009/22/EC, and repealing Directive 1999/44/EC (Second Consumer Sales Directive) [2019] OJ L 136/28.

295 Second Consumer Sales Directive, art 23; Digital Content Directive, art 24(1).

296 Mário Tenreiro and Soledad Gómez, 'La Directive 1999/44/CE Sur Certains Aspects de La Vente et Des Garanties Des Biens de Consommation' [2000] Revue Européenne de Droit de la Consommation 5; Robert Bradgate and Christian Twigg-Flesner, *Blackstone's Guide to Consumer Sales and Associated Guarantees* (Blackstone Press Limited 2003).

297 Some national laws already provide such extension, see e.g. the UK CRA.

298 Morais Carvalho (n 289).

299 Christian Twigg-Flesner, 'Disruptive Technology-Disrupted Law? How the Digital Revolution Affects (Contract) Law' in Alberto De Franceschi (ed), *European Contract Law and the Digital Single Market: The Implications of the Digital Revolution* (Intersentia 2016) 31.

300 Proposal for a Regulation on a Common European Sales Law (COM/2011/0635 final).

301 Giliker (n 290).

302 Second Consumer Sales Directive, art 4; Digital Content Directive, art 4. This means that, in principle, member states cannot deviate from the directives' requirements. 'EU Adopts New Rules on Sales Contracts for Goods and Digital Content' (*Consilium Europa*, 15 April 2019) <www.consilium.europa.eu/en/press/press-releases/2019/04/15/eu-adopts-new-rules-on-sales-contracts-for-goods-and-digital-content/>.

303 The objective of the First Consumer Sales Directive is to 'ensure a uniform minimum level of consumer protection in the context of the internal market' (art 1(1)).

304 Second Consumer Sales Directive, recital 21; Digital Content Directive, recital 16. Based on available evidence, I would suggest that the new directives be applied to microenterprises, but future research should gather more empirical evidence to this end.

imbalances in business-to-business relationships.[305] From this book's perspective, it is crucial to ascertain whether the reformed law relies on the tangible-intangible dichotomy and, relatedly, if the separate regulation of sale of tangible goods and provision of digital content/services is fit for the IoT.

The goal of this reform is 'to contribute to the *proper functioning of the internal market while providing for a high level of consumer protection.*'[306] This makes explicit what scholars[307] inferred from the First Consumer Sales Directive, namely, that consumers are protected as a means to the actual end to achieve a perfectly competitive single market.[308] The pursuit of a certain idea of market through consumer laws was epitomised by the First Consumer Sales Directive's hierarchy of remedies, whereby the remedies that preserve the validity of the contract prevail on remedies that make the contract void. For example, the consumer cannot choose to ask the termination of the contract: they have to first opt for the performance remedies (repair and replacement). As mentioned above, such approach reinforced the new consumeristic function of consumer sales.[309] Before the reform, member states were free to decide whether or not to introduce the hierarchy of remedies. With the reform, the original plan comes full circle as the principle of maximum harmonisation will force member states to introduce the remedial hierarchy.[310] This is one of the main reasons that the new law has been criticised and the EU has been called to withdraw it.[311]

Without the ambition of a comprehensive coverage of this reform, the following analysis will focus on the following aspects:

(i)   Express inclusion of 'goods with digital elements';
(ii) Definition of sale and inclusion of nonmonetary exchanges, namely, personal data, as consideration;
(iii) Changes in the presumptions of conformity that become requirements for conformity.

---

305 Guido Noto La Diega, 'Can the Law Fix the Problems of Fashion? An Empirical Study on Social Norms and Power Imbalance in the Fashion Industry' (2019) 14 Journal of Intellectual Property Law & Practice 18.

306 Second Consumer Sales Directive, art 1; Digital Content Directive, art 1.

307 Mazzamuto and Plaia (n 225); Nivarra (n 263).

308 A similar wording, though perhaps not as telling, can be found in the CRD, art 1.

309 Cf Mazzamuto and Plaia (n 225); Nivarra (n 263).

310 Second Consumer Sales Directive, art 13(2); Digital Content Directive, art 14(2). The only exception is the case of nonsupply of digital content, in which case consumers can terminate the contract immediately. See Rafał Mańko and DG for Parliamentary Research Services, *Contracts for Supply of Digital Content* (European Parliament 2016) <http://bookshop.europa.eu/uri?target= EUB:NOTICE:QA0116489:EN:HTML>.

311 Critical of the fact that member states will be obliged to introduce the aforementioned hierarchy of remedies, also Geraint Howells, 'Reflections on Remedies for Lack of Conformity in Light of the Proposals of the EU Commission on Supply of Digital Content and Online and Other Distance Sales of Goods' in Alberto De Franceschi (ed), *European Contract Law and the Digital Single Market – The Implications of the Digital Revolution* (Intersentia 2016).

3.3.2.1   *The Grey Area between Goods with Digital Elements and Mere Carriers*

The second innovation – the most important one, from an IoT perspective – is that while goods are still defined as necessarily tangible,[312] there is an express inclusion of '*goods with digital elements.*' These

> incorporate or are inter-connected with digital content or a digital service in such a way that the absence of that digital content or digital service would prevent the goods from performing their functions.[313]

From this book's standpoint, this is positive news because it seems clear that most Things can be regarded as goods with digital elements inasmuch as they have a tangible component and are entangled with software, service, and data that are necessary for the Thing to be 'smart' or altogether to work. This is not to say that the sale of Things would not fall under the First Consumer Sales Directive. As agued above, the previous regime could already be interpreted as meaning that the sale of goods applied to Things and 'goods with digital elements' more generally, as long as a tangible element was present. The new wording better reflects current IoT applications, where the good (Thing) is rarely just a medium; it is integrated with intangible components that are often vital to its functioning. It remains to be seen what will happen to goods that include digital elements but can perform their tasks without the latter. It will be assessed below whether the Digital Content Directive covers those Things that can perform their functions without a particular digital content or service, as it's not clear when 'the absence of (the) digital content or digital service would prevent the goods from performing their functions.'[314]

The Digital Content Directive leaves goods with digital elements expressly out of its scope if the content or service is provided 'with the goods under a sales contract concerning those goods.'[315] At a first look, one could think that if there is a tangible good (including one with digital elements), the Second Consumer Sales Directive will apply, whilst if there is no tangible good, the Digital Content Directive will apply. However, the matter is more complicated than this for a twofold reason.

First, the latter directive also applies to 'digital content which is supplied on a tangible medium, such as DVDs, CDs, USB sticks and memory cards, as well as to the *tangible medium itself,* provided that the tangible medium serves exclusively as a carrier of the digital content.'[316] Since legal certainty is one of the objectives of the reform,[317] provisions such as this hinder its achievement. Indeed,

---

312 Second Consumer Sales Directive, art 2(5)(a).
313 Second Consumer Sales Directive, art 2(5)(b).
314 Second Consumer Sales Directive, art 2(5)(b).
315 Digital Content Directive, art 3(4).
316 Digital Content Directive, recital 20, italics added.
317 Digital Content Directive, recitals 3–5; Second Consumer Sales Directive, recitals 3 and 5. See Giliker (n 290).

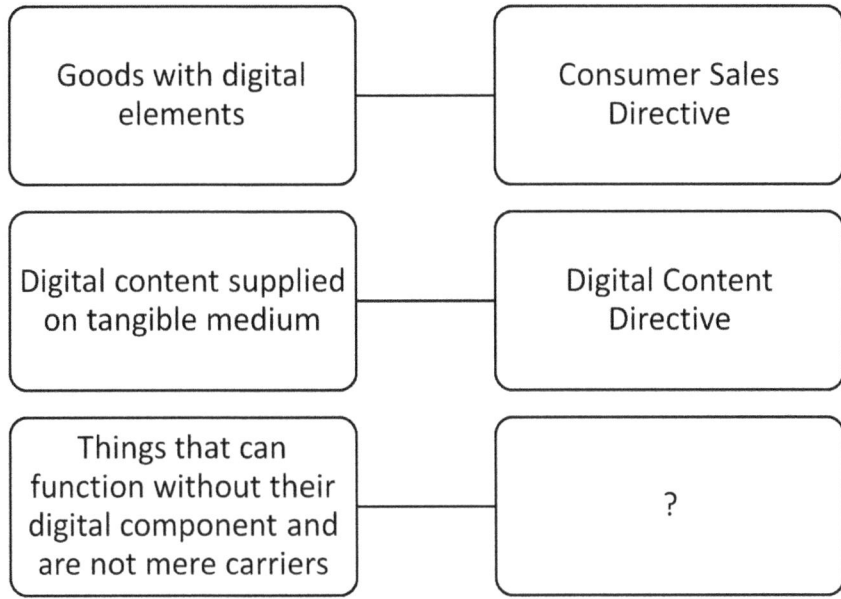

Figure 3.3 The 'smart' grey area left out of the scope of the new law of consumer sales.

there is a vast grey area between a good whose digital components are vital to its functioning – falling within the scope of the Second Consumer Sales Directive – and goods that are exclusively a carrier of the digital content, to which the Digital Content Directive will apply (Figure 3.3).

It is not clear what happens to all the Things that are embedded with digital components and yet can function without them but do now qualify as mere carriers of the digital content. Arguably, for example, Echo can function without Alexa (as a speaker), and it is not a mere carrier of Amazon's virtual assistant. Neither such Things qualify as goods with digital elements, or as mere carriers; therefore, there is no certainty as to which, if any, protections consumers will be able to rely on. Conversely, in some scenarios, both regimes may apply. For example, Echo Input – Thing that can 'bring' Alexa to any nonsmart speaker – cannot function without Alexa; hence, it is a good with digital elements, but it can also be seen as its mere carrier. This is not only a risk to consumers. Indeed, it may lead to conflicting compliance burdens to the detriment of IoT companies themselves.

A second reason that there is a grey area is that the Digital Content Directive excludes goods with digital elements only if the content or service is provided 'with the goods under a sales contract concerning those goods.'[318] Let us imagine

---

318 Digital Content Directive, art 3(4). See Second Consumer Sales Directive, art 3(3).

a smart function added to a good via an update released after the sales contract (e.g. an Alexa 'skill'). Does the exclusion of these particular goods with digital elements mean that the other goods with digital elements – when the content or service is *not* provided with the goods under a sales contract (e.g. after the contract) – fall under the Digital Content Directive that the latter will apply to the digital elements and the Consumer Sales Directive to the tangible component, or will they be left without protection? Different judges may consider Things as goods with digital elements, mere carriers, neither, or both, thus decreasing legal certainty and hampering the Digital Single Market. It will be up to national lawmakers, hopefully in a coordinated fashion, to ensure that the transposing measures will prevent this from happening.

A solution may build on the Digital Content Directive's provision, whereby

> *in the event of doubt as to whether* the supply of incorporated or interconnected digital content or an incorporated or inter-connected digital service forms *part of the sales contract*, the digital content or digital service shall be presumed to be covered by the sales contract.[319]

Whilst this provision may not apply to many scenarios falling within the aforementioned grey area (e.g. Things that can function without certain digital components), it can be seen as an expression of a more general preference for, and hence prevalence of, the sale of goods regime over the Digital Content Directive, in case of doubt. To further corroborate this view, the latter directive further provides that in the event of a contractual bundle – contracts bundling e.g. sale of goods, supply of digital content, and provision of nondigital services – the Digital Content Directive will 'only apply to the elements of the contract concerning the digital content or digital service.'[320] In this sense, this directive could be seen as playing an ancillary function, compared to the sale of goods regime that should apply to all scenarios falling within the grey area and when in doubt. While this may be regarded as a good, pragmatic provision, it may also be seen as a reflection of the hierarchy of values in a pre-IoT world, where tangible goods were considered more important than intangible ones.

3.3.2.2 The Definition of Sale and the Inclusion of Nonmonetary Prices

Another news in the reform is that the 'sales contract' is now defined as meaning 'any contract under which the seller *transfers or undertakes to transfer ownership of goods* to a consumer, and the consumer pays or undertakes to pay the *price* thereof.'[321] The limitation to distance contracts, originally provided in the Commission's proposal,[322] has been removed following criticism by businesses,

---

319 Digital Content Directive, art 3(4).
320 Digital Content Directive, art 3(6).
321 Second Consumer Sales Directive, art 2(1).
322 The Second Consumer Sales Directive covers 'all sales channels, in order to create a level playing field for all businesses selling goods to consumers' (recital 9). Under art 1(1) of the Proposal

consumers, and commentators.[323] A harmonised definition of sale increases legal certainty, especially in cross-border transactions. However, this definition is not IoT-friendly, for two reasons. First, as we will see in Chapter 6, the IoT ushers in the death of ownership – and if the consumer does not acquire the ownership of the Thing, the contract will not qualify as sale and the relevant remedies will not apply. Second, the reference to the price may be interpreted as excluding nonmonetary value transfers (e.g. personal data transfers), that under the previous regime might have been regarded as included in the directive, since there was no reference to the necessity of a price.[324] A large number of IoT-related transactions, where the Thing is exchanged for the consumer's data, would be left without protections. Arguably, the directive refers to 'price' because of the remedy of price reduction. However, it is my opinion that the 'price' should not be necessarily monetary, and in the event of a sales contract where personal data is used to purchase a good, the price reduction may be construed as meaning a reduction in the quantity of personal data transferred to the trader. An argument in favour of this position is that, to achieve the Digital Single Market in an IoT world, where the distinction between tangible and intangible is blurred, the same rules should apply to goods, digital content, and digital services, where possible.

The express inclusion of nonmonetary prices is the most visible difference between the Second Consumer Sales Directive and the Digital Content Directive. The latter does not require a monetary price to be paid; indeed, it also covers scenarios where '*the consumer provides or undertakes to provide personal data to the trader.*'[325] Data as contractual consideration or counterperformance has been regarded[326] as one of the most important challenges faced by private law in this era of digitalisation. This is also a key difference between the Digital Content Directive and the UK CRA,[327] which defines the price in monetary terms. Applying both directives to consumer contracts regardless of a monetary price not only would be conducive to the proper functioning of the internal market but would also take account of one of the most popular business models in the digital economy, where personal data instantiates the contractual consideration. However, the Digital Content Directive is no model of legislative perfection. The provision of personal data as consideration in consumer contracts has been criticised mainly for three reasons.[328] First, it has been seen as contrary to the GDPR. While it is

---

for a Directive on certain aspects concerning contracts for the online and other distance sales of goods (COM/2015/635 final), '[t]his Directive lays down certain requirements concerning distance sales contracts concluded between the seller and the consumer.'

323 Giliker (n 290).

324 The prevalent interpretation, however, would require monetary prices, since one of the remedies is the price reduction. cf Mak (n 232).

325 Digital Content Directive, art 3(1), italics added.

326 Sebastian Lohsse, Reiner Schulze and Dirk Staudenmayer (eds), *Data as Counter-Performance – Contract Law 2.0? Münster Colloquia on EU Law and the Digital Economy V* (Hart – Nomos 2020).

327 S 33, as noted by Giliker (n 290).

328 Laura Drechsler, 'Data As Counter-Performance: A New Way Forward or a Step Back for the Fundamental Right of Data Protection?' <cris.vub.be/files/36462976/IRIS2017_DRAFT_

possible to argue both ways, nothing in the GDPR prevents a data subject to treat their data as a commodity. On the contrary, innovations such as the right to data portability signal that personal data is useful to access many services, and the data subjects can dispose of them at their discretion.[329] Some issues may nevertheless arise, e.g. if the exercise of the right to erasure can lead to a breach of contract when personal data is the consideration. The second criticism is the concern that the nature of data protection as a fundamental right may be affected. It is possible to respond to this that the fundamental nature of a right is not affected by its transferability; for example, property is a fundamental right, and yet one can transfer it.[330] To exclude personal data from the concept of price would result in the nonapplication of the laws on consumer sales, which in turn would lead to a diminished protection of the consumer-data subject. A third criticism is that the lawmaker should not legitimise a business model that runs counter to data protection. The criticism misses the point, as proved by the fact that the UK government decided to define the price in monetary terms and excluded personal data as consideration as a result of lobbying by businesses that argued 'that inclusion might inhibit business development.'[331] I believe that the Digital Content Directive has positively taken a pragmatic approach that, taking account of a shift in contractual practices towards personal data as the default consideration, has broadened the scope of EU consumer law to strengthen the protection of consumers and advancing the harmonisation of the relevant rules to achieve the goal of the Digital Single Market.[332] In September 2020, Singapore announced a partnership with Apple whereby citizens would be paid to use Apple Watch.[333] Companies are increasingly willing to compensate data producers not only with services but also with money. Denying that data is a new currency seems futile: the point is how to prevent data abuses and strengthen data control in a market that relies on data monetisation.

From this book's perspective, the main issue with the Digital Content Directive's provision, including the contracts having personal data as consideration, is the reference to the 'provision' of personal data by the consumer. As confirmed by the GDPR, oftentimes personal data *is not provided by* the data subject; instead,

---

Drechsler_V3.pdf>; Alberto De Franceschi, *La Circolazione Dei Dati Personali Tra Privacy e Contratto*, vol 156 (Edizioni scientifiche italiane 2017); European Data Protection Supervisor, 'Opinion 4/2017 on the Proposal for a Directive on Certain Aspects Concerning Contracts for the Supply of Digital Content' (2017).

329 GDPR, art 20.
330 Whilst it is generally accepted that property is a fundamental right, this characterisation is controversial. See e.g. Gregory S Alexander, 'Property as a Fundamental Constitutional Right? The German Example' (2002) 88 Cornell Law Review 733.
331 Giliker (n 290) 121.
332 cf Madalena Barreto Torres de Mendonca Narciso, '"Gratuitous" Digital Content Contracts in EU Consumer Law' (2017) 6 Journal of European Consumer and Market Law 198.
333 Sareena Dayaram, 'Apple and Singapore to Reward Apple Watch Users for Keeping Healthy' (*CNET*, 16 September 2020) <www.cnet.com/news/singapore-to-reward-citizens-for-healthy-activity-apple-watch/>.

it can be collected from third parties (e.g. Facebook sharing user preferences with the advertisers)[334] or otherwise generated (e.g. inferred through observation of online behaviour).[335] This is particularly important in an IoT world, where surveillance capitalism manifests itself through ubiquitous and surreptitious monitoring, tracking, and profiling of users of smart technologies.[336] Accordingly, the GDPR deals separately with the information to be provided, where personal data are collected from the data subject,[337] and the one to be provided where personal data have not been obtained from the data subject.[338] Hopefully, the national measures implementing the EU reform will clarify that the latter covers all the contracts where the trader transfers or undertakes to transfer a good's ownership or digital content/service is provided in exchange for personal data, regardless of whether the consumer provided it. Thus, they would implement the European Parliament's recommendation[339] to expand the directive's scope to include digital content supplied against data that consumers provide passively.

The Digital Content Directive excludes those contracts where personal data is processed by the trader *exclusively* for the purpose of:

(i) Allowing the trader to comply with legal requirements to which the trader is subject,[340] or
(ii) Supplying the digital content or digital service in accordance with the directive.[341]

The directive illustrates the first scenario by referring to the example of mandated processing for security and identification purposes.[342] However, it does not clarify whether the 'legal requirements to which the trader is subject' refers only to laws obliging the trader to process certain data or whether it is sufficient that the law justifies the processing without making it mandatory. The distinction is subtle but crucial. As an example of obligatory processing, one can think of the strong authentication measures imposed by the PSD2. As an example of laws merely justifying personal data processing, one can refer to the so-called upload filter[343] under the DSM Copyright Directive. Whilst the draft directive contained

334 Guido Noto La Diega, 'Data as Digital Assets. The Case of Targeted Advertising: Towards a Holistic Approach?' in Mor Bakhoum and others (eds), *Personal Data in Competition, Consumer Protection and Intellectual Property Law. Towards a Holistic Approach?* (Springer 2018).
335 Sandra Wachter and Brent Mittelstadt, 'A Right to Reasonable Inferences: Re-Thinking Data Protection Law in the Age of Big Data and AI' [2019] Columbia Business Law Review 494.
336 cf Shoshana Zuboff, *The Age of Surveillance Capitalism: The Fight for a Human Future at the New Frontier of Power* (PublicAffairs 2019).
337 GDPR, art 13.
338 GDPR, art 14.
339 Rafał Mańko, 'Contracts for Supply of Digital Content to Consumers' (2016) European Parliamentary Research Service PE 581.980.
340 Digital Content Directive, art 3(1).
341 Digital Content Directive, art 3(1).
342 Digital Content Directive, recital 25.
343 DSM Copyright Directive, art 17.

an obligation for online platforms to ex ante filter user-generated content,[344] the final version incentivises the implementation of such filters; it does not mandate them, even though one can expect that providers will indeed implement them to minimise exposure. Indeed, Article 17 now provides that online content-sharing service providers are liable for unauthorised acts of communication to the public unless they show that they 'made, in accordance with high industry standards of professional diligence, best efforts to ensure the unavailability'[345] of the unauthorised content and have '*made best efforts to prevent their future uploads.*'[346] Arguably, an interpretation of 'legal requirement' as 'legal obligation' or duty is to be preferred because it is closer to the literal meaning of the provision and more conducive to its protective rationale. Therefore, laws like the upload filter, authorizing yet not mandating personal data processing, cannot be invoked to bring the matter outside of the scope of the Digital Content Directive.

Even more controversial is the exclusion of those contracts where personal data is '*exclusively processed by the trader for the purpose of supplying the digital content* or digital service in accordance with this Directive.'[347] The legals of most social media accounts would instantiate a nonexcluded contract as they typically involve data processing that goes beyond what is necessary for providing digital content or services, e.g. when 'personal data, such as photographs or posts that the consumer uploads, (are) processed by the trader for marketing purposes.'[348] Conversely, it is not easy to identify contracts that are excluded under this provision. There are mainly two problematic aspects in this exclusion. First, the notion of a processing that has exclusively a purpose shows unawareness of the IoT's repurposing capabilities, whereby Things and systems designed for a purpose often end up serving another purpose either automatically or for reasons that are not under the control of the original manufacturer or designer. These issues are exacerbated when the Thing or IoT systems are machine learning–powered and, accordingly, learn over time to perform new tasks and process for new purposes. In the IoT, the idea of an 'exclusive' purpose is untenable. Second, the processing of personal data obtained from third parties in the absence of a contract falls outside the scope of the directive.[349] For example, if I use Echo Show to watch video content provided by third parties that, in exchange, obtain my personal data, I will not be able to invoke the Digital Content Directive as I do not have a contract with these third parties. In implementing this directive, therefore, member states should take advantage of the option 'to extend the application of this Directive to such situations [where there is no contract], or to otherwise regulate such situations.'[350]

---

344 cf Proposal for a Directive on copyright in the Digital Single Market (COM/2016/0593 final – 2016/0280 (COD)), art 13.
345 DSM Copyright Directive, art 17(4)(b).
346 DSM Copyright Directive, art 17(4)(c).
347 Digital Content Directive, art 3(1).
348 Digital Content Directive, recital 24.
349 Digital Content Directive, recital 25.
350 Digital Content Directive, recital 25.

3.3.2.3 From the Presumptions of Conformity to the Requirements for Conformity

The final innovation brought about by this EU reform regards the presumptions of conformity that have become requirements for conformity. Whilst at a first glance there would seem to be no substantial changes in these requirements,[351] compared to the First Consumer Sales Directive, there are indeed five noteworthy additions: (i) reorganisation of the conformity requirements into subjective and objective; (ii) new interoperability requirement; (iii) new duty to update; (iv) ad hoc requirements for goods with digital elements; (v) duty not to let third-party rights limit the use of the product.

First, the requirements have been reorganised into 'subjective'[352] and 'objective.'[353] *Subjective* means that the good, content, or service must match the contract.[354] *Objective* requirements for conformity add to the subjective ones and concern what consumers can reasonably expect.[355] In principle, the objective requirements are more likely to be relevant in the IoT because they oblige traders to ensure that products are and remain as reasonably expected by consumers, regardless of the legals. Indeed, exploiting the power imbalance that characterises IoT transactions, these traders could have the consumers accept contractual terms that allow the trader to depart from the conformity requirements (e.g. by removing the smart features of a Thing). Regardless of such terms, consumers are entitled to have the product brought into conformity if there is a breach of the objective requirements.

This notwithstanding, in principle two of the subjective requirements are of relevance for IoT consumers: goods, digital content, and digital services must be interoperable and updated. In light of the importance of IoT interoperability to prevent the Internet of Silos, commendably the EU reform mandates that goods, digital content, and digital services must possess *functionality*, *compatibility*, and *interoperability*, as required by the contract.[356] The relevance of this provision – and of all the 'objective' requirements – is limited in a context of power imbalance and information asymmetry that the IoT exacerbates. Indeed, contracts are used to realise a private ordering of online transactions that penalises consumers. For example, Amazon informs consumers that 'devices that are Compatible Devices at one time may cease to be Compatible Devices in the future.'[357] Since the contract does not require Amazon to ensure the contents and services are compatible with the goods, the lack of compatibility cannot be ground for an action for breach of this subjective requirement.

Similar issues relate to the subjective requirement to supply updates 'as stipulated by the contract.'[358] The obsolescence of a product can be dangerous because

351 Morais Carvalho (n 289).
352 Second Consumer Sales Directive, art 6; Digital Content Directive, art 7.
353 Second Consumer Sales Directive, art 7; Digital Content Directive, art 8.
354 Second Consumer Sales Directive, art 6; Digital Content Directive, art 7.
355 Second Consumer Sales Directive, art 7(1)(a); Digital Content Directive, art 8(1)(a).
356 Second Consumer Sales Directive, art 6(a); Digital Content Directive, art 7(a).
357 Amazon Prime Video Terms of Use, point 2.
358 Second Consumer Sales Directive, art 6(d); Digital Content Directive, art 7(d).

it can make the product unsafe and vulnerable to attacks. Therefore, in principle it is positive that the nonprovision of updates qualifies as a lack of conformity. However, the reference to the contract means that IoT traders can impose imbalanced terms whereby they do not have an obligation to keep the Thing updated. For example, Amazon's Conditions of Use[359] provide that '[i]n order to keep the Amazon Software up-to-date, [Amazon] *may* offer automatic or manual updates at any time and without notice to you.' This is not an actionable obligation; it is left to the trader's discretion. Arguably, therefore, they could put in place that form of private ordering that goes by the name of planned obsolescence.

However, in addition to the conformity requirements that apply to all goods, digital content, and digital service, the EU reform also introduces an ad hoc requirement to update that applies to 'goods with digital elements,' hence to most Things. What is crucial is that this requirement is an objective one; therefore, IoT legals cannot be used to sidestep it. Traders of goods with digital elements must ensure that the consumer 'is informed of and supplied with *updates*, including security updates, that are necessary to keep those goods in conformity.'[360] This obligation can last for the period of time that the consumer can reasonably expect or, should the contract provide a continuous supply of the content or service, for as long as the supply is contractually provided. In striking a balance between consumer protection and the traders' interest to conduct a business, the EU reform also introduces a defence for traders; they will not be liable should the consumer fail to install, within a reasonable time, the updates.[361] This provision nudges consumers to look after their Things and counters the paternalism that many see as characterising consumer protection laws.[362] At a closer look, the provision confirms the current trend to move on from protecting consumers through law – consumer law in Europe was linked to the rise of the welfare state in the Sixties and Seventies[363] – to a world where '[c]onsumers are supposed to play an active role in European markets.'[364] From this standpoint, the expectation that consumers do not need top-down regulations and are active players in the market is an ideological one; in particular, it can be regarded as the expression of the neoliberal concepts of minimal state and free market.[365]

---

359 Additional Amazon Software Terms, point 4.
360 Second Consumer Sales Directive, art 7(3). Similar provisions can be found in the Digital Content Directive, art 8(2).
361 Second Consumer Sales Directive, art 7(4); Digital Content Directive, art 8(3).
362 cf Ana Odorović, 'The "New" Paternalism in Consumer Credit Regulation: When, Why, and How?' (2018) 66 Анали Правног факултета у Београду 156.
363 Dorota Leczykiewicz and Stephen Weatherill, *The Images of the Consumer in EU Law: Legislation, Free Movement and Competition Law* (Hart 2016).
364 Hans-W Micklitz and Geneviève Saumier, 'Enforcement and Effectiveness of Consumer Law' in Hans-W Micklitz and Geneviève Saumier (eds), *Enforcement and Effectiveness of Consumer Law* (Springer 2018) 31.
365 Anne L Alstott, 'Neoliberalism in US Family Law: Negative Liberty and Laissez-Faire Markets in the Minimal State' (2014) 77 Law & Contemporary Problems 25. The role of the neoliberal state

Fifth, building on a similar provision in the proposed Common European Sales Law,[366] conformity will cover also legal defects, namely, any 'restriction resulting from a violation of any right of a third party, in particular intellectual property rights.'[367] This phenomenon is epitomised by the infamous deletion of Orwell's *1984* and *Animal Farm* e-books from users' Kindles, since a third party had placed the e-books on Kindle without the permission of the author's estate.[368] Things are increasingly 'legal black boxes'[369] because their every aspect and layer is covered by some form of intellectual property, technological protection measure, or contractual right. This means that each 'layer of owner must rely on the owners above them'[370] through a complex system of licensing and sublicensing that has been criticised as 'the new subinfeudation.'[371] This is a contributing factor of the death of ownership, as will be seen in Chapter 6. Positively, when the EU reform will become effective, such third-party restrictions will qualify as a lack of conformity if they prevent or limit the use of the goods, digital content, or digital service; consumers, therefore, will be able to invoke the usual remedies of replacement, repair, etc.[372] However, member states may opt for the nullity or rescission of the contract instead of the remedies of the lack of conformity.[373] Commentators of the draft Digital Content Directive lamented the lack of 'clarification that End User Licence Agreements do not affect the consumer's legal position.'[374] Commendably, the final text expressly recognises that restrictions can arise also from such agreements that may prevent 'the consumer from making use of certain features related to the functionality of the digital content or digital service.'[375] It is to be hoped that national implementation measures will provide that contractual restrictions such as the aforementioned can qualify as lack of conformity also in domestic consumer sales law.

3.3.2.4 Private Ordering by Bricking Breaches the New Law of Consumer Sales

To conclude, the EU reform's objective to extend the remedies for lack of conformity to digital content and digital services is a positive one that – in constituting a stepping stone towards the realisation of a fully harmonised European contract

---

is contested, as pointed out by Linda Weiss, 'The State in the Economy: Neoliberal or Neoactivist?' [2010] The Oxford Handbook of Comparative Institutional Analysis 183.

366 Proposal for a Regulation on a Common European Sales Law, art 102.
367 Second Consumer Sales Directive, art 9; Digital Content Directive, art 10.
368 Brad Stone, 'Amazon Erases Orwell Books From Kindle Devices' *The New York Times* (17 July 2009) <www.nytimes.com/2009/07/18/technology/companies/18amazon.html?_r=0>.
369 Noto La Diega, 'Against the Dehumanisation of Decision-Making' (n 6).
370 Joshua AT Fairfield, *Owned: Property, Privacy, and the New Digital Serfdom* (CUP 2017) 40.
371 ibid.
372 Second Consumer Sales Directive, art 9; Digital Content Directive, art 10.
373 Second Consumer Sales Directive, art 9; Digital Content Directive, art 10.
374 Schulze (n 217) 137.
375 Digital Content Directive, recital 53.

law[376] – is likely to benefit the IoT and the digital economy more generally. Regrettably, the reform keeps relying on the tangible-intangible divide that the IoT is rendering outdated. If there is a sales contract regarding a good, including 'goods with digital elements,' the Second Sales of Goods Directive will apply; in turn, the Digital Content Directive covers the contracts for the supply of digital contents or services, including their tangible medium, as long as the latter is the mere carrier of the former. The qualification of Things as goods or services, therefore, will have profound practical consequences. Although similar in their content, the directives provide partly different rules for goods, contents, and services. For example, whereas the Second Consumer Sales Directive provides that the trader 'shall be liable . . . for any lack of conformity . . . which becomes apparent within two years'[377] of the delivery, no obligation to introduce such limit exists under the Digital Content Directive. Therefore, if national laws do provide a time limit, this cannot be under two years;[378] if they do not, national prescription rules will apply. As the latter rules are not subject to harmonisation, there will be 'variation in the period of applicability of the conformity requirement that is far from ideal in a maximum harmonization directive,'[379] and an unfortunate divergence between the regime of 'tangibles' and the regime of 'intangibles.' Although there is a vast grey area where it is not clear which regime, if any, will apply, this chapter suggests that, when in doubt, consumer sales law should control.

Many of the aforementioned legal innovations are likely to benefit IoT consumers. First, the express inclusion of goods with digital elements that must match the contract and the reasonable expectations of the consumers. These goods are defined as goods that incorporate digital content or service, with the latter being necessary for the good to function – this definition should cover most Things, since their 'smartness' is likely to be considered as their vital component. However, national lawmakers will have to make sure that Things that do not fall under this regime will be covered by the Digital Content Directive, which also includes the tangible medium of digital content or service, as long as it is the mere carrier of the intangible components. Second, since many IoT contracts have personal data, as opposed to a monetary price, as their consideration, it is commendable that the Digital Content Directive expressly covers the contracts where the consumer receives the content or service and provides personal data. Some shortcomings – such as the reference to the provision of data by the consumer, whilst in the IoT data, are inferred or obtained from other sources – can be fixed at the implementation stage. Finally, the revision of the conformity requirements is IoT-aware, in that interoperability, the provision of updates, and the absence

---

376 This extension to contracts beyond sales has been seen as giving 'rise to the chance to use the future *acquis communautaire* of the "digital internal market" to come closer to a more coherent general contract law, as Ole Lando and the earlier pioneers of European contract law strived to achieve, though on a different basis, before the digital revolution' (Schulze (n 217) 143).
377 Second Consumer Sales Directive, art 10.
378 Digital Content Directive, art 11(2).
379 Giliker (n 290) 111.

of restrictions stemming from third-party intellectual property rights have now become requirements under both the Second Consumer Sales Directive and the Digital Content Directive. Thus, the EU reform may provide incentives for a more open, secure, and trustworthy IoT.

Overall, it seems that, especially after the EU reform, consumer sales law, as complemented by digital content law, can provide an answer to private regulation 'by bricking.' IoT traders' attempts to remotely monitor consumers and automatically downgrade the Thing, discontinue the service, remove functionalities, determine the lifespan of the Thing, and 'brick' it may qualify as a lack of conformity, and therefore, consumers will be able to upgrade their Things and keep them smart by demanding that they match the contract and/or their reasonable expectations.

Despite the reform, consumer sales laws are of little use to track another major consumer threat, which is connected to the shift from e-commerce to IoT commerce. Consumer information becomes difficult when consumers make transactions while immersed in hyperconnected, interface-free environments. The next sections will assess whether other EU consumer laws may be invoked to protect consumers in the IoT commerce.

3.4 Precontractual Duties to Inform Under the CRD in a Hyperconnected, Interface-Free World

One of the main ways in which EU laws protect consumers is by introducing duties to communicate with consumers and inform them about rights, risks, and obligations stemming from a business-to-consumer transaction. This is epitomised by Directive 2011/83 ('CRD'),[380] as amended in 2020 by the Omnibus Directive, in the context of the 'New Deal for Consumers' package.[381] The CRD mandates the communication of certain information before the conclusion of a contract – precontractual information duties, also known as mandated disclosures and consumer notices.[382] Information is an enabler of consumer choice as it should put the consumer in the best position to make an informed transactional decision.

Whereas the IoT can benefit consumers by making the relevant communication more pertinent, engaging, and timely, it can also constitute a challenge to these information duties. On the one hand, the ubiquitous presence of Things means that traders have more opportunities to communicate with consumers. Amazon can inform me via its website's policy, the Alexa app's notification, and Echo's audio notices. By leveraging the granular information IoT traders hold about their customers, they can tailor their mandated disclosures and transmit the quantity

---

380 Directive 2011/83/EU of 25 October 2011 on consumer rights, amending Council Directive 93/13/EEC and Directive 1999/44/EC and repealing Council Directive 85/577/EEC and Directive 97/7/EC [2011] OJ L 304/64.

381 European Commission (n 11).

382 Christoph Busch, 'The Future of Pre-Contractual Information Duties: From Behavioural Insights to Big Data' in Christian Twigg-Flesner (ed), *Research Handbook on EU Consumer and Contract Law* (Elgar 2016) 221.

and quality of information that is more suitable for the consumer at hand, thus avoiding both insufficient disclosures and information overload.[383] For instance, Amazon knows that I am more active and attentive at a certain time (e.g. between 12:00 and 1:00 p.m.), that I respond better to communications in a certain format (e.g. video), and that being a relatively tech-savvy legal scholar, I need only a limited amount of information about my rights and obligations. Therefore, they can use IoT-powered big data to personalise their disclosures accordingly, as the trend of 'personalised law' suggests.[384]

On the other hand, the IoT renders compliance with information duties harder because it is ubiquitous, invisible, and often interface-free.[385] Things are increasingly used for e-commerce purposes, as exemplified by the purchases consumers can make through Amazon Echo and Google Home. This means that consumer contracts are concluded not only without any paper information but also without an accessible digital visual copy of the information. This is because, in the IoT, interfaces become smaller, change form, and even disappear.[386] With the advent of e-commerce, computer replaced physical shops. With the move to IoT commerce, there is a further shift because computers decrease in size and increase in numbers, to the point that consumers transact while immersed in a hyperconnected, always-, on interface-free environment. In this immersive, IoT-saturated environment, everything is connected and can potentially be used to conclude transactions, with little if any consumer awareness of whether a transaction is initiated, let alone the awareness of the associated rights, risks, and obligations. Therefore, this section will explore whether EU consumer laws' notice-and-consent approach is fit for a hyperconnected, interface-free world, where purchases are initiated by voice, buttons, and eye blinks. I will first briefly analyse the relevant legal framework and then present a German ruling about Amazon's Dash Button as a case study.

The CRD is arguably the most wide-ranging instrument of EU contract law, in that it applies to any contract concluded between a trader and a consumer after 13 June 2014.[387] This is unlike those directives that exclude some contracts based on the way they are concluded (online, offline, off-premises, etc.), namely, the Distance Selling Directive[388] and the Doorstep Selling Directive,[389] which were

---

383 Cf Christoph Busch, 'Implementing Personalized Law: Personalized Disclosures in Consumer Law and Data Privacy Law' (2019) 86 University of Chicago Law Review 309.

384 Ariel Porat and Lior Jacob Strahilevitz, 'Personalizing Default Rules and Disclosure with Big Data' (2014) 112 Michigan Law Review 1417.

385 Eliza Mik, 'The Disappearing Computer: Consent in the World of Smart Objects' [2020] REDC.

386 cf Mark Weiser, 'The Computer for the 21st Century' (1999) 3 SIGMOBILE Mobile Computing Communications Review 3.

387 CRD, art 28.

388 Directive 97/7/EC of 20 May 1997 on the protection of consumers in respect of distance contracts [1997] OJ L 144/19.

389 Council Directive 85/577/EEC of 20 December 1985 to protect the consumer in respect of contracts negotiated away from business premises [1985] OJ L 372/31.

repealed by the 2011 Directive. There are some contracts that are exempt,[390] e.g. transfer of immovable property, but such exemptions must be interpreted narrowly, as settled since *Heininger*.[391] This directive is IoT-friendly because it does not exclude some products based on their tangibility or lack thereof. Unlike the Product Liability Directive, the CRD applies expressly not only to goods but also to services[392] and implicitly to data and software. Indeed, it deals with digital content that is defined broadly as 'data which are produced and supplied in digital format.'[393] This may well include software, as corroborated by the fact that there is no right of withdrawal in respect of distance and off-premises contracts regarding 'sealed computer software which were unsealed after delivery.'[394] *A contrario*, other types of contracts and other types of software should be included in the scope of the directive. Therefore, as far as the scope is concerned, this directive appears to be IoT-ready.

The IoT-readiness will further increase once member states implement the Omnibus Directive; four changes point in this direction. First, this reform streamlined the definition of 'goods' under the CRD and the Second Consumer Sales Directive, namely, as meaning any tangible items, including goods with digital elements,[395] hence most Things. Second, the definition of sales contract has been amended, and it now reads, 'Any contract under which the trader transfers or undertakes to transfer ownership of goods to the consumer, including any contract having as its object both goods and services.'[396] The removal of the reference to the payment of price will make it easier to include those IoT transactions where products are purchased by means of one's personal data.[397] However, the amended CRD does not apply if personal data is provided exclusively to supply the digital content not on a tangible medium or the digital service in accordance with the directive itself or to comply with legal requirements.[398] The same critical remarks expressed above with regards to the analogous exclusions under the Second Consumer Sales Directive apply here. Third, the reformed CRD expressly includes digital services, which means (i) a service that allows the consumer to create, process, store or access data in digital form[399] or (ii) a

---

390 Certain contracts are excluded because they are regulated by sectoral laws e.g. financial services and gambling. See CRD, art 3(3).
391 Case C-481/99 *Heininger v Bayerische Hypo- und Vereinsbank AG* [2001] ECR I-9945 [31]; Case C-215/08 *Friz GmbH v von der Heyden* [2010] ECR I-2947 [32]; Case C-166/11 *González Alonso v Nationale Nederlanden Vida Cía de Seguros y Reaseguros SAE* [2012] 3 WLUK 11.
392 CRD, art 2(6).
393 CRD, art 2(11).
394 CRD, art 16(i).
395 CRD, art 2(3), as amended by the Omnibus Directive, art 4(1), refers to the definition of goods provided by the Second Consumer Sales Directive, art 2(5).
396 CRD, art 2(5) as amended by the Omnibus Directive, art 4.
397 However, as said with regards to consumer sales law, price can be interpreted as including non-monetary considerations.
398 CRD, art 3(1a), as inserted by the Omnibus Directive, art 4(2).
399 Digital Content Directive, art 2(2)(a) as referred to by the CRD, art 2(16), inserted by the Omnibus Directive, art 4(1).

service that allows the sharing of, or any other interaction with, data in digital form uploaded or created by the consumer or other users of that service.[400] Forth, member states now are obliged to implement effective remedies and fines of up to 4% of the annual turnover or EUR 2 million if the relevant information is not available.[401] This should provide stronger incentives for IoT traders to properly inform consumers.

The CRD aims to contribute to the proper functioning of the internal market by approximating certain aspects of the main EU consumer laws (maximum harmonisation)[402] while achieving a high level of consumer protection.[403] Information requirements – more stringent in distance and off-premises contracts,[404] less so in the others[405] – are the cornerstone of this instrument. When Things are used to conclude contracts, consumers are, in principle, entering into a distance contract, namely, a contract concluded 'under an organised distance sales or service-provision scheme without the simultaneous physical presence of the trader and the consumer, with the exclusive use of one or more means of distance communication.'[406] Therefore, the rules on distance contracts will be considered.

3.4.1 IoT Commerce and Information in Distance Contracts

The CRD provides the legal framework for precontractual information duties. *Precontractual* means that the information must be provided before the consumer is bound by the contract or any corresponding offer.[407] The usual transparency requirements are reiterated; the information must be provided in a clear and comprehensible manner.[408] In its notice-and-consent model, the required information is an 'integral part of the . . . contract and shall not be altered unless the contracting parties *expressly agree* otherwise.'[409] Should a dispute arise about compliance with these requirements, the burden of proof would be on the trader.[410] Limiting this section's analysis to the elements that are more likely to be relevant in the IoT, traders have to disclose the following information.

(i) The trader's identity and contact details.[411] This is important to successfully bring an action. Identifying the trader is less important when filing a

---

400 Digital Content Directive, art 2(2)(b) as referred to by the CRD, art 2(16), inserted by the Omnibus Directive, art 4(1).
401 CRD, art 24(1), (3), (4).
402 CRD, art 4.
403 CRD, art 1.
404 CRD, art 6.
405 CRD, art 5.
406 CRD, art 2(7).
407 CRD, art 6(1).
408 CRD, art 6(1).
409 CRD, art 6(5).
410 CRD, art 6(9).
411 CRD, art 6(1)(b)-(c).

complaint under product liability; indeed, as will be shown in the next chapter, the latter regime allows consumers to sue the supplier when the trader is not identified.

(ii) The good's or service's main characteristics.[412] For the aforementioned reasons, these have to be understood as including data and software.

(iii) The conditions that apply, including payment terms, delivery time, and performance,[413] as well as duration of the contract[414] and termination conditions.[415] These will typically be buried in long and obscure 'legals,' as seen in section 3.2.4.

(iv) The functionality of digital content, including applicable technical protection measures.[416] In an IoT context, this may prove difficult because of the Thing's complexity, which is an obstacle to explaining the underlying functionalities in layperson's terms.

(v) The interoperability of digital content with hardware and software. This will mean that the trader will have to underline if the Thing or system is open or 'proprietary' and hence closed. This is a strict requirement: it applies even when the trader is not aware of it but 'can reasonably be expected to have been aware.'[417] As noted above, interoperability is a subjective requirement for conformity under the Second Consumer Sales Directive. 'Subjective' means that IoT traders can use the contract to limit or even exclude interoperability. However, regardless of such a contract, the CRD obliges IoT traders to inform consumers about the Thing's interoperability or lack thereof.

In addition to the aforementioned elements, the trader will have to include in the disclosure twelve items, e.g. information about after-sale customer assistance, after-sale services, and commercial guarantees.[418] It is safe to say, therefore, that the notice to provide to consumers, especially IoT ones, is likely to be extremely long and complicated. Consequently, the way that the communication of this information is designed becomes crucial.

Under the CRD, the trader, before concluding a distance contract, has to '*give* the (required) information . . . or *make that information available* to the consumer in a way *appropriate to the means of distance* communication used in *plain and intelligible* language.'[419] 'Giving' the information refers to the more traditional forms of consumer notice, such as the paper leaflet contained in a product's packaging. There is also a legibility requirement for the information that is provided on a durable medium.[420] The references to 'legibility' is unfortunate because it

---

412 CRD, art 6(1)(a).
413 CRD, art 6(1)(g).
414 CRD, art 6(1)(o).
415 CRD, art 6(1)(h).
416 CRD, art 6(1)(r).
417 CRD, art 6(1)(s).
418 CRD, art 6(1)(m).
419 CRD, art 8(1), italics added.
420 CRD, art 8(1).

reflects a text-based paradigm that is not fit for the IoT and, more generally, for more modern consumer disclosures. This should be replaced by a comprehensibility requirement that can be derived from the principle of transparency, as noted by the advocate general in *Cofidis*.[421] However, 'legibility' is not required when the information is not *given* to the consumer, but it is *made available* to them, typically online ('appropriate to the means of distance communication'). In principle, the legals accessed on the Thing's website could comply with requirement as long as they are in plain and intelligible language. We have seen above that these 'legals' are hard to find, read, and understand.

In light of the currently poor contractual drafting practices, the importance of information and transparency for data protection, and the amount and quality of information that must be communicated to consumers, especially in an IoT context, it becomes imperative to rethink consumer information. One promising way to do so is to adopt a legal design methodology. Legal design is a nascent field of study focused on redesigning legal practices (e.g. contracts, policies, notices, etc.) in a way that is user-centric and multidisciplinary.[422] The key is to start by understanding who is the user, their expectations, their needs, their preferences. This may lead to the overcoming of traditional notices and to embrace more visual[423] and engaging means of consumer communications, such as videos, dashboards, story-based disclosures, smart disclosures, selective just-in-time alerts, and visual diagrams.[424] An Echo Show e.g. may inform consumers about the functionalities of its own digital content by showing a video rather than simply making available the Conditions of Use on Amazon's website. Given the rise of voice-user interfaces in the IoT,[425] one could witness a rise of the audio-notice-and-consent model. As consumers interact with Echo, Google Home, etc. using their voice, consumer notices should reflect this and be provided through audio messages. A lesson could be learned by the GDPR and its requirement that it must be as easy to withdraw consent as it is to give it.[426] The European Data Protection Board interpreted it as meaning that when 'consent is obtained through use of a *service-specific user interface*

---

421 Joint Cases C-616/18 and C-679/18 *Codifis v YU* (Advocate General Kokott, 14 November 2019) [54].

422 The pioneer of legal design is Margaret Hagan, Director of Stanford's Legal Design Lab. She has been followed by a number of outstanding women, in particular Rossana Ducato, Helena Haapio, Arianna Rossi, and Stefania Passera. See e.g. Margaret Hagan, 'Law By Design' (*Law By Design*, 2017) <www.lawbydesign.co/>.

423 Nonetheless, visualisation 'is almost always used in hybrid ways – combinations of words and images to enhance the effectiveness of communication' (Gerlinde Berger-Walliser, Thomas D Barton and Helena Haapio, 'From Visualization to Legal Design: A Collaborative and Creative Process' (2017) 54 American Business Law Journal 347).

424 cf Rossana Ducato, 'House of Terms: Fixing the Information Paradigm with Legal Design' (2018) *Conference: BILETA 2018.*

425 See e.g. patent US9811312B2 for a 'Connected device voice command support.' More generally, Pradeep Doss and others, 'Unified Voice Assistant and IoT Interface' (2018) 19061 International Journal of Engineering Science.

426 GDPR, art 7(3).

Figure 3.4 An illustration of the principle of interface continuity: a legal design approach to compliance with consumer information requirements using Amazon Echo Plus's voice-user interface.

(e.g. via . . . the interface of an IoT device . . .), there is no doubt a data subject must be able to withdraw consent via the *same electronic interface.*'[427] A similar meaning should be given to the CRD's requirement that, with respect to distance contracts, the trader has to inform the consumer 'in a way appropriate to the means of distance communication.'[428] I posit that these provisions signal the emergence of a more general principle: the principle of interface continuity. If I use the voice to give consent and interact with my Thing, it is reasonable to expect that the same interface will be used to transmit further information, as mandated by consumer and privacy laws. For an example of such an approach to consumer notices, see Figure 3.4, which follows.

Generally, consumer information has to be in plain and intelligible language; legibility is optional.[429] However, additional requirements apply in certain scenarios, as illustrated in the table that follows.

---

427 European Data Protection Board, 'Guidelines 05/2020 on Consent under Regulation 2016/679' (2020) v 1.1 24.
428 CRD, art 8(1).
429 CRD, art 8(1).

Table 3.1 Additional Formal Requirements for Distance Contracts Under the CRD

Scenario	Formal Requirements	Items of Information
Contracts with an obligation to pay (art 8(2))	Clear, prominent, directly before the consumer places the order	Main characteristics of the product, total price, duration[430]
Orders placed via buttons (art 8(2))	Easily legible label with the words 'order with obligation to pay' or similar	Obligation to pay
Trading websites (art 8(3))	Clear, legible, at the beginning of the ordering process	Delivery restrictions and accepted means of payment
Means of distance communication which allows limited space or time to display the information (art 8(4))	On that particular means and prior to the conclusion	Main characteristics of the product, trader's identity, total price, withdrawal, duration[431]

Certain information should be given or made available directly before the order, in a clear and prominent manner, if there is an obligation to pay. The main items to cover are the total price and, where the nature of the product is such that the price cannot reasonably be calculated in advance, the manner in which the price is to be calculated.[432] Prominence has been traditionally interpreted as meaning that the relevant contractual clause should be in capital letters, but the concept is broader than that.[433]

The meaning of 'prominence' has been further detailed for those instances where consumers place orders by activating a button or a similar function. This applies not only to buttons such as Amazon's Dash Button (both in its software and hardware versions) but also to all the Things used for e-commerce purposes. In these cases, 'the button or similar function shall be labelled in an easily legible manner only with the words "order with obligation to pay" or a corresponding unambiguous formulation.'[434] As noted by the European Commission,[435] words and phrases such as 'register,' 'confirm,' 'order now,' and unnecessarily long phrases are unlikely to meet the requirement. Whilst this is a positive legal innovation, the reference to a legibility requirement is likely to exclude voice-user interfaces, video consumer notices, and other unwritten means of communication[436] that would be more suitable for the IoT.

---

430 CRD, art 6(1)(a), (e), (o), (p).
431 CRD, art 6(1)(a), (b), (e), (h).
432 CRD, art 8(2).
433 cf Debra Kay Thomas Graves, 'The Consumer Protection Myth in Long-Distance Telephone Regulation: Remedies for the Caveat Dialer Attitude' (1996) 27 Texas Tech Law Review 383.
434 CRD, art 8(2).
435 DG JUSTICE, *Guidance Document Concerning Directive 2011/83/EU* (European Commission 2014) 32 <https://ec.europa.eu/info/sites/info/files/crd_guidance_en_0.pdf>.
436 Karin Sein, 'Concluding Consumer Contracts via Smart Assistants: Mission Impossible Under European Consumer Law?' (2018) 7 Journal of European Consumer and Market Law 179.

As shown in the table above, prominence is not a requirement for the information that trading websites have to provide at the beginning of the ordering process; this information must only be clear and legible. Trading websites are interactive websites that allow 'consumers to transfer an offer to the professional.'[437] These websites have to inform consumers about delivery restrictions and accepted means of payment.[438] *Legible* means that the relevant information must be provided in the form of a written text, which, again, may be interpreted as ruling out more engaging forms of consumer communication, such as audio notices and videos. And indeed this directive has been read[439] as preventing the conclusion of consumer contracts via smart assistants in that it is based on the premise that distance contracts are concluded by means that ensure the legibility of the information. This is an example of a provision that is not IoT-ready. In an age where interfaces are changing and at times disappearing, to adopt a text-based paradigm risks disenfranchising consumers that engage with their Things with their voice, movement, etc. but are expected to rely on traditional, written text to be informed. The other issue of this provision is that this legibility requirement is imposed on 'trading websites,' which might be interpreted as excluding the more complex platforms of the IoT commerce. Accordingly, *de lege ferenda* it has been suggested that the provision be amended to make it more technologically neutral and to remove the legibility requirement.[440] Meanwhile, as I argued above, it is possible to interpret the law as imposing interface continuity, that is, the requirement to use the same interface for normal Thing-user interaction and for the notices mandated by the law. Therefore, the Echo products that do not have a display and work with a voice-user interface should inform the consumers using Alexa's voice in plain and intelligible language.

Conversely, the EU lawmaker showed some awareness of the fact that many Things have small interfaces (mainly displays). In particular, when a contract is concluded through a means of distance communication which allows for limited space or time to display the information (i.e. most Things), the trader has to show only some of the required information 'on or through' that means before the transaction is completed.[441] In particular, the information to display on or through the Thing regards the main characteristics of the product, the identity of the trader, the price, the right of withdrawal, the duration of the contract, and if the contract is of indeterminate duration, the conditions for terminating it.[442] The rest of the precontractual information could be made available via hyperlink.[443] This provision was thought primarily for contracts concluded using technologies such as SMS which impose technical limits on the amount of information that can

---

437 Peter Kindler, 'The Law Applicable to Consumer Contracts in the Digital Single Market' in Alberto De Franceschi (ed), *European Contract Law and the Digital Single Market: The Implications of the Digital Revolution* (Intersentia 2016) 179.

438 CRD, art 8(3). This should be read in light of recitals 38 and 39.

439 Sein (n 435).

440 ibid.

441 CRD, art 8(4).

442 CRD, art 8(4).

443 CRD, recital 36.

be sent.[444] Nonetheless, the provision appears to be IoT-ready, and it can apply to all the Things that have small interfaces. It is not clear what happens if the means of distance communication does not allow any space to display the information. The European Commission considers the requirements in Article 8(2)-(4) as 'additional.'[445] Therefore, it seems reasonable to argue that for Things without displays, the general regime will apply, and therefore, the information will have to be provided or made available in plain and intelligible language.

3.4.2 Amazon Dash Button as a Fitness Check of Precontractual Information Duties

To have a better idea of whether the CRD and its precontractual information duties are fit for the IoT, this section will use Amazon's Dash Button as a case study. Indeed, this Thing was at the centre of the most relevant dispute in the field of precontractual information and the IoT, which was settled in 2018 by *Landgericht München* (Regional Court of Munich)[446] and upheld on appeal by the *Oberlandesgericht* (Higher Regional Court).[447]

For some time, a fridge that would order milk was the go-to example of consumer IoT.[448] When Amazon launched the Dash Button, it seemed that, by allowing potentially any product to order automatically new supplies, the IoT revolution was eventually coming to its realisation and would change forever the world of retail.[449] The consumer would set up the button through a mobile app, simply place the button on the washing machine (or similar product), and click it every time the, say, laundry detergent was running low. The button is a device that can connect to a user's WLAN and send signals to the wireless router via the WLAN connection. The sending of a signal is triggered by pressing an electromechanical button – this no longer applies to the 'virtual' Dash Buttons that are entirely intangible and have been replacing their hardware predecessors since February 2019.[450] Made available to consumers for free,[451] Dash Buttons were one of Amazon's fast-growing products in 2017.[452] By making the purchase carefree, the button was seen as 'the epitome of instant, impulsive buying,'[453] which may benefit

---

444 DG JUSTICE (n 434).
445 ibid [5.2].
446 LG München I, 1 March 2018–12 O 730/17 [2019] MMR 125.
447 OLG München, 10 January 2019–29 U 1091/18 [2019] GRUR-RR 372.
448 Alan Grau, 'Can You Trust Your Fridge?' (2015) 52 IEEE Spectrum 50.
449 Roger Aitken, 'Will Amazon's Internet of Things Device "Dash" UK Supermarket Fortunes?' *Forbes* (1 September 2016) <www.forbes.com/sites/rogeraitken/2016/09/01/will-amazons-internet-of-things-device-dash-uk-supermarket-fortunes/>.
450 See 'Instantly Reorder Your Favorite Products' (*Amazon.com*) <www.amazon.com/b?ie=UTF8& node=17729534011>.
451 Consumers would buy it for 4.99.
452 Leena Rao, 'Two Years After Launching, Amazon Dash Shows Promise' (*Fortune*, 25 April 2017) <https://fortune.com/2017/04/25/amazon-dash-button-growth/>.
453 Christoph Busch, 'Does the Amazon Dash Button Violate EU Consumer Law? Balancing Consumer Protection and Technological Innovation in the Internet of Things' (2018) 7 Journal of European Consumer and Market Law 78, 78.

Figure 3.5 Front and back of a Dash Button at the time of the dispute at hand. Source: OLG München, 10 January 2019–29 U 1091/18 [2019] GRUR-RR 372.

consumers in terms of time spent shopping, but at the same time, it may adversely affect them in terms of information and freedom of choice. Indeed, Dash Button was criticised[454] for introducing a form of 'brand loyalty by default' as it reduced switching behaviour. Whilst information overload has often been criticised as a consequence of paternalistic consumer regulation,[455] the opposite of information overload – that one may call 'information dearth' – risks being a real problem for consumers who are parties to IoT transactions.

At the time of the dispute, the Dash Button was labelled on the front with the logo of the manufacturer of the product to reorder, and on the back with the so-called CE safety mark and other technical details, as per Figure 3.5.

No other information could be found on the button or was otherwise provided through it. This made the Consumer Association of North Rhine-Westphalia (hereinafter NRW or the claimant) seek a prohibitory injunction[456] to prevent Amazon from selling Things that, by design and by default, did not provide the required precontractual information. In particular, the button was not labelled with the words 'order with obligation to pay' and did not inform the consumer, before the purchase, about the essential characteristics of the product and its total price. For the purposes of this section, it is not necessary to deal with the other ground of the injunction's request, namely, the alleged invalidity of the contractual clause whereby Amazon would reserve the right to change the price or deliver a different product.[457]

As is often the case with cyberdisputes – and this holds true also for the IoT – the preliminary point was jurisdiction. The Regional Court of Munich resolved the question by relying on the Brussels I Regulation on jurisdiction and the recognition

---

454 Busch, 'Does the Amazon Dash Button Violate EU Consumer Law? Balancing Consumer Protection and Technological Innovation in the Internet of Things' (n 452).

455 cf Cass R Sunstein, *Choosing Not to Choose: Understanding the Value of Choice* (OUP 2015).

456 This is 'an order with all due expediency, where appropriate by way of summary procedure, requiring the . . . prohibition of any infringement' (Directive 2009/22/EC of 23 April 2009 on injunctions for the protection of consumers' interests (Codified version) [2009] OJ L 110/30, art 2(1)(a)).

457 The button's terms whereby Amazon reserved the right to change the price or deliver a different item was found in violation of the principle of transparency under the Unfair Terms Directive, arts 4(2) and 5.

and enforcement of judgements in civil and commercial matters,[458] as well as on the principle of flying jurisdiction. The general principle is that persons domiciled in a member state shall be sued in the courts of that member state.[459] However, an entity domiciled in a member state (e.g. Amazon in Luxembourg) may be sued in another member state (e.g. Germany) in matters relating to tort, delict, or quasidelict if that is 'the place where the harmful event occurred or may occur.'[460] The Regional Court of Munich held that this provision applied because the preventive action by a consumer protection association to prohibit the use of allegedly abusive clauses by a trader regarded an unlawful act.[461] This is consistent with the *Henkel*[462] jurisprudence, whereby a preventive action brought by a consumer protection organisation for the purpose of preventing a trader from using unfair terms is a matter relating to tort, delict, or quasidelict. Like in *Henkel*, the effectiveness of class actions to stop the use of abusive clauses in consumer contracts would be significantly impaired if they could only be brought in the state of the trader's establishment. The Regional Court of Munich's conclusion is corroborated by the Rome II Regulation on the law applicable to noncontractual obligations.[463] In particular, by the provision whereby '[t]he law applicable to a non-contractual obligation arising out of an act of unfair competition shall be the law of the country where competitive relations or the collective interests of consumers are, or are likely to be, affected.'[464] From this intricate framework, as interpreted by Germany's Supreme Court,[465] follows the principle of 'flying jurisdiction,' whereby all German courts and thus also the Regional Court of Munich have jurisdiction in these types of disputes.[466]

After having asserted the jurisdiction, the court focused on the fact that the button was not labelled with the words 'order with obligation to pay.' As noted above, the CRD appears IoT-ready where it explicitly regulates button-enabled purchases by mandating forms of labelling that make explicit the obligation to pay that will accompany the transaction. The defendant disputed that purchases via the Dash Button can be regarded as 'placing an order that entails activating a button or a similar function.'[467] Amazon claimed that the provision would apply only to virtual buttons; otherwise, one should start labelling also a computer's mouse. The argument was not upheld. Indeed, although the provision was designed having website

---

458 Regulation (EU) No 1215/2012 of 12 December 2012 on jurisdiction and the recognition and enforcement of judgements in civil and commercial matters ('Brussels I Regulation') [2012] OJ L 351/1.
459 Brussels I Regulation, art 4.
460 Brussels I Regulation, art 7(2).
461 LG München I, 1 March 2018–12 O 730/17 [81].
462 Case C-167/00 *Verein für Konsumenteninformation v Karl Heinz Henkel* [2002] ECR I-8111.
463 Regulation (EC) No 864/2007 of 11 July 2007 on the law applicable to noncontractual obligations ('Rome II Regulation') [2007] OJ L 199/40.
464 Rome II Regulation, art 6(1).
465 BGH, Urteil vom 09.07.2009, Az. Xa ZR 19/08.
466 LG München I, 1 March 2018–12 O 730/17 [91].
467 CRD, art 8(2). In Germany, this was implemented by the German Civil Code (BGB, § 312 j(3), second sentence).

buttons in mind,[468] it was formulated in a technologically neutral way to ensure its longevity.[469] The provision applies to any mechanism that triggers a purchasing order.[470] Once again, the IoT confirms the untenability of the tangible-intangible dichotomy and calls for unified rules. Accordingly, the provision on labelling buttons applies both to virtual buttons (like the new generation of Dash Buttons) and tangible ones, like the one at issue. It follows that the button must carry an 'order with obligation to pay' label or a corresponding unambiguous formulation. The remedy for noncompliance with this requirement is that the consumer will not be bound by the contract resulting from pushing the unlabelled button.[471] The fact that the Dash Button's label contained only the logo of the manufacturer and some technical details (CE marking) did not meet the legal requirement. In passing, the court also noted that Dash Button's design would be in breach of the precontractual information duties even in the event that it was not considered a 'button' for the purposes of the CRD. This is because the button-labelling duties are to be seen as a specification of the general rule that the consumer must explicitly confirm before the order that they undertake to effect a payment.[472]

The Regional Court of Munich then moved on to consider whether there was a breach of the precontractual information duties, as the Dash Button did not timely inform the consumer about the essential characteristics of the product to be reordered and its overall price. This was held to be in breach of the trader's duty to inform the consumer about the main characteristics of the goods or services and the price in a clear and prominent manner and before the consumer places the order.[473] Indeed, the key information in a transaction not only has to be communicated clearly (in an 'unambiguous and comprehensible manner,' in the wording of the German Civil Code),[474] but this information must also be provided directly before the consumer submits the order. Therefore, to provide the information through Terms of Service at the moment of setting up the button is not enough.[475] In the IoT, this means that traders cannot rely on the contractual quagmire to inform consumers. The information must accompany the contract with which one purchases a product using the button, not the contract laying out the general conditions of use of the button (or Thing more generally). Whilst the literal meaning of the provision imposes a temporal vicinity between the information and the order,[476] the court took a purposive approach to its interpretation. Indeed, the information must be provided in close connection to the order also

---

468 See the Explanatory Memorandum accompanying the Law on Hidden Costs in e-Commerce BT-Drs. 17/7745, 12.

469 LG München I, 1 March 2018–12 O 730/17 [146].

470 ibid [148].

471 CRD, art 8(2).

472 First sentence of BGB, § 312 j(3), equivalent to the first sentence of CRD, art 8(2).

473 CRD, art 8(2), to be read jointly with art 6(1)(a),(e). See, for the national implementation measure, BGB, § 312 j(2) and Introductory Act to the Civil Code, § 246a(1) nn. 1 and 4.

474 BGB, § 312 j(2).

475 LG München I, 1 March 2018–12 O 730/17 [161].

476 The terms 'directly before' in Article 8(2) should cover, firstly, the temporal aspect and should be construed as meaning 'immediately before,' according to DG JUSTICE (n 434). This study

from a functional and spatial sense (*'Zusammenhang'*).[477] Practically, this means that the necessary information must be displayed on the button or, if not viable, in its immediate vicinity. The Dash Button did not display this information in the vicinity of both the order and the button itself. Amazon argued that consumers are informed of the order via a separate app that they may download on their phones, which would send them push notifications. However, this was not considered as a satisfactory way to comply with the vicinity requirement, for a twofold reason: the information is provided after the order, and one can place orders without having or using a phone. This has broader relevance as it means that all Things that are used for e-commerce purposes must provide the required information in close temporal, functional, and spatial vicinity to the order and to the Thing itself. Therefore, if one orders something using one's Amazon Echo, it is not enough that they are shown the necessary information on the Alexa app or on Amazon's website. Augmented reality, computer vision, and holograms are just some of the approaches that could be used to display the required information when it is not viable to display the information on the Thing itself.

For the aforementioned reasons, and for others that have less relevance from this book's perspective,[478] the Regional Court of Munich granted the consumer association an injunction prohibiting Amazon to sell Dash Buttons in Germany.[479] In January 2019, this decision was upheld by the *Oberlandesgericht München*, which reiterated the aforementioned arguments.[480] The main ground of appeal was that the CRD does not apply to the contracts concluded via the Dash Button because they fall under one of the directive's exclusions, namely, 'for the supply of foodstuffs, beverages or other goods intended for current consumption in the household, and which are physically supplied by a trader on frequent and regular rounds to the consumer's home, residence or workplace.'[481] However, the court held that in many scenarios, the button's orders will fall outside the scope of this exclusion because the trader relies on third-party delivery – and therefore the products are not physically supplied by the trader. In turn, when the contracts fall within its scope, national laws are not bound by the directive and cannot be impugned for alleged contrast to them.[482] As to the use of the terms of service as a means to communicate the mandated information, the court of appeals reiterated

---

recognises that the terms 'prominent manner' and 'close vicinity' (CRD, recital 39) suggest stronger requirements on presenting information compared to the general requirements.

477 ibid [148]. The court of appeals does not refer to *Zusammenhang*; it refers to *Unmittelbarkeit* or proximity (as in absence of obstacles); OLG München, 10 January 2019–29 U 1091/18 [75]

478 For the other reasons, see Busch, 'Does the Amazon Dash Button Violate EU Consumer Law? Balancing Consumer Protection and Technological Innovation in the Internet of Things' (n 452).

479 Consumer Injunctions Law (*Gesetz über Unterlassungsklagen bei Verbraucherrechts- und anderen Verstößen* or UKlaG), § 2(1)(1).

480 OLG München, 10 January 2019–29 U 1091/18.

481 CRD, art 3(3)(j).

482 Amazon had claimed that the German implementing provisions were in breach of the CRD because the latter is a full harmonisation instrument. The court referred to the *Vanderborght* jurisprudence, whereby national regulations on matters that are not covered by a fully harmonising directive are not called into question for their violation (Case C-339/15 *Criminal proceedings against Luc Vanderborght* [2017] GRUR 627).

the reasoning of the regional court and noted that it cannot 'be assumed that the consumer will remember the details of the goods when ordering – some time after setting up the button – especially since he uses several dash buttons for different products.'[483] This is of great importance in an IoT context. Indeed, since we are increasingly surrounded by several Things, with augmented ease of purchase, it becomes vital that traders not rely on the 'legals' and, instead, inform consumers in close temporal, functional, and spatial vicinity to the order.

The CRD, despite being only ten years old, mostly reflects a world in which information was provided in a written form (the leaflet inside the product's box, the 'legals' available on the trader's website, etc.). This is exemplified by the legibility requirement that applies when buttons are used to place orders and when the transaction is mediated by a trading website. However, the general rule is that the information needs to be provided in a clear and intelligible manner, which means not necessarily in a written form. Arguably, in an IoT world where there is a rise of audio-user and video-user interfaces, consumers should be given information in the same format as the one that is usually utilised to interact with the Thing (namely, audio or video). The directive's provisions are often forward-looking and IoT-friendly. This is exemplified by the provision whereby when a contract is concluded through a distance communication means which allows limited space or time to display the information (arguably, most Things, due to their small interfaces), the trader has to show only some of the required information on the display before the transaction is completed. This is also shown by the ad hoc provision about buttons, correctly interpreted as encompassing both virtual buttons and mechanical ones, thus confirming that the tangible-intangible divide is fading away. It seems to be that EU consumer laws are not in need of a radical overhaul to become fit for a world of IoT commerce, where consumers live immersed in a hyperconnected environment and transactions are concluded with the wink of an eye.[484] De lege ferenda, lawmakers should amend the CRD by (i) introducing special provisions for when transactions are concluded through interface-free Things, (ii) eliminating the legibility requirements, and (iii) embracing the principle of interface continuity. The ideal way to proceed is to amend the directive, but this will take a long time. In the meantime, the latter is flexible enough to allow the courts to keep the enforcement of the directive up to date and relevant; this may be done, like in *Codifis*, by looking at transparency as comprehensibility, as opposed to mere legibility.

3.5 Interim Conclusion

This chapter focused on three consumer issues in the IoT and critically assessed if they can be tackled invoking three EU laws that deal with power imbalances in business-to-consumer contracts.

First, it critically assessed if the Unfair Terms Directive is fit for the contractual quagmire. The unfairness 'of form' and 'of substance' of Amazon Echo's terms

---

483 OLG München, 10 January 2019–29 U 1091/18 [74].
484 cf Busch, 'Does the Amazon Dash Button Violate EU Consumer Law? Balancing Consumer Protection and Technological Innovation in the Internet of Things' (n 452).

has been analysed, and the conclusion is that they fall under both types of unfairness and that the IoT contributes to overcoming the form-substance dichotomy. Fairness demands better contractual design and more transparent transactions. IoT traders, in light of the complexity of the IoT and of the imbalances in terms of power and information, must comply with more stringer requirements of fairness, with a particularly urgent need to rethink the IoT legals to make them easy to find, read, and understand. De lege ferenda, EU regulators should, for once, learn from the US counterparts and introduce obligations to draft 'legals' that reach at least a Flesch-Kincaid readability score that reflects the literacy and cognitive resources of the average IoT user (e.g. 70, making the text readable to a 13-year-old). Policymakers wanting IoT traders to adopt fairer practices should be aware of the IoT's hierarchy of incentives, whereby traders are more likely to respond to public pressure (e.g. a public inquiry), less likely to respond to financial incentives (e.g. the subscription cost), and unlikely to protect consumers who 'pay' with their personal data. Any inquiry into IoT traders' contractual practices should also take account of the contractual quagmire; therefore, for instance, having traders changing their cloud contracts (like the Competition and Markets Authority did) without considering that they are only one element of an intricate web of legals constitutes an inadequate solution to the problem.

Second, the chapter explored the possibility of relying on consumer sales laws to counter the IoT traders' private ordering by bricking. It has been proposed that the First Consumer Sales Directive's right to repair can be interpreted as a right to have the Thing's smartness restored. The main limitation of this regime is that traders are liable 'for any lack of conformity which exists *at the time the goods were delivered.*'[485] Arguably, if a trader bricks the Thing after the delivery, that lack of conformity did not exist when the Thing was delivered. It has been suggested that 'delivery' be construed broadly. Indeed, since in the IoT the good's key components are intangible, and given that the intangible components are delivered throughout the Thing's life cycle, any deprivation of smartness will, by definition, take place at the time of delivery. This approach has been adopted by the Second Consumer Sales Directive. As of 1 January 2022, consumers will be able to rely on the fact that, where the contract provides for a continuous supply of a Thing's digital elements, the seller shall be liable for any lack of conformity of the digital content or digital service that occurs or becomes apparent within the period of time during the time of supply. Prima facie, this reform, which will see the First Consumer Sales Directive replaced and paired with a directive on the supply of digital content and digital services, is IoT-friendly. This can be seen in the express regulation of goods with digital elements, whose definition broadly coincides with the definition of a Thing. An ad hoc rule is that goods with digital elements must be kept updated. This may be used to counter one of the practices in the private-ordering-by-bricking spectrum, namely, planned obsolescence. The main issue with the reform is that there is the risk that certain Things will fall in

---

485 First Consumer Sales Directive, art 3(1), emphasis added.

a regulatory vacuum. If the digital element is necessary for the good to function, the Second Consumer Sales Directive will apply. If the tangible aspect is the mere carrier of the digital element, the Digital Content Directive will. National lawmakers, in implementing the reform, must make sure to regulate the grey area between the two.

Third, this chapter looked at IoT commerce and in particular at the challenges that an interface-free, hyperconnected environment poses to precontractual duties of information. It has been suggested that the general rule to inform consumers in a clear and intelligible manner should be interpreted in creative ways that go beyond the traditional terms of service available on the trader's website. In an IoT world where there is a rise of voice-user and video-user interfaces, consumers should be given information in the same format as the one that is usually utilised to interact with the Thing (namely, audio or video). This principle of interface continuity is emerging from both consumer contracts laws and data protection laws. However, its full implementation is hindered by the legibility requirement that the CRD set forth for some online transactions. This requirement clearly refers to a written paradigm and should be abandoned to future-proof the directive. Positively, there are special rules that apply to distance communication means that have some limitations, e.g. small displays, though they do not tackle the issue of the absence of a display or other traditional interface. It is recommended to introduce special provisions for when transactions are concluded through interface-free Things.

The regulation of the information that must be communicated in business-to-consumer contracts is at the very core of consumer contract laws.[486] However, building on insights from behavioural economics, scholars have increasingly underlined how the focus on information is often of limited value.[487] There is little recourse against information overload, whilst information omissions are prohibited.[488] Such a single-minded focus on the necessity to increase information is partly overcome by the rise of fairness in EU consumer laws,[489] as seen in particular in some laws that protect consumers regardless of a contractual relationship. This will be the focus of the next chapter.

---

486 Alongside the CRD, the Package Travel Directive, the Directive 2008/122/EC of 14 January 2009 on the protection of consumers in respect of certain aspects of timeshare, long-term holiday product, resale, and exchange contracts ('Timeshare Directive') [2009] OJ L 33/10, and the Directive 2008/48/EC of 23 April 2008 on credit agreements for consumers and repealing Council Directive 87/102/EEC ('Consumer Credit Directive') [2008] OJ L 133/66 all provide precontractual information duties. See Geraint Howells, Christian Twigg-Flesner and Thomas Wilhelmsson, *Rethinking EU Consumer Law* (Routledge 2017).

487 Geneviève Helleringer and Anne-Lise Sibony, 'European Consumer Protection through the Behavioral Lens' (2016) 23 Columbia Journal of European Law 607.

488 Unfair Commercial Practices Directive, art 7, referring to misleading omissions.

489 On the different meaning os 'fairness' in EU law, see Gianclaudio Malgieri, 'The Concept of Fairness in the GDPR: A Linguistic and Contextual Interpretation' *Proceedings of the 2020 Conference on Fairness, Accountability, and Transparency* (FAT 2020).

4 The Internet of Vulnerabilities

Tackling Human and Product Vulnerabilities through Noncontractual Consumer Laws

> *The less you eat, drink and buy books; the less you go to the theatre, the dance hall, the public house; the less you think, love, theorize, sing, paint, fence, etc., the more you save – the greater becomes your treasure which neither moths nor rust will devour – your capital.*
>
> K. Marx, *Economic and Philosophic Manuscripts of 1844*

4.1 Introduction

Although drafted in a pre-IoT world, the consumer laws analysed in the previous chapter can play a tactical role in empowering consumers who are negatively affected by issues such as the contractual quagmire, private ordering by bricking, and IoT commerce. Their main limitation, however, is that they are contract laws and therefore are of little help when (i) there is no contract (or no sales contract, if the issue is a faulty product), (ii) the contractual party cannot be identified, or (iii) the power imbalance manifests itself outside the contract. Therefore, this chapter will consider two consumer laws that look beyond the contract, namely, the Product Liability Directive and the Unfair Commercial Practices Directive.

The IoT-readiness of these laws will be tested by critically assessing whether they can be used to tackle the vulnerability of Things and of humans. First, I will focus on the Things that are vulnerable inasmuch as they are defective. Current legal regimes struggle to cope with new defects (e.g. software updates, inaccurate sensors, etc.) and vulnerabilities (e.g. the limitations stemming from software instructions and training datasets that affect the capacity to predict human behaviour in real-world scenarios). Second, I will deal with the vulnerability of IoT users through the lens of the so-called Internet of Personalised Things. In April 2021, the European Commission presented a proposal for an AI regulation (so-called AI Act) which prohibits the use of subliminal techniques to materially distort behaviours and likely cause harm.[1] The threat goes beyond AI, however. Things allow traders to personalise products, services, prices, and 'legals.' Situational data and granular knowledge of biases and human vulnerabilities allow

---

1 Proposed AI Act, art 5(1)(a).

DOI: 10.4324/9780429468377-5

these traders to manipulate consumers and even discriminate against them, thus hindering their trust. In Amazon's commitment – 'We seek to be Earth's most customer-centric company,'[2] – it is possible to find at once one of the key benefits and dangers of the IoT: personalisation.

One may think it accidental that Things and humans share vulnerability as a common trait. I would opine that this is no accident. Indeed, capitalism produces a double, convergent movement: the objectification of the subject and the subjectivation of the object.[3] Under capitalism, the commodity compensates for the lack of being of the subject and, at the same time, attributes a subjectivity to the objects. The production of vulnerable Things – programmed to be consumed as quickly as possible – and of vulnerable humans – prone to all sorts of manipulations – is one of the ways that the IoT realises the capitalistic enterprise. With this in mind, this chapter will answer the following subquestion: *can the laws on noncontractual business-to-consumer relationships tackle techno-human vulnerability?*

4.2 What's in a Product? EU Product Liability Laws and the Challenge of a Defective IoT

The analysis of Echo's legals confirmed the findings of previous research showing that a new legal conception of a 'product' may be required in the context of the IoT. As products become increasingly smart, they can no longer be reduced to their hardware   dimension: they have to be rethought as an amalgam of hardware, software, service, and data.[4] Even though the Conditions of Use regulate 'Amazon Services,' these are defined to include Amazon devices, products, services, apps, and software.[5] Similarly, Amazon Device Terms, despite having tangible products as their core subject, cover also digital content, services, and software.[6] In turn, the Alexa Terms deal mainly with the virtual assistant as encompassing services, digital content, and software but regards also Alexa-enabled products, meaning 'any *product or application* that enables access to Alexa, such as Amazon Echo devices and the Alexa App.'[7] What happens if an Echo consumer is in breach of Alexa Terms and, consequently, can no longer use the virtual assistant?[8] The end customer's ability to use the hardware's functions

---

2 Amazon.com, Inc., 'US Securities and Exchange Commission, Form 10-K No 000–22513 2020' 42 <www.sec.gov/ix?doc=/Archives/edgar/data/1018724/000101872420000004/amzn-20191231x 10k.htm>.

3 Federico Chicchi, 'Phantasmagoria of the Thing: Aporias of the New Capitalist Discourse' (2016) 9 Política Común.

4 Guido Noto La Diega and Ian Walden, 'Contracting for the "Internet of Things": Looking into the Nest' (2016) 7 European Journal of Law and Technology <http://ejlt.org/article/view/450>.

5 Conditions of Use & Sale, preamble.

6 Amazon Device Terms of Use, preamble.

7 Alexa Terms of Use, preamble.

8 'If you do not accept the terms of this Agreement, then you may not use Alexa' (Alexa Terms of Use, preamble).

will be profoundly affected. Despite attempts through the 'legals' to distinguish the different elements of the Thing (hardware, software, etc.), this fragmentation has become untenable. This convergence has implications for the applicability of EU product liability law.

Product liability is focused on the compensation for damage caused by defective products to the consumer or their property. Fitness for use is the not its benchmark; the safety which the public is entitled to expect is.[9] Product liability regimes address the allocation of liability between the producer of a product and its user.[10] These laws represent a departure from traditional contractual and tortious rules under which an injured party in litigation has to prove that the defendant is either in breach of contract or at fault and in breach of a duty of care towards the claimant.[11] By contrast, under product liability law, the injured person does not need to prove a fault or a breach of contract. Another key difference is that it will usually be possible to bring a claim against a broader category of persons.[12] Strict liability rules exist also beyond defective products, and they tend to protect vulnerable persons and allocate liability on those who are better positioned to prevent the harm.[13] By imposing strict liability, the law increases the risk of liability for the producer, enhances protection and the possibility of redress for the consumer, and as a by-product, should ensure the safety and quality of products sold on the market. The existence of strict liability regime is of vital importance in an IoT world because the characteristics themselves of the IoT – and in particular the high degree of autonomation – 'could make it hard to trace the damage back to a human behaviour,'[14] which renders ordinary, fault-based liability regimes unhelpful, as recently noted by the European Commission.

Ensuring the safety of the IoT is crucial because this sociotechnological phenomenon has led to an overcoming of the distinction between security and cybersecurity. Hacking would be traditionally seen as a cybersecurity issue, but if one hacks a Thing or an IoT system to control them and weaponise them (e.g. a 'smart' petrol station),[15] then the issue would become one of security. Vulnerable Things

---

9 Christoph Schmon, 'Product Liability of Emerging Digital Technologies : A Fitness Check of the 1985 Product Liability Directive' (2018) 6 IWRZ 257.

10 Thomas Kadner Graziano, 'The Law Applicable to Product Liability: The Present State of the Law in Europe and Current Proposals for Reform' (2005) 54 International & Comparative Law Quarterly 475.

11 cf Fabrizio Cafaggi and Horatia Muir Watt, *The Regulatory Function of European Private Law* (Edward Elgar 2009).

12 Geraint Howells and David G Owen, 'Products Liability Law in America and Europe' in Geraint Howells and others (eds), *Handbook of Research on International Consumer Law* (2nd edn, Edward Elgar 2018).

13 E.g. in jurisdictions such as Italy, there is strict liability for dangerous activity under *Codice Civile*, art 2050, and it falls within the scope of torts. cf Elspeth Reid, 'Liability for Dangerous Activities: A Comparative Analysis' (1999) 48 The International and Comparative Law Quarterly 731.

14 European Commission, 'Report on the Safety and Liability Implications of Artificial Intelligence, the Internet of Things and Robotics' (2020) COM/2020/64 final [3].

15 Danny Palmer, 'IoT Security' (*ZDNet*, 10 September 2019) <www.zdnet.com/article/iot-security-now-dark-web-hackers-are-targeting-internet-connected-gas-pumps/>.

can damage other Things and systems, often at scale, e.g. when an infected IoT botnet executed an unforeseen DDoS attack to bring down online servers.[16] More generally, potential IoT safety risks can be categorised into malfunction by defect or updates, loss of connectivity and product obsolescence, data quality and integrity concerns, and physical dangers.[17] Only some of the risks relate to the tangible components of the Thing.

In the EU, Directive 85/374 ('Product Liability Directive') was seen from the outset as a response to 'solving the problem, peculiar to our age of increasing technicality, of a fair apportionment of the *risks inherent in modern technological production.*'[18] With the increase in risks that the IoT carries with it, partly due to its being technically complex, the regime cannot be dismissed as not being intended to cover recent developments such as the IoT. However, the rules regarding liability for defective products seem to have been somewhat neglected over recent years.[19] Indeed, it has been critically noted that while the EU product liability model has been influential internationally, 'the practical impact of its ideas has been close to negligible.'[20] At least in part, this is due to the fact that these laws were written in a time when products were tangible, they would not change after the point of sale, and the defects were mostly mechanical. The IoT challenges each one of those assumptions, as products live on a continuum between tangible and tangible, dynamically change throughout their life cycle, and their defects are mostly intangible.

Although the Product Liability Directive has been relatively dormant, the CJEU has recently been asked to consider its application in a case involving health-related Things,[21] namely, 'pacemakers and implantable cardioverter defibrillators.'[22] In *Boston Scientific*,[23] products contained a defect that could result in premature battery depletion and subsequent loss of certain functionality, including telemetry, that is, the transmission of recorded data to an external device. Following identification of the defect, the supplier offered their replacement free of charge. However, claims were made for compensation in respect of the costs of the implantation of the original faulty products. The main issue was whether a 'product belonging to the same group or forming part of the same

16 Schmon (n 9).

17 OECD, 'Consumer Product Safety in the Internet of Things' (2018) OECD Digital Economy Paper no 267.

18 Product Liability Directive, recital 2, italics added.

19 European Commission, 'Fourth Report on the Application of Council Directive 85/374/EEC' (2011) COM(2011) 547 final 3.

20 Mathias Reimann, 'Product Liability in a Global Context: The Hollow Victory of the European Model' (2003) 11 European Review of Private Law 128, 129. It has also been noted that this Directive stands as a model of the process of legal integration in Europe (Simon Whittaker, 'European Product Liability and Intellectual Products' (1989) 105 LQR 125).

21 Since on the facts there is no mention of capability to connect, it would be more accurate to say that this product was an M2M one.

22 Cases C-503/13 and 504/13, *Boston Scientific Medizintechnik v AOK Sachsen-Anhalt* [2015] 3 CMLR 6 [12].

23 ibid.

production series'[24] could be said to be defective without the need to prove that the specific product was defective. The court held that it could, because users had high expectations of safety, 'in the light of (the product's) function and the particularly vulnerable situation of (the users).'[25] Such high expectations are likely to lower the evidentiary standard in most disputes regarding Things, because the latter endanger consumers in novel ways. As noted by the advocate general, 'making proof of a lack of safety subject to the *actual occurrence of damage would disregard the preventive function* assigned to EU legislation on the safety of products.'[26] Second, the court was asked to determine whether damage relating to death and personal injury[27] extended to the surgical procedure required to replace the defective device. The court held that it did, but only if the operation was necessary to overcome the defect.[28] This will have an impact on all those 'smart' implantables that require an operation to be removed – their cost of replacement will qualify as damage under product liability.

When *Boston Scientific* was decided, it was predicted that the implications of this decision for product liability regimes could be significant.[29] With the explosive growth of the IoT market and an expansive concept of 'product,' the possibility of a revival of product liability was foreseeable. Such revival has not materialised yet, which may suggest that the Product Liability Directive is unfit for purpose. On this basis, it is worth examining the EU regime and considering its applicability to the Echo case study and the IoT more generally.

4.2.1 Are Software, Service, and Data 'Products'?

The Product Liability Directive applies to 'products,' which are defined as all movables even when incorporated into another movable or immovable, and including electricity.[30] Further clarity around this definition may be found in the national implementation measures. In the UK e.g. a *product* includes 'a product which is comprised in another product, whether by virtue of being a component part or raw material or otherwise.'[31] In an Echo and IoT context, therefore, a key issue is to what extent the 'product' can be said to include its intangible component parts, specifically software, service, and data. The Commission saw the directive's definition as extending to software, with Lord Cockfield noting that the directive 'applies to software in the same way . . . that it applies to handicraft

---

24 ibid [28].
25 ibid [39].
26 Cases C-503/13 and C-504/13 *Boston Scientific* [2015] 3 CMLR 6, Opinion of AG Bot, para 38.
27 Product Liability Directive, art 9(a).
28 *Boston Scientific* (n 21) [55].
29 Barend Van Leeuwen and Paul Verbruggen, 'Resuscitating EU Product Liability Law? Contemplating the Effects of Boston Scientific Medizintechnik GmbH v. AOK Sachsen-Anhalt and Betriebskrankenkasse RWE (Joined Cases C-503/13 and C-504/13)' (2015) 23 European Review of Private Law 899.
30 Product Liability Directive, art 2.
31 Consumer Protection Act 1987, s 1(2).

and artistic products.'[32] Notwithstanding the Commission's statement, uncertainty about the application of the directive to software has persisted over the years, partly due to the fact that software may be considered a service in certain circumstances. While it is increasingly accepted that product liability applies at least to the physical media on which software is supplied and to the software encoded on that media, 'there is some doubt about whether they apply to software delivered online (although it is possible that the common law would imply).'[33] The concept encompasses those products whose 'essential characteristics . . . are attributable to an industrial or other process having been carried out.'[34] This would seem applicable to a product's integrated software and does not exclude intangible software products. It has been noted[35] that, since the directive does not establish whether products must be tangible and its *travaux préparatoires* focus on preventing risks stemming from industrially manufactured products, software products could be included. Including intangible products would have also the benefit of ensuring convergence between product liability and free movement of goods, since – as decided by the CJEU in *Jägerskiöld v Gustafsson*[36] – tangibility is not a requirement for items to be considered goods.[37] This inclusive stance is further corroborated by the circumstance that, in an IoT world, a large number of everyday objects is embedded with – and made vulnerable by – software components and that distinguishing between the components of a Thing is becoming increasingly difficult, if at all possible. However, it has been argued[38] that the directive would implicitly focus on tangibles by expressly including electricity as the only intangible product, and it would concentrate on damages that are typically associated with defective tangible goods rather than digital damages. It would follow that the directive applies to digital content supplied on a tangible medium and non-embedded software that fulfils a component function for a tangible product, but not to software without any tangibility. Whilst these arguments are not without merit, given the evolution of the market in a direction that was not predicable by the lawmakers in 1985, excluding software would mean condemning product liability law to irrelevance by obsolescence.

US-based commentators agree that this issue can be determined by deciding whether the reasons for imposing strict liability apply to software.[39] In considering

---

32 Answer given by Lord Cockfield on behalf of the Commission (15.11.1988) to the Written Question No 706/88 by Mr Gijs de Vries (LDR-NL) (5.7.1988) (89/C 114/76).
33 Chris Reed (ed), *Computer Law* (7th edn, OUP 2012) 176.
34 Consumer Protection Act 1987, s 1(2).
35 Schmon (n 9).
36 Case C-97/98 *Jägerskiöld v Gustafsson* [1999] ECR I-7319 [37].
37 Under the provisions on the free movement of goods, *goods* are 'products which can be valued in money and which are capable, as such, of forming the subject of commercial transaction's (Case 7/68 *Commission v Italy* [1968] ECR 423, 429).
38 Schmon (n 9).
39 Susan Lanoue, 'Computer Software and Strict Products Liability' (1983) 20 San Diego Law Review 439; Jim Prince, 'Negligence: Liability for Defective Software' (1980) 33 Oklahoma Law Review 848.

the expansion of the scope of strict liability beyond chattels, US courts identify a threefold rationale: the placing of a product into the stream of commerce, the producer's better position to control risks, and the latter's ability to spread the costs of accidents.[40] It has been claimed that product liability's rationale does not apply to software that is especially designed for the needs and to the order of the consumer; it would only apply to software which is a standard marketed package – both in the US and in the EU.[41] This may have been true in the eighties, but it is perhaps less convincing in an IoT world, where the distinction between hardware and software is blurred and IoT players remotely control products, including software, remotely and throughout their life cycle. Accordingly, they are better positioned to control the risks if compared to consumers who find themselves in a position that is weaker than consumers in a pre-IoT world. It can be said that the IoT challenges the distinction between especially designed software and standard marketed package.

Therefore, whilst current laws can already be interpreted as including software in the concept of product, *de lege ferenda* such concept should be redefined to expressly include software, regardless of whether it is embedded and whether it is a standard marketed package. Positively, the European Commission, recognising that software may often be classified as a service and not as a product, and that non-embedded software may be difficult to classify, recommended a clarification of the definition of product to 'ensure that compensation is always available for damage caused by products that are defective because of software or other digital features.'[42] This change would contribute to making the product liability regime fit for the IoT.

The same can be said for the exclusion of service and data from the concept of product. The directive is usually seen as not applicable to services; e.g. it has been observed that 'if the machine learning technology is hosted in the cloud, so that its users receive it as a service, the product liability regime will not apply.'[43] Positively, in its process of reviewing the directive, the Commission has noted that '[t]here are open questions about what separates a product from a service (e.g. for the *Internet of Things, where products and services interact*).'[44] Data has not been dealt with expressly, but it is reasonable to say that the directive was not designed to deal with hazards to the safety of people related personal and nonpersonal

---

40 Prince (n 39) 851. Similar considerations apply in European jurisdictions; see e.g. Whittaker (n 20).
41 Whittaker (n 20); Prince (n 39).
42 European Commission, 'Report on the Safety and Liability Implications of Artificial Intelligence, the Internet of Things and Robotics' (n 14) [3].
43 Chris Reed, Elizabeth Kennedy and Sara Silva, 'Responsibility, Autonomy and Accountability: Legal Liability for Machine Learning' [2016] Queen Mary School of Law Legal Studies Research Paper 6.
44 European Commission, 'Report from the Commission to the Parliament, the Council and the European Economic and Social Committee on the Application of the Council Directive on the Approximation of the Laws, Regulations, and Administrative Provisions of the Member States Concerning Liability for Defective Products (85/374/EEC)' (2018) COM/2018/246 final [5.4].

data.[45] Currently, defective service and defective data, as such, do not trigger the Product Liability Directive, though if they are embedded in a product, including software, they should. If Things are a mixture of hardware, service, software, and data, then the product's vulnerabilities should be considered holistically and include the Thing's intangible defects. De lege ferenda, the directive should be amended to expressly apply to service and data as such; otherwise, it risks becoming irrelevant in an IoT world.

It follows that some of Echo's terms are potentially unenforceable under product liability rules. For example, in the One-Year Limited Warranty, Amazon states that they 'warrant the Device against defects in materials and workmanship under ordinary consumer use'[46] and the warranty 'applies only to hardware components of the Device.'[47] These limitations are no longer justified. To make sure that the regime remains fit for the IoT and, more generally, of predictable application, it is to be hoped that the ongoing review of the directive will lead to a clarification that products also include software, service, and data.

4.2.2 Allocation of Liability in Complex Supply Chains

One of the main concerns of consumers of Things is that the multilayered structure of the supply chain could effectively shield IoT companies from liability. There is a risk that the manufacturer of the hardware could claim that the software developer is the party responsible for any defect or could try to shift responsibility to the service provider. The problem is exacerbated in complex ecosystems, such as Echo, where, as a result of an intricate and opaque corporate structure, consumers are contracting with several different traders whose identification is often arduous. Under product liability, invoking complex supply chains to disclaim liability should not be allowed. Under Article 3 of the Product Liability Directive, the concept of the 'producer' is multilayered, to prevent any shifting of responsibility. In the first instance, 'producer' means the manufacturer of the finished product, or the manufacturer of a component part, or any persons who present themselves as the producer, by putting the name, trademark, or other distinguishing feature on the product.[48] Additionally, where the product is imported and distributed in the territory, that person is deemed responsible as producer, which extends the territorial application of the directive to foreign products.[49] Finally, where neither the producer nor the importer can be identified, then the supplier is considered the responsible producer, unless they can identify the producer, the importer, or the supplier's supplier within a reasonable time.[50] However, the

---

45 Schmon (n 9).
46 One Year Limited Warranty for Amazon Devices.
47 One Year Limited Warranty for Amazon Devices.
48 Product Liability Directive, art 3(1).
49 Product Liability Directive, art 3(2). The majority of consumers are likely to buy direct from the producer's website or from an e-Commerce platform, as noted in Noto La Diega and Walden (n 4).
50 Product Liability Directive, art 3(3).

preference goes to the producer because, as pointed out by the CJEU in *Skov AEG v Bilka Lavprisvarehus*,[51] 'by obliging all suppliers to insure against such liability, it would result in products becoming significantly more expensive.'[52] Such an inclusive and broad concept would seem perfectly applicable to the characteristic of IoT markets, where nearly all Things are composite and the supply chain is incredibly complex. If the consumer cannot identify the producer, the supplier will be the defendant.

4.2.3 Defect, Damage, and Causal Link in the Liability for Defective Things

Under the Product Liability Directive, the injured person has to prove the defect, the damage, and the causal link between the two.[53] This allocation of the burden of proof is the stepping stone to compensation for damage, and on the face of it, it would favour consumers as they do not have to prove fault. However, there is empirical evidence that it is 'the most burdensome to consumers.'[54]

With regard to defects, the threshold is that the product does 'not provide the safety which a person is entitled to expect, taking all circumstances into account.'[55] This is an objective assessment, as courts will consider what the public are entitled to expect, not what they actually expect. This was clearly stated in *A v National Blood Authority*, where inflected blood had caused a group of people to contract hepatitis C, and the court – highlighting that there were no warnings and no publicity material – held that the blood was defective because 'the public at large was entitled to expect that the blood transfused to them would be free from infection.'[56] This expectation has to be evaluated as at the time the product was first introduced to the market, but as held in *Gee v DePuy International Ltd*,[57] courts can have regard to everything relevant known about the product, whether or not that information had been available when it was first put on the market.

What constitutes a general expectation of safety may vary considerably depending on many factors, including the market segment in which the Thing is deployed. In *Boston Scientific*, the court held that this expectation must be assessed on the basis of 'the intended purpose, the objective characteristics and properties of the product in question and the specific requirements of the group of users for whom the product is intended.'[58] With regard to the medical devices under consideration, the court felt that an expectation of a near-zero failure rate in an implantable device would be reasonable for patients, even though medical experts are aware

---

51 Case C-402/03 [2006] 2 CMLR 16.
52 ibid [28].
53 Product Liability Directive, art 4.
54 European Commission, 'Fifth Report' (n 44) [5.2.1].
55 Product Liability Directive, art 6(1) and recital 6.
56 *A v National Blood Authority (No.1)* [2001] 3 All E R 289 [80].
57 [2018] EWHC 1208 (QB).
58 *Boston Scientific* [38].

that such devices are not free of the risk of failure.[59] Following the rationale of the directive and the vague yet encompassing general expectation test, the producer may be held accountable also 'for a *lack of cybersecurity* where it is an expected product feature to be secured against such attacks.'[60] Whilst health-related Things are a field where one can foresee a rise in product liability cases connected to high expectations of safety, similar expectations apply to many other Things, such as driverless cars, as one can infer from *X BV v Staatssecretaris van Financiën*.[61] To date, the standard of proof has varied considerably across the member states.[62] However, following *Boston Scientific*, it now appears sufficient for the claimant to demonstrate the risk of a defect or the potential for failure rather than that a specific Thing has a defect, which significantly lowers the threshold.[63]

The concept of damage under the Product Liability Directive is limited to death, personal injury, and damage to any other item of property.[64] Damage to the device itself, so-called 'transaction damage,' is not covered.[65] However, in *Boston Scientific* the court took an expansive view of what damage should be compensated, including 'all that is necessary to eliminate harmful consequences and to restore the level of safety which a person is entitled to expect.'[66] Where the damaged property is for private use or consumption, a maximum recoverable threshold of €500 is imposed, which would apply to the Echo series.[67] For recovery of nonmaterial damages, such as distress, this is left for the member state's law to determine.[68] However, as recently confirmed in *Schmitt v TÜV Rheinland*[69] regarding breast implants, the Product Liability Directive 'does not preclude the application of other systems of contractual or non-contractual liability based on other grounds.'[70] Since the directive does not affect national laws on torts[71] and the vast majority of legal systems provide compensation for nonmaterial or moral damages, consumers will be able to claim such damages uncapped under general tortious liability. *De lege ferenda*, I echo the European Consumer Organisation's recommendation that the directive should be revised to expressly include nonmaterial damages.[72] Construing damage as broadly as possible is fundamental in an

---

59 ibid [26].
60 Schmon (n 9) 256.
61 Case C-661/15 (CJEU, 12 October 2017). See Safia Cazet, 'Détermination de La Valeur En Douane Dans l'hypothèse de Marchandises Défectueuses' [2017] Europe.
62 The Product Liability Directive did not harmonise the relevant procedural rules. For standard of proof in the UK, see *Ide v ATB Sales Ltd* [2008] EWCA Civ 424.
63 Opinion of AG Bot (n 26), para 3.
64 Product Liability Directive, art 9.
65 Product Liability Directive, art 9. See Case C-285/08 *Moteurs Leroy Somer v Dalkia France* [2009] ECR I-4733.
66 *Boston Scientific* (n 21) [49].
67 Product Liability Directive, art 9(b).
68 Product Liability Directive, art 9(2).
69 Case C-219/15 *Schmitt v TÜV Rheinland LGA Products GmbH* (CJEU, 16 February 2017).
70 ibid [58].
71 Product Liability Directive, art 13.
72 Christoph Schmon, 'Review of Product Liability Rules' (2017) BEUC Position Paper.

IoT world to avoid what happens to the US, where the lack of actual harm is the prevalent theme in IoT product liability cases.[73]

Finally, evidencing the causal relationship between the defect and damage is a major problem for consumers, and it can be a challenge particularly when complex technologies are involved.[74] The failure to prove the causal link is the main reason that courts reject product liability claims in Europe.[75] The directive relies on national rules on the evidence and the establishment of causation; therefore, it is useful to look at domestic case law. In *Hufford v Samsung Electronics (UK) Ltd.*[76] e.g. the claimant proved defect and damage but was unable to discharge the burden of proof that a fridge-freezer caused a fire in their home. Such difficulties led some member states and consumer groups to call for the Product Liability Directive to be amended either to reverse the burden of proof or to adopt a presumption of producer liability.[77] Recently, the Expert Group on Liability and New Technologies[78] has suggested that the burden of proof could be linked to compliance with specific cybersecurity obligations set by law: the noncompliance would lead to a reversal in the burden of proof. Perhaps unsurprisingly, producers and insurers contest these proposals.[79]

A related issue is whether consumers can only rely on uncontested scientific research to prove the causal link or if national laws can provide for a lower threshold. An answer can be found in the recent *N.W v Sanofi Pasteur* case,[80] where it was held that, despite medical research neither establishing nor ruling out the existence of a link between the administering of a vaccine and the occurrence of a disease, courts may find in favour of the consumer if 'certain factual evidence relied on by the applicant constitutes serious, specific and consistent evidence enabling it to conclude that there is a defect in the vaccine and that there is a causal link between that defect and that disease.'[81] Therefore, even though IoT consumers cannot rely solely on presumptions[82] and carry the burden to prove defect, damage, and causal link, the evidentiary threshold is a relatively low one.

---

73 See e.g. *Cahen v. Toyota Motor Corp* 3:15-cv-01104 (N.D. Cal. March 10, 2015).
74 See European Commission, 'Fifth Report' (n 44) [5.2.1].
75 European Commission, 'Evaluation of Council Directive 85/374/EEC of 25 July 1985 Accompanying the Document Report on the Application of the Product Liability Directive' (2018) Commission Staff Working Document SWD/2018/157 final.
76 [2014] EWHC 2956.
77 European Commission, 'Fourth Report on the Application of Council Directive 85/374/EEC' (n 19) 7.
78 Expert Group on Liability and New Technologies – New Technologies Formation, 'Liability for Artificial Intelligence and Other Emerging Digital Technologies' (2019) 48.
79 Chris Hodges, 'Reform of the Product Liability Directive' (*CMS*, 5 August 1999) <www.cms-lawnow.com/ealerts/1999/08/reform-of-the-product-liability-directive?cc_lang=en>.
80 Case C-621/15 *NW v Sanofi Pasteur* (CJEU, 21 June 2017).
81 ibid [43].
82 ibid [55]. This case, however, has been seen as introducing a defectiveness presumption by EY, Technopolis Group and VVA, *Evaluation of Council Directive 85/374/EEC* (EU 2018). The authors thought that 'the defectiveness presumption could apply to some new technological developments, such as smartphones or tablets or even robots' (ibid 36).

4.2.4 Product Liability Defences and IoT: Friends or Foes?

It is not permissible for a producer to limit or exclude their liability under the Product Liability Directive.[83] Therefore, contractual provisions such as Amazon Prime Terms accepting liability only 'for fraudulently concealed defects'[84] are unenforceable. Additionally, given the overlaps between the different consumer laws, such terms would likely be considered also an unfair commercial practice and an unfair term.[85] However, producers can raise various defences under this directive, namely:

  (i) They did not put the product into circulation;[86]
 (ii) The product was not made for sale or other distribution for economic purpose or not manufactured or distributed in the course of business;[87]
(iii) The defect was due to compliance with mandatory regulations;[88]
 (iv) The defect could be attributed to the product in which the component has been fitted;[89]
  (v) The 'development risk' or 'state-of-the-art' defence[90] – the state of scientific and technical knowledge when the product was put into circulation – was 'not such as to enable the existence of the defect to be discovered;'[91]
 (vi) The 'later defect' defence – the defect did not exist when the product was put into circulation.[92]

Defences *v* and *vi* are the most relevant in the context of the IoT. First, the development risk defence requires courts to consider whether the defect could be discovered based on all scientific and technical knowledge available at the time that it was put into circulation, including 'the most advanced available (to anyone, not simply to the producer in question).'[93]

As the *travaux préparatoires* show, the development risk defence was seen as a compromise between consumer protection and innovation.[94] Since 1985, debate has continued over its relative costs and benefits for both consumers and producers. It has been held that this provision does not require consideration of

---

83 Product Liability Directive, art 12.
84 Amazon Prime Terms and Conditions, point 6.
85 Reed (n 33).
86 Product Liability Directive, art 7(a).
87 Product Liability Directive, art 7(c).
88 Product Liability Directive, art 7(d).
89 Product Liability Directive, art 7(f).
90 Bernhard A Koch, 'The Development Risk Defence of the EC Product Liability Directive' (2018) 20 Pharmaceuticals Policy and Law 163.
91 Product Liability Directive, art 7(e).
92 Product Liability Directive, art 7(b).
93 *National Blood Authority* (n 56) [49].
94 Fondazione Rosselli, 'Analysis of the Economic Impact of the Development Risk Clause as Provided by Directive 85/374/EEC on Liability for Defective Products' (2014) Study for the European Commission Contract No. ETD/2002/B5.

the 'practices and safety standards in use in the industrial sector in which the producer is operating,'[95] which would be a consideration under a traditional negligence analysis.[96] Instead, it requires a more holistic perspective involving considerations of accessibility.[97] The EU lawmaker was aware that this defence could provide producers with too much wiggle room, especially in sectors such as ICTs, where states of industry knowledge change rapidly and can be difficult to determine with certainty. It therefore provided member states with an option to exclude this defence, such that a producer would be liable 'even if (they prove) that the state of scientific and technical knowledge at the time when (they) put the product into circulation was not such as to enable the existence of a defect to be discovered.'[98] Countries such as Luxembourg and Finland availed themselves of this option to the benefit of consumers of high-tech products.[99]

Technological advances such as the IoT have an ambiguous relationship to the development risk defence. Indeed, on the one hand, the increased complexity of the Things, especially of their software components, makes them more prone to vulnerabilities.[100] On the other hand, decisively, IoT and AI produce huge amounts of information, including information that can be used to predict the risks associated to a product.[101] All in all, the rise of the IoT is likely to be exploited tactically by IoT companies to argue the unpredictability of defects, thus avoiding liability, while consumers will be able to underline how the IoT calls for a lower threshold of predictability.

A second relevant defence is the later defect defence, whereby the defendant claims that the defect did not exist when the product was put into circulation.[102] Its rationale is that 'the manufacturer has control over the product until that moment.'[103] With the shift from analogue to digital and, finally, to 'smart,' producers do have control over Things also after the point of sale, and this is not currently reflected in the law. Not only producers can remotely control and monitor Things, but also, the IoT is often open to third-party additions and interventions.[104] The unfitness of the defence becomes even more palpable where Things

---

95　Case C-300/95 *Commission v United Kingdom* [1997] ECR I-2469, Opinion of AG Tesauro [20].

96　One of the leading authorities in the field of tortious liability is a product liability case: *Donoghue v Stevenson* [1932] AC 562.

97　*Commission v United Kingdom* (n 95) [26]–[28].

98　Product Liability Directive, art 15(1)(b).

99　Fondazione Rosselli (n 94).

100　Yasir Javed and others, 'Discovering the Relationship between Software Complexity and Software Vulnerabilities' (2018) 96 Journal of Theoretical and Applied Information Technology 4690.

101　Steve Kommrusch, 'Artificial Intelligence Techniques for Security Vulnerability Prevention' [2019] arXiv:1912.06796 [cs] <http://arxiv.org/abs/1912.06796>.

102　Product Liability Directive, art 7(b).

103　Gabriele Mazzini, 'A System of Governance for Artificial Intelligence through the Lens of Emerging Intersections between AI and EU Law' in A. De Franceschi, R. Schulze, M. Graziadei, O. Pollicino, F. Riente, S. Sica, P. Sirena (eds.), *Digital Revolution – New Challenges for Law : Data Protection, Artificial Intelligence, Smart Products, Blockchain Technology and Virtual Currencies* (Beck 2019) 22.

104　Mazzini (n 103).

embed AI and can therefore learn and change over time, with limited possibilities for the producer to predict the new defect.[105]

Finally, though it is not strictly speaking a defence, producers can rely on the argument that the consumer initiated proceedings after the time limit of three years that runs from 'the day on which the plaintiff became aware, or should reasonably have become aware, of the damage, the defect and the identity of the producer.'[106] In case of hidden defects, therefore, potentially no time limit will apply, other than the ten-year limitation period.[107] Such statute of limitations is arguably in violation of the human right of access to a court under the European Convention of Human Rights[108] in cases where it is scientifically proven that an individual could not know that they were suffering from a particular disease caused by a defective product within ten years, similarly to *Moor v Switzerland*.[109]

4.2.5 Product Liability's Interplay with Complementary Regimes

Product liability regimes are closely linked with the related field of product safety law, whose main instrument is Directive 2001/95 (General Product Safety Directive).[110] While the Product Liability Directive addresses liability for defects in a product that is already on the market, the General Product Safety Directive imposes controls on the quality of products before they can be placed on the market. A product can be 'secure' under the product safety regime and 'unsecure' under the product liability regime.[111] The main obligation of producers is to ensure that only safe products are placed on the market.[112] Products are safe if they do not present any reasonably foreseeable risk or only the minimum risks compatible with the product's use, 'considered to be acceptable and consistent with a high level of protection for the safety and health of persons.'[113] As an example of an unsafe Thing, in 2019 it was found that Mazda's braking system (Smart Brake Support) had been inappropriately programmed, and therefore, it might unexpectedly trigger the brakes, thus increasing the risk of accidents. Mazda was forced by the Romanian authorities to recall the product, and Belgium, Bulgaria, Estonia, Finland, Germany, Poland, Portugal followed suit.[114] This is no isolated incident, as the number of unsafe Things rise, e.g. smart watch

---

105 cf David C Vladeck, 'Machines without Principals: Liability Rules and Artificial Intelligence' (2014) 89 Washington Law Review 117.

106 Product Liability Directive, art 10.

107 Product Liability Directive, art 11.

108 ECHR, art 6.

109 *Moor v Switzerland* Apps no 52067/10 and 41072/11 (ECtHR, 11 March 2014).

110 Directive 2001/95/EC of 3 December 2001 on general product safety [2002] OJ L 11/ 4, art 1(1).

111 Giuseppina Pisciotta, 'La Responsabilità per Danno Da Prodotto e La Produzione Agricola Con Metodo Biologico' in Ezio Capizzano (ed), *Diritti fondamentali, qualità dei prodotti agricoli e tutela del consumatore* (Università degli Studi di Camerino 1993) 211.

112 General Product Safety Directive, art 1(1).

113 General Product Safety Directive, art 2(b).

114 Safety Gate: Rapid Alert System for dangerous non-food products, alert no A12/00491/20.

in Iceland that could allow anyone to track and contact the child wearing it,[115] to a connected car in Germany whose software security gaps could be exploited to hack the interconnected control systems in the vehicle.[116] The main shortcoming of product safety legislation is that it does not provide for specific mandatory cybersecurity requirements,[117] at least not expressly. However, if one accepts that the IoT disrupts the security-cybersecurity binary, it should follow that existing security requirements should be interpreted extensively to cover cyber threats.[118] Hopefully, three proposals – the new Machinery Regulation, the Directive on the Resilience of Critical Entities,[119] and the NIS 2 Directive[120] – will provide the perfect opportunity to abandon the obsolete binary.

With respect to the IoT, there is a range of potentially applicable product safety laws at an EU level, both horizontal and vertical. Indeed, the General Product Safety Directive is complemented by sector-specific laws, such as the directives on Machinery and Medical Devices,[121] particularly useful to maintain the safety of robots[122] and Things used in healthcare.[123] These provide for *ex ante* compliance procedures coupled with an *ex post* oversight mechanism. The compliance procedures may be carried out by external 'notified bodies' or through self-certification mechanisms. Once a product completes the 'conformity assessment procedure' (also known as 'type approval'), it can be placed on the European market. Once on the market, if a defect is subsequently identified, the associated exposure under the Product Liability Directive should create a positive feedback loop into the producer's product safety management systems.[124] This could benefit the IoT e.g. by incentivising producers to have software update procedures in place, to enable 'defects' to be addressed over-the-air, rapidly, and en masse.[125]

---

115 RAPEX notification from Iceland published in the EU Safety Gate's website (A12/0157/19).

116 RAPEX notification from Germany published in the EU Safety Gate (A12/1671/15).

117 European Commission, 'Report on the Safety and Liability Implications of Artificial Intelligence, the Internet of Things and Robotics' (n 14) [2].

118 This is in line with the European Commission's observation that product safety law embraces an extended concept of safety, which includes 'not only mechanical, chemical, electrical risks but also cyber risks and risks related to the loss of connectivity of devices' (ibid.) The Commission does recognise, however, that more explicit provisions would better protect consumers.

119 Proposal for a Directive on the resilience of critical entities (COM(2020) 829 final).

120 Proposal for a Directive on measures for a high common level of cybersecurity across the Union, repealing Directive (EU) 2016/1148 (COM/2020/823 final). On 13 May 2022, the Council and the European Parliament reached an agreement on the NIS 2 Directive.

121 Council Directive 93/42/EEC of 14 June 1993 concerning medical devices [1993] OJ L 169/1, as complemented by Commission Implementing Decision (EU) 2020/437 of 24 March 2020 on the harmonised standards for medical devices drafted in support of Council Directive 93/42/EEC [2020] OJ L 90I/1.

122 Guido Noto La Diega, 'Machine Rules. Of Drones, Robots and the Info-Capitalist Society' (2017) 2 Italian Law Journal 367.

123 EPFL International Risk Governance Center, 'Governing Cybersecurity Risks and Benefits of the Internet of Things: Connected Medical & Health Devices and Connected Vehicles' (2017) IRGC Expert Workshop.

124 See Van Leeuwen and Verbruggen (n 29) 14.

125 Updates may also be the cause of a defect. See Jane Wakefield, 'Nest Thermostat Bug Leaves Users Cold' *BBC News* (14 January 2016) <www.bbc.com/news/technology-35311447>.

Such obligation may be seen as stemming today from the requirements to deliver updates to avoid 'lack of conformity' disputes under the reformed EU consumer sales law and digital content law.[126] Since the lack of conformity covers both legal and factual defects and does not require a qualified damage (death, injury, damage to property), consumer sales law is likely to have broader application than product liability. However, consumer sales law has its own limitations, mainly due to its focus on the contractual relation and the requirement that the parties conclude a sales contract. Therefore, consumers will have to see on a case-by-case basis which strategy would more likely be successful.

4.2.6 Time for a Reform of Product Liability?

The Product Liability Directive has constituted a model for other countries and has been generally seen as striking a fair balance between consumer protection and competition.[127] However, technological developments such as the IoT are showing that a revision would now be timely. In 2018, the European Commission published its fifth report on the application of the directive.[128] There, it underlined that many *'products available today have characteristics that were considered science fiction in the 1980s*. The challenges we are facing now and even more acutely in the future (relate to) the Internet of Things.'[129] This is in line with this book's contention that the IoT calls for a rethinking of the concept of product. Moreover, the Commission noted that stakeholders have expressed concerns about the continued relevance of the directive's concepts and that, in particular, the good-service distinction is blurred.[130] As noted above, whilst the directive is flexible enough to deal with software products, the other digital components embedded in most Things, namely, service and data, are usually seen as currently escaping this strict liability regime, although more inclusive interpretations are possible.

In the context of the *Fifth Report*, the Commission carried out a formal evaluation of the Product Liability Directive with a focus on IoT and autonomous systems. There, they underlined that the IoT involves different actors in the value chain, 'which all enable the technology to function (product manufacturers, software producers, the connectivity service, sensor manufacturers, owners of the object, service providers etc.),'[131] and added that IoT applications 'have a very open ecosystem, where new features can be added by the user or even third parties to create a new one.'[132] Arguably, despite the IoT's relational black box, the product liability regime can be regarded as fit for purpose thanks to a

---

126 Second Consumer Sales Directive, art 7(3); Digital Content Directive, art 8(2).
127 Recently surveyed consumer associations do not think that 'the costs and benefits due to the Directive for consumers and producers are balanced' (European Commission, 'Product Liability Evaluation' (n 75) [5]).
128 European Commission, 'Fifth Report' (n 44).
129 ibid [1]. Emphasis added.
130 ibid [5.4]. Emphasis added.
131 European Commission, 'Product Liability Evaluation' (n 75) [5.4.2].
132 ibid.

broad definition of *producer* and to the possibility to bring an action against the supplier should the producer remain unidentified. The Commission's formal evaluation was supported by an external study[133] that inter alia gathered evidence that consumers experience product liability issues with regards to Things and that consumer organisations 'see difficulties in obtaining compensation for the damages suffered in case of defective products based on new technological developments.'[134]

In February 2020, the Commission published a report on the safety and liability implications of AI, IoT, and robotics.[135] There, alongside already-mentioned issues around the concept of product and defect, the Commission warned of the dangers of a likely rise in the defences of later defect and development risk. This is due to the fact that '[c]ybersecurity weaknesses . . . may also appear at a later stage, well after the product was put into circulation.'[136] To include post-sale defects in the scope of product liability would be justified by the increased risks and increased control that are connected to the IoT, as well as to the fact the (cyber)security risks are inherent to the IoT environment that requires openness and connectivity. IoT-friendly amendments will have to revolve around a revisitation of the concept of 'putting into circulation,' which is no longer justified as the be-all and end-all of product liability.

In light of this, and given the directive's partial unfitness for purpose, it would be crucial to see IoT-ready amendments and guidelines for interpretation and application. Guidance from the Commission was expected in mid-2019 with the promise to consider an update to the concepts of defect, damage, product, and producer,[137] but as of May 2021, it has not been published yet. Hopefully, it will help overcome distinctions that the IoT shows to be outdated, such as product-service, hardware-software, and cybersecurity-security.[138]

In the current stage of development of capitalism, the vulnerability of the Things cannot be fully comprehended without also considering the vulnerability of the consumers using them. Therefore, the second part of this chapter will critically assess how the law deals with that particular type of vulnerability that is generated by what we call 'the Internet of Personalised Things.'

4.3 Can We Trust the Internet of Personalised Things?

To carry out this assessment, I will focus on the Unfair Commercial Practices Directive, which aims at protecting consumers against unfair business-to-consumer commercial practices before, during, and after a commercial transaction in relation to

---

133 EY, Technopolis Group and VVA (n 82).
134 ibid 36.
135 European Commission, 'Report on the Safety and Liability Implications of Artificial Intelligence, the Internet of Things and Robotics' (n 14).
136 ibid [3].
137 European Commission, 'Fifth Report' (n 44) [6].
138 cf OECD (n 17).

a product.[139] The key point is to avoid that traders, through misleading or aggressive practices (e.g. by creating the impression that the consumer cannot leave the premises until a contract is formed),[140] prevent consumers from making informed and free choices.[141] We have already seen that the IoT constitutes a challenge to consumer decision-making. This section deals with how the IoT can curtail consumers' autonomy, freedom of choice, and self-determination through personalisation. This will constitute the basis for the next section's critical assessment of whether the Unfair Commercial Practices Directive provides an adequate response to the issues raised by the 'Internet of Personalised Things.'

In the Internet of Personalised Things, IoT data allows traders to personalise products, services, prices, and even 'legals.' Thanks to detailed and situational data about the consumer, context-specific targeting capabilities, and remote control over the Thing, IoT traders can go beyond the personalisation of their offers (targeted advertisements) and the innovation of their content delivery:[142] they can personalise the way products are built, priced, negotiated, sold, and interacted with by consumers. Things are dynamic products that can be remotely changed during their life cycle to respond to the consumer's preferences and behaviours. Echo learns about its users over time, and its answers become increasingly more relevant. Improved tracking and profiling capabilities allow IoT traders to target consumers with more relevant offers and at a price that mirrors their spending capabilities and is often determined automatically.[143] For example, research showed that the same search for holiday bookings can lead to different results, depending on whether or not one has deleted the cookies.[144] Whilst personalisation is a trend that goes beyond the IoT, there is evidence that, in this field, '[p]roduct data increasingly underpins finer-grain product personalization.'[145]

Personalisation is not all bad. Positive examples of personalisation come from personalised healthcare, where postoperation treatments can be provided remotely and at home using commercially available Things. One can stand up and walk in front of Kinect (Microsoft's motion-sensing Thing), which can automatically tell patients if they are regaining their strength.[146] IoT-powered personalised

---

139 Unfair Commercial Practices Directive, art 3(1).
140 Annex I to the Unfair Commercial Practices Directive, point 24.
141 Unfair Commercial Practices Directive, art 8; recitals 7, 14, 16; annex I point 7.
142 The 'IoT offers unlimited creativity for content creation as well as targeted delivery of content, as opposed to traditional advertising avenues' (Chloe E Spilotro, *Connecting the Dots: How IoT Is Going to Revolutionize the Digital Marketing Landscape for Millennials* (University of San Diego 2016).).
143 Gergely G Karácsony, 'Automated Personalised Pricing Practices Online' (2018) XVI Opolskie Studia Administracyjno-Prawne 75.
144 Aniko Hannak and others, 'Measuring Price Discrimination and Steering on E-Commerce Web Sites' (2014). In general, there is limited evidence of price discrimination practices (Morgan Wild and Marini Thorne, 'A Price of One's Own. An Investigation into Personalised Pricing in Essential Markets' (2018) Citizens Advice.).
145 Euan Davis, 'The Rise of the Smart Product Economy' (2015) Cognizant and EIU.
146 'Illinois Researchers Incorporating "Internet of Personalized Things" into World of Healthcare | Coordinated Science Laboratory' (n 144).

medicine is used not only for postoperation treatments but also for diagnosis, as exemplified by the smart toilet that, leveraging pressure and motion sensors, as well as computer vision and deep learning, analyses the colour, flow rate, and volume of a user's urine using 'with performance that is comparable to the performance of trained medical personnel.'[147]

Personalisation becomes negative when it leads to consumer manipulation in the form of decision-making that maximises the trader's profit and adversely affects the consumer's autonomy, freedom of choice, and self-determination. This is connected to a number of factors, such as the IoT-produced information overload. Indeed, there is evidence that 'an increase in the amount of personal information decreases information processing ability, and this hinders rational decision-making.'[148] The dynamic nature of Things, incrementally learning about their users, can also lead to lock-in effects. This is exemplified by Amazon's warning that, if we decide to protect our privacy by deleting Alexa's voice recordings associated with our account, this 'may degrade your experience.'[149] Ultimately, the IoT is changing the customer-trader relationship, which becomes far more direct and personalised,[150] hence Amazon's and other major IoT players' pledge to espouse customer-centrism as their philosophy. Such direct relationship, or its appearance, can provide IoT traders with unprecedented opportunities to manipulate consumers. IoT-powered analytics not only predicts consumer behaviours but also changes them and makes them more predictable – targeted ads can, over time, profoundly affect consumers' likes and dislikes.[151] One need only think of Facebook's experiment where the social networking site manipulated the newsfeed to see how this would affect the users' emotions.[152] Even the 'legals' can be personalised, as already happens in pay-as-you-drive car insurance models.[153] Personalised Things can be used to nudge consumers into changing their behaviour and shape their habits.[154] By monopolising our attention, our Things can make us into less-alert, more-e-commerce-ready consumers. Instead

---

147 Seung-min Park and others, 'A Mountable Toilet System for Personalized Health Monitoring via the Analysis of Excreta' [2020] Nature Biomedical Engineering 1.

148 Won-Hyun So and Ha-Kyun Kim, 'The Personal Information Overloads Effect Information Protective Responses in the Internet of Thing (IoT) Era' in James J Park and others (eds), *Advances in Computer Science and Ubiquitous Computing*, vol 474 (Springer 2018) 889.

149 'Review Your Alexa Voice History' <www.amazon.co.uk/gp/help/customer/display.html?nodeId =GHXNJNLTRWCTBBGW>.

150 Davis (n 148).

151 Guido Noto La Diega, 'Some Considerations on Intelligent Online Behavioural Advertising' (2018) 66 RDTI 53.

152 Catherine Flick, 'Informed Consent and the Facebook Emotional Manipulation Study' (2016) 12 Research Ethics 14.

153 Natali Helberger, 'Profiling and Targeting Consumers in the Internet of Things – A New Challenge for Consumer Law' in Reiner Schulze and Dirk Staudenmayer (eds), *Digital Revolution: Challenges for Contract Law in Practice* (Nomos 2016).

154 cf Cass R Sunstein, 'Impersonal Default Rules vs. Active Choices vs. Personalized Default Rules: A Triptych' [2012] <http://nrs.harvard.edu/urn-3:HUL.InstRepos:9876090>.

of using retail shelves, IoT consumers browse pages of search results – the 'digital shelves' – looking for answers to their questions and shopping opportunities. Space on the digital shelf is limited, e.g. if I ask Echo Show to search for boots, due to the size of the display, it will only show me few models and brands. Therefore, 'competition to capture the consumer's attention can be intense,'[155] and those who control the digital shelf control consumers' attention.[156] Thus, the IoT may play an important role in determining who will win the internet's attention wars, that is, the constant struggle to attract and monopolise the attention of increasingly distracted consumers.[157] Consumer manipulation can even alter our beliefs, as evidenced by how Russian hackers and trolls allegedly helped win the 2016 US election in Trump's favour.[158] Personalisation, finally, can hide forms of discrimination. This happens if e.g. Facebook does not show certain job opportunities to women and non-binary users.[159] Considering the practices of the 'attention markets'[160] as mere personalisation is giving a colourable face to manipulation and discrimination.[161]

Manipulation is a phenomenon that has been observed since the nineties. Back then, it was called 'market manipulation.'[162] It revolves around the fact that manufacturers have incentives to exploit cognitive biases 'to shape consumer perceptions throughout the product purchasing context . . . [a]dvertising, promotion and price setting all become means of altering consumer risk perceptions.'[163] With the digital revolution, market manipulation becomes pervasive and is increasingly

155 Matthew Rivard, 'How Brands Can Own the Digital Shelf (and Why They Should)' (*Think with Google*, June 2014) <www.thinkwithgoogle.com/advertising-channels/search/owning-the-digital-shelf/>.

156 See Pedro Bordalo, Nicola Gennaioli and Andrei Shleifer, 'Competition for Attention' (2016) 83 The Review of Economic Studies 481.

157 Sean Rintel, 'Is StumbleUpon Trumping Facebook in the Internet Attention Wars?' (*The Conversation*, 30 August 2011) <http://theconversation.com/is-stumbleupon-trumping-facebook-in-the-internet-attention-wars-3100>.

158 Kathleen Hall Jamieson, *Cyberwar: How Russian Hackers and Trolls Helped Elect a President: What We Don't, Can't, and Do Know* (OUP 2018).

159 Galen Sherwin and Esha Bhandari, 'Facebook Settles Civil Rights Cases by Making Sweeping Changes to Its Online Ad Platform' (*American Civil Liberties Union*, 19 March 2019) <www.aclu.org/blog/womens-rights/womens-rights-workplace/facebook-settles-civil-rights-cases-making-sweeping>.

160 Giuseppe Colangelo and Mariateresa Maggiolino, 'Data Protection in Attention Markets: Protecting Privacy through Competition' (2017) 8 Journal of European Competition Law & Practice 363.

161 Similarly, copyright was initially a right of the booksellers, who only later introduced the authors as parties in their claims 'to give a colourable face to their monopoly' (Attorney General Thurlow in 'Proceedings in the Lords on the Question of Literary Property, February 4 through February 22, 1774' (1774).).

162 Jon D Hanson and Douglas A Kysar, 'Taking Behavioralism Seriously: Some Evidence of Market Manipulation' [1999] Harvard Law Review 1420; Jon D Hanson and Douglas A Kysar, 'Taking Behavioralism Seriously: The Problem of Market Manipulation' (1999) 74 NYUL Review 630.

163 Hanson and Kysar, 'Taking Behavioralism Seriously: Some Evidence of Market Manipulation' (n 165) 1564–1565.

referred to as 'consumer manipulation'[164] or 'digital market manipulation.'[165] It combines for the first time what Ryan Calo calls 'a certain kind of personalization with the intense systematization made possible by mediated consumption.[166] Marketing is systematised as automated commercial messages flood mail and emails; 'online advertising platforms match hundreds of thousands of ads with millions of Internet users on the basis of complex factors in a fraction of a second.'[167] The shift comes with the systematisation of the personal. Traditionally, ads could exploit general consumer vulnerability (e.g. the 'price blindness' that makes most consumers perceive €9.99 as closer to €9.00 than to €10).[168] Now it is possible to change the digital environment of transactions to exploit each consumer's cognitive style, bias, vulnerability, and idiosyncrasy. We have already seen this when dealing with the IoT commerce's immersion in hyperconnected transacting environments. The IoT allows more refined forms of personalisation. Such enhanced personalisation can lead to manipulation, and as concluded by the European Data Protection Supervisor, 'online manipulation poses a threat to society.'[169]

IoT-enhanced personalisation, and hence manipulation, can affect autonomy, freedom of choice, and self-determination more profoundly than other ICTs because of the combined effect of five features of the IoT. First, being 'always on,' Things produce a wealth of granular data (e.g. UK smart meters generate 21.2 billion megabytes of data each year).[170] Second, thanks to its networked dimension, the IoT allows traders to track and profile users across Things and IoT systems and in increasingly sophisticated ways. For example, using signals that can be picked up by a consumer's Things but not heard by the consumer themselves, IoT traders can map all the Things used by the same consumer, which makes cross-device tracking easier.[171] Third, the IoT provides increased opportunities to target consumers. This derives from its being ubiquitous: around us when we walk (smart city), when we are in our own home (smart home), and it even invades the most private of spaces, that is, our body – the Internet of Bodies.[172] Therefore, consumers can be targeted with ads, political messages, or any type of

---

164 Kayleen Manwaring, 'Will Emerging Technologies Outpace Consumer Protection Law? The Case of Digital Consumer Manipulation' [2018] Competition and Consumer Law Journal 141. The author also uses the acronym DCM (digital consumer manipulation).

165 Helberger (n 156). The author takes the phrase from Ryan Calo, 'Digital Market Manipulation' (2013) 82 The George Washington Law Review 995.

166 Calo (n 168) 1021.

167 ibid.

168 Hanson and Kysar, 'Taking Behavioralism Seriously: Some Evidence of Market Manipulation' (n 165) 1441.

169 European Data Protection Supervisor, 'EDPS Opinion on Online Manipulation and Personal Data' (2018) Opinion 3/2018 22.

170 Wild and Thorne (n 147).

171 Haojian Jin, Christian Holz and Kasper Hornbaek, 'Tracko: Ad-Hoc Mobile 3D Tracking Using Bluetooth Low Energy and Inaudible Signals for Cross-Device Interaction' *Proceedings of the 28th Annual ACM Symposium on User Interface Software & Technology* (ACM 2015).

172 Guido Noto La Diega, 'Grinding Privacy in the Internet of Bodies. An Empirical Qualitative Research on Dating Mobile Applications for Men Who Have Sex with Men' in Ronald Leenes et al. (eds), *Data Protection and Privacy: The Internet of Bodies* (Hart 2018).

manipulative content at any given moment and anywhere. Fourth, targeting techniques become increasingly personalised. Thanks to the wealth of data produced by Things, the use of behavioural research 'to exploit the biases, emotions, and vulnerabilities of consumers,'[173] and new technologies allowing refined emotion recognition, IoT traders know what the best way is to target a consumer and when. They may know that consumer X is more susceptible to short video content when they are sad and target them using short video content when the data (e.g. one's tone of voice) suggests that the consumer is sad. Fifth, the IoT furthers the power imbalance between consumers and traders. Tackling this imbalance is the rationale for most consumer laws, designed to address an imbalance that has its roots in, but is not limited to, information asymmetries and economic power. The IoT exacerbates this, mainly because of the power to remotely control, downgrade, 'brick' the Thing throughout its life cycle. The consumer knows that the trader can take away any functionalities of the Thing or even make it unusable. This provides an incentive not to react to unfair practices.

4.3.1 IoT-Enhanced Consumer Manipulation as an Unfair Commercial Practice

The negative effects of personalisation that can be referred to as 'Internet of Personalised Things' have been correctly considered as inherently unfair.[174] They can harm consumers' trust in the IoT. As noted in a study on smart dolls,[175] to find out that free choice is illusory and that monitoring and data-sharing practices are invasive and hidden leads to a loss of trust. Without trust, the IoT will not unleash its potential. Since the Unfair Commercial Practices Directive is aimed at countering misleading and aggressive practices and at building trust in the internal market,[176] this section will inquire whether unfair trading law can provide an adequate response to the risks of the Internet of Personalised Things. In doing so, this section will analyse this directive as amended by Directive (EU) 2019/2161, that is, the Enforcement and Modernisation of Consumer Protection Directive. It has already been seen how the latter amended the Consumer Rights Directive and the Unfair Terms Directive. This reform, part of the 'New Deal for Consumers' package,[177] increases the effectiveness of consumer protection against unfair practices as now member states have to provide consumers not

---

173 Manwaring (n 167) 145.
174 Among the unfair effects that data processing can produce, manipulation and discrimination play a prominent role, according to Gianclaudio Malgieri, 'The Concept of Fairness in the GDPR: A Linguistic and Contextual Interpretation' *Proceedings of the 2020 Conference on Fairness, Accountability, and Transparency* (FAT 2020) 163.
175 Esther Keymolen and Simone Van der Hof, 'Can I Still Trust You, My Dear Doll? A Philosophical and Legal Exploration of Smart Toys and Trust' [2019] Journal of Cyber Policy 1.
176 European Commission, 'Communication on the Application of the Unfair Commercial Practices Directive Achieving a High Level of Consumer Protection Building Trust in the Internal Market' (2013) COM/2013/138 final.
177 European Commission, 'Communication "A New Deal for Consumers"' (2018) COM/2018/183 final.

only of the right to seek an injunction but also compensation, price reduction, and the termination of the contract.[178] The reform made the Unfair Commercial Practices Directive more IoT-ready thanks to a broader definition of *product* – 'any good or service *including* immovable property, *digital service and digital content*, as well as rights and obligations'[179] – and for the reasons detailed in the following passages.

A study on the implementation of the Unfair Commercial Practices Directive showed that it considerably improved consumer protection thanks to two of its specific features, namely, its horizontal safety-net character and its combination of principle-based rules with a 'blacklist' of specific prohibitions of certain unfair practices.[180] This full-harmonisation[181] directive strongly protects consumers in all sectors; in this sense, it provides a safety net that bridges the gaps that are left unregulated by other EU sector-specific rules.[182] Indeed, it applies to all unfair business-to-consumer commercial practices, specifically 'any act, omission, course of conduct or representation, commercial communication including advertising and marketing, by a trader, directly connected with the promotion, sale or supply of a product to consumer.'[183] The concept has been interpreted broadly by the CJEU; for instance, in *UPC*[184] the court stated that even individual acts and omissions amount to 'commercial practices,' thus overcoming more restrictive national rules epitomised by the UK case *R v X Ltd*,[185] where single incidents would fall within the scope of unfair trading laws only depending on the circumstances of the case.[186] Similarly, in *Vanderborght*, the CJEU confirmed a broad notion of commercial practice, which would cover the advertising of oral and dental care services 'whether through publications in advertising periodicals or on the internet, or through the use of signs.'[187] Even more explicitly,

---

178 Unfair Commercial Practices Directive, art 11a. Some member states had already introduced compensation as a remedy to unfair commercial practices when there was no EU obligation to do so (see e.g. the Consumer Protection from Unfair Trading Regulations 2008, reg 27J).

179 Unfair Commercial Practices Directive, art 2(1)(c). The previous definition did not expressly include digital service and digital content.

180 European Commission, 'Communication on the Application of the Unfair Commercial Practices Directive Achieving a High Level of Consumer Protection Building Trust in the Internal Market' (n 180).

181 On the effects of full harmonisation in this field, see Cases C-261/07 and C-299/07 *VTB-VAB NV v Total Belgium NV; Galatea BVBA v Sanoma Magazines Belgium NV* [2009] ECR I-2949; Case C-421/12 *European Commission v Belgium* [2015] 1 CMLR 13.

182 The filling-the-gap function of the directive is confirmed by its provision whereby '[i]n the case of conflict between the provisions of this Directive and other Community rules regulating specific aspects of unfair commercial practices, the latter shall prevail and apply to those specific aspects' (art 3(4).

183 Unfair Commercial Practices Directive, arts 2(d) and 3.

184 Case C-388/13 *Nemzeti Fogyasztovedelmi Hatosag v UPC Magyarorszag Kft* [2015] Bus L R 946.

185 [2013] EWCA Crim 818; [2014] 1 WLR 591.

186 ibid [22] (Leveson LG): '[i]n the circumstances, it is clear that a commercial practice can be derived from a single incident. It will depend on the circumstances.'

187 Case C-339/15 *Proceedings against Luc Vanderborght* [2017] 3 CMLR 37.

the CJEU in *Dyson v BSH*[188] gave 'commercial practice' a 'particularly broad formulation,'[189] including all practices that originate from traders and are directly connected with the promotion, sale, or supply of their products to consumers. This first feature – the horizontal safety-net character – suggests that the directive is fit for the IoT because it takes account of the latter's sectoral fragmentation as well as of the many forms that personalisation and manipulation can take. Amazon Echo e.g. may influence a consumer by manipulating the search results and not making it clear that the items recommended for purchase are shown because their manufacturer paid a fee for them to be ranked higher. These types of manipulation are becoming increasingly common and may not necessarily be captured by other consumer laws. Positively, the Enforcement and Modernisation of Consumer Protection Directive introduced specific provisions regarding e-commerce searches and rankings. In particular, first, it defined 'ranking' as the relative prominence given to products, as presented, organised, or communicated by the trader, irrespective of the technological means used for such presentation, organisation, or communication.[190] Second, it clarified that not to inform the consumers about the main parameters determining the ranking of products presented to them 'as a result of the search query and the relative importance of those parameters, as opposed to other parameters,'[191] is a misleading omission. Third, it blacklisted (i.e. made automatically unfair) the practice to provide search results in response to a consumer's online search query without clearly disclosing any paid advertisement or payment specifically for achieving higher ranking of products within the search results.[192] This is a commendable strengthening of consumer protection that builds on national best practices. Indeed, ranking manipulation was already considered misleading in Germany, where the *Landgericht Berlin* (Regional Court of Berlin) sanctioned a well-known comparison and booking service that enabled hotels to manipulate the ranking by paying higher commission fees.[193] Similarly, in France the *Conseil d'État* observed that the practice was unfair and noted that fairness means good faith in the provision of a ranking service, 'without trying to alter it or manipulate it for purposes that are not in the users' interest.'[194] The qualification of these practices being unfair will soon be complemented by a new obligation that the forthcoming Digital Markets Act will place on 'gatekeepers' (a provider of core platform

---

188 Case C-632/16 *Dyson Ltd, Dyson BV v BSH Home Appliances NV* [2018] 7 WLUK 574.
189 ibid [30], referring to Case C-391/12 *RLvS Verlagsgesellschaft mbH v Stuttgarter Wochenblatt GmbH* | [2014] 2 CMLR 7.
190 Unfair Commercial Practices Directive, art 2(1)(m), as inserted by the Enforcement and Modernisation of Consumer Protection Directive, art 3.
191 Unfair Commercial Practices Directive, art 7(4a), as inserted by the Enforcement and Modernisation of Consumer Protection Directive, art 3.
192 Annex I to the Unfair Commercial Practices Directive, point 11a, as inserted by the Enforcement and Modernisation of Consumer Protection Directive.
193 LG Berlin, 25 August 2011–16 O 418/11 [2012] MMR 683.
194 Conseil d'État, *Étude Annuelle 2014 – Le Numérique et Les Droits Fondamentaux* (EDCE 2014) 273.

services, such as search engines and social networking services).[195] Gatekeepers will have to refrain from treating more favourably in ranking services and products offered by the gatekeeper itself or by any third party belonging to the same undertaking compared to similar services or products of third party and apply fair and nondiscriminatory conditions to such ranking.[196] Such a clear and EU-wide protection against this form of consumer manipulation is of utmost importance in the IoT mainly because of the latter's limited interfaces. Most Things will be able to display only one or a few search results; therefore, consumer freedom of choice risks being severely curtailed by practices attempting to manipulate the way search results are ranked. This links back to the issues of the digital shelf and the attention wars seen above.

An objection to the application of unfair trading laws to IoT-enhanced manipulation could be that it is the Thing, not the trader (e.g. Amazon), that puts in place manipulative practices. Such an objection could be easily defeated by noting that the definition of 'commercial practice' does not require the promotion, sale, or supply to be done by the trader itself. As held in *R. v Scottish and Southern Energy Plc*,[197] a nontrading holding company can be regarded as a trader putting in place unfair commercial practices despite the latter being the direct responsibility of one of the subsidiary's employees. In that case, there was evidence that the training of the subsidiary's employees was done with the holding company's involvement and under its ultimate supervision and control, even if it was acting in conjunction with, and left the details to, the subsidiary. If a nontrading holding company can be held liable for the unfair practices of one of its subsidiaries' employees, then IoT traders will be liable for the unfair practices carried out by their Things, since they train, supervise, and ultimately control them.

The success of the Unfair Commercial Practices Directive derives also by the joint operation of principle-based rules and a 'blacklist' of specific prohibitions of some unfair practices. The former consists of outlawing:

   (i) The practices that are in contravention of professional diligence;[198]
  (ii) Misleading actions;[199]
 (iii) Misleading omissions;[200] and
  (iv) Aggressive practices.[201]

---

195 Proposal for a regulation on contestable and fair markets in the digital sector ('Digital Markets Act' or DMA) COM/2020/842 final, art 2(1).
196 Digital Markets Act, art 6(1)(d).
197 [2012] EWCA Crim 539; (2012) 176 JP 241.
198 Unfair Commercial Practices Directive, art 5; reg 3(3).
199 Unfair Commercial Practices Directive, art 6; Consumer Protection from Unfair Trading Regulations 2008, SI 2008/1277, reg 5.
200 Unfair Commercial Practices Directive, art 7; Consumer Protection from Unfair Trading Regulations 2008, reg 6.
201 Unfair Commercial Practices Directive, arts 8–9; Consumer Protection from Unfair Trading Regulations 2008, reg 7.

In doing so, the directive and its national implementations, e.g. the UK Consumer Protection from Unfair Trading Regulations 2008,[202] do not describe individual practices (e.g. price discrimination) but set out some requirements that, if made out, indicate that a practice is unfair. Whereas these rules require a case-by-case assessment of their unfairness, the blacklisted practices are considered unfair in all circumstances.

The principle-based rules can be beneficial to counter the negative effects of the Internet of Personalised Things. Indeed, they allow the directive to adapt to fast-evolving products, services, and sales methods and prevent unfair behaviour that is not covered by specific prohibitions.[203] Each rule will be analysed in turn.

4.3.1.1 Unfair Commercial Practices That Are Contrary to the Requirements of Professional Diligence: Vulnerable by Design?

Under Article 5 of the directive, a commercial practice is unfair if it is contrary to the requirements of professional diligence and is likely to materially distort the average consumer's economic behaviour. An unfair commercial practice of this type was at issue in *Office of Fair Trading v Ashbourne Management Services Ltd*,[204] where a gym described members who wished to terminate their agreements before the end of a minimum subscription period as 'defaulters' and threatened to register that information with credit reference agencies. This was contrary to professional diligence, because a gym's subscription is not a regulated credit agreement and the 'debt' was, in reality, nothing more than unliquidated damages. In the context of the IoT, one of the commercial practices that may be considered contrary to professional diligence would be the sale of a Thing with preinstalled software without any option for the consumer to purchase the same model of Thing not equipped with preinstalled software, as was the case in *Deroo-Blanquart*.[205] On this front, the proposed Digital Markets Act will strengthen consumer protection by obliging gatekeepers to allow end users to uninstall any preinstalled software applications on their core platform service.[206]

For a commercial practice to be found unfair and contrary to professional diligence, three requirements have to be made out. The practice must:

(i) Be contrary to professional diligence;
(ii) Likely lead to an unwanted transactional decision; and
(iii) Regard the average consumer.

---

202 SI 2008/1277.
203 European Commission, 'Communication on the Application of the Unfair Commercial Practices Directive Achieving a High Level of Consumer Protection Building Trust in the Internal Market' (n 180).
204 [2011] EWHC 1237 (Ch); [2011] ECC 31.
205 (n 51). It is up to the national courts to assess if such practice is contrary to diligence and likely to distort the average consumer's behaviour, taking into account the specific circumstances of the case.
206 Digital Markets Act, art 6(1)(b).

The first requirement is straightforward. The practice must be contrary to professional diligence, that is, the standard of special skill and care which a trader may reasonably be expected to exercise towards consumers, commensurate with honest market practice or good faith in the trader's field of activity.[207] Codes of conduct and professional bodies regulations will play a role in defining the relevant standards.[208]

Second, the practice must materially distort the economic behaviour of consumers by appreciably impairing their ability to make an informed decision, thus potentially causing them to make a transactional decision that they would not have taken otherwise.[209] *Transactional decisions* are defined as:

> Any decision taken by a consumer concerning whether, how and on what terms to purchase, make payment in whole or in part for, retain or dispose of a product or to exercise a contractual right in relation to the product, *whether the consumer decides to act or to refrain from acting.*[210]

It is settled case law that 'transactional decision' must be interpreted in a broad way. In *Trento Sviluppo*[211] it was held that this concept covers not only the decision whether or not to purchase a product but also decisions directly related to the former. In that case, the directly related decision was the decision to enter the shop; in the IoT, a similar situation would configure if the IoT trader manipulated the consumer into keeping the Thing 'always on.' This could be the result of design choices, e.g. if the Thing does not come with a button to switch it off (e.g. Google Home). This trend justifies calls for a right to be disconnected.[212]

Third, 'average consumer' refers to the consumer who is reached by the practice, to whom the practice is addressed, or when it is directed to a particular group of consumers, the reference will be to the average member of that group. The Unfair Commercial Practices Directive does not define the average consumer, but the CJEU[213] and the national authorities[214] tend to consider it as reasonably well-informed and reasonably observant and circumspect, taking into account social, cultural, and linguistic factors. As observed in *UPC*,[215] the average consumer is

207 Unfair Commercial Practices Directive, art 2(h).
208 See Unfair Commercial Practices Directive, recital 20.
209 Unfair Commercial Practices Directive, art 2(e).
210 Unfair Commercial Practices Directive, art 2(k), emphasis added.
211 Case C-281/12 *Trento Sviluppo s.r.l. v Autorità Garante della Concorrenza e del Mercato* [2014] 1 WLR 890.
212 Cláudia Toriz Ramos, 'Democracy and Governance in the Smart City' in Anna Visvizi and Miltiadis D Lytras (eds), *Smart Cities: Issues and Challenges. Mapping Political, Social and Economic Risks and Threats* (Elsevier 2019) 17.
213 Cases C-54/17 and C-55/17 *AGCM v Wind Tre* [2019] 1 CMLR 14 [51].
214 Office of Fair Trading and Department for Business Enterprise & Regulatory Reform, *Consumer Protection from Unfair Trading. Guidance on the Consumer Protection from Unfair Trading Regulations 2008* (OFT and BERR 2008) [14.32].
215 (n 184).

'economically weaker and less experienced in legal matters than the other party to the contract.'[216] In that case, it followed that it did not constitute a defence for the trader to prove that the consumer could have obtained the correct information by themselves. A more trader-friendly approach is taken in those jurisdictions, such as England, where the average consumer is seen as taking reasonable care of themselves rather than, to put it in Brigg J's emphatic words in *Office of Fair Trading v Purely Creative Ltd*,[217] 'the ignorant, the careless or the overhasty consumer.'[218] Leaving aside this perhaps caricatural representation of the EU concept of average consumer, one should wonder if pervasive sociotechnological phenomena such as the IoT affect the standard of 'average consumer' and make us all ignorant, or at least more vulnerable, compared to the average consumers of nonsmart products.[219] As Ugo Mattei recently put it, smart products are making us 'dumb' in the sense that the IoT is transforming us into commodities akin to cyborgs.[220]

Vulnerable consumers enjoy special protection in the context of the unfair practices that are in violation of professional diligence.[221] Indeed, Article 5(3) of the directive provides special rules that apply when the practice can affect a group of consumers who are particularly vulnerable.[222] They may be vulnerable either to a commercial practice or to the underlying product.[223] For example, one could be vulnerable to the practice consisting of the exploitation of every Thing in a consumer's smart home to deliver ads. Vulnerability to products may apply, for instance, to a scenario where Amazon uses its emotion-recognition technology[224] and its knowledge of the consumer behaviour to target them with ads regarding immune system boosters when the consumer is worried that they are about to get a cold. Traditionally, it has been recognised that vulnerability can be related to ignorance, necessity, or trust.[225] In a recent study regarding IoT targeting, it has been suggested that a fourth cause of vulnerability should be the susceptibility to digital market manipulation.[226] The argument could be put forward that the Internet of Personalised Things is making us all vulnerable. The matter has practical relevance because if a commercial practice is likely to distort a vulnerable consumer's

---

216 ibid [53].
217 [2011] EWHC 106 (Ch); [2011] ECC 20.
218 ibid [62].
219 Ugo Mattei, 'Smart' in *Parole Chiave del XXI Secolo* (Treccani 2020).
220 Ugo Mattei, 'Do Smart Things Make Us Dumb? Reflections on the Addiction Crisis of Cyborg Consummerism' (2020) 3 REDC 613.
221 The importance and complexities of the concept of vulnerability in consumer law are at the centre of Christine Riefa and Severine Saintier (eds), *Vulnerable Consumers and the Law: Consumer Protection and Access to Justice* (Routledge 2020).
222 Unfair Commercial Practices Directive, art 5(3).
223 Unfair Commercial Practices Directive, art 5(3).
224 USPTO 10,019,489.
225 Spence Nathan Thal, 'The Inequality of Bargaining Power Doctrine: The Problem of Defining Contractual Unfairness' [1988] Oxford Journal of Legal Studies 17.
226 Helberger (n 156).

behaviour, then it 'shall be assessed from the perspective of the average member of that group,'[227] which means a lower threshold for a finding of unfairness.

This provision does not tackle all types of vulnerability, at least not expressly. It deals only with consumers who are vulnerable because of their mental or physical infirmity, age, or credulity and only inasmuch as the trader could reasonably be expected to foresee the economic behaviour's distortion. The first two types of vulnerability are self-explanatory and are not particularly relevant from an IoT angle. They may nonetheless play a role in the fields of smart ageing and games because of the targeting of the elderly and of the children. It has been observed that '[m]illennials who adopt IoT offer their data more willingly to marketers and firms, which makes it easier for marketers to collect data and target customers more precisely.'[228] Less clear and more relevant is the concept of 'credulity.' As an example of unfair practice affecting credulous consumers, one could refer to the Finnish case[229] of a trader who had stated that for each candy bag sold, they would plant a tree, despite having already agreed to plant a certain number of trees independently of the number of candy bags sold. The Finnish Market Court found that this statement took advantage of the credulity of consumers that were concerned about the environment. This does not mean that 'green' consumers are credulous in general, but they are more likely to be vulnerable to certain practices.

'Credulity' is the most flexible of the categories considered by Article 5(3) in the context of the protection of vulnerable consumers, but it should be critically assessed whether it is flexible enough to counter the negative effects of the Internet of Personalised Things.

As observed by the European Commission in its guidance on the directive,[230] 'credulity' covers groups of consumers who may more readily believe specific claims. However, these are not groups that can be identified with certainty. The term is 'neutral and circumstantial. . . . *Any consumer could qualify as a member of this group.*'[231] Depending on the circumstances, anyone could be credulous, even just temporarily and with regards to a single product or practice. A study on consumer vulnerability[232] found that credulous people are less likely to complain when facing problems. Considering that one of the main reasons of the Enforcement and Modernisation of Consumer Protection Directive was to improve enforcement,[233] an interpretation of credulity and vulnerability that is as broad as possible would prevent the issue of consumers not reacting to unfair practices, thus furthering the aims of the reformed directive. Another argument towards a

---

227 Unfair Commercial Practices Directive, art 5(3).
228 Spilotro (n 145).
229 *Kuluttaja-asiamies v Leaf Suomi Oy* (Markkinaoikeus 8 August 2011 MAO 157/11).
230 European Commission, 'Guidance on the Implementation/Application of Directive 2005/29/EC' (2016) Staff Working Document SWD/2016/163 final.
231 ibid [2.6.1].
232 London Economics, VVA Consulting and Ipsos Mori, 'Consumer Vulnerability across Key Markets in the European Union' (2016) European Commission EAHC 2013/CP/08.
233 Enforcement and Modernisation of Consumer Protection Directive, recital 16.

broad interpretation of credulity and vulnerability is that this is consistent with insights from behavioural studies, which EU consumer laws increasingly draw on.[234] These studies[235] confirm that a vulnerable consumer is one who, as a result of sociodemographic characteristics, behavioural characteristics, personal situation, or market environment:

(i) Is at higher risk of experiencing negative outcomes in the market;
(ii) Has limited well-being maximisation capabilities;
(iii) Struggles to obtain or assimilate information;
(iv) Is less able to access and select suitable products; *or*
(v) Is more susceptible to certain marketing practices.

Arguably, as a consequences of the aforementioned IoT-generated wealth of granular data, improved targeting capabilities, and remote control throughout the life cycle of the Thing, consumers are likely to find themselves vulnerable to an insidious market environment where it is difficult to obtain and assimilate information (the contractual quagmire) and where several IoT traders contend the user's attention, thus reducing the consumers' capabilities to maximise their well-being and choose the most suitable products. A recent study[236] on the dark side of the behaviour of IoT traders shed light on a number of exploitative and extractive practices where the complexity of the technology is used to spread confusion among the consumers. This study mentions the examples of complex pricing alternatives of IoT subscriptions and complicated usage rates that make comparisons of price and fees among IoT service providers rather arduous. This renders well-informed decision-making difficult for consumers; not only the young and the elderly are vulnerable, but also the 'technologically unsavvy are particularly susceptible to this type of dark-side behaviour.'[237] These are all good reasons to widen the scope of vulnerability to tackle the issues on the Internet of Personalised Things. The IoT may lead to a more intense application of the special regime on unfair commercial practices affecting vulnerable consumers, which in practice means that it will be easier for consumers (and consumer organisations) to prove that the Internet of Personalised Things is unfair. Indeed, by virtue of this special regime, the likelihood of the practice distorting a vulnerable consumer's behaviour will be assessed from the perspective of the average IoT consumer, who can hardly be described as reasonably well-informed, reasonably observant, and circumspect.

---

234 Geneviève Helleringer and Anne-Lise Sibony, 'European Consumer Protection through the Behavioral Lens' (2016) 23 Columbia Journal of European Law 607.
235 London Economics, VVA Consulting and Ipsos Mori (n 237).
236 David De Cremer, Bang Nguyen and Lyndon Simkin, 'The Integrity Challenge of the Internet-of-Things (IoT): On Understanding Its Dark Side' (2017) 33 Journal of Marketing Management 145.
237 ibid 151. Citing Pennie Frow and others, 'Customer Management and CRM: Addressing the Dark Side' (2011) 25 Journal of Services Marketing 79.

4.3.1.2 *Misleading Actions and Confusing Practices*

Another set of principle-based rules deals with misleading actions. These rules are distinct from those that apply to the practices in violation of professional diligence. As the CJEU pointed out in *CHS Tour Services GmbH v Team4 Travel GmbH*,[238] there is no automatic infringement of the requirements of professional diligence if a commercial practice is categorised as a misleading action. These actions may, however, be also contrary to professional diligence. As an example of such a misleading action, one can think of Italy's injunction[239] against a website that invited consumers to purchase drug Kaletra, falsely advertised as 'the only remedy to the Coronavirus (COVID-19).'[240]

Under Article 6 of the Unfair Commercial Practices Directive, misleading actions can be divided into two types: information-related and behaviour-related.

For an information-related action to be regarded as misleading, it must:

  (i) Likely deceive the average consumer;
 (ii) Likely cause the consumer to make an unwanted transactional decision;
(iii) Concern certain items of information that are considered 'material.'

The first requirement is that the misleading action must be likely to deceive the average consumer.[241] This can depend on the provision of false information or of factually correct information that is nonetheless deceitful, for instance, due to its overall presentation. As held in *Competition and Markets Authority v Care UK Health and Social Care Holdings Ltd*,[242] a misleading action does not inherently require a dishonest action, as the offence is one of strict liability.[243] As an example of deceitful false information, Poland's Office of Competition and Consumer Protection[244] sanctioned a trader for falsely claiming that its loans to consumers had the lowest interest rates on the market. As an example of truthful yet deceitful actions, Malta's Consumer Claims Tribunal[245] considered as misleading a mobile phone operator's advertisement where the mobile rates were claimed to be 30% cheaper than those of the competitors. Indeed, it ambiguously presented the offer as it did not make clear that the first minute of phone conversation was not on a per-second basis. In an IoT context, e.g. a statement that Echo can be used to listen to music for free when in fact a consumer needs to purchase additional

---

238 Case C-435/11 [2014] 1 All ER (Comm).
239 Autorità Garante della Concorrenza e del Mercato, decision 16 April 2020 no 28226 (2020) XXX(18) Bollettino 11.
240 ibid 11.
241 Unfair Commercial Practices Directive, art 6(1).
242 [2019] EWHC 2828 (Ch).
243 The court followed *R v X Ltd* (n 185).
244 Urząd Ochrony Konkurencji i Konsumentów (UOKiK), decision No RPZ 4/2015 – RPZ-61/2/13/ JM, cited by European Commission, '2016 Guidance on Unfair Commercial Practices' (n 234) [3.3.1].
245 Consumer Claims Tribunal, decision 17 April 2013 (*Melita*) as cited ibid.

subscriptions (e.g. Prime), may be regarded as an action likely to deceive the average consumer.

Second, the misleading action must be likely to cause the consumer to take a transactional decision that they would have not taken otherwise.[246] This requirement applies also to practices in contravention of professional diligence, misleading actions, misleading omissions, and aggressive practices. Therefore, the same broad concept of 'transactional decision' applies here. On the point, national courts have followed the CJEU's approach. E.g. an English court stated in *R v X Ltd*[247] that concept of transactional decision is such that it may be affected by statements made *after the transaction* has been completed. In that case, the statement, provided after the installation of a CCTV system, that the system as fitted was fit for purpose was considered misleading. Linking back to our case study, if a consumer buys a product and, during the time when they could have returned it, Alexa convinces them that the product is fit for purpose, such practice may be regarded as unfair regardless of the fact that, strictly speaking, it occurred once the transactional decision had already been taken.

Third, the information must regard one of seven items expressly listed by the directive.[248] These are the existence or nature of the product; its main characteristics; the extent of the trader's commitments; the price; the need for a service, part, replacement, or repair; the nature, attributes, and rights of the trader; and the consumer's rights. These items are called 'material information,' that is, as noted in *Office of Fair Trading v Purely Creative Ltd*,[249] the information which is necessary to enable the average consumer to take an informed transactional decision. A key question in the IoT is whether presenting the Thing as provided for free, when in fact it is 'paid for' using the consumer's personal data, can be regarded as a misleading action. In other words, it can be posited that such an action qualifies as a false statement regarding material information, in particular the price. Whilst there is disagreement on the point, it can be argued that, in light of the growth of the business model having personal data as contractual consideration,[250] the notion of price 'must be interpreted broadly, including non-monetary forms of exchanges, such as data.'[251] Whilst this inference appears correct, a better way to tackle the practice is to invoke the breach of Article 7 of the directive ('misleading omissions') and of its blacklist; therefore, we will expand on the matter later in the chapter.

The directive does not limit the notion of misleading action to the provision of information. Behaviour-related misleading actions include confusing

---

246 Unfair Commercial Practices Directive, art 6(1).

247 (n 185) [25].

248 Unfair Commercial Practices Directive, art 6(1)(a)-(g).

249 (n 217).

250 E.g. in June 2021, Google changed YouTube's Terms of Service to provide that YouTube has the right to monetise all content on the platform (*content* is not defined and therefore could include *data*). See YouTube Terms of Service, available at <www.youtube.com/t/terms>.

251 Helberger (n 156) 10.

marketing,[252] noncompliance with codes of conduct,[253] and the marketing of goods as being identical to goods that are marketed in other member states whilst they are significantly different.[254] Compared to the misleading actions regarding false or otherwise deceitful information, these three behaviour-related actions have to meet partly different requirements to be found unfair. The likelihood to lead to an unwanted transactional decision applies here as well. Conversely, unlike the information-related misleading actions, the assessment here will have to be conducted in the 'factual context (of the practice), taking account of all its features and circumstances.'[255]

Confusing marketing is the marketing of products that creates confusion with the competitors' products (e.g. copycat branding).[256] Whilst the use of a sign that is similar to an existing mark can qualify as trademark infringement,[257] if the trademark is dissimilar but the more general branding is similar, this could fall outside the scope of trademark infringement.[258] That is when the Unfair Commercial Practices Directive[259] can step in.[260] An example may be the deployment of a virtual assistant whose voice resembles Siri and thus may lead consumers to trust it.[261]

Noncompliance with codes of conduct can qualify as unfair only when two requirements are met. First, the trader has breached the code's commitments, which are firm and capable to be verified.[262] Second, the trader indicated in its practice that they were bound by the code.[263] Let us imagine that a trader advertises its Things as being secure pursuant to the Code of Practice for Consumer IoT Security.[264] The code's first commitment is that Things' passwords have to be unique and not resettable to any universal factory default value. If the trader sells Things with default passwords such as 'admin' or 'password,' then they are committing an unfair, misleading action.

---

252 Unfair Commercial Practices Directive, art 6(2)(a).

253 Unfair Commercial Practices Directive, art 6(2)(b).

254 Unfair Commercial Practices Directive, art 6(2)(c).

255 Unfair Commercial Practices Directive, art 6(2).

256 European Commission, '2016 Guidance on Unfair Commercial Practices' (n 234).

257 Directive (EU) 2015/2436 of 16 December 2015 to Approximate the Laws of the Member States Relating to Trade Marks ('Trade Marks Directive') [2015] OJ L 336/1, art 10.

258 In common law jurisdictions, in addition to the remedies afforded by trademark registration, companies can rely on the economic tort of passing off. Claimants have to prove that their goodwill has been damaged by the defendant's misrepresentation and that the misrepresentation was likely to deceive the public (*Reckitt & Colman v Borden* [1990] RPC 341 HL).

259 Art 6(2)(a).

260 See Marknadsdomstolen No MD 2009:36 of 19 November 2009 on similar-looking invoices.

261 Voice misappropriation may be unlawful under other regimes. For an example applying the right to publicity, see *Tom Waits v Frito-Lay* 978 F.2d 1093 (9th Cir. 1992), cert. denied, 113 S. Ct. 1047 (1993).

262 Unfair Commercial Practices Directive, art 6(2)(b)(i).

263 Unfair Commercial Practices Directive, art 6(2)(b)(ii).

264 Department for Digital, Culture, Media & Sport, *Code of Practice for Consumer IoT Security* (UK Gov 2018) <www.gov.uk/government/publications/code-of-practice-for-consumer-iot-security/code-of-practice-for-consumer-iot-security>.

Finally, the marketing of goods as being identical to goods that are marketed in other member states whilst they are significantly different is an addition of the Enforcement and Modernisation of Consumer Protection Directive.[265] Whilst the reference to 'goods' implies a focus on tangible products, it should be underlined that in the IoT tangible goods can be rendered different through a variation of their intangible components. Things may embed lower-quality software or provide more limited digital contents if compared to Things used in another member state. Thus, this directive would complement the Cross-Border Service Portability Regulation. Indeed, whilst the latter does not apply to the lack of portability of online content services when they are not paid for,[266] the former may fill the gap and cover also free services. More generally, it is useful to keep in mind that, although this particular provision regards goods, the Unfair Commercial Practices Directive applies to products. These are defined as 'any good or service including immovable property, digital service and digital content;'[267] therefore, it is fit for the IoT as it applies to all those Things that escape the good-service dichotomy.

4.3.1.3 Misleading Omissions and the Limitations of the Communication Medium

Traders can mislead consumers not only through their actions but also through their omissions. An example of misleading omission regards planned obsolescence, that is, a common practice in an IoT context.[268] Planned obsolescence refers to the practice of designing a product so that it will become obsolete or nonfunctional after a certain period of time; it has been observed that obsolescence 'sits uneasily with the current prescriptions of the law.'[269] This practice is not in itself unfair. However, the European Commission[270] noted that a trader who omits to clearly inform about planned obsolescence (e.g. that a software is likely to be discontinued after a number of years) may be in breach of the directive's provision on misleading omissions. This could reduce IoT traders' control over their Things' life cycle, thus partly correcting the power imbalance between them and their consumers.

Article 7 of the Unfair Commercial Practices Directive considers misleading those omissions that:

 (i) Are likely to lead to an unwanted transactional decision; and *either*
 (ii) Omit material information, *or*
 (iii) Hide it.

---

265 Art 3(3).
266 Cross-Border Service Portability Regulation, art 3.
267 Unfair Commercial Practices Directive, art 2(c).
268 Marcus Foth and others, 'Submission to the Australian Council of Learned Academies Internet of Things Report 2020' (2010) QUT.
269 Pierre-Emmanuel Moyse, 'The Uneasy Case of Programmed Obsolescence Part III: Forum – Legal Issues in the Modern Economy' (2020) 71 University of New Brunswick Law Journal 61, 114.
270 European Commission, '2016 Guidance on Unfair Commercial Practices' (n 234).

The first requirement is not problematic as it is the same that has been previously analysed with regards to unfair practices in contravention of professional diligence and misleading actions. It means that the practice causes or is likely to cause the consumer to make a transactional decision that they would have not otherwise taken.[271] It includes one-off omissions concerning an individual consumer, as was the case in *UPC*.[272]

The second requirement is that the trader omitted 'material information,' that is, the information that the average consumer needs, according to the context, to take an informed transactional decision.[273] In *Office of Fair Trading v Purely Creative Ltd*,[274] Briggs J stated that the 'question is not whether the omitted information would assist, or be relevant, but whether its provision is necessary to enable the average consumer to take an informed transactional decision.'[275] There are four types of material information.

First, the information is 'material' depending on the context ('contextual materiality'). This is a flexible category that can be better understood considering the distinction set forth in *Secretary of State for Business, Innovation and Skills v PLT Anti-Marketing Ltd*.[276] The court of appeals distinguished between inward-facing information and publicly accessible information. The former is information about a trader's product that is likely to be known only to the trader – in that case, the consumer needs to obtain the information from the trader and its omission is likely to qualify as misleading. Not all inward-facing information about a product is material; in *PLT Anti-Marketing* e.g. a trader was not required to disclose to consumers its markup or the cost of obtaining the product from a supplier. Conversely, if the information is publicly accessible and the consumer could obtain the information by making enquiries in the marketplace (e.g. looking it up online), then the information would likely be regarded as immaterial and its omission not misleading.

A second type of material information refers to Annex II to the directive. This provides a nonexhaustive list[277] of EU law instruments that set out obligations to provide information that is deemed material for the purposes of the provision on misleading omissions. These include the information requirements imposed by the Consumer Rights Directive[278] and the e-Commerce Directive.[279]

A third type was introduced by the Enforcement and Modernisation of Consumer Protection Directive, which provided more stringent requirements for consumer reviews. When a trader provides access to consumer reviews, information

---

271 Unfair Commercial Practices Directive, art 7(1).
272 (n 184).
273 Unfair Commercial Practices Directive, art 7(1).
274 (n 217).
275 ibid [74].
276 [2015] EWCA Civ 76; [2015] Bus L R 959.
277 Unfair Commercial Practices Directive, art 7(5).
278 Arts 5–6.
279 Unfair Commercial Practices Directive, arts 5–6.

about whether and how the trader ensures that the reviews originate from consumers who have actually used or purchased the product is material.[280]

Finally, Article 7(4) provides a list of information items that are material in the case of an invitation to purchase, if their 'materiality' is not already apparent from the context. Limiting ourselves to the items that are more directly relevant from an IoT perspective:

a) *The main characteristics of the product, 'to an extent appropriate to the medium and the product. '*[281] More will be said later on about the importance of the medium, but suffice it to say now that it is important to distinguish between the use of a Thing for e-commerce purposes – Thing as a medium – and the purchase of a Thing regardless of the medium – Thing as a product. In the former scenario, the physical limitations of the Thing may provide a justification for the trader to provide less information regarding the product purchased through the Thing. In the latter, conversely, traders will have to be careful to provide thorough and clear information to offset the intrinsic complexity of the Thing as a product.

b) *The address and the identity of the trader.* This is important in an IoT context because we have seen that, as a result of a complex supply chain and of an intricate web of legals, it is not easy for the consumer to identify who is the trader.

c) *The price and the manner in which the price is calculated.* It can be argued[282] that 'price' should be interpreted broadly as encompassing nonmonetary exchanges (e.g. personal data as consideration). If a trader omits to inform that the price of the service or product is paid for by the consumer's data, the practice may count as a misleading omission. This will depend not only on the courts' readiness to consider personal data as a currency but also on their assessment of whether the consumer needs such information to take an informed transactional decision and whether its omission would be likely to lead to an unwanted transactional decision. This will have to be seen on a case-by-case basis, but arguably in an IoT context that increasingly relies on data monetisation, this information should be regarded as material.

d) *The existence of a right of withdrawal, when applicable.* This has been strengthened by the Enforcement and Modernisation of Consumer Protection Directive. Indeed, member states have been empowered to adopt stronger rules on the right of withdrawal to better protect their consumers in the context of unsolicited visits by a trader to a consumer's home (doorstep selling) and commercial excursions.[283] Since these practices may qualify as aggressive, they will be dealt with in the next section. Suffice it to say, however, that

---

280 Unfair Commercial Practices Directive, art 7(6).
281 Unfair Commercial Practices Directive, art 7(4)(a).
282 Helberger (n 156).
283 Consumer Rights Directive, art 9(1a).

the concept of home should include the smart home and IoT traders should therefore be careful to avoid unsolicited virtual visits.

e) *Whether the third party offering the products on an online marketplace is a trader or not.* This is an important innovation of the Enforcement and Modernisation of Consumer Protection Directive, and it can be useful in an IoT context. IoT traders can allow third parties to integrate their apps into the former's Things. Most of these third parties are likely to qualify as traders. In any event the IoT trader will have an obligation to inform about their quality as traders (or as consumers); otherwise, they are likely to be in breach of this provision on misleading omissions.

As ruled in *Deroo-Blanquart*,[284] the aforementioned is an 'exhaustive list of the material information that must be included in an invitation to purchase.'[285] However, the fact that a trader provides, in an invitation to purchase, all the information listed above does not preclude that invitation from being regarded as a misleading action or a misleading omission of the 'hiding' sort, to which we now turn.

The third requirement for the omission to be found misleading is that information is hidden, as opposed to being altogether omitted. This requirement is alternative to the second one. It rarely happens that a trader simply omits material information that is mandated to allow the consumer to make informed transactional decisions. Positively, therefore, the directive[286] addresses the more usual scenario where the information is hidden or provided in an unclear, unintelligible, ambiguous, or untimely manner. This comes with the proviso of the likelihood to lead to an unwanted transactional decision. This provision is of utmost importance to counter the contractual quagmire in which IoT consumers find themselves. If IoT traders bury the mandated information in legals that are long, difficult to find, or difficult to understand, this would be likely to count as a misleading omission of this type. The directive expressly mentions a particular category of 'hiding' practice, that is, the failure to identify the commercial intent of the commercial practice, if this intent is not already apparent from the context.[287] The European Commission's official guidance deals with the issue of whether traders who provide 'free' services where the consumers' personal data is monetised should inform consumers – and, correspondingly, whether omitting this information would be a misleading omission. Hiding the purpose of data processing is, in principle, in breach of the GDPR,[288] but a trader's violation of data protection laws does not necessarily mean that the practice is also in breach of the Unfair Commercial Practices Directive.[289] However, data protection violations 'should

---

284 (n 51).
285 ibid [73].
286 Unfair Commercial Practices Directive, art 7(3).
287 Unfair Commercial Practices Directive, art 7(2).
288 See the principle of purpose limitation under the GDPR, art 5(1)(b) and the right to be informed about the purposes of the data processing under arts 13(1)(c) and 14(1)(c).
289 European Commission, '2016 Guidance on Unfair Commercial Practices' (n 234) [1.4.10].

be considered when assessing the overall unfairness of commercial practices,'[290] and if the trader does not inform a consumer that the data that is required to access the service will be used for commercial purposes, this may qualify as a misleading omission of material information.[291]

Along the same line as confusing marketing and other non-information-related misleading actions, the assessment of whether omissions are misleading has to look at the factual context of the practice, taking account of all its features and circumstances. However, a specific requirement is that courts that assess the unfairness of misleading omissions need also consider the limitations of the communication medium.[292] This is of great importance in an IoT context, given the aforementioned limitations in terms of size of interfaces, lack of displays, etc. The directive[293] clarifies that, where the medium used to communicate the practice imposes limitations of space or time, these limitations and any measures taken by the trader to make the information available to consumers by other means shall be considered in deciding whether information has been omitted. This means that, when a Thing is used as a medium to communicate commercial practices, its limitations (e.g. small display) provide a justification for the IoT trader not to provide certain information through the Thing itself. The display of a biometric wristband may not provide the required information but simply tell consumers where they can find such information (e.g. the terms of service available on the manufacturer's website). Unlike the provision on information to be regarded as material in an invitation to purchase,[294] the directive does not expressly provide a general obligation for courts to consider both the limitations of the 'Thing as a medium' and the complexity of the 'Thing as a product.' However, the CJEU in *Deroo-Blanquart* stated that it is up to national courts to determine if there has been a misleading omission, taking into account also 'the nature and characteristics of the product.'[295] Therefore, also the complexity of the 'Thing as a product' can be taken into account to decide whether there has been a misleading omission of material information. While the use of a Thing as an IoT commerce medium may provide a justification for certain omissions, when the Thing is (also) the object of the transaction, more stringent information duties will apply. Additionally, unfair trading laws should not be considered in isolation. A Thing's display showing the website where information can be found, or an audio notice to the same effect, may comply with the Unfair Commercial Practices Directive but not necessarily with other regimes. Since this directive has a 'safety net' character, should other instruments provide clear duties to inform regardless of the medium, these instruments will prevail. For example, under the Consumer Rights Directive, even when the medium has limitations of space, the trader has to provide

---

290 ibid.
291 This would be in violation of both Article 7 and No 22 of Annex I.
292 Unfair Commercial Practices, art 7(1).
293 Art 7(3).
294 Unfair Commercial Practices, art 7(4)(a).
295 (n 51) [73].

some key information before the conclusion of the contract (e.g. the total price).[296] Its omission will be in breach of the latter directive, though it will not count as an unfair practice. This is an IoT-friendly provision that considers the physical limitations and the complexity of Things when assessing misleading omissions. Currently, under *Deroo-Blanquart*,[297] courts are expressly prevented from taking into account the constraints of certain media when assessing misleading actions. *De lege ferenda*, therefore, the duty to consider the limitations of Things as medium and Things as product should be extended also to practices in contravention of professional diligence, misleading actions, as well as the fourth type of unfair practices, that is, aggressive practices, to which the next section is dedicated.

4.3.1.4 Aggressive Commercial Practices: IoT Traders' Undue Influence Over Consumers' Freedom of Choice

Aggressive commercial practices are not limited to the use of physical threats and intimidation to force consumers to enter into a transaction. For example, in Latvia, Air Baltic's use of preticked boxes to have the consumers inadvertently request ancillary services was considered aggressive.[298] In turn, in *Office of Fair Trading v Ashbourne Management Services Ltd*,[299] an English court held that threatening to report a gym's consumer to a credit reference agency could be regarded as aggressive. These practices can result in high fines, as was the case with Italy's Antitrust Authority handing Ryanair an EUR550,000 fine for the high costs of the phone calls to its customer centre.[300] In some countries, an aggressive practice may lead to a prison sentence. For example, in *R v Montague*,[301] the defendant was sentenced to 42 months' imprisonment after he accompanied an elderly woman to her bank, where she withdrew a princely sum for work in respect of which the trader had already been paid. The Enforcement and Modernisation of Consumer Protection Directive has strengthened the protection against aggressive practices because it has allowed member states to introduce more stringent rules about unsolicited visits by a trader to a consumer's home (doorstep selling) and excursions organised by a trader with the aim or effect of promoting or selling products to consumers (commercial excursions).[302] This is important from this book's perspective because the argument can be put forward that these unsolicited visits to a consumer's home do not have to be physical: also, virtual visits to the consumer's smart home may trigger the provisions on aggressive practices. Member states cannot altogether ban such sales channels, but they can

---

296 Consumer Rights Directive, art 8(4).
297 (n 51).
298 Latvian Consumer Rights Protection Centre, decision No E03-PTU-K115–39 of 23 October 2012.
299 [2011] EWHC 1237 (Ch); [2011] ECC 31.
300 Autorità Garante della Concorrenza e del Mercato, decision 19 January 2015 no 25247 (2015) XXIV(52) Bollettino 14.
301 *(Derek George)* [2015] EWCA Crim 902.
302 Unfair Commercial Practices Directive, art 3(5).

restrict them, e.g. by defining the time of day when visits to consumers' homes – including smart homes – without their express request are not allowed.[303] This is in line with the case law of the ECtHR that has interpreted the concept of 'home' broadly to include inter alia mobile abodes.[304]

Under Article 8 of the Unfair Commercial Practices Directive, a practice is aggressive if it meets two requirements:

i   It significantly impairs or is likely to significantly impair the average consumer's freedom of choice or conduct with regard to the product by means of harassment, coercion, or undue influence; and
ii   As a result of such impairment, it causes the average consumer or is likely to cause them to make an unwanted transactional decision.

In assessing whether a practice occurring before, during, or after[305] a transactional decision is aggressive, courts will have to consider its factual context, taking account of all its features and circumstances.[306] These could include, e.g. the physical limitations of the Thing and the power held by the IoT trader as a consequence of the granular data regarding each consumer. It has been noted that manipulation will rarely take the form of incorrect or incomplete information; consumers are 'put in a situation where they are more likely to agree to buy . . . due to their own vulnerabilities.'[307] The exploitation of the vulnerabilities is more likely to take an aggressive form. This regime has been successfully used to counter 'business models whose very operating premise relies upon taking advantage of the reduced ability of the consumers . . . to protect their own interests.'[308] As such, it lends itself to be used in the IoT, where traders know of and can exploit consumers' vulnerabilities.

For the purposes of this book, it should be explored whether IoT-enabled manipulation can qualify as harassment, coercion, or undue influence. There is no definition of 'harassment' or specific guidance, but the UK Competition and Markets Authority provides the example of threatening language and behaviour in an attempt to intimidate consumers into accepting the services or agreeing the terms of service.[309] Harassment is primarily concerned 'with the invasion of an individual's private space.'[310] Using Things that are present in the most private

303 Enforcement and Modernisation of Consumer Protection Directive, recital 55.
304 *Chapman v UK* (2001) 33 E.H.R.R. 18 [71-[74].
305 European Commission, '2016 Guidance on Unfair Commercial Practices' (n 234) [3.1.5].
306 Unfair Commercial Practices Directive, art 8.
307 Manwaring (n 167) 165.
308 Jeannie Marie Paterson and Gerard Brody, '"Safety Net" Consumer Protection: Using Prohibitions on Unfair and Unconscionable Conduct to Respond to Predatory Business Models' (2015) 38 Journal of Consumer Policy 331, 332.
309 Office of Fair Trading and Department for Business Enterprise & Regulatory Reform (n 218).
310 Geraint Howells, 'Aggressive Commercial Practices' in Geraint Howells, Hans-W Micklitz and Thomas Wilhelmsson (eds), *European Fair Trading Law: The Unfair Commercial Practices Directive* (Ashgate 2006) 178. Geraint Howells, 'Aggressive Commercial Practices' in Geraint

spaces around the consumer (smart home, wearables, etc.) to constantly serve advertisements and invitation to purchase based on the consumers' vulnerabilities may be regarded as harassing. Harassment encompasses both physical and non-physical (including psychological) pressure; this applies also to coercion, that is, the second method to impair consumer freedom.[311]

Coercion is more focused on the use of physical force, as suggested by the wording of Article 8 ('coercion, including the use of physical force'). Although *coercion* is not defined, the Competition and Markets Authority provides the example of a trader starting to work without the explicit permission of the consumer; indeed, 'consumers may be discouraged from shopping around, or from deciding not to have the work done.'[312] From this book's perspective, it has been shown that IoT traders seek consent through a mountain of unreadable and scattered legals: providing services on the basis of such weak consent may be regarded as coercion, and therefore as an aggressive practice, provided that the other requirements are met.

Harassment and coercion are the most blatant forms of aggressive practices that attempt to pressurise the consumer into a transactional decision. Undue influence, conversely, addresses more subtle ways to unduly influence consumers;[313] as such, it better lends itself to be used to counter the sophisticated practices used in the Internet of Personalised Things. It is not by chance that the study[314] commissioned by the European Commission in view of the adoption of the Unfair Commercial Practices Directive exemplified undue influence by referring to emotional advertising, that is, advertising that plays on emotions or fears and the exploitation of trust in third parties. Things can report back to the manufacturers about the emotions and feelings of the consumer, thus providing IoT traders with powerful weapons. However, the European Commission[315] pointed out that if the information gathered through profiling is used to exert undue influence (e.g. a trader knows that the consumer is running out of time to buy a flight ticket and falsely claims that only a 'few tickets are left available'), then these practices may be regarded as aggressive.

'Undue influence' is the only impairing technique that is expressly defined in the directive,[316] possibly because it is the concept where common law and civil

---

Howells, Hans-W Micklitz and Thomas Wilhelmsson (eds), *European Fair Trading Law* (Ashgate 2006) 167–195, 178.

311 Office of Fair Trading and Department for Business Enterprise & Regulatory Reform (n 218) [8.3].

312 Office of Fair Trading and Department for Business Enterprise & Regulatory Reform (n 218) [A3(2)].

313 Reiner Schulze and Hans Schulte-Nölke, 'Analysis of National Fairness Laws Aimed at Protecting Consumers in Relation to Commercial Practices' (2003) European Commission DG Sanco. *Contra*, Howells (n 316).

314 Schulze and Schulte-Nölke (n 320).

315 European Commission, '2016 Guidance on Unfair Commercial Practices' (n 234) [5.2.13].

316 Unfair Commercial Practices Directive, art 2(j).

law jurisdictions most diverge.[317] There is exercise of undue influence when the trader exploits a position of power vis-à-vis the consumer so as to apply pressure in a way which significantly limits the ability to make an informed decision. The imbalance of power can have economic or intellectual causes and derive from social ties that go beyond the professional one.[318] The power to put pressure on the consumer can be derived from the fact that the latter depends on the cooperation of the trader or on the fact that the trader has psychological tools to convince the consumer to make a transaction.[319] To better understand when the pressure can be deemed to significantly limit the ability to make an informed decision, one can refer to the guidance recently provided by the CJEU in *Orange Polska*.[320] In that case, the deciding factor was the circumstance that the consumer had to take the transactional decision in the presence of the courier who delivered the standard-form contract, without being able 'to take cognisance of the content of that contract while the courier (was) present.'[321] This was a form of undue influence that would make the 'consumer feel uncomfortable or confuse (their) thinking concerning the transactional decision to be taken.'[322] The fact that the provision on aggressive practices tackles more subtle psychological techniques that confused consumers makes this regime likely to be applied to the Internet of Personalised Things. This is corroborated by Article 9 of the directive, which provides courts with the criteria to consider when determining if these forms of impairment took place.[323] The main criterion is to look at the timing, location, nature, and persistence of the practice.[324] In light of this, to exploit IoT data about preferences, biases, and vul-nerabilities to target consumers when, where, and in the way that the trader knows to be more likely to lead to a transactional decision may qualify as aggressive. For example, by combining geolocation data, calendar entries, browsing history, and face recognition data, an IoT trader may know that the consumer is sad because they have been to a funeral and that when they are sad they binge on YouTube videos of grumpy cats. Accordingly, this trader may target this consumer when they are back from the funeral and have a sad facial expression, by showing them grumpy-cat-themed 'advertorials' (portmanteau of *advertisement* and *editorial*) that convince them to purchase a certain film or a medicine.

In assessing undue influence, courts need also to consider 'any onerous or dis-proportionate non-contractual barriers imposed by the trader where a consumer

---

317 cf Howells (n 316).
318 H Köhler and T Lettl, 'Das Geltende Europäische Lauterkeitsrecht, Der Vorschlag Für Eine EG – Richtlinie Über Unlautere Geschäftspraktiken Und Die UWG – Reform' [2003] Wettbewerb in Recht und Praxis 1019.
319 Helberger (n 156).
320 Case C-628/17 *Prezes Urzedu Ochrony Konkurencji i Konsumentow v Orange Polska SA* [2019] Bus LR 1882.
321 ibid [50].
322 ibid.
323 Unfair Commercial Practices Directive, art 9.
324 Unfair Commercial Practices Directive, art 9(a).

wishes to exercise rights under the contract, including rights to . . . switch to another product or another trader.'[325] It is not sufficient to give the consumer some rights under the contract if factually they cannot exercise them, as was the case with a Bulgarian trader that made it burdensome to terminate the contract, which led to unwanted renewals of the service.[326] Therefore, linking back to the issue of the 'Internet of Silos' and the lack of interoperability in proprietary IoT systems, it can be said that the factual lock-in that these types of barriers create can be countered by invoking the Unfair Commercial Practices Directive's provisions on aggressive practices. This is not to say that all advertising and profiling leads to unfair consumer manipulation. This will depend on a number of factors, including 'the persuasive potential of the personalised message and the extent to which the practice reduces the autonomous decision-making process.'[327] However, it is fair to say that the IoT furthers the power imbalance that characterises most business-to-consumer relationships and creates new opportunities to exploit it to limit consumer freedom and lead to unwanted transactional decisions.

The aforementioned principle-based rules on aggressive practices may operate as a counterweight as they can be invoked to rebalance the consumer-to-business relationship, thus rebuilding the trust in the IoT. The main weakness of this strategy is that it relies on a case-by-case assessment of unfairness and on the requirement of the likelihood to lead to unwanted transactional decision. These drawbacks can be overcome by relying on the so-called blacklist, which is the focus of the next section.

4.3.1.5 Commercial Practices That Are Unfair in All Circumstances: The Blacklist

As said above, the benefits of the Unfair Commercial Practices Directive are connected to its horizontal 'safety net' character and the joint operation of principle-based rules (e.g. misleading omissions) and a 'blacklist' of specific prohibitions of certain unfair practices. This blacklist of practices that are considered unfair in all circumstances is particularly useful to tackle the negative effects of the Internet of Personalised Things. The meaning of 'unfair in all circumstances' was clarified in *European Commission v Belgium*,[328] where the CJEU held that blacklisted practices are altogether banned: national authorities do not have to assess their unfairness on a case-by-case basis using criteria set forth by the directive. Annex I to the directive lists them, and as stated in *Plus Warenhandelsgesellschaft*,[329] this list is exhaustive. The blacklist provides national authorities with an effective tool to tackle common practices,[330] such as targeting of children, hidden advertising,

---

325 Unfair Commercial Practices Directive, art 9(d).
326 Supreme Administrative Court of Bulgaria, decision No 15182 of 3 November 2011.
327 Helberger (n 156) 20.
328 (n 181).
329 Case C-304/08 *Plus Warenhandelsgesellschaft* [2010] ECR I-217.
330 European Commission, '2016 Guidance on Unfair Commercial Practices' (n 234).

and fake free offers. Originally, there were 31 practices; they are now 35. The Enforcement and Modernisation of Consumer Protection Directive added ranking manipulation, resale of tickets acquired by automated means in circumvention of limits on the number of tickets that a person can buy, not checking that the consumer reviews originate from consumers who used or purchased the product, and false or misleading consumer reviews (e.g. social influencers posting content where they commend a certain brand without making it clear that they are paid to promote that brand).[331] The blacklist is useful in the IoT context because it provides for a stricter regime (compared to the principle-based rule under Articles 5–9) that can better protect vulnerable consumers. And indeed, as noted by the European Commission, this list epitomises the directive's endeavour to protect vulnerable consumers 'from the risks deriving from the effects of the economic crisis *and the complexity of digital markets*.'[332]

Some manipulative practices that are common in the Internet of Personalised Things are well represented in the blacklist. A first example is the business model, where services are provided in exchange for personal data. It has already been shown that they might qualify as misleading actions or omissions, but the application of those principle-based rules has its shortcomings. In particular, the requirement to prove that the practice led to an unwanted transactional decision is not easily made out. It will be onerous for the consumer to prove they would have not taken the decision if they knew their data would be commercialised. The blacklisted practices are banned as such, and therefore consumers do not need to prove anything apart from the fact that the practice took place. The opaque monetisation of personal data in this popular business model could be attacked through a combined reading of Nos 20 and 22 of Annex I. These provisions prevent traders from presenting their services as free when they are not[333] and from creating the impression that the trader is not acting for commercial purposes.[334] This applies also to IoT traders that do not inform consumers about the commercialisation of their data, regardless of any assessment of the unfairness of the practice in the individual case.[335] It has been convincingly argued[336] that these provisions are fit for IoT-enabled profiling and targeting also because they are illegal, regardless of the effect on the consumer's choice, a decision to perform a transaction or not, and the existence of a monetary price. Moreover, the first report on the application of

---

331 See CAP and CMA, *An Influencer's Guide to Making Clear That Ads Are Ads* (ASA 2018); Rossana Ducato, 'One Hashtag to Rule Them All? Mandated Disclosures and Design Duties in Influencer Marketing Practices' in Sofia Ranchordas and Catalina Goanta (eds), *The Regulation of Social Media Influencers* (Edward Elgar 2020) 232.
332 European Commission, 'Communication on the Application of the Unfair Commercial Practices Directive Achieving a High Level of Consumer Protection Building Trust in the Internal Market' (n 180) [2.1]. Emphasis added.
333 Unfair Commercial Practices Directive, annex I, no 20.
334 Unfair Commercial Practices Directive, annex I, no 22.
335 See European Commission, '2016 Guidance on Unfair Commercial Practices' (n 234).
336 Helberger (n 156).

the directive[337] presented evidence that these provisions deal with practices 'targeting mainly vulnerable consumers.'[338] The report referred to the example of websites offering mobile phone ringtones that were presented as 'free' but that would, in reality, trigger a paid-for subscription. A year later, Consumer Protection Cooperation, the network of consumer protection authorities in the EEA, relied on these provisions to have traders change their practices, whereby games were presented as free but it was not possible to play without 'in-app' purchases.[339] Arguably, these provisions are fit also for more subtle practices that, powered by the IoT, exploit consumer vulnerabilities in novel ways to monetise their data.

Another practice that IoT traders can put in place when they target consumers and that can ultimately manipulate them is the use of always-on and ubiquitous Things to constantly offer services or products for purchase or paid-for access. Echo Show may show you a video about a new gadget that you never thought you may want to purchase, Echo Dot may reiterate the message in audio form, the advert may follow you in the bathroom, where you have an Echo Look, and it could be finally repeated when you go to bed by Echo Spot. These types of practices should be considered aggressive and unfair in all circumstances under No 26 of Annex I, which tackles 'persistent and unwanted solicitations by . . . remote media.'[340] The threshold of what is 'persistent' is low. Austria's Supreme Court e.g. excluded from the definition a single letter to a person.[341] This provision is complemented by No 29 of Annex I on inertia selling, namely, the unsolicited supply of products accompanied by the demand of immediate or deferred payment.[342] As pointed out by the CJEU in *Toplofikatsia*,[343] the absence of a response from the consumer following an unsolicited supply does not constitute consent.[344] This practice falls foul also of the Consumer Rights Directive, which exempts the consumer targeted by these type of practices from providing any consideration.[345] The rationale is that traders should not be allowed to impose 'a contractual relationship on a consumer to which (they have) not freely consented.'[346] Therefore, in addition to any injunction and compensation granted under the Unfair Commercial Practices Directive, consumers will have the right not to pay for unsolicited products. Additionally, if the practice takes the form of unsolicited direct marketing by means of automatic calling machines, fax, or email, they will be illegal if not previously consented to, regardless of whether or not they are persistent. This is because the e-Privacy Directive provides detailed rules applicable

---

337 European Commission, 'First Report on the Application of Directive 2005/29/EC' (2013) COM/ 2013/139 final.

338 ibid [3.3.6].

339 Consumer Protection Cooperation Network, 'Single Market Scoreboard' (2018) 01/2018–12/2018.

340 Unfair Commercial Practices Directive, annex I, no 26.

341 Oberster Gerichtshof (Supreme Court), decision No 4 Ob 174/09f of 19 January 2010.

342 See *Wind Tre* (n 213) [43].

343 Cases C-708/17 and C-725/17 *EVN v Dimitrova, EAD v Dimitrov* (CJEU, 5 December 2019).

344 ibid [63]. In terms, Consumer Rights Directive, art 27.

345 Consumer Rights Directive, art 27.

346 *EVN* (n 343) [65].

to these scenarios;[347] they will prevail on the Unfair Commercial Practices Directive, given the latter's safety-net character. The blacklisted practices, therefore, will be particularly useful in the context of printed marketing and, more importantly, unsolicited communications via unconventional media, which includes IoT-mediated communications.

4.3.2 The Limitations and the Potential of the Unfair Commercial Practices to Counter the Internet of Personalised Things

Two factors would appear to militate against the use of the Unfair Commercial Practices Directive to counter the negative effects of the Internet of Personalised Things. First, this directive is seen as focusing chiefly, if not exclusively, on the economic interests of the consumers.[348] For example, in *Wamo*[349] the CJEU held that national laws that prohibit price reductions during presales periods are not compatible with the directive insofar as their goal is to protect the consumers' economic interests.[350] Correspondingly, in *Pelckmans*,[351] national laws that prevent traders from opening their shop seven days a week and require them to choose a weekly closing day were found to be in line with the directive as long as they did not pursue objectives related to consumer protection.[352] An example of an objective falling outside the scope of this directive is the regulation of relations between competitors, as was the case in *Inno*.[353] The European Commission observed that the directive does not cover national rules intended to protect 'interests which are not of an economic nature,'[354] such as human dignity, preventing sexual, racial, and religious discrimination, and antisocial behaviour. Second, it has been noted that this directive may not be fit for IoT-powered consumer manipulation because, even though it provides some room to consider broader societal implications of unfair marketing practices, 'societal interests are primarily viewed through the lens of a consumer who is about to take an economic transaction.'[355] This argument is based on the fact that, usually, a practice can be regarded as unfair if it is likely to cause the consumer to take a transactional decision that they would not have taken otherwise.[356]

The aforementioned criticisms about the fitness of the Unfair Commercial Practices Directive to deal with consumer manipulation are not without merit, but

347 E-Privacy Directive, art 13.
348 This is one of the arguments put forward by Helberger (n 156).
349 Case C-288/10 *Wamo v JBC* [2011] ECR I-5835.
350 Similarly, with regards to national prohibitions on sales at loss, Case C-343/12 *Euronics Belgium v Kamera Express* [2013] 83 Revue Lamy droit des affaires 35.
351 Case C-559/11 *Pelckmans v Van Gastel Balen* [2014] 3 CMLR 49.
352 It is for the national authorities to decide whether a national provision intends to protect consumer interests (Case C-13/15 *Cdiscount* [2015] 11 Europe 44).
353 Case C-126/11 *Inno v UNIZO* (CJEU, 15 December 2011).
354 European Commission, '2016 Guidance on Unfair Commercial Practices' (n 234) [1.2.1].
355 Helberger (n 156) 23.
356 Unfair Commercial Practices Directive, art 5(2)(b), 6(1), 7(1), 8.

they are not insurmountable. Four considerations can be made about the first criticism; they revolve around the suitability of the directive to protect noneconomic interests against manipulation.

First, there is not a clear divide between economic and noneconomic interests. This can be seen in the *Mediaprint* case,[357] when the CJEU held that the directive precludes a general national ban on sales with bonuses designed to achieve consumer protection as well as other noneconomic interests; in that case, the law also pursued the maintenance of pluralism of the press in Austria. Similarly, in *Köck*[358] it was found that national laws allowing clearance sales to be announced only if authorised by the competent district administrative authority fall within the scope of the directive despite being aimed at protecting both consumers and competitors. It should also be noted that the directive considers unfair the omission of information mandated not only by consumer laws but also by laws protecting noneconomic interests, such as the environment and health.[359]

Second, it is not by chance that one of the main cases of unfair practices regards a form of manipulation with a noneconomic impact. The reference is to the 'Dieselgate,' when Volkswagen installed 'defeat devices' in their diesel cars to manipulate emission test results.[360] Over 11 million consumers were misled by untruthful claims about the environmental performance of the cars. The Italian and the Dutch antitrust authorities issued fines for a total of EUR5.5M to the manufacturer for breaching the Unfair Commercial Practices Directive.[361]

Third, when the European Commission in 2016 updated its 2009 guidance[362] on the directive, it did so also to incorporate the key principles developed by the multistakeholder group on false claims about products' environmental credentials.[363] The directive can be used to counter practices, such as 'greenwashing,' that can affect consumers well beyond their economic interests, as exemplified by the Romanian actions against providers of cleaning products and services that were unduly advertised as ecological.[364]

---

357 Case C-540/08 *Mediaprint v Osterreich-Zeitungsverlag* [2010] ECR I-10909.
358 Case C-206/11 *Köck v Schutzverband gegen unlauteren Wettbewerb* [2013] 2 CMLR 21.
359 European Commission, '2016 Guidance on Unfair Commercial Practices' (n 234) [1.4.3]. See, e.g. Regulation (EU) 2017/1369 of 4 July 2017 setting a framework for energy labelling and repealing Directive 2010/30/EU ('Energy Labelling Regulation') [2017] OJ L 198/1.
360 European Commission, 'Impact Assessment Accompanying the Document Proposals for Directives (1) Amending Council Directive 93/13/EEC, Directive 98/6/EC, Directive 2005/29/EC and Directive 2011/83/EU as Regards Better Enforcement and Modernisation of EU Consumer Protection Rules and (2) on Representative Actions for the Protection of the Collective Interests of Consumers, and Repealing Directive 2009/22/EC' (2018) Staff Working Document SWD/2018/096 final-2018/089 (COD).
361 Autorità Garante della Concorrenza e del Mercato, decision no 26137 of 4 August 2016; Autoriteit Consument & Markt, decision no ACM/UIT/230480 of 18 October 2017.
362 European Commission, 'Guidance on the Implementation/Application of Directive 2005/29/CE' (2009) Commission Staff Working Document SEC(2009)1666 final.
363 'Unfair Commercial Practices Directive' (*European Commission*) <https://ec.europa.eu/info/law/law-topic/consumers/unfair-commercial-practices-law/unfair-commercial-practices-directive_en>.
364 European Commission, '2016 Guidance on Unfair Commercial Practices' (n 234).

Fourth, the impact assessment of the Enforcement and Modernisation of Consumer Protection Directive of unfair trading law underlined that this regime brings about broader societal benefits. It is no coincidence that the European Commission links the societal impact of the reform to the issue of tackling consumer vulnerability. Traders' compliance with the directive improves the situation of vulnerable consumers because they are more likely than average to be victims of unfair commercial practices.[365] However, this is not just an economic vulnerability. Explicitly building on behavioural insight,[366] the Commission underlines that consumer vulnerability patterns are 'complex (multi-dimensional), have multiple drivers and are highly context-dependent. It is not possible to strictly associate consumer vulnerability with specific groups or socio-demographic characteristics.'[367] For these reasons, the directive's focus on the consumer's economic interest does not prevent consumers from invoking this regime to counter the negative effects of IoT-enhanced personalisation.

The second criticisms about the fitness of the Unfair Commercial Practices Directive to deal with consumer manipulation[368] revolves around the observation that the directive would view societal interests exclusively through the lens of a consumer who is about to take a transaction and, therefore, would be unsuitable for the forms of consumer manipulation that are not directly linked to a transaction. Three counterarguments can be put forward.

First, as noted before, 'transaction' has been interpreted in a broad way, e.g. by encompassing the decision *not to* enter into a transaction or exercise a right[369] and also those decisions that are not transactional but are directly related to the transactional decision.[370] Therefore, for example, designing a virtual assistant to be 'always on' and to target the consumer with frequent ads could fall within the scope of the directive because it would be likely to affect the decision to enter or not the online shop.

Second, consumers do not have to prove that the IoT-enabled manipulation led to a transactional decision. Indeed, the requirement is not subjective – the question that courts need to answer is not whether the claimant took an unwanted transactional decision. The requirement is objective and abstract – given the nature of the practice and of the product, would the hypothetical average consumer be likely to make a transactional decision? As IoT consumers are arguably re-engineered to become impulsive, or even compulsive, purchasers,[371] and since we have underlined their increased vulnerability, it would seem that the requirement of the likelihood to lead to an unwanted decision would be easily made out in most IoT scenarios.

---

365 European Commission, *Consumer Conditions Scoreboard: Consumers at Home in the Single Market* (European Union 2019).

366 The Commission refers to London Economics, VVA Consulting and Ipsos Mori (n 237).

367 European Commission, 'New Deal for Consumers' Impact Assessment' (n 369) [6.1.1].

368 Helberger (n 156) 23.

369 This follows directly from the definition of 'transactional decision' under art 2(k) of the Unfair Commercial Practices Directive.

370 *Trento Sviluppo* (n 211).

371 cf Spilotro (n 145). On the manifold ways new technologies are re-engineering us, see Brett M Frischmann and Evan Selinger, *Re-Engineering Humanity* (CUP 2018).

Third, we have seen that the directive's Annex I provides a blacklist of practices that 'shall in all circumstances be regarded as unfair,'[372] regardless of their likelihood to lead to an unwanted transactional decision. This means that the 35 practices listed in Annex I can be invoked by IoT consumers who are victims of manipulation even when the practice is not likely to lead to any transactional decision. For example, as Things by definition embed digital content, they lend themselves to being a medium for the surreptitious use of editorial content in the media to promote a product. Some particularly savvy consumers may be unlikely to be misled by such 'advertorials' and would therefore be unlikely to be able to prove that they made a transactional decision that they would have not otherwise taken. Nonetheless, the directive outlaws all blacklisted practices, and the ban is not accompanied by a proviso of likelihood of transactional decision. Therefore, Annex I is likely to be particularly useful to counter those manipulative practices that are not connected to transactions.

In conclusion, the Unfair Commercial Practices Directives, despite its limitations, can be invoked to resist against the Internet of Personalised Things. The blacklisted practices and the provision on vulnerable consumers may be of great help. This is mainly due to special provisions that protect credulous consumers, the provisions that address power imbalance, and those that tackle unfairness even when it is not linked to a transaction. However, as noted by the European Commission,[373] much remains to be done to strengthen the protection of vulnerable consumers. Especially in an IoT world, these are not just the elderly and the youth; also, other categories of citizens can 'find themselves in a situation of weakness.'[374] As outlined in the European Consumer Agenda,[375] it must be ensured that vulnerable consumers are protected from the risks deriving from the increased complexity of digital markets and from the difficulty many may encounter in mastering the digital environment. This is urgent because the IoT can act as a powerful tool to manipulate consumers thanks to the power imbalance that is furthered by the trader's remote control over the Thing throughout its life cycle, the increased quantity of data generated by Things that are 'always on', the better quality of this data produced by cross-device tracking and profiling, the increased opportunities to target consumers anywhere (ubiquitous computing), and bespoke delivery of ads, political messages, and other potentially manipulative content thanks to technologies such as emotion recognition. We have reached the point that predictive analytics, opaque algorithms, and sophisticated forms of persuasion have turned the normally 'average' consumer into a vulnerable one.[376] Therefore, unfair trading laws should be applied in a behaviourally savvy way, which means also interpreting vulnerability as inclusive of IoT-induced manipulability.

---

372 Unfair Commercial Practices Directive, art 5(5).
373 European Commission, 'First Report on the Unfair Commercial Practices Directive' (n 345).
374 ibid [3.3.2].
375 European Commission, 'A European Consumer Agenda – Boosting Confidence and Growth' (2012) COM(2012)225 final.
376 This question was asked by Helberger (n 156).

It has been opined that no changes in the law would be needed as long as governments promote digital literacy programs in schools discussing how the IoT works and how personalisation can lead to manipulation. However, awareness raising is hindered by the 'real disincentive, for service providers to reveal details of these practices.'[377] In *A New Deal for Consumers*,[378] communication that presented the reform instantiated by the Enforcement and Modernisation of Consumer Protection Directive and the Representative Actions Directive, the European Commission clarified that the IoT and mobile e-commerce are major challenges for which consumer policy needs to prepare, as they 'can make consumers vulnerable in different ways.'[379] *De lege ferenda*, building on the model of the blacklist in Annex I to the directive, amendments should be introduced to tackle unfair practices affecting consumers regardless of the likelihood of unwanted transactional decision and shifting the focus from the consumer's economic interests to the broader societal impact of unfairness in the Internet of Personalised Things.

4.4 Interim Conclusion

This chapter considered whether two consumer laws that look beyond the contract – the Product Liability Directive and the Unfair Commercial Practices Directive – can address techno-human vulnerability by tackling defective Things and the Internet of Personalised Things.

The new concept of product as an amalgam of hardware, software, service, and data may lead to more inclusive interpretations of the scope of the Product Liability Directive, which may in turn see the revival of this oft-forgotten legal regime. *De lege ferenda*, it would be important to redefine the concept of product to expressly include software – regardless of whether it is embedded in a tangible medium – as well as service and data. Otherwise, the prospect of the harm coming from defective Things may reduce consumer trust in the IoT, which may not in turn unleash its potential. The review of the directive is ongoing, and hopefully it will reflect the overcoming of those binaries that the IoT is challenging, such as product-service, hardware-software, and cybersecurity-security.

The IoT provides enhanced means to manipulate consumers and create new needs, expectations, and beliefs. Thus, it can be regarded as a powerful capitalistic device. Indeed, capitalism requires the manipulation of workers and the creation in them of new needs. This is because it is aimed at the maximisation of profit, not at the satisfaction of existing needs.[380] Capitalistic growth in productivity and division of labour produces not only wealth but also new needs. It produces

---

377 Manwaring (n 167) 165.
378 European Commission, 'Communication "A New Deal for Consumers"' (n 181).
379 ibid [7].
380 Karl Marx, *Il capitale (1894)*, vol 3 (Bruno Maffi tr, Bruno Maffi, UTET 2009).

selfish needs that are a manifestation of alienation.[381] As Marx puts it in his *Economic and Philosophic Manuscripts*:[382]

> Under private property . . . every person speculates on creating a *new* need in another, so as to drive him to a fresh sacrifice, to place him in a new dependence, and to seduce him into a new mode of gratification . . . The less you are, the less you express your life, the more you have, the greater is your alienated life and the greater is the saving of your alienated being.[383]

It has been convincingly argued that Marx 'actually discovered the problem of "manipulated needs" and indeed of the "manipulation of needs."'[384] Capitalism manipulates needs in that it creates consumption needs which silence those deeper needs that shape the human personality and hinder the valorisation of capital, e.g. the need for free time. Free time and authentic needs[385] are appropriated and manipulated by IoT traders – 'smartness' becomes the ultimate neoliberal tool to make us 'dumb.'[386] It is no accident that vulnerability has become a key common trait that Things and humans share. The Unfair Commercial Practices Directive can be invoked to counter the Internet of Personalised Things. However, it should not come as a surprise that, being a neoliberal instrument focused on the economic dimension of the consumer and on the internal market, its response to IoT-enhanced consumer manipulation is not entirely satisfactory. It is starting to emerge the feeling that in the age of cyborg consumers, the 'smart' internet is 'a space whose organisation does not require lawyers since it does not need any laws different from the *de facto* power of the smartest.'[387] If the law is supplanted by engineering and by self-programming Things, one can doubt that we can still do something to force our values upon the capitalist project. As the new extractive practises of the IoT are mostly data-led, it becomes necessary to turn our gaze to data protection – or what is left of it – in the 'Internet of Loos.'

381 On alienation in Marx see A Wendling, *Karl Marx on Technology and Alienation* (Springer 2009).
382 Karl Marx, *Economic and Philosophic Manuscripts of 1844* (Martin Milligan tr, first published 1932, Foreign Languages Publishing House 1961).
383 ibid 115, 119. This volume was translated from the German text contained in Marx-Engels, *Gesamtausgabe*, Abt I, Bd 3.
384 Agnes Heller, *The Theory of Need in Marx* (Verso Books 2018) 51.
385 See PT Grier, *Marxist Ethical Theory in the Soviet Union* (Springer Science & Business Media 2012); Heller (n 393).
386 Mattei (n 223).
387 Mattei (n 224) 628.

5 The Internet of Loos, the General Data Protection Regulation, and Digital Dispossession Under Surveillance Capitalism

[T]he only necessary wage rate is that providing for the subsistence of the worker for the duration of his work and as much more as is necessary for him to support a family and for the race of labourers not to die out. . . . The demand for men necessarily governs the production of men, as of every other commodity.

Marx, *Economic and Philosophic Manuscripts of 1844* (1)

5.1 Introduction: The Erosion of Privacy and Data Protection in the Global Private-Public Surveillance Network

The IoT constitutes an unprecedented challenge to privacy and data protection.[1] Despite a growing body of literature, many aspects of the relationship between IoT, privacy, and data protection require further exploration.[2] Whereas privacy and data protection are distinct concepts and deserve separate attention,[3] for the sake of brevity I will merely touch upon the former in this introduction, while the chapter will focus on the latter.

The IoT 'could undermine such core values as privacy'[4] as it is progressively eroding the area of what can be regarded as private. Traditionally, the home and

---

1 EU Charter, arts 7 and 8.
2 The relationship between IoT and privacy can be and has been analysed from manifold perspectives. See e.g. Lilian Edwards, 'Privacy, Security and Data Protection in Smart Cities: A Critical EU Law Perspective' (2016) 2 EDPL 28; Guido Noto La Diega, 'Clouds of Things: Data Protection and Consumer Law at the Intersection of Cloud Computing and the Internet of Things in the United Kingdom' (2016) 9(1) Journal of Law & Economic Regulation 69; Sandra Wachter, 'Normative Challenges of Identification in the Internet of Things: Privacy, Profiling, Discrimination, and the GDPR' (2018) 34 CLSR 436; Lachlan Urquhart, 'White Noise from the White Goods? Privacy by Design for Ambient Domestic Computing' in Lilian Edwards, Burkhard Schafer and Edina Harbinja (eds), *Future Law* (EUP 2019).
3 There are activities that comply with data protection legislation while constituting a disproportionate interference with the right to privacy, and vice versa. The fact that information is in the public domain and therefore no longer private does not mean that the right to data protection will not apply, as was the case in *Satakunnan Markkinapörssi Oy and Satamedia Oy v. Finland* (2018) 66 EHRR 8 [133]–[134].
4 William H Dutton, 'Putting Things to Work: Social and Policy Challenges for the Internet of Things' (2014) 16 info 1.

DOI: 10.4324/9780429468377-6

the body were the most sacred of private spaces.[5] This assumption may have to be revisited as smart home and IoT health are becoming commonplace.[6] The IoT risks becoming a global private-public surveillance network. To exemplify this, one need only think that since Amazon acquired smart video doorbell Ring, it brokered nearly 2,000 partnerships with local law enforcement agencies, who 'can request recorded video content from Ring users without a warrant.'[7] The IoT is normalising the idea that ubiquitous cameras, microphones, and sensors track citizens'[8] behaviour and transform it into structured data flows that are sent back to our Things' manufacturers. This is perhaps best illustrated by Amazon's Echo Spot and Echo Look – respectively an alarm clock and a style assistant –which are equipped with cameras and are designed to be used in the bedroom and even in the bathroom, hence the 'Internet of Loos.' As the ability to be alone with oneself is pivotal to human flourishing, the IoT – with its erosion of the private/public boundaries – launches a most concerning attack on the self.

Alongside being a threat to privacy, the IoT challenges the right to data protection. Indeed, the focus of this chapter will be to critically assess whether the IoT is intrinsically inconsistent with the GDPR or whether the most advanced European data protection law can tackle the emerging issues in the IoT. After an introduction to the GDPR, this chapter will present the main data protection issues in the IoT. It will then zoom in on one of them that is usually overlooked: 'digital dispossession.' This refers to IoT companies' (ab)use of intellectual property rights (especially trade secrets) to appropriate citizens' data and prevent them from exercising their data subject rights, including the right(s) of access.[9] Digital dispossession is part of a wider context that has seen the shift from the knowledge economy to the data economy.[10] This is leading to the private appropriation of both the IoT's infrastructure and data.[11] Digital dispossession will be analysed as a tenet of the theory of surveillance capitalism.[12] To understand what practically happens to IoT users' data, the chapter will move on to analyse Echo's data practices by means of a subject access request, interactions with Amazon's customer support staff, and text

---

5 *Ismayilova v Azerbaijan (No.3)* [2020] 5 WLUK 42; *Solska and Rybicka v Poland* App nos 30491/17 and 31083/17 (ECtHR, 20 September 2018).

6 See Ian Kerr, 'The Internet of Things? Reflection on the Future Regulation of Human-Implantable Radio Frequency Identification' in Ian Kerr, Valerie Steeves and Carole Lucock (eds), *Lessons from the Identity Trail: Anonymity, Privacy and Identity in a Networked Society* (OUP 2009) 335.

7 Lauren Bridges, 'Amazon's Ring Is the Largest Civilian Surveillance Network the US Has Ever Seen' (*The Guardian*, 18 May 2021) <www.theguardian.com/commentisfree/2021/may/18/amazon-ring-largest-civilian-surveillance-network-us>.

8 This chapter refers to citizens and users rather than consumers because, unlike the consumer laws analysed in the previous chapters, data protection law does not apply only to consumers but also to all natural persons.

9 See Václav Janeček, 'Ownership of Personal Data in the Internet of Things' [2018] CLSR 1039.

10 Josef Drexl, 'Designing Competitive Markets for Industrial Data. Between Propertisation and Access' (2017) 8 JIPITEC 257.

11 Edwards (n 2).

12 Shoshana Zuboff, *The Age of Surveillance Capitalism: The Fight for a Human Future at the New Frontier of Power* (PublicAffairs 2019).

analysis of the relevant privacy policy. This evidence base will be used to carry out a fitness check, namely to explore whether the rights of access, to portability, to be informed, and not to be subject to solely automated decisions can be successfully invoked to counter IoT companies' digital dispossession, or whether trade secrets may give these companies a weapon to effectively nullify GDPR rights.

While some features of the IoT render GDPR compliance difficult (e.g. the tension between 'repurposing'[13] and the principle of purpose limitation), I will argue that there is no intrinsic trade-off between the IoT in its technological dimension and the GDPR; rather, the problems stem from the IoT companies' exploitative and proprietary business models centred on opaque data practices whose epitome is digital dispossession. Against this backdrop, this chapter will answer the following subquestion: *how does the law cope with data being at once a fundamental human right and a commodity?*

5.2 The GDPR: From Confidentiality to Data Control

When every Thing that is *around*, *on*, and *in* us collects granular data about us, sends it back to the manufacturer, and shares it with an unknown number of third parties, there is no doubt that our rights to privacy and data protection are at stake. Despite its shortcomings (e.g. excessive compliance burdens for smaller businesses),[14] the GDPR constitutes a progress in the protection of personal data insofar as it attempts to restore users' control over their own data. In light of the complex data flows that characterise IoT sensing and actuating – and the associated likelihood that data will be used in unforeseeable ways and by unknown parties – data control has become more important than data confidentiality. As the IoT heralds 'a data-sharing storm where there are no controls or safeguards on what data is shared, who it is shared with, or for what purposes data is used or re-used,'[15] the GDPR can be regarded as a safe port.

Effective as of May 2018, the GDPR replaced the Data Protection Directive[16] and increased the protection of personal data throughout the EU. It applies to personal data processed by entities that are either established in the EU or target EU residents.[17] Although it mostly codifies best practices that developed under the previous regime,[18] the GDPR is usually regarded as an advancement

---

13 Noto La Diega (n 2).

14 Craig McAllister, 'What about Small Businesses: The GDPR and Its Consequences for Small, U.S.-Based Companies Notes' (2017) 12 Brooklyn Journal of Corporate, Financial & Commercial Law 187. cf CMS, 'GDPR Enforcement Tracker' (*Enforcement Tracker*) <www.enforcement-tracker.com>.

15 Nóra Ni Loideain, 'A Port in the Data-Sharing Storm: The GDPR and the Internet of Things' (2019) 4 Journal of Cyber Policy 178, 178.

16 Directive 95/46/EC of 24 October 1995 on the protection of individuals with regard to the processing of personal data and on the free movement of such data ('Data Protection Directive') [1995] OJ L 281/31.

17 GDPR, art 3.

18 See Paul De Hert and Vagelis Papakonstantinou, 'The Proposed Data Protection Regulation Replacing Directive 95/46/EC: A Sound System for the Protection of Individuals' (2012) 28 CLSR 130.

in data protection for a twofold reason. First, high fines incentivise its compliance. France's data protection authority CNIL e.g. imposed a EUR50M fine on Google over the company's opaque privacy policy and lack of legal basis for personalised ads.[19] Recent research shows, however, that GDPR fines have limited, if any, deterrence effect.[20] Second, the GDPR is a regulation as opposed to a directive. This means that it is directly applicable in all member states;[21] the latter have adopted implementing measures to regulate those aspects where the GDPR left room for national tailoring.[22] Some countries, e.g. Italy[23] and France,[24] proceeded by amending their existing data protection statutes. Others, such as the UK and Spain, repealed the pre-existing statutes[25] and replaced it with new, GDPR-compliant legislation.[26] To dispel any confusion related to the effect of Brexit on UK data protection law, the Data Protection Act 2018 incorporated and supplemented the GDPR.[27] The retention of the same rules as the EU after Brexit through the so-called UK GDPR should guarantee the continuity of EU-UK data flows.[28] There are strong incentives to maintain convergence, since EU personal data-enabled services exports to the UK are worth approximately £42bn, and exports from the UK to the EU are worth £85bn.[29] Accordingly, the UK government is seeking an adequacy decision, i.e. the European Commission's confirmation that a non-EEA country provides an adequate level of personal data protection.[30] Since the IoT, where Things are composite and provided through a complex supply chain, is intrinsically international, ensuring smooth data flows will be of utmost importance for the functioning of the IoT.

19 CNIL, Deliberation of the Restricted Committee SAN-2019–001 of 21 January 2019 pronouncing a financial sanction against Google LLC.
20 W Gregory Voss and Hugues Bouthinon-Dumas, 'EU General Data Protection Regulation Sanctions in Theory and in Practice' (2020) 37 Santa Clara High Technology Law Journal.
21 Treaty on the Functioning of the European Union (TFEU) [2008] OJ C 115/171, art 288.
22 cf Denise Amram, 'Building up the "Accountable Ulysses" Model. The Impact of GDPR and National Implementations, Ethics, and Health-Data Research: Comparative Remarks' (2020) 37 CLSR 1.
23 *Decreto legislativo* 20 June 2003 n° 196.
24 *Loi* n° 78–17 of 6 January 1978 *relative à l'informatique, aux fichiers et aux libertés.*
25 Data Protection Act 1998 and *Ley Orgánica* 15/1999.
26 Data Protection Act 2018 and *Ley Orgánica* 3/2018.
27 Data Protection Act 2018, s 4; European Union (Withdrawal) Act 2018, s 3.
28 Karen Mc Cullagh, 'Post-Brexit Data Protection in the UK' in Rosamunde van Brakel, Paul de Hert and Gloria González Fuster (eds), *Research Handbook on Privacy and Data Protection Law: Values, Norms and Global Politics* (Edward Elgar 2021).
29 Department for Digital, Culture, Media & Sport, 'Explanatory Framework for Adequacy Discussions' (*GOV.UK*, 13 March 2020) <www.gov.uk/government/publications/explanatory-framework-for-adequacy-discussions>.
30 GDPR, art 15; Directive (EU) 2016/680 of 27 April 2016 on the protection of natural persons with regard to the processing of personal data by competent authorities for the purposes of the prevention, investigation, detection, or prosecution of criminal offences or the execution of criminal penalties, and on the free movement of such data, and repealing Council Framework Decision 2008/977/JHA ('Law Enforcement Directive') [2016] OJ L 119/89, art 36.

The GDPR is not as much about privacy as it is about control. Especially if privacy is interpreted as secrecy. This may seem counterintuitive. Indeed, pseudonymisation is one of the measures that the GDPR recommends,[31] and companies tend to anonymise data as an attempt to bring the processing outside of the scope of the GDPR.[32] Such a strategy is based on the fact that principles of data protection should not apply to anonymous information.[33] However, it does not consider that anonymisation alleviates companies of the burden of GDPR compliance only inasmuch as the data subject is no longer identifiable.[34] The IoT, however, ushers is an era of reidentification, as Things provide new ways to deanonymise data flows.[35]

The misunderstanding of the GDPR as a privacy – and even secrecy – law has led to risks for citizens. The reliance on anonymisation and other forms of confidentiality-focused, privacy-enhancing technologies is leaving data 're-identifiable by capable adversaries while heavily limiting controllers' ability to provide data subject rights, such as access, erasure and objection, to manage this risk.'[36] The point is that the GDPR espouses a concept of data protection that focuses on control rather than on privacy as confidentiality.[37] Data control is exercised through rights such as access, rectification, and portability. This is consistent with the GDPR's goal to facilitate the free flow of personal data within the Union[38] and eliminate the differences between national laws that are regarded as an obstacle to the pursuit of economic activities at the level of the Union and distort competition.[39] In this sense, the argument is put forward that the GDPR is underpinned by a philosophy of openness and control rather than of secrecy and privacy. Such philosophy is pivotal to using the GDPR to tackle the main data protection issues in the IoT.

5.3 Data Protection Issues in the IoT

The Article 29 Working Party's opinion on the IoT[40] provides an analytical framework for the main data protection issues in the IoT. Although the opinion

---

31 GDPR, art 6(4)(e).
32 Michael Veale, Reuben Binns and Jef Ausloos, 'When Data Protection by Design and Data Subject Rights Clash' (2018) 8 IDPL 105.
33 GDPR, art 4(1).
34 GDPR, recital 26.
35 Jose Luis Canovas Sanchez, Jorge Bernal Bernabe and Antonio F Skarmeta, 'Towards Privacy Preserving Data Provenance for the Internet of Things' *2018 IEEE 4th World Forum on Internet of Things (WF-IoT)* (IEEE 2018) <https://ieeexplore.ieee.org/document/8355229/>.
36 Veale, Binns and Ausloos (n 32).
37 Article 29 Working Party and Working Party on Police and Justice, 'The Future of Privacy: Joint Contribution to the Consultation of the European Commission on the Legal Framework for the Fundamental Right to Protection of Personal Data' (2009) WP 168; Seda Gürses, 'Can You Engineer Privacy?' (2014) 57 Communications of the ACM 20. The Article 29 Working Party, pan-European advisory group in matters of data protection, has been replaced by the European Data Protection Board on 25 May 2018.
38 GDPR, recitals 6 and 9.
39 GDPR, recital 9.
40 Article 29 Working Party, 'Opinion 8/2014 on the Recent Developments on the Internet of Things' (2014) WP 223.

considered the data protection issues in the IoT with reference to the Data Protection Directive, the framework needs only minor adapting. Indeed, for the most part, the GDPR can be regarded as the codification of best practices that developed under the Data Protection Directive;[41] therefore, most of the considerations that the Article 29 Working Party made retain their validity. The framework has also been adapted to take account of phenomena on which only recently the scholarly debate has started developing, namely, the status of inferences and the threat of digital dispossession.

The main data protection issues in the IoT relate to:

  (i) Lack of control and information asymmetry;
 (ii) Quality of consent;
(iii) The contested status of inferential data;
 (iv) The chimera of anonymisation;
 (v) The shift of the compliance burden from the IoT company to the end user; and
(vi) Digital dispossession.

5.3.1 Lack of Control and Information Asymmetry

First, lack of control[42] and information asymmetry[43] are intertwined issues. The difficulty to control how Things interact and to know which data the Thing sends back to the manufacturer makes it difficult to assert data control, especially because IoT companies keep these practices secret. Similar issues arise with big data and cloud computing, but as noted by the Article 29 Working Party, the possibility to combine data from multiple sources exacerbates the loss of control.[44] This is perhaps best illustrated by IoT-enabled third-party monitoring, which may lead to the user losing control over how their data is processed. IoT systems are characterised by a high level of automation. Thing-to-Thing communication can take place automatically, without the end user being aware of it. As an example of lack of control in the IoT, digital advertising company Improve Digital points out in its privacy policy that its clients sell advertising space on Things and that 'for most of such devices it is *not possible to generally not allow cookies or opt-out*, although you can often remove all cookies.'[45] Whilst direct marketing can act as a legitimate interest under the GDPR[46] – and therefore controllers would not

---

41 See e.g. De Hert and Papakonstantinou (n 18).
42 On whether the lack of control can be overcome through data ownership, see Janeček (n 9).
43 The problem of information asymmetry in the IoT has been analysed from a US consumer contracts' perspective by Stacy-Ann Elvy, 'Contracting in the Age of the Internet of Things: Article 2 of the UCC and Beyond' (2015) 44 Hofstra Law Review 839.
44 Article 29 Working Party, 'Opinion 8/2014 on the Recent Developments on the Internet of Things' (n 40) 6.
45 Improve Digital Platform Privacy Policy, 3 <www.improvedigital.com/platform-privacy-policy/> accessed 20 December 2018.
46 GDPR, recital 47.

need to seek the data subject's consent when processing data for direct market-ing purposes – the use of cookies or similar identifiers requires consent under the e-Privacy Directive.[47] Moreover, even though the legitimate interests of third parties may justify the relevant monitoring, data subjects (including IoT users) have a right to object to that processing of their personal data. In principle, this is not an absolute right, because data controllers could demonstrate compelling, overriding, and legitimate grounds for the processing.[48] However, data subjects have an absolute right to object to processing, including third-party monitoring, if this is for direct marketing purposes: IoT companies will have to immediately stop processing for such purposes.[49] It would be regrettable if IoT data control-lers could invoke the limitations and complexities of the Things as an excuse to deprive end users of the control over their data.

5.3.2 The Quality of Consent

A closely interwoven issue has to do with the quality of the IoT user's consent.[50] From a technical point of view, consent in the IoT is problematic mainly for two reasons.[51] A first technical issue is that '[r]esource heterogeneity and limitations are found in connectivity, computational power, storage,'[52] as well as in input/output, which refers to devices used to communicate with computers, e.g. keyboards and monitors. As an example of such limitations, one can think of the limited size of Things' screens or the lack of screens. Chapter 3 has already shown that this limitation hinders the compliance with precontractual duties of information. This limitation makes it also hard for IoT companies to provide appropriate privacy notices and for their users to input privacy choices.[53] Accordingly, it has been con-vincingly argued that the 'existing privacy frameworks that rely heavily on a notice and choice model do not effectively safeguard consumers in the IoT setting.'[54] A second technical issue that makes consent in the IoT problematic is device identity. Traditional authorisation systems used to decide whether a requester of a resource

47 Art 5.
48 GDPR, art 21(1).
49 GDPR, art 21(2)-(3).
50 See e.g. Yvonne O'Connor and others, 'Privacy by Design: Informed Consent and Internet of Things for Smart Health' (2017) 113 Procedia Computer Science 653: 'the first phase for universal usability of IoT within the smart health domain is to ensure that digital health citizens [. . .] are fully aware of what they are consenting to when they register an account with such technological artefacts' and accordingly suggest privacy by design solutions.'
51 Cigdem Sengul, 'Privacy, Consent and Authorization in IoT' *2017 20th Conference on Inno-vations in Clouds, Internet and Networks (ICIN)* (IEEE 2017) <https://ieeexplore.ieee.org/document/7899432/>.
52 ibid.
53 On the lack of opportunity in a smart city environment for the giving of meaningful consent, see Edwards (n 2).
54 Stacy-Ann Elvy, 'Commodifying Consumer Data in the Era of the Internet of Things' (2018) 59 Boston College Law Review 423.

has sufficient permissions are not entirely applicable to the IoT.[55] A privacy policy needs to state exactly who interacts with what data, when, where, how, and why. This conflicts with the objective of easy-to-understand policies, especially in the IoT context. Pointing out all possible data interactions is challenging at best and detrimental to understanding at worst. However, consent can be regarded as 'informed' only if the user has sufficient knowledge of the risks and benefits of disclosing information to make a reasonable evaluation.[56]

The GDPR set a high standard of consent, which has to be informed, freely given, specific, unambiguous, granularity, easy to withdraw, and demonstrable. Consent can hardly be regarded as informed in most IoT scenarios, where users are unlikely to be aware of their Things' processing activities. Informed consent has been regarded as unattainable in the IoT because one of its key features is sensor fusion, which consists of 'combining sensor data or data derived from different sources in order to get better and more precise information than would be possible when these sources are working in isolation.'[57] Sensor fusion contributes to 'the near impossibility of truly de-identifying sensor data.'[58] Therefore, data controllers had better not rely on consent as a valid justification for processing.[59] This is also due to the fact that Things are ubiquitous and tend to disappear, while the relational black box makes it arduous to map the players involved in the data flows. This is all the more true when data controllers state that the alternative to consenting is not to access certain services or features.[60]

Consent must be freely given, and this does seem the case here. Especially because, when assessing whether consent is freely given, account has to be given to whether the performance of the contract 'is conditional on consent to the processing of personal data that is not necessary for'[61] the performance. IoT companies cannot make the functioning of their virtual assistant conditional to consenting to interest-based advertising.

The requirements for consent to be informed and freely given is not an innovation of the GDPR. The Data Protection Directive already imposed these requirements, alongside requiring consent to be specific and unambiguous.[62] *Specific* means that consent must be given in relation to 'one or more specific

55 Sengul (n 51) 320.
56 Robert H Sloan and Richard Warner, 'Beyond Notice and Choice: Privacy, Norms, and Consent' (2014) 14 Journal of High Technology Law 370.
57 Article 29 Working Party, 'Opinion 8/2014 on the Recent Developments on the Internet of Things' (n 40) 7, fn 6.
58 Scott R Peppet, 'Regulating the Internet of Things: First Steps Toward Managing Discrimination, Privacy, Security, and Consent' (2014) 93 Texas Law Review 85, 85.
59 Article 29 Working Party, 'Opinion 8/2014 on the Recent Developments on the Internet of Things' (n 40) 7.
60 Cf. Natasha Tusikov, 'Regulation through "Bricking": Private Ordering in the "Internet of Things"' (2019) 8 Internet Policy Review.
61 GDPR, art 7(4).
62 Data Protection Directive, arts 2(h) and 7(a).

purposes'[63] and that a data subject has a choice in relation to each of them. This requirement is closely interwoven with the principle of purpose limitation,[64] whereby personal data has to be 'collected for specified, explicit and legitimate purposes and not further processed in a manner that is incompatible with those purposes.'[65] IoT's 'repurposing' challenges both the requirement that consent be specific and the principle of purpose limitation. Repurposing is a critical characteristic of IoT systems, dependent on their (inter)connectivity and system-of-systems dimension.[66] It can be understood as the phenomenon whereby an IoT system ends up being used for purposes other than those originally foreseen in two scenarios:

(i) The communication within the relevant subsystem and among subsystems can lead the system to perform actions and produce information which the single Thing was incapable of or that could not be foreseen by its manufacturers; and

(ii) Under certain conditions (e.g. an emergency), the system may reconfigure either in an automated fashion or a user-initiated one.

IoT's repurposing has an ambiguous relationship to the purpose limitation principle. On the one hand, it is virtually impossible for data controllers to foresee and therefore specify all the purposes the Thing may process data for. On the other hand, controllers may argue that as repurposing is core feature of the IoT, when using Things consumers expect the reuse of their data. In other words, the IoT could be seen as pushing the boundaries of what is to be regarded as a compatible purpose under the purpose limitation principle.

For consent to be valid, it also needs to be unambiguous. Under the Data Protection Directive, 'unambiguous' meant the 'indication of wishes by which the data subject signifies his agreement to personal data relating to him being processed.'[67] In theory, this meant that opt-out mechanisms (e.g. preticked boxes) would have complied with this requirement. In practice, the Article 29 Working Party clarified that a clear affirmative action was needed.[68] This position was finally adopted by the GDPR.[69] Silence, preticked boxes, or inactivity cannot be regarded as meeting the standard.[70] Accordingly, IoT companies that give users the possibility 'to

63 European Data Protection Board, 'Guidelines 05/2020 on Consent under Regulation 2016/679' (2020) v 1.1 13.
64 ibid 14.
65 GDPR, art 5(1)(b).
66 On the repurposing of big data drawn from the IoT in smart cities, see Edwards (n 2).
67 Data Protection Directive, art 2(h).
68 Article 29 Working Party, 'Opinion 15/2011 on the Definition of Consent' (2011) WP187 26. This opinion was replaced by Article 29 Working Party, 'Guidelines on Consent under Regulation 2016/679' (2018) WP259 rev.01. They have been superseded by European Data Protection Board, 'Guidelines 05/2020 on Consent under Regulation 2016/679' (n 63).
69 GDPR, art 4(11).
70 GDPR, recital 32.

opt out of certain other types of data processing by updating your settings on the applicable . . . device'[71] are not relying on a valid consent.[72]

The innovations of the GDPR as far as consent is concerned are – alongside clearer rules regarding the pre-existing requirements – the new requirements of granularity, ease of withdrawal, and demonstrability. The heightened standard for consent under the GDPR and the 'increase of personal data collection, use and re-use, will make consent a major problem for IoT players.'[73]

'Granular' means that there should be separate consent options for different types of processing, and if the data subject's consent is given in the context of a written declaration which also concerns other matters, 'the request for consent shall be presented in a manner which is clearly distinguishable from the other matters, in an intelligible and easily accessible form, using clear and plain language.'[74] Practically, this means that IoT companies cannot bury consent in a long document that deals also with non-privacy-related matters (e.g. the terms of service).[75]

IoT users should be free to withdraw their consent at any time and with the same ease that characterised the giving of the consent.[76] This means that when consent is obtained via electronic means 'through only one mouse-click, swipe, or keystroke,'[77] IoT companies cannot impose more cumbersome procedures to withdraw consent.

Finally, consent must be demonstrable. Indeed, the controller – the IoT company in our scenario – must be able to 'demonstrate that the data subject has consented to processing of (their) personal data.'[78] This is an application of the overarching principle of accountability that the GDPR introduced to make clear that compliance as such is not enough: controllers must keep accurate records of their processing activities and of the ways they comply with the GDPR.[79] Accordingly, IoT companies must retain proof of a valid consent as long as the processing lasts, and after the processing ends, for as long as it is necessary for compliance with a legal obligation or for the exercise of legal claims.[80] The lack of accountability in the IoT precludes meaningful engage-

---

71 Amazon Privacy Notice <www.amazon.co.uk/gp/help/customer/display.html?nodeId=201909010> accessed 22 March 2019.

72 Amazon tends to rely, as a legal basis for processing, on legitimate interest, contractual necessity, and legal obligation. However: 'We may also ask for your consent to process your personal information for a specific purpose that we communicate to you.' (Amazon Privacy Notice).

73 Leonie Tanczer et al., 'IoT and Its Implications for Informed Consent' (PETRAS IoT Hub, STEaPP, 2017) <https://papers.ssrn.com/sol3/papers.cfm?abstract_id=3117293>.

74 GDPR, art 7(2).

75 ICO, 'Lawful Basis for Processing: Consent' (2018) 1.0.65 4.

76 GDPR, art 7(3).

77 European Data Protection Board, 'Guidelines 05/2020 on Consent under Regulation 2016/679' (n 63) 23.

78 GDPR, art 7(1).

79 GDPR, art 5(2).

80 GDPR, art 17(3)(b),(e); European Data Protection Board, 'Guidelines 05/2020 on Consent under Regulation 2016/679' (n 63) 22–23.

ment by users with their personal data and 'poses a key challenge to creating user trust in the IoT and the reciprocal development of the digital economy.'[81] Accountability is rendered difficult by IoT's inadequate consent mechanisms, opaque distributed data flows, and lack of adequate interfaces; therefore, IoT companies have to invest sufficient resources in finding creative solutions to demonstrate compliance.[82]

In the context of wearables and the related processing of sensitive personal data, it has been observed[83] that too rigid an interpretation of consent may stifle innovation; accordingly, self-regulation has been recommended as a solution. However, as noted in Chapter 1, self-regulation does not appear to be the best regulatory approach when private entities have incentives to behave in ways that are not conducive to the common good. Conversely, at least some of the issues of consent in the IoT can be overcome by moving 'past reliance on contractual T&C (and) use the concept of trajectories.'[84] The concept of trajectories has been developed by human-computer interaction (HCI) scholars.[85] HCI is a domain of technology design that 'prioritises understanding the social context of technology, questioning the interactions and relationships between end users and technology.'[86] Trajectories are a 'conceptual framework for understanding cultural user experiences'[87] and for designing interactive user experiences. Trajectories share in common that 'they take their participants on journeys (that) may pass through different places, times, roles and interfaces.'[88] IoT designers could adopt this framework to embed a GDPR compliance in the users' trajectory, thus improving the overall experience. Trajectories' designers have to consider factors such as the interfaces, the physical space, and the actors.[89] This means e.g. that as opposed to providing all information upfront, 'information can be spread over the lifetime'[90] of the user-Thing relationship. This multidisciplinary approach is certainly promising, although it is still unclear how to provide incentives to push IoT companies to embrace HCI principles in the design of their GDPR compliance.

---

81 Lachlan Urquhart, Tom Lodge and Andy Crabtree, 'Demonstrably Doing Accountability in the Internet of Things' (2019) 27 International Journal of Law and Information Technology 1.

82 One such solution is the so-called IoT Databox presented ibid 15.

83 Syagnik Banerjee, Thomas Hemphill and Phil Longstreet, 'Wearable Devices and Healthcare: Data Sharing and Privacy' (2018) 34 The Information Society 49.

84 Lachlan Urquhart and Tom Rodden, 'New Directions in Information Technology Law: Learning from Human – Computer Interaction' (2017) 31 International Review of Law, Computers & Technology 150, 164.

85 Steve Benford and others, 'From Interaction to Trajectories: Designing Coherent Journeys through User Experiences' *Proceedings of the 27th International Conference on Human Factors in Computing Systems – CHI 09* (ACM Press 2009) <http://dl.acm.org/citation.cfm?doid=1518701.1518812>.

86 Urquhart and Rodden (n 84) 150.

87 Benford and others (n 85) 710.

88 ibid 712.

89 Urquhart and Rodden (n 84) 161.

90 ibid 162.

5.3.3 The Contested Status of Inferential Data

The value in IoT data stems often not from the data itself but from the inferences IoT companies can make from it.[91] The status of inferences as personal data is contested.[92] The IoT requires pervasive collection and 'linkage of user data to provide personalised experiences based on potentially *invasive inferences.*'[93] The joint operation of IoT-produced big data, improved data-mining techniques, and combination of data from multiple sources leads to the creation of highly valuable inferences about the user's behaviour and vulnerabilities. This is problematic for a twofold reason. Analytics is moving from being merely predictive to giving IoT companies the power to change the way the individual actually behaves. There is evidence that people censor themselves when they know that they feel that they are being watched.[94] Moreover, these inferences may not necessarily be regarded as personal data, which would bring the processing outside of the scope of the GDPR. If this thesis prevails, IoT companies may sidestep the principle of purpose limitation and reuse inferred data for purposes that go beyond the original purpose for which data had been collected, thus giving rise to the threat of function creep.[95] Besides, users could not invoke the right to rectify[96] inaccurate and unreasonable inferences, which is alarming, as inferences are unverifiable and 'create new opportunities for discriminatory, biased, and invasive decision-making.'[97] Accordingly, it has been argued[98] that a new 'right to reasonable inferences' is needed to help close the accountability gap currently posed by high-risk inferences. The proposal has two drawbacks. First, it is characterised by the same rights-based approach that negatively affects the GDPR; the effectivity of data protection ends up depending on the individual citizen, who has scarce resources and knowledge to sue IoT big tech.[99] Second, albeit imperfect, the GDPR provides tools against abuses regarding inferred data. The starting point is that inferential data is personal data, and therefore the GDPR applies. Indeed, personal data includes information that even potentially and indirectly identify a natural person; such a broad interpretation predates the GDPR and dates

---

91 Sandra Wachter and Brent Mittelstadt, 'A Right to Reasonable Inferences: Re-Thinking Data Protection Law in the Age of Big Data and AI' [2019] Columbia Business Law Review 494.

92 ibid.

93 Sandra Wachter, 'The GDPR and the Internet of Things: A Three-Step Transparency Model' (2018) 10 Law, Innovation and Technology 266.

94 Jonathon W Penney, 'Chilling Effects: Online Surveillance and Wikipedia Use' (2016) 31 Berkeley Technology Law Journal 117.

95 Loideain (n 15) 182.

96 GDPR, art 16.

97 Wachter and Mittelstadt (n 91) 494.

98 Wachter and Mittelstadt (n 91).

99 See Rachel Allsopp, 'Levelling the Odds? Big Data Analytics in the Online Gambling Industry and the Application of the GDPR' in MM Carvalho (ed), *Law & Technology. E.Tec Yearbook* (University of Minho 2018) 135.

back to the Convention 108 of 1981.[100] The CJEU, ECtHR, and national courts tend to interpret the concept broadly, including inter alia IP addresses[101] and the body temperature recorded by portable thermal cameras.[102] Although the right not to be subject to automated decisions[103] is unlikely to apply to inferences, lacking a significant 'decision,' the rules on profiling apply regardless of a solely automated decision.[104] Profiling consists of any form of automated processing of personal data to analyse an individual's personality, behaviour, interests, and habits to make predictions or decisions about them.[105] The definition is broad enough to encompass most inferences. And indeed, as noted by the Article 29 Working Party, profiling is 'often used to make predictions about people, using *data from various sources to infer something* about an individual, based on the qualities of others who appear statistically similar.'[106] This means that IoT companies whose business model relies on inferences have to actively inform the data subject about profiling and carry out a Data Protection Impact Assessment.[107] Moreover, the principle of accuracy will apply[108] and IoT companies will have to put in place appropriate processes to check that personal data, including inferences, is correct and not misleading.[109] The importance of accurate inferences was also underlined by the Council of Europe, which stressed the importance of data quality and recommended that the data controller 'periodically and within a reasonable time reevaluate the quality of the data and of the statistical inferences used.'[110] Accordingly, IoT companies should be proactive in correcting data inaccuracy factors and in limiting the risks of errors inherent to profiling.

5.3.4 The Chimera of Anonymisation

There are intrinsic limitations on the possibility to remain anonymous when using Things. This is problematic since anonymisation is identified as a best practice

---

100 GDPR, art 4(1); Council of Europe Convention no 108 for the protection of individuals with regard to automatic processing of personal data ('Convention 108'), art 1.
101 Case C-582/14 *Breyer* [2017] 1 WLR 1569 (codified in GDPR, recital 30); *Benedik v Slovenia* App no 62357/14 (ECtHR, 24 April 2018) [107]-[108].
102 Conseil d'État, ordonnance no 441065 of 26 June 2020, unreported.
103 GDPR, art 22.
104 Article 29 Working Party, 'Guidelines on Automated Individual Decision-Making and Profiling for the Purposes of Regulation 2016/679' (2018) WP251rev.01 7.
105 GDPR, art 4(4).
106 Article 29 Working Party, 'Guidelines on Automated Individual Decision-Making and Profiling for the Purposes of Regulation 2016/679' (n 104) 7. Emphasis added.
107 ICO, 'Automated Decision-Making and Profiling' (2018) v. 1.1.49 4–5.
108 GDPR, art 5(1)(d).
109 See ICO, 'Guide to the GDPR' (ICO 2019) v. 1.0.711 33.
110 Council of Europe, *The Protection of Individuals with Regard to Automatic Processing of Personal Data in Context of Profiling: Recommendation CM/Rec(2010)13* (Council of Europe 2011) 11.

in data processing, especially when profiling.[111] The IoT makes robust anonymisation difficult for a fourfold reason. First, Things and IoT systems produce an abundance of data, as exemplified by the fact that UK smart meters generate 21.2 billion megabytes of data each year.[112] Second, this data is more granular because of the possibility to recombine data coming from multiple sources, also thanks to more refined tracking techniques. Using signals that can be heard from a user's Things but not from the user themselves, IoT traders can map all the Things used by the same user, which makes cross-device tracking easier.[113] Third, the data produced by Things and IoT systems provides information that relates to the most intimate aspects of an individual's life. This is because they are ubiquitous and can access the most private spaces, including the home and the body. Finally, Things that are in close proximity to the data subject (e.g. wearables) result in the availability of stable identifiers (e.g. multiple MAC addresses)[114] that lead to the creation of a unique fingerprint.[115] In light of the above – and thanks to the ensuing data power[116] that IoT companies hold – anonymous data can be easily linked back to individuals.[117]

5.3.5 The Shift of the Compliance Burden from the IoT Company to the End User

The burden of compliance with the GDPR is gradually shifting from IoT companies to other players, including the end user. Connected to the issue of lack of control over one's own data, this shift is the result of the convergence of two jurisprudential trends regarding joint controllership and the household exemption.[118] On the one hand, as noted in Chapter 1, we are witnessing the rise of joint controllership, that is, the situation where two or more controllers jointly determine the purposes and means of processing. As seen in *Wirtschaftsakademie*

---

111 ICO, 'Guide to the GDPR' (n 109) 157.
112 Morgan Wild and Marini Thorne, 'A Price of One's Own. An Investigation into Personalised Pricing in Essential Markets' (2018) Citizens Advice.
113 Haojian Jin, Christian Holz and Kasper Hornbaek, 'Tracko: Ad-Hoc Mobile 3D Tracking Using Bluetooth Low Energy and Inaudible Signals for Cross-Device Interaction' *Proceedings of the 28th Annual ACM Symposium on User Interface Software & Technology* (ACM 2015) 147.
114 Media access control (MAC) address is the hardware address of a device connected to a network. Jeff Rutenbeck, *Tech Terms: What Every Telecommunications and Digital Media Professional Should Know* (3rd edn, Routledge 2012) 161.
115 Article 29 Working Party, 'Opinion 8/2014 on the Recent Developments on the Internet of Things' (n 40) 8.
116 Orla Lynskey, 'Grappling with "Data Power": Normative Nudges from Data Protection and Privacy' (2019) 20 Theoretical Inquiries in Law 189.
117 Lilian Edwards and Michael Veale, 'Slave to the Algorithm: Why a Right to an Explanation Is Probably Not the Remedy You Are Looking For' (2017) 16 Duke Law & Technology Review 18.
118 See Jiahong Chen and others, 'Who Is Responsible for Data Processing in Smart Homes? Reconsidering Joint Controllership and the Household Exemption' [2020] IDPL ipaa011.

Schleswig-Holstein (the Facebook fan page case),[119] joint controllership means that data subjects / end users will increasingly be recognised as data controllers and therefore bound by the GDPR's principles and obligations.[120] Whilst joint controllership may increase the level of data protection in the IoT by making it easier to find someone accountable in the complex IoT supply chain, it could also have negative effects. It has been noted[121] e.g. that developers of privacy-enhancing technologies for the smart home may fall within the definition of joint controllers even when they do not have access to any personal data.[122] On the other hand, one needs to consider the strict interpretation given by courts to the household exemption. Under this exemption, the processing of personal data 'by a natural person in the course of a purely personal or household activity'[123] falls outside the scope of the GDPR. To escape liability under the joint controllership scheme, an IoT user may invoke the household exemption. However, the CJEU has been interpreting it rather narrowly.[124] In *Ryneš*[125] it was held that the user of a CCTV that recorded the entrance to his home, the public footpath, and the entrance to the house opposite could not invoke the household exemption. Indeed, since the video surveillance covered 'even partially, a public space,'[126] it could not be regarded as a purely personal or household activity. This is despite the Data Protection Directive, applicable at that time, clarifying that household activities can be exempt despite the incidental inclusion of third parties' personal data.[127] More recently, *Jehovan todistajat* clarified that the exemption is precluded not only when the processing extends to public spaces but also when there is access by an 'unrestricted number of people.'[128] Amazon-owned Ring has launched the 'Always Home Cam,' an indoor security drone to scare off burglars.[129] The drone may end up recording the burglar before and after the break-in, outside the home. It would seem that the household exemption would not apply to this scenario. Similar considerations are likely to apply to the Things that we wear (wearables) and carry with us, thus allowing them to potentially record data in public spaces.

---

119 Case C-210/16 *Unabhangiges Landeszentrum fur Datenschutz Schleswig-Holstein v Wirtschaft-sakademie Schleswig-Holstein GmbH* [2019] 1 WLR 119.
120 The trend was confirmed in Case C-25/17 *Proceedings brought by Tietosuojavaltuutettu* [2019] 4 EDPLR 391 ('*Jehovan todistajat*') and Case C-40/17 *Fashion ID GmbH & Co.KG v Verbr-aucherzentrale NRW eV* (2019) GRUR Int 1023.
121 Chen and others (n 118) 6–7.
122 *Wirtschaftsakademie* (n 119) [38]; *Jehovan todistajat* (n 120) [69]; *Fashion ID* (n 120) [82].
123 GDPR, art 2(2)(c).
124 Chen and others (n 118) 8. The authors refer to Case C-101/01 *Lindqvist* [2003] ECR I-12971; Case C-73/07 *Tietosuojavaltuutettu v Markkinaporssi* [2008] ECR I-9831; Case C-212/13 *Ryneš* [2014] 12 WLUK 430; *Jehovan todistajat* (n 120).
125 (n 124).
126 ibid [33].
127 Data Protection Directive, recital 18.
128 *Jehovan todistajat* (n 120) [42].
129 Evan Ackerman, 'Why You Should Be Very Skeptical of Ring's Indoor Security Drone – IEEE Spectrum' (*IEEE Spectrum*, 25 September 2020) <https://spectrum.ieee.org/automaton/robotics/drones/ring-indoor-security-drone>.

As to the issue of the accessibility of the data by an unrestricted number of people, one could argue that Things designed to routinely send back data to the manufacturer provide opportunities for such an unrestricted access and therefore pre-empt the applicability of the exemption. The above considerations, combined with the fact that the CJEU has 'never ruled in favour of a claim of the exemption,'[130] make it unlikely that an IoT user could successfully invoke the household exemption, even when it comes to smart home processing, and that, in turn, the application of the joint controllership regime will lead to a shift of the burden in GDPR compliance from the IoT company to the data subject-user.

5.3.6 Digital Dispossession

Finally, digital dispossession is another issue that the Article 29 Working Party overlooked.[131] IoT companies attempt to appropriate and otherwise control both the algorithms that underpin the IoT system and the data that this system produces. Leveraging a portfolio of big data and intellectual property rights (especially trade secrets), IoT companies put in place novel extractive practices that can negatively affect citizens, who are often unaware of them due to a technical and legal secrecy. 'Technical' secrecy results from the opacity of the algorithms that underpin the IoT, especially when AI-enabled. 'Legal' secrecy, in turn, come from a combination of trade secrets, proprietary software, and contracts that keep IoT data practices secret. Thanks to the data power that IoT big players hold, they can take advantage of their dominant position to impose contracts that purport to justify unfair and opaque practices, including the appropriation and reuse of personal as well as nonpersonal data. As a study of the neoliberal smart city showed, 'data lies at the heart of most power relations today.'[132] IoT companies' proprietary strategy can harm citizens in manifold ways. It can affect their privacy because it allows for surreptitious forms of monitoring and surveillance. It can also affect their autonomy and self-determination because IoT data allows companies to exploit users' biases and vulnerabilities to manipulate them.[133] It can even affect their dignity, when IoT data includes protected characteristics that allow companies to discriminate against certain categories of citizens.[134] Following the brutal killing of George Floyd, tech companies started announcing that they would stop selling facial-recognition software to law enforcement because

---

130 Chen and others (n 118) 8.

131 Zuboff, Surveillance Capitalism (n 12); Guido Noto La Diega and Cristiana Sappa, 'The Internet of Things at the Intersection of Data Protection and Trade Secrets. Non-Conventional Paths to Counter Data Appropriation and Empower Consumers' [2020] REDC 419.

132 Evgeny Morozov and Francesca Bria, 'Rethinking the Smart City. Democritizing Urban Technology' (2018) Rosa Luxemburg Stiftung New York Office 53 <www.rosalux-nyc.org/rethinking-the-smart-city/>.

133 As the ECtHR held in *Satakunnan* (n 3) [137], art 8 of the ECHR 'provides for the right to a form of informational self-determination.'

134 It has been noted that the fact that Things tell us more and more about ourselves and each other will permit racial, economic, as well as new forms of discrimination. Peppet (n 58).

it's inherently biased against BAME people.[135] However, the same companies often kept entering into agreements with the police, allowing for forms of biased policing and surveillance. This was well illustrated by Amazon's Ring – 'smart' home doorbell –which allowed (and still does) users to share concerning video footage with the police: reports[136] have found that a disproportionate number of incidents involve people of colour. A most pressing and understudied issue, the next section will shed light on the concept of digital dispossession in the context of IoT-enabled surveillance capitalism.

5.4 Surveillance Capitalism and IoT Apparatus: From Prediction to Execution

The role of private corporations in appropriating private resources (e.g. labour) and the commons (e.g. natural resources) has long been the subject of investigations. A particular contribution has been provided by Marxist scholars, including legal scholars, who underlined how the law enabled and facilitated the processes of capitalistic accumulation and exploitation.[137] Conversely, until recently, most ignored that a new variant of capitalism is on the rise, and it has to do with private corporations' exploitation of personal data. This is the focus of one of the few law books to recently acquire the status of bestsellers, *Surveillance Capitalism* by Shoshana Zuboff,[138] which was considered, perhaps emphatically, '*Das Kapital* of the digital age.'[139]

'Surveillance capitalism' is a concept that Zuboff coined in 2014.[140] It illuminates a new form of power generated by big data, an unprecedented threat to democratic values as it operates through 'unexpected and often illegible mechanisms of extraction, commodification, and control that effectively exile persons from their own behaviour.'[141] While not only about the IoT, this book underscores that 'although it may be possible to imagine something like the "internet of things" without surveillance capitalism, it is *impossible to imagine surveillance capitalism*

---

135 Emily Birnbaum and Issie Lapowsky, 'Amazon, Facing Pressure, Won't Provide Facial Recognition to Police for a Year' (*Protocol*, 10 June 2020) <www.protocol.com/amazon-facial-recognition-police>; 'IBM Abandons "biased" Facial Recognition Tech' *BBC News* (9 June 2020) <www.bbc.com/news/technology-52978191>.

136 Caroline Haskins, 'Amazon's Home Security Company Is Turning Everyone Into Cops' (*Vice*, 7 February 2019) <www.vice.com/en_us/article/qvyvzd/amazons-home-security-company-is-turning-everyone-into-cops>.

137 David Harvey, *The New Imperialism* (OUP 2003).

138 Zuboff, Surveillance Capitalism (n 12).

139 Hugo Rifkind, 'Review: The Age of Surveillance Capitalism by Shoshana Zuboff – Das Kapital for the Digital Generation' *The Times* (18 January 2019) <www.thetimes.co.uk/article/review-the-age-of-surveillance-capitalism-by-shoshana-zuboff-das-kapital-for-the-digital-generation-mb39mjk2s>.

140 Shoshana Zuboff, 'A Digital Declaration' *Frankfurter Allgemeine* (15 September 2014) <www.faz.net/1.3152525>.

141 Shoshana Zuboff, 'Big Other: Surveillance Capitalism and the Prospects of an Information Civilization' (2015) 30 Journal of Information Technology 75.

without something like the "internet of things."[142] At a higher level, *Surveillance Capitalism* is a book about power. Specifically, it is a book about the way big techs exercise power. As such, it can be seen as complementary to another notable contribution to contemporary scholarship, namely, *Re-engineering Humanity* by Brett Frischmann and Evan Selinger,[143] who focus on how these companies use new technologies, including the IoT –which the authors rebranded 'smart techno-social environment'[144] – to change those subjected to power: us. The IoT risks erasing the '*freedom to be off*, to be free from systemic, environmentally architected human engineering.'[145] Alongside power and its subjects, the law is the third element of the equation. This is at the centre of a third germinal book, *Between Truth and Power* by Julie E. Cohen,[146] who focuses on how the law is changing in the networked information age.[147] The law is closely intertwined with code (or design) and political economy: 'through their capacities to authorize, channel, and modulate information flows and behavior patterns, code and law *mediate* between truth and power.'[148] Whilst these books beautifully complement each other and are of great importance, this chapter will focus on *Surveillance Capitalism* because it analyses more closely the IoT as an expression of capitalistic power and contributes to the understanding of digital dispossession. Zuboff has been criticised because she would fail to appreciate the critical role that law plays in the construction and persistence of private power; conversely, informational capitalism would be 'contingent upon specific legal choices.'[149] This argument is based on the optimistic assumption that anticapitalistic resistance can be built into the law, whilst I would argue that the solution can only be found beyond the law.

In adopting Zuboff's book as an analytical framework, this chapter will depart from it to the limited extent required by my belief that surveillance capitalism is a mere variant of industrial capitalism and that both should be criticised for the exploitation of the vulnerable: yesterday the factory's workers, today the IoT's 'smart' users. Although Zuboff does not attempt a critique of capitalism as a whole, it can be argued that surveillance capitalism is a continuation of information capitalism that goes back to the Sixties, when American economists[150] started analysing the knowledge industry and understood that our society was already transitioning to an economy based on knowledge. Informational capital-

---

142 Zuboff, Surveillance Capitalism (n 12) 195. Emphasis added.
143 Brett M Frischmann and Evan Selinger, *Re-Engineering Humanity* (CUP 2018).
144 ibid esp 102 ff.
145 ibid 124. Italics in the text.
146 Julie E Cohen, *Between Truth and Power: The Legal Constructions of Informational Capitalism* (OUP 2019).
147 For a comparison between Cohen's and Zuboff's books, see Amy Kapczynski, 'The Law of Informational Capitalism' (2020) 129 Yale Law Journal 1460.
148 Cohen (n 146) 1. Italics in the text.
149 Kapczynski (n 147) 1460.
150 Fritz Machlup, *The Production and Distribution of Knowledge in the United States* (PUP 1962); Peter F Drucker, *The Age of Discontinuity: Guidelines to Our Changing Society* (Harper and Row 1969).

ism evolved out of industrial capitalism in the seventies, when computer technologies became common in the most developed countries, and it boomed in the nineties when investments in information technologies contributed to productivity increases on a grand scale.[151] Information technologies led to what Castells called the network logic; networks were seen as constituting 'the new social morphology of our societies, and the diffusion of networking logic substantially modifies the operation and outcomes in processes of production, experience, power, and culture.'[152]

Surveillance capitalism can be regarded as the current developmental stage of informational capitalism,[153] where the 'capture, rendering and analysis of behavioural data allow private companies to modify citizens' behaviour by cultivating 'radical indifference . . . a form of observation without witness.'[154] The focus on the production of 'new markets of behavioural prediction and modification'[155] is what differs. Whilst many had already studied the legality of predictive analytics, the element of behavioural modification had been mostly ignored. That is where the real danger lies – and that is where the IoT, with its combination of sensors and actuators, shows to be pivotal to surveillance capitalism. In the IoT, data is the main commodity, and the users can be regarded as data producers.[156] By appropriating this commodity and controlling the means of production, surveillance capitalists treat us as industrial capitalists treat their workers – except that now we are not even aware of being workers.[157]

Surveillance capitalists regard citizens as the by-product of the data they and their Things produce. Companies such as Google and Facebook rely on a continual process of 'digital dispossession.' This concept is rooted in the social theory of 'accumulation by dispossession' developed by David Harvey.[158] Though Zuboff refers to Harvey without much elucidation, it is worth keeping in mind that the social theorist criticised Marx[159] and Rosa Luxemburg[160] for relegat-

151 D Jorgenson, 'Information Technology and the U.S. Economy' (2001) 91 The Americal Economic Review 1.

152 Manuel Castells, *The Rise of the Network Society* (Blackwell 2000) 500.

153 In a regime of informational capitalism, 'market actors use knowledge, culture, and networked information technologies as means of extracting and appropriating surplus value, including consumer surplus' (Cohen (n 146) 6).

154 Zuboff, Surveillance Capitalism (n 12) 379.

155 Zuboff, 'Big Other' (n 141).

156 With the proliferation of complex Things, 'consumers become increasingly important as data producers, whether as operators of "smart cars" or carriers of "wearables"' (Herbert Zech, 'Data as Tradeable Commodity' in Alberto De Franceschi (ed), *European Contract Law and the Digital Single Market. The Implications of the Digital Revolution* (Intersentia 2016) 51.).

157 See Dominique Cardon and Antonio A Casilli, *Qu'est-ce que le Digital Labor?* (INA 2015).

158 Harvey (n 137).

159 Karl Marx, *Il Capitale (1867)*, vol 1 (Bruno Maffi tr, Aurelio Macchioro and Bruno Maffi, UTET 2008) ch 24.

160 Rosa Luxemburg, 'The Accumulation of Capital: A Contribution to an Economic Explanation of Imperialism (1913)' in Peter Hudius and Paul Le Blanc (eds), Nicholas Gray (tr), *The Complete Works of Rosa Luxemburg*, vol II: Economic Writings 2 (Verso 2016) 7.

ing accumulation based upon predation and violence to an 'original stage' that they considered outside of the capitalistic system – the so-called primitive accumulation.[161] In Marxist terms, primitive accumulation is the prehistory of capital as it is the '*historical process of divorcing the producer from the means of production.*'[162] The capitalist system presupposes the 'complete separation of the labourers from all property in the means by which they can realize their labour.'[163] To achieve such separation – in other words, to allow capitalists to own the means of production and subjugate labourers – one need consider the history of violent dispossessions that is rooted in the enslavement of feudalism, colonialism, and the enclosures that created a landless proletariat.[164] This primitive accumulation, albeit important to understand capitalism, is not the result of the capitalistic mode of production; according to Marx, it is its starting point.[165] This is where Harvey differs, and I would concur. His phrase 'accumulation by dispossession' intends to underline the persistence of predatory practices of accumulation of capital: it is a call for a 'general re-evaluation of the continuous role and persistence of the predatory practices of "primitive" or "original" accumulation within the long historical geography of capital accumulation.'[166] Contemporary capitalism is all about predation, fraud, and thievery, as epitomised by the wave of financialisation that set in after 1973 and its '[s]tock promotions, ponzi schemes, structured asset destruction through inflation, asset-stripping through mergers and acquisitions, and the promotion of levels of debt incumbency that reduce whole populations . . . to debt peonage.'[167] Accumulation by dispossession had one of its most tragic moments with the collapse of Enron dispossessing many of their pension rights, and the financial crisis of 2007–2008, which shed light on the new proletariat of subprime mortgagors.

Zuboff builds on the idea of accumulation by dispossession to present the concept of digital dispossession. To give it some context, she refers to Google's cofounder Larry Page's answer to the question 'What is Google?':

> If we did have a category, it would be *personal information*. . . . The places you've seen. Communications. . . . *Sensors are really cheap.* . . . Storage is cheap. Cameras are cheap. People will generate enormous amounts of

---

161 Harvey (n 137) 145. Cf Jim Glassman, 'Primitive Accumulation, Accumulation by Dispossession, Accumulation by "Extra-Economic" Means' (2006) 30 Progress in Human Geography 608.
162 Marx (n 159) 898.
163 ibid 897.
164 Unlike Marx, Coulthard argued that dispossession was not a singular event but a set of persistent and enduring practices of state violence that multiply coerced Indigenous peoples into the nation-state's colonial project. See Glen Sean Coulthard, *Red Skin, White Masks: Rejecting the Colonial Politics of Recognition* (University of Minnesota Press 2014).
165 Marx (n 159) 896.
166 Harvey (n 137) 144. Such persistence was also noted by Michael Perelman, *The Invention of Capitalism: Classical Political Economy and the Secret History of Primitive Accumulation* (DUP 2000).
167 Harvey (n 137) 147.

data. . . . Everything you've ever heard or seen or experienced will become searchable. *Your whole life will be searchable.*[168]

The IoT, with its ubiquitous and cost-effective sensors, allow surveillance capitalists to extract information about any aspect of the human experience at virtually no cost, and this can be 'rendered as behavioral data, producing a surplus that forms the basis of a wholly new class of market exchange.'[169] Surveillance capitalism 'originates in this act of *digital dispossession*.'[170] While surveillance capitalists acquire this data, we, as citizens, lose it without gaining anything meaningful in return. Indeed, market power is protected by 'moats of secrecy, indecipherability, and expertise. . . . [W]e are exiles from our own behavior, *denied access to or control over knowledge derived from its dispossession* by others for others.'[171] The IoT overlords observe us to generate detailed profiles about our beliefs, preferences, vulnerabilities. These profiles, created by means of digital dispossession, are kept secret by means of technical, organisational, and legal secrecy,[172] as technologies, such as machine learning and cryptographic techniques, are used to shield algorithms and other dispossessed data (e.g. inferences) from the public eye. There are also issues of organisational secrecy, as big tech companies operate under minimum transparency requirements. This chapter's main concern regards legal secrecy, defined as a combination of intellectual property rights (mainly trade secrets), and contracts are used to prevent citizens from knowing what surveillance capitalists do with the dispossessed data.

As the quote in this chapter's epigraph suggests, the IoT is at the centre of surveillance capitalism. As Zuboff notices, the IoT is characterised by a vision: 'the everywhere, always-on instrumentation, datafication, connection, communication, and computation of all things, animate and inanimate, and all processes.'[173] Of these terms, the crucial one – and perhaps the least accessible one – is instrumentation. Surveillance capitalists exercise instrumentarian power: the '*instrumentation and instrumentalization of behaviour* for the purposes of modification, prediction, monetization, and control.'[174] Its theoretical basis can be identified in Skinner's behaviourism.[175] His so-called operant conditioning approach stemmed from the belief that behaviour could be re-engineered through reinforcement. In the same way as a pigeon can learn to peck a button twice in order to receive a pellet of grain, a pervasive 'technology of behaviour' could condition the entire

---

168 Douglas Edwards, *I'm Feeling Lucky* (Houghton Mifflin Harcourt 2011) 291. Italics added.
169 *Corruption of Capitalism: Why Rentiers Thrive and Work Does Not Pay* 99.
170 ibid. Italics in the text.
171 ibid 100. Italics added.
172 I called this the 'triple black box' in Guido Noto La Diega, 'Against the Dehumanisation of Decision-Making – Algorithmic Decisions at the Crossroads of Intellectual Property, Data Protection, and Freedom of Information' (2018) 9 JIPITEC 3. Please see said paper for bibliographic references.
173 Zuboff, Surveillance Capitalism (n 12) 194.
174 ibid 352.
175 BF Skinner, *Beyond Freedom and Dignity* (Knopf/Random House 1971).

human populations.[176] Instrumentarianism 'erodes [democracy] from within, eating away at the human capabilities and self-understanding required to sustain a democratic life.'[177] Its imperative is to collect information about any aspect of the human behaviour so that the power of surveillance capitalists can most effectively pursue the behavioural re-engineering of citizens.

The IoT is pivotal to this end. As a distributed network of sensors, the IoT transforms all real-world activities into computational streams. This data, in turn, is subject to a two-dimensional transformation. One dimension is prediction. From this point of view, the IoT shares the stage with other technologies and techniques, such as machine learning and data mining.[178] However, it is the second dimension that sees the IoT as the real, albeit not the only, protagonist: execution. Indeed, the 'extraction architecture is combined with a new execution architecture, through which hidden economic objectives are imposed upon the vast and varied field of behavior.'[179] This architecture is provided by the IoT, which gives surveillance capitalists that real-world 'knowing and doing'[180] presence that is required from the prediction imperative. Zuboff sees the convergence between IoT and economic imperatives of surveillance capitalism as the shift '*from a thing that we have to a thing that has us*.'[181] Thanks to the IoT, Things are creating invaluable secondary data markets; Things – and, potentially, the people who carry them or are in their proximity – become 'as easily *indexed, searched and traded* as any online commodity [in what IBM calls] the *liquification of the physical world*.'[182] In other words, a major challenge in the regulation of the IoT is that the addition of billions of sensors to the internet's network is allowing individual behaviour in the physical world to be 'as closely tracked as online activity.'[183] This is in line with the more general tendency of capitalism to subjectify the object and objectify the subject, as seen in Chapter 4.

With its mix of sensors and actuators, the IoT is the perfect arm of this prediction-execution vision to make everything computable – and thus open to re-engineering. The rhetorical device used to allow the digital dispossession that is integral to this vision is subtle, and it goes by the names of data exhaust and raw data. As a by-product of our life, both online and offline, we generate huge amounts of data that, if not harnessed, risk going to waste, the tale goes. This is perhaps best illustrated through the ideas of Harriet Green, the woman behind the

---

176 For a critique, see Noam Chomsky, 'The Case Against B.F. Skinner' (1971) 17 The New York Review of Books 18.

177 Zuboff, Surveillance Capitalism (n 12) 381.

178 See Dean Abbott, *Applied Predictive Analytics: Principles and Techniques for the Professional Data Analyst* (Wiley 2014).

179 Zuboff, Surveillance Capitalism (n 12) 194.

180 ibid 195.

181 ibid.

182 IBM Institute for Business Value, 'The Economy of Things. Extracting New Value from the Internet of Things' (2015) 2.

183 Ian Brown and Christopher T Marsden, *Regulating Code: Good Governance and Better Regulation in the Information Age* (The MIT Press 2013) 47.

attempt to transform IBM into 'the Google' of the IoT. According to Green,[184] the single major obstacle to digital omniscience would be that most of the data companies' hold is unstructured and therefore difficult to code. This data is framed as 'dark,' evil data that prevents IoT companies from being more efficient and creative. Accordingly, the IoT is intended to be all-encompassing: 'any behavior of human or thing absent from this push for universal inclusion is dark: menacing, untamed, rebellious, rogue, out of control.'[185] Surveillance capitalists present digital dispossession as a service that gives value to otherwise-useless data – what we may refer to as 'Dispossession-as-a-Service.' Only by shedding light on this darkness, by illuminating every aspect of individuals' private sphere, will the IoT unleash its potential. In line with this, the recently adopted Data Governance Act has put forward the concept of data altruism, whereby data subjects are encouraged to share their data for the common good.[186] While not without merit, this concept reinforces the idea that if we do not give up control over our data, we are being selfish as we are wasting data. In this light, the IoT becomes the best solution to counter data selfishness and data waste by transforming everything into a computer, be it a fridge or a hospital bed.[187] Thus, the IoT offers the phenomenal opportunity to 'translate ubiquitous data into *ubiquitous knowledge and action*.'[188]

IoT's digital dispossession, in appropriating our data with the promise of optimisation, extracts value from us with little in return if not the prediction and transformation of our behaviour. By exercising new forms of conditioning and by translating us into 'an objective and measurable, indexable, browsable, searchable "it",'[189] IoT companies treat us like Skinner's pigeons – by-products of behavioural experiments – thus perpetuating the primitive violence of capitalism and fully realising its panoptic vision. This is perhaps the main shortcoming of *Surveillance Capitalism*, which can be criticised for not dealing with the continuity between industrial capitalism and surveillance capitalism,[190] for depicting the emerging regime of governance for the political economy of informationalism as

---

184 Bryan Glick, 'Executive Interview: Harriet Green, IBM's Internet of Things Chief' (*Computer Weekly*, 7 April 2016) <www.computerweekly.com/news/450280673/Executive-interview-Harriet-Green-IBMs-internet-of-things-chief>.

185 Zuboff, Surveillance Capitalism (n 12) 202.

186 Regulation (EU) 2022/868 of the European Parliament and of the Council of 30 May 2022 on European data governance and amending Regulation (EU) 2018/1724 (Data Governance Act or DGA) [2022] OJ L 152/1, art 2(16) and ch IV. Effective as of June 2022, the Data Governance Act will apply from September 2023.

187 Glick (n 184).

188 Zuboff, Surveillance Capitalism (n 12) 202.

189 ibid 203.

190 Sam di Bella, 'Book Review: The Age of Surveillance Capitalism: The Fight for a Human Future at the New Frontier of Power by Shoshana Zuboff' (*LSE Review of Books*, 4 November 2019) <https://blogs.lse.ac.uk/lsereviewofbooks/2019/11/04/book-review-the-age-of-surveillance-capitalism-the-fight-for-the-future-at-the-new-frontier-of-power-by-shoshana-zuboff/>; Evgeny Morozov, 'Capitalism's New Clothes | Evgeny Morozov' (*The Baffler*, 4 February 2019) <https://thebaffler.com/latest/capitalisms-new-clothes-morozov>.

lawless,[191] and for tending to ignore global South perspectives.[192] However, her 'thoroughly researched, rigorously argued'[193] monumental work has the merits of bringing back at the centre of the public debate ubiquitous corporate surveillance and, more generally, capitalism's efforts to appropriate every aspect of our being, as well as the role of the IoT in this context. The issues in surveillance capitalism go beyond privacy and data protection, having to do also with other fundamental rights, such as self-determination and dignity. A separate book should be written to deal with all this. However, this chapter will more modestly focus on how to use data protection legislation to protect ourselves from digital dispossession by means of legal secrecy.

5.5 Looking into Alexa's Black Box

To illustrate how digital dispossession plays out in the IoT, this section will investigate Alexa's black box. To do so, I will analyse the data obtained through a subject access request, the interactions with Amazon's customer support centre, and Alexa's privacy policy.

It is a common misunderstanding to think that IoT data escapes data protection laws. This belief is rooted in the assumption that all IoT data is 'machine data,' thus counting as nonpersonal data.[194] For example, GEA, one of the largest technology suppliers for food processing industries, declares to deploy the IoT to monitor and analyse data in relation to its products with the caveat that '*[t]ypically, no personal data is processed* in connection with any such technologies.'[195] This misunderstanding is based on two incorrect notions. First, it assumes that all IoT data is machine data. On the contrary, especially in the context of consumer IoT (e.g. smart home), the Thing can send back to manufacturers not only data about the Thing itself (e.g. when a movement sensor is activated) but also granular data about the user's behaviour. As held by the ECtHR in *PG v UK*,[196] voice samples are valuable personal data. Second, even machine data can count as personal data, either in isolation or after recombination. An example of the first type is provided by *Uzun v Germany*,[197] where data about a GPS device placed in a car was regarded as personal data. More often, through aggregation and recombination of data from multiple Things and other sources, data that, considered

191 Julie E Cohen, 'Review of Zuboff's The Age of Surveillance Capitalism' (2019) 17 Surveillance & Society 240.

192 Rafael Evangelista, 'Review of Zuboff's The Age of Surveillance Capitalism' (2019) 17 Surveillance & Society 246.

193 Mark Whitehead, 'Book Review of Shoshana Zuboff, The Age of Surveillance Capitalism' (*Antipode*, 2 October 2019) <https://antipodeonline.org/2019/10/02/the-age-of-surveillance-capitalism/>.

194 Amongst others, Daniar Supriyadi, 'Personal and Non-Personal Data in the Context of Big Data' (Tilburg University 2017).

195 Data Protection Notice <www.gea.com/en/info/legal/privacy-policy/index.jsp>.

196 *P.G. and J.H. v United Kingdom* (2008) 46 EHRR 51 [59]-[60].

197 (2011) 53 EHRR 24.

individually, would be nonpersonal can become personal.[198] Thus, the IoT corroborates the idea that 'the distinction between personal and nonpersonal data is likely to vanish over time.'[199] The argument can be further developed by claiming that one should not distinguish between 'ordinary' personal data and special categories of sensitive data (e.g. health data) because new technologies allow for the inference of sensitive data from ordinary personal data.

As evidence of the fact that digital dispossession practices are mostly kept private, one can consider Alexa as a case study. Amazon, Alexa's provider, does not tell users which data they collect about them. They only disclose '*the types* of information [they] gather.'[200] They merely provide '*examples* of information collected.'[201] This includes data provided by users (e.g. account information), automatic information (e.g. cookies), and data from unspecified 'other sources' (e.g. when users authorise a third-party website, such as Facebook, to interact with the Thing). This is inconsistent inter alia with the principle of transparency,[202] the requirements for consent,[203] and the right to be informed[204] as enshrined in the GDPR.

Moreover, in defiance of the principle of purpose limitation,[205] Amazon does not disclose for which purposes data are collected and processed: they only list examples of such purposes, which include advertising and unspecified 'purposes for which [they] seek your consent.'[206] Additionally, Amazon shares users' personal data with Amazon.com Inc.'s subsidiaries. When I initially wrote this chapter, Amazon relied on the Privacy Shield to transfer data to the US, but only five of its subsidiaries were Privacy Shield–certified, which meant that it was unclear whether the transfers of EU residents' personal data to the US had a legal basis. Recently, such uncertainty was made worse by the *Schrems II* case,[207] which invalidated the Privacy Shield and called into question also the other ways to justify international data transfers.[208] Indeed, the only ways private companies[209] can justify these transfers to non-EEA countries are as follows.

(i) Adequacy decision, that is, a finding by the European Commission that the non-EEA country where the data importer is based provides adequate

198 See Allsopp (n 99) 135.
199 Michèle Finck, *Blockchain Regulation and Governance in Europe* (CUP 2018) 93.
200 Amazon Privacy Notice; emphasis added.
201 ibid. Emphasis added.
202 GDPR, arts 5(1)(a) and 12.
203 GDPR, art 7.
204 GDPR, arts 13–14.
205 GDPR, art 5(1)(b).
206 ibid.
207 Case C-311/18 *Data Protection Commissioner v Facebook Ireland and Schrems* (CJEU, 16 July 2020).
208 The main reasons for invalidating the Privacy Shield were that the US legal system neither set out clear limits on the activities of the intelligence services nor provided effective remedies for individuals whose data has been exported (*Schrems II* (n 207) [174]–[176], [180]–[182], [191]).
209 On the transfers between public bodies, see GDPR, art 46(2)(a) and 46(3)(b).

protection.[210] As far as the US is concerned, the Commission originally found their level of data protection adequate in the so-called Safe Harbour decision,[211] which was found invalid in the *Schrems I* case.[212] It 2016, it was succeeded by the EU-US Privacy Shield,[213] which was a partial finding of adequacy of the level of data protection in the US.[214] The CJEU annulled it in July 2020, and as there is currently no adequacy decision covering EU-US data transfers, one should assess whether Amazon's data exports are otherwise justified.[215]

(ii) Binding corporate rules, a group document to which both the data exporter and the data importer are signatories.[216] Being internal code of conduct within corporate groups, it would lend itself to being used in our scenario. However, binding corporate rules have to be submitted to a data protection authority for approval, and Amazon is not among the few companies availing themselves this possibility.[217]

(iii) Standard contractual clauses (also known as model clauses or standard data protection clauses) have been adopted by the European Commission and must be entered into by the data exporter and the data importer.[218] The validity of the standard contractual clauses has been recently confirmed in *Schrems II*.[219] However, the CJEU underlined that additional safeguards may be necessary depending on the law and practice of the country of the data importer, especially if the foreign authorities may have access to the data.[220] If the controller or the processor cannot take these additional measures, they have to suspend or end the transfer.[221] In particular, this will be the case when domestic law imposes obligations that run counter

210 GDPR, art 45; recitals 103–107.
211 Commission Decision 2000/520/EC of 26 July 2000 pursuant to Directive 95/46 on the adequacy of the protection provided by the safe harbour privacy principles and related frequently asked questions issued by the US Department of Commerce [2000] OJ 2000 L 215/7.
212 Case C-362/14 *Maximillian Schrems v Data Protection Commissioner* [2016] QB 527.
213 Commission Implementing Decision (EU) 2016/1250 of 12 July 2016 pursuant to Directive 95/46/EC on the adequacy of the protection provided by the EU-U.S. Privacy Shield [2016] OJ L 207/1.
214 ICO, 'Guide to the GDPR' (n 109) 262.
215 Amazon's privacy policy states that the company does not rely on the Privacy Shield, but it does not clarify how international transfers are justified (see Privacy Notice, point 12).
216 GDPR, arts 46–47; recitals 108–110.
217 In the UK, the ICO has approved only the binding corporate rules submitted by Equinix Inc.
218 GDPR, arts 46(2)(c) and 93(2); recitals 108–109, 114.
219 (n 207). The CJEU held that Commission Decision of 5 February 2010 on standard contractual clauses for the transfer of personal data to processors established in third countries under Directive 95/46/EC of the European Parliament and of the Council, as amended by Commission Implementing Decision (EU) 2016/2297 of 16 December 2016 [2016] OJ L 344/100, includes effective mechanisms that make it possible, in practice, to ensure compliance with the level of protection required by EU law and that transfers of personal data pursuant to such clauses are suspended or prohibited in the event of the breach of such clauses or it being impossible to honour them.
220 *Schrems II* (n 207) [134].
221 ibid [135].

to the content of the standard contractual clauses. An example of this is provided by US and UK authorities having access to the undersea fibre-optic cables that make internet communications possible.[222] The passage of Amazon's Privacy Notice whereby '[w]e may be required to disclose personal information that we handle under the Privacy Shield in response to lawful requests by public authorities'[223] corroborates the concern. There is no indication that Amazon relies on these clauses or that it has put in place additional safeguards.

(iv) Code of conduct approved by a data protection authority, if the data importer is a signatory.[224] However, no approved codes of conduct are yet in use.[225]

(v) Certification under a certification mechanism that has been approved by a data protection authority.[226] Similarly to the codes of conduct, no approved certification scheme is in use.

(vi) Bespoke contract between data importer and data exporter to govern a specific transfer.[227] No data protection authority has authorised any such contract yet.[228]

(vii) The GDPR sets out 'derogations for specific situations'[229] in the absence of an adequacy decision or of the appropriate safeguards detailed in ii–vi. They include explicit consent[230] and contractual performance.[231] However, these are true exceptions, and therefore data controllers, including IoT companies, could rely on them only for occasional transfers.[232] Therefore, Amazon could not rely on the derogations for the constant data flows that Alexa-enabled Things send to the US.

Finally, as discovered through a subject access request I submitted in March 2019, Amazon grants users access only to some of their personal data, mainly the data that the user provided and the times when they interacted with Amazon's Things and services. To my surprise, the company thought to comply with my request by sending me hundreds of obscure spreadsheets, without any explanation and in a format that is hard to decipher, as seen in Table 5.1 below.[233]

---

222 Roxana Vatanparast, 'The Infrastructures of the Global Data Economy: Undersea Cables and International Law' (2020) 61 Harvard International Law Journal Frontiers 1.

223 Amazon Privacy Notice, point 12.

224 GDPR, arts 40 and 46(2)(e), recitals 108–109 and 114. See European Data Protection Board, 'Guidelines 1/2019 on Codes of Conduct and Monitoring Bodies under Regulation 2016/679' 679.

225 ICO, 'Guide to the GDPR' (n 109) 266.

226 GDPR, arts 42, 43, 46(2)(f), recitals 108–109 and 114; European Data Protection Board, 'Guidelines 1/2018 on Certification and Identifying Certification Criteria in Accordance with Articles 42 and 43 of the Regulation' (2019).

227 GDPR, art 46(3)(a).

228 ICO, 'Guide to the GDPR' (n 109) 267.

229 GDPR, art 49.

230 GDPR, art 49(1)(a).

231 GDPR, art 49(1)(b).

232 ICO, 'Guide to the GDPR' (n 109) 268–269.

233 This is an extract from one of the spreadsheets that Amazon sent to me when I requested access to my personal data.

Table 5.1 Extract from Amazon's Reply to One of the Coauthors' Subject Access Request

Device Record Time	Data Source Name[234]	Country of Residence	Software Version
21/03/2019 01:24	G070L8118454139U	GB	288.6.3.2_user_632552020
21/03/2019 01:24	G070L8118454139U	GB	288.6.3.2_user_632552020
21/03/2019 00:28	G090RF04743204M2	GB	288.6.3.1_user_631550720
21/03/2019 00:28	G090RF04743204M2	GB	288.6.3.1_user_631550720
20/03/2019 20:50	G070L8118454139U	GB	288.6.3.2_user_632552020
20/03/2019 20:25	G090RF04743204M2	GB	288.6.3.1_user_631550720
19/03/2019 20:04	G070L8118454139U	IT	288.6.3.2_user_632552020

The data I was granted access to did not include, e.g. my 'digital twin,' namely, the profile that Amazon has been building about me – and about any other customer – based on my personal data.[235] Importantly, the copy of my data obtained upon request under Article 15 GDPR excluded those precious inferences that should be recognised as personal data, as said prior.[236] Amazon stores the recording of the user's interactions with Alexa.[237] Thanks to its emotion-recognition technologies, Amazon can extract from users' voice valuable information about their feelings. Information that can be utilised to target them more effectively. This is exemplified by the patent Amazon was granted in 2018 under the ostensibly innocuous title 'Indirect feedback systems and methods.'[238] Thanks to this patent, Amazon has a monopoly on a technology that allows the company to detect users' physical, emotional, and behavioural states. These states are 'shown, heard, or otherwise detected in the sensed data. . . . [A] user's facial expression and/or body language can provide indirect feedback as to how the user is feeling (e.g. mood).'[239] As Figure 5.1 illustrates, Amazon uses its IoT sensors to extract data about our emotions to serve us with ads and offers that reflect those emotions.

Our face and our voice are rich data sources. It is crucial to keep this in mind when reflecting on the fact that our voice interactions with Alexa are recorded and thousands of Amazon employees transcribe, annotate, and feedback the recordings

---

234 In the spreadsheet that was sent as a reply to our subject access request, Amazon uses the obscure acronym 'DSN' that interpret as referring to an equally obscure concept, that is 'data source name'. This is a 'means of identifying, and connecting to, a database (...) required for many Web applications that interact with and query databases' (F Botto, *Dictionary of E-Business* (2nd edn, Wiley 2003) 109.). This would suggest that Amazon has a database that includes all users' personal data, which begs the question of whether the sui generis right could be used to appropriate said data.

235 While Amazon does not expressly say that it profiles customers, this can be inferred by its privacy policy that states that the company tracks users within and beyond the service and uses that information for personalisation and advertising purposes (Amazon Privacy Notice, points 2 and 3).

236 Wachter and Mittelstadt (n 91).

237 Amazon's Privacy Policy.

238 USPTO 10,019,489, 10 July 2018.

239 USPTO 10,019,489, abstract.

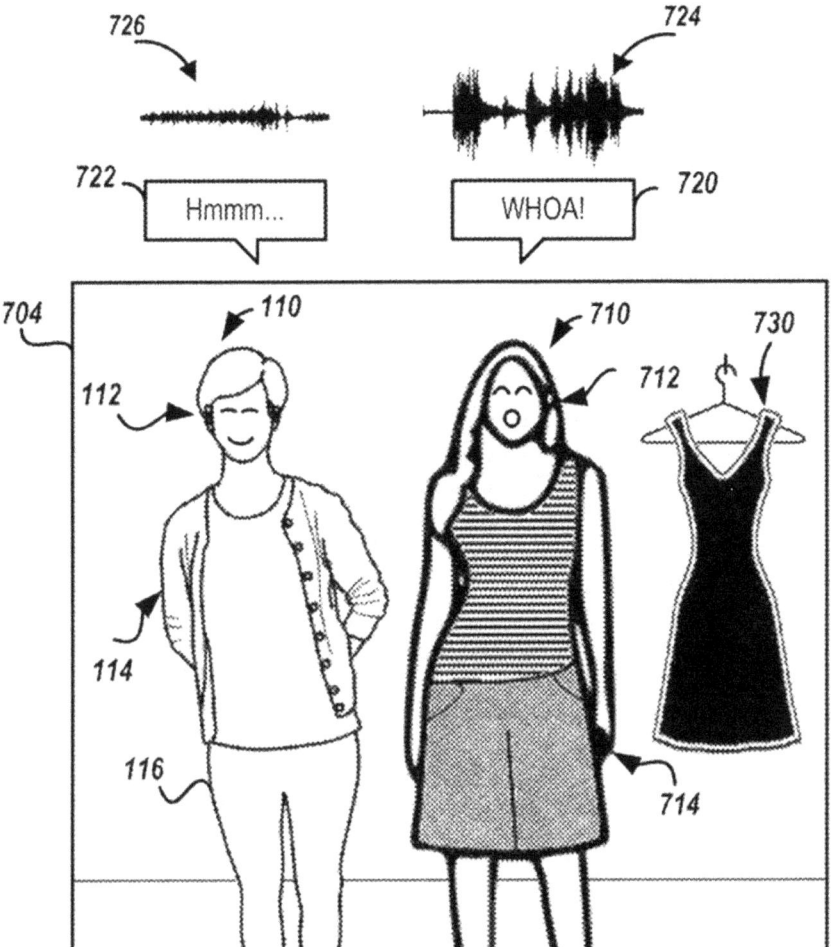

Figure 5.1 Drawing no 7, USPTO 10,019,489.

into the software.[240] This patent is only one of the many worrying applications of affective computing, a field that infers people's emotions, traits, and behaviours by exploiting intelligent machine learning methods and data acquired through Things.[241] This is a threat to citizens' privacy, data protection, autonomy, and

240 Matt Day, Giles Turner and Natalia Drozdiak, 'Amazon Workers Are Listening to What You Tell Alexa' (*Bloomberg.com*, 12 April 2019) <www.bloomberg.com/news/articles/2019-04-10/ is-anyone-listening-to-you-on-alexa-a-global-team-reviews-audio>.
241 Eugenia Politou, Efthimios Alepis and Constantinos Patsakis, 'A Survey on Mobile Affective Computing' (2017) 25 Computer Science Review 79.

self-determination. Interpreted in a future-proof and technologically neutral way, the GDPR should allow IoT users to access these inferences and to stop their use when in the context of solely automated decisions. Regrettably, Amazon keeps our emotional profile secret. Once interrogated to obtain more information about my data, Amazon did not comply with my requests. One may conjecture that this is because Amazon's Privacy Notice subjects the rights to access, rectification, portability, and erasure to the 'applicable law,'[242] and the applicable law includes intellectual property law and trade secrets. Therefore, the next section will investigate under which circumstances IoT companies can invoke this 'legal secrecy' to prevent the exercise of those GDPR rights that may otherwise help citizens fight against digital dispossession.

5.6   Can the GDPR Counter IoT-Powered Digital Dispossession?

To understand whether IoT users can invoke the GDPR to counter IoT-powered digital dispossession, one need critically analyse the relationship between trade secrets and personal data protection. Indeed, trade secrets appear to be the main tool used by IoT companies to digitally dispossess their users.[243] Other intellectual property rights – namely, patents on computer-implemented inventions and software copyright – do play a role and will be accounted for in the next chapter. Tensions over the control of IoT data arise at the confluence of data protection laws and trade secrets. Nonetheless, there has been little effort to investigate the interplay between these two regimes.[244] The same data could be covered by both data protection rights and trade secrets; this begs the question if and to what extent trade secrets can be invoked by IoT companies to reject users' claims based on the GDPR.[245] In other words, it will be questioned whether the GDPR's philosophy of data control and openness can prevail on trade secrecy or whether, by contrast, closed, siloed systems are the (present and) future of the IoT.

5.6.1   The Conflict between Trade Secrets and Data Protection

Transposed by member states in June 2017, the Trade Secrets Directive contains a commitment to respect the right for private and family life, the right to protection of personal data, as enshrined in the Charter of Fundamental Rights of the EU.[246] It further clarifies that the GDPR[247] governs the processing of personal data that takes place whilst taking steps to protect a trade secret and, in proceedings on the

---

242 Amazon Privacy Notice, 'What Choices Do I Have?'
243 See Noto La Diega and Sappa (n 131).
244 See Drexl (n 10).
245 Gintare Surblyte, 'Data Mobility at the Intersection of Data, Trade Secret Protection and the Mobility of Employees in the Digital Economy' [2016] GRUR International 1121.
246 TS Directive, recital 34; Charter of Fundamental Rights of the EU, arts 7 and 8.
247 TS Directive, recital 35. This Directive refers to the Data Protection Directive but I will replace the references to it with references to the GDPR.

unlawful acquisition, use or disclosure of trade secrets.[248] The conclusion is that the Trade Secrets Directive 'should not affect the rights and obligations laid down in'[249] the GDPR. Considering the GDPR's underlying philosophy, the assumption that the two regimes converge is debatable. An IoT company may seek its users' consent to collect their data and commercialise them, but it is unclear what happens if the users want to access that data, especially once it has been aggregated with other secret information and it has become difficult to isolate. Regardless of the directive's statement of principle that no conflicts will arise, trade secrets and personal data protection do and will indeed clash. Therefore, it is crucial to understand how to govern such conflict.

It should be noted that the directive's aforementioned provisions about the relationship to data protection are not binding as they are found in the Trade Secrets Directive's recitals. The only binding provision is Article 9(4), whereby the processing of personal data in the course of legal proceedings relating to the unlawful acquisition, use, or disclosure of a trade secret must comply with the GDPR. This is significant for two reasons. First, it shows a single-minded conception of the GDPR as a confidentiality law as opposed to a data control law. Indeed, the legal proceedings this provision refers to are the proceedings for the '[p]reservation of confidentiality.' The national implementation measures confirm this by imposing obligations of confidentiality, but not an express duty to comply with the GDPR.[250] Second, the fact that this is the only binding provision that refers to data protection may be interpreted as meaning that the rest of the trade secret–related processing, e.g. acquisition of the trade secret, must not necessarily comply with the GDPR. An analysis of the latter instrument militates against this interpretation, as will be shown later on.

Finally, whilst the Trade Secrets Directive does not provide unambiguous arguments to conclude on which regime will prevail – trade secrets or data protection – a pro-GDPR argument can be made starting from the exceptions that the directive provides. In particular, defendants can claim that the acquisition, use, or disclosure of the secret was carried out 'for exercising the right to freedom of expression and information'[251] as well as for a 'legitimate interest.'[252] The next chapter will delve into these exceptions. For the purposes of this section, suffice it to say that the GDPR can be seen as an application of the freedom to access information and that data protection is a legitimate interest in the EU.[253] Therefore, the unauthorised access to one's personal data held by an IoT company may be regarded as lawful inasmuch as it falls within the scope of these exceptions.

248 TS Directive, recital 35.
249 TS Directive, recital 35.
250 See Italy's Industrial Property Code, art 121-ter; France's Code of Commerce, art L 153–2; and the UK's Trade Secrets Regulations, reg 30.
251 TS Directive, art 5(a).
252 TS Directive, art 5(d).
253 Noto La Diega and Sappa (n 131).

Unlike the Trade Secrets Directive, the GDPR provides clearer arguments to conclude that in most scenarios, data protection will prevail on trade secrets. It is possible to construe the GDPR as meaning that IoT companies cannot use intellectual property rights as an excuse not to comply with the right to data protection. The starting point is Recital 63, whereunder the right of access '*should not adversely affect the rights or freedoms of others including trade secrets or intellectual property.*'[254] Thus, the GDPR recognises that trade secrets and data protection may clash and that a balance should be struck between the right to maintain the secrecy of valuable commercial information and the right to access that information when it includes personal data. Concerns have been expressed that the trend to appropriate algorithms by means of trade secrets may render transparency unfeasible.[255] However, Recital 63 should not be interpreted as a blanket preference for trade secrets over data protection. To prove this point, three observations can be made.

First – and this is a key difference between the GDPR and the Data Protection Directive[256] – Recital 63 of the GDPR clarifies that the result of trade secrets considerations '*should not be a refusal to provide all information to the data subject.*' The Article 29 Working Party pointed out that the provision whereby trade secrets should not be adversely affected is to be interpreted narrowly; indeed, 'controllers cannot rely on the protection of their trade secrets as an excuse to deny access or refuse to provide information to the data subject.'[257] When it comes to the right of access, the GDPR recommends data controllers offer remote access to a secure self-service system which would, in turn, provide data subjects with direct access to their data.[258] The Information Commissioner's Office – the UK's data protection authority – suggests that such a self-service system should not include trade secrets.[259] And indeed, allowing automated, remote access would not be consistent with the reasonable steps that the holder has to take to keep the commercial information secret; indeed, without these steps, the information would fall beyond the definition of trade secret.[260] Therefore, the indication that the right of access should not adversely affect trade secrets should be interpreted as a right not to allow remote automated access to the personal data that the company holds. However, IoT companies, and all data controllers, must grant access through nonautomated means. Companies should rigorously distinguish the data whose disclosure would nullify the secrecy of the relevant commercial information and the data that can be

---

254 GDPR, recital 63.
255 This was an interpretation of recital 63 that was suggested, albeit in passing, by Giulia Schneider, 'European Intellectual Property and Data Protection in the Digital-Algorithmic Economy: A Role Reversal(?)' (2018) 13 Journal of Intellectual Property Law & Practice 229, 237.
256 Gianclaudio Malgieri, 'Trade Secrets v Personal Data: A Possible Solution for Balancing Rights' (2016) 2 IDPL 102, 103.
257 Article 29 Working Party, 'Guidelines on Automated Individual Decision-Making and Profiling for the Purposes of Regulation 2016/679' (n 104) 17.
258 GDPR, recital 63.
259 ICO, 'Guide to the GDPR' (n 109) 105.
260 Trade Secret Directive, art 2(1)(c).

disclosed without nullifying said secrecy. Should this disclosure not satisfy the user, a broader disclosure can be obtained through administrative or judicial proceedings. In these venues, access to personal data covered by a trade secret can be granted and will be accompanied by measures that safeguard the commercial value of the trade secret, for instance an order not to disclose the trade secret outside the courtroom.[261]

Second, it is crucial to keep in mind that the GDPR refers to trade secrets as an example of third-party rights that one should consider when responding to subject access requests. The right of access should not adversely affect the 'rights or freedoms of others, *including* trade secrets.'[262] This is crucial because Article 15 of the GDPR, which deals with the right of access, provides that rights and freedoms of others should not be adversely affected by the 'right to obtain a copy'[263] of the data undergoing processing. This is a right to obtain a free-of-charge copy of one's personal data, and it is only one of the powers that the right of access gives data subjects.[264] This means that rights and freedom of others, including trade secrets, can only adversely affect the right to obtain a copy, not the right of access as a whole. Indeed, under Article 15,[265] the right of access gives the data subject a wide range of powers:

   (i) A right to obtain confirmation as to whether one's personal data is processed;
  (ii) A right to access the data that is being processed;
 (iii) A right to obtain a free-of-charge copy of the data;
 (iv) A right to obtain information about some key features of the processing. These include the purposes of the processing, their sources, and the existence of – and the logic involved in – automated decision-making.[266]

I am of the view that IoT companies cannot invoke their trade secrets to deny subject access requests. The only derogation that the joint operation regards the right to obtain a copy of the data. Accordingly, IoT companies can only leverage trade secrets to exclude from the free-of-charge copy data that cannot be isolated from the confidential information. Conversely, I would argue that these companies, and more generally companies that use trade secrets for digital dispossession purposes, must:

   (i) Release a copy of the data that can be isolated from the confidential information;

---

261 Noto La Diega (n 172) [87].
262 GDPR, recital 63.
263 GDPR, art 15(4), that refers back to art 15(3).
264 ICO, 'Guide to the GDPR' (n 109) 102. ICO, *Guide*, cit., p. 102. Cf M Di Martino, 'Personal Information Leakage by Abusing the GDPR "Right of Access"' *Proceedings of the Fifteenth Symposium on Usable Privacy and Security* (Usenix 2019) 271.
265 In particular, GDPR, art 15(1)(a), (g), (h), and 15(3).
266 See L Mendoza and Lee A Bygrave, 'The Right Not to Be Subject to Automated Decisions Based on Profiling' in Tatiana – Eleni Synodinou et al. (eds), *EU Internet Law: Regulation and Enforcement* (Springer 2017) 77.

(ii) Confirm that personal data – including data that cannot be isolated from confidential information – is being processed;
(iii) Grant access to key information, including the purposes of the processing, e.g. the inclusion in information covered by trade secrets; and finally, more importantly,
(iv) Grant access to all the data, including the data covered by trade secrets, although in a 'view only' mode.

For example, if the data appropriated by an IoT company can play a role in the data subject's defence in legal proceedings – and such data cannot be isolated from the rest of the information covered by the trade secret – the company may decide not to release a copy of the data, but at least it should allow the parties' representatives and the court to view the relevant data.

Third, there is one other data subject right whose exercise should not affect the rights and freedoms of others under the GDPR.[267] The only other data protection right on which trade secrets can, under certain circumstances, prevail is the right to portability under Article 20 GDPR. This is the right to receive one's personal data in a structured, commonly used, and machine-readable format and to transmit it to another controller.[268] Article 20 does not refer to trade secrets, but it seems reasonable to interpret its reference to 'the rights and freedoms of others'[269] as inclusive of them. The right to data portability 'is the cornerstone of the right to control.'[270] In principle, Echo users who would like to switch to Google Home have an interest in transmitting the data that Echo has been collecting about them to Google. Thanks to this data, the new virtual assistant would learn more quickly about the user's preferences and habits and would provide a more personalised service.[271] Data portability is also pivotal to the right to repair. It is a common practice in the IoT to prevent users from using third-party services to repair or update the Thing.[272] The right to data portability – especially used in combination to the rights of service portability and nonpersonal data portability seen in Chapter 1 – is particularly useful to tackle such lock-in practices.[273] Under Amazon's Privacy Notice, users can 'ask for data portability . . . subject to applicable law.'[274] The reference to the applicable law surely includes Article 20(4) of the GDPR, whereby the right to data portability 'shall not adversely affect the rights and freedoms of others.' Accordingly, users should not be advised

---

267 cf Article 29 Working Party, 'Guidelines on the Right to Data Portability' (2017) WP242 rev.01 12.
268 GDPR, art 20.
269 GDPR, art 20(4).
270 Marco Ricolfi, 'Il Futuro Della Proprietà Intellettuale Nella Società Algoritmica' [2019] Giur it 10, 31.
271 See Article 29 Working Party, 'Guidelines on the Right to Data Portability' (n 267).
272 See e.g. the famous case of the John Deere 'smart' tractors whose manufacturer tried to force farmers to only repair their tractors at a John Deere–approved mechanic. Joshua AT Fairfield, *Owned: Property, Privacy, and the New Digital Serfdom* (CUP 2017) 14.
273 See Ricolfi (n 270) 30.
274 Amazon's Privacy Notice, 'What Choices do I Have?'.

to rely on the right to data portability to counter IoT companies' digital dispossession practices. Indeed, unlike the right of access, the right to data portability would appear to be excluded as such if its exercise adversely affects trade secrets. Nonetheless, the result of trade secrets considerations 'should not be the refusal to provide all information.'[275] Therefore, IoT companies should endeavour to isolate the requesting data subject's personal data and facilitate its portability.

The rights to obtain a free-of-charge copy and to portability are the only data subject's rights that can be, to some extent, compressed if they adversely affect the rights and freedoms of others, including trade secrets. Therefore, relying on an *argumentum a contrario*, I would opine that IoT companies cannot invoke their trade secrets to neutralise other data subject rights and their obligations as controllers. With the exception of the rights to obtain a copy and to portability, trade secrets will not be a valid legal basis for any exceptions or limitations. This means that trade secrets will not limit the rights to be informed, to rectification, to erasure, to restrict processing, to object, and not to be subject to automated decision-making. Two of these rights are best placed to empower citizens who are victims of IoT-powered digital dispossession: the right to be informed and the right not to be subject to automated decisions.

5.6.2 The Rights to be Informed and Not to Be Subject to Automated Decisions in the Arsenal of the Digitally Dispossessed

The right to be informed[276] is an expression of the first data protection principle, namely, lawfulness, fairness, and transparency.[277] Transparency operates as the chief counterweight to secrecy in that it creates an obligation to be clear, open, and honest with users about how and why their personal data is processed.[278] As we have seen in the analysis of the Unfair Terms Directive,[279] transparency is intrinsically linked to fairness. In the field of data protection, it applies to three central areas:

(i) The provision of the information about which data is processed and how it is processed;
(ii) The provision of information about data subject rights;
(iii) The way data controllers facilitate the exercise of data subjects' rights.[280]

For the purposes of this chapter, it is sufficient to focus on *i*, as it is the most likely to apply to a scenario where an IoT company attempts to appropriate its users' personal data by trade secrecy means.

---

275 Article 29 Working Party, 'Guidelines on the Right to Data Portability' (n 267).
276 GDPR, arts 13–14.
277 GDPR, arts 5(1)(a) and 12.
278 ICO, 'Guide to the GDPR' (n 109) 22.
279 See Chapter 3 of this book.
280 Article 29 Working Party, 'Guidelines on Transparency under Regulation 2016/679' (2018) WP260 rev.01 4.

IoT companies that process personal data must inform users in a concise, transparent, intelligible, and easily accessible way.[281] The information – to be provided at the time when personal data is obtained[282] or within a month[283] – include the purposes of the processing, the entities with whom the data is shared, the existence of the right to access the data, as well as the existence and the logic involved in automated decision-making.[284] Since Things have unconventional, limited, or no interfaces, it is crucial that IoT companies follow a Data Protection by Design[285] approach, whereby the GDPR principles are embedded in the design on the Thing from the outset (e.g. holograms to provide privacy notices).[286] The study of Amazon Echo's contractual quagmire showed that the GDPR-mandated information is only partly provided – and certainly not in an accessible way. Amazon e.g. declares that they process personal data to 'operate, provide, and improve the Amazon services'[287] and enclose a list of purposes that are supposed to exemplify this triad. However, they include also advertising that, strictly speaking, is not necessary to operate, provide, or improve the services. Advertising is one of the purposes that are behind Amazon's digital dispossession practices through affective computing technologies.

Informing users in a transparent way means that they should be able to '*determine in advance what the scope and consequences of the processing* entails and that they should not be taken by surprise at a later point about the ways in which their personal data has been used.'[288] Therefore, the IoT company should be clear about the consequences that appropriating personal data can have on the user. Digitally dispossessed data can be used for targeted advertising at best, for manipulation and discrimination at worst.

There are limited exceptions to the obligation to inform, and they apply only when personal data is obtained from sources other than the user (e.g. data brokers).[289] When this is the case, data controllers do not have to inform users if the latter already has the information, providing it would be impossible, require a disproportionate effort, or render impossible the achievement of the objectives of the processing; the processing is required by law; or an obligation of professional

281 GDPR, art 12.
282 GDPR, art 13(1).
283 GDPR, art 14(3)(a).
284 GDPR, arts 13–14.
285 GDPR, art 25. See European Data Protection Board, 'Guidelines 4/2019 on Article 25 Data Protection by Design and by Default' (2019).
286 From a US perspective, Julie Brill, 'The Internet of Things: Building Trust and Maximizing Benefits through Consumer Control' (2014) 83 Fordham Law Review 205.
287 Amazon Privacy Notice, 'For What Purposes Does Amazon Europe Process Your Personal Information?'
288 Article 29 Working Party, 'Guidelines on Transparency under Regulation 2016/679' (n 282) 7. Italics added.
289 Chris Hoofnagle, 'Big Brother's Little Helpers: How ChoicePoint and Other Commercial Data Brokers Collect and Package Your Data for Law Enforcement' (2004) 29 North Carolina Journal of International Law 595.

secrecy covers the data.[290] *Inclusio unius, exclusio alterius*: the reference to professional secrecy means that trade secrecy, as such, does not constitute an exception to the right to be informed and that, as a rule, IoT companies that hold trade secret must fully comply with the obligations to inform. Conversely, said companies may try to argue that informing the user would make impossible the achievement of the objectives of the processing. This does not provide a blanket exemption to IoT companies holding trade secrets. They have to prove that the provision of information 'would *nullify* the objectives of the processing.'[291] Whereas one could argue that the disclosure of the trade secret as such might nullify said objectives, informing that the data is being appropriated e.g. to create profiles with the data inferred from the observation of the user's behaviour would not. At any rate, IoT companies relying on this exception would still need to satisfy all the data protection principles, including fairness and lawfulness.[292]

In most cases, IoT companies will not be able to adduce trade secrets as an exception to the right to be informed. Accordingly, they will have to thoroughly inform users about their digital dispossession practices. The principle of transparency, which underpins the obligations to inform, may offset trade secrecy. Being informed of digital dispossession is the prerequisite for the users to act and attempt to stop it or minimise its risks. Users can rely on another right to actively defend themselves from IoT companies who weaponise their appropriated personal data, e.g. by using their algorithms to take automated decisions that can have profound consequences, e.g. automated screening of job applications.[293] The main tool that the GDPR makes available in this sort of scenarios is the right not to be subject to an automated decision.[294]

Under Article 22 of the GDPR, the right not to be subject to an automated decision instantiates a general prohibition for data controllers to subject individuals to a (i) decision that is (ii) based solely on automated processing and (iii) produces legal effects concerning the individual or, similarly, significantly affect them.[295] Amazon e.g. should not be allowed to automatically exclude from its IoT platforms some users based on their ethnicity. Such automated systems should never be put in place if their decision can profoundly affect data subjects.

The restriction on solely automated decision-making can be lifted on three grounds: contractual necessity, statutory authorisation, and explicit consent.[296] The restriction cannot be lifted if the controller processes special categories of

---

290 GDPR, art 14(5).

291 Article 29 Working Party, 'Guidelines on Transparency under Regulation 2016/679' (n 282) 31. Italics added.

292 ibid.

293 TC Sandanayake et al., 'Automated CV Analyzing and Ranking Tool to Select Candidates for Job Positions' *Proceedings of the 6th International Conference on Information Technology: IoT and Smart City* (ACM 2018) 13.

294 GDPR, art 22.

295 GDPR, art 22(1). These concepts are problematic, but they are of little relevance from this paper's perspective, and therefore they will not be analysed. For more information on this, see ibid 20.

296 GDPR, art 22(2).

data (e.g. health data), unless special circumstances apply, e.g. the processing is necessary for substantial public interest reasons.[297]

Contractual necessity, statutory authorisation, and explicit consent do not operate as a *carte blanche*; an IoT company wishing to rely on them would have to implement suitable safeguards for the data subject's rights, freedoms, and legitimate interests. They include, at least, the right to obtain human intervention on the part of the controller, to express their point of view, and to contest the decision.[298] It is debated whether one of the safeguards is the right to obtain an explanation of the decision. On the one hand, it can be argued that since such right is only referred to in a nonbinding recital and not in Article 22 itself, there would be no right to an explanation.[299] On the other hand, based on a more systematic interpretation that takes into account the principle of transparency and the obligations to inform, it can be argued that a right to an explanation exists.[300] And indeed, the fact that the right to an explanation is referred to in a nonbinding recital should not be overstated. The pivotal role of recitals in interpreting the provisions of an EU act has been expressly recognised by the Commission.[301] Therefore, the reference to the right of explanation in the recital shall be used to properly construe Article 22 to reflect the context of the provision and the overall purpose of the GDPR, that is, increasing the protection of the data subjects' rights. Even though applying the literal rule of Article 22 would not entail a right to explanation, a purposive approach and a correct valorisation of the role of recitals make it clear that data subjects are entitled to such a right. In any event, should one be of the view that the right to an explanation does not exist, the right to inform expressly includes the obligation to inform about the existence of automated decision-making and to provide meaningful information about the 'logic involved, as well as the significance and the envisaged consequences of such processing for the data subject.'[302] This means that IoT companies that hold trade secrets should not use algorithmic or otherwise-automated systems to take decisions that can negatively affect the user. If they do so, e.g. because the user gave them explicit consent, they still need to put in place some safeguards that at least include an obligation to explain the logic involved in the algorithmic decision and the right to a human being reviewing the decision. Whereas under certain conditions IoT companies may trigger their trade secrets to limit the rights to obtain a copy of the data and to portability, they will not be able to oppose their trade secrets as a valid reason not to provide

---

297 GDPR, arts 22(4) and 9.

298 GDPR, art 22(3).

299 Sandra Wachter, Brent Mittelstadt and Luciano Floridi, 'Why a Right to Explanation of Automated Decision-Making Does Not Exist in the General Data Protection Regulation' (2017) 7 IDPL 76, 76.

300 Gianclaudio Malgieri and Giovanni Comandé, 'Why a Right to Legibility of Automated Decision-Making Exists in the General Data Protection Regulation' (2017) 7 IDPL 243.

301 Roberto Baratta, 'Complexity of EU Law in the Domestic Implementing Process' *19th Quality of Legislation Seminar "EU Legislative Drafting: Views from Those Applying EU Law in the Member States* (European Commission 2014) 4.

302 GDPR, arts 13(2)(f) and 14(2)(g).

meaningful information about their algorithmic decisions and to deny the right to human review. Thus, there is a major difference to the US approach in *State v Loomis*,[303] when Mr Loomis had been considered dangerous by an algorithmic system and had not been able to contest the decision because the system was proprietary. In the EU, higher data protection standards[304] and the right to a fair trial[305] would not allow such an outcome.

This should be caveated with the observation that the GDPR does allow member states to introduce restrictions to all data protection rights – not just to the rights of access and of portability – 'when such a restriction respects the essence of the fundamental rights and freedoms and is a necessary and proportionate measure in a democratic society to safeguard . . . the protection of the data subject or the rights and freedoms of others.'[306] This option could be used to allow wider limitations to data subjects' rights based on trade secrecy. As far as I know, France is the only member state that took advantage of this option. Indeed, the *Loi informatique et libertés* – France's data protection statute – provides that when an automated decision is justified by contractual necessity or explicit consent, the data controller, alongside ensuring human intervention, the right to express one's point of view, and the right to contest the decision, must communicate the rules that define the processing and the main characteristics of its implementation 'with the exception of the secrets protected by the law.'[307] It is fair to infer that these secrets protected by the law encompass trade secrets. This does not mean, however, that users who are based in France cannot rely on Article 22 of the GDPR to counter IoT digital dispossession. It merely means that in informing about the automated system, the controller does not have to disclose trade secrets. Nonetheless, all IoT companies, including those who are based in France, will have to:

  (i) Abide by the general ban on solely automated decisions, unless they have secured user consent or demonstrated contractual necessity or statutory authorisation;
 (ii) Respect the other GDPR rights, including the right to be informed about the logic involved in the automated decision; and
(iii) Endeavour to isolate users' personal data from the rest of the information that is covered by trade secrets and inform users accordingly.

---

303 881 N.W.2d 749 (Wis. 2016).
304 Cf. Han-Wei Liu, Ching-Fu Lin and Yu-Jie Chen, 'Beyond State v Loomis: Artificial Intelligence, Government Algorithmization and Accountability' (2019) 27 International Journal of Law and Information Technology 122.
305 Under the ECHR, art 6, there is not an absolute obligation to disclose all evidence. However, preventing the full disclosure of evidence is allowed only to the limited extent that it is strictly necessary to preserve an important public interest or the fundamental rights of another individual (*Paci v Belgium* App no 45597/09 (ECtHR, 17 April 2018) [85]).
306 GDPR, art 23(1)(i).
307 Loi n° 78–17 of 6 January 1978 *relative à l'informatique, aux fichiers et aux libertés*, art 47(1) (*à l'exception des secrets protégés par la loi'*).

5.7 Interim Conclusion: Data Protection Law and the 'Smart' Proletariat

Overall, the GDPR does provide adequate tools to counter IoT-powered digital dispossession. Prima facie, this might be interpreted as meaning that the GDPR is an anticapitalistic instrument. This is not the case. The theory of surveillance capitalism underlines how the violence of dispossession is not limited to those histories that precede capitalism: digital dispossession is a continuous process, and its violence is disguised in multifarious ways. Capitalists need to sell the commodities produced by the workers in order to recover the original outlays and the surplus value extracted from the labour force.[308] By leveraging IoT data, including inferential data, surveillance capitalists can exploit users' vulnerabilities to do precisely this – what the previous chapter called 'the Internet of Personalised Things.' However, the convergence between IoT and capitalism also takes another, more subtle form. With her characteristic lucidity, Rosa Luxemburg defined the essence of capitalism as a system that uses the fruits of exploitation 'to increase exploitation itself':[309] this is seen as the way to achieve not only profit but also constantly growing profit. For exploitation to take place, capitalists need a sufficient quantity of labour power. To ensure this, they have to make sure that workers can maintain themselves (typically through wages) 'so that they will be available for future exploitations.'[310] Data subjects are data producers and hence unwitting workers of the data economy.[311] The GDPR gives this new 'smart' proletariat some rights that can be relied on to reacquire some control over the data. In doing so, the GDPR allows us data subjects / unwitting workers to maintain ourselves, thus being available for future exploitations. This is in line with the more general observation that the '[l]aw for the information economy is emerging . . . via the ordinary, uncoordinated but self-interested efforts of information economy participants and the lawyers and lobbyists they employ.'[312] In this sense, both the GDPR and the IoT can be framed as neoliberal weapons that enable the perpetuation of surveillance capitalism.

308 Rosa Luxemburg, 'The Accumulation of Capital, Or, What the Epigones Have Made Out of Marx's Theory – An Anti-Critique (1921)' in Peter Hudius and Paul Le Blanc (eds), George Shriver (tr), *The Complete Works of Rosa Luxemburg*, vol II: Economic Writings 2 (Verso 2016) 350.
309 ibid 349.
310 ibid.
311 Algorithms have been regarded as the new employers in Antonio Aloisi and Valerio De Stefano, *Your Boss Is an Algorithm. Artificial Intelligence, Platform Work and Labour* (Hart 2022).
312 Cohen (n 146) 9.

6   The Internet of Things (You Don't Own) under Bourgeois Law

An Integrated Tactic to Rebalance Intellectual Property

Science, generally speaking, costs the capitalist nothing, a fact that by no means prevents him from exploiting it.

Marx, *Das Kapital* (1)

6.1 Introduction: Intellectual Property and Rentier Capitalism

It is a commonly held view that intellectual property (IP) is a policy bargain whereby exclusive rights and monopolies are granted as a reward to intellectual labour and investments in order to incentivise innovation and creativity.[1] The idea that IP rights (IPRs) would be a necessary incentive has been largely debunked.[2] Law and economics studies demonstrated that IP is just another product of capitalism aimed at creating new enclosures of the 'commons.'[3] This notwithstanding, a number of national and international laws have kept expanding its scope and augmenting the relevant level of protection. Most IP-stemming monopolies are temporary[4] on paper but end up producing revenues that are regarded as rents on a virtually permanent basis. The elevation of IP to perpetual rent is rendered possible by complex strategies that rely on cumulation of IPRs, factual control over data and service, contracts, and technical protection measures. Favoured by a legal environment that is 'heavily tilted in favour of IP rent-seekers,'[5] IP has become the key ideological device of rentier capitalism. Traditionally, the phenomenon of rentiers refers to the fact that landowners would exploit their monopoly power over the land to impose a rent that was a monopoly price. As noted by Marx in *The Poverty of Philosophy*, '[r]ent, in the Ricardian sense, is patriarchal agriculture

---

1 Robert P Merges, *Justifying Intellectual Property* (HUP 2011).

2 Andreas Von Gunten, *Intellectual Property Is Common Property: Arguments for the Abolition of Private Intellectual Property Rights* (buch et netz 2015).

3 N Stephan Kinsella, *Against Intellectual Property* (Ludwig von Mises Institute 2008); James Boyle, 'The Second Enclosure Movement and the Construction of the Public Domain' in *Copyright Law* (Routledge 2017) 63.

4 Trade secrets and trademarks constitute the exception as they can potentially last forever as long as, respectively, they are kept secret and they are renewed.

5 Brett Christophers, *Rentier Capitalism. Who Owns the Economy, and Who Pays for It?* (Verso 2020) 178.

DOI: 10.4324/9780429468377-7

transformed into commercial industry, industrial capital applied to land, the town bourgeoisie transplanted into the country.'[6] Marx and Ricardo could not foresee that new forms of rent-seeking would become an essential component of capitalism: rent-seeking through IPRs.[7] The IoT is pivotal to rentier capitalism as it generates 'new sources of rent, new infrastructures of rentier relations, and new mechanisms of extraction and enclosure.'[8] While the IoT is not rentier in nature, the historically existing IoT is indeed rentier also thanks to IP abuses. According to Jathan Sadowski, data extraction, capital convergence, and digital enclosure are the main mechanisms of rentier capitalism.[9] IP is key to digital enclosure, as instantiated by the use of software licenses to control access and collecting rents over the physical world, regardless of the ownership of the underlying tangible assets.[10]

The IoT ushers in an era of ubiquitous computing and ubiquitous IPRs. IP is everywhere and lends itself to monopolise virtually anything.[11] One may be naively inclined to think that one's own phone is one's own property. That is not the case. One's phone belongs to the holders of the copyright on the code running on it, the manufacturers owning its design, and the patents on how it works, as well as trademarks not only on logos but also on things such as the way one 'swipes.'[12] What happens when being embedded with software and other IP-protected digital contents is no longer an exclusive feature of computers and phones? What happens when proprietary Things and closed systems are everywhere: in one's bedroom, in one's bathroom, in one's body? Our behaviour becomes heavily restricted by the factual, legal, and technical control that IoT companies retain over their Things – and that we correspondingly lose. We have become digital tenants, not owning or controlling any of the objects around us and data about us.[13] To the point that, one can argue, we no longer own: *we are owned*.[14]

This chapter will present the main IP issues in the IoT and concentrate on one of them that has been framed as 'death of ownership' by Joshua Fairfield in

---

6 Karl Marx, *The Poverty of Philosophy. Answer to the Philosophy of Poverty by M. Proudhon (1847)* (Herr 1913) 174. On the relationship between Marx and David Ricardo see Giovanni A Caravale, 'On Marx's Interpretation Of Ricardo: A Note' (1989) 17 Atlantic Economic Journal 6.

7 David Harvey, *Marx, Capital and the Madness of Economic Reason* (Profile 2017) 37.

8 Jathan Sadowski, 'The Internet of Landlords: Digital Platforms and New Mechanisms of Rentier Capitalism' (2020) 52 Antipode 562, 564.

9 ibid 570.

10 ibid 576.

11 Gustavo Ghidini, 'Prospettive "Protezioniste" Nel Diritto Industriale' [1995] Rivista di diritto industriale 73; Marco Ricolfi, 'Il Futuro Della Proprietà Intellettuale Nella Società Algoritmica' [2019] Giur it 10.

12 *Match Group, LLC v Bumble Trading Inc.*, No. 6:18-cv-00080 (W.D. Tex, Mar. 16, 2018). The dispute was settled in June 2020.

13 Zeynep Tufekci, 'We Are Tenants on Our Own Devices' [2019] *Wired* <www.wired.com/story/right-to-repair-tenants-on-our-own-devices/>.

14 Christina Mulligan, 'Personal Property Servitudes on the Internet of Things' (2015) 50 Georgia Law Review 1121; Joshua AT Fairfield, *Owned: Property, Privacy, and the New Digital Serfdom* (CUP 2017). This book has been consulted as an e-book, and since its digital pages were not numbered, pinpointing was not possible.

Owned,[15] a germinal book that will provide an initial framework to understand this issue. Ownership (of Things) is dying either because of the shift from sale to subscription or because users only formally own their Things but they cannot exercise any of the powers traditionally associated to property as IoT companies control every layer of the Thing. This 'tethered economy'[16] has been seen as an attack on the concept of property reminiscent of feudal times, when 'serfs of feudal Europe . . . lacked rights in the land they worked.'[17] Similarly, users of Things would not own them but simply manage them on behalf of the IoT overlords – in this sense, they would be digital serfs. In reality, as will be argued in this chapter, the death of ownership – and IP abuses in the IoT more generally – has its roots in the individualistic outlook of 'bourgeois' law under capitalism, rather than resembling the medieval legal system.

Alongside desk-based research of EU laws, UK laws will be taken into account when national implementations can shed light on whether it is possible to rely on IP's internal and external limitations to protect the IoT user affected by the death of ownership. This will be complemented by qualitative research, namely, text analysis of some 'legals' that are deemed representative of IoT-typical contractual practices.

With this in mind, this chapter will answer the following subquestion: *can IP and antitrust counter the death of ownership?*

6.2 An Overview of the IP Issues and Themes in the IoT

A review of the relevant literature and case law identifies the following themes and issues at the intersection of IP and IoT:

   (i) Death of ownership and digital serfdom;
  (ii) Antitrust control over standard essential patent (SEP) licensing to achieve a standardised and interoperable IoT;
 (iii) The 'Internet of Secrets';
  (iv) Patentability of IoT inventions;
   (v) The 'Internet of Digital Locks';
  (vi) Data ownership;
 (vii) Smartness and distinctiveness;
(viii) Overcoming Western-centrism; and
  (ix) Commons for an open IoT.

Points i and ii will be the main focus of this chapter and therefore will be expanded upon in the next sections; point iii refers to the legal, technical, and organisational secrecy that we have analysed in the previous chapter.

---

15 Fairfield (n 14).
16 Chris Jay Hoofnagle, Aniket Kesari and Aaron Perzanowski, 'The Tethered Economy' (2019) 87 George Washington Law Review 783.
17 Fairfield (n 14).

Patentability of IoT inventions. The IoT challenges the identification of the subject pattern that is excluded from patentability (hereinafter also 'excluded subject matter').[18] The European Patent Convention excludes software as such from patentability.[19] As shown in the *travaux préparatoires* to the Convention, the rationale of the exclusion is that 'patent protection is reserved for creations in the technical field'[20] and that software is already protected by copyright. The exclusion of software only 'as such' means that the latter is patentable if it has a technical character, that is, if it produces a further technical effect when run on a computer or other Thing.[21] *HTC v Apple*[22] provides some useful signposts to understand what this technical effect is: (a) whether the claimed technical effect has a technical effect on a process which is carried on outside the computer; (b) whether it operates at the level of the architecture of the computer; (c) whether it results in the computer operating in a new way; (d) whether it makes the computer run more efficiently or effectively; or (e) whether the perceived problem is overcome by the invention rather than merely circumvented. A common way to circumvent the software exclusion is to frame the invention as a computer-implemented invention. This is seen as distinct from a computer program because it refers to 'computers, computer networks or other programmable apparatus wherein at least one feature is realised by means of a computer program.'[23] Unlike software inventions, they cannot be objected 'as any method involving the use of technical means (e.g. a computer) and any technical means itself (e.g. a computer or a computer-readable storage medium) have technical character.'[24] By issuing guidance on computer-implemented inventions and examples of 'further technical effect,' the European Patent Office has made it easier to apply for software patents, including IoT patents.[25] Moreover, a competent draftsperson 'can usually present a claim as a computer-implemented method . . . rather than as a "computer program."'[26] Even before the IoT, the exclusion of software 'as such' from patentability had done little to slow down the monopolisation of software innovation. The situation risks worsening with the IoT. Indeed, the European Patent Convention's exclusion is based on the hardware-software dichotomy, but as argued in this book, the IoT disrupted this dichotomy. The same applies to the North-American exclusion of

18 Patent issues that I will not deal with include joint infringement, connected to the interactive nature of the IoT, and patent quality. On them, see W Keith Robinson, 'Patent Law Challenges for the Internet of Things' (2015) 15 Wake Forest Intellectual Property Law Journal.

19 Art 52(2)(c) and 52(3).

20 Administrative Council, 'Basic Proposal for the Revision of the EPC (MR/2/00)' (2000) 43. For the debate around the reform of this exclusion, see President of the European Patent Office, 'Revision of EPC: Article 52(1)-(3)' (1999) CA/PL 6/99.

21 European Patent Office, *Guidelines for Examination* (EPO 2019) [G, II, 3.6].

22 *HTC Europe v Apple* [2013] EWCA Civ 451.

23 European Patent Office (n 22) [G, II, 3.6].

24 ibid.

25 See Yahong Li, 'The Current Dilemma and Future of Software Patenting' (2019) 50 IIC 823.

26 Mateo Aboy and others, 'How Does Emerging Patent Case Law in the US and Europe Affect Precision Medicine?' (2019) 37 Nature Biotechnology 1118.

abstract ideas,[27] whose historical rationale is that patents were intended to cover devices and things.[28] Although the inclusion of a Thing in a software claim does not necessarily make it admissible, and even though software claims may still fail for lack of inventive step,[29] there is the undeniable risk that the overcoming of the hardware-software dichotomy will lead to the factual overcoming of the software exclusion.[30] When all software becomes embedded in a Thing – in other words, when no software is purely software, software 'as such' – we must be alert and prevent IoT companies from monopolising software innovation at the expenses of smaller businesses, consumers, and society at large. An ambitious solution could be a software treaty that would provide for a limited scope and length of software protection, 'allowing only the means of implementation but not the function to be patented; and granting 10 years of utility-model-type or sui generis protection.'[31] Or even, perhaps more radically, to exclude all software inventions from patentability – removing the 'as such' proviso – and to rely exclusively on the copyright protection of software.[32] Indeed, although the duration of copyright is excessive for a rapid market such as the software one, I would argue that pure copyright protection would instantiate a more balanced approach to the legal protection of software as, unlike patents, copyright is not a monopoly right which allows for independent creations and thus encourages follow-on innovation.

The Internet of Digital Locks. Technological protection measures and digital rights management (DRM),[33] exemplified by the digital locks that prevent gamers from running counterfeit games on their consoles, are problematic for at least three reasons. First, they leave it to the IP owner to decide whether a use is permitted by one of the exceptions, with no or limited possibility for the user to argue otherwise. This goes hand in hand with the de facto privatization of internet governance – and ultimately of justice – that is a recent trend in digital regulation.[34] For example, under the Copyright

---

27 The leading cases are *Alice v CLS*, 573 U.S. 208 (2014) and *Mayo v Prometheus*, 566 U.S. 66 (2012).

28 Miriam Bitton, 'Patenting Abstractions' (2014) 15 NCJL & Tech 153, 162.

29 Indeed, features that fall within Art. 52(2) categories (e.g. software) 'can contribute to the assessment of non-obviousness only if they contribute to the technical character' (Aboy and others (n 27) 1124).

30 This was my main thesis in Guido Noto La Diega, 'Software Patents and the Internet of Things in Europe, the United States and India' (2017) 39 EIPR 173.

31 Li (n 26) 823.

32 'Member States shall protect computer programs, by copyright, as literary works' (Software Directive, art 1(1)). The TRIPS Agreement is often referred to as the legal basis of the alleged obligation for contracting states to protect software patents as it provides that 'patents shall be available for any inventions . . . in all fields of technology' (art 27). However, software is a type of technology, not a field and software patentability under TRIPS 'remains an open question' (Robert Tomkowicz, *Intellectual Property Overlaps: Theory, Strategies and Solutions* (Routledge 2012) 45).

33 Infosoc Directive, art 6; DMCA, s 1201.

34 Alongside the provision at hand, one need only think of the proposed Digital Services Act that provides a mixed public-private system of oversight and enforcement where platforms and users themselves are called to an active role in policing compliance and handling complaints (arts 6, 8, 17, and 19).

in the Digital Single Market Directive,[35] online content-sharing providers have to prevent the sharing of infringing material (so-called upload filter). In doing so, they have to 'put in place an effective and expeditious complaint and redress mechanism.'[36] Thus, not only it is up to the IoT company to deploy technological locks and filters to pre-empt ex ante potentially infringing behaviour, but they are also judges in the disputes arising therefrom. This is likely to lead to a further compression of the user freedoms enshrined in IP exceptions and limitations. This can be inferred by the fact that this directive openly provided that 'Member States shall ensure that users have access to a court or another relevant judicial authority to assert the use of an exception or limitation to copyright and related rights.'[37] Traditional judicial process is better positioned to account for the conflicting interests at play and understand whether the digital lock regarded as infringing activities that would fall within the scope of IP exceptions and limitations. However, in a fast-paced, opaque, and asymmetrical environment such as the IoT, it is unlikely that end users will resort to legal action to open the digital locks. This is regrettable as IP exceptions and limitations are pivotal to achieving a fair balance between the rightsholders' and the users' interest. As the US Supreme Court put it, copyright 'protection has never accorded the copyright owner complete control over all possible uses of (the) work.'[38] Conversely, DRM may accord complete control. Second, digital locks delegate to automated or partly automated systems complex assessments that do not lend themselves to being translated into code – e.g. how is one to translate the concepts of 'fairness' and 'substantiality'?[39] Third, the circumvention of DRM measures is unlawful even when there is no proof of underlying copyright infringement.[40] In this sense, DRM gives rise to forms of overprotective 'paracopyright'[41] and runs counter to fundamental use freedoms, including freedom of expression. With the IoT, copyright works such as software and databases become embedded in virtually any object that surrounds us; with multimedia products becoming commonplace and with every layer of a Thing being locked, 'the effect of DRM systems in economic and social processes may be pervasive.'[42] There is little, if

---

35 C-DSM Directive, art 17.

36 C-DSM Directive, art 17(9).

37 C-DSM Directive, art 17(9).

38 *Sony v Universal Studios*, 464 U.S. 417, 432 (1984).

39 Léo Pascault and others, 'Copyright and Remote Teaching in the Time of Covid-19: A Study of Contractual Terms and Conditions of Selected Online Services' (2020) 42 EIPR 548. cf Niva Elkin-Koren, 'Fair Use by Design' (2017) 64 UCLA Law Review 22.

40 The DMCA, and arguably the Infosoc Directive, forbid 'these circumventions regardless of the purpose of the circumvention' (Lawrence Lessig, *Code* (Version 20, Basic Books 2006) 186.) Whilst circumventing a DRM system does not involve copyright infringement, it is less clear whether the circumventions need to have some relationship to copyright infringement.

41 Guido Westkamp, 'Code, Copying, Competition: The Subversive Force of Para-Copyright and the Need for an Unfair Competition Based Reassessment of DRM Laws after Infopaq' (2010) 58 Journal of the Copyright Society of the USA 665.

42 Michèle Finck and Valentina Moscon, 'Copyright Law on Blockchains: Between New Forms of Rights Administration and Digital Rights Management 2.0' (2019) 50 IIC 77.

any,[43] recourse against IoT companies that implement DRM systems to prevent 'users and the government from ever finding out what data is collected and how it is used by device manufacturers.'[44] As the Internet of Digital Locks rises, the postsale control over our Things throughout their life cycle is a threat not only to our property but also to our autonomy.

Data ownership. Trade secrets do not, strictly speaking, instantiate a property right: they implement a tort law approach that outlaws certain specific uses of the confidential information.[45] Therefore, they have been seen as suitable to protect firms in the data economy whilst balancing the potentially conflicting interests in data protection and in the free flow of information.[46] Their widespread use to protect IoT data, coupled with factual control over data, supported by DRM-like measures, corroborates the thesis that the case for a new property right on the data as such has not been convincingly made.[47] Such a proposal – dubbed 'data producer's right' – is contained in the European Commission's Free Flow of Data initiative.[48] On the debatable assumption that the Database Directive's sui generis right[49] would not be fit for machine-generated data and that new incentives are needed for the data economy to thrive,[50] the Commission proposed a data ownership right, that is, a 'right to use and authorise the use of nonpersonal data'[51] granted to the data producer, that is, 'the owner or long-term user (i.e. the lessee) of the device.'[52] Thus, users would 'utilise their data and thereby contribute to unlocking machine-generated data.'[53] However, law and economics studies have abundantly proved that big data is generated despite the absence of proprietary incentives.[54] Moreover, the unfitness of the sui generis right for IoT data can be called into question.[55] More on this will be said later in the chapter, when dealing with the exceptions to the sui generis right. For the purposes of this

43 As seen in the previous chapter, data protection laws can prevail on IP, with limited exceptions regarding the rights to access and portability.

44 Lidiya Mishchenko, 'The Internet of Things: Where Privacy and Copyright Collide' (2016) 33 Santa Clara High Technology Law Journal 90, 90.

45 cf Mark A Lemley, 'The Surprising Virtues of Treating Trade Secrets as IP Rights' (2008) 61 Stanford Law Review 311.

46 Josef Drexl, 'Designing Competitive Markets for Industrial Data. Between Propertisation and Access' (2017) 8 JIPITEC 257 [183].

47 ibid.

48 European Commission, 'SWD on the Free Flow of Data And Emerging Issues of the European Data Economy' (2017) COM(2017) 9 final.

49 Directive 96/9/EC of 11 March 1996 on the legal protection of databases [1996] OJ L 77/20, arts 7 ff.

50 A majority of studies tend to agree on this. See Andrea Ottolia, *Big Data e Innovazione Computazionale* (Giappichelli 2017).

51 European Commission, 'SWD on the Free Flow of Data and Emerging Issues of the European Data Economy' (n 50) 13.

52 ibid.

53 ibid.

54 '[N]o incentives are needed for generating and commercialising data' (Drexl (n 47) [183].).

55 Guido Noto La Diega, 'Artificial Intelligence and Databases in the Age of Big Machine Data' (2019) 25 AIDA 2018 93.

section, suffice it to say that this right provides some protection to IoT data. With this in mind – and considering the protection already afforded by trade secrets, factual control, and DRM – one can hardly say that the production of data needs further incentives. This said, we are still far from reaching a consensus on critical questions, such as whether and how IoT data can be (and should be) the subject of property, how trade secrets and sui generis right interact in governing IoT data, and whether ownership should rest with the owner of the Thing, its user, its manufacturer, or the manufacturer of the relevant sensor.[56] It seems, however, that scholars and policymakers are shifting their focus from issues of ownership to questions of access – which in the IoT are closely connected to interoperability. Pragmatically, it would appear more useful to take account of the fact that IoT companies already treat data like property, regardless of their formal qualification. Accordingly, we should endeavour and find ways to govern access to IoT data flows in a transparent, fair, and balanced way.[57]

Smartness and distinctiveness. The only EU ruling that expressly deals with the IoT is the trademark case *Bosch v EUIPO*.[58] In recent years, Bosch has been making investments to become an IoT leader. This effort resulted in Bosch IoT Suite, an open-source-based platform for IoT solutions with over ten million sensors, devices, and machines connected to it.[59] Bosch launched its '*Simply.Connected.*' series of 'smart' tools that can be controlled via a mobile app – and attempted to register the relevant logo as an EU trademark (Figure 6.1)

For the purposes of this book, it is sufficient to focus on two aspects of the case. The application regarded a wide range of goods and services, from sensors through sanitary devices to products that were either directly connected

Figure 6.1 Figurative mark at issue in *Bosch v EUIPO*.

56 See e.g. Stacy-Ann Elvy, 'Commodifying Consumer Data in the Era of the Internet of Things' (2018) 59 Boston College Law Review 423; Mehmet Bilal Ünver, 'Turning the Crossroad for a Connected World: Reshaping the European Prospect for the Internet of Things' (2018) 26 International Journal of Law and Information Technology 93.
57 See e.g. Martina Barbero and others, *Study on Emerging Issues of Data Ownership, Interoperability, (Re-)Usability and Access to Data, and Liability* (European Commission 2018); Thomas J Farkas, 'Data Created by the Internet of Things: The New Gold without Ownership?' [2017] Revista La Propiedad Inmaterial 5.
58 Cases T-251/17 and T-252/17 *Bosch v EUIPO* (CJEU, 28 March 2019).
59 'Bosch IoT Suite' <www.bosch-iot-suite.com/>.

to a network or embedded into connected objects.[60] EUIPO's Board of Appeal rejected the application as the sign was deemed devoid of any distinctive character. Indeed, the words 'simply connected' were seen as a mere slogan meaning 'just connected,' and the figurative elements were considered customary and nondistinctive. The Board, in particular, referred to the concept of IoT, which they defined as 'the interconnection of physical objects in a network comparable to the Internet, so as to allow them to be controlled at a distance or to make them capable of communicating and exchanging information.'[61] In light of this, 'simply connected' meant 'just connected to a network' or 'above all connected to a network'; as such, it was to be regarded as '*desirable characteristic*'[62] and a '*laudatory indication*'[63] for Things, as such nondistinctive. Therefore, IoT companies attempting to register connectivity-related signs should be aware that their signs may be regarded as descriptive and devoid of distinctiveness.

A second aspect that is of relevance from this book's perspective has to do with the examiners' discretion when it comes to considering signs that are applied to a diverse range of IoT products. Bosch attempted to demonstrate that, even if the relevant public would understand 'Simply.Connected.' as just connected to a network, this would be meaningless in relation to the majority of the products to which the sign referred. In particular, whereas consumers know that laptops, mobile phones, tablets, and earphones can be connected to the internet – and therefore the sign may be descriptive with regard to these products – they would not be aware that other, everyday objects or their components (e.g. antennas for radios and television receivers, batteries, etc.) can be connected to a network.[64] Moreover, the defence went on arguing that a number of services (e.g. training and instruction services) were not limited to connectivity. In principle, when assessing distinctiveness, examiners should look at each good and service separately. Conversely, the Board of Appeal assessed jointly products that were prima facie diverse – this was at the core of Bosch's appeal. However, the CJEU confirmed that examiners do have the power to use the same general reasoning for a group of products if 'goods and services . . . are interlinked in a sufficiently direct and specific way, to the point where they form a *sufficiently homogenous category*.'[65] The concept of IoT provided this homogenizing factor. Indeed, the court stated that:

> In view of the development of the Internet of Things, the Board of Appeal was correct to state that the relevant public would see the signs at issue as

---

60 *Bosch* (n 59) [4], [81].
61 ibid [43].
62 ibid.
63 ibid [45].
64 ibid [71], [72].
65 ibid [50]. Italics added.

indicating the ability of the goods at issue to be connected and would perceive the services at issue as relating to such connections.[66]

Therefore, the existence and pervasiveness of the IoT makes the examiners' work easier as they can assess jointly all the 'smart' goods and services, and it renders connectivity-related signs nondistinctive well beyond the realm of traditionally connected objects to encompass all Things.

Overcoming Western-centrism. Reflecting a road-to-Damascus moment in legal scholarship, it has occurred to some authors that Western-centric IP studies do not reflect the socio-economic, cultural, and legal importance of Eastern and Southern countries (the 'global South').[67] This is particularly the case with China. Once an imitator, China has for some time taken on the role of innovator.[68] The country has an established manufacturing industry, and many IoT start-ups rely on it. Much of the value of these start-ups is in their IP; nonetheless, they do not properly assess the IP risks and opportunities of having their Things manufactured in China. Some scholars have been studying ways in which IP law can be leveraged to strengthen the position of foreign IoT start-ups in China.[69] The Chinese information economy is now as important as its manufacturing: this is evidenced by its being a top IP holder and by the gradual strengthening of its IP laws.[70] This can be seen in the latest statistics of the European Patent Office, where China is the fastest-growing patent applicant in the world (+9.9%).[71] In light of the growth of China-based IoT and of the modernisation of its laws on innovation, IP scholars and practitioners should avoid their Western-centric habits. China is no longer a mere rule-taker in global lawmaking,[72] including in the field of internet regulation and IT law. The awareness of China's rulemaking power should permeate contemporary legal scholarship. In turn, consumers should be aware that at least some components of their Things are provided by China-based companies, which can leverage their national IP laws to control the Thing's software, hardware, service, and data, thus affecting the Thing as a whole.

Commons for an open IoT. While IP excesses tend to create a closed and noninteroperable IoT, there are many attempts to open the IoT to make it more socially just and user-centric. Some of these attempts revolve around the concept of 'commons.' Information is a common and a public good because it is difficult 'to exclude people from knowledge once someone had made a discovery. One person's use of knowledge . . . does not subtract from another person's capacity to use

---

66 ibid [80].
67 Yun Zhao and Michael HK Ng, *Chinese Legal Reform and the Global Legal Order Adoption and Adaptation* (CUP 2018).
68 Jingxi Ding and others, 'From Imitation to Innovation: A Study of China's Drug R&D and Relevant National Policies' (2011) 6 Journal of Technology Management & Innovation 1.
69 Carr and Harris (n 68).
70 Li (n 68).
71 'Patent Index 2020' (*European Patent Office*, 2021) <www.epo.org/about-us/annual-reports-statistics/statistics.html#patentees>.
72 Peter K Yu, 'The Middle Kingdom and the Intellectual Property World' (2011) 13 Oregon Review of International Law 209.

it.'[73] Information is a nonrivalrous and nonexclusionary good. The status of data as a commons *extra commercium* has been recently convincingly argued.[74] New technologies, including the IoT, make the commons more vulnerable due to their 'ability to *capture the previously uncapturable.*'[75] In the field of software, the commons increasingly take the form of free and open-source licenses.[76] Some studies focused on the importance of free and open-source software (FOSS) and hardware to ensure a fully-functioning, inclusive, and interoperable IoT.[77] IoT software is increasingly developed under open-source innovation models and combined with proprietary ones, giving rise to hybrid business models. IoT commons are instantiated amongst other things by open patent strategies, such as patent pools and patent pledges.[78] Around the knowledge commons, including open software and hardware, forms of antiproprietary collective resistance can develop.[79] In the next chapter, I will expand on how the commons can provide a solution to many of the problems of the IoT in two senses: on the one hand, as a practice of collective resistance to new extractive practices; on the other hand, as the foundation for free and open-source software, hardware, standards, data, and platforms.

Current IP scholarship tends to focus on the practical question of how to govern the IoT as in how to protect its components and the related inventions. However, I felt it was more urgent to explore whether IP laws can be leveraged to re-empower IoT users who, increasingly affected by the death of ownership, struggle to cope with their diminished status as digital tenants. This chapter aims to fill this gap.

6.3 Death of Ownership: To Strengthen Property Rights and Empower IoT Users-Digital Peasants or to Counter Bourgeois Property?

By selling consumers hardware while retaining ownership of software, service, digital content, and data, IoT companies 'are treating users like digital tenants.'[80]

---

73 Charlotte Hess and Elinor Ostrom, 'Introduction: An Overview of the Knowledge Commons' in Charlotte Hess and Elinor Ostrom (eds), *Understanding Knowledge as a Commons. From Theory to Practice* (MIT Press 2007).

74 Chiara Angiolini, *Lo statuto dei dati personali: uno studio a partire dalla nozione di bene* (Giappichelli 2020).

75 Hess and Ostrom (n 74) 10.

76 Shubha Ghosh, 'How to Build a Commons: Is Intellectual Property Constrictive, Facilitating, or Irrelevant?' in Charlotte Hess and Elinor Ostrom (eds), *Understanding Knowledge as a Commons: From Theory to Practice* (MIT Press 2007).

77 Ovidiu Vermesan and Peter Friess (eds), *Building the Hyperconnected Society* (River 2016).

78 Mariateresa Maggiolino and Maria Lillà Montagnani, 'From Open Source Software to Open Patenting – What's New in the Real of Openness?' (2011) 42 IIC 804; Natacha Estèves, 'Open Models for Patents: Giving Patents a New Lease on Life?' (2018) 21 The Journal of World Intellectual Property 2.

79 Peter Levine, 'Collective Action, Civic Engagement, and Knowledge Commons' in Charlotte Hess and Elinor Ostrom (eds), *Understanding Knowledge as a Commons* (MIT Press 2007).

80 Jathan Sadowski, 'Landlord 2.0' (*OneZero*, 4 April 2019) <https://onezero.medium.com/landlord-2-0-techs-new-rentier-capitalism-a0bfe491b463>.

These companies are the new prophets of 'rentier capitalism' as they are monopolising access to property (including IP) to extract value from users often without providing any actual service, let alone innovating or contributing to society.[81] Being demoted to tenants of one's own Things has practical consequences. E.g. in the UK there is an implied term that the purchaser of a good, as opposed to its tenant, will enjoy its quiet possession.[82] This means that a trader who transfers ownership over a good promises the owner that the possession and use will be uninterrupted.[83] Owners can avail themselves of this implied term when the trader transfers IPRs on the Thing to third parties[84] as well as to counter the deletion of software that makes the Thing inoperable.[85] Conversely, digital tenants cannot invoke such legal protections.

The concept of 'death of ownership' originated in the 'new servitudes'[86] that Molly Shaffer Van Houweling described in her study on the usage restrictions that courts recognise on software-embedded goods. The 'death of ownership' transforms end users into digital tenants in a twofold way. First, IoT traders may retain ownership of the Thing as such. This trend sees the shift from the contract of sale to a mere subscription: in the tethered economy,[87] we have a right to access the 'device-as-a-service'[88] as opposed to outright owning it. Cost saving is not the only justification for this phenomenon. IoT users may lease the Thing under the condition that, at the end of the life cycle, the Thing be returned to them for them to dispose of it responsibly. Perhaps surprisingly, the 'green' imperatives of the circular economy could contribute to the death of ownership.[89] Second – and this is the focus of this section – the death of ownership can be caused by IoT companies retaining control over the Thing by factual, legal (IPRs and contracts), and technological means. IoT users remain owners, though only formally, as they cannot exercise the powers that are traditionally associated to property. These two forms of death of ownership are not mutually exclusive. For example, in June 2021 owners of smart treadmill Tread+, which retails for thousands of dollars, were notified that if they wanted to keep having access to the smart functionalities of the product, they had to pay a monthly

---

81 Guy Standing, *Corruption of Capitalism* (Biteback 2016); Carlo Vercellone, 'Il Ritorno Del Rentier. Salario, Rendita, Profitto Nel Capitalismo Cognitivo' (2006) Autunno Posse 97.

82 CRA, s 17(2)(c).

83 Christopher Millard, W Kuan Hon and Jatinder Singh, 'Internet of Things Ecosystems: Unpacking Legal Relationships and Liabilities' [2017] IC2E 286.

84 *Microbeads v Vinhurst* [1975] 1 WLR 218.

85 *Cox v Riley* (1986) 83 Cr App Rep 54, [1986] Crim LR 460.

86 Molly Shaffer Van Houweling, 'The New Servitudes' (2007) 96 Georgetown Law Journal 885.

87 Hoofnagle, Kesari and Perzanowski (n 17).

88 See e.g. the subscription plans offered by Microsoft to lease devices certified for Teams meetings. 'What's New in Microsoft Teams' (*Microsoft TechCommunity*, 2 March 2021) <https://techcommunity.microsoft.com/t5/microsoft-teams-blog/what-s-new-in-microsoft-teams-microsoft-ignite-2021/ba-p/2118226>.

89 Sean Thomas, 'Law, Smart Technology, and Circular Economy: All Watched Over by Machines of Loving Grace?' (2018) 10 Law, Innovation and Technology 230.

subscription fee.[90] Nonetheless, the focus of this chapter is on the second type of death in its pure form, while the issues of the subscription economy will be the subject of future research.

IoT companies factually, technologically, and legally control the Thing – and ultimately its users – by controlling virtually each of its components and layers.

Factual control regards mostly data and services: they do not lend themselves to being appropriated through IPRs but are de facto subject to the jurisdiction of the IoT overlord. The latter can factually prevent access to one's own data and roll back services at its discretion. A telling illustration of factual control was provided in the previous chapter, where I showed that although in theory we have a right to access our data under the GDPR, Amazon does not grant meaningful access to the data subject's profile, including the inferences that the company makes about one's preferences, biases, and vulnerabilities.

IoT companies also retain technological control over the Thing. This is exemplified by the aforementioned issue of the 'Internet of Digital Locks.' A group of farmers was surprised to find out that they did not have a right to repair their own tractors, purchased from John Deere, a heavy equipment manufacturer. The service could only be provided by John Deere–approved technicians.[91] John Deere argued to the Copyright Office that because the tractor was equipped with software and the copyright on the software was merely licensed to the farmer, it was within the manufacturer's powers to prevent farmers from modifying or even repairing their own equipment.[92] Any independent repair would have qualified as an illegal DRM circumvention. This led to widespread criticism and some emphatic calls not to let IoT companies 'eviscerate the notion of ownership.'[93] As such, the evisceration of ownership does not necessarily harm IoT users; the loss of control does.

'Legal control' refers to a combination of contracts and IPRs. As seen in Chapter 2, the user of as simple a Thing as a speaker would hardly expect to be confronted with a mountain of hundreds of terms of service, privacy policy, warranties, etc. These 'legals' are often used to affect those exclusive rights that are quintessential to the property right, at least in its traditional, i.e. tangible, form.[94]

---

90 Ax Sharma, 'Peloton's $3,000 Treadmill Now Comes with Surprise "Subscription Fee"' (*Bleeping-Computer*, 22 June 2021) <www.bleepingcomputer.com/news/technology/pelotons-3-000-tread mill-now-comes-with-surprise-subscription-fee/>.

91 Kit Walsh, 'John Deere Really Doesn't Want You to Own That Tractor' (*Electronic Frontier Foundation*, 20 December 2016) <www.eff.org/deeplinks/2016/12/john-deere-really-doesnt-want-you-own-tractor>.

92 Laura Sydell, 'DIY Tractor Repair Runs Afoul Of Copyright Law' (*NPR.org*, 17 August 2015) <www.npr.org/sections/alltechconsidered/2015/08/17/432601480/diy-tractor-repair-runs-afoul-of-copyright-law>.

93 Kyle Wiens, 'We Can't Let John Deere Destroy the Very Idea of Ownership' (*Wired*, 21 April 2015) <www.wired.com/2015/04/dmca-ownership-john-deere>.

94 This exacerbates a phenomenon that was already taking place previously, e.g. in the field of cloud contracting. See Guido Noto La Diega, 'Il Cloud Computing. Alla Ricerca Del Diritto Perduto Nel Web 3.0' (2014) 2 Europa e diritto privato 577.

The analysis of Echo's contractual quagmire also shed light on how a number of IPRs protect Amazon's speaker. Echo is protected by 84 patents and 427 trademarks that monopolise virtually any aspect of the Thing.[95] On top of this, IoT companies can leverage a rich portfolio of unregistered and registered IPRs from trade secrets through copyright to database rights. A perspicuous illustration of the death of ownership caused by the incorporation of numerous IP works in all 'our' Things is provided by the recent *Tom Kabinet* case,[96] which dealt with the legality of a virtual market for second-hand e-books. The resale of IP-protected products without the rightsholder's permission is allowed by the principle of exhaustion. This principle applies to all IPRs,[97] and it provides that, once an IP-protected product has been lawfully put on the market within the European Economic Area by the rightsholder or with their consent, the rights conferred by that IPR in relation to the commercial exploitation of the good become exhausted.[98] This means that, once exhaustion occurs, the rightsholder can no longer invoke the IPR in question to prevent the further resale (including parallel imports), rental, lending, or other forms of commercial exploitation of the product by third parties.[99] In the EU, exhaustion can be regarded as a limitation on IP imposed by the fundamental freedom of movement of goods.[100] The right to distribution – the right to issue copies of the work to the public, i.e. to put the work into circulation – is one of the copyright owner's exclusive rights to which exhaustion applies.[101] Conversely, the right to communication to the public – that is, the right to make the works available to the public in such a way that the public may access them from a place and at a time individually chosen by them – is not subject to exhaustion. The key question in *Tom Kabinet* was whether the supply by downloading, for permanent use, of an e-book was covered by the concept of 'communication to the public' or by that of 'distribution to the public.' In the former event, the IP holder could prevent the resale of the e-book; in the latter, the resale would be lawful as exhaustion applied. As stated by the CJEU in *UsedSoft*,[102] the right to distribution of a computer program is subject to exhaustion regardless of whether it is incorporated in

---

95 I sourced the data from WIPO's Patentscope and Global Brand Database on 1 June 2021.

96 Case C-263/18 *Nederlands Uitgeversverbond v Tom Kabinet* [2020] Bus LR 983.

97 Infosoc Directive, art 4(2), and other references in Guido Noto La Diega, 'Can the Law Fix the Problems of Fashion? An Empirical Study on Social Norms and Power Imbalance in the Fashion Industry' (2019) 14 JIPLP 18.

98 See Irene Calboli and Edward Lee (eds), *Research Handbook on Intellectual Property Exhaustion and Parallel Imports* (Edward Elgar 2016).

99 IPO and Government Digital Service, 'Exhaustion of IP Rights and Parallel Trade from 1 January 2021' (2020) Guidance <www.gov.uk/guidance/exhaustion-of-ip-rights-and-parallel-trade-after-the-transition-period>.

100 Guido Westkamp, 'Intellectual Property, Competition Rules, and the Emerging Internal Market: Some Thoughts on the European Exhaustion Doctrine' (2007) 11 Marquette Intellectual Property Law Review 291.

101 Berdien BE van der Donk, 'CJEU Rules the Right to Distribution Only Applies to Tangible Digital Works – UsedSoft Doctrine of Exhaustion Does Not Apply to e-Books CJEU C-263/18 (Tom Kabinet)' (2020) 42(8) EIPR 516, 517.

102 Case C-128/11 *UsedSoft v Oracle* [2012] 3 CMLR. 44.

a tangible medium. Accordingly, lawfully downloaded software may be resold.[103] In *Tom Kabinet*, the CJEU considerably narrowed the scope of the *UsedSoft* doctrine by arguing that:

(i) The right to distribution of computer programs is indeed subject to exhaustion regardless of the existence of a tangible medium. However, the concept of 'computer program' does not include e-books, which can be regarded as digital copyright products governed by the Infosoc Directive as opposed to the Software Directive.[104]

(ii) Unlike the Software Directive, the Infosoc Directive would rely on the tangible-intangible divide; therefore, tangible items distributed by tangible means are covered by the right to distribution and can be resold without the rights-holder's permission under the principle of exhaustion. Conversely, intangible copyright products such as e-books are not distributed; they are communicated to the public, and since this right is not subject to exhaustion, the resale of used e-books requires the copyright holder's permission.[105]

This decision is open to a twofold criticism. First, the growth of IoT and converged devices has led to an erosion of the distinction between software and digital products. Arguably, an e-book – similar to the digital content and the service embedded in a Thing (e.g. e-sport played on a 'smart' console) – falls within the commonly accepted definition of software, that is, a collection of instructions that can be executed by a computer to perform a specific task.[106] With *Tom Kabinet*, it is unclear when a set of instruction leaves the realm of computer programs and enters that of digital product. Second, perhaps more importantly, given the amalgam of hardware, software, service, and data in the IoT, the *Tom Kabinet* doctrine risks leading to an 'exhaustion of exhaustion.' Things are sold intact with software preinstalled and not removable or changeable under the license agreement – software is not bundled separately anymore. To predicate that the exhaustion of IPRs depends on the tangible-intangible divide may reflect the wording of the Infosoc Directive and, in particular, of Recital 28, whereby '(c)opyright protection under this Directive includes the exclusive right to control distribution of the work incorporated in a tangible article.' However, it is an outdated approach that is at odds with the smart reality we live in. Such binary doctrine may be exploited by IoT companies that own the IPRs on the intangible components of the Thing to prevent further resale or other commercial exploitation despite the exhaustion of the right to distribution, ultimately breaching the fundamental freedom of movement of goods in the EU. This is in line with other attacks on the principle

---

103 This rule comes with two provisos: (i) the licence is for an unlimited period of time, and (ii) the acquirer has paid a fee that responds to the economic value of the copy of the work.

104 *Tom Kabinet* (n 97) [53]–[59].

105 ibid [42], [56].

106 See e.g. JB Dixit, *Fundamentals of Computer Programming and Information* (Firewall Media 2005) 59.

of exhaustion, as exemplified by *Coty v Akzente*.[107] In this case, a luxury brand was allowed to impose restrictive distribution agreements excluding third-party e-commerce platforms. De lege ferenda, two recommendations can be made. First, the Software Directive should be amended to expressly define computer programs in line with commonly accepted computer science ontologies, while providing that every time software is involved, this directive will prevail on general copyright rules. Second, in light of the right to communication to the public becoming ubiquitous (most recently in *VG Bild*[108] about 'framing'), copyright law should be amended to provide that this right too – not just the right to distribution – be subject to exhaustion. Otherwise, as most Things include content that is communicated to the public, there is the risk of reducing the principle of exhaustion to irrelevance, thus sterilising a limitation to IP that would otherwise be pivotal to ensuring the free movement of Things.

The combination of these factual, technological, and legal controls that the IoT company retains over the Thing results in the death of ownership. In turn, this manifests itself in decreased user power over the Thing, whilst the IoT company increases its power over the Thing, leading to its after-sale modification throughout its life cycle, and over usergenerated content. I will analyse each manifestation in turn.

Decreased User Power Over the Thing. Linking back to Echo's scenario, its legals warn that 'Service, Software and the Digital Content embody intellectual property that is protected by law.'[109] Virtually any aspect of Amazon's apps and Things is covered by patents, trademarks, copyright, trade secrets, and other IPRs.[110] Amazon's control over Echo's IP-embedding components prevents users from exercising their proprietary prerogatives. Under Alexa Terms of Use, e.g. users can utilise it only for personal and noncommercial purposes.[111] Under Amazon's Conditions of Use and Sale, users can only share content via 'their' Thing to the limited extent that they 'own or otherwise control all of the rights.'[112] This begs the question whether they can share contents by relying on IP exceptions or defences.[113] The question is of crucial importance because Amazon can suspend and terminate those accounts that they deem to carry out infringing activities.[114]

---

107 Case C-230/16 *Coty Germany v Parfümerie Akzente* [2018] 4 CMLR 9.
108 Case C-392/19 *VG Bild-Kunst v Stiftung Preußischer Kulturbesitz* [2021] ECDR 9, criticised for its 'dangerous extension of the right to communication to the public' (Roberto Caso, 'Diritto d'autore, Comunicazione al Pubblico e Misure Tecnologiche Di Protezione Contro Il Framing: VG Bild-Kunst e l'ultimo Cioccolatino Della Corte Di Giustizia' (2021) 45 Trento Law and Technology Research Group Research Papers 1.).
109 Amazon Prime Video Terms of Use, last updated 27 May 2020, 6f.
110 Inter alia Amazon App Suite Legal Notices; Amazon App Legal Notice; Alexa Built-In Trademark Usage Guidelines; Works with Alexa – Trademark Usage Guidelines; etc.
111 Alexa Terms of Use, last updated on 31 January 2020, 1.2.
112 Conditions of Use & Sale, last updated on 29 January 2020, 8.
113 Similar problems, in the context of distance learning platforms, have been observed by Pascault and others (n 40).
114 Amazon Intellectual Property Policy.

Amazon's approach is clearly against allowing users to exercise their fundamental freedoms as conveyed by the copyright exceptions. This can be seen in the Additional Amazon Software Terms that prohibit to 'copy, modify, reverse engineer, decompile or disassemble, or otherwise tamper'[115] with Echo's software. This provision is likely to qualify as 'null and void'[116] under the Software Directive as it is contrary to the study and decompilation exceptions.[117] More on the potential of IP exceptions to tackle the death of ownership will be said in the next section.

This cumulation of IPRs affects the degree of control that we have over the Thing as a whole and signals a shift from ownership to tenancy. Indicative of this shift are also those provisions whereby users do not own the digital content embedded in Echo: users have only a 'non-exclusive *right to view*'[118] the content. Indeed, the latter is merely 'licensed, not sold, to you.'[119] Amazon exercises a form of techno-legal power that is epitomised by its use of Microsoft PlayReady,™ a copy prevention technology embedded in software and hardware that allows control over the video content displayed on Amazon's Things.[120] Users remain owners of the Thing, but their right does not even resemble that absolute power over goods that is at the core of the traditional concept of property.

Increased Corporate Power Over the Thing. The death of ownership is not limited to the reduced power that users can exercise over 'their' Things. It is also connected to the IoT companies' increased contractual power that leads to the possibility to modify the Thing unilaterally throughout its life cycle. Users must be aware that their Thing may vary over time and possibly become radically different to what it was when they purchased it. This is evidenced by the fact that the services and the digital content provided through Echo may become unavailable over time and contain errors, without Amazon being liable for it.[121] This can be seen with even more clarity in that contractual provision that allows Amazon to cease providing Echo's software and to terminate the user's right to use the software at any time: '[y]our rights to use the Amazon Software will automatically terminate without notice from us if you fail to comply with any of these Software Terms, the Conditions of Use or any other Service Terms.'[122] The unavailability of the software makes the Thing as a whole unusable, including its hardware, service, digital content, and data components.

Increased Corporate Power Over User-Generated Content. Alongside decreased user power over the Thing – and, correspondingly, increased corporate power over it – the death of ownership manifests itself through IoT companies claiming control over the content generated by users via the Things. Users typically retain

---

115 Additional Amazon Software Terms, last updated on 29 January 2020, 3.
116 Software Directive, art 8.
117 Software Directive, arts 6 and 5(3).
118 Kindle Store Terms of Use, last updated on 22 May 2018, 1. Similar provisions apply to the video content under Amazon Prime Video Terms of Use, 4h.
119 Kindle Store Terms of Use, 1.
120 Third Party Software, last updated on 26 July 2019.
121 ibid 13; Amazon Prime Video Terms of Use, 4i and 6d.
122 Additional Amazon Software Terms, 1.

ownership over the contents they generate, but they effectively lose control over them by granting Amazon a worldwide sublicensable, royalty-free license over that content.[123] This can only partly be countered through the exercise of moral rights and image rights, but their protection is, in practice, weak and piecemeal.[124] The shift from ownership to control is a feature of contemporary IP that goes beyond the IoT. We have seen it occur in the context of the platformisation of education during the COVID-19 pandemic, when most universities adopted third-party proprietary platforms that de facto dispossessed teachers and students of their data.[125] The IoT brings the irrelevance of formal ownership to the physical world and renders it ubiquitous.

The power dynamics that underpin the death of ownership result in a fundamental shift in 'the traditional conceptions of ownership'[126] that goes beyond Echo's case study: it is a core characteristic of the IoT as a whole, as noted in a significant and comprehensive book on ownership in a 'smart' world: *Owned* by Joshua Fairfield.[127] Previous research had already underlined how the dematerialisation of traditional goods was leading to a shift in the concepts of ownership and property.[128] Conversely, less explored had been the opposite move, that is, when goods remain tangible but are embedded with software, service, and data. This is the gap filled by *Owned*, which shows that IP law has usurped a role traditionally delegated to property law when it comes to governing Things. Through IP-enabled postsale control over the Things – and ultimately over their 'owners' – IoT companies are responsible for a system that Fairfield sees as reminiscent of the feudal times, when people would only manage property subject to the ruler's will. The feudal lord's power was exemplified by the infamous *ius primae noctis*, the right to have sexual intercourse with his peasants' brides on the night of the wedding. While there is no hard evidence that the *ius primae noctis* actually existed,[129] *Owned* refers to it as a powerful metaphor: 'as the owner of the intellectual property embedded in the device, and as the drafter of clauses buried deep within its license agreement,'[130] IoT companies may be

---

123 Conditions of Use & Sale, 8.

124 See e.g. Huw Beverley-Smith, Ansgar Ohly and Agnes Lucas-Schloetter, *Privacy, Property and Personality: Civil Law Perspectives on Commercial Appropriation* (CUP 2005) esp 207.

125 Pascault and others (n 40).

126 Natasha Tusikov, 'Precarious Ownership of the Internet of Things in the Age of Data' in Blayne Haggart, Kathryn Henne and Natasha Tusikov (eds), *Information, Technology and Control in a Changing World* (Springer International Publishing 2019) 140. Tusikov's main contention is that 'companies that own the knowledge integral to the IoT's functionality (the software) control that knowledge through intellectual property laws, especially copyright, and the ubiquitous surveillance of their customers.'

127 Fairfield (n 14).

128 M Scott Boone, 'Ubiquitous Computing, Virtual Worlds, and the Displacement of Property Rights' (2008) 4 ISJLP 91; Aaron Perzanowski and Jason M Schultz, *The End of Ownership: Personal Property in the Digital Economy* (The MIT Press 2016).

129 Jörg Wettlaufer, 'The Jus Primae Noctis as a Male Power Display. A Review of Historic Sources with Evolutionary Interpretation' (2000) 21 Evolution and Human Behavior 111.

130 Fairfield (n 14). No pinpointing is provided as this e-book's pages are not numbered.

regarded as digital lords who blatantly invade the property and privacy of the users, who are demoted to digital peasants.

Fairfield goes as far as to claim that '[l]ike the serfs of feudal Europe who lacked rights in the land they worked, without digital property rights, we aren't owners – *we're owned*.'[131] The solution to the death of ownership is found in the extension of the property rights that people have traditionally enjoyed over their things. Alongside the rights to modify, sell, use, and exclude – traditionally associated to 'ordinary' property – Fairfield claims that we should have the rights to hack, sell, run, and ban.[132] To some extent, this has been already recognised by the Library of Congress's Copyright Office, which has introduced new exemptions to the Digital Millennium Copyright Act in order to recognise a right to hack one's own Thing without the fear of being liable for copyright infringement for the unauthorised use of the software embedded in the Thing.[133] These include exemptions to 'unlock' the Thing to connect it to alternative wireless networks and to 'jailbreak' it to make the Thing interoperable. It also includes more specific, IoT-friendly exemptions for purposes of diagnosis, repair, and lawful modification of motorised land vehicles.[134] Whilst stronger IP exceptions may play a role as part of a strategy to re-empower IoT users, they are not as such sufficient. More importantly, their revitalisation can be hindered by a strengthening of the property right over the Thing. IP exceptions are not grounded in the right to property: they reflect the public interest to ensure freedom of expression and information, as well as the right to self-determination. Extended property rights do not achieve much; they inherently foster the private interest, whose all-absorbing character in the IoT threatens the public and collective interests.

The parallel between IoT and feudalism, whilst a potent metaphor, does not fully account for the power dynamics at play in feudal times and today. In the current stage of capitalistic development, IoT companies leverage their IP and data power to impose their private interests on the end users' rights and freedoms – not only on their property, but also on their fundamental freedoms that is in the public interest to protect e.g. expression and information. Under medieval law, the lord could not wield property as a weapon: the power over the land depended on – and could be limited in view of – the collective interest, mainly to 'a more abundant and higher-quality agricultural harvest,'[135] which would ultimately bind both the lord and the peasants. As revolutionary Paul Lafargue put it, the feudal landlord 'has obligations and is *far from enjoying the liberty of the capitalist – the right to use and abuse. The land is not marketable; it is burdened with conditions.*'[136] In

---

131 ibid.

132 ibid.

133 US Copyright Office, Library of Congress, 'Exemption to Prohibition on Circumvention of Copyright Protection Systems for Access Control Technologies (83 FR 54010)' (26 October 2018).

134 ibid.

135 Paolo Grossi, *A History of European Law* (Laurence Hooper tr, Wiley-Blackwell 2010) 17.

136 Paul Lafargue, *The Evolution of Property from Savagery to Civilization (1890)* (New Park 1975) 48.

a sense, the public interest could be seen as able to limit private power, that is, the opposite to what appears to be happening under IoT capitalism.[137] Property, the private interest, and IP become the real protagonists of the market dynamics with the passage from feudal society to bourgeois society.[138] That was the moment when the ownership of goods started to be branded as 'natural,' as if it emanated from the ownership over oneself.[139] Thus, property became the most significant contributor to a person's individuality, and the bourgeoisie, by accumulating 'sacred'[140] property, reorientated society towards profit and accumulation of wealth. I would posit that the individualist outlook of bourgeois society – as opposed to medieval property – is the real precursor of the current state of things. The death of ownership is not the death of property: in the IoT, property thrives in the forms of IP, data power, contractual and technical control. Under their weight, citizens' freedoms, their collective interests, and the public interest risk succumbing. Compared to this, the feudal communities, based on collective property and the feudal hierarchy where everyone 'from the serf upwards to the king . . . were bound by the ties of reciprocal duties,'[141] become a rather alluring prospect.

Even though the metaphor of digital serfdom has its drawbacks, it is possible to trace a parallel between feudalism and IoT economy. It has been noted that the 'most distinctive feature of villein tenures was *labour rent*, i.e. the obligation to perform unpaid labour-service'[142] on the manorial demesne. The demesne was the land that the lord retained for his own use and under his own management. From this viewpoint, an echo of this unpaid labour is present in the increasingly widespread practices of digital labour that see IoT users becoming unwitting workers. E.g. to extract value from images, companies need to annotate them, namely, they need to add tags that say, 'This image contains a cat, a person, etc.' In this way, image datasets can be used to train image-recognition AI models. However, manual annotation is slow and expensive. The solution Facebook came up with was to use user-generated hashtags as a proxy to human annotations for training purposes.[143] Thus, by 'using a dataset comprised of 3.5 billion Instagram photos, Facebook was able to achieve an all-time record-high score of 85.4 percent on

---

137 This statement comes with the caveat that in medieval times, larger parts of society were marginalised, and therefore their interests would be unlikely to be subsumed under the public interest.

138 Grossi (n 136) esp 63.

139 James Tully, *A Discourse on Property: John Locke and His Adversaries* (Re-issued, Cambridge University Press 2006).

140 Declaration of the Rights of Man [1789], art 17.

141 Lafargue (n 137) 48.

142 Chris Middleton, 'Peasants, Patriarchy, and the Feudal Mode of Production in England: A Marxist Appraisal: 1 Property and Patriarchal Relations within the Peasantry' (1981) 29 The Sociological Review 105, 109.

143 Manohar Paluri and others, 'Advancing State-of-the-Art Image Recognition with Deep Learning on Hashtags' (*Facebook Engineering*, 2 May 2018) <https://engineering.fb.com/ml-applications/advancing-state-of-the-art-image-recognition-with-deep-learning-on-hashtags/>.

image recognition accuracy.'[144] I would argue that this free labour that Instagram users provide resembles the unpaid labour provided by the peasant on the manorial demesne. As data is the main commodity in the IoT market and it is produced in large quantities by IoT users, the latter necessarily qualify as unwitting workers and should therefore be protected both in their individual and collective dimension.

Private property, by definition, will always be a means to protect the capitalist's private interest. Part of the capitalist strategy has been presenting IP as a form of nearly absolute property, as opposed to a policy bargain between the public and the rightsholders.[145] Against this backdrop, extending property rights is a dangerous path to take. By contrast, an answer may be found in the limitations to property. These can be intra-IP (exceptions), extra-IP (competition), and even extralegal limitations (the commons). The next sections will critically assess whether intra-IP limitation can be at the centre of a strategy to re-empower IoT users affected by the death of ownership.

6.4 Intra-IP Limitations: IP Exceptions or the Piecemeal Protection of Public Interest

Our Things being protected by a plurality of IPRs and embedding of a variety of IP works, combined with the strategic use of contractual, technical, and factual controls, leads to an imbalanced relationship between the IoT company/rightsholder and the end user. The death of ownership is the epitome of this imbalance. The principle of exhaustion is a key way IP law ensures a fair balance is achieved. However, we have seen that the principle is itself 'exhausted' in light of the *Tom Kabinet* doctrine with its outdated tangible-intangible divide, arbitrarily narrow interpretation of 'software,' and expansion of the right of communication to the public. Therefore, it becomes even more important to assess whether IP law provides effective tools to maintain a balance between public interest and private interest, as well as between the rightsholders' interest and the end user's ones: this is the realm of IP exceptions, also known as permitted acts or defences.[146] These exceptions allow users of IP works to carry out certain activities without the permission of the rightsholder. They can be invoked by the defendant in infringement proceedings and can be regarded as a way to inject public interest into IP, albeit in a piecemeal way.[147] As held in *Deckmyn*,[148] it is in the public interest to

---

144 Paige Tsai, 'Image Recognition at Facebook' (*HBS Digital Initiative*, 13 November 2018) <https://digital.hbs.edu/platform-rctom/submission/image-recognition-at-facebook-how-machine-learning-is-helping-computers-and-people-who-are-blind-see-digital-photos/>.

145 David Bollier, *Viral Spiral: How the Commoners Built a Digital Republic of Their Own* (New Press 2008) esp 49.

146 cf Laurence R Helfer, 'The New Innovation Frontier – Intellectual Property and the European Court of Human Rights' (2008) 49 Harvard International Law Journal 1.

147 Ruth L Okediji, 'Le Système International de Droit d'Auteur. Restrictions, Exceptions et Considérations En Matière d'Intéret Public Pour Les Pays En Développement' (2006) ICTSD 15.

148 Case C-201/13 *Johan Deckmyn and Vrijheidsfonds VZW v Helena Vandersteen and Others* [2014] Bus L R 1368.

protect freedom of expression, and this includes the unauthorised use of IP works for parody purposes.[149] The role of exceptions as devices inject the public interest into IP has become more evident in parallel to the increased awareness of the importance of a commitment to sustainability in a time of climate emergency. To adopt a more flexible and balanced approach to exceptions, as epitomised by the fair use doctrine, would '*préserver pour les pays la flexibilité de continuer à élaborer des limitations et exceptions selon leurs besoins, dans leur propre contexte local.*'[150] Sustainable – and, more generally, fair – IP needs to have strong in-built limitations.

My starting point is that, regardless of the manifold ways IoT users attempt to neutralise the end users' proprietary prerogatives, the latter could still use their Things without the former's permission as long as the relevant activity falls within the scope of one of the IP exceptions. On the face of it,[151] the IP exceptions that more clearly lend themselves to give back (some) control to the end user in the context of the IoT are:

  (i) Observation, study, and test of the functioning of a computer program;[152]
 (ii) The decompilation (or reverse engineering) exception;[153]
(iii) Private copy of copyright works;
 (iv) Insubstantial extraction and reutilisation of databases protected by the sui generis right;
  (v) Use of a trade secret for freedom of information purposes;[154]
 (vi) Use of a trademark not 'in the course of trade'[155] and with 'due cause';[156]
(vii) Acts done privately and for noncommercial purposes in respect of objects protected by design rights.

An IoT user with some IT skills may want to inspect the Thing's software to understand how it works, e.g. to comprehend the logic of the black box algorithm that runs in the Thing. In principle, this falls within the scope of exception that the Software Directive sets forth 'to observe, study or test the functioning of the program.'[157] However, to successfully invoke it, the defendant must meet

149 Christophe Geiger and others, 'Limitations and Exceptions as Key Elements of the Legal Framework for Copyright in the European Union: Opinion of the European Copyright Society on the CJEU Ruling in Case C-201/13 Deckmyn' (2015) 46 IIC 93.
150 Okediji (n 148) 52.
151 This selection is, by its nature, discretionary. Other exceptions may play a role in consumer empowerment, see, e.g. Rossana Ducato and Alain Strowel, 'Limitations to Text and Data Mining and Consumer Empowerment: Making the Case for a Right to "Machine Legibility"' (2019) 50 IIC 649.
152 Software Directive, art 5(3).
153 Software Directive, art 6.
154 TS Directive, art 5(a).
155 TM Directive, art 10(2).
156 TM Directive, art 10(2)(c).
157 Software Directive, art 5(3).

the following requirements: (a) they must be a lawful acquirer, that is, a 'person having a right to use a copy of a computer program';[158] (b) the purpose has to be the determination of the 'ideas and principles which underlie any element of the program';[159] (c) the activity must be carried out 'while performing any of the acts of loading, displaying, running, transmitting or storing the program which (they are) entitled to do.'[160] The first requirement has to be interpreted broadly as encompassing anyone having a right to use the program based on a license or otherwise.[161] This is straightforward as the owner of a Thing is likely to qualify as a lawful user despite being a mere licensee of the embedded software, unless the Thing as a whole is held under a subscription contract. The second requirement can constitute more of a hurdle because it can be interpreted as excluding activities that go beyond the mere understanding of the ideas to e.g. repair or improve the software. The third requirement is the most problematic because it might be construed as meaning that the IoT company can use the EULA or one of the other 'legals' to restrict the types of acts that end users can put in place while studying, testing, etc. the program. Even though this is a grey area, IoT companies cannot go as far as to exclude this exception altogether, directly or indirectly. Indeed, under Article 8 of the Software Directive, any contractual provision contrary to this exception is null and void. Arguably, this should extend also to those technical measures aimed at restricting user freedoms in the 'Internet of Digital Locks.'

The right to decompile the embedded software is a complementary exception that IoT users affected by the death of ownership can trigger.[162] Decompilation is a method of reverse engineering whereby a program's code is analysed and the program is translated from a low level of abstraction to a higher level. Reverse engineering is a more general concept that goes beyond software (hardware can be reverse engineered) and has to do with the extrapolation of the underlying logic of a system based on the observation of its visible behaviour. Like the observation exception, the right to decompile cannot be overridden contractually; therefore, it can be useful to counter the power imbalance between IoT companies and end users by neutralising the contractual quagmire seen in Chapter 2. Decompilation is particularly important from this book's perspective given the vital role interoperability plays in preventing the Internet of Silos. Practically, this right gives IoT users the power to reproduce and translate the software's code to obtain

---

158 Software Directive, art 5(3).
159 Software Directive, art 5(3).
160 Software Directive, art 5(3).
161 The concept of lawful acquirer has been interpreted broadly as a 'purchaser, licensee, renter, or a person authorized to use the program on behalf of one of the above' (European Commission, 'Report on the Implementation and Effects of Directive 91/250/EEC' (2000) COM(2000)199 final para 10.) *UsedSoft* (n 103) included in the concept of lawful acquirer those who use a computer program based on a license resold by the original licensee. Moreover, national implementations (e.g. UK Copyright, Designs, and Patents Act 1988 (CDPA), s 50A) often refer to 'user' rather than 'acquirer.'
162 Software Directive, art 6.

the information necessary to achieve the interoperability of an independently created computer program. Defendants will have to prove:

(i)   To be a lawful user (typically a licensee);[163]
(ii) That the information necessary to achieve interoperability had not been previously made readily available;[164]
(iii) That reproduction and translation of the code are confined to the parts of the original program which are necessary in order to achieve interoperability;[165]
(iv) That the three-step test is made out, namely, that the exception does not unreasonably prejudices the rightsholder's legitimate interests or conflicts with a normal exploitation of the computer program.[166]

The main limitation of this exception is that reverse engineering is possible only to obtain interoperability-related information. This is likely to require skills that most users will not have. It could nonetheless benefit them indirectly by allowing developers to design interoperable Things. Additionally, in the case of complex software, reverse engineering 'does not provide a viable means for achieving interoperability,'[167] and this will usually be the case with IoT software, due to its intrinsic complexity and its being fused with hardware.[168] A more IoT-friendly copyright and patent law would entail a positive obligation for developers to disclose the interoperability information.[169]

Whilst the embedded software falls clearly within the scope of that subcategory of copyright that is regulated by the Software Directive, other components of our Things are covered by 'general' copyright law, as enshrined in the Infosoc Directive and the Copyright in the Digital Single Market Directive, which was transposed by member states in June 2021. Under *Nintendo v PC Box*,[170] complex multimedia products fall within the scope of both general copyright and software copyright when the CJEU interprets the provisions on the rightsholder's rights and remedies. The law of complex multimedia products is far from settled, however. *Tom Kabinet*[171] is indicative of this issue as the court held

---

163   Software Directive, art 6(1)(a).
164   Software Directive, art 6(1)(b).
165   Software Directive, art 6(1)(c).
166   Software Directive, art 6(3); Berne Convention, art 9(2). The third step is that exceptions should be provided in 'special cases,' which is usually interpreted as meaning that they should be statutorily listed; decompilation instantiates such special case.
167   Ulla-Maija Mylly, 'An Evolutionary Economics Perspective on Computer Program Interoperability and Copyright' (2010) 41 IIC 284, 315.
168   See Zhi-Kai Zhang and others, 'IoT Security: Ongoing Challenges and Research Opportunities' *2014 IEEE 7th International Conference on Service-Oriented Computing and Applications* (IEEE 2014).
169   Mylly (n 168).
170   Case C-355/12 *Nintendo v PC Box* [2014] 1 WLUK 506; cf Dan L Burk, 'Owning E-Sports: Proprietary Rights in Professional Computer Gaming' (2013) 161 University of Pennsylvania Law Review 1535.
171   (n 97).

that e-books are attracted under 'general' copyright as opposed to 'special' software copyright. Whilst the code of the embedded program is covered by 'literary' copyright, the original interface of the Thing, should the Thing have one, may be protected as an artistic work.[172] The original sounds emitted by the Thing, either downloaded or streamed, may qualify as musical works.[173] Accordingly, the IoT company's exclusive rights are limited by a number of exceptions to 'general' copyright. In particular, the private copy exception appears to be the most suitable to re-empower the IoT user who is affected by the death of ownership. Under the Infosoc Directive, member states may allow the unauthorised reproduction of copyright material for private and noncommercial use, by natural persons, on condition that the rightsholders receive fair compensation, unless the prejudice caused to them is minimal.[174] Positively, this exception applies to the reproduction on any medium.[175] Therefore, e.g. a Thing's user could make a copy of the Thing's digital content accessed through the cloud and save it on a computer or other device.[176] However, the private copy exception has three shortcomings. First, it is optional. Unlike the aforementioned exceptions to software copyright and unlike the new exceptions under the Copyright in the Digital Single Market Directive, member states have discretion when it comes to the implementation of most of the exceptions under the Infosoc Directive.[177] This explains why the UK does not provide the private copy exception[178] and the Republic of Ireland only partly implemented it.[179] Second, unlike the Software Directive, the exception can be overridden by means of contracts and technological protection measures.[180] Therefore, IoT companies can contract it out and technologically exclude it. Third, the CJEU interprets the concept of communication to the public broadly, thus leading to the excessive monopolisation of intangible assets and, ultimately,

---

172 Case C-393/09 *BSA v Ministerstvo Kultury* [2010] 12 WLUK 773. Conversely, the graphic user interfaces are not protected under the Software Directive.

173 Nigel Davies, 'The Digital Music Revolution – How Will Traditional Rights Operate in the on-Line Music World?' (2005) 16 Entertainment Law Review 137.

174 Infosoc Directive, art 5(2)(b) and recital 35; Case C-463/12 *Copydan Båndkopi v Nokia Danmark* [2015] 3 WLUK 142 [96(4)].

175 Infosoc Directive, art 5(2)(b).

176 Case C-265/16 *VCAST v RTI* [2017] 11 WLUK 694.

177 Apart from the exception for transient and incidental inclusion, all the exceptions under the Infosoc Directive are optional.

178 The High Court quashed the Copyright and Rights in Performances (Personal Copies for Private Use) Regulations 2014 because of a defect in the consultation process (*BASCA and others v Secretary of State for Business, Innovation and Skills* [2015] EWHC 2041 (Admin)). See Guido Noto La Diega, 'In Light of the Ends. Copyright Hysteresis and Private Copy Exception after the British Academy of Songwriters, Composers and Authors (BASCA) and Others v Secretary of State for Business, Innovation and Skills Case' in Alberto M Gambino (ed), *Studi giuridici europei 2014* (Giappichelli 2016).

179 Copyright and Related Rights Act 2000, ss 101–102.

180 Estelle Derclaye and Marcella Favale, 'Copyright and Contract Law: Regulating User Contracts: The State of the Art and a Research Agenda The Relationship between Copyright and Contract Law' (2010) 18 Journal of Intellectual Property Law 65.

the death of ownership.[181] The *Vcast* case[182] well illustrates the point. The dispute regarded an online recording service of television broadcasts in which Vcast captured the television signal by its own antennas and recorded the time slot of the selected broadcast signal in the user's cloud storage. The private copy exception applies to the right of reproduction and not to the right of communication to the public.[183] The CJEU argued that the concept of communication to the public must be interpreted broadly as 'covering any transmission or retransmission of a work to the public by wire or wireless means, including broadcasting.'[184] Since the 'active involvement' of Vcast in the realization of the private copies required some form of transmission – and hence, according to the court, of communication to the public – it followed that the private copy exception would not apply. This links back to the aforementioned issue of the 'exhaustion of exhaustion': since Things are interactive objects that are embedded with content that is often transmitted and retransmitted, there is the risk that the private copy exception will not be available to IoT users. De lege ferenda, alongside being subject to the principle of exhaustion, the private copy exception should be rendered mandatory and binding.

IP, however, is not only about the protection of intangible assets. After some recent jurisprudential developments at the EU level, three-dimensional copyright is of growing importance. Traditionally, the only three-dimensional works to be protected by copyright were artistic works, and in particular sculptures, works of architecture, and works of artistic craftsmanship.[185] Arguably, most Things cannot be regarded as any of these 'works.' Sculptures are protected irrespective of artistic quality, but the UK Supreme Court interpreted narrowly the concept of 'sculpture' in *Lucasfilm v Ainsworth*.[186] There, the Imperial Stormtrooper's helmet (Figure 6.2) was deemed not to fall within the scope of copyright protection because it was a mere prop, not a sculpture.[187]

It is fair to say that most Things are closer to props than they are to sculptures. Works of architecture, e.g. buildings, may be embedded with Things, but they are not a Thing as such, following this book's approach. Finally, works of artistic craftsmanship refer to things such as handcrafted jewellery and hand-knitted mittens. Regardless of the fact that most Things are industrially produced and cannot be regarded as a work of artistic craftsmanship, they are unlikely to meet the additional requirements of being of artistic quality and of craftsmanship.[188]

181　See Giancarlo Frosio, 'It's All Linked: How Communication to the Public Affects Internet Architecture' (2020) 37 Computer Law & Security Review 105410.

182　(n 177).

183　Infosoc Directive, art 5(3).

184　*VCAST* (n 177) [40].

185　CDPA, s 4.

186　[2011] UKSC 39.

187　The Supreme Court underlined the importance to refer to the ordinary use of the word 'sculpture' and observed that not every three-dimensional representation of a concept qualifies (ibid [36], [37]).

188　*Hensher v Restawile Upholstery* [1976] AC 64.

Figure 6.2 Imperial Stormtrooper helmet. Copy created from the original mouldings used in the first Star Wars film *A New Hope*.

Source: RS Prop Masters.

This approach is consistent with the traditional assumption that copyright protects only an exhaustive list of 'works,' namely, literary, dramatic, musical, artistic works, films, sound recordings, typographical arrangements, and broadcasts.[189] This theory of the *numerus clausus* (closed number) has been arguably abandoned by the CJEU notably in *Levola Hengelo*[190] and *Cofemel*.[191] In the former case, regarding the taste of cheese, it was held that for something to be a work, it must be original and it must be expressed in a manner which makes it identifiable with

189 *Creation Records v News Group Newspapers* [1997] EMLR 444.
190 Case C-310/17 *Levola Hengelo v Smilde Foods* [2018] 11 WLUK 155.
191 C-683/17 *Cofemel – Sociedade de Vestuario v G-Star Raw* [2019] 9 WLUK 110.

sufficient precision and objectivity.[192] In *Cofemel*, a case about the protection of the design of a line of jeans, the court applied *Levola Hengelo* and further clarified that all works that are original and identifiable with precision and objectivity are protected by copyright: no additional and subjective requirements are allowed.[193] This means that the tangible components of the Things may be protected even though they do not fall under any of the categories of 'works' as long as they are the author's own intellectual creation and if the subject matter of protection can be identified with precision and objectivity. If that is the case, the aforementioned considerations on the private copy exception apply.

The tangible components of a Thing may be protected as well by means of patents, trademarks, and design rights. For the purposes of this book, it is possible to ignore patents since they – and their exceptions – have not been harmonised at the EU level. Trademarks need only touching upon because, although one can register a shape as a trademark, the vast majority of these applications fail because consumers are unlikely to think of a shape as being indicative of a particular undertaking's goods.[194] Moreover, applications for three-dimensional marks have to overcome three absolute grounds for refusal that before the 2015–2017 reform applied only to shapes:[195] it will not be possible to register a shape that depends on the nature of the goods, is necessary to achieve a technical result, or adds substantial value to the good.[196] The latter would most likely apply here. Indeed, as Advocate General Szpunar noted in *Hauck*,[197] the rationale of this exclusion is to demarcate the protection conferred by trademarks and that conferred by industrial designs and copyright, which are usually seen as better suited for the external features of goods that 'substantially enhance (their) attractiveness . . . and strongly influence consumer preferences.'[198] I would argue that the shape of the Things influences consumer preferences and thus cannot be registered as a trademark as it adds substantial value to the Thing. There is evidence that consumer purchase Things based on emotional factors rather than rational ones related to the functionalities of the Thing as such.[199] Design plays a key role in eliciting consumer emotions based on a product's attractiveness.[200] I would conclude that

---

192 *Levola Hengelo* (n 191) [37], [40].

193 *Cofemel* (n 192) [35].

194 'Average consumers are not in the habit of making assumptions about the origin of goods based on the shape' (Case C-218/01 *Henkel KGaA v Deutsches Patent- und Markenamt* [2004] ECR I-1725 [52]). Recently, the General Court has held that the shape of a lipstick can be distinctive in Case T-488/20 *Guerlain v EUIPO* (General Court, 14 July 2021).

195 The EU reform of trademark extended the absolute grounds for refusal that once applied only to shape marks to 'another characteristic' (TM Directive, art 4(1)(e)).

196 TM Directive, art 4(1)(e); Case T-508/08 *Bang & Olufsen v OHIM* [2011] ECR II-6975.

197 Case C-205/13 *Hauck v Stokke* [2014] 9 WLUK 444, Opinion of AG Szpunar.

198 ibid [80].

199 Luis Hernan Contreras Pinochet and others, 'The Influence of the Attributes of "Internet of Things" Products on Functional and Emotional Experiences of Purchase Intention' (2018) 15 Innovation & Management Review 303.

200 Ravindra Chitturi, 'Emotions by Design: A Consumer Perspective' (2009) 3 International Journal of Design 7.

the fact that the design of a Thing affects the decision to purchase it suggests that IoT companies are unlikely to be successful in registering the shape of their Things as a trademark as that shape would add substantial value to the goods. Nonetheless, should a Thing's shape be registered as a trademark, its private use would not constitute infringement because 3D mark owners can only prevent uses 'in the course of trade.'[201] A trademark is used in the course of trade if it performs one of functions of trademarks, mainly, if it acts as a 'badge of origin'[202] of the good or service. Most private uses of IoT shape marks will not qualify as infringement because a private use of a Thing is unlikely to signal to third parties a claim that the Thing originates from the end user. Moreover, in line with ECtHR jurisprudence, freedom of expression can operate as an external limit to trademark law.[203] Some have argued that it is not necessary to introduce external freedom-of-expression limits because 'EU trade mark law itself provides for limits that guarantee respect of the freedom of expression.'[204] This applies especially to well-known marks, such as Amazon's arrow. Their protection is stronger than ordinary marks, but their unauthorised use does not constitute infringement if it is supported by 'due cause.'[205] There is no definition of *due cause*, but as held in *Leidseplein v Red Bull*,[206] it includes ante-registration uses and uses that are in good faith. The CJEU underlined that the concept of due cause is intended to strike a balance between the proprietor's interests and either objective or subjective interests of a third party using the identical sign. Although the court does not couch this as freedom of expression, it is not unfounded to see the concept through this lens. Whilst it is contested whether freedom of expression creates an autonomous defence to trademark infringement, it is clear that existing exceptions must be interpreted broadly. Indeed, the new Trade Marks Directive and the EU Trade Marks Regulation,[207] for the first time, provide that their application must ensure 'full respect for fundamental rights and freedoms, and in particular the freedom of expression.'[208] Accordingly, in the unlikely event that the shape of a Thing is registered as a trademark, freedom of expression will breathe life into the

---

201 TM Directive, art 10(2); Regulation (EU) 2017/1001 of 14 June 2017 on the European Union trade mark ('EUTM Regulation') [2017] OJ L 154/1, *art 9*.

202 *Unilever v Griffin* [2010] EWHC 899 (Ch) [11]-[14].

203 *Österreichische Schutzgemeinschaft für Nichtraucher v Austria*, App no 17200/90 (Eur. Comm'n on H.R., 2 December 1991) as interpreted by Christophe Geiger and Elena Izyumenko, 'The Constitutionalization of Intellectual Property Law in the EU and the Funke Medien, Pelham and Spiegel Online Decisions of the CJEU: Progress, But Still Some Way to Go!' (2020) 51 IIC 282, 63.

204 Michal Bohaczewski, 'Conflicts Between Trade Mark Rights and Freedom of Expression Under EU Trade Mark Law: Reality or Illusion?' (2020) 51 IIC 856.

205 TM Directive, art 10(2)(c).

206 Case C-65/12 *Leidseplein Beheer v Red Bull* [2014] Bus LR 280.

207 TM Directive, recital 27; EUTM Regulation, recital 21.

208 No such reference was present in the previous directive (Directive 2008/95/EC of 22 October 2008 to approximate the laws of the Member States relating to trade marks ('Second TM Directive') [2008] OJ L 299/25).

aforementioned defences and most acts carried out by IoT users will not qualify as infringement.

Design rights[209] appear to be the most suitable form of IP protection for the shape of a Thing and, more generally, its tangible components.[210] *Design* means the 'appearance of the whole or a part of a product resulting from the features of, in particular, the lines, contours, colours, shape, texture and/or materials of the product itself and/or its ornamentation.'[211] In light of the composite nature of most Things, many of them will likely qualify as 'complex products,' which design law defines as products 'composed of multiple components which can be replaced permitting disassembly and reassembly of the product.'[212] If a Thing's design – or the design of its visible component parts if we are dealing with a complex product[213] – is novel[214] and has individual character,[215] the rightsholder can prevent anyone, including the IoT user, from using the product.[216] However, although the 'delineation of rights is not restricted to commercial uses,'[217] design rights cannot be exercised in respect of acts done for private and noncommercial purposes.[218] This exception – that applies also to Community Design Rights[219] – is mandatory, and therefore, member states must provide it in their national laws.[220] It is unclear whether the exception can be overridden by means of a contract, e.g. via the terms of service linked to the purchase of a Thing. On the one hand, the Design Directive is without prejudice of other forms of protection, including civil liability and unfair competition, whilst contract law is not mentioned.[221] On

---

209 Design rights can be registered or unregistered, but this chapter will only consider the former because there has been no harmonisation of unregistered designs in the EU.

210 Design rights can also protect two-dimensional articles. The unregistered design right has not been harmonised; therefore, some countries, e.g. the UK, apply unregistered design rights only to two-dimensional articles. See CDPA, s 213.

211 Directive 98/71/EC of 13 October 1998 on the legal protection of designs ('Design Directive') [1998] OJ L 289/28, art 1(a).

212 Design Directive, art 1(c).

213 Design Directive, art 3(3).

214 A design is novel if no identical design has been made available to the public before the date of filing of the application or if the variant differs only in immaterial details (Design Directive, art 4).

215 A design has individual character if the 'overall impression it produces on the informed user differs from the overall impression produced on such a user by any design which has been made available to the public before the date of filing of the application' (Design Directive, art 5).

216 Design Directive, art 12(1).

217 Lionel Bently and others, *Intellectual Property Law* (5th edn, OUP 2018) 797.

218 Design Directive, art 13(1)(a). Some unauthorised commercial uses are lawful as well. E.g. the citation exception refers to commercial citation (Community Design Regulation, art 20(1)(c); Joined Cases C-24/16, C-25/16 *Nintendo Co Ltd v BigBen Interactive GmbH* [2018] Bus LR 1245).

219 Council Regulation (EC) No 6/2002 of 12 December 2001 on Community designs ('Community Design Regulation') [2002] OJ L 3/1, art 20(1)(a).

220 This can be inferred by the use of 'shall' in art 13 of the Design Directive. E.g. in the UK, the Intellectual Property Act 2014 introduced a series of exceptions which mirror patent and copyright exceptions, including the private and noncommercial defence under the CDPA, s 244A.

221 Design Directive, art 14.

the other hand, no specific provision on the contractual overridability is made. The exception is further narrowed by national laws imposing requirements of (i) no undue prejudice to the normal exploitation of the design, (ii) compatibility with fair trade practices, and (iii) acknowledgement of the source.[222] However, the interpretation of design law and of its exceptions should never lead to a disproportionate interference of freedom of expression, as the ECtHR held in *Plesner v Louis Vuitton*.[223] This should empower the IoT user to utilise their Things as freely as possible regardless of their design protection. Moreover, design rights should not be used to stifle innovation and suppress competition. This was made clear by the CJEU in *Nintendo v BigBen*,[224] where the citation exception – hitherto regarded as narrowly applicable – was 'transformed into a far more expansive right for third-party competitors to re-produce designs to explain or demonstrate product compatibility.'[225] These human rights–orientated interpretations of the exceptions are fit for the IoT and should be welcomed as a positive approach to balancing IP and competing interests.[226]

It is of little doubt that the value of the IoT is intrinsically linked to the value of the big data produced by our Things, also known as machine data or industrial data.[227] Whilst data as such and in isolation is not covered by IP, it can be protected under certain circumstances by an oft-forgotten right, namely, the sui generis right under the Database Directive (also known as 'the database right').[228] This is of particular relevance in the context of machine-generated datasets that are at the core of the IoT. The sui generis right is not confined to physical databases where documents are systematically archived (e.g. the Wiener Holocaust Library) and to online databases (e.g. WestLaw). Under this directive, a database is any collection of 'independent works, data or other materials arranged in a systematic or methodical way and individually accessible by electronic or other means.'[229] In principle, an air company's website that allows users to search and book flights can be regarded as a database.[230] The collection of voice recordings of the users' interactions with Google Home could be an example of IoT database.

222 CDPA, s 244A(c)(i), (ii).
223 *Plesner v Louis Vuitton* [2011] E.C.D.R. 14.
224 (n 218) [86].
225 Jane Cornwell, 'Nintendo v BigBen and Acacia v Audi; Acacia v Porsche: Design Exceptions at the CJEU' (2019) 14 JIPLP 51, 53.
226 Natalia Kapyrina, 'Limitations in the Field of Designs' (2018) 49 IIC 41, 58. *Contra*, David Stone, 'Design Law Misplayed in Nintendo AG Opinion' (2017) 12 JIPLP 558, 560.
227 Nastaran Hajiheydari, Mojtaba Talafidaryani and SeyedHossein Khabiri, 'IoT Big Data Value Map: How to Generate Value from IoT Data' *Proceedings of the 2019 the 5th International Conference on e-Society, e-Learning and e-Technologies – ICSLT 2019* (ACM Press 2019).
228 Database Directive, arts 7–11.
229 Database Directive, art 1.
230 In Case C-30/14 *Ryanair v PR Aviation* [2015] 2 All E.R. (Comm) 455, however, the database fell outside the scope of the directive because it did not meet the further requirements of originality and substantial investment. See Tatiana – Eleni Synodinou, 'Databases and Screen Scraping: Lawful User's Rights and Contractual Restrictions Do Not Fly Together' (2016) 38 EIPR 312.

Indeed, these recordings are stored systematically and made available in an individually retrievable way.[231]

A database may be protected by copyright or by the sui generis right. I will overlook the former as only a minority of IoT databases will attract copyright. Indeed, for a database to be copyright protected, the selection and arrangement of the contents must be original, that is, the author's own intellectual creation.[232] Copyright is not fit for IoT databases because of the prevalence of automation in selecting and arranging the contents; in other words, the setting up of these databases 'is dictated by technical considerations, rules or constraints which leave no room for creative freedom.'[233] IoT databases, nonetheless, could be protected by the sui generis right, since the latter does not require originality. The maker of a database has the right to prevent extraction and reutilisation of the contents of the database if the investment in obtaining, verifying, or presenting its contents was substantial.[234] One could object that IoT companies do not need to invest substantially to set up their databases, since they are mostly machine-generated. However, in reality, the threshold of substantiality accepted by courts throughout Europe is low. In practice, any investment is regarded as substantial as long as it is 'more than minimal.'[235] IoT companies will not struggle to identify even a limited amount of 'human, technical and financial resources'[236] invested in the database, and therefore, this requirement is unlikely to constitute a hurdle. An investment will be needed e.g. for human beings to label the data, especially if the database relies on supervised or semisupervised learning techniques.[237]

The sui generis right is often regarded as unfit for IoT data.[238] The unfitness is mostly based on *British Horseracing Board v William Hill*[239] and the three *Fixtures Marketing* cases,[240] where the CJEU took the debatable decision that the investment into newly created – as opposed to already existing, 'obtained' – data does not attract sui generis protection. Many have interpreted this obtaining-creating dichotomy as an endorsement of the so-called spin-off theory, whereby 'databases which are the by-products of the main activities of an economic undertaking ('spin-off'

---

231 'Google – My Activity' <https://myactivity.google.com/activitycontrols/webandapp>.
232 Database Directive, art 3(1); Case C-604/10 *Football Dataco v Yahoo! UK* [2012] Dir com sc int 269.
233 *Football Dataco* (n 232) [39].
234 Database Directive, art 7.
235 European Commission, 'SWD "Evaluation of Directive 96/9/EC on the Legal Protection of Databases"' (2018) SWD(2018)147final 27.
236 Database Directive, recital 7.
237 Noto La Diega, 'Artificial Intelligence and Databases in the Age of Big Machine Data' (n 56).
238 Matthias Leistner, 'Big Data and the EU Database Directive 96/9/EC: Current Law and Potential for Reform' in Sebastian Lohsse, Reiner Schulze and Dirk Staudenmayer (eds), *Trading Data in the Digital Economy: Legal Concepts and Tools* (Nomos 2017) 25.
239 Case C-203/02 *British Horseracing Board v William Hill* [2004] ECR I-10415.
240 Case C-338/02 *Fixtures Marketing v Svenska Spel* [2004] ECR I-10497; Case C-444/02 *Fixtures Marketing v OPAP* [2004] ECR I-1549; Case C-46/02 *Fixtures Marketing v Oy Veikkaus Ab* [2004] ECR I-10365.

databases) are in principle not protected by the *sui generis* right.'[241] The example of such spin-off databases made by the Commission was 'the automated creation of machine-generated data (e.g. Internet of Things data).'[242] However, the spin-off theory has no sound basis in the four aforementioned cases. Indeed, the CJEU held that the creation of a database can be 'linked to the exercise of a principal activity in which the person creating the database is also the creator of the materials contained in the database'[243] as long as the obtaining, verification, or presentation 'required *substantial investment . . . independent of the resources used to create* those materials.'[244] Accordingly, although most IoT databases may be regarded as spin-off databases, they could nonetheless be protected by the sui generis right. More generally, the CJEU cases – and their postulation of an obtaining-creating dichotomy – can be criticised for three reasons. First, *British Horseracing* and *Fixtures Marketing* overemphasise the relevance of some recitals of the Database Directive that could be invoked to reach the opposite conclusion. In particular, they can lead to conclude that databases of 'created' data are in fact protected by the sui generis right. As pointed out in Recital 9, databases are a vital tool in the development of an information market. Given that the majority of the investments made by the database makers regard data collection rather than the setting up of the database itself,[245] this recital can be construed as providing an argument in favour of the relevance of investments in 'created' data for the sui generis right to subsist. Second, a comparative analysis of domestic case laws shows that the same data can be treated as 'created' in some jurisdictions and 'obtained' in others,[246] with live football data deemed to be 'created' in Germany and 'obtained' in the UK.[247] Third, the Fourth Industrial Revolution shows the untenability of the creating-obtaining dichotomy. This is well illustrated by the use of AI-powered data mining in predictive analytics: it leads to inferences, identification of patterns, and discovery of correlations between existing data; one could argue both ways, that this data is created or, as seems more reasonable, obtained.

Given that, consequently, it can be argued that the sui generis right provides some protection to IoT data,[248] it becomes important to assess whether the excep-

---

241 European Commission, 'SWD "Evaluation of Directive 96/9/EC on the Legal Protection of Databases"' (n 236) 15.

242 ibid.

243 *British Horseracing* (n 239) [35].

244 ibid [35].

245 European Commission, 'SWD "Evaluation of Directive 96/9/EC on the Legal Protection of Databases"' (n 236) 36.

246 In the literature, there is no consensus on where to draw the line between creation and obtaining. See Estelle Derclaye, *The Legal Protection of Databases: A Comparative Analysis* (Edward Elgar 2008); Ottolia (n 51).

247 *Football Dataco Ltd v Stan James Ltd* (No 2) [2013] EWCA Civ 27; European Commission, 'SWD "Evaluation of Directive 96/9/EC on the Legal Protection of Databases"' (n 236) 25.

248 The sui generis protection will depend on a number of factors, e.g. if the learning model utilised is a supervised one (i.e. requiring human intervention), if the IoT system is created with the purpose of setting up a database, or if it produces databases serially, etc. More on this in Noto La Diega, 'Artificial Intelligence and Databases in the Age of Big Machine Data' (n 56).

tions to this right can be successfully invoked by IoT users who find themselves affected by the death of ownership. There are two exceptions that may come into play in these scenarios. First, database makers cannot prevent lawful users from extracting or reutilising insubstantial parts of the database's contents.[249] Importantly, this is expressly qualified as a user right rather than an exception, and therefore, any narrow interpretation should be excluded. This is further corroborated by the generous wording of the directive, whereby insubstantial extraction and reutilisation can be carried out 'for any purposes whatsoever';[250] therefore, commercial and mixed uses are included. It is mandatory for member states to provide this right in the national implementation measures,[251] and companies may not override it contractually.[252] The limit to this is that only a lawful user can exercise this right, which means that if the terms of service prevent all access and use of the database, the term will prevail on the exception. However, if the use is permitted, then the terms of service (and the other 'legals') cannot be used to prevent the insubstantial extraction of the database's contents. Conversely, the private use exception to the sui generis right is rather narrow. First, it is optional, and therefore, member states can decide not to implement it.[253] Second, contracts can be used to override it,[254] which is worrying in the IoT's contractual quagmire and associated power imbalance. Third, the private use exception applies only to the extraction (and not to the reutilisation) of the contents of nonelectronic databases, which makes it useless in an IoT context. The main weakness in any strategy that would rely on the exceptions to the sui generis right is the narrow interpretation given to this regime in *Ryanair v PR Aviation*.[255] There, the defendant's screen scraping, i.e. the automated extraction of data from a website,[256] was considered to be in violation of Ryanair website's terms and conditions. In particular, the low-cost airline put in place an exclusive distribution system and prevented unauthorised websites to sell Ryanair flights.[257] The use of the website was limited to private, noncommercial purposes. The defendant's argument was

---

249 Database Directive, art 8.

250 Database Directive, art 8(1).

251 This is clear from the working of Article 8, especially if compared with Article 9 and the latter's use of the verb 'may.'

252 Any contractual provision that would be contrary to this right would be null and void (Database Directive, art 12).

253 This is made clear by the wording of Article 8, whereby: 'Member States may stipulate' as noted by David I Bainbridge, *Information Technology and Intellectual Property Law* (7th edn, Bloomsbury 2019) 242.

254 The Database Directive considers binding only the aforementioned right to insubstantial extraction and the right to perform those acts that are necessary to access the database and its normal use (the latter applies to original databases protected by copyright).

255 (n 230).

256 Marco Caspers and others, 'Baseline Report of Policies and Barriers of TDM in Europe' (2016) Future TDM D3.3+ 9.

257 The current version of the Terms and Conditions, as updated on 5 September 2018, no longer contains such provisions. See Ryanair General Terms & Conditions of Carriage, effective as of 9 September 2020 <www.ryanair.com/gb/en/useful-info/help-centre/terms-and-conditions>.

that what they did was covered by exceptions that contracts could not override. The CJEU held that if a database does not meet the requirements of originality or substantial investment, they are outwith the scope of the directive, and therefore the relevant exceptions cannot be invoked.[258] This decision can be criticised on three grounds. First, the directive's scope is identified by reference to the definition of database;[259] therefore, as long as the materials are independent, arranged systematically or methodically, and individually accessible, we are within the scope of the directive and the exceptions should be available. The assessments regarding originality and substantiality should not be conflated with the issue of the scope of protection. Second, making the exceptions unavailable to users of databases where neither substantial investment nor originality can be proved is unreasonable. Indeed, it would lead to recognising a stronger protection to those databases where the author did not put in place any intellectual effort or any meaningful investment. Finally, the main justification of the Database Directive is to stimulate investments in the database industry to bridge the gap between the US and the EU market.[260] This goal cannot be achieved applying *Ryanair* because this ruling incentivises the database makers not to invest significantly in obtaining, verifying, and presenting contents. By reducing investments, they can circumvent the database's user rights and exceptions. The joint operation of the obtaining-creating dichotomy and the *Ryanair* jurisprudence confirms the need to revitalise the sui generis rights and, in particular, its exceptions: otherwise, IoT companies and other database makers can accumulate vast amounts of data and increase their data power by contractual and technical means, thus cementing the death of ownership.

IoT data is of tremendous value especially when used to train the algorithms that constitute the IoT's hidden architecture. Much of their value comes from being secret.[261] Indeed, as seen in the previous chapter, an increasingly important role is played by the (ab)use of trade secrets on IoT's algorithms and machine data. The Trade Secrets Directive has clarified that, for a trade secret to subsist, the information has to be (i) not generally known or readily accessible, (ii) of commercial value because it is secret, and (iii) subject to reasonable steps to keep it secret.[262] One may argue that the information that is embodied in a Thing, being easily accessible by third parties, can be accessed or reverse engineered and is therefore not secret.[263] Accordingly, one may say, the data and the algorithms that are embodied in Things are not secret, as long as they can be easily accessed by means of reverse engineering or decrypted. However, courts have become, over

258 *Ryanair* (n 230) [49].
259 Database Directive, art 1(2).
260 Database Directive, recital 11.
261 This is not limited to IoT's algorithms. See more generally Guido Noto La Diega, 'Against the Dehumanisation of Decision-Making – Algorithmic Decisions at the Crossroads of Intellectual Property, Data Protection, and Freedom of Information' (2018) 9 JIPITEC 3.
262 TS Directive, art 2(1).
263 *Saltman Engineering v Campbell Engineering* (1948) 65 RPC 203.

time, more amendable to the idea of considering Thing-embedded algorithms as secret. In *Volkswagen v Garcia*,[264] the court e.g. granted an interim injunction to prevent the disclosure of an algorithm. This algorithm was embedded in a car's immobiliser, and the defendants had accessed it by reverse engineering a computer program that they had found online.[265] Whilst theoretical objections can be moved to the idea of IoT algorithms and machine data as trade secrets, pragmatically one needs to take account of the fact that IoT companies do keep this information secret, and this is part of its value. For example, the algorithm that allows Alexa to be a powerful tool of the 'Internet of Personalised Things' constitutes commercially valuable confidential information.[266]

Trade secret protection is dangerous because IoT companies could keep the information secret potentially forever. Although users may counter it by invoking exceptions and GDPR rights (e.g. right to be informed),[267] the likelihood that this happens in practice is limited due to the secrecy of these practices. Under Article 5 of the Trade Secrets Directive, user freedom can be ensured by a number of exceptions that allow the unauthorised acquisition, use, or disclosure of a trade secret. These exceptions are in place to ensure the interest of circulation of knowledge.[268] This is particularly the case with the exception 'for exercising the right to freedom of expression and information as set out in the Charter (of Fundamental Rights of the EU).'[269] Whilst the emphasis of the directive is on press freedom and media pluralism, these are not the only applications of freedom of expression and information that are protected as a human right in Europe. This is evidenced by the ECtHR jurisprudence that balances IP against higher values and, in particular, freedom of expression and information under Article 10 ECHR.[270] Although this case law regards copyright,[271] the same rationale applies to all IPRs, including trade secrets.[272] It is not by chance that *N.V. Televizier v The*

---

264 [2013] EWHC 1832.

265 The court did not consider *Saltman* and ignored the issue of whether, once decrypted, the algorithms could still be regarded as secret. Moreover, a crucial role was played by the practical consideration that the disclosure may have led to mass car theft. Nonetheless, *Volkswagen v Garcia* remains an important victory for those who consider IoT-embedded data and algorithms as secret.

266 Guido Noto La Diega and Cristiana Sappa, 'The Internet of Things at the Intersection of Data Protection and Trade Secrets. Non-Conventional Paths to Counter Data Appropriation and Empower Consumers' [2020] REDC 419.

267 GDPR, arts 13–14.

268 cf Andrea Ottolia, 'Il D. Lgs n. 63/18 Di Attuazione Della Direttiva Sulla Protezione Dei Segreti Commerciali Fra Tutela e Bilanciamenti' [2019] NLCC 1091.

269 TS Directive, art 5(a).

270 Peggy Ducoulombier, 'Interaction between Human Rights: Are All Human Rights Equal?' in Christophe Geiger (ed), *Research Handbook on Human Rights and Intellectual Property* (Edward Elgar 2015) 45–46.

271 Christophe Geiger and Elena Izyumenko, 'Shaping Intellectual Property Rights Through Human Rights Adjudication. The Example of the European Court of Human Rights' (2020) Centre for International Intellectual Property Studies Research Paper No 2020–02 44.

272 The nature of trade secrets is contested; they have been considered as a 'creature of contract, of tort, of property, or even of criminal law' (Lemley (n 46).).

Netherlands[273] – the first-ever ECHR case about the balance of IP and human rights – regarded Article 10.[274] The first 'balancing' rulings in the seventies and in the nineties did not find violations of Article 10.[275] The 'real breakthrough'[276] was in 2013, when the court started dealing with online copyright infringement and its impact on free flow of information in the digital environment. This change in direction started with the rulings in *Donald v France*[277] and *The Pirate Bay*.[278] The facts were quite different, the former dealing with the unauthorised publication of some photographs taken at a fashion show, the latter with a notorious file-sharing platform that enabled the illegal download of music, films, and computer games. Importantly, the court held that the applicants' convictions for copyright infringement constituted an interference with Article 10. The interference was not considered disproportionate as the expression the applicants were seeking to protect had commercial character.[279] This means that the abuse of IP, including trade secrets, to prevent an IoT user from utilising their Things for noncommercial purposes may be regarded as disproportionately interfering with freedom of expression.[280]

In considering the scope of the Trade Secrets Directive's freedom of expression exception, one needs to account for the ECtHR's practice to view IP 'as an exception to freedom of expression (which) must hence be narrowly interpreted.'[281] Even more progressive in its recognition of the limits of IP is the CJEU jurisprudence, which has been balancing IP and freedom of expression – in particular, freedom of information – in a way that allows the interpreter to requalify IP exceptions as proper user rights as opposed to mere 'exceptional' defences available only passively, should the rightsholder claim infringement.[282] The CJEU has been gradually recognising the importance of a fair balance between the rightsholders' interests and the competing rights and interests in the context of IP disputes that are examined 'mainly from the angle of fundamental rights.'[283] It follows that courts need to interpret trade secrets exceptions in a way that pursues a fair balance between the IPRs and the '*rights of the users* of protected subject matter.'[284]

---

273 App no 2690/65 [1968] Y B Eur Conv on H R 782.
274 Geiger and Izyumenko (n 272).
275 *D.G.P.N.V. v Netherlands*, App no 5178/71 (1976) 44 Eur Comm'n H R Dec & Rep 13; *Société Nationale de Programmes FRANCE 2 v. France*, App no 30262/96 [1997] Eur Comm'n on H R 15.
276 Geiger and Izyumenko (n 272) 52.
277 App no 36769/08 (ECtHR, 10 January 2013).
278 *Kolmisoppi v Sweden*, App no 40397/12 (ECtHR, 19 February 2013).
279 Geiger and Izyumenko (n 272). The other reason being that the information contained in the shared material did not contribute to the general debate of public interest.
280 cf *Akdeniz v Turkey*, App no 20877/10 (ECtHR, 11 March 2014).
281 Elena Izyumenko, 'The Freedom of Expression Contours of Copyright in the Digital Era: A European Perspective: The Freedom of Expression Contours of Copyright' (2016) 19 The Journal of World Intellectual Property 115.
282 ibid.
283 Case C-70/10 *Scarlet v SABAM*, Opinion of AG Cruz Villalón [5].
284 *Deckmyn* (n 148) [26], italics added.

As stated inter alia in *Deckmyn*[285] and elaborated in the literature,[286] IP and user rights should be regarded as having equal standing.

At first glance, more recent cases *Funke Medien*,[287] *Pelham*,[288] and *Spiegel Online*[289] would seem to go in the opposite direction. Indeed, they deny that member states can create exceptions beyond those listed in the relevant directives. This notwithstanding, these cases have been seen as the confirmation of the 'liberal, "*freedom-of-expression-driven*" approach of the CJEU'[290] to IP balancing. Accordingly, the awareness that 'freedom of expression and information give a substantive content to the rights of users'[291] must inform the understanding of the exceptions under all IP laws, including the Trade Secrets Directive. Therefore, I would opine that under the freedom of information exception, trade secrets cannot be used to prevent IoT users from handling their Things unencumbered, especially so as to allow them to understand how their Things work and to comprehend their underlying logic, including by accessing the Things' intangible components.

The prospect of relying on a combination of exceptions-user rights to regain control over one's Things is appealing. However, its potential to tackle the death of ownership in the IoT is thwarted by five factors. First, exceptions may counter only abuses that are perpetrated by means of IP rights. IoT companies can find ways to strategically bring their conduct outwith the scope of IP laws. If IP laws do not apply, IP exceptions will be unavailable, as was the case in *Ryanair v Aviation PR*.[292] In practice, most of IoT data is likely to fall outside the scope of the Database Directive, and IoT users are therefore unlikely to be able to invoke the relevant exceptions. Second, although IP law discourages rightsholders from using technological protection measures to compress the exceptions,[293] however, this may prove to be immaterial in practice. Indeed, the IoT is a high-speed and low-focus environment, and therefore technical defaults can influence user behaviour more than traditional legal rules. Third, contractual abuses may be tackled only by those exceptions that expressly override contracts. De lege ferenda, it is crucial to streamline all IP exceptions to render them binding. Fourth, IP excep-

285 ibid, referring to Case C-467/08 *Padawan v SGAE* [2011] ECDR 1.

286 Lionel Bently and Tanya Aplin, *Global Mandatory Fair Use: The Nature and Scope of the Right to Quote Copyright Works* (CUP 2020).

287 Case C-469/17 *Funke Medien v Germany* [2020] 1 WLR 1573 about the unauthorised communication to the public of periodic briefing reports on the operations of the federal armed forces abroad.

288 Case C-476/17 *Pelham v Hutter* ('Metall auf Metall') [2019] 7 WLUK 462 about music sampling.

289 Case C-516/17 *Spiegel Online GmbH v Beck* [2019] 7 WLUK 458 about hyperlinks, news reporting, quotation, and freedom of expression.

290 Geiger and Izyumenko (n 204) 286. The authors recognise, however, that whilst freedom of expression could be used to overcome a rigid approach to the three-step test and embrace an open-ended copyright exception, the CJEU did not go as far.

291 Izyumenko (n 282) 118.

292 (n 230).

293 Infosoc Directive, art 6(4); C-DSM Directive, art 17(9).

tions can do little to empower IoT users affected by factual control over the Thing, in particular over services and data. Abuses of data power are under increased scrutiny of antitrust authorities, but competition law remains unfit for these new forms of power.[294] The recent inquiry of the European Commission into the antitrust issues of the IoT confirmed this inadequacy.[295] It remains to be seen whether unconventional interventions such as the Data Governance Act, the Digital Services Act, and the Digital Markets Act will be able to curb IoT power. Finally, the viability of exception-focused strategies is limited by the issue of IP overlaps. The latter predates the IoT but is exacerbated by this sociotechnological phenomenon. To test the viability of the proposed exception-focused strategy, the next section will give a closer look at IP overlaps.

6.5 IP Overlaps and the Erosion of IP Exceptions in the 'Smart' World

The IoT provides an excellent illustration of the problem of the cumulation of rights. As IPRs overlap, any strategy aimed at countering the death of ownership by leveraging the potential of IP exceptions is called into question. Indeed, what constitutes an exception under one IP subsystem (e.g. copyright) may constitute infringement under another (e.g. design rights). The IoT ushers in an era of ubiquitous computing and ubiquitous IPRs. The more these rights expand, the more user rights contract.

Despite some similarities, the exceptions analysed in the previous section are rather diverse. Some are mandatory; others are left to the discretion of member states as to whether to implement them. Some are binding; others can be overridden contractually. Some cover commercial uses; others do not. Some are regarded as user rights; others are not.[296] The joint operation of overlapping IPRs covering virtually any aspect of a Thing and the misalignment between IP exceptions hampers any strategy to counter the death of ownership in the IoT by invoking IP exceptions.

The question of IP overlaps may be perceived as niche, but it is of great theoretical and practical importance.[297] Countless laws have been passed – and numerous rulings have been handed in – in the 310 years of the history of copyright legislation, from the Statute of Anne to the Copyright in the Digital Single

---

294 The shift in focus can be seen, e.g. in Case AT.39740 *Google Search* (C(2017) 4444 final.

295 'Antitrust: Initial Findings of Consumer IoT Sector Inquiry' (*European Commission*, 9 July 2021) <https://ec.europa.eu/commission/presscorner/detail/en/IP_21_2884>.

296 Even when a limitation to an IP right is qualified as an exception and not as a right, it should nonetheless be interpreted in a way that does not undermine its effectiveness and that takes into account the exception's purpose. In this sense, *Nintendo v BigBen* (n 218) [74].

297 As shown by the following in-depth analyses: Estelle Derclaye and Matthias Leistner, *Intellectual Property Overlaps: A European Perspective* (Hart 2011); Neil Wilkof and Shamnad Basheer (eds), *Overlapping Intellectual Property Rights* (OUP 2012); Tomkowicz (n 33); Nuno de Araújo Sousa e Silva, *The Ownership Problems of Overlaps in European Intellectual Property* (Nomos 2014).

Market Directive. These laws and rulings have enlarged the types of subject matters eligible for protection (e.g. databases),[298] widened and strengthened the owners' exclusive rights (e.g. the all-encompassing right of communication to the public),[299] and provided discrete IPRs for their protection (e.g. the new publishers' right that adds to already-existing author rights on the same subject matter).[300] The fact that the 'expansion of (IP) rights at the international level is more extensive than ever'[301] is at the root of this phenomenon and of the subsequent issue of overlaps. If a country wishes to be a member of the WTO, they have to accept to be bound by Agreement on Trade-Related Aspects of Intellectual Property Rights (TRIPS). This agreement obliges contracting states to protect all the rights covered by the treaty, that is, copyright and related rights,[302] trademarks,[303] geographical indications,[304] industrial designs,[305] patents,[306] topographies of integrated circuits,[307] and protection of undisclosed information.[308] The lack of adequate protection of these rights would expose the country to a breach of the TRIPS obligations falling under the jurisdiction of the WTO Dispute Settlement Body. Conversely, it is left to the states' discretion whether to introduce IP exceptions. If they do introduce them, they need to comply with the three-step test. As touched upon in the previous section, exceptions need to be limited to certain special cases, not to conflict with the normal exploitation of the work and not unreasonably prejudice the legitimate interest of the owner.[309] Whilst a fair and balanced interpretation of the three-step test could be put forward,[310] the WTO favours a strict interpretation that regards the limbs as cumulative.[311] The situation is worsened by the so-called TRIPS-plus provisions: free trade agreements that introduce stronger IP protection in exchange for trade opportunities.[312] TRIPS-plus provisions further tilt the IP balance in favour of rightsholders, especially those based in developed countries. This is exemplified by the data exclusivity provisions that, by allowing pharmaceutical test data submitted by companies to drug regulatory

---

298   Database Directive (although databases were arguably protected also before the directive; see Derclaye (n 247) 45).

299   We have seen above this phenomenon as epitomised by *Tom Kabinet* (n 97).

300   C-DSM Directive, art 15(1).

301   Wilkof and Basheer (n 298) ivii.

302   TRIPS, arts 9 ff.

303   TRIPS, arts 15 ff.

304   TRIPS, arts 22 ff.

305   TRIPS, arts 25 ff.

306   TRIPS, arts 27 ff.

307   TRIPS, arts 35 ff.

308   TRIPS, art 39.

309   See e.g. TRIPS art 13.

310   Christophe Geiger and others, 'Declaration. A Balanced Interpretation Of The "Three-Step Test" In Copyright Law' (2010) 1 JIPITEC 119.

311   WTO Panel, 'United States – Section 110(5) of the US Copyright Act' (2000) WT/DS160/R.

312   S Frankel, 'Challenging Trips-Plus Agreements: The Potential Utility of Non-Violation Disputes' (2009) 12 Journal of International Economic Law 1023.

authorities to remain secret, factually and substantially extend the duration and the scope of the monopoly granted by the relevant patent.[313] This is one of the reasons that a COVID patent waiver may not suffice and more courageous, open innovation models should be adopted.[314] Stronger and pervasive IPRs led to their overlaps becoming commonplace. This also depends on technological development producing a 'diversity of goods and services and ever-more powerful platforms to deliver them.'[315] Existing IP laws are often claimed not to be fit for these innovations, which typically leads to additional protection being provided in legislation or case law, with judicial expansions being often crystallised in legislation.[316]

The negative effects of this accumulation can be seen most clearly in the IoT, where virtually every aspect and component of even simple Things are protected by some form of IP. This risks neutralising the potential of IP exceptions because many of the acts covered by an IPR's exceptions constitute infringement of another IPR.[317] Most countries, including all EU countries, allow or even impose partial overlap and cumulation of IPRs.[318] There are three scenarios where IPRs overlap.[319] First, two (or more) rights may cover the entirety of the subject matter. Artistic works e.g. can be the domain of copyright, design, and trademarks. Second, the subject matters of the IPRs may overlap in part. This is the case with plant-related inventions that are protected by patents and plant breeders' rights.[320] Third, an article may be protected by a range of IPRs, but each of them protects different aspects of the article; e.g. a product's aesthetic aspects are covered by design rights, its functional aspects by patents.[321] In the IoT, all three scenarios occur. There are instances where the two sets of IP laws will dictate clear rules

313 Lisa Diependaele, Julian Cockbain and Sigrid Sterckx, 'Raising the Barriers to Access to Medicines in the Developing World – The Relentless Push for Data Exclusivity' (2017) 17 Developing World Bioethics 11.

314 Enrico Bonadio and Filippo Fontanelli, 'Push for COVID-19 Vaccine Patent Waiver Isn't a Panacea: But It Could Nudge Companies to Share' (*The Conversation*, 12 May 2021) <http://theconversation.com/push-for-covid-19-vaccine-patent-waiver-isnt-a-panacea-but-it-could-nudge-companies-to-share-160802>.

315 Wilkof and Basheer (n 298) ivi.

316 E.g. the US Digital Millennium Copyright Act 1998 codified the approach to secondary liability of ISPs set forth in *Religious Technology Center v Netcom Online Communications Services* 907 F Supp 1361 (ND Cal, 1995) as noted by Chris Reed (ed), *Computer Law* (7th edn, OUP 2012) 460.

317 Derclaye and Leistner (n 298) 92.

318 Estelle Derclaye, 'Overlapping Rights' in Rochelle Dreyfuss and Justine Pila (eds), *The Oxford Handbook of Intellectual Property Rights* (OUP 2018) 629.

319 This distinction is adapted by Wilkof and Basheer (n 298).

320 The overlap is partial because patent protection is geared towards the methods to breed the plants, and the patentability of plants as such is excluded unless 'the technical feasibility of the invention is not confined to a particular plant or animal variety' (Directive 98/44/EC of 6 July 1998 on the legal protection of biotechnological inventions ('Biotech Directive') [1998] OJ L 213/13, art 4(2)).

321 David Musker, 'The Overlap between Patent and Design Protection' in Neil Wilkof and Shamnad Basheer (eds), *Overlapping Intellectual Property Rights* (OUP 2012) 23.

on mutual exclusion. This is not a common occurrence. Usually, interplay and demarcation rules are unclear and more than one IP law will apply.[322] The resulting overlaps can be criticised due to their leading to uncertainty and overprotection.[323] Indeed, when overlaps occur – and in the IoT they are the rule rather than the exception – the 'strictest regime overrides the more generous one.'[324] In a context where the exceptions to the IPRs vary so greatly from one IP subsystem to another, this renders any strategy that centres on these exceptions unlikely to be successful, especially in an IoT world.

An in-depth analysis of IP overlaps is beyond the scope of this chapter. Three examples will suffice: (i) the cumulation of copyright and patents in protecting software, (ii) the troubled relationship between general copyright and special copyright in complex multimedia products, and (iii) the copyright-design interface.[325] They are, at once, the most relevant from an IoT perspective and the most topical in current IP jurisprudence. A particularly fitting scenario regards the copyright-patent interface in the protection of software.[326] At an international, European, and national level, attempts to draw a clear line between the domain of software copyright and software patents have not led to clarity.[327] In Europe, software is excluded from patentability only 'as such.'[328] This criterion of prevention of overlaps becomes irrelevant in an IoT world, where the boundaries between software and hardware are blurred.[329] In Europe, whilst there is a harmonized right to reverse engineer that users can invoke without the copyright holder's permission,[330] IoT companies may block it by qualifying it as patent

---

322 Araújo Sousa e Silva (n 298).

323 G Moschini and O Yerokhin, 'The Economic Incentive to Innovate in Plants: Patents and Plant Breeders' Rights' in Jay P Kesan (ed), *Agricultural Biotechnology and Intellectual Property: Seeds of Change* (CAB International 2007) 161.

324 Derclaye (n 319) 622.

325 However, similar considerations apply to the other overlaps. E.g. most countries do not have rules to resolve the issue in the copyright-trademark overlap, and since these regimes diverge (trademark law providing more limited exceptions), the stricter regime will prevail over the other, whose exceptions will be practically unavailable (see Ellen Gredley and Spyros Maniatis, 'Parody: A Fatal Attraction' (1997) 19 EIPR 339.).

326 Although patent law has not been harmonised at the EU level, it will be analysed because the lack of harmonisation is a key factor to consider when analysing the problem created by IP overlaps. EU harmonisation of patent law, including the streamlining of exceptions, would benefit the IoT.

327 Andrew P Bridges, 'Navigating the Interface Between Utility Patents and Copyrights' in Neil Wilkof and Basheer (eds), *Overlapping Intellectual Property Rights* (OUP 2012) 6.

328 European Patent Convention, art 52(2)(c). 'As such' means that computer programs that produce a further technical effect and have therefore technical character are not excluded. In Europe, software patents claims are typically drafted as claims to a computer-implemented invention, that is, a method performed by a computer, computer network, or other programmable apparatus where one or more of the features of the invention is realised by means of a computer program. European Patent Office (n 22) G, II, 3.6.

329 Noto La Diega, 'Software Patents and the Internet of Things in Europe, the United States and India' (n 31).

330 Software Directive, art 6.

infringement[331] since the relevant defences have not been harmonised.[332] E.g. in the UK there is no reverse engineering defence in patent infringement proceedings.[333] Equally, copyright holders' power to control derivative software is at odds with the right to patents derivative nonobvious inventions.[334] More generally, there are fewer and divergent exceptions in patent law, and this allows patent law to override copyright exceptions.[335] It has been noted that, consequently, software patent holders are in a stronger position compared to companies that hold copyright.[336] However, it has been overlooked that IoT companies may at the same time be patent holders and copyright holders; accordingly, they can leverage their multiple IPRs to neutralise IP exceptions. Law and economics studies have shown that the copyright-patent overlap is overprotective, anticompetitive, and undesirable,[337] with some commentators convincingly arguing for a resolution of the conflict by abolishing software copyright or significantly limiting its scope.[338] More moderate proposals[339] include a call for reconsidering the balance between freedom of use and protection of the right owner via a patent fair use defence that could be invoked irrespective of commercial motivations. A reform that would be necessary from an IoT perspective would be to make sure that patents and copyright provide for the same exceptions and that these are qualified as user rights.

The second scenario has to do with the relationship between software copyright and general copyright in multimedia products. The composite nature of Things has been mainly explored with regard to its amalgam of software, hardware,

---

331 When copyright and patents overlap, the infringement of the former will normally constitute an infringement also of the latter. Indeed, 'since copying copyright expressions includes copying the underlying ideas, the patent will typically be infringed' (Derclaye and Leistner (n 298) 93.).

332 In the UK e.g. there is a private use defence in patent infringement proceedings, but there is no homologous defence in copyright infringement proceedings (Patents Act 1977, s 60(5)(a); *BASCA* (n 179)). Conversely, in Austria there is no private use defence in patent infringement proceedings, but a copyright private use defence is available (Bundesgesetz über das Urheberrecht an Werken der Literatur und der Kunst und über verwandte Schutzrechte (Austria's Copyright Act), §§ 42, 42a, 42b; WIPO Standing Committee on the Law of Patents, 'Certain Aspects of National/Regional Patent Laws. Revised Annex II of Document SCP/12/3 Rev.2: Report on the International Patent System' (2020).).

333 Joachim Weyand and Heiko Haase, 'Patenting Computer Programs: New Challenges' (2005) 36 IIC 647, 653.

334 Gustavo Ghidini and Emanuela Arezzo, 'One, None or a Hundred Thousand: How Many Layers of Protection for Software Innovations?' in Josef Drexl (ed), *Research Handbook on Intellectual Property and Competition Law* (Edward Elgar 2008) 358.

335 Derclaye (n 319) 644.

336 Bridges (n 328) 16.

337 Christian Le Stanc, Gustavo Ghidini and Luis Mariano Genovesi, 'Logiciels Entre Droit d'Auteur et Brevet: Implications Juridiques et Economiques' in *Intellectual Property and Market Power* (Eudeba 2008) 309. However, there is no consensus on this, see Robert Hart, Peter Holmes and John Reid, 'The Economic Impact of Patentability of Computer Programs. Report to the European Commission' (2000) Intellectual Property Institute Study Contract ETD/99/B5–3000/E/106.

338 Le Stanc, Ghidini and Genovesi (n 338) 295; Ghidini and Arezzo (n 335) 372.

339 Martin Senftleben, 'Overprotection and Protection Overlaps in Intellectual Property Law – the Need for Horizontal Fair Use Defences' in Annette Kur and Vytautas Mizaras (eds), *The Structure of Intellectual Property Law: Can One Size Fit All?* (Edward Elgar 2011) 21.

service, and data. However, it goes beyond it. The analysis of *Tom Kabinet* has already shown that as e-books are composite products – computer programs and digitised literary works – the stronger protection afforded by general copyright law prevails, in that case rendering de facto irrelevant the principle of exhaustion on the basis of a non-IoT-friendly tangible-intangible dichotomy and an unjustifiably narrow interpretation of the concept of software.

Tom Kabinet is no isolated incident. In *Nintendo v PC Box*,[340] for the claimant's video games and consoles to work, they would have to exchange encrypted information, thus 'recognising' each other and confirming that the game was not counterfeit. Although the nature of this pairing mechanism was contested, Nintendo regarded it as a form of technological protection measures. Their circumvention is forbidden under the Infosoc Directive.[341] The defendant manufactured devices that enabled video games other than Nintendo and Nintendo-licensed games to be played on the claimant's consoles. The latter accused the former of thusly circumventing their technological protection measures. The defendant put forward two contentions. First, Nintendo's 'locks' could not be regarded as a technological measure because they were present both in the hardware of the console and in the video games. This argument was rejected by the CJEU that accepted the advocate general's broad interpretation of technological protection measure as including the application of an access control or protection process, such as encryption, scrambling, or other transformation of the work or other subject matter or a copy control mechanism.[342] Importantly, this interpretation was supported by the observation that 'the principal objective of (the Infosoc Directive) is to establish a high level of protection in favour, in particular, of authors, which is crucial to intellectual creation.'[343] Such an approach is at odds with a key tenet of copyright law, whereby copyright is a policy bargain, a delicate balance between the rightsholder's interests and competing private and public interests.[344] The second contention that PC Box put forward was that Nintendo's true purpose was to prevent the use of independent software and to compartmentalise markets by rendering games purchased in one geographical zone incompatible with consoles purchased in another.[345] The referring court itself had found that the effect of Nintendo's protective measures was not limited to allowing only Nintendo and Nintendo-licensed games to be played on Nintendo consoles; it 'prevented such games from being played on any other console, thus restricting interoperability and consumer choice.'[346] Accordingly, PC Box's devices would favour independent software and the internal market in a way that was lawful under the Software Directive and

---

340 (n 171).
341 Art 6.
342 *Nintendo v PC Box* (n 171) [27].
343 ibid [27]
344 See e.g. Rebecca Tushnet, 'Intellectual Property as Public Interest Mechanism' in Rochelle Dreyfuss and Justine Pila, *The Oxford Handbook of Intellectual Property Law* (OUP 2018) 95.
345 *Nintendo v PC Box* (n 171) [24].
346 AG Sharpston in *Nintendo v PC Box* (n 171) [25].

aligned to the principle of free movement of goods. In particular, the defendant was relying on the decompilation exception;[347] the decompilation was 'confined to the parts of the programme strictly necessary in order to ensure interoperability between Nintendo consoles and "homebrew" games which did not infringe any copyright or related right.'[348] The advocate general rejected this argument, and the CJEU followed suit. The starting point was that video games are complex multimedia products. Indeed, they constitute 'complex matter comprising not only a computer program but also graphic and sound elements.'[349] Since a video game is not (only) a computer program but is also a complex multimedia work, the Software Directive – and, with it, the decompilation exception – was seen as inapplicable. The advocate general argued that the Software Directive would take precedence over the Infosoc Directive 'only where the *protected material falls entirely within the scope* of the former.'[350] Such prevalence was justified by saying that, by reason of its exceptions, the protection afforded by the Software Directive is 'slightly less generous'[351] than that which the Infosoc Directive affords. From this, the controversial inference was that where 'complex intellectual works comprising both computer programs and other material are concerned – and where the two cannot be separated – . . . the *greater, and not the lesser, protection* should be accorded.'[352] Therefore, users of most Things could not rely on the Software Directive's exceptions because Things are composite and cannot fall exclusively within the scope of this directive.

The prevalence of stronger proprietary regimes over weaker, user-focused regimes in the event of overlaps is open to criticism. The propertarianism that underpins this approach is incompatible with the public interest dimension of IP. The CJEU recognises that technological protection measures must be proportionate and that their circumvention cannot be invoked to 'prohibit devices or activities which have a commercially significant purpose or use other than to circumvent the technical protection.'[353] However, the court bases this conclusion on the need to protect competitors' private interests rather than on the public interest. Although *Nintendo v PC Box* illustrates the prevalence of stronger general copyright on weaker special regimes, whose exceptions are neutralised, it also indicates that external considerations – the imperatives of free market – can play a role in limiting IP excesses, at least in principle. The next section will delve into the drawbacks of the reliance on external limitations.

Similar overprotection issues can be seen when reflecting on the copyright-design interface. As seen in the preceding passages, Things may be protected by

---

347 Software Directive, art 6.
348 AG Sharpston in *Nintendo v PC Box* (n 171) [32].
349 *Nintendo v PC Box* (n 171) [23].
350 AG Sharpston in *Nintendo v PC Box* (n 171) [32].
351 ibid [35].
352 ibid.
353 *Nintendo v PC Box* (n 171) [30].

both rights. This is all the more true after recent EU cases *Cofemel*[354] and *Brompton*.[355] In the former,[356] the court observed that the Berne Convention left it to the contracting parties to decide whether to exclude cumulative protection of designs under both copyright and registered designs (or industrial designs).[357] However, the CJEU opined that 'the EU legislature opted for a system in which the protection reserved for designs and the protection ensured by copyright are not mutually exclusive.'[358] This conclusion is inferred from both the Design Directive and the Community Design Regulation, whereby a registered design can also be protected in other ways, including copyright.[359] The court does not adequately account for the fact that design law leaves it to member states to decide the conditions under which this cumulation should operate, 'including the level of originality required.'[360] As to the Infosoc Directive, the argument appears even less convincing because it is based on Article 9, whereby this directive 'shall be without prejudice to provisions concerning . . . design rights.'[361] Being without prejudice does not necessarily mean that EU law provides, let alone mandates, a cumulation of IPRs.

Even more recently, in the *Brompton Bicycle* case,[362] the CJEU held that copyright protects original functional shapes. This case is in line with the rise of the role of copyright in protecting the three-dimensional aspect of Things, as seen in prior paragraphs.[363] Commentators have warned that 'cumulation may have adverse effects if it is absolute and unrestricted in such a way as to become the norm.'[364] With the IoT, cumulation is indeed becoming the norm. This is problematic because, on the one hand, IoT companies will be able to rely on copyright's longer protection; on the other hand, copyright exceptions may be overridden by relying on design rights. Indeed, as there are far fewer exceptions in the design right regimes, this mismatch can adversely affect the public interest that permeates copyright exceptions. This was the case, e.g. in a decision of the Tribunal de Grande Instance of Paris,[365] where the parody exception to copyright was deemed

---

354 (n 192).

355 C-833/18 *SI v Chedech/Get2Get* [2020] 6 WLUK 135.

356 (n 192).

357 Berne Convention, art 2(7).

358 *Cofemel* (n 192) [43].

359 Design Directive, art 17; Community Design Regulation, art 96.

360 Design Directive, art 17; Community Design Regulation, art 96(2).

361 Infosoc Directive, art 9.

362 (n 356).

363 We have seen the limits traditionally encountered by copyright when protecting 3D objects. A reflection on the impact of *Brompton Bicycle* (n 356) on the category of works of artistic craftsmanship is proposed by Neil Wilkof, 'The CJEU Brompton Bicycle Case: A UK View' (*The IPKat*, 5 July 2020) <https://ipkitten.blogspot.com/2020/07/the-cjeu-brompton-bicycle-case-uk-view.html>.

364 Daniel Inguanez, 'A Refined Approach to Originality in EU Copyright Law in Light of the ECJ's Recent Copyright/Design Cumulation Case Law' (2020) 51 IIC 797.

365 TGI Paris, 18 March 2005 [2005] Propriétés Intellectuelles 339.

unavailable because of the cumulation with design rights. Thus, design law ends up overriding 'the public-regarding aspects of copyright law.'[366]

The problems created by IP overlaps to exception-focused strategies are exacerbated in the IoT, where the overlaps become ubiquitous. *De lege ferenda*, this brings further evidence to support a change in IP laws to better govern the relationships between IP subsystems and ensure convergence between the regimes of exceptions.[367] Such convergence would be consistent with international law and, in particular, TRIPS and WTO case law.[368] An open-ended exception along the lines of fair use – as opposed to enumerated and rigid exceptions – may provide an effective way to prevent clashes and avoid overprotection of IP.[369] A study of the drafting history of the three-step test – whose narrow interpretation has led to the current EU approach to copyright exceptions – shows that the test can and ought to be regarded as a 'flexible formula (with) its roots in the Anglo-American copyright tradition.'[370] Properly understood, based on the *travaux préparatoires* of the WIPO Copyright Treaty,[371] the three-step test would allow states to devise new exceptions that are fit for the IoT and for the digital environment more generally.[372] A new international treaty establishing a core of minimum mandatory IP exceptions would provide further guarantees, compared to an approach that relies on judicial interpretation of existing provisions. In this sense, I would welcome as a positive effort the International Instrument on Permitted Uses in Copyright Law,[373] a project launched by the Max Planck Institute for Innovation and Competition in February 2021. If adopted, this treaty would counterbalance the traditional 'minimum protection' approach of international copyright law, and it would constitute a model that should be followed in other IP fields, else the problem of overlaps would not be resolved. A second-best and perhaps more pragmatic solution may be to retain the current approach and its reliance on exhaustive lists of exceptions, but either to provide the same exceptions across the board or to provide that the overlap will not prevent the application of all the exceptions that

---

366   Derclaye (n 319) 630.
367   Annette Kur, 'Harmonization of the Trademark Laws in Europe. An Overview' (1997) 28 IIC 1; Irene Calboli, 'Betty Boop and the Return of Aesthetic Functionality: A Bitter Medicine Against "Mutant Copyrights"?' (2014) 36 EIPR 80; Derclaye (n 319).
368   Senftleben (n 340).
369   A pragmatic solution may be to recognise that European fair use would lead to remuneration at least in some cases, as argued ibid 138.
370   ibid 8. The author refers to the observations submitted by the United Kingdom, Doc. S/13, *Records of the Intellectual Property Conference of Stockholm*, 11 June – 14 July 1967, Geneva: WIPO 1971, 630.
371   Agreed Statements concerning the WIPO Copyright Treaty adopted by the Diplomatic Conference on 20 December 1996, art 10.
372   The degree to which the three-step is flexible is contested because a fair use system is regarded as contrary to the first step of the test, namely, 'certain special cases.' See Herman Cohen Jehoram, 'Restrictions on Copyright and Their Abuse' (2005) 27 EIPR 359.
373   Reto M Hilty and others, 'International Instrument on Permitted Uses in Copyright Law' (2021) 52 IIC 62.

may come into play.[374] A third option would be the clarification that, despite the divergence, each IP subsystem safeguards the other subsystems' exceptions. This was the approach of the proposed Directive on Computer-Implemented Inventions.[375] This proposal is now defunct, but the IoT shows that a harmonised and balanced approach to the propertisation of software calls urgently for an EU intervention to prevent clashes and protect the public interest. Such an intervention should ensure the convergence between the regimes of exceptions so as to cover similar acts as well as being mandatory, binding, and include both commercial and noncommercial uses as long as they are fair. Since these processes of legislative harmonisation are slow, my hope is that human rights–infused interpretations of IP exceptions as proper user rights will prevail, thus achieving a more balanced and open approach to innovation governance.

This analysis shows the drawbacks of any attempts to find a solution to IP abuses within IP itself. Looking through the looking glass, external limitations could play a role in resolving the overlaps or at least reducing the clashes. We have seen above the slow and steady rise of freedom of expression to rebalance IP.[376] Other external limitations may come from the principle of free competition, including free movement of goods and services.[377] Whilst exceptions – as in-built

---

374 With regards to the copyright-patent interface in the protection of software, Gustavo Ghidini and Emanuela Arezzo, 'Dynamic Competition in Software Development: How Copyrights and Patents, and Their Overlapping, Impact on Derivative Innovation' (2013) 3 Queen Mary Journal of Intellectual Property 278. Similarly, with a call for a 'network of corresponding fair use limitations in different IP domains', Senftleben (n 340) 30.

375 Proposal for a Directive on the Patentability of Computer-Implemented Inventions (COM(2002)92 final – 2002/47(COD)) [23]: 'the exercise of a patent covering a computer-implemented invention should not interfere with the freedoms granted under copyright law to software developers by the provisions of the (Software) Directive.'

376 Although freedom of expression does not constitute, as such, a separate, open-ended defence in civil law, member states under *Funke Medien* (n 288), *Pelham* (n 289), and *Spiegel Online* (n 290). In the UK, alongside the statutory defences that mirror the Infosoc Directive and the Copyright in the Digital Single Market, there is an open-ended public interest defence whereby copyright infringement – and a breach of confidence – will not be enforced if the unauthorised use of the work or disclosure of the information was in the public interest, which includes freedom of expression. When freedom of expression is involved, interim injunctions are unlikely to be granted under *Kennard v Levis* [1983] FSR 346. However, English courts tend to deny that the Human Rights Act 1998, implementing the ECHR, imposes a different interpretation of the CDPA (*Ashdown v Telegraph Group Ltd* [2001] RPC 34). Whilst they accept that they must have particular regard for freedom of expression, they interpret the limit as not necessarily meaning that 'injunctive or any other relief in respect of the copyright claim should be refused' (*Imutran Ltd v Uncaged Campaigns Ltd* [2002] FSR 2 [33]). Some commentators thought that the Infosoc Directive had killed the public interest defence in copyright infringement proceedings (William Cornish and David Llewelyn, *Intellectual Property: Patents, Copyright, Trade Marks and Allied Rights* (5th edn, Sweet & Maxwell 2003) [13.5].) However, there is evidence that the defence is alive and well (Alexandra Sims, 'The Public Interest Defence in Copyright Law: Myth or Reality?' (2006) 28 EIPR 335.), and the potential conflict with EU law has become less relevant with the UK's withdrawal from the EU.

377 Derclaye (n 319) 650. The author notes that other external mechanisms include the misuse doctrine (US), the theory of abuse of rights (civil law countries), and the doctrine of public interest (UK).

limitations to the powers of the IP holder – are of little help, a more successful strategy may rely on the EU fundamental freedoms of movement. A good illustration of this point can be found in *Parfums Christian Dior SA v Evora BV*,[378] where the CJEU held that if the commercialisation of a product was lawful due to the exhaustion of the relevant trademarks, copyright could not be invoked to undermine the objectives of the single market.

I will therefore venture to test the potential of external limitations – and in particular of competition law – to curb IP excesses and counter the death of ownership in the IoT. Such potential, or lack thereof, is well illustrated by the antitrust control over the licensing of SEPs. This will be the focus of the next section.

6.6 Extra-IP Limitations: Are Standard Essential Patents on Fair, Reasonable, and Nondiscriminatory Terms IoT-FRANDly?

For IoT (inter)connectivity to work, standardisation is necessary. Standardisation bodies such as the European Telecommunications Standards Institute ('ETSI') require their members to commit to license their patents on fair, reasonable, and nondiscriminatory (FRAND) terms if they are essential to one of ETSI's standards. This mechanism is of utmost importance because it reduces the risk of litigation, thus incentivising the sharing of technologies and the growth of open, standardised, and interoperable innovation. For this system to work, it needs to be assisted by antitrust interventions to prevent SEP holders that are in a dominant position from abusing it by suing their technologies' implementers, despite their FRAND commitment. From this book's perspective, the reference to technology implementers is to be construed as referring to companies wanting to enter the IoT market. To untangle this complex issue, this section will focus on *Huawei v ZTE*[379] and its aftermath, including the 2020 decision of the UK Supreme Court in *Unwired Planet International v Huawei*.[380]

A SEP is a patent that protects technology that is essential to a standard.[381] The anticompetitive relevance of licensing practices in the field of SEPs is the currently most-debated area of friction between IP and competition law as well as the most relevant competition law issue in IoT regulation.[382] Although, in general,

---

378   Case C-337/95 [1997] ECR I-6013 [58].

379   Case C-170/13 *Huawei Technologies Co Ltd v ZTE Corp* [2015] Bus LR 1261.

380   *Unwired Planet International Ltd and another v Huawei Technologies (UK) Co Ltd and another* [2020] UKSC 37.

381   European Commission, 'Communication "Setting out the EU Approach to Standard Essential Patents"' (2017) COM/2017/712 final 1.

382   Jason R Bartlett and Jorge L Contreras, 'Rationalizing FRAND Royalties: Can Interpleader Save the Internet of Things' (2017) 36 Review of Litigation 285; Beatriz Conde Gallego and Josef Drexl, 'IoT Connectivity Standards: How Adaptive Is the Current SEP Regulatory Framework?' (2019) 50 IIC-IIC 135; Luke McDonagh and Enrico Bonadio, 'Standard Essential Patents and the Internet of Things' (2019) European Parliamenti (JURI); Rupprecht Podszun, 'Standard Essential Patents and Antitrust Law in the Age of Standardisation and the Internet of Things: Shifting

it is still 'controversial whether the (IP)-antitrust interface should be viewed as a conflict or a finalistic convergence,'[383] it would seem that from the viewpoint of SEP abuses, IP and competition law diverge. Engaging with SEPs is pivotal to understanding the economic relevance of patents more generally, as SEPs are the most valuable type of patents. Indeed, they are more frequently traded, more frequently litigated, more frequently renewed, and more frequently cited as prior art compared to non-SEP patents.[384]

If SEPs are not adequately governed, IoT standardisation cannot be achieved. It is not an exaggeration to say that '[w]ithout access to SEPs the whole IoT would not work.'[385] European organisations play an active role in the development of standards. As seen in Chapter 1, standardisation is a form of self-regulation of the IoT. European standard setting 'may serve to ameliorate the problems of over-lapping IPRs in those industries in which IP is most problematic for innovation, particularly semiconductors, software, and telecommunications,'[386] that is, the sectors that are key to the IoT. Under the EU Standardisation Regulation, a standard consists of technical specifications, 'adopted by a recognised standardisation body, for repeated or continuous application, with which compliance is not compulsory.'[387] A technical specification, in turn, is a document that prescribes technical requirements to be fulfilled by a product, process, service, or system.[388] The most important of these requirements, especially from an IoT perspective, is the laying down of the characteristics required of a product and of a service, including levels of quality, performance, and interoperability.[389] There are several standard-developing organisations, from the international level through the European level to the national one.[390] The European standardisation organisations are the European Committee for Standardisation (CEN), the European Committee

---

Paradigms' (2019) 50 IIC 720; Francesca Gennari, 'Internet Protocol Standards for IoT Interoperability in the House. Open Issues in EU Competition Law' in Carlos A Iglesias and others (eds), *Intelligent Environments 2020* (IOS 2020) 95.

383 Giuseppe Colangelo and Roberto Pardolesi, 'Intellectual Property, Standards, and Antitrust: A New Life for the Essential Facilities Doctrine? Some Insights from the Chinese Regulation' in Gustavo Ghidini, Hanns Ullrich and Peter Drahos (eds), *Kritika: Essays on Intellectual Property*, vol 2 (Edward Elgar 2017).

384 Tim Pohlmann and Knut Blind, 'Landscaping Study on Standard Essential Patents (SEPs)' (2016) IPlytics GmbH and TU Berlin 2.

385 Podszun (n 385) 730.

386 Mark A Lemley, 'Intellectual Property Rights and Standard-Setting Organizations' (2002) 90 California Law Review 1889, 1892.

387 Regulation (EU) No 1025/2012 of 25 October 2012 on European standardisation, amending Council Directives 89/686/EEC and 93/15/EEC and Directives 94/9/EC, 94/25/EC, 95/16/EC, 97/23/EC, 98/34/EC, 2004/22/EC, 2007/23/EC, 2009/23/EC and 2009/105/EC and repealing Council Decision 87/95/EEC and Decision No 1673/2006/EC [2012] OJ L 316/12, art 2(1).

388 Standardisation Regulation, art 2(4).

389 Standardisation Regulation, art 2(4)(a), (c).

390 'International standardisation body' means the International Organisation for Standardisation (ISO), the International Electrotechnical Commission (IEC), and the International Telecommunication Union (ITU). The UK's national standardisation body is the British Standards Institution (BSI).

for Electrotechnical Standardisation (Cenelec), and the ETSI.[391] The focus of this section will be on the latter because *Huawei v ZTE*[392] – the leading EU authority on SEPs – regards a standard adopted by ETSI.

In their ensuring interoperability, connectivity, and safety of technologies, standards are pivotal to the IoT.[393] These standards frequently refer to technologies that are protected by patents. A patent is essential to a standard 'if it is not possible on technical grounds to make equipment which complies with the standard without infringing the intellectual-property right.'[394] Examples of SEPs that are instrumental to the IoT include patents on Wi-Fi and Bluetooth. More than 23,500 patents have been declared essential to GSM and 3G.[395] Thanks to the 5G standard, currently being developed, users will enjoy interoperable, high-performance, and affordable Things.[396] The share of declared SEPs from Chinese and Korean companies has been growing over time, reflecting their role in the telecommunications sector and the global economy more generally.[397] With currently 334,680 SEPs,[398] standardised patented technologies make interconnectivity, and therefore the IoT, a reality.

IoT companies face a dilemma. In order to maximise the potential for value extraction, they may be inclined to exclude everyone from their closed proprietary systems. This strategy risks transforming the IoT into a noninteroperable 'Internet of Silos'; without seamless data flows and interoperability, the IoT will fail – and proprietary IoT companies will fail with it. However, the prospect of licensing patents that are essential to standards on an industry-wide scale provides an incentive for patent holders not to leverage their monopolies to prevent the standards from being available to all for public use.[399] To this end, ETSI and other standard setting organisations develop IP policies, demanding that their members declare whether their patented invention is essential to a standard and commit to licensing it on FRAND terms.[400] Other standard-developing organisations do not require their members to commit to a license at all; others require default license commitments under royalty-free terms or non-assertion agreements. A limited number

---

391 Annex I to the Standardisation Regulation.

392 (n 380).

393 CEN and Cenelec, 'Standard Essential Patents and Fair, Reasonable and Non-Discriminatory (FRAND) Commitments' (2016); European Commission, 'Communication "Setting out the EU Approach to Standard Essential Patents"' (n 384).

394 ETSI IPR Policy, Clause 15.6.

395 Alison Jones, 'Standard Essential Patents: FRAND Commitments, Injunctions and the Smartphone Wars' (2014) 10 European Competition Journal 5.

396 Frederik Nilsson, 'Appropriate Base to Determine a Fair Return on Investment: A Legal and Economic Perspective on FRAND' [2017] GRUR International 1017.

397 Pohlmann and Blind (n 387) 1.

398 ETSI's database <https://ipr.etsi.org/>.

399 Chryssoula Pentheroudakis and Justus A Baron, 'Licensing Terms of Standard Essential Patents. A Comprehensive Analysis of Cases' (2017) RC Science for Policy Report EUR 28302 EN 10.

400 See e.g. ETSI Intellectual Property Rights Policy, Annex 6 to Rules of Procedure, 4 December 2019.

of organisations rely on patent pools.[401] The focus of this section is on the ETSI model. Once a standard is established and the holders of the relevant SEPs commit to license them on FRAND terms, the technology included in the standard should be available to any potential user of the standard. What is FRAND – especially which royalties are fair and reasonable – is open to debate. The vagueness of these concepts made commentators observe that '[w]ithout some idea of what those terms are, reasonable and non-discriminatory licensing loses much of its meaning.'[402] Whilst SEP holders allege that technology users free ride on their innovation, there is evidence that the former charge excessive licensing fees based on weak patent portfolios and use litigation threats as a negotiation tool.[403] This conflict is worsened in the IoT in light of the relational black box as presented in Chapter 1. As noted in a European Commission report, the evolution of the IoT, with its need for wider connectivity, has led to a variety of SEP owners and implementers with different business models and to greater diversity of licensing practices.[404] The IoT's diversity is exemplified by the large numbers of alliances and consortia that try to shape IoT standardisation, e.g. the Industrial Internet Consortium, Open Interconnect, Thread, and Allseen.[405] This diversity is making it 'more difficult to identify a consensual interpretation of FRAND licensing principles,'[406] which is in turn leading to a proliferation of disputes that can be framed as patent holdup. *Patent holdup* refers to the practice of waiting for a company to include a standardised technology in their products and either seeking remedies or imposing a settlement because, once the technology has been implemented, 'it is too late for the company to change course.'[407] The most common form of patent holdup is when patent holders that had made FRAND commitments seek injunctive relief to exclude willing licensees.[408] Another IoT-related issue is that it is not clear whether SEP holders can decide to demand that the licensee be the end-product manufacturer as opposed to the supplier of the relevant component. In November 2020, the Düsseldorf Regional Court asked this question to the CJEU in *Nokia v Daimler*,[409] as Nokia refused to license its SEP to the suppliers of connectivity components for connected cars and required to license it only to car manufacturer

---

401 Pohlmann and Blind (n 387) 2.
402 Lemley (n 389) 1891.
403 European Commission, 'Communication "Setting out the EU Approach to Standard Essential Patents"' (n 384) 2.
404 Pentheroudakis and Baron (n 403) 10.
405 Aref Meddeb, 'Internet of Things Standards: Who Stands out from the Crowd?' (2016) 54 IEEE Communications Magazine 40.
406 Pentheroudakis and Baron (n 403) 10.
407 Colleen V Chien, 'Holding Up and Holding Out' (2014) 21 Michigan Telecommunications & Technology Law Review 1.) In other words, holdup arises when a patent owner extracts 'a larger royalty ex post than it could have obtained in an arm's length transaction ex ante' (Thomas F Cotter, Erik Hovenkamp and Norman Siebrasse, 'Demystifying Patent Holdup' (2019) 76 Washington & Lee Law Review 1501.).
408 Sonia Kuester Pfaffenroth, Peter J Levitas and Dylan S Young, 'DOJ Changing Its Antitrust Approach to FRAND and SEPs' (2019) 31 IP & Technology Law Journal 1.
409 LG Düsseldorf, 26 November 2020–4c O 17/19 [2021] MMR 276.

Daimler. As Things are inherently composite, and in light of the relational black box, it is to be hoped that the CJEU decides in favour of Daimler. Indeed, to allow SEP holders to require a license at every level of the supply chain would be in violation of both the principle of exhaustion and Article 102 TFEU.

In the US, the prevalent approach is that SEP enforcement – including patent holdup and injunctions against technology users – should not be regarded as an antitrust violation.[410] There seems to be some divergence between the Department of Justice, against antitrust interventions in these scenarios, and the Federal Trade Commission (FTC), more open to them.[411] However, *FTC v Qualcomm*,[412] a case that the FTC was using to affirm the antitrust relevance of SEP abuses, has been adjudicated in favour of the modem chips monopolist.[413] Although in theory in the EU the antitrust relevance of SEP abuses is not contested, in practice the reasons of property tend to prevail. This means that the distance between the US and the EU is more apparent than real. This also means that the death of ownership does not equate to the death of property. The right to property is as strong as it has always been, as illustrated by *Huawei v ZTE*.[414]

Huawei v ZTE deserves a closer look for a twofold reason. First, it is the leading EU authority in the field of antitrust control over SEP licensing.[415] Second, it exemplifies the CJEU's habit to, on the one hand, declare that IP must be balanced with other fundamental rights under the Charter of Fundamental Rights of the EU and the ECHR and, on the other hand, to refer to fundamental rights as a mere rhetoric device to strengthen 'already strong IP protection.'[416] This ruling directly

---

410 See Terrell McSweeny, 'Holding the Line on Patent Holdup: Why Antitrust Enforcement Matters' (*FTC*, 21 March 2018) <www.ftc.gov/public-statements/2018/03/holding-line-patent-holdup-why-antitrust-enforcement-matters>.

411 Kuester Pfaffenroth, Levitas and Young (n 412).

412 *Federal Trade Commission v Qualcomm Incorporated*, No 19–16122, D.C. No 5:17-cv-0020-LHK (9th Cir., August 11, 2020).

413 The FTC contended that Qualcomm violated the Sherman Act, 15 U.S.C. §§ 1, 2, by unreasonably restraining trade in and unlawfully monopolising the code division multiple access (CDMA) and premium long-term evolution (LTE) cellular modern chip markets. The breach of the SEP commitments played an important role in this conduct.

414 (n 380); Roberto Grasso, 'Selected Issues in SEP Licensing in Europe: The Antitrust Perspective' in Ashish Bharadwaj, Vishwas H Devaiah and Indranath Gupta (eds), *Complications and Quandaries in the ICT Sector: Standard Essential Patents and Competition Issues* (Springer 2018) 79.

415 Timothy McIver, Andrea Pomana and Judith Schmidt, 'Between Patent Protection and Abuse of Dominance: Highest EU Court Issues Landmark Decision on Standard-Essential Patents' (2015) 36 ECLR 533; Markus Gampp, 'Huawei v ZTE – CJEU Landmark Decision Provides New Ground Rules for Asserting Standard-Essential Patents in Europe.' (2015) 31 CLS Rev 810; Reto M Hilty and Peter R Slowinski, 'Standardessentielle Patente – Perspektiven außerhalb des Kartellrechts' (2015) 64 GRUR International 781.

416 Tuomas Mylly, 'The Constitutionalization of the European Legal Order: Impact of Human Rights on Intellectual Property in the EU' in Christophe Geiger (ed), *Research Handbook on Human Rights and Intellectual Property* (Edward Elgar 2015) 104. *Contra*, Peter Oliver and Christopher Stothers, 'Intellectual Property Under the Charter: Are the Court's Scales Properly Calibrated?' (2017) 54 Common Market Law Review 517, 564.

impacts the extent to which external limitations can be invoked to re-empower the IoT user affected by the death of ownership.

Amongst other SEPs, Huawei owns the patent 'Method and apparatus of establishing a synchronisation signal in a communication system'[417] and notified it to ETSI as essential to 'Long Term Evolution,' a wireless broadband communication standard.[418] This notification included, as per ETSI's IPR Policy, the commitment to license the patent on FRAND terms.[419] ZTE, the defendant, marketed products equipped with software linked to the aforementioned standard. Therefore, they engaged in negotiations with Huawei by indicating the royalty which they considered fair and reasonable to reach a cross-licensing agreement.[420] Although the agreement was not finalised, ZTE kept marketing the products at issue. It followed that Huawei brought an action for infringement seeking a prohibitory injunction, account of profits, delivery-up, and damages.[421] The Landgericht Düsseldorf (Court of First Instance) decided to stay the proceedings and ask the CJEU whether Huawei's conduct qualified as an abuse of dominant position under Article 102 TFEU. Such an abuse occurs when a dominant undertaking resorts to methods different from those governing normal competition, thus (i) hindering the maintenance of the degree of competition still existing in the market where competition is weakened because of the presence of the dominant undertaking, or (ii) hindering the growth of that competition.[422] A dominant position is:

> [A] position of *economic strength* enjoyed by an undertaking which enables it to *prevent effective competition* being maintained on the relevant market by affording it the power to *behave to an appreciable extent independently* of its competitors, customers and ultimately of its consumers.[423]

On the abusive qualification of Huawei's conduct, two views could be taken. On the one hand, in line with the European Commission's position in *Samsung/UMTS*,[424] to seek an injunction when the defendant shows willingness to negotiate a license would constitute an abuse of dominant position, regardless of whether the parties could not agree on the content of certain clauses in the licensing agreement,

---

417 European Patent EP 2090050 B 1/.

418 LTE is a standard for wireless broadband communication for mobile devices and data terminals. See 'ETSI – 4G – Long Term Evolution' (*ETSI*) <www.etsi.org/technologies/mobile/4g>.

419 *Huawei v ZTE* (n 380) [22]; ETSI Intellectual Property Rights Policy, Clause 6.1.

420 *Huawei v ZTE* (n 380) [23], [24].

421 EPC, art 64, on the rights of the European patent owner and the applicability of national law to infringement proceedings; Patentgesetz (PatG or Germany's Patent Act), § 139 on the injunction (*Unterlassung*).

422 Case 85/76 *Hoffmann-La Roche v Commission* [1979] ECR 461 [91].

423 ibid [38].

424 Case AT.39939 *Samsung* C(2014)2891 final [2014] OJ C 350/8. Samsung had sought injunctive relief in various member states' courts against competing mobile device makers based on alleged infringements of certain of its patent rights which it has declared essential to implement European mobile telephony standards.

including the royalty.[425] On the other hand, the Bundesgerichtshof (Germany's Federal Court of Justice)[426] held that this conduct would be abusive only under certain circumstances. First, the defendant must have made an unconditional offer to conclude a licensing agreement not limited exclusively to cases of infringement. Second, the defendant must account for past acts of use and to pay the sums resulting therefrom.[427] The first view relied on a pro-competitive approach to IP, the second view, a pro-proprietary one. The CJEU decided to espouse the latter approach on the following grounds.

As *Volvo*,[428] *Magill*,[429] and *IMS Health*[430] exemplify, it is settled case law that the exercise of an IP can qualify as an abuse of dominant position in 'exceptional circumstances.'[431] The essential facility doctrine[432] set forth in these cases means that a refusal to grant an IP licence may constitute an abuse when:

(i) The undertaking requesting a licence intends to offer new products for which there is potential consumer demand;
(ii) No objective considerations justify a refusal to license;
(iii) Through the refusal, the IP holder reserves the market to itself, thus eliminating all competition.[433]

The difference between this jurisprudence and the current dispute does not escape the court. First, SEPs are, by definition, 'essential,' as opposed to normal patents, in which case excluded third parties can 'manufacture competing products

---

425 The Commission accepted legally binding commitments by Samsung whereby the company will not seek injunctions in Europe on the basis of its SEPs for smartphones and tablets against licensees who sign up to a specified licensing framework. Under this framework, any dispute over what are FRAND terms for the SEPs in question will be determined by a court, or, if both parties agree, by an arbitrator. Thus, 'Samsung will not be able to seek injunctions on the basis of its Mobile SEPs against any potential licensee willing to enter into a licence agreement on FRAND terms and conditions' (*Samsung* (n 425) [19]).
426 Urteil 6 May 2009 – KZR 39/06 (*Orange Book*).
427 *Huawei v ZTE* (n 380) [30]–[33].
428 Case 238/87 *Volvo AB v Erik Veng (UK) Ltd* [1988] ECR 6211 about the refusal by the proprietor of a registered design to grant to third parties a licence for the supply of parts.
429 Joined Cases C-241/91 P and C-242/91 P *Radio Telefis Eireann v Commission* [1995] ECR I-743 on the refusal to grant a copyright licence regarding TV guides in Ireland.
430 C-418/01 *IMS Health v NDC Health* [2004] ECR I-5039 about the refusal to grant a copyright licence regarding a database.
431 *Volvo* (n 429) [9]; *Magill* (n 430) [50]; *IMS Health* (n 431) [35].
432 This doctrine was developed with regards to the owners of physical facilities or infrastructure, although it can apply to intangible facilities, such as IP. Pursuant to this doctrine, the owner may, by virtue of this facility or infrastructure, have a dominant position on a market, and the refusal to give access to it to competitors on nondiscriminatory terms may constitute an abuse under Article 102 TFEU. See *Sealink/B&I* [1992] 5 CLMR 255.
433 See Thomas F Cotter, 'Intellectual Property and the Essential Facilities Doctrine' (1999) 44 The Antitrust Bulletin 211; Roberto Pardolesi and Massimiliano Granelli, 'Licenza Obbligatoria Ed Essential Facilities Nell'antitrust Comunitario' (2004) 2 Riv dir ind 323; Colangelo and Pardolesi (n 386).

without recourse to the patent concerned and without compromising the essential functions of the product in question.'[434] It follows that SEP holders can prevent competitors' Things from appearing or remaining on the market and reserve to themselves their manufacture. Second, FRAND commitments create a legitimate expectation that the SEP holder will grant a FRAND licences. Therefore, 'a refusal by the proprietor of the SEP to grant a licence on those terms may, in principle, constitute an abuse.'[435] This defence can be raised in infringement proceedings if the claimant refuses to grant a FRAND licence. There is disagreement, however, as to what is required for a term to be FRAND.

To resolve the disagreement as to the meaning of 'FRAND,' *Huawei v ZTE* set forth a procedure that the parties must comply with to achieve a fair balance of interests. In elaborating on the balance, the CJEU referred to the EU Charter of Fundamental Rights and, in particular, to Article 17(2) on the protection of IP and Article 47 on the right to an effective remedy. Both rights can be invoked by the SEP holder against technology implementers. Surprisingly, the court ignores the competing fundamental rights that could play a role in rebalancing the protection of IP. In particular, the right to conduct a business,[436] the right to consumer protection,[437] and freedom of expression.[438] Similarly, the ruling disregards that, whilst protecting property, the charter recognises that the law can limit it on public interest grounds.[439] One may object that the public interest limitation is expressly stated with regard to property, and it is not repeated in paragraph 2 that cryptically provides, 'Intellectual property shall be protected.'[440] However, the rules on property are increasingly applied to IP, at least by analogy.[441] *Luksan*[442] e.g. referred not only to Article 17(2) but also to the first paragraph of the provision, whereby one may be deprived of one's possessions, if this is in the public interest. If one rejects the qualification of IP as property, limitations would nonetheless stem from Articles 52 and 54 of the EU Charter. Under the former, limitations to the Charter rights may be made if they are proportionate, necessary, and 'genuinely meet objectives of general interest recognised by the Union or the need to protect the rights and freedoms of others.'[443] In *ZZ (France)*,[444] the CJEU confirmed that

434 *Huawei v ZTE* (n 380) [50].

435 ibid [53].

436 EU Charter, art 16. The AG himself had noted that a SEP injunction 'places a significant restriction on (the freedom to conduct business) and is therefore capable of distorting competition' (Opinion of AG Wathelet in *Huawei v ZTE* (n 380) [59]). The CJEU overlooked this point.

437 EU Charter, art 38.

438 EU Charter, art 11.

439 EU Charter, art 17(1).

440 See Christophe Geiger, 'Intellectual Property Shall Be Protected!? Article 17 (2) of the Charter of Fundamental Rights of the European Union: A Mysterious Provision with an Unclear Scope' (2009) 31 EIPR 113.

441 Opinion of AG Wathelet in *Huawei v ZTE* (n 380) [66], fn 41; *R. (on the application of British American Tobacco UK Ltd) v Secretary of State for Health* [2016] EWCA Civ 1182.

442 Case C-277/10 *Martin Luksan v Petrus van der Let* [2013] ECDR 5 [68].

443 EU Charter, art 52(1).

444 Case C-300/11 *ZZ (France) v Secretary of State for the Home Department* [2013] QB 1136.

Article 52 permits limitations on the exercise of the right to an effective remedy.[445] This right includes the right to an injunction.[446] The advocate general in *Huawei* confirmed that this provision can be leveraged also to introduce limitations to IP, although this point was overlooked by the court.[447] The right to conduct business, consumer protection, and freedom of expression can justify limitations either as 'general interest' or as 'rights and freedoms of others.' Under Article 54 of the Charter, the abuse of rights is prohibited. This doctrine is popular in civil law jurisdictions, and it prevents rightsholders from using their rights to impinge in third parties' rights to a greater extent than provided by the law.[448] This means that SEP holders cannot weaponise their IP to engage in activities aimed at the limitation of the Charter rights and freedoms beyond what the Charter allows.[449] None of these considerations figure in the court's reasoning, which – whilst declaring the importance of a fair balance – focused only on the proprietary interests of the SEP holder. Indeed, the CJEU used the Charter to argue that a high level of IP protection and effective enforcement must be ensured. Accordingly, it held the fact that any use of the patent must be preceded by a license and that FRAND commitments 'cannot negate the substance of the rights guaranteed to that proprietor.'[450] This is not an isolated incident. A recent analysis of the EU case law has indeed showed that 'Article 17(2) (is) essential in order to strengthen the discipline of intellectual property protection.'[451] It could be said that the more user ownership dies, the more the right to property thrives. In an IoT world, where standards are vital and each comprises countless SEPs, this imbalanced stance is not socially just as it prevents smaller IoT business and newcomers from entering the market while reducing consumer freedoms.

In *Huawei v ZTE*, the CJEU does not regard Article 102 as a source of fundamental rights that the defendant could rely on. Instead, it regards it as the source

---

445 This was also noted by the AG, who, however, seemed to give more importance to the right of access to the courts rather than Article 52, despite the statement of principle whereby 'the Charter does not create a hierarchy among the fundamental rights which it recognises' (Opinion of AG Wathelet in *Huawei v ZTE* (n 380) [67]).

446 Case C-314/12 *UPC Telekabel Wien GmbH v Constantin Film Verleih GmbH and Wega Film-produktionsgesellschaft mbH* [2014] Bus LR 541 [63].

447 Opinion of AG Wathelet in *Huawei v ZTE* (n 380) [66], fn 41, that refers, by analogy, to Case 44/79 *Hauer v Land Rheinland-Pfalz* [1979] ECR 3727, where it was held that the interference in the right to property stemming from the EU rules that had prevented a German citizen from planting new vines on her land were justified in the public interest.

448 In Scots law, that is a mixed common-civil law system, the *aemulatio vicini* – a doctrine aimed at preventing neighbours from abusing their property rights (e.g. by depriving them of light in *Ross v Baird* (1829) 7 S 361) – can be regarded as a limited abuse of rights doctrine. See Elspeth Reid, 'Strange Gods in the Twenty-First Century: The Doctrine of Aemulatio Vicini' in Elspeth Reid and David Carey Miller (eds), *A Mixed Legal System in Transition: T. B. Smith and the Progress of Scots Law* (EUP 2005) 239.

449 EU Charter, art 54.

450 *Huawei v ZTE* (n 380) [59].

451 Alain Strowel, 'Copyright Strengthened by the Court of Justice Interpretation of Article 17(2) of the EU Charter of Fundamental Rights' in Oreste Pollicino, Giovanni M Riccio and Marco Bassini (eds), *Copyright and Fundamental Rights in the Digital Age* (Edward Elgar 2020) 28.

of a limited obligation for the SEP holder to 'comply with specific requirements when bringing actions against alleged infringers.'[452] Therefore, it would constitute an abuse if the SEP holder brought an action for a prohibitory injunction or for the recall of products 'without notice or prior consultation with the alleged infringer,'[453] regardless of whether the latter has already used the SEP. Instead of the flexible and balanced approach of the European Commission in *Samsung*[454] and its focus on the defendant's willingness to negotiate, the court opts for a rather-rigid and imbalanced step-by-step procedure that the parties are expected to follow to escape liability (the '*Huawei* protocol'). The steps are as follows.

(i) The SEP holder has to alert the technology implementer of the alleged infringement by identifying the SEP and specifying the way in which it has been infringed.[455]

(ii) It is for the alleged infringer to express its willingness to conclude a licensing agreement on FRAND terms.[456]

(iii) The SEP holder has to present a specific written offer for a FRAND licence, in accordance with the undertaking given to the standardisation body. This has to include the amount of the royalty and how it has been calculated.[457] The court justifies this by noting that the SEP holder has access to previous agreements and is better placed to check whether the offer is nondiscriminatory.[458] *De lege ferenda*, it would be important that transparency is ensured: if these agreements were to be made public, the implementer would be in a better position to judge which terms are nondiscriminatory.

(iv) The implementer has to respond to the offer diligently, in accordance with recognised commercial practices in the field, and in good faith. Delaying tactics would be expression of bad faith.[459] In case of nonacceptance, the counteroffer must be prompt, specific, in writing, and FRAND.[460]

(v) If the rightsholder rejects it, the alleged infringer has to provide appropriate security to cover for the past acts of use of the SEP, and an account must be rendered of those acts.

(vi) Optionally, an independent third party will be appointed to determine the amount of the royalties.[461]

It is for national courts to refer to the criteria of the so-called Huawei protocol 'insofar as they are relevant, in the circumstances, for the purpose of resolving

452 ibid [59].
453 ibid [60].
454 (n 425).
455 *Huawei v ZTE* (n 380) [61, [62].
456 ibid [63].
457 ibid.
458 ibid [64].
459 ibid [65].
460 ibid [66].
461 ibid [68].

the dispute.'[462] The decision of the CJEU is affected by the drawbacks of the positions of both the European Commission and the Bundesgerichtshof. On the one hand, it is affected by the same lack of certainty of the former, as the criteria set forth appear to be of merely advisory nature.[463] This was confirmed in *Unwired Planet v Huawei*,[464] where the UK Supreme Court was asked whether courts should refuse to grant a SEP injunction on grounds of noncompliance with the *Huawei* protocol. The Supreme Court rejected 'the argument that the CJEU's scheme was mandatory.'[465] On the other hand, the ruling of the CJEU is affected by the lack of flexibility of the German approach, as it focuses on a step-by-step procedure rather than the open formula of the willingness to negotiate. On a positive note, *Huawei v ZTE* shows that the 'exceptional circumstances' required by the essential facility doctrine[466] do not apply to SEP licensing, which means that, compared to the IP-competition conflict resolved under *Volvo*,[467] *Magill*,[468] and *IMS Health*,[469] the defendant is more likely to escape liability. This is important because the essential facility doctrine requires the identification of a new product that could be produced by accessing the facility, but in IoT markets that rely on large quantities of industrial data, it is extremely difficult for the potential licensor to even imagine what the new product would look like. Indeed, to imagine it, they would need access to the IoT data that constitute the essential facility.[470]

As the case law stands, *Huawei* has 'blunted the sword of antitrust law,'[471] and it is not by chance that, after *Huawei*, the European Commission has not intervened to temper patent abuses. This is in line with the Competition Commissioner's statement whereby 'the best way to solve those issues is sometimes to change the regulations, not to apply the competition rules.'[472] This stance further strengthens the case for the need of an EU harmonisation of patent law to set forth a single and balanced framework for SEP licensing without the need for competition law interventions that do not appear to be fit for the IoT. Such a harmonised framework would centre on the adoption of the 'willingness to negotiate' doctrine, the clear

---

462 ibid [70].
463 *Huawei* has also been interpreted as setting forth 'strict obligations' (Enrico Bonadio and Luke McDonagh, '2020 Is Set to Be a Crucial Year for Standard-Essential Patent Litigation in Europe' (*Kluwer Patent Blog*, 17 January 2020) <http://patentblog.kluweriplaw.com/2020/01/17/2020-is-set-to-be-a-crucial-year-for-standard-essential-patent-litigation-in-europe/>).
464 (n 381).
465 ibid [158].
466 These are the conditions to be met: (1) the potential licensor intends to offer a new product on a secondary market, (2) lack of objective justification for the refusal to license, (3) the refusal reserves a secondary market by eliminating all competition on that market, and (4) the product or service is indispensable for enabling the undertakings to carry on business in a particular market.
467 (n 429).
468 (n 430).
469 (n 431).
470 Drexl (n 47).
471 Podszun (n 385) 729.
472 Margrethe Vestager cited ibid.

definition of FRAND terms, and the streamlining of exceptions, ideally modelled on fair use.

Future research should critically assess if the Competition Commissioner's caution is to be applauded, considering how national courts are interpreting *Huawei*. At a cursory look, it would seem that domestic approaches are converging in assuring a pro-proprietary application of *Huawei*. The UK Supreme Court in *Unwired Planet* declared English courts' jurisdiction to determine a FRAND global licence for a multinational SEP portfolio. An approach sensitive to the necessity to strike a balance between IP and competing interests would have led to the clarification that the market value should not be the be-all and end-all of royalty determination when SEPs are involved. Instead, the Supreme Court imposed 'fair market price'[473] to technology implementers.[474] The pro-monopolist favour is also confirmed by the fact that the court regarded damages inadequate, opting for an injunction – a discretionary remedy that constitutes an indirect form of specific performance.[475] They did so on the untested assumption that compensation would give implementers an incentive to hold out country by country until compelled to pay damages in each country.[476] This preference for 'property rules' (injunction) over 'liability rules' (damages) well illustrates the imbalance of the SEP framework.[477] Similarly, Germany's Supreme Court[478] held that (i) a willing licensee is one who is willing to accept a license on FRAND terms, however FRAND may be construed, and (ii) *nondiscriminatory* does not mean that the rate should be the same as previous comparable agreements. Finally, in the Netherlands, the Court of Appeal of The Hague granted injunctions allowing Philips to stop alleged infringements by Asus and Wiko and reiterated that the *Huawei* protocol is not binding.[479]

---

473   *Unwired Planet* (n 381) [114].

474   A similar evolution can be seen with regard to the compensation offered to landowners subject to expropriation in the public interest. The compensation was originally much lower than the market value, but also through the rhetoric reference to the human right to property, the compensation now has to match the market value of the expropriated land. See, critically, Luca Nivarra, 'La Funzione Sociale Della Proprietà: Dalla Strategia Alla Tattica' (2014) 31 Riv crit dir priv 503.

475   Like specific performance, an injunction is an equitable remedy that is awarded if damages do not adequately compensate the claimant, as the latter needs to restrain the defendant from starting or continuing a breach of a negative contractual undertaking (prohibitory injunction) or needs to compel performance of a positive contractual obligation (mandatory injunction). See *Lumley v Wagner* [1852] 1 DM & G604. On injunction as indirect specific performance, see James T Brennan, 'Injunction against Professional Athletes Breaching Their Contracts' (1967) 34 Brooklyn Law Review 61.

476   *Unwired Planet* (n 381) [169].

477   For this distinction, see the germinal Guido Calabresi and A Douglas Melamed, 'Property Rules, Liability Rules and Inalienability: One View of the Cathedral' (1972) 85 Harvard Law Review 1089.

478   Urteil des Kartellsenats 5 May 2020 – KZR 36/17 (*Sisvel v Haier*).

479   Gerechtshof Den Haag, 9 January 2020–200.219.487/01 (*Koninklijke Philips N.V. v Wiko SAS*); Gerechtshof Den Haag, 14 May 2019–200.221.250/01 (*Koninklijke Philips N.V. v Asustek Computers Inc. and others*).

Despite these shortcomings, the *Huawei* approach was endorsed by the European Commission in its Communication 'Setting out the Approach to Standard Essential Patents,'[480] and it has been welcomed by those scholars who see it as satisfying 'in an effective manner the interests of all stakeholders.'[481] In general, the Commission follows *Huawei* in refusing a one-size-fits-all approach, which leaves an important role for national courts. In practice, this is leading to SEP overprotection.

The first pillar of the Commission's framework is transparency. Technology implementers – including companies wishing to enter the IoT market – can hardly predict their exposure if they cannot easily access information about the existence and scope of SEPs. Ironically, SEP databases held by standard-developing organisations are not standardised and lack transparency. The main standards are covered by hundreds of thousands of SEPs held by dozens of parties.[482] Uncertainty stems also on the fact that ETSI members can submit their declarations of essentiality before the actual grant of the patent, which may ultimately not be granted. As a consequence of this overdeclaration issue, the 'current declaration practices do not convey reliable information on the essentiality of declared patents.'[483] Essentiality is self-assessed, without external scrutiny. Nor is clarity provided at the licensing stage. The Commission notes that this is especially problematic in the context of IoT, where new players with little experience of SEPs licensing are 'continually entering the market for connectivity.'[484] Therefore, the Commission:

(i) Called on standard-developing organisations to improve the quality of their databases by making them user-friendly, searchable on the basis of the standardisation project, synchronised with patent offices' databases.[485]
(ii) Called on these organisations to transform the current declaration system into a tool that provides up-to-date and precise information in a way that helps technology implementers assess patent infringement exposure;
(iii) Committed to the launch of a pilot project for SEPs in selected technologies with a view of facilitating the introduction of an appropriate mechanism to scrutinise their essentiality to a standard.[486]

The second pillar is a framework for FRAND licensing. The Commission's starting point is that the parties are best placed to achieve a common understanding of what is a fair rate. This consensus is hindered by conflicting interpretations

---

480 European Commission, 'Communication "Setting out the EU Approach to Standard Essential Patents"' (n 384).
481 McDonagh and Bonadio (n 385) 6.
482 Bartlett and Contreras (n 385).
483 Pohlmann and Blind (n 387) 3.
484 European Commission, 'Communication "Setting out the EU Approach to Standard Essential Patents"' (n 384) [1].
485 ibid [1.1].
486 ibid [1.2.2].

of 'FRAND,' especially in the IoT sectors, where '[d]ivergent views and litiga-tion over FRAND licensing risk delaying the uptake of new technologies.'[487] To overcome this, the Commission invites negotiating parties to consider efficiency considerations, mutual expectations, and importance of the uptake by implement-ers to promote the diffusion of the standard. Worryingly, the Commission takes a pro-monopolist stance that seems even more extreme than the CJEU's. Indeed, the value to consider is not the market value: it is the nebulous concept of 'value added of the patented technology (which is) irrespective of the market success of the product.'[488] Nonetheless, the Commission seemed aware that this liberal approach of leaving the FRAND determinations to party autonomy does not work in the IoT, due to its complex supply chain and imbalanced relationships. Accord-ingly, it called on standard-developing organisations and SEP holders to develop effective, transparent, and predictable solutions 'to facilitate the licensing of a large number of implementers in the IoT environment,'[489] via patent pools or other licensing platforms.[490] Meanwhile, it committed to monitor licensing prac-tices, in particular in the IoT sector.

The third pillar is a predictable enforcement environment. SEP patents are more litigated than regular patents, and this can result in barriers to entry.[491] This is particularly true for IoT stakeholders that report that 'uncertainties and imbal-ances in the enforcement system have serious implications for market entry.'[492] Once again, the Commission prefers to leave the solution to party autonomy on the premise that good faith will be a guiding principle and that injunctions can be granted against implementers in bad faith. Leaving aside the limited role of good faith in common law jurisdictions,[493] this approach has four shortcomings. First, it ignores that the corrective virtues of good faith are of limited relevance in the con-text of imbalanced business-to-business relationships that are commonplace in the IoT, especially if the implementer cannot enter a market without using a SEP.[494]

---

487 ibid [2].

488 ibid [2.4].

489 ibid.

490 E.g. Ericsson launched Avanci, an IoT licensing platform that promises to be 'the first market-place for licensing patented cellular technology to the Internet of Things' ('Licensing on FRAND Terms' (*Ericsson*, 25 January 2017) <www.ericsson.com/en/patents/frand>) This platform allows technology implementers to access SEPs under one agreement and for one fair, flat per-unit rate.

491 Pohlmann and Blind (n 387).

492 European Commission, 'Communication "Setting out the EU Approach to Standard Essential Patents"' (n 384) [3].

493 Although in some cases in recent years UK courts have not found the idea of good faith as repugnant as they once did, there is considerable divergence between common law and civil law countries in this matter. See David Campbell, 'Good Faith and the Ubiquity of the "Relational" Contract: Good Faith and the Ubiquity of the "Relational" Contract' (2014) 77 The Modern Law Review 475.

494 In business-to-business relationships, the stronger company can (i) impose contracts that are unfair, relying on the fact that the economic dependence and reputational factors will deter the weaker company from suing them, and (ii) set aside the contract and impose a relationship that is factually unfair. More on this in Noto La Diega (n 97). The laws controlling the fairness of the

Second, the *Unwired Planet* 'saga has shown that different views on the way the parties should negotiate are always just around the corner.'[495] Therefore, it is hard to understand why the Commission, the CJEU, and national courts share the view that parties to a SEP licensing agreement are in the best position to determine the terms that are most appropriate for their specific situation. Third, it disregards that implementers may be in good faith and yet infringe e.g. because the SEP holder is unilaterally imposing unfair 'FRAND' terms or because they cannot afford to pay the market value or the added value for each of the thousands of patents that are declared essential to a standard. Fourth, it lacks detail with regard to the 'precise terms of FRAND licensing and the exact meaning of good faith.'[496] This means that FRAND terms will be determined in a fragmented way, patent holder by patent holder, patent by patent, usually in separate proceedings: this can harm the IoT 'as *technology convergence* continues to impact standardisation in key areas such as next-generation wireless communication and the Internet of Things.'[497] The Commission declared that it would improve the enforcement environment by working 'with stakeholders to develop and use methodologies, such as sampling, which allow for efficient and effective SEP litigation.'[498] This confirms the coregulatory preference of the EU, the dangers of which have been underlined in Chapter 1. The statement also corroborates the idea that the Commission wants to achieve an 'efficient and effective' outcome as opposed to a balanced outcome.[499] Imbalanced efficiencies are likely to come from implementers passively accepting FRAND terms and injunctions being given the antitrust green light. This can also be seen in the Commission's ambiguous treatment of the concept of open

---

terms of business-to-business contracts are still underdeveloped. See Simon Whittaker, 'Unfair Terms in Commercial Contracts and the Two Laws of Competition: French Law and English Law Contrasted' (2019) 39 Oxford Journal of Legal Studies 404. Good faith in business-to-consumer transactions plays a crucial role, as epitomised by the Unfair Terms Directive, which considers a contractual term to be unfair unfair 'if, contrary to the requirement of good faith, it causes a significant imbalance in the parties' rights and obligations.' This gives corrective powers to courts that can weigh up the fairness of a term in a consumer contract. See Simon Whittaker and Reinhard Zimmerann, 'Good Faith in European Contract Law: Surveying the Legal Landscape' in Reinhard Zimmerann and Simon Whittaker (eds), *Good Faith in European Contract Law* (CUP 2000) 7, esp 53. The corrective function of good faith is disputed. Cf Carmelo Restivo, *Contributo Ad Una Teoria Dell'abuso Del Diritto* (Giuffrè 2007); Claudio Scognamiglio, 'Abuso Del Diritto, Buona Fede, Ragionevolezza (Verso Una Riscoperta Della Pretesa Funzione Correttiva Dell'interpretazione Del Contratto?)' (2010) 2 NGCC 139.

495 Giuseppe Colangelo and Gianluca Scaramuzzino, 'Unwired Planet Act 2: The Return of the FRAND Range' (2019) 40 ECLR 306.

496 McDonagh and Bonadio (n 385) 7.

497 Bartlett and Contreras (n 385) 285. Italics added. The authors recommend a mechanism of statutory interpleader be used to join the holders of all patents covering a particular technology standard into a single proceeding in which an aggregate FRAND royalty may be determined.

498 European Commission, 'Communication "Setting out the EU Approach to Standard Essential Patents"' (n 384) [3.6].

499 This is in spite of emphatic declarations whereby 'a balanced IPR framework is needed that supports a sustainable and efficient standardisation ecosystem and SEP licensing environment' (ibid [5]). For a more optimistic appraisal, see McDonagh and Bonadio (n 385).

source. On the one hand, it recognises that open source is important to improve standard development, standard take-up, and interoperability. On the other hand, it concludes with the concerning notation whereby we need to 'pay *attention to the interaction between open source community projects and (standardisation)*'[500] due to the divergences between the former and the latter in terms of IPR policies and balance. It is this book's conviction that, as opposed to looking at free and open-source Things with scepticism or even hostility, open-source community projects should be convincingly supported – in them lies the hope to take back control of the IoT.

This area of law will have to be kept under observation as changes are in sight. At the end of 2020, the European Commission published its *IP Action Plan*,[501] where it declared that new technologies such as the IoT provide an opportunity to modernise the IP framework by intervening in five areas. These include the proposal for action to 'facilitate access to and sharing of intangible assets while guaranteeing a fair return on investment.'[502] The Commission implicitly admits that the Communication 'Setting out the Approach to Standard Essential Patents'[503] was not a success as '[d]espite the guidance provided in the SEPs Communication . . . some businesses continue to find it difficult to agree on SEP licensing,' as agreeing on what is fair remains controversial. However, instead of learning from its own mistakes (the focus on self- and coregulation as well as on party autonomy), the Commission reiterates that, at least in the short term, the solution will be provided by industry-led initiatives. Positively, reforms will be considered, including third-party checks on whether the SEP declarations actually regard 'essential' patents.[504] Hopefully, the reform will include a harmonisation of patent laws, including SEPs licensing and streamlining of IP exceptions, so as to rebalance the IP framework, currently tilted in favour of monopolists and deaf to the arguments of fairness.

Overall, competition law appears to be an ineffective tool in the regulation of the IoT and in curbing the underlying power imbalance. This was confirmed in June 2021, when the Commission published the initial findings of its inquiry into the consumer IoT sector.[505] The respondents reported difficulties in competing with vertically integrated companies, such as Amazon, Google, and Apple, which have built their own ecosystems within and beyond the consumer IoT sector. In particular, they complained about (i) exclusivity and tying practices; (ii) big tech role as bottlenecks controlling user relationships; (iii) use of data by

---

500 European Commission, 'Communication "Setting out the EU Approach to Standard Essential Patents"' (n 384) [4]. Emphasis attention.
501 European Commission, 'Making the Most of the EU's Innovative Potential. An Intellectual Property Action Plan to Support the EU's Recovery and Resilience' (2020) COM(2020)760 final.
502 ibid 3.
503 European Commission, 'Communication "Setting out the EU Approach to Standard Essential Patents"' (n 384).
504 The plan is based on Rudi Bekkers and others, 'Pilot Study for Essentiality Assessment of Standard Essential Patents' (2020) JRC119894.
505 'Antitrust: Initial Findings of Consumer IoT Sector Inquiry' (n 296).

voice assistant providers not only to improve the market position of their general-purpose voice assistants but also to allow them to leverage more easily into adjacent markets; and (iv) 'the prevalence of *proprietary technology*, leading at times to the creation of "*de facto standards*", together with technology fragmentation and lack of common standards, raise concerns as to the *lack of interoperability*.'[506] Unlike ownership, property is alive and well, and it prevails on those 'official' standards that – overburdened with SEPs and not helped by the lack of decisive antitrust interventions – struggle to play a meaningful role in the realisation of an interoperable and open IoT.

6.7 Interim Conclusion

'Smart' capitalism equates rentier capitalism. Increasingly, IoT companies leverage their intangible assets – and their integration in proprietary hardware – to impose monopolistic prices, inaccessible barriers to access, and behavioural constraints, thus harming newcomers, consumers, and society as a whole. The death of ownership is the chief manifestation of the underlying imbalance of power. In a way that, on the face of it, would resemble medieval times, we exercise our rights on 'our' property subject to the control of the digital lords. However, as the collective interest and reciprocal duties played an important role in limiting property in the feudal system, the real precursor of the current state of things ought to be found in the individualist outlook of bourgeois society. Under IoT capitalism, the death of ownership does not amount to a death of the right to property, which has never been stronger, at least in its IP species. Hypertrophic IP portfolios held by few multinational IoT corporations are a threat both to individual ownership and to the commons. This is well illustrated by the phenomenon of IP overlaps and by the prevalence of patents on competition in the context of FRAND licensing.

In the IoT, IP overprotection and the death of ownership are the result of a combination of overlapping IPRs and corporate control over the Thing exercised by factual, technological, and legal means. IP overlaps hamper any attempt to rely on IP's internal limitations to protect the IoT user. For instance, an act that falls under a copyright exception (e.g. reverse engineering) may qualify as infringement under patent law. My recommendation to courts is to leverage European fundamental rights – mainly freedom of expression and prohibition of abuse of rights – to (i) interpret existing exceptions as user rights that are of equal standing as the IP holder's rights; (ii) recognise an autonomous, open-ended defence along the lines of fair use in the US. As IPRs become ubiquitous and sterilise IP exceptions, the case for a fair use approach has never been more convincing. Such an approach would allow the public interest to play more of a role in IP governance, and it would make sure that the IoT unleashes its sustainability potential. A more generous approach to exceptions would be robustly grounded in the ECHR jurisprudence that regards IP as an exception to human rights, and the CJEU freedom-of-expression-driven jurisprudence. Should a flexible approach be rejected, a second-best solution would see EU lawmakers streamlining existing defences across the different IP subsystems to make sure that they are framed explicitly as user rights, as well as being mandatory, binding, and covering commercial and mixed purposes.

Private power, including the power of IoT platforms and consortia, is the traditional domain of competition law interventions. In the IoT, the IP-competition conflict is mainly resolved through the qualification of SEP holders' actions as an abuse of dominant position. Regrettably, the CJEU took an imbalanced, pro-SEP holder stance that has been worsened by national courts. Rather than the flexible pro-competitive approach taken by the Commission in *Samsung*, a rigid and pro-proprietary, step-by-step protocol has prevailed in *Huawei v ZTE* and its aftermath. The Commission has unquestioningly accepted this new turn and, in keeping with its coregulatory preference, is leaving to public and private stakeholders to codefine a licensing and enforcement framework that revolves around party autonomy and good faith. These are unlikely to work in the IoT, with its complex supply chain, the abundance of players that are new to the technicalities of SEP licensing, and its ubiquitous power imbalance. One can only hope that the Commission takes a braver approach and adopts a binding instrument that would harmonise patent law in the EU, thereby embracing the willingness to negotiate as a more flexible method and clearly defining FRAND terms as opposed to leaving the definition of fairness to market dynamics. As things stand, similarly to Ricardo's and Marx's rentiers that would exploit their monopoly power over the land to impose a rent that was a monopoly price, SEP owners aggressively patrol the gates to IoT innovation and seek monopolistic rents in the form of licensing fees that are only nominally fair.

IP law and competition provide an unsatisfactory solution to the death of ownership. This is partly due to the increasing influence of private superpowers. Thanks to them – and to the lawmakers that accommodated their demands – IP has become pervasive and imbalanced, whilst market forces no longer erode their monopolies.[507] Antitrust itself has not yet developed adequate ways to address data power, with the end result that both internal and external limitations are unlikely to play an effective role in rebalancing IoT relationships, at least if relied upon in isolation. Legal arguments based on exceptions and competition have failed, but where the law fails, collective action may succeed. Free and open source, open hardware, open data, and open standards – in a word, the commons – may provide the opportunity to organise new forms of resistance and address the IoT struggle.[508] This will be the ambitious task of the next chapter, which will attempt to draw some conclusions.

---

507 Ricolfi (n 11) 26.
508 Evgeny Morozov and Francesca Bria, 'Rethinking the Smart City. Democritizing Urban Technology' (2018) Rosa Luxemburg Stiftung New York Office <www.rosalux-nyc.org/rethinking-the-smart-city/>.

Conclusion

When the Law Fails Us: The Commons for a Collectivised and Open IoT

> *The product ceases to be the direct product of the individual, and becomes a social product, produced in common by a collective labourer.*
>
> Marx, *Das Kapital* (2)

In the three years and a half that have passed since I started writing this book, much has changed. Pandemics, overthrowing of dictators, secessions, and anti-racist uprisings have been affected by increased access to the internet and digital technologies, leading to the wider adoption of connected devices, to more information being shared online, and to more action being organised in a continuum between the cyber and the physical.[1]

In this world where information and action have become progressively more intertwined, and where the online-offline divide is a thing of the past, the IoT is destined to be one of the protagonists of our times. As such, understanding this sociotechnological phenomenon and its laws is pivotal to the comprehension of internet governance more generally, its recent trends, and its main challenges.

Not having reached technological maturity when I commenced this book, the IoT is now past its hype as there are an average of five Things per person globally.[2] Surprisingly, the ubiquity of the IoT has not led to an augmented scrutiny by legal scholars, unlike more popular phenomena, such as AI and the blockchain. With the recent publication of *A Commercial Law of Privacy and Security for the Internet of Things* by Stacy-Ann Elvy,[3] alongside this book, I hope for a renewed interest in and wider discourse around the IoT.

To regulate capitalism has always been an onerous task as capital routinely find ways to either sidestep regulation or to influence the drafting of the rules. In the IoT, the former has been rendered possible by laws that were already obsolete

---

1 See e.g. Muhammad Umair and others, 'Impact of COVID-19 on IoT Adoption in Healthcare, Smart Homes, Smart Buildings, Smart Cities, Transportation and Industrial IoT' (2021) 21 Sensors 3838.
2 'Internet of Things (IoT)' (*Statista*, 11 May 2021) <www.statista.com/topics/2637/internet-of-things/>.
3 Stacy-Ann Elvy, *A Commercial Law of Privacy and Security for the Internet of Things* (CUP 2021). Unfortunately, I could not get ahold of Professor Elvy's book before the completion of this book, but her previous research has significantly influenced my understanding of the legal issues in the IoT.

DOI: 10.4324/9780429468377-8

when they were adopted as they relied on untenable binaries (hardware-software, good-service, personal-nonpersonal, online-offline), by the difficulty to pin down a definition of the phenomenon, and by some of its core characteristics – namely, its sectoral fragmentation, relational black box, and global nature. The latter strategy has been traditionally pursued through organised lobbying aimed at preventing the passing of legislation or at watering it down. While this still stakes places, more refined tactics include the support to coregulation and self-regulation, in particular by means of 'ethical' initiatives and regulation 'by design.' While often praiseworthy, these soft approaches do not provide sufficient incentives for IoT corporations to change their behaviour and adopt more responsible, open, human-centric, and socially just practices. Ethics, design, self-regulation, and coregulation have to complement a core of hard laws and regulations that need updating to take account of the non-binary nature of the IoT as well as of the novel risks that come with it. To account for the IoT's sectoral fragmentation, relational black box, and global nature, these laws will have to be implemented by multiple regulators and on multiple levels in a coordinated fashion. To this end, we do not need an 'IoT Act' or a specific IoT authority. Rather, I have proposed the setting up of International Regulation Coordination Organisation for the IoT (IRCOIOT) to bring together existing horizontal and vertical regulators in a cross-sector and cross-border way.

The changes in substantive law need to be evidence-based; notably, they have to start from a thorough understanding of the sociotechnological dimension of the IoT. To do so, the IoT must be first framed as a subcategory of the internet: IoT and internet share similar issues in terms of software, service, data, concentration of power, and extraterritoriality. At the same time, the IoT differs due to the role played by the Things within it. The physicality is crucial in the sense of accounting for both the hardware component of the Things and the action that the latter perform on the physical world. This is not to say that the internet does not have a physical dimension. In fact, the physicality has only a more visible role in the IoT, with its injection of connectivity, sensors, and actuators in every object around, on, and in us. One would misrepresent the internet should one overlook the importance of its tangible dimension, as exemplified by the issues around the ownership of the undersea cables, access to the servers, etc.

The hybrid (cyber-physical) nature of the IoT – and to some extent of the internet - has implications as to private power and territoriality. While in the late nineties power became extraterritorial as it could move with the speed of the electronic signal, as Bauman put it,[4] with the IoT power becomes fluid as it is both territorial and extraterritorial at the same time. To define the boundaries of the IoT is pivotal to assessing how existing laws apply to it and whether new laws should be introduced. While I accept that there will always be a degree of discretion in any definitory attempt, I propose to account for both dimensions of the Thing by defining it as *an inextricable mixture of hardware, software, service, digital content, and data with (inter)connectivity, sensing, and actuating capabilities and interfacing the physical world.*

---

4 Zygmunt Bauman, *Liquid Modernity* (Polity Press; Blackwell 2000) 10–11.

While understanding the technology behind connectivity, sensing, and actuating is a necessary prerequisite for good regulation and legal analysis, technology should be considered in its social and even political dimension. To frame the IoT as a sociotechnological phenomenon means to explore the role of IoT companies as rule-setters and to critically assess the relationship between their private ordering and the law, at least in its traditional version of democratically created rules. At the end of 2020, the European Commission presented the Digital Services Package. For the first time, the Commission expressly acknowledged that 'a few large platforms . . . act as *private rule-makers*'[5] and that these gatekeepers circumvent the law by 'contractual, commercial, technical'[6] means. The package recognises the role of the terms and conditions (and other 'legals')[7] in regulating business-to-consumer relationships and in 'contracting out' legal requirements.[8] Positively, it states that the law should be able to limit big tech contractual power in the interests of transparency, consumer protection, and fairness.[9] This confirms my initial methodological option to illuminate the consumer issues in the IoT by analysing the legals of one of its main gatekeepers, i.e., Amazon. As Langdon Winner would put it,[10] technological artefacts have politics, and to understand the politics of the IoT, one needs to focus on its private ordering, starting from its contracts.

The exploration of Amazon's contractual quagmire left me baffled as no one would expect that the use of a simple product such as a speaker ends up triggering a complex web of 246 legals, which are difficult to find and read, let alone understand. The low readability coefficient of the legals, their length, and the fact that they are scattered around the web rather than systematically grouped are only some of the reasons that render it impossible for IoT users to fully comprehend the relationship to the company as well as the risks and obligations associated to the use of the Thing. The lack of transparency is also due to the fact that Amazon relies on hundreds of subsidiaries and affiliates who are responsible – and liable – for some of the functionalities and services incorporated in the Thing. Two common, and concerning, characteristics of the contractual quagmire are that one can hardly identify the contractual parties – which adversely affects the possibility to

---

5 'The Digital Services Act Package' (*European Commission*, 26 April 2021) <https://digital-strategy. ec.europa.eu/en/policies/digital-services-act-package>. Emphasis added. There is a growing body of literature that reflects on the role of private legislators of platform operators in this 'new technologically-supported centrally planned economy' (Christoph Busch, 'Regulation of Digital Platforms as Infrastructures for Services of General Interest' (2021) 09 9.).

6 Proposed Digital Markets Act, art 11(1). A *gatekeeper* is a provider of a core platform service which serves as an important gateway for businesses to reach end users (e.g. search engine), provided that it has significant impact on the internal market, as well as enjoying an entrenched and durable position (arts 2(1)(2), and 3(1)).

7 Indeed, the proposed Digital Services Act defines *terms and conditions* broadly as 'all terms and conditions or specifications, irrespective of their name or form, which govern the contractual relationship between the provider of intermediary services and the recipients of the services' (art 2(q)).

8 Proposed Digital Services Act, art 12(1).

9 Proposed Digital Services Act, recital 38 and art 12(2).

10 Langdon Winner, 'Do Artifacts Have Politics?' (1980) 109 Daedalus 121.

successfully bring an action – and the fluidity of the contractual subject matter. Some legals purport to regulate the Thing by separating its hardware, software, service, and data components, but the way these components are on each occasion (re)defined – often by qualifying as 'service' what would normally count as software, data, or hardware – confirms the initial thesis that Things are an inextricable mixture of these components.

The practices exemplified by the contractual quagmire of Amazon are by no means specific to this company or to the IoT but are particularly pernicious in this context due to the fact that the Things' ubiquitous sensing and actuating capabilities – and their being weaved in the fabric of virtually any object and environment, to the point of disappearing – worsen consumer vulnerabilities and empower IoT companies to exploit them. Based on my analysis and on my experience of discomfort while mapping and studying the legals, my recommendation is that these companies apply web design principles to the legals, namely, the principle of least astonishment, whereby '[i]f a necessary feature has a high astonishment factor, it may be necessary to redesign the feature.'[11] This will mean to redesign the legals to reduce their number, group them in one place, increase their readability, decrease their length, improve their clarity, consistency and fairness.

The study of these legals – coupled with other 'law in context' methods, including subject access requests, interactions with customer advisers, and autoethnography – led me to the identification of some major consumer issues in the IoT. In assessing whether the law can play a role in tackling these issues, I started off from traditional consumer law, namely, those laws that apply exclusively to business-to-consumer relationships, be they contractual or noncontractual. I then embraced a looser concept of consumer law and critically assessed the role of data protection and IP.

First, I considered that the contractual quagmire itself – regardless of the content of the legals – is a fundamental threat to consumers. The fact that, by using a Thing, consumers are forced to accept a plethora of poorly designed and incomprehensible legals struck me as something that the Unfair Terms Directive would tackle. In light of the complexity of the IoT and of the imbalances in terms of power and information, this directive imposes on IoT companies more stringent requirements of fairness, with a particularly urgent need to rethink the IoT legals to make them easy to find, read, and understand. While legal design approaches can be useful, it is important that they are not left to the company's discretion. EU regulators may learn from the US counterparts and introduce obligations to draft 'legals' that reach at least a Flesch-Kincaid readability score that reflects the literacy and cognitive resources of the average IoT user. In choosing the best way to make IoT legals fairer, regulators and policymakers should become aware of what I called the 'hierarchy of incentives.' This means that IoT companies are more likely to improve their legals in response to public pressure, less likely to do so in response to financial incentives, and unlikely to do so if purely motivated by the goal of protecting those consumers who 'pay' for the Thing with their

---

11 MF Cowlishaw, 'The Design of the REXX Language' (1984) 23 IBM Systems Journal 326, 333.

personal data. While keeping public pressure high on IoT companies' contractual practices is of the utmost importance to achieve a fairer ecosystem, any inquiry into these practices should take account of the specific characteristics of the contractual quagmire. For example, enforcement actions or inquiries that target some contracts in isolation, thus overlooking the relationships with the other contracts in the quagmire, would be unlikely to achieve their purposes. The analysis of the relation between the contractual quagmire and the Unfair Terms Directive generated also new learnings about the role of this directive in the digital world more generally. Indeed, this regime is predicated on the form-substance binary. Conversely, unfairness of form can lead to unfairness of substance, and the opposite is also true, to the point that the dichotomy becomes untenable. Additionally, the IoT is a reminder that unfairness is to be assessed at the systemic level, not analysing individual terms in vitro. Individual terms as well be per se fair, there is no doubt that one needs to consider the interrelations within the web of contracts: to submerge the consumers with thousands of legals that are impossible to find, read or understand is in itself unfair and will contribute to findings of unfairness of otherwise-fair individual terms.

Second, I explored the realm of private ordering 'by bricking,' that is, the IoT company's ability to remotely monitor consumers and automatically downgrade the Thing, discontinue the service, remove functionalities, determine the lifespan of the Thing, and even deactivate or 'brick' it. I put forward the argument that many of these bricking practices can be regarded as a lack of conformity under sale of goods law and that the right to repair can be interpreted as a right to have the 'smartness' of the Thing restored. This is all the more true now that the Second Consumer Sales Directive has passed its transposition deadline and that it has been paired with the Digital Content Directive. At a first examination, the reform is IoT-friendly. This can be seen in the introduction of the category of 'goods with digital elements,' whose definition broadly coincides with that of a Thing. The main issue with the reform is that there is the risk that certain Things will fall in a regulatory vacuum. If the digital element is necessary for the good to function, the Second Consumer Sales Directive will apply. If the tangible aspect is the mere carrier of the digital element, the Digital Content Directive will. There remains a grey area between the two poles and future research will need to assess whether national implementations are dealing with it appropriately.

Third, I looked at 'IoT-commerce' and in particular at the challenges that an interface-free, hyperconnected environment poses to precontractual duties of information. The general rule to inform consumers in a clear and intelligible manner should be interpreted in creative ways that go beyond the traditional terms of service available on the company's website. In an IoT world where there is a rise of voice-user and video-user interfaces, consumers should be given information in the same format as the one that is usually utilised to interact with the Thing (namely, audio or video). This principle, which I called 'interface continuity,' is emerging from both consumer contracts laws and data protection laws. However, its full implementation is hindered by the legibility requirement that the Consumer Rights Directive set forth for some online transactions. This requirement clearly presupposes a written text paradigm and should be abandoned to make the directive future-proof. De lege ferenda, special provisions should be introduced for when transactions are concluded through interface-free Things.

While the significance of contracts should not be underestimated, it is of the utmost importance to comprehend how power imbalance and new extractive practices shape up beyond or regardless of a contractual nexus. Moreover, information and transparency – the traditional pillars of consumer contract law – are not the only thing that matters to IoT end users. With this in mind, I framed the noncontractual consumer issues in the IoT as issues of vulnerability – both of Things and of the human beings that use them: the former affects the latter, and vice versa.

With this in mind, the fourth consumer issue I explored was the vulnerability of Things. In particular, I zoomed in on product liability law, which was conceived for tangible products and mechanical or chemical defects. On the face of it, this is at odds with mixed hardware-software products, whose defects are often intangible (e.g. software updates, inaccurate sensor data, etc.). The Product Liability Directive has been influential as a model for product liability laws around the world, but in recent years it has been only seldom enforced. I would argue that the IoT provides an opportunity to rethink the concept of product as an amalgam of hardware, software, service, and data. More inclusive interpretations of the scope of the Product Liability Directive may, in turn, see the revival of this oft-forgotten legal regime. While it is possible to future-proof the law by interpretative means, in the interest of legal certainty, it would be important to expressly redefine the concept of product to expressly include software – regardless of whether it is embedded in a tangible medium – as well as service and data. Similarly, intangible defects and postsale defects should be accounted for. Otherwise, the prospect of the harm coming from defective Things may reduce consumer trust in the IoT. The review of the directive is ongoing, and hopefully it will overcome those binaries that the IoT is disrupting, such as product-service, hardware-software, and cybersecurity-security.

Fifth, I critically evaluated the impact of the 'Internet of Personalised Things' on human vulnerability, The granular, situational, and often sensitive data collected by Things and their ability to follow the consumer and target them at the best time and in the best context allow IoT companies to personalise ads, products, prices, and even terms of service. These features can be exploited for nefarious reasons, including manipulation and discrimination. This is in line with the fact that capitalism itself revolves around the manipulation of workers to create new needs, in particular selfish ones. Capitalism manipulates needs in that it creates consumption needs which silence those deeper needs that shape the human personality and hinder the valorisation of capital, e.g. the need for free time. Free time and authentic needs are appropriated and manipulated by IoT companies – 'smartness' becomes the ultimate neoliberal tool to make us 'dumb.'[12] It is no accident that vulnerability has become a key common trait that Things

---

12 Ugo Mattei, 'Smart', *Parole Chiave del XXI Secolo* (Treccani 2020).

and humans share. I argued that at least some of the practices that fall within the scope of the Internet of Personalised Things can be regarded as running counter to the Unfair Commercial Practices Directive. However, as this directive is a neoliberal instrument focused on the economic dimension of the consumer and on the internal market, its response to IoT-enhanced consumer manipulation is not entirely satisfactory. In the age of 'cyborg consumers,' the IoT becomes 'a space whose organisation does not require lawyers since it does not need any laws different from the *de facto* power of the smartest.'[13] If the law is supplanted by engineering and self-programming Things, one can doubt that we can still do something to force our values upon the capitalist project.

The profit-maximising function of manipulation, an individualistic outlook on life, and the limited role of the law in constraining capital are only some of the features that industrial capitalism shares with IoT capitalism. This appears with clarity when analysing a sixth consumer issue in the IoT, namely the 'Internet of Loos.' As Things collect data in our most intimate spaces, including the home and the body, one should question whether IoT users retain any reasonable expectation of privacy. In this sense, the IoT challenges also the private-public dichotomy. If data is the main commodity in the IoT market, then IoT users are to be regarded as unwitting workers and the manifold corporate strategies to appropriate data are to be considered as a form of digital dispossession. In line with Shoshana Zuboff's theory of surveillance capitalism,[14] my study confirms that the violence of dispossession is not limited to a pre–industrial capitalism stage: digital dispossession is a continuous process, and in the IoT dispossession is no less violent than pre-industrial dispossession: it is only better hidden. A subtle way IoT capitalists utilise to disposses data is to take steps to keep the data secret or to aggregate it with existing trade secrets. To find a solution to this problem, one needs to grapple with conundrum of the twofold nature of data, at once the object of fundamental rights and an asset to monetise. To do so, I considered how the Trade Secrets Directive and the GDPR deal with the potential conflict. This presupposes the debunking of two myths: that IoT data cannot be the object of trade secrets and that the GDPR does not apply to IoT data. IoT data can be and is kept secret, as confirmed by Amazon's response to my subject access request, which left out crucial information related to inferential data and affective computing. Equally, denying that IoT data is personal data presupposes the acceptance of a personal-nonpersonal dichotomy that the IoT contributes to render untenable. Even raw, aggregated, and anonymised data can be recombined and traced back to the identifiable individuals, especially when sensitive data is included and AI-powered mining techniques are used. Whilst the Trade Secrets Directive is of little help, the GDPR deals with the conflict in a mysterious recital, about the right of access:

---

13 Ugo Mattei, 'Do Smart Things Make Us Dumb? Reflections on the Addiction Crisis of Cyborg Consummerism' (2020) 3 REDC 613, 628.
14 Shoshana Zuboff, *The Age of Surveillance Capitalism: The Fight for a Human Future at the New Frontier of Power* (1st edn, PublicAffairs 2019).

That right should not adversely affect the rights or freedoms of others, including trade secrets or intellectual property and in particular the copyright protecting the software. However, the result of those considerations should not
be a refusal to provide all information to the data subject.[15]

This has been often read by companies as justifying blanket rejections of subject
access requests where there is the potential for IP to be affected. Instead, I put forward that all GDPR rights and obligations still apply (e.g. information, data protection by design, etc.) and that even the right of access itself applies. Indeed, on
closer inspection, this is a quadripartite right that is subdivided into (i) a right to
obtain confirmation as to whether personal data is processed; (ii) a right to obtain
information about some key features of the processing; (iii) a right to access the
data that is being processed; and (iv) a right to obtain a free-of-charge copy of
the data. Trade secrets can limit only this fourth right, not the right of access as
a whole. In practice this will mean that IoT companies that appropriate data can
use trade secrets to justify why they do not offer a self-service facility for users
to download their data. Otherwise, IoT users should be able to count on the full
armoury of the GDPR to counter digital dispossession.

It would be hasty to conclude that the GDPR can be regarded as anticapitalistic instrument solely because it can play a role in tackling of the most insidious
practices of IoT capitalism. It would be hasty to conclude that the GDPR can be
regarded as anticapitalistic instrument solely because it can play a role in tackling
of the most insidious practices of IoT capitalism. Quite the opposite. For exploitation to take place, capitalists need a sufficient quantity of labour power. To this
end capital makes sure that workers can maintain themselves (typically through
wages) 'so that they will be available for future exploitations.'[16] The GDPR gives
the new 'smart' proletariat of IoT users / data producers some rights that can be
relied on to reacquire some control over the data. In doing so, it allows us data
subjects / unwitting workers to maintain ourselves, thus being available for future
exploitations. In this sense, both the GDPR and the IoT are neoliberal weapons
that enable the perpetuation of surveillance capitalism.

The final issue analysed in this book is the death of ownership. We are digital
tenants, as opposed to owners, of our Things for two reasons. First, the 'death'
may be related to the shift from the sale contract to the subscription – in the 'subscription economy,' we never formally own our Things. This may be for good
reasons, e.g. sustainability in the circular economy, but it does adversely affect the
protections that the law affords consumers. Second, ownership dies when users
formally buy a Thing, but IoT companies retain factual, legal, and technical control over it throughout its life cycle. This trend has been seen as sort of return to
medieval times, when peasants did not own the land they worked; they merely

---

15 GDPR, recital 63.
16 Rosa Luxemburg, 'The Accumulation of Capital, Or, What the Epigones Have Made Out of Marx's
    Theory – An Anti-Critique (1921)' in Peter Hudius and Paul Le Blanc (eds), George Shriver (tr),
    The Complete Works of Rosa Luxemburg, vol II: Economic Writings 2 (Verso 2016) 349.

managed it on behalf of the lord. Related to the power imbalance epitomised by the death of ownership, the lord would be entitled to the infamous yet never proved *ius primae noctis*. The idea that IoT users have become digital peasants as the IoT company retains full postsale control over the Thing is a powerful metaphor, and it does contribute to the understanding of an actual problem. However, it seems to be predicated on the idea of current capitalism being radically different to industrial capitalism – a capitalism of the origins that was good as it tackled the medieval problem of the death of ownership by celebrating private property. However, I believe that there is a lot to be learned from land management in medieval times and that industrial capitalism is at the root of the current issue. The collective interest and reciprocal duties played an important role in limiting property in the feudal system – such limitations on the altar of the collective interest are what is missing in the current laws that fail to regulate the IoT. The real precursor of the current state of things ought to be found in the individualistic outlook of bourgeois society. In fact, the death of ownership does not equate the death of the right to property, which has never been stronger, at least in its IP species. Hypertrophic IP portfolios held by few multinational IoT corporations are a threat both to individual ownership and to the commons. This can be inferred by the phenomenon of IP overlaps and by the prevalence of patents on competition in the context of FRAND licensing.

Every component of 'our' Things is covered by some IPR. IP overlaps are caused by the creation of new types of subject matter eligible for protection, wider exclusive rights, and novel IPRs. This tendency should be read jointly with the increase in cases that interpret IP exceptions narrowly. Thus, IP overlaps hinder the ability to rely on IP exceptions and limitations to counter the death of ownership. When IPRs overlap, the stricter regime will prevail on the more permissive one. An act that falls under a copyright exception (e.g. reverse engineering) may qualify as infringement under patent law. These rights converge on the same Thing and may be held by the same IoT company. Accordingly, the latter will attempt to regard as infringement virtually any activity of the end user, regardless of the fact that in principle these activities would be lawful, as covered by an IP exception. My recommendation to courts is to leverage European fundamental rights – mainly freedom of expression and prohibition of abuse of rights – to (i) interpret existing exceptions as user rights that are of equal standing as the IP holder's rights and (ii) recognise an autonomous, open-ended defence along the lines of fair use in the US or the Japanese open exception. As IPRs become ubiquitous and sterilise IP exceptions, the case for a fair use approach has never been more convincing.

The point that death of ownership is not the same as the death of property – and the fact that external limitations can do little to tackle this issue – is most clearly shown by the failures of antitrust control over SEP abuses. In order to enter the IoT market, companies have to abide by national, regional, and international standards. Set by organisations that are heavily influenced by big tech, these standards contain thousands of patents (e.g. Wi-Fi, Bluetooth, etc.). Without them, it is impossible to achieve connectivity and interoperability; thus, without access to patented inventions included in standards, smaller businesses cannot enter the market. In the IoT there is a variety of players, many of them are not used to the complicated negotiations required to obtain the relevant licenses. The situation is worsened by the fact that incumbent big IoT companies wait for smaller, new entrants to adopt the technology included in the standard and, when the product is launched, sue for infringement. Until recent times, these patent holdup practices were often regarded as an abuse of dominant position as long as the technology implementer could show the willingness to negotiate a licence. However, in recent years, a pro-proprietary approach has prevailed, and it has become nearly impossible to escape liability and obtain a licence that is actually fair, reasonable, nondiscriminatory. With a single-minded focus on the right to property – effectively ignoring the need to balance it with competing interests, including freedom of expression and consumer protection – the CJEU, the European Commission, and some national courts ignore the power imbalance that is exacerbated in the IoT and leave the definition of what is fair to party autonomy and good faith. In keeping with the coregulatory trend in internet governance, the law provides only a general and flimsy framework, while the actual rules are set by private parties, usually unilaterally, by the incumbent, typically a big IoT company. My recommendation is that a binding instrument be adopted to harmonise patent law in the EU, thereby embracing the willingness to negotiate as a more flexible method and clearly defining FRAND terms as opposed to leaving the definition of fairness to market dynamics.

Reflecting back on these years of study of the IoT and its laws, I am left with the conviction that, on the one hand, it is possible to interpret the law tactically and to reform it to counter the key issues of the IoT; on the other hand, at a higher level, the law will never be enough to steer the development of the IoT in a human-centric, open, responsible, and socially just direction. This is in line with a Marxist theory of law, whose main tenet is the belief that the rule of law is not an essential component of social order ('legal fetishism') and that it acts as 'a subtle and pervasive ideology which serves to obscure the structures of class domination within the State.'[17] A Marxist legal theory does not deny that the law and its reform can help the working classes – including, today, the 'smart proletariat' – but the fact remains that the law is mainly an instrument of class oppression and it can do little to heighten class consciousness.[18] Indeed, Marx shone a light on the fact the law helps capitalists in preventing workers from understanding their own interests and from acting in common.[19] I would put forward that where the law fails us, the commons may succeed.

---

17 Hugh Collins, *Marxism and Law* (OUP 1984) 3.
18 ibid 129. It has been noted that 'by failing to account for the extralegal and coercive origins of property right, the law . . . functions to secure the asymmetrical domination of the few over the many' (Daniel Bensaïd, *The Dispossessed: Karl Marx's Debates on Wood Theft and the Right of the Poor* (University of Minnesota Press 2021) 10.).
19 A paradigmatic example was the decree of 14 June 1791 ('Le Chapelier Law') outlawing the right to strike as intrinsically incompatible with the free enterprise. See Karl Marx, *Il Capitale (1867)*, vol 1 (Bruno Maffi tr, Aurelio Macchioro and Bruno Maffi, UTET 2008) 813.

The concept of 'commons' predates Marx, but the underlying idea is central in Marx's reflection, and the contemporary category is indebted to Marxist theory.[20] Marx's article on the law on the theft of wood has been the subject of recent attention as an important contribution to understanding – and fighting against – the enclosure of the commons.[21] In analysing this law – which abruptly privatised the forest of the Rhineland, thus transforming the local farmers into thieves – Marx underlined the anxiety of the bourgeois legislator about the relation between natural and artificial; the difficulty of a categorical distinction reveals a crisis of the labouring subject, and it ultimately reveals that all labour is social.[22] A popular theory to justify the existence of property and IP is based on John Locke's *Of Civil Government*[23]. The Lockean justification is that every person has a right to own property, including IP, because they have a right to own their person and, hence, what their body produces through labour.[24] Accordingly, individuals who fail to produce value have no claim to property. Marx unmasked the Lockean fiction:[25] as in the factory, labour is collectively organised; if there were any property rights to be derived from this form of labouring, they would have to be collective rights. Similarly, Engels claimed that it would be in the interests of the proletariat to replace the state with the *Gemeinwesen*,[26] which can be translated as commonalty, community, and polity.[27] Collectivising the IoT and embracing the commons in this context means free and open source, open hardware, open data, open standards, open platforms, as well as extralegal collective resistance.

From an economic point of view, the concept of 'commons' refers to nonrivalrous and nonexcludable goods or resources.[28] Knowledge is a commons as it can be the object of collective simultaneous consumption, and one cannot prevent or exclude nonpaying consumers from accessing it. From this angle, IP and technological protection measures have been invented to render knowledge and information artificially scarce. Thanks to IP, information goods become excludable.[29] The

---

20 See Luca Basso, *Marx and the Commons: From Capital to the Late Writings* (Haymarket 2016).

21 Bensaïd (n 20). While at a first glance an episode of little importance, it has been noted that 'the mass illegal appropriation of forest products represented an important moment in the development of German capitalism' (Peter Linebaugh, 'Karl Marx, the Theft of Wood, and Working-Class Composition: A Contribution to the Current Debate' (2014) 40(1/2) Social Justice 131, 140).

22 Karl Marx, 'Proceedings of the Sixth Rhine Province Assembly. Third Article Debates on the Law on Thefts of Wood' in *Marx & Engels Collected Works*, vol 1 Karl Marx 1835–43 (Lawrence & Wishart 2010) 224.

23 John Locke, *Two Treatises of Government* (Awnsham Churchill 1690).

24 Herman T Tavani, 'Locke, Intellectual Property Rights, and the Information Commons' (2005) 7 Ethics and Information Technology 87.

25 David Harvey, 'The Future of the Commons' (2011) 2011 Radical History Review 101.

26 Friedrich Engels, Correspondence with August Bebel (London, 18–28 March 1875).

27 For Marx too 'communism meant going beyond the state' (Basso (n 22) 203.).

28 David Bollier, *Silent Theft: The Private Plunder of Our Common Wealth* (Routledge 2003).

29 Tom G Palmer, 'Are Patents and Copyrights Morally Justified – the Philosophy of Property Rights and Ideal Objects Symposium on Law and Philosophy' (1990) 13 Harvard Journal of Law & Public Policy 817.

economic understanding of the commons is rather narrow and does not account for the polysemous nature of the term.[30] For example, in her new book *Owned, An Ethological Jurisprudence of Property*,[31] Johanna Gibson uses the commons as a way to rethink the nature of property and IP as uniquely human. From an IoT perspective, the commons are relevant in two senses. First, the commons are intrinsically alternative to private and public property: they refer to goods and resources that can be collectively used or managed in anticapitalistic and even extralegal ways. This is in line with what Engels sees as the only possible solution to the problems of the dispossessed. Namely, the dispossessed should realise that 'a revolution by peaceful means is impossible and that only a forcible abolition of the existing unnatural conditions, a radical overthrow of the nobility and industrial aristocracy, can improve the material position of the proletarians.'[32] As Luca Nivarra noted, the laws limiting private property – e.g. the mechanisms of compulsory purchase or eminent domain – are insufficient to realise a world of commons.[33] These laws can be used tactically, as a support for defences in disputes brought by property owners. However, a commons-oriented strategy cannot rely on such limited tools. The antagonistic potential of the commons can express itself only through extralegal action. One can think of the Gezi Park uprisings in Turkey, when people resisted the government's plans to replace the park with a shopping centre and collectively organised to 'reclaim, repurpose, and reimagine the park's space as a venue that belonged to and was used by everyone who spent time there, engaging with each other outside capitalist, commercial, or state-led governance.'[34] The collective reappropriation of the commons may technically be illegal, but this begs the question whether its enclosure was legal in the first place: as Marx put it in the *Debates on the Law on Thefts of* Wood, '[y]ou will never succeed in making us believe that there is a crime where there is no crime, you will only succeed in converting crime itself into a legal act.'[35] My call to civic engagement – a call for citizens to 'organise (their) "forces propres" as social forces'[36] to pursue human emancipation and social justice will benefit the law itself and the public governance structures that underpin it. Indeed, 'the state is held together by civil life.'[37] Similar examples of collective organising to regain

---

30 Luca Nivarra, 'Quattro Usi Di "beni Comuni" per Una Buona Discussione' (2016) 1 Rivista critica di diritto privato 43.

31 Johanna Gibson, *Owned, An Ethological Jurisprudence of Property. From the Cave to the Commons* (Routledge 2021).

32 Frederick Engels, 'The Internal Crises' (1842) 344 Rheinische Zeitung, now in *Marx & Engels Collected Works* 2 (Lawrence & Wishart 2010) 370, 374.

33 Luca Nivarra, 'La Funzione Sociale Della Proprietà: Dalla Strategia Alla Tattica' (2014) 31 Riv crit dir priv 503.

34 Cenk Özbay and Evren Savcı, 'Queering Commons in Turkey' (2018) 24 GLQ: A Journal of Lesbian and Gay Studies 516, 517.

35 Marx (n 24) 227.

36 Karl Marx, 'On the Jewish Question' in *Marx & Engels Collected Works*, 3 (Lawrence & Wishart 2010) 168.

37 Karl Mark, 'The Holy Family' in *Marx & Engels Collected Works* 4 (Lawrence & Wishart 2010) 121.

access or control over underused resources, regardless of their legality, abound. Even though the commons applies to the tangible and the intangible world, these extralegal collective practices of resistance have usually applied to real property, not to the immaterial world.[38] This is partly the result of the practical and theoretical difficulty of conceiving an occupation of an intangible space. I would argue that the limited uptake of the commons as a practice of resistance in the world of immaterial property is also connected to the evocative power of the traditional right to property and the emotional attachments that people tend to have to tangible property.[39] In a sense, the rematerialisation heralded by the IoT – with its return of tangible property to the centre of the stage (be it in the form of a cyber-physical amalgam) – could provide an unparalleled opportunity for a mobilisation that will go beyond the occupation of parks, theatres, and other tangible resources. As all the reality that surrounds us becomes networked, the fight may organically extend from the land to the network. In the IoT, the commons create opportunities for collective forms of resistance.[40] We have seen how a manufacturer of smart tractors leveraged the IP on the software and the technological protection measures embedded in the machinery to prevent some farmers from repairing their tractors. These abuses have led to practices of resistance, such as the illegal download of the Ukrainian version of the software to circumvent the IoT master's orders.[41] Examples of collective forms of resistance and organisation abound. One need only think of Barcelona's digital plan that revolved around 'citizen-led movements to reclaim'[42] the smart city, with the ultimate goal of building a data commons. IoT users experiment in new forms of cooperativism, responsible IoT, and socialisation of data in a number of ways, many of which revolve around the idea of an 'open' IoT.

This leads to a second sense in which the commons the commons are relevant from an IoT viewpoint. As Things become commonplace and are routinely used even in sensitive domains (healthcare, national security, etc.), it becomes of the utmost importance to open the IoT for at least two reasons. First, proprietary 'black

---

38 While the theoretical analysis increasingly centres on intangible commons, the commons as a practice continues to be mainly concerned with the tangible world. It is important to keep in mind that the return to the commons epitomised by the book *Commonwealth* by Hardt and Negri emerged from the move in focus from industrial capitalism to biopolitical and immaterial forms of production. See Michael Hardt and Antonio Negri, *Commonwealth* (HUP 2009) 132–133.

39 See e.g. Diego Salzman and Remco CJ Zwinkels, 'Behavioral Real Estate' (2017) 25 Journal of Real Estate Literature 77.

40 On the link between the commons and collective resistance, see e.g. Denise Wilkins, Bashar Nuseibeh and Mark Levine, 'Monetize This? Marketized-Commons Platforms, New Opportunities and Challenges for Collective Action' in Masaaki Kurosu (ed), *Human-Computer Interaction. Design Practice in Contemporary Societies* (Springer International Publishing 2019).

41 Jason Koebler, 'Why American Farmers Are Hacking Their Tractors With Ukrainian Firmware' (*Vice*, 21 March 2017) <www.vice.com/en_us/article/xykkkd/why-american-farmers-are-hacking-their-tractors-with-ukrainian-firmware>.

42 Evgeny Morozov and Francesca Bria, 'Rethinking the Smart City. Democritizing Urban Technology' (2018) Rosa Luxemburg Stiftung New York Office 26 <www.rosalux-nyc.org/rethinking-the-smart-city/>.

box' Things are dangerous: openness allows users to regain control over their Things, and by underlying interoperability, it makes IoT systems safer. Second, the manufacturers of proprietary Things often discontinue security updates or no longer support the Thing. One need only think of smart medicine: one should feel confident that a medical device implanted in your body will be supported and updated throughout one's lifetime. Therefore, it is imperative to either create Things that are open from the get-go or to release the code once the Thing is discontinued. The most immediate application of the commons to the IoT is free and open-source software. Indeed, at the basis of the information commons, there is 'an organization of the production and distribution of knowledge that ensures open access.'[43] The victory of the open-access model over the proprietary one depends on a number of factors which go beyond the IoT but are here more visible. First, free and open-source software has a political, activist dimension aiming at organising bottom-up forms of resistance to big tech. However, the rise of pure, open-source software – as opposed to *free and open* – ushers in an era of depoliticised openness. This can be seen particularly clearly in the fact that big tech, such as Google and Microsoft, are sponsoring numerous open-source projects. These are ways to exploit the allure of open source to drive adoption while taming its political potential. Second, as Things are an amalgam of software, hardware, service, and data, free and open-source software per se is not enough to achieve an open IoT. We need to open standards, data, hardware, and platforms. The ambition of open standards is thwarted by big tech–led consortia lobbying standard-developing organisations and becoming effectively standard-setting entities themselves. Open data is vital as the long-term impact of IoT data is unimaginable. Open data is hard to achieve in context of increasing technical and legal secrecy. The Data Governance Act provides some incentives to open up data. However, it relies on an individualistic model of governance that ignores the interests of those affected by the decisions based on the data altruistically donated.[44] Preferences around data governance vary as they are political in nature; therefore, more participative approaches to the relevant design process should be adopted.[45] Important open data projects include the European Tracking Network, which integrates all aquatic animal tracking in Europe (fish tags) in one network. Open hardware has been pivotal to the growth of the IoT. One need only think of the Arduino boards, whose plans are published under a Creative Commons license. Open hardware meets the resistance of all those that see it as a threat to security. However, there are a number of promising projects that are making the idea of open hardware more widely accepted. An example is provided by the Databox, 'an

---

43 Shubha Ghosh, 'How to Build a Commons: Is Intellectual Property Constrictive, Facilitating, or Irrelevant?' in Charlotte Hess and Elinor Ostrom (eds), *Understanding Knowledge as a Commons: From Theory to Practice* (MIT Press 2007) 210.

44 Salomé Viljoen, 'Democratic Data: A Relational Theory For Data Governance' (2021) 131(2) YLJ 370.

45 Jeni Tennison, 'Individual, Collective and Community Interests in Data' (*Jeni's Musings*, 27 December 2020) <www.jenitennison.com/2020/12/27/individual-collective-community.html>.

open-source personal networked device, augmented by cloud-hosted services'[46] that mediates access to one's personal data by audited third-party applications. A nonacademic illustration is offered by Arribada, which codevelops open, customisable, and impact-driven conservation technologies. Its open platform provides the building blocks necessary to develop low-cost wireless sensors and biologging tags. Arribada's plug-and-play satellite connectivity can be added to any Thing, and this openness has enabled a number of green projects ranging from the tracking of plastic in the Ganges to avoiding human-elephant conflict in India.[47] Based on interviews with leaders in the field, it seems clear that the security concerns are overstated, but open hardware is still often regarded as not commercially attractive, as suggested by the fact that many make open hardware but rebrand it as 'future-proof' IoT and 'customisable' IoT. Finally, the openness of platforms is of utmost importance, and this brings us back to the first meaning of commons. An example is provided by the collective organisation of Google's employee in June 2020 to fight and end the company's practice to provide its AI to law enforcement agencies,[48] despite the visible failures of predictive policing and facial recognition, which has often perpetuated and exacerbated racism and other forms of discrimination. Finally, the openness of platforms depends on various regulatory factors. One the one hand, the rise of monitoring obligations epitomised by the upload filter is an incentive for platforms to 'close' themselves and become more secretive to reduce exposure to liability. On the other hand, recently proposed EU legislation is embracing the idea of auditing platforms. For example, under the draft Digital Services Act, very large online platforms are subject to yearly independent audits to assess compliance with the Act and the codes of conduct.[49] Similarly, under the proposed AI Act, providers of high-risk AI systems are audited to evaluate the maintenance of a quality management system that ensures compliance with this Act.[50] Audits are likely to be pivotal to opening all platforms, including IoT ones. In opening software, hardware, standards, data, and platforms, an important role will be played by the design of Things. For years now, human-centred design has been the prevalent approach, but it has often adopted an individualistic outlook: those who are not the direct users of the Thing and the collective interests that could not be linked to a specific human being would often be overlooked.[51] Against this backdrop, More-

---

46 'Databox Project' (*Imperial College London*) <www.imperial.ac.uk/a-z-research/systems-algorithms-design-lab/research/databox-project/>. See Andy Crabtree and others, 'Building Accountability into the Internet of Things: The IoT Databox Model' (2018) 4 Journal of Reliable Intelligent Environments 39.

47 'Blog' (*Arribada Initiative | Open Source Conservation Technology*) <https://arribada.org/blog/>.

48 Megan Rose Dickey, 'Google Employees Demand Company Stop Selling Tech to Police' (*TechCrunch*, 22 June 2022) <www.techcrunch.com/2020/06/22/google-employees-demand-company-stop-selling-tech-to-police/>.

49 Digital Services Act, art 28.

50 AI Act, art 17 and annex VII, point 5.3.

51 Elisa Giaccardi and Felipe Pierantoni, 'The Repertoire of Meaningful Voice Interactions. How to Design Good Smart Speakers' in *The State of Responsible IoT 2020* (ThingsCon 2020) 53.

Than-Human Design should be preferred as a methodology to design Things that take into account the consequences that decrease the well-being of all the inhabitants of the relevant natural and social systems.[52] While I would warn of the consequences of framing this new design approach as Thing-centred[53] or Post-Human-Centred[54] – as I still believe that human beings, albeit in their collective dimension, should be the core concern of regulation (including regulation 'by design') – I do think that, especially in a time of climate emergency and social unrest, we can no longer afford an individualistic IoT.

Overall, there are some reasons to remain hopeful that through free and open-source software, standards, data, hardware, and platforms, we will one day realise the dream of an open and socially just IoT. This is likely to depend more on collectively organised citizens than on big tech–lobbied governments. Such collective forms of organised resistance can be formal or informal. Trade union action is a prime example of the former. In December 2020, the Tribunale di Bologna upheld the motion of trade union CGIL to consider Deliveroo's algorithm discriminatory as it would penalise riders who would be less productive due to sickness or exercise of the right to strike.[55] Equally important are informal forms of collective resistance, especially popular in the IoT space. The most famous one is the Open Internet of Things Certification Mark. This was a community-led project initiated in 2017 by the IoT meetup. It led inter alia to 'Better IoT,' a free, accessible, open assessment tool aimed at start-ups and SMEs to help them design better-connected products. From talking to one its founders, it appeared clear that collective and community-led projects are vital for at least two reasons. first, ethics is often pushed by professional bodies, but the IoT does not have one; second, IoT makers come from diverse background, and if they do not talk to each other, there is a risk of reducing responsible innovation to mere issues of security. Some initiatives work within the capitalistic horizon, trying to reform the system from within. Certification schemes like BCorp[56] and Responsible 100,[57] as well as the

---

52 Maximilian Brandi and Philipp Kaltofen, 'Entangled Interfaces – The Design of Post Human-Centered Interfaces' in *The State of Responsible IoT 2020* (ThingsCon 2020) 58.

53 Elisa Giaccardi and others, 'Thing Ethnography: Doing Design Research with Non-Humans' *Proceedings of the 2016 ACM Conference on Designing Interactive Systems* (ACM 2016); Wen-Wei Chang and others, '"Interview with Things": A First-Thing Perspective to Understand the Scooter's Everyday Socio-Material Network in Taiwan' *Proceedings of the 2017 Conference on Designing Interactive Systems* (ACM 2017).

54 Jan Rod, 'Post Human-Centered Design Approach for Ubiquity' <https://escholarship.org/uc/item/7nx6199f>; Brandi and Kaltofen (n 53).

55 Tribunale di Bologna, Sezione Lavoro, ordinanza 31 December 2020 (*Filcams CGIL Bologna, NIDIL CGIL Bologna, FILT CGIL Bologna v Deliveroo Italia srl*).

56 Certified B Corporations are businesses that meet the highest standards of verified social and environmental performance, public transparency, and legal accountability to balance profit and purpose. 'About B Corps' (*BCorp*) <https://bcorporation.net/about-b-corps>.

57 Responsible 100 is a catalyst for better business; it provides tools to assess and improve businesses' performance on social and environmental issues. 'Responsible 100' (*Responsible 100*) <www.responsible100.com/>.

Zebra movement,[58] are part of this trend. For example, BCorp-certified Mycroft has been successful at developing an open, customisable, and private alternative to Echo but has since been busy with patent litigation.[59] The most promising realities operate through anticapitalistic models. Hubs such as the Platform Cooperativism Consortium facilitate the creation of jointly owned and democratically controlled enterprises with a commitment to open-source development and open data.[60] Similarly, CoTech is a network of digital worker cooperatives that believe that technology can make the world fairer as 'workers who collectively own their companies and control their destinies make better workplaces, better suppliers and better digital products.'[61] More IoT-specific, the Things Network provides a set of open tools and a global, open network to build IoT applications that have so far included a range of community projects ranging from cattle tracking to smart irrigation.[62] While IoT cooperatives seem to me the most attractive model, they are not the only one and they are not necessarily the best approach in every sector and geographical area. Other models include membership associations, such as ThingsCon, known for its Trustable Technology certification mark, whereby IoT companies undergo an assessment to evaluate if they are developing fair, responsible, and human-centric technologies.[63] ThingsCon also contributes through an annual collection of essays to explore the challenges, opportunities, and questions surrounding the creation of a responsible IoT.[64] Similarly, think tank Doteveryone developed TechTransformed – now adopted by the Open Data Institute – a set of open practical resources to help organisations be more technologically responsible day-to-day.[65] Another relevant organisational structure is the action group; for example, INTEROPen adopts such a model to accelerate the development of open standards for interoperability in the health and social care sector, while putting commercial interests to one side.[66] Some projects are more institutional than others e.g., OpenUK is a not-for-profit company and industry advocacy organisation that promotes open software, open hardware, and open data while representing the UK in the development of Gaia-X.[67] The latter is a

58 A cooperatively owned movement that pushes alternative business models that aim to balance profit and purpose inter alia by incentivising the sharing of power and resources. Astrid Scholz, 'Where Unicorns Fear to Tread' (*Medium*, 2 February 2020) <https://medium.com/zebras-unite/where-unicorns-fear-to-tread-building-businesses-that-are-better-for-the-world-35190e632c9e>.

59 Joshua Montgomery, 'Mycroft Defeats Patent Trolls . . . Again . . . For Now' (*Mycroft*, 15 October 2020) <https://mycroft.ai/blog/mycroft-defeats-patent-trolls-again/>.

60 'Platform Cooperativism Consortium' (*Platform Cooperativism Consortium*) <https://platform.coop/>.

61 'Our Manifesto' (*CoTech*) <www.coops.tech/manifesto.html>.

62 'The Things Network' <www.thethingsnetwork.org/>.

63 ThingsCon, 'Trustable Technology' (*TrustableTech*) <https://trustabletech.org/>.

64 ThingsCon, 'The State of Responsible IoT 2020' (ThingsCon eV 2020) <www.thingscon.org/publications/the-state-of-responsible-iot-2020/>.

65 doteveryone, 'Five Years Fighting for Better Tech for Everyone' (2020).

66 'Vision Mission Values' (*INTEROPen*) <www.interopen.org/about-us/>.

67 'OpenUK Joins Euro Data Infrastructure Gaia-X Project' (*OpenUK*, 20 November 2020) <https://openuk.uk/press-posts/openuk-joins-euro-data-infrastructure-gaia-x-project/>.

project to develop a European federated data infrastructure where openness and transparency are declared to be central aims. It is unclear how the ultimate goal of data sovereignty can be achieved involving US companies closely tied to the military and intelligence apparatus, such as Palantir.[68] While most of these initiatives are local, some are international. For instance, openEHR International is the nonprofit organisation behind a community-led campaign for e-health, consisting of open specifications, clinical models, and software that can be used to create standards and build information and interoperability solutions for healthcare.[69] During the pandemic, this community released open-source components to assist software developers in creating applications to fight COVID-19.

Upon interviewing some of these projects' founders, three common threads emerged. First, they do not hold much hope that legal interventions will do much to improve the IoT, although specific reforms in support of the right to repair, corporate transparency, and data control seem to be the top priorities for those working in the field. Second, they are convinced that on a level playing field, open models would be a winner, and therefore antitrust authorities should do more against incumbents that can sell Things at a loss because they monetise sensor data in opaque ways. Ensuring a level playing field would also mean preventing IoT big tech from externalising costs especially by neglecting the IoT's sustainability footprint. Third, perhaps most importantly, what they expect from governments is mostly the convinced backing of different ownership and control model that have potential to scale and, unlike venture capitalist–backed organisations, do not aim for growth. This support can take many forms, from public funding through procurement to tax relief. Recommendations for governments include the backing of cooperatives with a model to raise investment which is not from a venture capitalist, and need-based projects. Instead of more IoT gadgets, Things that help people with their basic needs, e.g. food, safe shelter, health. Currently, there are nearly 2,000 IoT meetups around the world – a vast number of which is in the Global South – with a million and a half active participants. In their collective, organised, bottom-up participatory action – not in bourgeois law, not in the ethical turn, not in the idea of regulation 'by design' – lies the hope for a better, human-centric, open, responsible, and socially just IoT.

Future research should be dedicated to more systematically comprehending the convergence between the commons and the IoT, including from queer and black perspectives. *Queer* here means a radical critique of society and culture put forward by nonnormative, oppressed, and 'othered' subjects.[70] Much of the impact of the IoT on the law and on power can be framed as a form of 'queering,' as

---

68 Ed Targett, 'Palantir and GAIA-X: Data Miner "Joins" EU Sovereign Cloud Project' (*The Stack*, 21 December 2020) <https://thestack.technology/palantir-and-gaia-x/>.

69 'OpenEHR Community Rises to the Challenge of Coronavirus' (*open EHR*, 11 March 2020) <www.openehr.org/news_events/openehr_news/311>.

70 *Queer* is often understood as an umbrella term for the LGBTQ+ community, but it has developed into a way of understanding the world that is not limited to the sexual dimension. Whilst queer is a polysemous concept, one should be wary not to entirely disconnect it from gender and sexuality.

in overcoming and troubling binary representations of the world (good-service, human-thing, consumer-worker, etc.) and celebrating forms of power that are fluid, both virtual and physical, public and private. Queer theory gives a meaningful contribution to the understanding of the commons and to activating its political potential.[71] Queer activism is a resource to be harnessed to imagine, experiment with, and enact 'the improvisational infrastructures necessary for managing the unevenness of contemporary existence.'[72] Not by accident, Gezi Park – where the 'largest and most public performance of commons in the history of the country'[73] took place – was a place where trans and queer people would have clandestine sexual encounters. The queer commons intersects with critical race theory and Global South voices, which can most notably be seen in the idea of 'brown commons' proposed by queer theorist José Esteban Muñoz: the brown commons is '*not about the production of the individual but instead about a movement*, a flow, and an impulse, to move *beyond the singular and individualized subjectivities*.'[74] To queer the laws of the IoT means to rethink them in a way that accommodates the non-binary nature of this sociotechnological phenomenon and that incentivises bottom-up collective action. Whether this approach will be taken by future legislative, regulatory, and jurisprudential innovations – e.g. the proposed Data Act,[75] or the antitrust interventions that will ensue from the Commission's inquiry into consumer IoT[76]– will be the subject of close scrutiny. To queer the IoT and its laws and to embrace the commons is no easy pursuit, but it is one whereupon the future of our society depends.

---

71 José Esteban Muñoz, *The Sense of Brown* (Tavia Amolo Ochieng' Nyongó and Joshua Takano Chambers-Letson eds, DUP 2020).

72 Nadja Millner-Larsen and Gavin Butt, 'Introduction' (2018) 24 GLQ: A Journal of Lesbian and Gay Studies 399, 400. With a reference to Lauren Berlant, 'The Commons: Infrastructures for Troubling Time' (2016) 34(3) Environment and Planning D: Society and Space 393.

73 Özbay and Savcı (n 36) 517.

74 José Esteban Muñoz, 'Preface: Fragment from the Sense of Brown Manuscript' (2018) 24 GLQ: A Journal of Lesbian and Gay Studies 395, 397. Emphasis added. However, one should not forget that the commons has also been criticised as 'steeped in colonial structures' (Macarena Gómez-Barris, 'How to Block the Extractive View' (2018) 24 GLQ: A Journal of Lesbian and Gay Studies 527, who refers to a 2013 lecture by J. Kēhaulani Kauanui). Therefore, in arguing for an IoT as a commons, we should also queer the commons, which means understanding its racial and gendered origins and embracing an antiracist and feminist concept of commons.

75 Proposal for a Regulation of the European Parliamento and of the Council on harmonised rules on fair access to and use of data ('Data Act') (COM/2022/68 final). Not to be confused with the Data Governance Act, the Data Act promises to clarify 'rights on non-personal Internet of Things data stemming from professional use' ('Data Act & Amended Rules on the Legal Protection of Databases' (*European Commission*, 3 June 2021) <https://ec.europa.eu/info/law/better-regulation/have-your-say/initiatives/13045-Data-Act-including-the-review-of-the-Directive-96-9-EC-on-the-legal-protection-of-databases-/public-consultation_en>).

76 'Antitrust: Initial Findings of Consumer IoT Sector Inquiry' (*European Commission*, 9 July 2021) <https://ec.europa.eu/commission/presscorner/detail/en/IP_21_2884>.

Index

Note: Page numbers in *italics* indicate a figure and page numbers in **bold** indicate a table on the corresponding page.

2016 US election 203
3G 20n74, 325
4G technologies 20n74, 56
5G technologies 38n211, 55–56, 325
6LowPAN 20–21, 21n76

abuse of dominant position 21, 328–329, 340, 350
abuse of rights 331, 331n448, 349; theory of 322n377
accountability 14, 48, 63, 246; legal 356n58; principle of 244–245
accumulation by dispossession 253–254
actuators 2, 6, 12–13, 253, 256, 342
adequacy decisions 93, 93n151, 238, 259–261
advertising ; interest-based **86**, 242
advertorials 226, 232
affective computing 263, 270, 347
affiliate **85–89**, 92–97, 95n161, 99, **100–105**, **108**, **110**, **111–112**, 115, 127, 343
aggressive practices 201, 205, 209, 215, 222, 224–226; *see also* coercion; harassment; undue influence
Agreement on Technical Barriers to Trade 13
Agreement on Trade-Related Aspects of Intellectual Property Rights (TRIPS) 279n32, 314, 321; TRIPS-plus provisions 314–315
AI *see* artificial intelligence (AI)
Alexa 70, **85**, **87–88**, 95, 107, **108**, **111**, 113, 116, 121, 136, 146, 148–149, 152, 157–158, 167, 175, 180, 185, 185n8, 202, 215, 236, 310; Black Box 258–264; Alexa Terms of Use **85**, 95,

115, 128–129, 131–132, 136, 148, 152, 185, 290
algorithms 1, 50, 54, 69, 118, 146, 250, 255, 266, 271–273, 274n311, 296, 309–310, 309n261, 310n265, 356; black box 296; opaque 78, 117, 233; Thing-embedded 310
Alibaba 34, 53
Alliance for Internet of Things Innovation (AIOTI) 23, 45, 62, 66
Amazon 54n351, 60, 70–71, 84, **85–90**, 92–99, 95n161, **100–105**, 107, **108**, 109, **110**, **111–112**, 113–116, 118, 120, 126–131, 136–140, 148–149, *150*, 151–152, 157, 163–164, 167–168, 172, 176–178, 180–181, 180n482, 185, 191, 202, 208, 211, 236, 249, 251, 258–260, 262, **262**, 262n234, 262n235, 264, 270–271, 287–288, 290–292, 338, 343–344, 347; Amazon Chime 113; Amazon Now 99; arrow 303; 'Buy Box' 54, 54n351; cloud services 70; Conditions of Use 131; 'Core Legals' 84, **85–90**, 91–92, 98, 115–116, 135; fine under GDPR 71; license information *72*; multilayered supply chain 92–98; privacy policy 260n215, 268; shopping interface 32; *VKI v Amazon* 120, 140; *see also* Alexa; Amazon.com Inc.; Amazon Dash Button; Amazon Device Terms of Use; Amazon Drive; Amazon Echo; Amazon EU S.à r.l.; Amazon Kindle; Amazon Media EU S.a.r.l.; Amazon Prime; Amazon Web Services (AWS); Ring
Amazon.com Inc. 71, *72*, 94, **102**, 259

Amazon Dash Button 81, 168, 174, *177*;
and precontractual information duties
176–181
Amazon Device Terms of Use 84, **85**, **100**,
115, 115n310, 128, 136, 151, 185
Amazon Drive (now Photos): Terms of
Use **89**, 127–128, 131
Amazon Echo 21, 29, 37, 58, 68, 70,
81, 84, 95, 109, 115–116, 121, 137,
148–149, 151–152, 157, 168, 172, 175,
180, 185, 188, 191, 193, 201, 207, 215,
268, 288, 290–292, 357; audio notices
167; cloud-related legals **111–112**,
113; conditions of sale 152; consumers
92–93, 97, 109, 116, 136, 149, 185;
contractual quagmire of 83–84, 91–99,
106–109, 113–115, 270, 288; core legals
85–90, 135; developer legals 107, **108**;
Echo Button **87**, 70; Echo Dot 70, 228;
Echo Flex 70; Echo Input 70, 146, 157;
Echo Look 70, 228, 236; Echo Plus
70, *173*; Echo Show 32, 70, **104**, 149,
149n261, *150*, 162, 172, 203, 228; Echo
Spot 70, 228, 236; Echo Wall Clock 70,
87; legals 70, 94, 98–99, **100–105**, 116,
118, 120, 129, 131, 135–136, 139, 151,
185; legals for prosumers **110**; software
291; terms 141, 182, 191; users 268,
291; *see also* Alexa
Amazon EU S.à r.l. (Amazon EU SARL)
71, **85**, **87–88**, 94, **100**, **104–105**, 151;
see also Amazon Media EU S.a.r.l.
Amazon Kindle 37, **85**, **88**, **90**, **102**, **104**,
149, 165
Amazon Media EU S.a.r.l. **85**, **88–89**, 94,
97, **102–105**, **108**, 127
Amazon Prime 95, **104**, 131–132, 137,
215; Prime Now *106*; Prime Terms **88**,
100–101, 128, 131–132, 195; Prime
Video **89**
Amazon Web Services (AWS) **87**, 94,
111–112, 113
anonymisation 38, 239–240, 247–248
antiproprietary collective resistance 285
antitrust control 277, 327, 349
antitrust jurisprudence 52
Apple 21, 53, 142, 160, 338; *HTC v Apple*
278; *see also* Apple Pay; Apple Watch
Apple Pay 19n65
Apple Watch 49, 160
apps 32, 77, **85**, 95, **102–105**, 107, **108**,
113, 151, 180, 185, 220, 282, 290
'arbitrary will' 69
Arduino IoT Manifesto 48

Aristotle 25, 25n110
Article 29 Working Party 62, 239–240,
239n37, 243, 247, 250, 266
artificial intelligence (AI) 3, 12, 15,
37n204, 38n211, 38n217, 47, 61, 118,
184, 196–197, 200, 294, 341, 355;
algorithms 118; *see also* Artificial
Intelligence (AI) Act
Artificial Intelligence (AI) Act 40, 40n230,
47, 66, 184–185, 355
'as described' 143, 148–149
Ashton, Kevin 11
'as reasonably expected' 148–149, 163
audiovisual content 29–30, 35
Austria 126, 140, 230, 317n332; Supreme
Court 228
autoethnography 7, 71–72, 344
automated decisions 237, 247, 264, 267,
269–273
autonomation 186
autonomous systems 38n211, 199
autonomy 25, 117, 201–202, 204, 250,
263, 281; energy 19; party 336, 338,
340, 350; principle of 69
average consumers 94, 132, 135–136,
209–211, 209n205, 214–215, 218, 223,
232, 302n194

BAME people 251
BATX (Baidu, Alibaba, Tencent, and
Xiaomi) 53–54
behaviour: technology of 255
behaviour(al) modification 4, 53, 253
behavioural prediction 4, 253
Belcher, Jennifer 82–83
Belgium 126, 197; *European Commission
v Belgium* 227
Berne Convention 320
big data 4, 10, 12, 26n120, 38n217, 53, 73,
82, 168, 243n66, 246, 250–251, 281, 305
big machine data 26, 26n120
binaries 55, 61–65, 233, 342, 346; *see also
specific binaries*; dichotomies
binary code 5
binding corporate rules 93, **112**, 260,
260n217
binding ethical instruments 47
'black box' AI algorithms 118
blacklists 126, 131, 206–209, 216,
226–228, 229, 232–233
blockchain 16n53, 49n308, 74, 341; energy
consumption of 2n5; technologies 12
Bluetooth 325, 349; *see also* Low Energy
Bluetooth (LEB)

Board of European Regulators for
  Electronic Communications (BEREC)
  59
Bosch 282–283; *Bosch v EUIPO* 149,
  282–283, *282*; 'Simply.Connected.'
  282–283, *282*
bots 2
'bourgeois law' 141, 141n212, 275–340, 358
bourgeois property 285–295
bourgeois society 294, 349
'brand loyalty by default' 177
breach of contract 130, 160, 186
Brexit 238
bricking 116; and consumer sales 165–167;
  definition 78; and lack of legals
  conformity 147–150; private ordering
  by 74, 78–79, **90**, 117, 142–167, 182,
  184, 345; regulation by 78
British Standards Institution (BSI)
  324n390
Brownsword, Roger 5, 15, 69, 78;
  technological management 69
Brussels effect 70
Bulgaria 126, 197, 226
burden of proof 143n220, 153, 170, 192,
  194
business-to-business relationships 37, 155,
  336, 336–337n494
business-to-consumer relationships 117,
  185, 226, 343
Buttarelli, Giovanni 65

capital convergence 276
capitalism *see* industrial capitalism;
  informational capitalism; rentier
  capitalism; surveillance capitalism
case law 26, 34, 121, 194, 210, 223, 277,
  307, 310, 315, 321, 329, 331, 333
causation 194
Center for Data Innovation 42
Children's Privacy Disclosure 84
China 42, 66, 284
circular economy 78–79, 114, 286, 348
civil society 1, 7, 61, 63
CJEU 76, 93, 120–122, 124, 135–136,
  138, 140, 144, 147n249, 149, 153, 187,
  189, 192, 206–207, 211, 214–215, 221,
  225, 227–230, 247, 249–250, 260,
  260n219, 283, 288–289, 298–301,
  303, 305–307, 309, 311–312, 312n290,
  318–320, 323, 326–331, 330n436, 333,
  336–337, 340, 350
class consciousness 7, 350
'click-wrap' 139

climate change 2n5, 79, 113
cloud computing 1n2, 12, 19, 98, 109, 113,
  240
Cloud of Things 37, 92, 109, 113, 147
cloud storage 37, 300; unfair terms and
  incentives hierarchy 127–133, *132*
clusters 44
code (or design) 5, 41–54, 76, 78, 252,
  276, 280, 297–299, 355; binary 5; as
  law 41, 69, 76; QR 44; as self-regulation
  49n307
codes of conduct 37, 84, 93, 216, 260–261;
  industry 41
coercion 223–224
Cohen, Julie E. 5, 252; *Between Truth and
  Power* 5, 252
collective interest 119, 119n12, 178,
  293–294, 339, 349, 355
collective property 294
collective resistance 285, 351, 353n40, 356
colonialism 46n284, 254
commercial excursions 220, 223
commercial exploitation 288–289
Common European Sales Law 154, 165
common good 245, 257
common law 6, 145n233, 189, 216n258,
  225, 336, 336n493
commons 251, 275, 295, 339–340,
  341–359, 353n38, 353n40, 359n74;
  concept of 284, 359n74; data as 285; for
  an open IoT 277, 284–285
communication to the public (right of)
  289–290
Community Design Regulation 304n218,
  320
compatibility 15, 163, 305
compensatory remedies 145
competition 27, 31, 31n159, 41, 59, 63–65,
  199, 203, 239, 295, 305, 328–329,
  330n436, 333, 333n466, 339–340,
  349; free 322; unfair 178, 304; *see also*
  competition law
Competition and Market Authority 120,
  127–133
Competition Commissioner 333–334
competition law 3, 65, 313, 323–324, 333,
  338, 340
complaint and redress mechanism 280
compliance burden(s) 40, 75–76, 157, 237,
  240, 248–250
comprehensibility 135, 181; requirement 172
computer program 13, 146, 278, 279n32,
  288–290, 296–298, 297n161, 310,
  316n328, 318–319

computer-implemented invention 264, 278, 316n328, 322, 322n375
conditioning 257
conditions of sale 84, 128, 151–152
conditions of use 84, **85**–86, 95, 97, 99, **102**, 128–132, 139, 151, 164, 172, 179, 185, 290–291
confidentiality 237–239; *see also* confidentiality law
confidentiality law 265
conformity 143–145, 147–150, 152–155, 153n283, 163–167, 171, 182, 198–199, 345; objective requirements 163; presumptions of 163–165; requirements for 163–165; subjective requirements 163; *see also* 'conformity assessment procedure'
'conformity assessment procedure' ('type approval') 198
connectivity 11–12, 19–21, 56–57, 72, **85**, 148, 187, 198n118, 199–200, 241, 243, 283–284, 323, 325–326, 335, 342–343, 349, 355; fragmented 21n79; high-speed 55–61; hyper- 10, 74, 81, 118, 167–181, 183, 204, 345; inter- 12, 325; IoT 21n79
consent 38n216, 76, 172–173, 224, 229, 259, 265, 273, 288; affirmative action 243–244; demonstrability 244; ease of withdrawal 244; explicit 261, 271–273; freely given 242; granularity 242, 244; informed 242; notice-and- 81, 118, 168, 170, 172; quality of 240–245, 244n72; specific 242–243; unambiguous 242–243
consumer benefits 72–74
consumer contract law(s) 116, 117–118, 153, 183, 345
consumer contracts 31, 81, 97, 117, 119, 137, 159, 175, 178, 240n43, 336–337n494; business-to- 181, 183; *see also* consumer contract laws
consumer empowerment 116, 142, 233, 296n151
consumer law(s) 30, 31n159, 37, 74–75, 81, 84, 109, 141, 153, 155, 160, 164, 167–168, 170, 181, 183, 236n8, 344; noncontractual 184–234, 211n221
consumer manipulation 82, 185, 202–229, 231–234, 347
consumer preferences 302
Consumer Protection Cooperation 228
consumer protection law(s) 127, 164
consumer rights 77, 107; *see also* Consumer Rights Act; Consumer Rights Directive (CRD)

Consumer Rights Act 13n23, 126
Consumer Rights Directive (CRD) 75, 81, 118–119, 153n293, 155n308, 167–181, 180n482, 183, 183n486, 205–206, 222, 229, 345
consumer risks 74–83; vulnerabilities 200, 205, 211–213, 227–228, 232
consumer sales 153n293, 155, *157*; *see also* consumer sales law(s)
Consumer Sales Directive 74, 158; *see also* First Consumer Sales Directive; Second Consumer Sales Directive
consumer sales law(s) 117, 142–167, 169n397, 182, 199
consumers' safety 117
consumer-to-business relationships 226
consumer-trader binary 5, 109
content *see* audiovisual content
contract law(s) 77, 92, 97, 138, 143, 153, 166n376, 168, 184, 304; *see also* consumer contract law(s)
contract of sale 144, 150–152, 286
contracts 7, 23, 31, 68–70, 74, 77–78, 83–84, 92–93, 97–98, 106, 109, 113, 117, 121, 123, 133, 135, 138–139, 145, 147, 153n293, 158, 160–163, 166, 166n376, 168–170, 169n190, 180, 182, 250, 255, 275, 286–287, 299, 308–309, 312, 336–337n494, 343, 346; business-to-consumer 31, 74, 181, 183; cloud 131, 133, 182; cloud storage 131; consumer 31, 81, 97, 117, 119, 137, 159, 168, 175, 178, 183, 240n43; distance 158, 170–176, **174**; IoT 68, 117, 126, 145, 150–153, 166; market-based 50; networks of 84, 84n99, 94, 123; standard 120; web of 127, 345; *see also* contract law(s); contract of sale; consumer contract law(s); dual-purpose contracts; Internet of Contracts
contractual necessity 244n72, 271–273
contractual parties 84, **86–87**, 99, 108, **111**, 115–116, 184, 343–344
contractual performance 261
contractual quagmire 40, 68–116, 117–118, 126–127, 132–133, 138–140, 142, 152, 181–182, 184, 213, 220, 297, 308, 343–345; of Amazon Echo 83–84, 91–99, 106–109, 113–115, 270, 288; and Unfair Terms Directive 119–123
contractual transparency: as fairness issue 92
controlled interoperability 92, 106–109
controllers 23, **87**, 93–4, 239–240, 243–244, 248, 260, 266, 268–269,

271–273; data 50, 76, 241–243, 247, 249, 261, 266, 269–271, 273; joint 249; *see also* controllership
controllership: joint 248–250
Convention on the International Sale of Goods 140, 144, 151
cookies 82, **86**, **102–103**, 201, 240–241, 259
cooperativism 356, 357
copycat branding 216
copyright 203n161; 3D objects 320n363; content 29, 35; designs 320; duration of 279; exceptions 291, 312n290, 317, 320–321, 339, 349; general 290, 298, 316–318; holders 289, 317; infringement **104**, 280, 280n40, 293, 311, 317n332, 322n376; law 30, 290, 298, 318, 321, 322n375; 'literary' 299; 'para-' 280; parody exception to 320–321; -patent overlap 317, 317n331; protection 279, 300, 320; reform of 28–30, 30n158; territoriality of 1, 9, 29–30, 35; three-dimensional 300; *see also* Berne Convention; Copyright in the Digital Single Market Directive; Digital Millennium Copyright Act; software copyright; WIPO Copyright Treaty
Copyright in the Digital Single Market Directive 298–299, 313–314, 322n376
Core Conventions of the International Labour Organization (ILO) 114n304
coregulation 40, 45, 50, 61–66, 338, 342
corporate power: over the Thing 291; over user-generated content 291–295
corporate social responsibility (CSR) 92, 113–114
cost-benefit analysis 61
Council of Europe 247
COVID-19 (Coronavirus) 214, 292, 315, 358
creating-obtaining dichotomy 307
Creative Commons license 354
credulity 212
Cross-Border Service Portability Regulation 29–32, 35–36, 217
cross-device tracking 204, 233, 248
cumulation 275, 291, 313, 315–316, 320–321
customer-centrism 202
customer-trader relationship 202
cybernetics 50
cybersecurity 3, 63, 79–80, 186, 193–194; issues 42n248; vs security 80, 186, 200, 233, 347; *see also* Cybersecurity Act; hacking

Cybersecurity Act 45, 80
cyberspace 2, 24, 24n106, 49–50, 76, 78
cyber threats 198
cyborg consumers 234, 347
Czech Republic 126

damage(s) 12n19, 125, 186, 188–190, 192–194, 197, 199–200, 209, 216n258, 328, 334, 334n475; concept of 193; moral 193; nonmaterial 193; 'transaction' 193
data: AI-powered mining 307, 347; altruism 257; biometric 6; brokers 270; collection 84, 244, 307; commercialisation of 227, 236; as commodity 4, 160; as commons 285; control 160, 237–240, 264–265, 358; control law(s) 265; controllers 50, 76, 241–243, 247, 249, 261, 266, 269–271, 273; created 307; 'dark' data 257; defective 191; dispossessed 255, 270; ethics 6; exhaust 256; exporters 93n155, 260–261; extraction 276; facial recognition 6; importers **86**, 93n155, 191, 259–261; inaccuracy 247; inferred/inferential 240, 246–247, 274, 347; international transfers of 93, 113, 116, 259, 344; IoT 20, 36, 76, 137, 166, 201, 225, 241, 246, 250, 258, 264, 274, 281–282, 305–307, 309, 312, 333, 347, 354; localisation laws 36–40; management 6; mining 31n164, 256; monetisation 160, 219, 228; nonpersonal 26, 28, 36–40, 38n217, 66, **105**, 250, 258–259, 268; obtained 307; open 109, 340, 351, 354, 357–358; ownership 277, 281–282; personal 12n18, 22–23, 32, 38–39, 38n217, 46, 58, 76, **85–86**, 99, **105**, 107, 147, 155, 159–162, 166, 169, 182, 215, 219–220, 227, 237–239, 241–247, 249, 251, 258–259, 260n219, 261–262, 261n233, 262n234, 264–271, 273, 345, 347, 355; portability 36, 38, 268–269; power 76, 76n50, 124, 149, 248, 250, 294, 309, 313; producers 4, 6, 160, 253, 274, 281; raw 38, 256; science 6; security 42; selfishness 257; socialisation of 353; subjects 36, 76–77, **105**, 160–161, 173, 236, 239, 241, 243–244, 247–250, 257, 266–269, 271–274, 287, 347–348; vs trade secrets 264–269; transfers **86**, 93, **112**, 113, 116, 159, 259–260, 344; ubiquitous 257; waste 257; *see also* Data Governance Act; data protection;

health data; industrial data; inferential data; machine data; open data; personal data; sensitive data

Data Governance Act 257, 313, 354, 359n75

data protection: anonymisation 38, 239–240, 247–248; by design 22, 50, 50n317, 270; digital dispossession 235–274; as fundamental right 160; information asymmetry 118, 135, 137, 163, 240–241, 240n43; issues in IoT 239–251; lack of control 240–241; quality of consent 240–245, 244n72; shifting compliance burden 248–250; status of inferential data 240, 246–247, 274, 347; *see also* Data Protection Directive; Data Protection Impact Assessment; data protection law(s)

Data Protection Directive 237, 240, 242–243, 264n247

Data Protection Impact Assessment 247

data protection law(s) 22–23, 26, 76, **111**, 183, 236, 236n8, 238, 258, 274, 281n43

database(s): contents 306, 308; definition 305; extraction and reutilisation of 296, 306; IoT 305–307; makers 307–309; nonelectronic 308; originality of 309; spin-off 306–307; substantiality of 309; *see also* Database Directive; database right

Database Directive 281, 305, 308n254, 309, 312, 314n298

database right 288, 305

datafication 255

death of ownership 74, 76–78, **89–90**, 99, 106, 159, 276–277, 285–295, 297, 299–300, 308–309, 313, 323, 327–328, 339–340, 348–349

decision-making 202, 213, 246; automated 267, 269–272; autonomous 226; consumer 201; rational 202

decompilation 23, 23n97, 296–297, 298n166, 319; exception 291, 319

defective products 13, 13n25, 75n39, 186–187, 197, 200

defects 13, 74, 79, **87**, 117, 184, 187, 191–192, 198, 346; chemical 346; factual 199; fraudulently concealed 195; hardware **88**; hidden 197; intangible 191, 346; IoT 13n24; legal 165, 199; liability for 197; mechanical 346; nonhardware 13n25; postsale 200, 346; unpredictability of 196

dematerialisation 1–2, 98, 292

democratic values 4, 251

Denmark 37; Danish Bookkeeping Act 37

derogations 261, 267

Deroo-Blanquart v Sony Europe 76, 209, 220–222

de Sade, Marquis 25

Design Directive 304, 320

design law 304–305, 320–321

design rights 296, 302, 304, 304n209, 304n210, 305, 313, 315, 320–321, 348

developers 22, 46, 107–108, 107n246, 115, 249, 298; legals of 107; software 322n375, 358

'development risk' defence 195–196, 200

dichotomies *see specific dichotomies/ divides*

'Dieselgate' 230

'Digital Clearinghouse' 65

digital content 11, 13, 13n23, **85**, **104**, **108**, 144, 147, 153–167, 153n293, 155n310, 169, 171–172, 182, 185, 189, 217, 232, 289–291, 299; *see also* Digital Content Directive; digital content law

Digital Content Directive (Directive 2019/770) 40, 40n228, 55, 75, 75n36, 118, 118n2, 153–154, 156–162, 165–167, 183, 345

digital content law 167, 199

digital dispossession **103**, 235–274, 347–348, 353; IoT-powered 264–273

digital economy 1, 27–28, 159, 166, 245

digital enclosure 276

digital environment 204, 232, 311, 321

digitalisation 1, 159

digital labour 6, 294

digital literacy 233

digitally dispossessed 269–273

digital market(s) 65, 227, 232; manipulation 204; *see also* Digital Markets Act

Digital Markets Act 28, 208, 209, 313, 343n6

Digital Millennium Copyright Act 293, 315n316

digital platforms 68, 76n50, 340

digital revolution 98, 154, 166n376, 203

digital rights management (DRM) 279–282, 280n40, 287

digital serfs/serfdom 277, 294

digital services 9, 40n228, 75n36, 118n2, 153–167, 169, 182; *see also* Digital Services Act; Digital Services Package

Digital Services Act 28, 279n34, 313, 343n7, 355

Digital Services Package 343, 343n5

digital shelf 54, 203, 208

Digital Single Market (DSM) 27–28, 30, 32–36, 35n193, 39–40, 55, 60n402, 66, 154, 158–160, 322n376; *see also* Digital Single Market (DSM) Directive; Digital Single Market (DSM) strategy; DSM Copyright Directive
Digital Single Market (DSM) strategy 27–28, 55, 154
digital supply laws 153–167
digital tenants 74, 74, 276–277, 285–286, 348
'digital twin' 262
Digitising European Industry initiative 45
dignity 3, 114, 229, 250, 258
direct marketing 148, 229, 240–241
Directive 93/13/EEC 119, 119n9
Directive on Computer-Implemented Inventions 322
Directive on the Resilience of Critical Entities 198, 198n119
dishonest action 214
'dissuasive effect' 121
distance contracts 158, 170–176, *174*
Distance Selling Directive 168
distinctiveness 277, 282–284
dominant position 21, 250, 328–329, 329n432, 340, 350; *see also* abuse of dominant position
domotics 16, 18, 18n57, 21n81
doorstep selling 220, 223; *see also* Doorstep Selling Directive
Doorstep Selling Directive 168
Draft Common Frame of Reference 151
Draft ePrivacy Regulation 59
driverless cars 16, 73, 79, 193
drones 3, 18, 18n62
DSM Copyright Directive 28, 161
dual-purpose contracts 109
due cause 296, 303
duties of pre-contractual information 92

e-books **84**, **104**, 165, 288–289, 299, 318
Echo *see* Amazon Echo
ECHR 273n305, 310–311, 322n376, 327, 339
Ecodesign Directive 79
e-commerce 34, 81–82, 167–168, 174, 180, 191n49, 202, 207, 219, 233, 290; *see also* e-Commerce Directive
e-Commerce Directive 14, 28n143, 219
economic interests 229–231, 233; non- 230
ECtHR 223, 247, 250n133, 258, 303, 305, 310–311
edge computing 12

Edinburgh Initiative 48–49
emotion recognition 205, 211, 233, 262–264
End User Licence Agreements 165
Enforcement and Modernisation of Consumer Protection Directive (Directive 2019/2161) 119, 205, 207, 213, 217–220, 223, 227, 231
Engels, Friedrich 351–352
England 145, 211
ENISA 80, 81n80
Enron 254
entities 22n86, 22n87, 23, 25, 55, 64, 93, 119, 134, 237, 245, 270, 354
ePrivacy Directive 59–60
equality 3, 121
Estonia 197
ethical turn 47–49, 52, 358
'ethics bashing' 48
ethics by design 48n299
ethics charters 47
Ethics Guidelines for Trustworthy AI 15, 47
'ethics washing' 48
EU 11, 22n91, 27, 29, 31, 36, 36n201, 60n406, 69, 78, 118n7, 150, 175, 187–188, 196, 211, 237–238, 300, 302, 309, 316n326, 320, 323, 331, 331n447; ban on geoblocking 32–36; Charter of Fundamental Rights 141, 264, 327, 330; consumer sales law 143–153; 'EU reform' 28, 153–167, 302n195; European Digital Strategy 28; hard law approach 55–61; IoT strategy 40–67; product liability laws 185–200; reform of laws on consumer sales and digital supply 153–167; regulatory and policy options 40–61; Standardisation Regulation 324; Trade Marks Regulation 302n195, 303; Treaties 29; *see also* General Data Protection Regulation (GDPR)
EULA 76–77, 107, 107n246, 297
Europe 4, 27, 56–57, 71, 79, 84, 96, 137, 164, 187n20, 194, 306, 310, 316, 316n328, 329n425, 354; feudal 277, 293
European Alliance for Internet of Things Innovation (AIOTI) 23, 45, 62, 66
European Commission 13n25, 15, 27, 34, 36, 38n217, 39, 44–45, 47, 54n351, 55–56, 62, 64, 93, 93n151, 123, 139, 174, 176, 184, 186, 190, 198n118, 199, 212, 218, 221, 225, 227, 229–231, 233, 238, 259–260, 281, 313, 326, 328, 332–

333, 335–338, 343, 350; Communication 'Setting out the Approach to Standard Essential Patents' 338; *European Commission v Belgium* 227; *see also* European Commission High-Level Expert Group on Artificial Intelligence

European Commission High-Level Expert Group on Artificial Intelligence 15; *Ethics Guidelines for Trustworthy AI* 15, 47

European Committee for Electrotechnical Standardisation (CENELEC) 324–325

European Committee for Standardisation (CEN) 324

European Consumer Agenda 232

European Consumer Organisation 193

European Convention of Human Rights 141, 197

European Data Protection Board (EDPB) 62, 93n155, **112**, 172, 239n37, 243n68

European Data Protection Supervisor (EDPS) 65, 132, 204

European Economic Area (EEA) 30–31, 30n155, 36, **111**, 228, 238, 259, 288

European Electronic Communications Code (EECC) 55–61

European Parliament 60n406, 65, 161, 260n219

European Patent Convention (EPC) 278

European Patent Office (EPO) 278, 284

European Research Cluster on the Internet of Things (IERC) 43–44, 43n262

European Telecommunications Standards Institute (ETSI) 51, 81, 323, 325–326, 328, 335; TS103645 81

European Tracking Network 354

European values 43, 46

EU-US Privacy Shield **86**, 93, 93n151, **111**, 259m 259n208, 260–261

Everyware Principles 48

evidentiary standard 188

evidentiary threshold 194

exceptions ; decompilation 291, 319

'excluded subject matter' 278

execution 251–258

exemption ; household 248–250

exhaustion, principle of 38, 38n216, 288–290, 295, 300, 318, 323, 327

Expert Group on Liability and New Technologies 194

extractive practices 4, 10, 213, 250, 285, 346

extra-IP limitations 295, 323–339

extraterritoriality 40, 66, 342

Facebook 53–54, 161, 202–203, 249, 253, 259, 294

Facebook Australia 118

facial recognition 355; data 6; software 250

factual control 275, 281–282, 287, 295, 313

fair, reasonable, and nondiscriminatory terms *see* FRAND terms

fair trade practices 305

fair use doctrine 78, 296, 317, 321, 321n369, 321n372, 322n374, 334, 339, 349

Fairfield, Joshua 77, 276–277, 292–293; *Owned* 77, 277, 292

fairness 54n355, 92, 116, 126, 128–129, 131, 133, 141–142, 182–183, 207, 269, 271, 336–337n494, 338, 340, 343–344, 350

Federal Trade Commission (FTC; US) 41–43, 53–54, 327, 327n413

feudalism 254, 293–294

feudal society 294

financial crisis of 2007–2008 254

financialisation 254

fingerprint, unique 248

Finland 196–197

fintech world 62

First Consumer Sales Directive (Directive 1999/44/EC) 143, 145–146, 145n233, 148, 150–156, 154n303, 163, 182, 345

fit for purpose 200, 215

Flesch-Kincaid test 135, 142, 182, 344

Floyd, George 250

flying jurisdiction, principle of 178

foreseeability, concept of 12, 12n19, 27, 149

Fourth Industrial Revolution 3, 70, 307

France 33n178, 79, 94, 126, 207, 238, 273; CNIL 238; *Conseil d'État* 207–208; *Loi informatique et libertés* 273

FRAND licensing and terms 323–340, 329n425, 337n497, 349–350

free and open-source software (FOSS) 285, 354, 355

free competition, principle of 31, 322

freedom of expression 3, 265, 280, 293, 296, 303, 305, 310–312, 322, 322n376, 330–331, 339, 349–350

freedom of information 265, 293, 296, 310–312

Free Flow of Data initiative 281

free flow of non-personal data 26, 28, 40, 66; *see also* Free Flow of Non-Personal Data Regulation

Free Flow of Non-Personal Data Regulation 37–40, 37n204

free market 164, 319; imperatives 38
Frischmann, Brett 4, 252; *Re-engineering Humanity* 4, 252
functionality 21n81, 51, 78, **89**, 99, 115, 163, 165, 171, 187, 292n126
function creep 246
fundamental freedoms 289, 293, 323

GAFA (Google, Apple, Facebook, and Amazon) 53–54
gatekeepers 207–209, 343, 343n6
GDPR *see* General Data Protection Regulation (GDPR)
General Agreement on Tariffs and Trade (GATT) 13
General Agreement on Trade in Services (GATS) 13
general contract law *see* contract law(s)
General Data Protection Regulation (GDPR) 6, 12, 22, 27, 31, 36, 38–40, 50, 66, 71, 75, 77, 80, 92, **112**, 125, 159–161, 172, 221, 235–274, 287, 310, 347–348; and digital dispossession 264–273; extraterritorial application clause 27; Recital 63 266, 266n255
General Product Safety Directive (Directive 2001/95) 197
geoblocking 26, 28, 32–36, 32n171, 38–40; *see also* Geoblocking Regulation
Geoblocking Regulation 32–33, 35n193, 36, 39, 39n223
Germany 94, 126, 153, 178, 178n467, 180, 197–198, 207, 307; Bundesgerichtshof 329, 333; Civil Code 133, 178n467, 179; *Landgericht Berlin* (Regional Court of Berlin) 207; *Landgericht München* (Regional Court of Munich) 176–180; *Oberlandesgericht München* 180, 180n477; Supreme Court 178, 334; Uzun v Germany 258
Global Cities Challenge programme 63
global private-public surveillance network 235–237
Global South 258, 284, 358
good faith 120, 123–127, 124n55, 133, 210, 303, 332, 336–337, 336n493, 336–337n494, 340, 350
goods 13, 13n23, 27–28, 32–33, 35–37, 38n216, 39–40, 39n223, 78, 98, 118, 124–125, 134, 143–147, 149–155, 159, 163–166, 169, 179–182, 189, 189n17, 216–217, 235, 282–284, 286, 288–289, 291–292, 302–303, 302n194, 315, 319, 322, 345, 351–352; vs carriers 156–158;

consumer 70, **100**, 143, 145, 147, 150–151; definition 169; digital 27; with digital elements 153, 155–158, 163–164, 166, 182, 345; free movement of 189, 189n37, 319, 322; information 109, 351; intangible 147, 154; ownership of 158, 169, 294; tangible 147, 154–155, 158, 189, 217; Things as 145–147, 150, 166; *see also* goods-services dichotomy/divide
goods-services dichotomy/divide 13, 39–40
Google 21n81, 53, 216n250, 238, 253–254, 257, 268, 338, 354–355; *see also* Google Home; Google Nest; Google Nest Thermostat; Google Pay
Google Home 33, 81, 168, 172, 210, 268, 305
Google Nest 21n81, 70, 116, ; legals 137n179
Google Nest Thermostat 21n81, 70, 107
Google Pay 19n65
Greece 126
Green, Harriet 256–257
green technologies 45
greenwashing 231
grey lists 126–127, 133
growth economy 109
GS1 43, 43n258; Electronic Product Code 43
GSM 20n74, 325

hack 198, 293
hackers 2, 12, 203
hacking 186
Hagan, Margaret 172n422
harassment 223–224
hard law(s) 53–54, 66, 342; approach 55–61
hardware 11, 13–14, 19, 24–25, 49, 51, 83, **85**, **87**, **90**, 99, **100**, 109, 113, 115–116, 134, 142, 146, 148, 171, 174, 176, 185–186, 190–191, 200, 233, 248n114, 284–285, 289, 291, 297–298, 316–318, 339–340, 342, 344, 346, 351, 354–357; defects **88**; open 109, 340, 351, 355, 357; proprietary 339; *see also* hardware-software dichotomy; open hardware
hardware-software dichotomy 5, 40, 66, 200, 233, 278–279, 342, 346
harmonisation 59–60, 126, 145, 154–155, 160, 166, 170, 180n482, 206, 304n209, 316n326, 322, 333, 338
Harvey, David 253–254
hashtags 294

health data 259, 272
Hegel, G. W. F. 69
'hiding' practice 220
hierarchy of remedies 144–145, 155
home automation 70
Huawei protocol 332–334
Huawei v ZTE 323, 325, 327, 330–331, 333–335, 333n463, 340
human engineering 4, 252
human rights 51, 70, 113–115, 305, 311, 322, 339; *see also* Human Rights Act
Human Rights Act (1998) 322n376
human trafficking 115
human vulnerability(ies) 74, 184–234, 346
human-computer interaction (HCI) 245
Hungary 126
hyperconnected, interface-free world 167–181
hyperservitisation 92, 98–99, 106, 142

i2010 27
IBM 256–257
Iceland 198
ICTs 196, 204
industrial capitalism 4, 6, 252–253, 257, 347–349, 353n38
industrial data 26n120, 37, 305, 333
Industrial Internet Consortium (IIC) 24, 326
inferences 246
inferential data 240, 246–247, 274, 347
information: age 5, 252; asymmetry 118, 135, 137, 163, 240–241, 240n43; 'dearth' 177; encrypted 318; incorrect 223; incomplete 223; inward-facing 218; IoT-produced 202; mandated 180, 220; material 215, 218–219, 220–221; networked 5, 252; omitted 218; overload 168, 177, 183; personal 42, 244n72, 254, 261; publicly accessible 218; required 170, 175, 180–181, 221; secret 265; technologies 253, 253n153; technologies law 4; *see also* data; informational capitalism; informationalism; information asymmetry; 'information dearth'; information technologies
informational capitalism 252–253, 253n153
informationalism 257
informed decision 210, 213, 225
Infosoc Directive 280n40, 289, 298–299, 299n177, 318–320, 322n376
infosphere 25

infrastructure(s) 329n432; federated data 358; global 6; hidden 70; improvisational 359; internet 25; IoT 44, 48, 236; networked communication 62; of rentier relations 276; -as-a-service 98; technological 5
infringement 55, 119, 177n496, 214, 295, 303–304, 311, 313, 315, 317, 317n331, 317n332, 328–330, 328n421, 328n424, 332, 334, 339, 349, 350; copyright **104**, 280, 280n40, 293, 311, 317n332, 322n376; IP **111**; joint 278n18; patent 317, 317n331, 317n332, 335; trademark 216, 303
injunction 119, 177, 177n456, 180, 206, 214, 229, 310, 322n376, 327–328, 329n425, 330n436, 331–334, 334n475, 336–337; SEP 330n436, 333
Instagram 294–295
instrumentalization 255
instrumentarianism 256
instrumentation 255
intangible assets 299–300, 338–339, 347
intellectual property (IP) 1, 165, 266, 275–277, 292, 330–331, 348; addresses 26n121, 58, 247; -competition conflict 333, 340; erosion of in 'smart' world 313–323; exceptions 280, 290–291, 293, 295–313, 338–339, 349; infringement **111**; overlaps 313–323, 316n326, 339, 349; *see also* intellectual property law; intellectual property (IP) rights (IPRs)
intellectual property (IP) rights (IPRs) 23, 34–35, 69, 74, 77, **90**, 99, 167, 236, 250, 255, 264, 266, 275–276, 286–291, 295, 310–317, 320, 324, 339, 349; third-party 167
intellectual property law 32–36, 75, 264, 292n126
interconnected world 9; regulatory and policy options for 40–61
interface continuity, principle of 173, *173*, 181, 183, 346
interface-free world 81, 167–181
international data transfers 93, 113, 116, 259, 344
International Electrotechnical Commission (IEC) 324n390
International Instrument on Permitted Uses in Copyright Law 321
International Organisation for Standardisation (ISO) 22, 324n390
International Regulation Coordination Organisation for the IoT (IRCOIOT) 65, 67, 342

International Telecommunication Union (ITU) 324n390
International Telecommunications Union Joint Coordination Activity on Internet of Things and Smart Cities and Communities (ITU-T) 24
international trade 13; law 13, 13n32
Internet access services 57
internet governance 4, 40, 47, 65, 341, 350; privatisation of 279–280
Internet of Bodies 204
Internet of Contracts 117–183
Internet of Digital Locks 277, 279–281, 287, 297
Internet of Loos 234, 235–274, 347
Internet of Personalised Things 74, 82, 201–234, 274, 310, 346; *see also* unfair commercial practices
Internet of Secrets 277
Internet of Silos 20–22, 38, 107, 109, 163, 226, 297
Internet of Things (You Don't Own): under bourgeois law 275–340
Internet of Things *see* IoT
Internet of Vulnerabilities 184–234
internet protocol (IP) 21n76, 41
interoperability 12, 20–23, 37–38, 40, 44, 92, 148, 163, 166, 171, 226, 282, 297–298, 318–319, 324–325, 338–339, 349, 354, 357–358; controlled 92, 106–109
interpersonal communications services 58
intra-IP limitations 295–313
IoT *17*; actors 83; Bill of Rights 48; collectivised 341–359; commerce 74, 81, 118, 167–168, 170–176, 181, 183, 184, 204, 222, 345; contracts 68, 117, 126, 145, 150–153, 166; data 20, 36, 76, 137, 166, 201, 226, 241, 246, 250, 258, 264, 274, 281–282, 305–307, 309, 312, 333, 347, 354; data protection issues in 239–251; defective 185–200; defects 13n24; definition 11–15; economy 294; -enhanced consumer manipulation 205–229, 234, 347; global nature of 64, 66, 342; infrastructures 44, 48, 236; innovation 44, 54, 340; inventions, patentability of 277–279; IP issues and themes in 277–285; law 9–67; open 277, 284, 339, 341–359; patents 4; regulation 52, 323; relational black box 16, 40, 66, 83, 199, 242, 326, 342; safety risks 187; sectoral fragmentation 16, 18–24, 40, 56, 66–67, 342; security 51, 80–81; and standard essential patents 323–339; standardisation 23, 45, 324, 326; taxonomy 15, 19, 24, 66; traders 69, 74–75, 76n50, 78–80, 82–83, 92, 114, 116, 124, 126, 129, 131, 134, 138, 140, 142–167, 170–171, 182, 201–202, 204–205, 208, 213, 217, 220, 222–228, 234, 248, 286; undue influence over consumers' freedom of choice 222–226; users 4, 6, 10, 36, 60, 69, 92, 184, 236, 241, 244, 264, 296–297, 300, 304, 308, 312–313, 343, 347–348, 353–354; users as data producers 4; users-digital peasants 285–295, 348–349; *see also* IoT European Platform Initiative (IoT-EPI); IoT High Level Architecture; IoT LSP Standard Framework Concepts; IoT regulation difficulties
IoT European Platform Initiative (IoT-EPI) 44
IoT High Level Architecture 45
IoT LSP Standard Framework Concepts 45
IoT regulation difficulties 15–40; EU ban on unjustified geoblocking 32–36; free-flow of nonpersonal data regulation 36–40; Netflix Law: cross-border service portability regulation and indirect reform of copyright's territoriality 29–32; non-binary approach to 40–67; overcoming regulatory binaries, coregulation, and supervisory authority 61–65; regulation, law, and jurisdiction in intrinsically transnational systems 24–40; sectoral fragmentation and enabling technologies 16–24
Ireland, Republic of 299
ISO/IEC JTC 1 (Working Group 10 on the Internet of Things) 24
Italy 29, 32, 64–65, 94, 96, 125–126, 145, 186n13, 214, 222, 238; Antitrust Authority 222; *Codice Civile* 186n13; Communications Authority (AGCOM) 65; Digital Italy Agency (AGID) 65; Electric Energy, Gas, and Water Authority (AEEGSI) 65; Ministry for the Economic Development (MISE) 65; Permanent Committee on M2M Communication 64–65; Transportation Authority (ART) 65

'jailbreak' 293
Japan 79, 349
John Deere 268n272, 287
joint controllership 248–250

jurisdiction 1n2, 23n93, 24–40, 26n123,
83–84, 93, 97, 124n55, 138, 141,
145n233, 177–178, 186n13, 190n40,
211, 216n258, 225, 287, 307, 314, 331,
334, 336; flying 178

killer petrol stations 74
Kindle *see* Amazon Kindle
knowledge distribution 354; open-access
model 354; proprietary model 354
knowledge industry 252

labour 4, 6, 10, 234, 254, 274, 348, 351;
digital 6, 294, 353; free 295; intellectual
275; rent 294; unpaid 294–295
labourers 10, 235, 254, ; collective 341;
-machine relationship 10
lack of conformity 143–153, 164–167,
182, 199, 345
'later defect' defence 195–196, 200
Latvia 222
law by design 22, 41
lawful acquirer 297, 297n161
lawfulness 269, 271
law(s): code as 41, 69, 76; copyright
30, 290, 298, 318, 321, 322n375;
information technology 4; international
trade 13, 13n32; personalised 168;
private 119, 151, 159; public 62, 119;
sale of goods 146; unfair terms 93,
118; *see also* 'bourgeois law'; case
law; common law; competition law;
confidentiality law; consumer contract
law(s); consumer law(s); consumer
protection law(s); contract law(s);
consumer sales law(s); data control
law(s); data localisation laws; data
protection law(s); design law; digital
content law; digital supply laws; hard
law(s); intellectual property law; law by
design; Nazi law; patent law; privacy
law(s); product liability law(s); product
safety laws/legislation; soft laws; tort
law
least astonishment, principle of 116, 344
least privilege, principle of 51
legal control 287, 290
legal defects 165
legal design 172, 172n422, *173*, 344
legals 69, 71, 74, 78, 81–116, 118,
120–124, 126–129, 131, 133–139,
142–153, 162–164, 171–172, 181–182,
185–186, 201–202, 219–220, 224, 277,
287, 290, 297, 308, 343–345; controlled

interoperability 92, 106–109; design of
133–142; incontrollable multiplication
of 92–99, 106–109, 113–115; and
sustainability 113–115; trader-consumer
dichotomy and prosumers 92, 109;
see also Amazon; Amazon Echo; Cloud
of Things; codes of conduct; conditions
of sale; conditions of use; terms of
service; Things-as-a-Service
legal secrecy 118, 250, 255, 258, 264, 354
legibility requirement 171–172, 175, 181,
183
legitimate interest 76, 124, 240–241,
244n72, 265, 272, 298
Lessig, Lawrence 5, 49, 69, 76; code as
law 41, 69, 76
liability 11–14, 26, 38, 41, 107, 126–127,
129–131, 138–139, 145, 186, 186n13,
189–192, 195–197, 199–200, 214,
249, 332–334, 350, 355; civil 304;
consumer's 136; contractual 193;
criminal 2–3n8; defences 195–197; for
defective Things 192–194; for defects
13, 13n25, 187, 197; disclaimer of
14, 21n81, 83, 92, 95, 95n161, 97,
129–131, 147, 152; non-contractual
193; secondary 315n316; tortious 193,
196n96; trader's 126, 131, 137–138; *see
also* product liability; Product Liability
Directive; product liability law(s);
product liability rules
Library of Congress's Copyright Office
287, 293
license agreements 70, **104**, 289, 292
licenses 56, 84, **90**, **104**, 276, 285, 350;
royalty-free 292; sub- 292; *see also*
license agreements; licensing
licensing 20, **102**, 165, 277, 323, 325–329,
329n425, 332–333, 335–340, 349;
FRAND 326, 335–337, 339, 349; IoT
336n490; SEP 327, 333, 337–338,
337n499, 340; sub- 165; *see also* license
agreements; licenses; licensing agreements
licensing agreements 328–329, 337
liquification of physical world 256
Locke, John 351; *Of Civil Government* 351
lock-in effects 202
Low Energy Bluetooth (LEB) 19
low-power wide area networking
(LPWAN) 20n75, 21n78
Low-Power Wireless Personal Area
Networks 21, 21n76
low-range wireless area network
(LoRaWAN) 20, 20n75

Luxembourg 93–94, 126, 140–141, 178, 196
Luxemburg, Rosa 253, 274

machine data 258, 305, 310; big 26, 26n120
machine learning 37n204, 162, 190, 255–256, 263; technology 190
Machinery Directive 80
Machinery Regulation 198
Malta: Consumer Claims Tribunal 215
manipulation 7, 82, 185, 203–204, 230, 232–233, 270, 347; digital market(s) 204; Internet of Personalised Things and consumer 82; IoT-enabled 232; IoT-enhanced consumer 205–229, 205n174; of needs 234; online 65, 204; *see also* consumer manipulation; market manipulation
manipulative toasters 74
market dominance 41
market forces 73, 340
market manipulation 203–204; digital 204, 212
Marx, Karl 1, 9–10, 275–276; *Capital* 9; *Economic Manuscript 1861–63* 9–10; *The Poverty of Philosophy* 275–276
Marxism 6–7, 141, 251, 254, 350–351
materiality 2n5, 218–219
Mazda 197
media pluralism 310
Microsoft 132–133, 201, 286n88, 354; Cloud Computing Research Centre 11; Kinect 202; Online Services Terms 133; PlayReady™ **90**, 291
minimal state 52, 164
misleading practices 201, 205
misuse doctrine 322n377
mobile apps *see* apps
monetary price 147, 158–166, 159n324, 228
monopoly(ies) 54, 202–203, 203n161, 262, 275–276, 278–279, 286, 288, 299, 315, 325, 327, 327n413, 334, 336, 338–340
More-Than-Human Design 355–356
multilayered supply chain 92–98, 134
multitenancy 19

national courts 121–122, 122n45, 140, 209n205, 221, 247, 332, 334–335, 337, 340, 350
National Institute of Standards and Technology (NIST; US) 43, 63

national prescription rules 166
Nazi law 47
Near-Field Communication (NFC) 19, 19n65
neocolonial digital imperialism 46
Netflix Law 29–32
Netherlands, the 94, 126, 153; Civil Code 153n293; Court of Appeal of The Hague 334; Implementation Law on CRD 153n293; *N.V. Televizier v The Netherlands* 310–311
Network Information Security (NIS) Directive 47, 80
network logic 253
Neul 21, 21n77
'New Deal for Consumers' package 119, 167, 205, 233
'new servitudes' 286
Nintendo v PC Box 298, 318–319
NIS 2 Directive 198
non-binary approach to regulation 61
non-binary sociotechnological phenomenon 5, 9–67
noncontradiction, principle of 25, 25n110
noneconomic interests 230
non-fungible tokens (NFTs) 1
nonmonetary exchanges 155, 219
nonmonetary prices 158–162
nonpersonal data 26, 28, 36–40, 38n217, 66, **105**, 250, 258–259, 268
North America 41, 278
Northern Ireland 145
notice and choice model 241
notice-and-consent: approach 81, 168; mechanisms 118; model 170, 172
numbering 55–61
numerus clausus (closed number), theory of 301

objective justification 33, 333n466
obsolescence 68, 163, 187, 189, 217; planned 164, 182, 217; programmed 78–79
Ofcom 18, 18n59
Ofgem 18
Omnibus Directive (Directive 2019/2161) 119, 205, 167, 169
online activity 256
online-offline dichotomy/divide 5, 13, 33, 66, 341–342
open data 109, 340, 351, 354, 357–358
open hardware 109, 340, 351, 354, 355, 357
Open Internet of Things Certification Mark 356

open IoT 277, 284, 339, 341–359
open source **90**, 109, 337–338, 340, 351, 354
open standard formats 37
operant conditioning 255
opt-out mechanisms 243
Organization for Economic Co-operation and Development (OECD) 64
over-the-top services 55–61
ownership 98, 151–152, 158–159, 291–292, 294, 339, 342, 349, 358; data 277, 281–282; of goods 158, 161, 169, 276–277, 285–287, 294; privatisation of 236; property 77; vs subscription 286; *see also* death of ownership

Page, Larry 254
particular purpose 143, 148–149
patentability 13, 277–279, 279n32, 315n320, 316
patent law 298, 316n326, 317, 333, 338–340, 349–350
patent(s) **103**, **110**, 264, 276, 279, 288, 290, 302, 314–317, 317n331, 323–339, 349; abuses 52, 333; holders 317, 325–326, 337; holdup 326, 326n407, 350; infringement 317, 317n331, 317n332, 335; IoT 4, 278; software 278, 279n32, 316, 316n328; *see also* patentability; patent law; standard essential patents (SEP)
paternalism 164
pay-as-you-drive car insurance model 202
personal data 12n18, 22–23, 32, 38–39, 38n218, 46, 58, 76, **85–86**, 99, **105**, 107, 147, 155, 159–162, 166, 169, 182, 215, 219–220, 227, 237–239, 241–247, 249, 251, 258–259, 260n219, 261–262, 261n233, 262n234, 264–271, 273, 345, 347–348, 355
personalisation 82, 185, 201–205, 207, 231, 233, 262n235
personalised ads 82, 238
'personally identifiable information' (PII) 22–23, **102**
personal/nonpersonal data binary 36–40, 342, 347
physicality 11, 74, 145, 342
physical world 2, 11, 80, 256, 276, 342
Platform to Business Regulation 31
platform-as-a-service 98
playground *see* regulatory sandbox
Poland 94, 197; Office of Competition and Consumer Protection 214
political economy 5, 9, 252, 257

Portugal 126, 197
power asymmetries 135
power-humans-law triad 5
power imbalance 32, 117–118, 126, 142, 144, 163, 181, 184, 218, 226, 232, 297, 308, 338, 340, 346, 349, 350
precontractual duties to inform 118, 167–181
precontractual information 175–177; duties 92, 167, 170, 176, 179; *see also* precontractual duties to inform
prediction 4, 129, 247, 253, 255–257
predictive analytics 233, 253, 307
predigital 'offline' technologies 1
press freedom 310
price discrimination 201n144, 209
Price Indication Directive 119
price reduction, remedy of 159, 159n324, 206, 229
primitive accumulation 254
privacy 3, 18, 19n68, 23n93, 25, 26n123, 31, 36, 41–43, 49, 53, 53n346, 54n350, 62–63, 74–78, **85–87**, 95, **101–105**, **111–112**, 117, 133, 138, 202, 235, 235n2, 236, 239, 241, 244, 249, 250, 258, 260n211, 263, 293, 347; notices **85**, 93, **101–105**, **111–112**, 261, 264, 268, 270; rights 93n155, 235n3, 237; *see also* ePrivacy Directive; privacy by design; privacy impact assessments (PIA); privacy law(s); privacy policy(ies); Privacy Shield
privacy by design 50, 50n318, 241n50
privacy impact assessments (PIA) 62, 66
privacy law(s) 26n123, 173
privacy policy(ies) 69–70, **85**, **105**, 125, 138, 236, 238, 240, 242, 258, 260n215, 262n235, 287
private copy exception 296, 299–300, 302
private interest 293–295, 319
private ordering 31, 68–116, **90**, 131, 141–167, 182, 184, 343, 345; through Amazon Echo's contractual quagmire 83–115; by bricking 74, 78–79, **90**, 117, 142–167, 182, 184, 345; consumer benefits 72–74; consumer risks 74–83; contracting in immersive, hyperconnected, interface-free environments 81; death of ownership in new rentier capitalism 77–78; Internet of Personalised Things and consumer manipulation 82; legal 117; legals 83–115; surveillance capitalism and insufficiency of privacy-only approach 75–77; technological 117; vulnerability

of Things 79–81; *see also* contractual
quagmire; legals
private power 78, 252, 294, 340
private resources 251
private use exception 308
producers 191, 194–199, 199n127; data 4,
    6, 160, 253, 274, 281
product(s) commercialisation of 323;
    compatibility 305; complex 304;
    composite 318; concept of 190,
    199–200, 233, 346; data as 188–191;
    intangible 153, 189; service as 188–191;
    software as 188–191; tangible 185,
    189, 217, 346; Things as 219, 222;
    vulnerability 346; *see also* defective
    products; product liability; product
    vulnerability(ies)
product liability 171, 186–191, 193–194,
    196n96, 197, 200; and complementary
    regimes 197–199; defences 195–197; EU
    laws 185–200; reform of 199–200; *see
    also* Product Liability Directive; product
    liability law(s); product liability rules
Product Liability Directive (Directive
    85/374) 13n25, 75, 75n39, 80, 169,
    184, 187–188, 191–193, 193n62, 195,
    197–199, 233, 346
product liability law(s) 185–200, 346
product liability rules 13n24, 13n25, 191
product safety laws/legislation 197–198,
    198n118
Product Security and Telecommunications
    Infrastructure Bill 42n248
product vulnerability(ies) 184–234
professional diligence 162, 208–215, 222
profiling 82, **86**, 161, 201, 225, 226–228,
    233, 247–248
proletariat 254, 351; landless 254; *see also*
    'smart' proletariat
prominence 139, 174–175, 207
property rights 285–295, 331n448, 351;
    see also intellectual property (IP) rights
    (IPRs)
proprietary system 21, 109, 276
prosumers 92, 109, **110**, 115, 154
PSD2 161
public interest 31, 58, 63, 235n3, 272,
    273n305, 293–294, 318–320, 322,
    322n376, 330, 331n447, 334n474,
    339; doctrine of 322n377; piecemeal
    protection of 295–313, 311n279
purpose limitation, principle of 12,
    221n288, 237, 243, 246, 259

queer perspective 359; theory 359

Radio Equipment Directive 14, 15n44, 80
radio frequency identification (RFID) 11,
    16, 19, 19n65, 43n259, 62, 66, 73
readability coefficient 135, 343
reasonable expectation 149, 152, 166–167,
    347
regulation by bricking 78
regulation by design 43, 49, 51–52
regulatory and policy options 40–61
regulatory binaries 61–65
regulatory sandbox 62–63
reidentification 38, 239
relational black box 16, 40, 66, 83, 199,
    242, 326, 342
rematerialisation 2, 5
rentier capitalism 77–78, 275–277, 286,
    339
rentiers 275, 340
Representative Actions Directive 119, 233
repurposing 12, 12n18, 12n19, 18–19, 49,
    148–149, 162, 237, 243, 243n66
research funding 41, 43–44
Ricardo, David 276, 276n6, 340
Rifkin, Jeremy 3n11, 109; *Zero Marginal
    Cost Society* 3n11, 73
rights: of access 197, 266–267, 269,
    347; author 314; to be informed
    259, 269–273, 310; broadcasting
    29; community design 304; of
    communication to public 162, 288,
    290, 290n108, 299–300, 314; to contest
    a decision 272; data ownership 281;
    data producer's 281; to data portability
    268–269; to data protection 235–236,
    235n3, 266; digital property 293; to
    distribution 288–290; to erasure 160,
    269; exclusive 275, 287–289, 291,
    299, 314, 349; to an explanation 272;
    to express point of view 272; to fair
    trial 273; -holder 332; image 292; to
    insubstantial extraction 308n254; *ius
    primae noctis* 292, 349; moral 292;
    neighbouring 35; non-exclusive 291; of
    nonpersonal data portability 268; not to
    be subject to automated decision-making
    269; to object 241, 269; to obtain a
    free-of-charge copy 267, 269; to obtain
    human intervention/review 272–273;
    owners' 314; to perform those acts that
    are necessary to access database and its
    normal use 308n254; privacy 93n155,
    235, 235n3, 237; to property 1, 293,
    327, 331, 331n447, 334n474, 339,
    349–350, 353; to rectification 239, 264,
    269; to repair 79, 144, 148, 152–153,

182, 268, 287, 358; of reproduction
300; to restrict processing 269; to self-
determination 293; of service portability
268; statutory 126, 130–131; third-party
163, 267; user 308–309, 311–313,
317, 322, 339–340, 349; to view 291;
of withdrawal 169, 175, 220; *see also*
abuse of rights; consumer rights;
copyright; database right; design rights;
human rights; intellectual property (IP)
rights (IPRs); sui generis right
Ring 236, 249, 251
roaming charges 28
robotics 200
robots 16, 18, 46n286, 50n317, 194n82,
198
Romania 197, 231
royalties 326, 332

Safe Harbour decision 260
safe harbours 14, 14n36, 260n211; *see also*
Safe Harbour decision
safety, general expectation of 192–193
sale: definition 151, 158–162; *see also*
contract of sale; sales contract
sale of goods98, 118–119n1, 154n294,
156, 158; law 146; *see also* Sale of
Goods Act; Sale of Goods Directive;
sales contract
Sale of Goods Act 1979 146
Sale of Goods Directive 40, 40n229, 55
sales contract 153, 157–159, 158–
159n322, 166, 169, 184, 199
Samsung 107, 328n424, 329n425; *Hufford
v Samsung Electronics* 194; Powerbot
107; *Samsung* 332, 340; *Samsung/
UMTS* 328
Schumpeter, Joseph A. 54
Scotland 145
Scotland Act (1998) 70
screen size 49, 241
Second Consumer Sales Directive
(Directive 2019/771) 40n229,
117–118n1, 153–154, 154n294, 157,
158–159n322, 159, 166–167, 169, 171,
182–183, 345
Second Sales of Goods Directive 166
secrecy 239, 266–267, 269, 310; corporate
93; legal 118, 250, 255, 258, 264, 354;
organisational 255; professional 271;
technical 118, 250, 255, 354; trade 264,
269, 271, 273, 347
security 3, 18, 21, 21n78, 27, 41–42, 51,
51n322, 79–80, 127, 161, 186, 198, 249,
354–356; data 42; vs cybersecurity 80,

186, 200, 233, 346; IoT 51, 80–81; laws
43; physical 51; updates 164, 354
self, attack on the 235–237
self-determination 3, 25, 117, 201–202,
204, 250, 250n133, 258, 264, 293
self-driving cars 2–3n8, 18; *see also*
driverless cars
self-regulation 40–41, 60–63, 66, 245, 324,
342; code as 49n307, 50; market-led
41–54
Selinger, Evan 4, 252; *Re-engineering
Humanity* 4, 252
sensitive data 51, 82, 259, 346–347
sensors 2, 2–3n8, 12, 14, 74, 79–80, 184,
202, 236, 253–256, 262, 282, 342, 355;
fusion 242
service: defective 191; as product(s)
188–191; software as 190; *see also*
goods-services dichotomy/divide;
service portability; Service Terms;
servitisation; Thing-as-a-Service
service portability 36, 38, 40, 268; cross-
border 29–32; *see also* Cross-Border
Service Portability Regulation
Service Terms 99, **104**, 110n275, **111–112**,
151, 291
servitisation 98; hyper- 92, 98–99, 106, 142
Sigfox 21, 21n78
signals transmission services 58
sign-in-wrap agreements 135
Singapore 160
Skinner, B. F. 255, 257; behaviourism 255;
operant conditioning approach 255
Skype 57
Slovakia 126
smart city 204, 241n53, 250, 353
smart devices 2; non- 143; *see also names
of individual devices*
'smart' economy 109
smart environments 5
smart home 16, 70, 145n242, 204, 211,
220, 223–224, 236, 249–250, 258;
unfairness of substance and unfairness
of form in 118–142
'smart' internet 234
'smart' machines 10
smart medicine 354
smartness 3, 5, 35, 78, 121, 142–167, 182,
234, 277, 282–284, 345, 346
smartphones 14, 29, 194n82, 329n425
'smart' platforms 7
'smart' proletariat 274, 348, 350
smart technologies 2, 19n64, 161; *see also
names of individual devices*
smart toilet 202

smart watch 197–198
'smart' world 292, 313–323
SMS technology 175
social robots 46n286
sociotechnological phenomenon 2, 5,
    9–67, 68, 113, 117, 186, 313, 341, 343,
    359
soft initiatives 52
soft laws 4, 41–54, 60
software 1, 2n8, 11, 13, 20, 23–25, 49,
    78, 80–81, 83–84, **85–86**, **89–90**, 92,
    98–99, **100**, **102**, **104**, 106, **108**, 109,
    112, 115–116, 123, 134, 143, 145–146,
    147n249, 151, 156, 164, 169, 171, 174,
    185–186, 191, 217, 233, **262**, 263,
    276, 278–279, 279n29, 279n32, 280,
    284–287, 289–292, 295–298, 316–318,
    316n328, 322n374, 324, 328, 342, 344,
    346, 348, 353–358; components 49,
    189, 196; derivative 317; developers
    322n375, 358; downloaded 289;
    embedded 77, 189–190, 293, 297–298;
    facial-recognition 250; innovation
    278–279; instructions 74, 184; integrity
    51; inventions 278–279; legal protection
    of 279; licenses **90**, 276; non-embedded
    190; open 109, 285, 358; open-source
    45, **104**, 108, 354; patents 278, 279n32,
    316–317, 316n328; preinstalled 209;
    producers 199; as product 188–191;
    products 189, 199, 346; propertisation
    of 322; proprietary 23, 250; security
    198; as service 190; third-party **90**,
    102; updates 45, 74, 78–79, 184, 198,
    346; vulnerabilities 80; *see also* free
    and open-source software (FOSS);
    hardware-software dichotomy; software-
    as-a-service; software copyright;
    Software Directive; software-hardware
    dichotomy
software-as-a-service 98, 147, 190
software copyright 264, 298–299, 316–317
software-defined networking (SDN) 20,
    20n73
Software Directive 23, 23n96, 289–291,
    296–299, 299n172, 318–319
software-hardware dichotomy 13
solutionism: techno- 52; techno-legal 7, 20
Spain 94, 126, 238
spectrum 18, 18n59, 20n74, 41, 182;
    management 55–61, 56n370
spin-off theory 306–307
Spotify 30
spying sex toys 74, 77

standard contractual clauses (model
    clauses or standard data protection
    clauses) 93, **112**, 260–261, 260n219
standard essential patents (SEP) 21,
    323–339, 329n425, 336n490; licensing
    277, 327, 333, 337–338, 337n499, 340
'state-of-the-art' defence 195
Statute of Anne 313
statute of limitations 197
statutory authorisation 271–272
sticky policies 19, 19n68
subinfeudation 165
subject access request 7, 236, 258, 261,
    262, 262n234, 267, 344, 347
subscription economy 287, 348
subsidiaries 52, 71, 93–97, 94n157, **112**,
    115, 127, 132, 208, 259, 343
subsidiarity, principle of 52
substantiality 280, 306, 309
sui generis protection 306, 307n248
sui generis right 262n234, 281–282,
    305–309; *see also* database right
supervisory authority 61–65
suppliers 114, 118, 118n7, 120, 135, 171,
    187, 191–192, 200, 219, 258, 326, 357;
    energy 18n60
supply chains 11, 16, 24, 26, 71, 74,
    76n50, 115, 219, 249, 327, 336, 340;
    allocation of liability in 191–192; *see
    also* multilayered supply chain
Supply of Digital Content Directive 118
supply of digital content 147, 153n293,
    158, 182; non- 155n310; *see also*
    Supply of Digital Content Directive
surveillance capitalism 70, 74–77, 161,
    235–274, 347, 348; and IoT apparatus
    251–258
surveillance capitalists 4, 253, 255–257,
    274
surveillance scandals 6
sustainability 2n5, 45, 49, 64, 79, 92,
    113–115, 296, 339, 348, 358
system-of-systems 14, 19, 243

tablets 29, **85**, **88**, 194n82, 283, 329n425
tangibility 169, 189
tangible-intangible dichotomy/divide 5,
    153, 155, 166, 179, 181, 289, 295, 318
tangible property 1, 353
tangible wealth 1
targeted advertising **86**, 201, 270
techno-human vulnerability 185
technological control 287
technological determinism 6n31

technological management 5, 15, 69
technology convergence 337
technology of behaviour 255
techno-regulation 5, 41, 50, 78
techno-solutionism 52
tenancy 291; multi- 19
terms of service 21n81, 69–70, 82, 84, **112**, 179–180, 183, 216n250, 221, 224, 287, 304, 308, 346
territoriality 32; of copyright 9, 29–30, 35; extra- 40, 66, 342
Tesla, Nikola 11
Tesla 2–3n8, 79
'tethered economy' 277, 286
text and data mining 31n164
Thing-as-a-Service 92, 98–99, **100–105**, 106, 115; era 98
Thing(s): composite nature of 14, 317; defective 192–194, 233; definition 11, 342; as goods 145–147, 150, 166; health-related 187–188, 193; immovable 145n242; lack of conformity to 'legals' 143–153; as medium 219, 222; as product 219, 222; smartness of 142–167; vulnerability of 79–81, 200; *see also* Thing-as-a-Service; ThingsCon; Things Network
Things Network 357
ThingsCon 48, 357
third-party monitoring 240–241
three-step test 298, 312n290, 314, 321, 321n372
Tom Kabinet 288–289, 298, 314n299, 318
tort law 12, 281; of negligence 12n19
torts 186n13, 193
trademark 33n178, **101**, **103**, 107, **110**, **112**, 191, 216, 275n4, 276, 282, 288, 290, 296, 302–303, 302n195, 314–315, 316n325, 323; ingringement 303; registration 216n258; *see also* Trade Marks Directive
Trade Marks Directive 303
trader-consumer dichotomy 92, 109
trade secrets 23, 118, 236–237, 250, 255, 264, 271–273, 275n4, 281–282, 288, 290, 309–311, 310n272, 347; vs data protection 264–269; *see also* Trade Secrets Directive
Trade Secrets Directive 264–266, 309–312, 347
Trading Standards Services 120
trading website **174**, 175, 181
trajectories, concept of 245

transactional decision 134, 167, 210, 214–220, 223–227, 230, 231–233, 231n369
transparency 48, 57, 92, 123, 128, 130, 133–135, 137, 139, 141, 170, 172, 181, 255, 266, 269, 332, 335, 343, 346, 356n56, 358; principle of 91, 136, 172, 177n457, 259, 271–272
'triple black box' 255n172
Trump, Donald 203
Turkey: Gezi Park 352, 359

Uber 2–3n8, 35n193, 71, 79–80
ubiquitous computing 29–32, 233, 276, 313
UK 4, 29, 33–34, 33n173, 65, 69–70, 84, 94–96, **110**, 115, 118n7, 123, 125–126, 133, 138, 145, 153, 188, 193n62, 206, 238, 260n217, 286, 304n210, 304n220, 307, 317, 317n332, 322n376, 357; Centre for Connected and Autonomous Vehicles (Department for Transport) 18; Civil Aviation Authority 18; *Code of Practice for Consumer IoT Security* 4, 50, 80, 217; Competition and Markets Authority 65, 120, 127–128, 131, 137, 214, 224; Consumer Protection from Unfair Trading Regulations 2008 206n178, 209; Consumer Rights Act 2015 (CRA) 13n23, 123n46, 126, 144, 146–147, 154n297, 159; Data Protection Act 2018 238; Financial Conduct Authority 65; government 42, 50, 160, 238; government's *Code of Practice for Consumer IoT Security* 4, 50–51, 80, 217; Information Commissioner's Office 65, 266; Modern Slavery Act 114; Office of Communications 65; Parliament 70; Plan for Digital Regulation 42; Supreme Court 300, 323, 333–334
UN 114; Guiding Principles on Business and Human Rights 114, 114n304; Sales Convention (CISG) 140; Security Council 3; Universal Declaration of Human Rights 114n304
unfair commercial practices 92, 117, 144, 206n178, 206n182, 208–214, 231; aggressive practices 222–226; blacklist 227–229; and Internet of Personalised Things 229–233; IoT-enhanced consumer manipulation as 205–229; and limitations of communication medium 217–222; misleading actions and confusing practices 214–217;

misleading omissions 217–222; undue influence 222–226; 'unfair in all circumstances' 126, 226–229; *see also* Unfair Commercial Practices Directive

Unfair Commercial Practices Directive 75, 119, 184, 201, 205–206, 208, 211, 214, 216–217, 221, 223, 226, 229–230, 232, 234, 347

unfairness of form 118–142, 345

unfairness of substance 118–142, 345

unfairness test 123–124, 133; lack of good faith 123–124, 124n55; significant imbalance 123–127, 133, 140, 336–337n494

unfair terms 92, 117, 119–122, 127, 137, 141, 144, 178; laws 93, 118; *see also* Unfair Terms Directive

Unfair Terms Directive 75, 117, 119–123, 133, 138, 141, 177n457, 181, 205, 269, 336–337n494, 344–345

'unlock' 293

Unwired Planet v Huawei 323, 333–334, 337

updates 163–164, 166, 187, 199, 199n125; security 164, 354; software 74, 78, 184, 346

upload filter 28, 162, 280, 355

US 3, 22n91, 41–43, 56, 62, 79, 84, **90**, 93–96, 141–142, 182, 190, 194, 259–261, 273, 309, 327, 339, 344, 349; Department of Commerce 63, 260n211; Department of Justice 327; legal system 259n208; Securities and Exchange Commission (SEC) 71; Sherman Act 327n413; Supreme Court 82, 280; *see also* Digital Millennium Copyright Act; Federal Trade Commission

user-Thing relationship 245

usual purpose 143, 148–149

vagueness, rules on 97

value-sensitive design 47

voice assistants 338–339

Voice over IP 57

Volkswagen 230; *Volkswagen v Garcia* 310, 310n265

vulnerability(ies): concept of 184, 211n221; of consumers 200, 205, 211–213, 227–228, 232; by design 209–213; human 74, 184–185, 346; of IoT users 184; product 346; software 80; techno-human 185; of Things 79–81, 200

Wales 145

wearables 16, 224, 245, 248–249, 253n156

Web of Data 61

Weiner, Norbert 50

welfare state 164

Western-centrism 277, 284

WhatsApp 57

Wi-Fi 55, 149, 325, 349

WIPO Copyright Treaty 321

World Commission on Environment and Development 113

World Trade Organization (WTO) 64, 314, 321; Dispute Settlement Body 314

World Wide Web consortium (W3C) 24

Zebra movement 357

ZigBee 19, 19n66

Zuboff, Shoshana 4, 70, 75, 251–256, 347; *Surveillance Capitalism* 4, 251–252, 257

Ingram Content Group UK Ltd.
Milton Keynes UK
UKHW050002080323
418222UK00005B/18